¡YA BASTA!

TEN YEARS OF THE ZAPATISTA UPRISING

Writings of Subcomandante Insurgente Marcos

Forewords by Noam Chomsky and Naomi Klein

Edited and with a contribution by Žiga Vodovnik

¡YA BASTA! - TEN YEARS OF THE ZAPATISTA UPRISING.

Proceeds from the sale of this book will go to the autonomous rebel communities in Chiapas, Mexico.

The original works of Subcomandante Marcos are not copyrighted.

Foreword: "Chiapas: Symbol of Resistance" © 2003 by Noam Chomsky

Foreword: "The Unknown Icon" © 2001 by Naomi Klein

Introduction: "The Struggle Continues" © 2004 by Žiga Vodovnik

ISBN: 1-904859-13-5

Library of Congress Control Number: 2004105035

First edition to the United States/United Kingdom 2004

AK Press
674-A 23rd St.
Oakland, CA 94612
www.akpress.org
akpress@akpress.org
(510) 208.1700

AK Press
PO Box 12766
Edinburgh
Scotland EH89YE
www.akuk.com
ak@akedin.demon.co.uk
(0131) 555.5165

We're grateful to all unknown translators from Spanish, especially to Irlandesa...

Editor: Žiga Vodovnik

Graphic Design & Layout: Jaka Modic

Printed in Canada

CONTENTS

CHAPTER II: Subcomandante Marcos: 1997-1999 – Building the World

CHAPTER III: Subcomandante Marcos: 2000-2003 – (R)evolution Continues...

CHAPTER IV: EZLN Communiqués

Acknowledgments

About the Contributors

Permissions

This book is dedicated to all victims of
neoliberalism and corporate greed.
Especially to those in Chiapas, Mexico,
who showed us how to fight back!
This one is for you...

When spiders unite they can tie down a lion.
-Ethiopian proverb

First they ignore us. Then they laugh at us.
Then they fight us. Then we win.
                                    -Mahatma Gandhi

FOREWORDS

Noam Chomsky

Chiapas - Symbol of Resistance

The Zapatistas appeared suddenly almost ten years ago like a meteor flashing across a dark sky, instantly capturing the imagination of the world. The moment could hardly have been more dramatic. The most powerful state in history was just about to implement a critically important international economic agreement, NAFTA, designed to place the fate of North Americans in the hands of US-based multinationals, agribusiness, and financial institutions, as a step towards much grander plans. Just as the agreement of elite's - over strong popular opposition - was to go into effect, some of the most oppressed people in the region, descendants of the earliest victims of European imperialist triumphs, forgotten and unknown, stood up and said "Enough": we demand our elementary rights, our land, our dignity, our freedom; we reject your project of subordinating people and resources to the interests of the "de facto world government" of the "masters of the universe", as they are called in the business press, with only a touch of irony.

The initial expectation - mine at least - was that the insolent rebels calling for freedom and justice would be subjected to a devastating attack by the Mexican military, backed by US power. I think that would have happened, had it not been for the resonance of the brave stand of the people of Chiapas throughout North America, and beyond. Its impact quickly spread beyond support for the Zapatistas, invigorating the rising popular movements for global justice. Chiapas became a symbol of resistance to the peculiar form of "globalization" that grants priority to capital and the private tyrannies that control it, leaving the interests of people to the side, as incidental.

The influence of the rebels of Chiapas grew as they carried forward their efforts to take control of their lives and their lands, and as the harmful effects of NAFTA on the people of the affected region became more difficult to conceal. The effects have been particularly severe in Mexico, the weakest of the three countries. That had been anticipated by the planners, despite their fine words. The US-Mexico border, like most borders, is the result of brutal conquest. In the century and a half since, it had remained a porous border, crossed regularly by people on both sides for whom it was largely artificial. Along with the passage of NAFTA, the Clinton administration instituted Operation Gatekeeper, militarizing the border for the first time. The reason, no doubt, is that they expected an "economic miracle" in Mexico, meaning that the poverty level would increase as fast as the number of billionaires. Since then hundreds die every year seeking to escape the "miracle". NAFTA is one of those rare international agreements that has apparently harmed the populations in all three of the participating countries, most severely Mexico.

There is a good deal of ritual worship at the shrine of Adam Smith, the patron saint of NAFTA. As in much organized religion, the words may be chanted, but they do not pass through the mind. For Adam Smith, the foundation of free trade is free movement of labor, and capital movement is a serious danger, which would have pernicious consequences, he recognized, for England in particular. But these consequences would be overcome, he believed, because for their own self-interest, investors would prefer to use their capital at home, even if profits were greater abroad. Therefore, as if "by an invisible hand", the harmful effects of free capital movement would be overcome - the only use of the phrase "invisible hand" in Smith's classic Wealth of Nations. NAFTA, and the other agreements like it, succeeds in reversing the doctrines it pretends to revere, barring free movement of people and encouraging free movement of capital, another indication of the priorities of the designers.

Meanwhile the Zapatista struggle continues, in the face of bitter difficulties, but with indomitable courage and inspiring achievements. It is difficult to exaggerate the significance of the conflict between the ideals for which Chiapas has become a symbol, and the forces of domination and oppression that hold the levers of power, and will wield them until such time as the people of the world learn the lessons of Chiapas and apply them in their own circumstances and lives.

Naomi Klein
The Unknown Icon

I've never been to Chiapas. I've never made the pilgrimage to the Lacandon jungle. I've never sat in the mud and the mist in La Realidad. I've never begged, pleaded or posed to get an audience with Subcomandante Marcos, the masked man, the faceless face of Mexico's Zapatista National Liberation Army. I know people who have. Lots of them. In 1994, the summer after the Zapatista rebellion, caravans to Chiapas were all the rage in north American activist circles: friends got together and raised money for secondhand vans, filled them with supplies, then drove south to San Cristobal de las Casas and left the vans behind. I didn't pay much attention at the time. Back then, Zapatista-mania looked suspiciously like just another cause for guilty lefties with a Latin American fetish: another Marxist rebel army, another macho leader, another chance to go south and buy colourful textiles. Hadn't we heard this story before? Hadn't it ended badly? Last week, there was another caravan in Chiapas. But this was different. First, it didn't end in San Cristobal de las Casas; it started there, and is now criss-crossing the Mexican countryside before the planned grand entrance into Mexico City on March 11. The caravan, nicknamed the "Zapatour" by the Mexican press, is being led by the council of 24 Zapatista commanders, in full uniform and masks (though no weapons), including Subcomandante Marcos himself. Because it is unheard of for the Zapatista command to travel outside Chiapas (and there are vigilantes threatening deadly duels with Marcos all along the way), the Zapatour needs tight security. The Red Cross turned down the job, so protection is being provided by several hundred anarchists from Italy who call themselves Ya Basta! (meaning "Enough is enough!"), after the defiant phrase used in the Zapatistas' declaration of war. Hundreds of students, small farmers and activists have joined the roadshow, and thousands greet them along the way. Unlike those early visitors to Chiapas, these travellers say they are there not because they are "in solidarity" with the Zapatistas, but because they are Zapatistas. Some even claim to be Subcomandante Marcos himself - they say we are all Marcos.

Perhaps only a man who never takes off his mask, who hides his real name, could lead this caravan of renegades, rebels, loners and anarchists on this two-week trek. These are people who have learned to steer clear of charismatic leaders with one-size-fits-all ideologies. These aren't party loyalists; these are members of groups that pride themselves on their autonomy and lack of hierarchy. Marcos - with his black wool mask, two eyes and pipe - seems to be an anti-leader tailor-made for this suspicious, critical lot. Not only does he refuse to show his face, undercutting (and simultaneously augmenting) his own celebrity, but Marcos' story is of a man who came to his leadership, not through swaggering certainty, but by coming to terms with political uncertainty, by learning to follow.

Though there is no confirmation of Marcos' real identity, the most repeated legend that surrounds him goes like this: an urban Marxist intellectual and activist, Marcos was wanted by the state and was no longer safe in the cities. He fled to the mountains of Chiapas in southeast Mexico filled with revolutionary rhetoric and certainty, there to convert the poor indigenous masses to the cause of armed proletarian revolution against the bourgeoisie. He said the workers of the world must unite, and the Mayans just stared at him. They said they weren't workers and, besides, land wasn't property but the heart of their community. Having failed as a Marxist missionary, Marcos immersed himself in Mayan culture. The more he learned, the less he knew. Out of this process, a new kind of army emerged, the EZLN, the Zapatista National Liberation Army, which was not controlled by an elite of guerrilla commanders but by the communities themselves, through clandestine councils and open assemblies. "Our army," says Marcos, "became scandalously Indian." That meant that he wasn't a commander barking orders, but a subcomandante, a conduit for the will of the councils. His first words said in the new persona were: "Through me speaks the will of the Zapatista National Liberation Army." Further subjugating himself, Marcos says that he is not a leader to those who seek him out, but that his black mask is a mirror, reflecting each of their own struggles; that a Zapatista is anyone anywhere fighting injustice, that "We are you". He once said, "Marcos is gay in San Francisco, black in South Africa, an Asian in Europe, a Chicano in San Ysidro, an anarchist in Spain, a Palestinian in Israel, a Mayan Indian in the streets of San Cristobal, a Jew in Germany, a Gypsy in Poland, a Mohawk in Quebec, a pacifist in Bosnia, a single woman on the Metro at 10pm, a peasant without land, a gang member in the slums, an unemployed worker, an unhappy student and, of course, a Zapatista in the mountains."

"This non-self," writes Juana Ponce de Leon, "makes it possible for Marcos to become the spokesperson for indigenous communities. He is transparent, and he is iconographic." Yet the paradox of Marcos and the Zapatistas is that, despite the masks, the non-selves, the mystery, their struggle is about the opposite of anonymity - it is about the right to be seen. When the Zapatistas took up arms and said Ya Basta! in 1994, it was a revolt against their invisibility. Like so many others left behind by globalization, the Mayans of Chiapas had fallen off the economic map: "Below in the cities," the EZLN command stated, "we did not exist. Our lives were worth less than those of machines or animals. We were like stones, like weeds in the road. We were silenced. We were faceless." By arming and masking themselves, the Zapatistas explain, they weren't joining some Star Trek-like Borg universe of people without identities fighting in common cause: they were forcing the world to stop ignoring their plight, to see their long neglected faces. The Zapatistas are "the voice that arms itself to be heard. The face that hides itself to be seen."

Meanwhile, Marcos himself - the supposed non-self, the conduit, the mirror-writes in a tone so personal and poetic, so completely and unmistakably his own, that he is constantly undercutting and subverting the anonymity that comes from his mask and pseudonym. It is often said that the Zapatistas' best weapon was the Internet, but their true secret weapon was their language. In <u>Our Word Is Our Weapon</u>, we read manifestos and war cries that are also poems, legends and riffs. A character emerges behind the mask, a personality. Marcos is a revolutionary who writes long meditative letters to Uruguayan poet Eduardo Galeano about the meaning of silence; who describes colonialism as a series of "bad jokes badly told", who quotes Lewis Carroll, Shakespeare and Borges. Who writes that resistance takes place "any time any man or woman rebels to the point of tearing off the clothes resignation has woven for them and cynicism has dyed grey". And who then sends whimsical mock telegrams to all of "civil society": "THE GRAYS HOPE TO WIN. STOP. RAINBOW NEEDED URGENTLY."

Marcos seems keenly aware of himself as an irresistible romantic hero. He's an Isabelle Allende character in reverse - not the poor peasant who becomes a Marxist rebel, but a Marxist intellectual who becomes a poor peasant. He plays with this character, flirts with it, saying that he can't reveal his real identity for fear of disappointing his female fans. Perhaps wary that this game was getting a little out of hand, Marcos chose the eve of Valentine's Day this year to break the bad news: he is married, and deeply in love, and her name is La Mar ("the Sea" - what else would it be?)

This is a movement keenly aware of the power of words and symbols. Rumour has it that when the 24-strong Zapatista command arrive in Mexico City, they hope to ride downtown on horseback, like indigenous conquistadors. There will be a massive rally, and concerts, and they will ask to address the Congress. There, they will demand that legislators pass an Indigenous Bill of Rights, a law that came out of the Zapatistas' failed peace negotiations with president, Ernesto Zedillo, who was defeated in recent elections. Vincente Fox, his successor who famously bragged during the campaign that he could solve the Zapatista problem "in 15 minutes", has asked for a meeting with Marcos, but has so far been refused - not until the bill is passed, says Marcos, not until more army troops are withdrawn from Zapatista territory, not until all Zapatista political prisoners are freed. Marcos has been betrayed before, and accuses Fox of staging a "simulation of peace" before the peace negotiations have even restarted. What is clear in all this jostling for position is that something radical has changed in the balance of power in Mexico. The Zapatistas are calling the shots now - which is significant, because they have lost the habit of firing shots. What started as a small, armed insurrection has in the past seven years turned into what now looks more like a peaceful, and mass movement. It has helped topple the corrupt 71-year reign of the Institutional Revolutionary Party, and has placed indigenous rights at the center of the Mexican political agenda.

Which is why Marcos gets angry when he is looked on as just another guy with a gun: "What other guerrilla force has convened a national democratic movement, civic and peaceful, so that armed struggle becomes useless?" he asks. "What other guerrilla force asks its bases of support about what it should do before doing it? What other guerrilla force has struggled to achieve a democratic space and not take power? What other guerrilla force has relied more on words than on bullets?"

The Zapatistas chose January 1, 1994, the day the North American Free Trade Agreement (NAFTA) came into force, to "declare war" on the Mexican army, launching an insurrection and briefly taking control of the city of San Cristobal de las Casas and five Chiapas towns. They sent out a communiqué explaining that NAFTA, which banned subsidies to indigenous farm co-operatives, would be a "summary execution" for four million indigenous Mexicans in Chiapas, the country's poorest province.

Nearly 100 years had passed since the Mexican revolution promised to return indigenous land through agrarian reform; after all these broken promises, NAFTA was simply the last straw. "We are the product of 500 years of struggle . . . but today we say Ya Basta! Enough is enough." The rebels called themselves Zapatistas, taking their name from Emiliano Zapata, the slain hero of the 1910 revolution who, along with a rag-tag peasant army, fought for lands held by large landowners to be returned to indigenous and peasant farmers.

In the seven years since, the Zapatistas have come to represent two forces at once: first, rebels struggling against grinding poverty and humiliation in the mountains of Chiapas and, on top of this, theorists of a new movement, another way to think about power, resistance and globalization. This theory - Zapatismo - not only turns classic guerrilla tactics inside out, but much of leftwing politics on its head.

I may never have made the pilgrimage to Chiapas, but I have watched the Zapatistas' ideas spread through activist circles, passed along second- and third-hand: a phrase, a way to run a meeting, a metaphor that twists your brain around. Unlike classic revolutionaries, who preach through bullhorns and from pulpits,

Marcos has spread the Zapatista word through riddles. Revolutionaries who don't want power. People who must hide their faces to be seen. A world with many worlds in it. A movement of one "no" and many "yesses".

These phrases seem simple at first, but don't be fooled. They have a way of burrowing into the consciousness, cropping up in strange places, being repeated until they take on this quality of truth - but not absolute truth: a truth, as the Zapatistas might say, with many truths in it. In Canada, where I'm from, indigenous uprising is always symbolized by a blockade: a physical barrier to stop the golf course from being built on a native burial site, to block the construction of a hydroelectric dam or to keep an old growth forest from being logged. The Zapatista uprising was a new way to protect land and culture: rather than locking out the world, the Zapatistas flung open the doors and invited the world inside. Chiapas was transformed, despite its poverty, despite being under constant military siege, into a global gathering place for activists, intellectuals, and indigenous groups.

From the first communiqué, the Zapatistas invited the international community "to watch over and regulate our battles". The summer after the uprising, they hosted a National Democratic Convention in the jungle; 6,000 people attended, most from Mexico. In 1996, they hosted the first Encuentro (or meeting) For Humanity And Against Neo-Liberalism. Some 3,000 activists travelled to Chiapas to meet with others from around the world.

Marcos himself is a one-man-web: he is a compulsive communicator, constantly reaching out, drawing connections between different issues and struggles. His communiqués are filled with lists of groups that he imagines are Zapatista allies, small shopkeepers, retired people and the disabled, as well as workers and campesinos. He writes to political prisoners Mumia Abu Jamal and Leonard Peltier. He is pen-pals with some of Latin America's best-known novelists. He writes letters addressed "to the people of world".

When the uprising began, the government attempted to play down the incident as a "local" problem, an ethnic dispute easily contained. The strategic victory of the Zapatistas was to change the terms: to insist that what was going on in Chiapas could not be written off as a narrow "ethnic" struggle, and that it was universal. They did this by clearly naming their enemy not only as the Mexican state but as the set of economic policies known as "neo-liberalism". Marcos insisted that the poverty and desperation in Chiapas was simply a more advanced version of something happening all around the world. He pointed to the huge numbers of people who were being left behind by prosperity, whose land, and work, made that prosperity possible. "The new distribution of the world excludes 'minorities'," Marcos has said. "The indigenous, youth, women, homosexuals, lesbians, people of colour, immigrants, workers, peasants; the majority who make up the world basements are presented, for power, as disposable. The distribution of the world excludes the majorities."

The Zapatistas staged an open insurrection, one that anyone could join, as long as they thought of themselves as outsiders. By conservative estimates, there are now 45,000 Zapatista-related websites, based in 26 countries. Marcos' communiqués are available in at least 14 languages. And then there is the Zapatista cottage industry: black T-shirts with red five-pointed stars, white T-shirts with EZLN printed in black. There are baseball hats, black EZLN ski masks, Mayan-made dolls and trucks. There are posters, including one of Comandante Ramona, the much loved EZLN matri-arch, as the Mona Lisa.

It looked like fun, but it was also influential. Many who attended the first "encuentros" went on to play key roles in the protests against the World Trade Organization in Seattle and the World Bank and IMF in Washington DC, arriving with a new taste for direct action, for collective decision-making and decentralized organizing. When the insurrection began, the Mexican military was convinced it would be able to squash the Zapatistas' jungle uprising like a bug. It sent in heavy artillery, conducted air raids, mobilized thousands of soldiers. Only, instead of stan-ding on a squashed bug, the government found itself surrounded by a swarm of int-ernational activists, buzzing around Chiapas. In a study commissioned by the US military from the Rand Corporation, the EZLN is studied as "a new mode of con-flict - 'netwar' - in which the protagonists depend on using network forms of organ-ization, doctrine, strategy and technology." This is dangerous, according to Rand, because what starts as "a war of the flea" can quickly turn into "a war of the swarm".

The ring around the rebels has not protected the Zapatistas entirely. In Decem-ber 1997, there was the brutal Acteal massacre in which 45 Zapatista supporters were killed, most of them women and children. And the situation in Chiapas is still desperate, with thousands displaced from their homes. But it is also true that the situation would probably have been much worse, potentially with far greater inter-vention from the US military, had it not been for this international swarm. The Rand Corporation study states that the global activist attention arrived "during a period when the United States may have been tacitly interested in seeing a force-ful crackdown on the rebels".

So it's worth asking: what are the ideas that proved so powerful that thousands have taken it upon themselves to disseminate them around the world? A few years ago, the idea of the rebels travelling to Mexico City to address the congress would have been impossible to imagine. The prospect of masked guerrillas (even masked guerrillas who have left their arms at home) entering a hall of political power signals one thing: revolution. But Zapatistas aren't interested in overthrowing the state or naming their leader, Marcos, as president. If anything, they want less state power over their lives. And, besides, Marcos says that as soon as peace has been negotiated he will take off his mask and disappear.

What does it mean to be a revolutionary who is not trying to stage a revolution? This is one of the key Zapatista paradoxes. In one of his many communiqués, Marcos writes that "it is not necessary to conquer the world. It is sufficient to make it new". He adds: "Us. Today." What sets the Zapatistas apart from your average Marxist guerrilla insurgents is that their goal is not to win control, but to seize and build autonomous spaces where "democracy, liberty and justice" can thrive.

Although the Zapatistas have articulated certain key goals of their resistance (control over land, direct political representation, and the right to protect their language and culture), they insist they are not interested in "the Revolution", but rather in "a revolution that makes revolution possible".

Marcos believes that what he has learned in Chiapas about non-hierarchical decision-making, decentralized organizing and deep community democracy holds answers for the non-indigenous world as well - if only it were willing to listen. This is a kind of organizing that doesn't compartmentalize the community into workers, warriors, farmers and students, but instead seeks to organize communities as a whole, across sectors and across generations, creating "social movements". For the Zapatistas, these autonomous zones aren't about isolationism or dropping out, 60s-style. Quite the opposite: Marcos is convinced that these free spaces, born of reclaimed land, communal agriculture, resistance to privatization, will eventually create counter-powers to the state simply by existing as alternatives.

This is the essence of Zapatismo, and explains much of its appeal: a global call to revolution that tells you not to wait for the revolution, only to stand where you stand, to fight with your own weapon. It could be a video camera, words, ideas, "hope" - all of these, Marcos has written, "are also weapons". It's a revolution in miniature that says, "Yes, you can try this at home." This organizing model has spread throughout Latin America, and the world. You can see it in the anarchist squats of Italy (called "social centers") and in the Landless Peasants' Movement of Brazil, which seizes tracts of unused farmland and uses them for sustainable agriculture, markets and schools under the slogan "Ocupar, Resistir, Producir" (Occupy, Resist, Produce). These same ideas were forcefully expressed by the students of the National Autonomous University of Mexico during last year's long and militant occupation of their campus. Zapata once said the land belongs to those who work it, their banners blared, WE SAY THAT THE UNIVERSITY BELONGS TO THOSE WHO STUDY IN IT.

Zapatismo, according to Marcos, is not a doctrine but "an intuition". And he is consciously trying to appeal to something that exists outside the intellect, something uncynical in us, that he found in himself in the mountains of Chiapas: wonder, a suspension of disbelief, myth and magic. So, instead of issuing manifestos, he tries to riff his way into this place, with long meditations, flights of fancy, dreaming out loud. This is, in a way, a kind of intellectual guerrilla warfare: Marcos won't meet his opponents head on, but instead surrounds them from all directions.

A month ago, I got an email from Greg Ruggiero. He wrote that when Marcos enters Mexico City next week, it will be "the equivalent of Martin Luther King Jr's March on Washington". I stared at the sentence for a long time. I have seen the clip of King's "I have a dream" speech maybe 10,000 times, though usually through adverts sellingmutual funds, cable news or computers and the like. Having grown up after history ended, it never occurred to me that I might see a capital-H history moment to match it.

Next thing I knew, I was on the phone talking to airlines, canceling engagements, making crazy excuses, mumbling about Zapatistas and Martin Luther King. Who cares that I dropped my introduction to Spanish course? Or that I've never been to Mexico City, let alone Chiapas? Marcos says I am a Zapatista and I am suddenly thinking, "Yes, yes, I am. I have to be in Mexico City on March 11. It's like Martin Luther King Jr's March on Washington." Only now, as March 11 approaches, it occurs to me that it's not like that at all. History is being made in Mexico City this week, but it's a smaller, lower-case, humbler kind of history than you see in those news-clips. A history that says ,"I can't make your history for you. But I can tell you that history is yours to make."

It also occurs to me that Marcos isn't Martin Luther King; he is King's very modern progeny, born of a bittersweet marriage of vision and necessity. This masked man who calls himself Marcos is the descendant of King, Che Guevara, Malcom X, Emiliano Zapata and all the other heroes who preached from pulpits only to be shot down one by one, leaving bodies of followers wandering around blind and disoriented because they lost their heads.

In their place, the world now has a new kind of hero, one who listens more than speaks, who preaches in riddles not in certainties, a leader who doesn't show his face, who says his mask is really a mirror. And in the Zapatistas, we have not one dream of a revolution, but a dreaming revolution. "This is our dream," writes Marcos, "the Zapatista paradox - one that takes away sleep. The only dream that is dreamed awake, sleepless. The history that is born and nurtured from below."

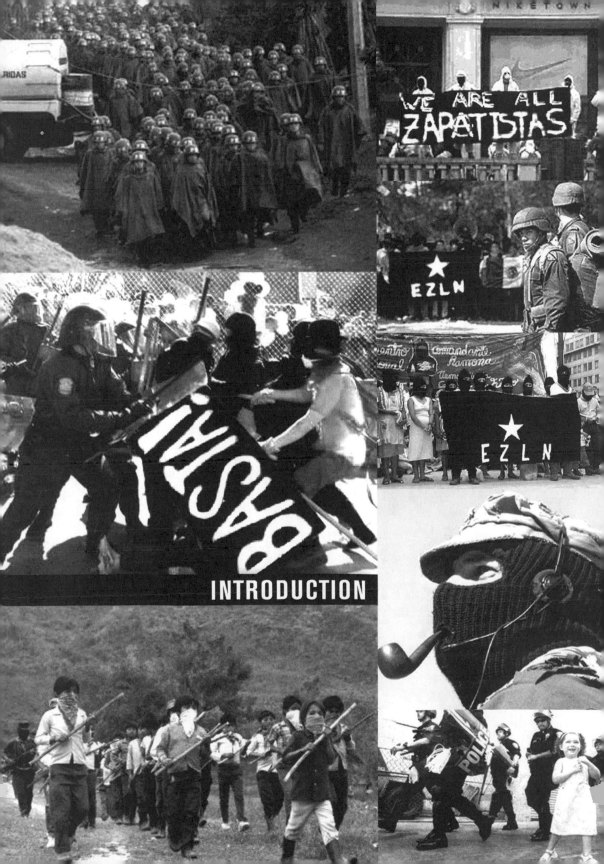

WE ARE ALL ZAPATISTAS

EZLN

¡YA BASTA!

INTRODUCTION

EZLN

Žiga Vodovnik
The Struggle Continues...

1. CONQUEST AND HUMAN PROGRESS

Howard Zinn, one of the most engaging social critics (of neoliberalism) alive, wrote his bestseller, A People's History of the United States, on the premise that *"the cry of the repressed, the poor and the exploited is not always just, but if you don't listen to it, you will never know what justice really is…"*

His book is probably one of the best available concerning the cruel fate of indigenous people in the New World. On the beginning of colonialism in Americas, Zinn precisely writes how an ambitious young Genoese sailor Columbus had persuaded the King and the Queen of Spain to finance his expedition to the lands of the wealth - the Indies and Asia with all their gold and spices. For, like other informed people of his time, he knew the world was round and he could sail west in order to get to the Far East. In return for bringing back gold and spices, he negotiated ten percent of all profits for himself, governorship over new-found lands, and the fame that would go with a new title - Admiral of the Ocean Sea. The first man to sight the land was supposed to get a yearly pension of 10,000 *maravedis* for lifetime. On October 12, 1492, a sailor called Rodrigo saw the early moon shining on the white sands of the island in the Bahamas, the Caribbean Sea. But Rodrigo never got it. Columbus claimed he had seen a light the evening before, therefore he also got that reward…

When Columbus and his sailors first came ashore carrying swords, speaking oddly, the Arawaks ran to greet them, bringing them food, water and gifts. The Arawak Indians lived in village communes, developing agriculture of corn, yams, cassava. They could spin and weave, but had no horses or work animals. They enjoyed a far more "civilized" life-style than any society in Europe; the natives only worked the equivalent of a few days per week, pulling fish from the sea, taking fruits from the trees; their children often accompanied them during their work; they displayed no shame, wearing little or no clothing; they had no guilt, making love openly; and they were so generous that anything Europeans showed interest in, was promptly given to them. You should expect Columbus to say, "We should send here our best scholars to study these people and learn from them." Instead, Columbus writes in his diary:

"...They do not bear arms, and do not know them, for I showed them a sword, they took it by the edge and cut themselves out of ignorance. They would make fine servants... With fifty men we could subjugate them all and make them do whatever we want."

The Arawaks had no iron, but they wore tiny gold ornaments in their ears. This had enormous consequences, it led Columbus to take some of them aboard as prisoners, because he insisted that they would guide him to the source of gold. Columbus writes:

"As soon as I arrived in the Indies, on the first island I found, I took some of the natives by force in order that they might learn our language and might give me information of whatever there is in these parts."

He then sailed to what is now Cuba, then to Hispaniola - the island, which today consists of Haiti and the Dominican Republic. He took more Indian prisoners and put them aboard his three ships. The Indians, Columbus wrote:

"...are so naive and so free with their possessions that no one who has not witnessed them would believe it. When you ask for something they have, they never say no. To the contrary, they offer to share with anyone..."

At one part of his first voyage he got into a fight with indigenous people who refused to trade as many bows and arrows as he and his men wanted. They were run through with swords and bled to death...

Because of Columbus' exaggerated reports and promises, his second expedition was given seventeen ships and more than twelve hundred men. There was only one goal, more slaves and more gold. They went from island to island in the Caribbean, taking Indians for captives. But as word (of the "humanity") of Europeans spread around, they found more and more villages empty.

As they found no gold fields, they had to fill up the ships returning to Spain with some kind of dividend. Zinn notes that in the year 1495, Columbus went on a great slave raid, rounded up fifteen hundred Arawak men, women and children, put them in pens guarded by Spaniards and dogs, then picked five hundred best "specimens" to load onto ships. Out of five hundred, two hundred died en route. The rest arrived to Spain and were put up for sale (men for labor, women and children for sex) by the archdeacon of the town, who reported that although the slaves were "naked as the day they were born," they showed "no more embarrassment than animals".

Bartolomé de las Casas is the chief source (and on many matters the only one) of information about what happened on the islands after Columbus came. Las Casas, as a young priest, participated in the conquest of Cuba, for a time owned a plantation on which Indian slaves worked, but finally gave that up and became a vehement critic of Spanish cruelty. In his book *History of the Indies*, las Casas precisely describes the treatment of the indigenous people by the Spaniards:

> "Endless testimonies... prove the mild and pacific temperament of the natives... But our work was to exasperate, ravage, kill, mangle and destroy; small wonder, then, if they tried to kill one of us now and then... The admiral, it is true, was blind as those who came after him, and he was so anxious to please the King that he committed irreparable crimes against the Indians..."

Columbus, desperate to pay back dividends to those who had invested in his voyages, had to make good promise to fill the ships with gold. Therefore, he ordered all persons fourteen years or older to collect a certain quantity of gold every three months - impossible task, considering that the only gold around was bits of dust garnered from the streams. When they brought it, they were given copper tokens to hang around their necks, but those found without a copper token, had their hands cut off and bled to death. Some obeyed - they suffered and died in the mines and other labors. After each six or eight months' work in the mines, which was the time required of each crew to dig enough gold for melting, up to a third of the men died. Others fled, made mass suicides, and killed their infants to save them from Spaniards. Las Casas writes how so-called Christians were knifing Indians by tens and twenties, and cutting slices off them to test the sharpness of their blades. The Spaniards also grew more conceited and lazy every day, and after a while refused to walk any distance. They were carried on hammocks by Indians running in relays - in that case they also had Indians carrying large leaves to shade them from the sun and others to fan them with goose wings. And if they were in a hurry? No, they didn't run... They rode the backs of Indians running for them...

In two years, in which they went through murder, mutilation and suicide, half of whole 250,000 indigenous population was dead. By the year 1515, there were fifty thousand Indians left. By 1550, there were five hundred. A report of the year 1650 shows none of the original Arawaks or their descendants were alive. Human progress? I don't think so...

2. Ceteris Paribus or Little Has Changed

What Columbus did to Arawaks of the Bahamas, Pizzaro to the Incas of Peru, the English settlers of Virginia and Massachusetts to the Powhatans and the Pequots, ..., Cortés did to the indigenous people of Mexico.

In Mexico, five hundred years later, little has changed for indigenous people in state of Chiapas, although the state is one of Mexico's richest in natural resources. As Marcos noted in his first public essay *Chiapas, The Southeast in Two Winds A Storm and a Prophecy*, this land continues to pay tribute to the imperialists, above all with oil, gas, timber, electricity, cattle, coffee, etc ...

In Chiapas, the national oil company Pemex sucks out enormous quantities of barrels of *petroleum* and cubic feet of *gas* every day. They take away the petroleum and gas, and in exchange leave behind the mark of capitalism - ecological destruction, agricultural plunder, hyperinflation, alcoholism, prostitution and poverty. Marcos writes that "the beast" is still not satisfied, and has extended its tentacles to the Lacandon jungle - eight petroleum deposits are under exploration. The paths are made with machetes by the same campesinos that are left without land by the insatiable beast. The trees fall down and dynamite explodes on land where campesinos are not allowed to cut down trees to cultivate. Every tree that is cut down costs them a fine that is ten times the minimum wage, and a jail sentence. The poor cannot cut down trees, but the petroleum beast can, a beast that every day falls more and more into foreign hands. The campesinos cut them down to survive the beast to plunder.

Chiapas also bleeds *coffee*. Thirty-five percent of the coffee produced in Mexico comes from this area. The industry employs 87,000 people. Forty-seven percent of the coffee is for national consumption and fifty-three percent is exported abroad, mainly to the United States and Europe. More than 100,000 tons of coffee are taken from this state to fatten the beast's bank accounts; in 1988 a kilo of pergamino coffee was sold abroad for 8,000 pesos. The Chiapaneco producers were paid 2,500 pesos or less.

The second most important plunder after coffee is *beef*. Three million head of cattle wait for middlemen and a small group of businessmen to take them away to fill refrigerators in Arriaga, Villahermosa and Mexico City. The cattle is sold for 400 pesos per kilo by the poor farmers, and resold by the middlemen and businessmen for up to ten times the price they paid for them.

Three major dams produce fifty-five percent of national hydroelectric energy, along with 20 percent of Mexico's total *electricity*. However, only a third of the homes in Chiapas have electricity... Where do the 12,907 kilowatts produced annually by hydroelectric plants in Chiapas go?

In spite of the current trend toward ecological awareness, the plunder of *wood* continues in Chiapas' forests. Between 1981 and 1989, 2,444,777 cubic meters of precious woods, conifers and tropical trees were taken from Chiapas. They were taken to Mexico City, Puebla, Veracruz and Quintana Roo. In 1988, wood exports brought revenue of 23,900,000,000 pesos, 6,000 percent more than in 1980.

The *honey* that is produced in 79,000 beehives in Chiapas goes entirely to European markets and US. The 2,756 tons of honey produced annually in the Chiapaneco countryside is converted into dollars, which the people of Chiapas never see. Of the *corn* produced in Chiapas, more than half goes to the domestic market. Chiapas is one of the largest corn producers in the country. *Sorghum* grown in Chiapas goes to Tabasco. Ninety percent of the *tamarind* goes to Mexico City and other states. Two-thirds of the *avocados* and all of the *mameys* are sold outside of the state. Sixty-nine percent of the *cacao* goes to the national market, and 31 percent is exported to the US, Holland, Japan and Italy. The majority of the *bananas* produced are exported.

Yet despite these resources and profits made from them, over 70 percent of the population (approximately 2,200,000 indigenous and mestizo peasants) still live below the poverty line, compared to 6 percent nationwide average. The lack of basic services for population places Chiapas "on top" also within the group of poverty-stricken Third World countries. In spite of the state's energy resources, between 70 and 80 percent of the houses in the villages and towns of eastern Chiapas have no access to electricity or gas, 62 percent have no clean drinking water, more than 85 percent no drainage, but over 80 percent *have* mud floors. Sadly...

Chiapas also has the lowest level of health services in whole Mexico. 1.5 million people have no medical services at their disposal. There are 0.2 clinics for every 1,000 inhabitant, one-fifth of the national average. There are 0.3 hospital beds for every 1,000 Chiapaneco, one-third the amount in the rest of Mexico. There is one operating room per 100,000 inhabitants, one half of the amount in the rest of the Mexico. There are 0.5 doctors and 0.4 nurses per 1,000 people, one half of the national average. Infant mortality rate in the rain forest is over 10 percent. Fifty-four percent of the Chiapas population suffers from malnutrition, and in the highlands and forest this percentage increases to 80 percent. These statistics only confirm the fact that the major cause of death in the Indian villages of Chiapas are poverty-related, easily curable diseases, which account for an estimated 15,000 Indian deaths each year.

One of Mexico's richest states can also be "praised" for its other achievements - maybe for the highest unemployment rate (50 percent) in the whole region, maybe for the lowest salaries paid to rural workers (where 6 out of 10 employed work in agriculture), or maybe for overall negation of Chiapanecos not only in their condition as Mexican citizens, but even in their condition as human beings? I think you get it by now... In the present neo-colonial period, Indians (for most part) are still viewed as they were 500 years ago. As they were viewed in the time of Columbus and Pizzaro. Not only as children of diminished intellectual capacity, but also as ignorant, lazy, drunken, inferior beings...

Mexican government found excellent solution for all the problems of indigenous people in Chiapas listed above. In San Cristóbal de las Casas, the city where the Zapatista rebellion started, government built eleven million dollars worth theater and opera house. With 1,000 seats and sunken pit for a 100 members of symphonic orchestra, the theater was built to serve a city and several surrounding Indian towns that together had fewer than 100,000 residents, and most of them couldn't even afford the pair of shoes required to enter it. The government also remodeled city's old theater at a cost of more than one million dollars. So San Cristóbal can be nominated for cultural center of the world, with more theater seats per capita than Paris, New York, ..., you-name-it...

The Indians in Chiapas are certainly not the only people in the world to be humiliated and oppressed. In every age and every place, we have divided humanity into irreconcilable categories, rich and poor, masters and slaves, superior and inferior, true believers and heathens. But we should bear in mind that "we" are those who are responsible for their human progress - for inventing things otherwise not found in their nature - cruelty, torture, contempt and exploitation. We should bear in mind that issue fought in Chiapas is just another episode in terrible tragedy that began in 1492 with arrival of the conquistadors. For 500 years the indigenous people in Chiapas have been passed from pillar to post - from soldiers who hunted and then killed them, to the masters who exploited them and to the Catholic church which took away their gods but could not crush their spirit. Despite centuries of slaughter and oppression, these people still found courage to put an end to the reign of evil inflicted upon them. They found out that they no longer have to chose between two evils (evils of two lessers), but that there is another road, road less traveled by, and if they choose it, it will make all the difference. In First Declaration from the Lacandon Jungle, the rebels of Chiapas addressed the people of Mexico and rest of the world:

> "We are a product of 500 years of struggle: first against slavery, then during the War of Independence against Spain led by insurgents, then to avoid being absorbed by North American imperialism, then to promulgate our constitution and expel the French empire from our soil, and later the dictatorship of Porfirio Diaz denied us the just application of the Reform laws and the people rebelled and leaders like Villa and Zapata emerged, poor men just like us. We have been denied the most elemental preparation so they can use us as cannon fodder and pillage the wealth of our country. They don't care that we have nothing, absolutely nothing, not even a roof over our heads, no land, no work, no health care, no food nor education. Nor are we able to freely and democratically elect our political representatives, nor is there independence from foreigners, nor is there peace nor justice for ourselves and our children.

But today, we say ENOUGH IS ENOUGH!

We are the inheritors of the true builders of our nation. The dispossessed, we are millions and we thereby call upon our brothers and sisters to join this struggle as the only path, so that we will not die of hunger..."

What was driving Columbus? What drove major colonial powers to violently subjugate most of Africa, Asia and America? What drove the slave trade? What drove the "civilizers" of America to exterminate the Native Americans? What is driving today's conquerors - multinational-corporations, whose swords and fire are replaced with policies of International Monetary Fund (IMF), World Bank, World Trade Organization (WTO), Organization for Economic Cooperation and Development (OECD), and those of the President of the United States? It was and still is, only power and money, which are very seldom separated, because either money buys power, or power seizes wealth. The system of global inequality thus began five centuries ago, when ships mounted with cannons left Europe (the Canary Islands), and headed to forcibly integrate other parts of the planet into the first really global economic system - system obsessed with money.

Today's *conquistadores*, corporate managers, generally measure progress by indicators of their own financial wealth, such as rising stock prices and indicators of the total output of goods and services available to those who have money to pay. With few exceptions of occasional cyclical setbacks in some parts of the world (Latin America) and declining per capita incomes in the poorest African countries, these indicators generally perform well, confirming *élite's* premise that their program is enriching the world. In contrast, ordinary citizens measure progress by indicators of their well being, with particular concern for the lives of those most in need. As Robert Kennedy once pointed out:

"Gross National Product measures neither the health of our children, the quality of their education, nor the joy of their play. It measures neither the beauty of our poetry, nor the strength of our marriages. It is indifferent to the decency of our factories and the safety of our streets alike. It measures neither our wisdom nor our learning, neither our wit nor our courage, neither our compassion nor our devotion to our country. It measures everything in short, except that which makes life worth living. It can tell us everything about our country, except those things that make us proud to be part of it."

These "people's" indicators are deteriorating at a frightening pace, suggesting that in terms of what really matters, things are not so bright after all. In fact, world is rapidly growing poorer. Economic globalization creates wealth, but only for the elite who benefits from the surge of consolidations, mergers, global scale technology and financial activity (gambling in currency speculation) in this "casino econo-my". The rising tide of free trade and globalization is supposed to "lift all boats", and finally end poverty. But in the half century since this big tide began, the world has more poverty than ever before, and the situation is getting even worse. UNICEF estimates that every hour (!), 1000 children die from easily preventable disease, and almost twice as many women die or suffer from serious disability in pregnancy or childbirth for lack of simple remedies and care. In Final Report to the UN Commission on Human Rights, Special Rapporteur Leandro Despouy cites the World Health Organization's characterization of extreme poverty as the world's most ruthless killer and the greatest cause of suffering on earth: *"No other disease compares to the devastation of hunger which had caused more deaths in the past two years than were killed in the two World Wars together."* To make the end to this tragedy, only 10 percent of U.S. military spending would be enough...

Similarly, the UN Food and Agriculture Organization (FAO) reports that the number of chronically hungry people in the world, declined steadily during the 1970s and 1980s, but has been increasing steadily since the early 1990s. In a world which a few enjoy unimaginable wealth, two hundred million children under age of five are underweight because of a lack of food. Some fourteen million children die each year from hunger-related disease. A hundred million children are living or working in the streets. Three hundred thousand children were conscripted as sol-diers during the 1990s, and six million were injured in armed conflicts. Just imag-ine that eight hundred million people go to bed hungry each night! And keep in mind that while so many people all over the world struggle just to survive, Alex Rodriguez of the Texas Rangers baseball team has a 10-year contract for $252 mil-lion. His contribution to the human race is hitting a ball with a stick...

But this human tragedy is not confined to poor countries only. Even in a coun-try as wealthy as the United States, about 10 percent of U.S. households, account-ing for 31 million people, do not have access to enough food to meet their basic needs, so they experience outright hunger. On other hand, the richest 5 percent of the U.S. population owns 81.9 percent of corporate stock and controls 57.4 percent of the net worth of all people in the United States. The maxim that "the rich get richer and the poor get poorer", is thus not just a cliché, but also a fact. A fact, which makes real democracy - equal access to power, obviously impossible.

To put the hint from above in a different way, it means that by the time you fin-ish reading this page 100 people will have died from easily preventable and hunger-related disease. Half of them will be children aged under five... So much for the ris-ing tide that lifts all boats... Don't be fooled! It lifts only yachts...

After visiting Chiapas and meeting Subcomandante Marcos, Portuguese novelist and Nobel Prize winner José Saramago wrote: *"The issue that is being fought out in the mountains in Chiapas extends beyond frontiers of Mexico. It touches the hearts of all those who have not abandoned their simple demand for equal justice for all."* Mainly because, at one level, the particular history in Chiapas illustrates how remorseless and pervasive was the process of globalization, and on the other hand, the same history exposes in the harshest light the actual consequences of the same process nowadays. Within this conquest, which is today masked in term "structural adjustment", indigenous people did and do not have time to engage from within their cultural identity in a dialogue with a (Western) world outside. They lost and are still losing not only their identity, but also their right to have an identity.

There is also a lesson that we all should learn from this... But which? Perhaps that democracy is not our government, not our constitution, not our legal structures. They are too many times its worst enemies. That we should strive towards small acts of resistance to authority, which, if persisted in, may lead to large social movements. That ordinary people, just like you and me, are capable of extraordinary acts of courage. That those in power who confidently say "never!" to possibility of change, may live to be embarrassed by those words... Chiapas, Seattle, D.C., Quebec, Prague, Genoa, ... It's up to you to join this struggle for just and peaceful world. To join the struggle for bringing democracy alive!

3. BEFORE THE DAWN

There were many who argued that the fall of Berlin Wall and collapse of Soviet Block would mark the beginning of a new era, in which a full blow of capitalism allowed freely to roam across the globe, would certainly mark "the end of history". Ten years later, we can claim with certainty that they were wrong. In the first place, that guy called Francis Fukuyama, although he succeeded to sell quite a lot of his incorrect "Bibles" of neoliberalism, and also a lady named Margaret Thatcher, who claimed few years earlier that *"there is no alternative"* to the rise of neoliberalism (a phrase so common that was often appreviated to TINA).

On January 1, 1994, Subcomandante Marcos explained to the surprised tourists on their Christmas holiday in Chiapas: "We apologize for the inconveniences, but this is a revolution." On that morning, the indigenous people of Chiapas came from the deepest reaches of the jungle, from the deepest reaches of abandonment, with rifles high, crying out that Indians and peasants also have the right to live. The Zapatistas chose to start their "war" on the day the North American Free Trade

Agreement (NAFTA) took effect. Dressed in handmade blankets, rough sandals, woolen ski-masks to hide their faces, and many of them armed only with wooden facsimiles of guns, they took over the Plaza de Armas in San Cristóbal de las Casas and five Chiapas towns. They sent out communiqué explaining that NAFTA (the reforms to Article 27 of the Constitution), which enabled buying communal land in Chiapas and on other side banned subsidies to indigenous farm cooperatives, would be a "summary execution" of all indigenous people in Mexico.

Who are they? How many of them are there? Where did they come from? What do they want? These are just few questions that were being raised few days after uprising, as the international press spread the news about situation in Chiapas. The name the Zapatistas suggest that the movement has its roots in the name and work of Mexico's famous Insurgent Emiliano Zapata. It certainly has.

Emiliano Zapata distributed the land of Morelos in 1910, after building an army out of a bunch of peasants. "The land belongs to the farmer", he said to poor and hacienda owners. So he was hated by the rich, and venerated by the poor. For Emiliano Zapata and his comrades, *"Tierra y Libertad!"* (Land and Liberty) - the rallying call of the peasant army - was no rhetoric slogan. By giving the indigenous land and the freedom to decide at the local village level how it should be cultivated, Zapata aimed to preserve the essential features of the indigenous agrarian tradition. On April 10, 1919, Emiliano Zapata rode into the hacienda at the end of the Cuautla Valley in Morelos State, where he had fought the military to a standstill for nearly 10 years. He had come to pick up a load of ammunition and guns promised to him by an alleged turncoat federal officer Jesús Guajardo. When Zapata rode through the archway of the hacienda, Guajardo's troops opened fire, cutting one of the greatest revolutionary leaders down. Today's Zapatista rebellion is rising exactly from these roots of Mexico's past. Their goals are firmly rooted in the lost democratic agrarian ideal for which Emiliano Zapata died, and which was appropriated and betrayed after his death by the Institutional Revolutionary Party (PRI).

But the real birth of "neo-Zapata" movement meant savage repression of student protests on the eve of the Olympic Games in 1968, when more than 500 students were killed during a public meeting at Three Cultures Square, Tlatelolco in Mexico City. After "Olympic massacre", cities were not safe anymore for any Left intellectual or activist. Many of them fled abroad and many in distant parts of rural Mexico. In 1970s one of those groups, the Fuerzas de Liberación Nacional (FLN), went to Mexico's Southeast State of Chiapas. Their leaders were university graduates, Marxist revolutionaries, who in the early 1970s had tried to create a guerilla foco within the Lacandon jungle. In 1974, the Mexican Army attacked and almost completely destroyed their force. There are speculations that one of the guerillas who survived, Fernando Yañez (the brother of the movement's founder), took refuge in the north of Mexico for few years and then returned to Chiapas, using code name Germán. He was accompanied by a dozen of others, among them a second-year medical student, who had been captured in a raid on another FLN camp, but after spending a few months in jail, she had been granted a presidential amnesty. In Chiapas, she took the code name Elisa - presumably in honor of the killed guerilla from the Ocosingo camp. Among them there was also a student of philosophy born in Tampico, probably in 1957.

In the early 1980s, the group revived their organization and began recruiting local Indians. They became known as the EZLN, the Zapatista Army of National Liberation. Formally established in November 1983, the Zapatista Army of National Liberation had about 100 members five years later, and was almost unknown elsewhere in the country. After the electoral fraud of 1988 (on July 6, presidential election opposition candidate Cárdenas is ahead in polling when vote-counting computers suddenly crash and three days later PRI candidate Carlos Salinas is declared winner), repeated in the 1989 state elections, the EZLN's membership grew over the course of the next year to some 1,300 people. In one of his interviews Subcomandante Marcos states:

> "We came to the forest like a classic revolutionary elite in search of that subject - the proletariat in the classic Marxist-Leninist sense. But that initial approach was not adequate to deal with the reality of the indigenous communities. They have a different substratum, a complex prehistory of uprisings and resistances. So we modified our approach 'interactively'. There is 'before' and 'after' of the Zapatista movement in relation to 1994. The EZLN was not born from approaches deriving exclusively from the indigenous communities. It was created out of mixture, a Molotov cocktail, out of a culture shock which then went on to produce a new discourse, a mestizo movement that is critical and emancipatory."

These "whites" came to convert the Indians to the revolution, as their ancestors did in the old days to the Gospel, but, in fact, it is the Indians who have converted them to another conception of the world. Those who came from the city, brought with them a sense of individuality, of the nation, and of the wider world; the natives a sense of harmony, of real democracy, and of listening. This crossbreeding of two microcosms has meant the progress for both of them. The new, sui generis conception of a world was born - conception of *a world in which many worlds fit...*

Yet the Zapatista uprising cannot be understood fully without examining its roots in Catholic liberation theology. Before there was an EZLN, there were catechist in Chiapas who had chosen the "preferential option for the poor", the slogan of liberation theology proclaimed at the 1969 Medellin conference, Columbia. The new theology incorporated some aspects of Marxist analysis, the class struggle as an objective fact, capital as the product of alienate labor, and especially the explanation of the underdevelopment of the so-called Third World as a direct product of the development of the so-called First World. That meeting was attended by a conservative young priest Samuel Ruíz, who would become in his time the best-known defender of the Indians since his predecessor in Chiapas, Bartolomé de las Casas, five centuries before. The apostles of liberation theology learned to give organizational energy to the existing Mayan culture of resistance, which continued to flicker in the mountains of Chiapas and throughout Central and Latin America. Instead of imposing their version of Christianity, they realized that Christianity had to respect and adapt to the religious traditions of the indigenous. Despite all disagreements between the Church and the EZLN in the past (Cardenismo versus Zapatismo; evolution versus revolution; "the electoral route" versus "the insurrectional route"), and the fact that the Zapatistas usurped the Church's exiting network of priests and deacons to promote "self-defense brigades", Bishop Ruíz's opinion about the Zapatista rebellion is ten years later slightly different:

> "I disagree with armed struggle, but I understand the causes. The Zapatistas are fighting for the same thing that we do. If I would reason as a theologian, I would talk of a 'just war'. The social situation was unbearable."

At the end of December 1991, the state police dispersed a gathering of Indians in Palenque with the usual violence. These Indians were protesting against the corruption of their municipal presidents, demanding the construction of public works and distribution of land as promised, and expressing their opposition to the reforms to Article 27 of the Constitution. The state government also reformed the Chiapas Penal Code that was then used as the legal basis for the (illegal) police action. Articles 129 and 135 of the new Penal Code stated that participation in unarmed collective protest constituted a threat to public order punishable by two to four years in prison.

On October 12, to commemorate 500 years of Indian resistance in America, thousands of Indians coming from all the towns in the surrounding region, occupied the city of San Cristóbal in an orderly demonstration. Thousands of Indians, who later joined the ranks of the EZLN, were in large part the very same group that had demonstrated on that day. Marcos explains:

> "I don't know, we don't want to know what's happening in the rest of the world, we are dying and you got to ask the people. Don't you all say that you must do what the people say? Well... yes. Well then, let's go ask them. And they sent me to ask around in the towns.

Yeah, I went to most of the pueblos to explain things. I told them, 'Here is the situation like this: it's a situation of misery and all that; this is the national situation, and that's the international situation. Everything is lined up against us. What are we gonna do?'

They kept on discussing for days, for many days, until they took a vote and drew up the results that said, 'So and so many children, so and so many men, so and so many women, so and so many say yes to war, and so and so many still say no.' And the result, by several tens of thousand, was that the war would have to start, in October of 1992, with the quincentenary."

Thus October 12, 1992, was the last call for peaceful, civil struggle. After that, there were more and more meetings in the settlements, and in a recount done in November 1992, the decision to launch rebellion was ratified. In January 1993 the Clandestine Revolutionary Indigenous Committee (CCRI) was formed "to formalize the real power they had in the communities and the no less real subordination of the EZLN to the CCRI." The CCRI, whose members had the title of comandante, then decided to wage a war and put Marcos in charge of military command.

In May 1993, there was an armed confrontation with the federal army at an EZLN training camp in the pueblo of Corralchén. Although the national press published the news, the government said it was unimportant and denied that there was any revolutionary activity. An image of prosperity and internal peace had to be maintained in order not to awaken worries before Mexico's entrance into NAFTA on January 1, 1994. Therefore, the grand spectacle of the next New Year's Eve...

4. WAGING WAR

After centuries of tyranny, tradition of Indian autonomy resistance was still alive in Chiapas. The natives had learned to survive under many forms of oppression, but in early 1990s their world became more threatened than ever. The preparations for NAFTA included cancellation of Article 27 of Mexico's constitution, the cornerstone of Zapata's revolution of 1910-1919. Under the (historic) Article 27, Indian communal landholdings were protected from sale or privatization. But under NAFTA this guarantee was defined as a barrier to investment. With the removal of Article 27, Indian farmers would be threatened with loss of their remaining lands, and also flooded with cheap imports (substitutes) from the US. Thus, the Zapatistas labeled NAFTA as "a death sentence" to Indian communities all over Mexico.

After the Zapatistas started rebellion against a situation that they need not, could not, and ought not to endure, the government responded to the Zapatista offensive with violence. The war lasted 12 days, the army going so far as to drop bombs; afterward, they razed the land to get rid of any supplies with which civilians might support the Zapatistas. The ten years between 1994 and 2004 have brought highs and lows to the Zapatista movement. Technically, the cease-fire has been held in Chiapas to this day, in which the Zapatistas have not fired a single shot. In February 1996, the government and the Zapatistas signed the San Andres Accords, allowing indigenous communities to control their form of governance, maintain justice systems in accordance with indigenous law, and to provide education in native languages. It gave indigenous people at least part of what they were fighting for - autonomy. But the Mexican government under President Zedillo refused to implement what it had signed. Instead, Zedillo chose to pursue a strategy of "low-intensity war" - a strategy of civilian-targeted warfare. The Zapatistas cut off talks with the government in November 1996, but held steady and organized their communities autonomously. They withstood the militarization. In 2001, the Zapatista caravan rode from Chiapas to the heart of Mexico City, and eventually spoke in front of the Mexican Congress. Hope for the implementation of the Accords had never been greater. Although newly elected President Vincente Fox declared that he can resolve "the Chiapas problem" in 15 minutes, things are still deadlocked.

To sum up, everything yet nothing had changed... The Mexican Senate and Congress overlooked the original bill, and passed one that denied the core guarantees agreed upon in the San Andres Accords - autonomy and democracy for indigenous communities. The National Indigenous Congress and the Zapatistas immediately rejected the bill, claiming that it represents a betrayal of the democratic will of the Mexican people by the Congress. As of time of this writing, people throughout the world are still fighting for the implementation of the San Andres Accords, as a first step toward justice in Chiapas.

First counter-offensive by the government troops (in January 1994) stopped demonstration by students, professors, housewives, workers, ordinary people all over the world, demanding the end to the army's genocidal attacks against the Zapatista Indians. Responding to public pressure, president Salinas even declared he would pardon the rebels. Marcos replied president Salinas with his famous communiqué:

> "Why should we ask for pardon? What are they to pardon us for? For not dying in hunger? For not being quiet about our misery? For not humbly accepting the gigantic historic burden of contempt and abandonment? For having taken up arms when all other ways were closed to us?
> For ignoring the Penal Code of Chiapas, the most absurd and repressive penal code in living memory? For having demonstrated to the rest of the country and to the whole world that human dignity is alive and can be found in its poorest inhabitants?

For having prepared ourselves well and conscientiously before we began? For carrying guns into battle instead of bows and arrows? For having previously learned how to fight? For all of us being Mexicans? For most of us being Indians? For calling on Mexicans to fight in every way possible to defend what is theirs? For fighting for freedom, democracy, and justice? For not following the patterns of previous guerilla groups? For not giving up? For not selling out? For not betraying each other?

Who should ask for pardon, and who is to grant it? ... Those who filled their pockets and their souls with declarations and promises? The dead, our dead, so mortally dead of a 'natural' death - that is, of measles, whooping cough, dengue, cholera, typhoid, mononucleosis, tetanus, pneumonia, malaria, and other gastrointestinal and pulmonary delights? ... Those who treat us like foreigners in our own land and ask us for our papers and our obedience to a law of whose existence and justice we know nothing? Those who torture us, put us in jail, murder us, or made us disappear for the serious 'infraction' of wanting a piece of land, not a big one, just a piece of land on which we could produce something to fill our stomachs?

Who should ask pardon, and who is to grant it?"

At that time the Zapatistas realized that they are only a symptom, a fragment of a movement much larger than they are, a movement that stretches overseas, although origins of the Zapatismo lie in specific local conditions. In short ten years the Zapatista movement has generated movements for social change all across the world. At one level, it has coalesced around a defense of the oppressed - the exemplary victims of neoliberalism and corporate greed. That is their symbolic power as representatives of a new politics, who are fighting for something that extends the mountains of Chiapas, also the frontiers of Mexico. Marcos explains:

"We see ourselves as a group that posed a series of demands and was lucky because those demands happened to coincide with and mirror the demands arising elsewhere in the country and in other parts of the world. The merit of the EZLN is that it has succeeded in finding the wavelength to produce this set of reverberations. The slogan '¡Ya Basta!' found a sympathetic echo in other places. We were lucky that we were able to tune in and communicate with those groups, and also because those groups felt themselves involved in and strengthened by what we were saying.

...The Zapatista indigenous movement is a symbol of resistance to being sacrificed in a world that is becoming standardized. In this world other differences are taken on board and so cease to be differences, or they are eliminated. That's why the indigenous movement has won sympathy of sectors that are seemingly very different, such as young people, anarchists, immigrants, the displaced people of our world..."

On the other hand, the reason for their popularity should be sought in new technologies, particularly the Internet. What began as a violent insurgency in an isolated region, mutated into a nonviolent though no less disruptive "social net-war" that engaged the attention of activists from far and wide. With 50,000 government troops still deployed in the state, the Zapatistas were forced to change a set of rules for the game - forced to change their strategy. Over the past ten years the Zapatistas became masters of the art of never being where it is expected. While wearing traditional Indian dress and presenting themselves to the world through multiple languages of indigenous Mexico, the Zapatistas have used the Internet as their "weapon", with "bullets" taking the form of faxes and e-mails and bombs in the shape of communiqués and letters.

But there is one other fact that makes the Zapatista movement so attractive. Yes, it is certainly the enigmatic *man with the mask*…

5. BENEATH THE MASK

The mystery surrounding the name and face of Subcomandante Insurgente Marcos, the spokesperson of the EZLN, has made him a living legend. Yet the main reason should rather be sought beneath the mask. Inside of this master of *the society of the spectacle*…

Marcos had come forth from the jungle as if from a grand historical obscurity, as if from a revolt founded on insult, propelled by a thirst and hunger for justice that really exists in Chiapas. As a sudden myth, he invaded television screens, the front pages of newspapers and magazines, the Internet, … Aside from the mask and pseudonym (many suggest that the name "Marcos" is made up of the initials of the towns in Chiapas that the Zapatistas took on January 1: Margaritas, Altamirano, La Realidad, Chanal, Ocosingo, and San Cristóbal), Marcos' corporeal decoration is a constellation of symbolic objects - the cartridge belts worn in an X (like that of Emiliano Zapata), the lit pipe as a distinctive amulet of an intellectual, the handkerchief tied about his neck, the barrel of shotgun at his shoulder, indicating that he is serious about whole thing, and some new age technology attached to his belt, signaling that the media are his battlefield. He knows that with 50,000 government soldiers deployed in the state, their (only) lethal weapon is their word. *"Nuestras fuerzas, nuestra palabra!"*

In July 1994, he sent out a facetious communiqué in which he both mocked journalist, and revealed his knowledge of their trade - *"Everything You Wanted to Know About El Sup but Were Afraid to Ask"*. It provides journalists with a format and multiple choices for their reports on Marcos.

"At last we were at (a valley/ a forest/ a clearing/ a bar/ a Metro station/ a pressroom). There we found (El Sup/ a transgressor of the law/ a ski mask with a pronounced nose/ a professional of violence). His eyes are (black/ coffee/ green/ blue/ red/ honey-colored/ oatmeal-colored/ yogurt-colored/ granola-colored). He lit his pipe while he sat on a (rocking chair/ swivel chair/ throne)..."

Marcos understands the power of the word and the image better than most of the people. He uses allegories and anecdotes, old saws and folk tales to convey his message. Marcos tells stories everybody can understand. He talks to those around him - the children, the men and women who followed him to the mountains to become Zapatistas, the peasants, philosopher-beetle Durito, Old Antonio, ... His writings reflects their thoughts thus helping the poorest and most downtrodden to be heard. This is his revolution! Thus disproving Hannah Arendt's claim that *"under conditions of tyranny it is far easier to act than to think"*.

When Marcos went to the Chiapas jungle and joined a group of armed rebels in August 1983, he carried a dozen books in his backpack which were one by one left behind, as the 27-year-old city kid learned the first rule of life as "guerilla": *"One kilo weights two after an hour. After two hours, it weights four and you just want to dump the whole f-king lot."* Marcos' skill in bringing books to life around the campfire, eventually led to a change of heart among his companions. *"Everytime I left book behind, someone would offer to carry it for me. 'A story is going to come out of that', they would say."* Marcos was soon in demand as a rent-a-scribe, writing letters for his lovesick compañeros.

His enigmatic identity and his poetic communiqués began to obsess people, making him a superstar - he was better known than any politician. He commanded more attention than any of the soap operas on Mexican TV, the opiate of the Mexican masses. People began asking who Marcos really is, or better, who he was? Honestly, for me is sufficient a fact that he is El Sup. Although he conceals his face with a ski mask, an essential part of his charisma, he shows himself through his letters, his famous communiqués, and thus reveals much more than his mask hides. For those, who are not satisfied with this, we can add the story of a Rafael Guillén.

The Rafael Sebastián Guillén Vincente, born in 1957, is a native of Tampico, Tamaulipas, the son of a wealthy part-time poet and full-time furniture salesman. Rafael and his four brothers attended Jesuit school, and later won a scholarship at the Universidad Autónoma Metropolitana (UNAM), where he took his doctorate in the early 1980s with a thesis championing the thought of Louis Althusser, a French structuralist. Guillén thesis, written at the university, bears an uncanny resemblance to the mocking tone and colorful epithets of the Subcomandante's communiqués. In his thesis, which was ostensibly about Althusser and really more about himself, Guillén wrote:

"One thing is certain: the philosopher is 'different'; he belongs to a strange lineage of 'sensibilities that keep themselves at a prudent distance from the trite'; he can reflect with a brilliant phrase that will eventually pass into posterity on the death of an ant squashed as it tries to cross a busy street at 8 p.m. ... His hair is disorderly and his beard unkempt, his gaze is continually ecstatic, as in an orgasm not yet achieved; cigarettes and coffee are part of his persona."

Rafael Guillén's last known place of employment was as a professor of communication philosophy at UNAM's Xochimilco campus in the far south of the capital. Before he and his comrades at his department left school, they did a wonderful mural for the auditorium, which is still there today. There are some other clues as well: most reporters who have interviewed Marcos, have noticed how Marcos talks like one of Guillén's brothers - Alfonso Guillén, a university professor in Baja California Sur. Last but not least, before the army incursion, the "capital" of the Zapatistas' *territorio liberado* was an impressively large performance space built in a clearing in the jungle, and presided over by an amphitheater, whose benches covered the entire face of a steep triangular hill, and whose rostrum was fronted with paintings. Needless to say, they recalled the mural at the university...

So the mask... The object which has transformed Rafael Sebastián Guillén into the myth, the living hero. The masks signify many things. When Marcos is asked about the EZLN masks, he replies with a mixture of humor and philosophy, that handsome ones like himself have to be protected. Moment later, he takes the statement back, and explains that one thing about masks is to be anonymous, to avoid cult of personality. And finally, "the black woolen ski mask", is in fact a symbol and a message. Everyone, no matter how degraded, how (il)literate, whatever their physical physique, can feel that it is enough to have dignity and put on a mask. Marcos tells:

"Marcos is gay in San Francisco, black in South Africa, an Asian in Europe, a Chicano in San Ysidro, an anarchist in Spain, a Palestinian in Israel, a Mayan Indian in the streets of San Cristóbal, a Jew in Germany, a Gypsy in Poland, a Mohawk in Quebec, a pacifist in Bosnia, a housewife alone on a Saturday night, a single woman on the Metro at 10 p.m., a peasant without land, a gang member in the slums, an unemployed worker, an unhappy student, a Zapatista in the mountains. Marcos is all the exploited, marginalize, and oppressed, resisting and saying, '¡Ya Basta!'"

Marcos is certainly a "guerilla" with a difference. He criticizes the Cuban and Central American revolutionaries, and chooses Martin Luther King, Gandhi and Mandela as figures who better represent what they want to achieve. His best book on political theory is Don Quixote, followed by Hamlet and Macbeth. *"They are much better than any column of political analysis,"* he explains.

His popularity (he even got an offer for *"ad"* by Italian clothing company Benetton, nevertheless he rejected it) made him more and more dangerous for the political system. Therefore, in 1995, the Zedillo administration tried to unmask Marcos and strip him of his power and mystique with the revelation of his true identity. And also with the warrant for his arrest... The plan to disillusion Marcos' admirers with the revelation that the ski masked revolutionary is a young academic full of Marxist dogma, worked for 72 hours. Three days later, Mexico newspaper received the first communiqué from Marcos since he and his campesino followers retreated from their villages into the hills. It had three of his trademark postscripts:

> **P.S.** That rapidly applauds this new 'success' of the government police: I heard they've found another 'Marcos', and that he's from Tampico. That doesn't sound bad, the port is nice. I remember when I used to work as a bouncer in a brothel in Ciudad Madero near Tampico, in the days when a corrupt oilworkers'-union leader used to do the same thing to the regional economy that Salinas did with stock market; inject money into it to hide poverty...
>
> **P.S.** That despite the circumstances does not abandon its narcissism: So... Is the new Subcomandante Marcos good-looking? Because lately they've been assigning me really ugly ones and my feminine correspondence gets ruined.
>
> **P.S.** That counts time and ammunition: I have 300 bullets, so try to bring 299 soldiers and police to get me. (Legend has it that I don't miss a shot, would you like to find out if it's true?)...
>
> Vale again. Salud, and can it be that there will be a little spot for me in her heart? The Sup, rearranging his ski mask with macabre flirtatiousness.
>
> *The myth was born once again...*

6. Marcos on Neoliberalism

Marcos' philosopher-beetle Durito once explained: *"Neoliberalism is not in crisis, neoliberalism is a crisis!"* The Zapatista rebellion is in its core exactly a spontaneous outburst against neoliberalism. Why? The indigenous population in Chiapas was a population who had struggled to function within the neoliberal system of capital, to which these people are superfluous. Firstly, they have not any purchase power to buy things. Secondly, they settle the land, rich in its natural resources, so wanted by multinational corporations. And thirdly, they are indigenous and thus do not fit in one-dimensional nature of the present (which is direct result of the cultural offensive conducted by neoliberalism during the past 15 years).

According to Marcos, nowadays the planet is a battlefield of the Fourth World War (the Third was so-called Cold War). The aim of the war is a conquest of the entire world through the market. Today's arms are financial, though millions of people are maimed or killed every moment. Those waging the war are aiming to convert whole planet into one big business company, with World Bank, IMF, WTO, OECD, and the President of the United States as the *board of directors*. Thanks to computers and the technological revolution, the financial markets operating from their office and answerable to nobody but themselves, have been imposing their laws and worldview on the planet as whole. Globalization is merely the totalitarian extension of the logic of the financial markets to all aspects of life. Meanwhile, nine-tenths of world's population live with "the jagged pieces that do not fit". Marcos writes:

> "What we have here today is a puzzle. When we attempt to put this pieces together in order to arrive at an understanding of today's world, we find that a lot of the pieces are missing. Still, we can make a start with seven of them, in the hope that this conflict won't end with the destruction of humanity. Seven pieces to draw, color in, cut out, and put together with others, in order to try to solve this global puzzle."

1. The first piece has the shape of a dollar sign and is green. This piece consists of the new concentration of global wealth in fewer and fewer hands, and the unprecedented extension of hopeless poverty.
2. The second piece is triangular (depicts the pyramid of worldwide exploitation), and consist of a lie. The new (world) order claims to rationalize and modernize production and human endeavor. In reality, it is a return to the barbarism of the beginnings of the industrial revolution with important difference, that the barbarism is unchecked by any opposing ethical consideration or principle.
3. The third piece is round like a vicious circle, and consists of enforced migration. Those who have nothing are forced to emigrate to survive. Yet the new order works according to the market principle, that anybody who doesn't produce and doesn't consume and has no money to put into a bank, is redundant. So the emigrants, the jobless, the landless, the homeless, are treated as the waste that should be eliminated.
4. The fourth piece is rectangular like a mirror, and consists of an ongoing exchange between the commercial banks and the world's modern soldiers - financial globalization is enforcing globalization of a crime.
5. The fifth piece is more or less like a pentagon, and consists of physical repression. The nation-states under the new order have lost their economic independence, their political initiative, and their sovereignty. Nowadays, the nation states are just departments of the

corporation known as the world, and politicians only local managers. The new task of nation-states is to manage what is allowed to them, to protect the interests of the market and to control and police the redundant.

6. The sixth piece is in the shape of a scribble, and consists of breakages. On the one hand, the new order does away with frontiers and distances by telecommunication of exchanges, and deals by obligatory free-trade zones, and by imposing everywhere law of the market.

7. The seventh piece has the shape of a pocket, and consists of all the various pockets of resistance against the new order that are developing around the world. The many pockets do not have a common political program *per se*. How could they, existing as they do in the broken puzzle, but exactly their heterogeneity may be a promise.

As you can see, these seven pieces will never fit together to make any sense, even if you try as hard as you can. This lack of sense, this absurdity, is endemic to the new order. Marcos warns, that the war which neoliberalism is conducting against humanity, is a planetary war and the worst and most cruel war ever seen. Therefore, it is necessary to fight neoliberalism back. Only then, we will be able to build a new world, a world capable of containing many worlds, capable of containing all worlds!

Yet, there the question may arise, what is an alternative to neoliberalism and corporate greed? One of plausible answers is certainly - Zapatismo - a new kind of politics. Zapatismo does not seek power, only justice; Zapatismo does not acknowledge leaders, but it is democratic to the extreme; Zapatismo is not a party, but a living and changing (world) movement, which coalesce around the defense of the oppressed, the victims of neoliberalism and corporate greed. As Marcos writes:

> "Zapatismo is not an ideology, it is not a bought and paid for doctrine. It is... an intuition. Something so open and flexible that it really occurs in all places. Zapatismo poses the question, 'What is that has excluded me?', 'What is that has isolated me?'... In each place the response is different. Zapatismo simply states that question and stipulates that the response is plural, that the response is inclusive...
> We do not want a revolution imposed from the top: It always turns against itself. We are not a vanguard. We are not here to close things down but to start renewing our efforts. Our aim is to give voice to civil society, everywhere, under all its forms, in all its forms. We are neither the only ones nor the best ones. We do not have the truth or the answer to everything. Provided we raise good questions, that is enough for us..."

We could say that Zapatismo is a non-falsifying mirror not only to Mexico, but also for the rest of the world, helping us understand and denounce the trick that "McMirror" offers us: a happy ending and a globalization that is made to suit the globalizers. Zapatismo is a catalyst, an instigator, and a creator of possibilities. It provides a platform for the widest possible convergence of democratic forces, ageless, classless, all contributing to a vast, inchoate movement that would return power to the people. Zapatismo aspires towards a democratic dialogue, not a violent rebellion. This makes Zapatismo so threatening to its enemies and so challenging and attractive to its supporters, although the only thing Zapatismo proposes is to change the world...

7. It's up to You

On the day of "the end of history", the world woke up with the rebellion of the damned. They declared war against neoliberalism as manifested in NAFTA and economic globalization *per se*. The Zapatistas demands as expressed in their Lacandon Jungle declarations were work, land, housing, food, health, education, independence, freedom, democracy and peace. They demanded that their rights and dignity as indigenous peoples be respected, and that their cultures and traditions should be taken into consideration. They wanted the discrimination and contempt they have suffered for centuries to stop. They demanded the right to organize and govern themselves autonomously, because they do not want to be subject of the will of powerful Mexicans and foreigners. They want their justice to be administrated by the indigenous people themselves, according to their customs and traditions, without intervention from illegitimate, corrupt government.

In 2003 the Zapatistas celebrated two important anniversaries: 20th anniversary of the foundation of the Zapatista Army of National Liberation - EZLN and 10th anniversary of their uprising against neoliberalism, both with quiet celebrations that were a sharp contrast to the show of force they displayed in the past. *"Chiapas is at peace, as you can see,"* President Vicente Fox said on the eve of the anniversary. *"The state has taken the lead in electronic government, and we've just opened a majestic new bridge that cuts four hours off the trip to Mexico City."* But not far away, a masked rebel leader, who identified himself only by his first name Isaac, warned at the "20/10" anniversary celebration: *"There could be another January 1, like the one in 1994, if the government doesn't listen to us! Nobody can say when, but it's possible."*

Anniversary celebrations were rather nostalgic occasions, with about 1,000 masked Zapatista rebels and supporters dancing to the vibes of the *marimba* and remembering the old days of struggle. Fireworks lit the night sky, but the verbal pyrotechnics of Subcomandante Marcos were absent. Marcos also didn't issue any of his customary poetry-laden communiqués. But this is no surprise, since earlier that year the EZLN gave full power and sovereignty to autonomous municipalities of Chiapas, which are now "autonomous" from the EZLN itself.

The Zapatistas are inspiring people all over the world for whole 10 years. The Zapatista Meeting Centers or *Aguascalientes*, in particular, as models of communication with national and international civil society (the way they invited and accepted the help of outsiders willing to share genuine solidarity), were examples from which movements all over the world tried to learn. It was therefore a surprise for many when, on August 8, 2003, the Zapatistas announced the "death" of the Aguascalientes, to be followed by a "birth" of something new on August 9 - all of which was to coincide with a big party. Supporters from all over Mexico and the world traveled to the Zapatista rebel municipality of Oventic, in the highlands of Chiapas, to witness the birth of the Caracoles and the Good Government Juntas (*Juntas del buen gobierno*). These five committees represent each of the five regions that the Zapatistas have demarcated within their "territories in rebellion", representing 30 autonomous municipalities. The Good Government Juntas *"will be seated in the 'Caracoles', with one junta for each rebel region, and it will be formed by 1 or 2 delegates from each one of the Autonomous Councils of that region. The following will continue to be the exclusive government functions of the Rebel Zapatista Autonomous Municipalities: the provision of justice; community health; education; housing; land; work; food; commerce; information; culture; and local movement. The Clandestine Revolutionary Indigenous Committee in each region will monitor the operations of the Good Government Juntas in order to prevent acts of corruption, intolerance, injustice and deviation from the Zapatista principle of 'Governing by Obeying.'"*

With the creation of the Caracoles the EZLN has also announced their intention to wield tighter control over what kind of outside support they will accept. In his series of communiqués in July 2003, Marcos wrote that in the past, some outside organizations have decided for themselves what the Zapatista communities need. To illustrate the problem he described a pink, high-heeled shoe (size 6 1/2) that arrived, without its pair, as part of an "aid package", and said the Zapatistas didn't wish to continue to be a dumping ground for broken computers and expired medicines. He wrote of communities that need clean water and get a library instead. Another problem with aid was that the best known Zapatista centers got the most visitors and the most support. With the creation of the Caracoles as the doorways, and overseen by the Committees of Good Government, the Zapatistas hope to manage a more equitable distribution of outside support, and to decide which projects serve the best in the various localities. Donations from the outside aren't allowed any longer to be earmarked to anyone in particular, to a specific community, or to a particular municipality. And only people and organizations registered with a Good Government Junta have been recognized as Zapatistas, preventing swindles from occurring where non-Zapatistas pose as Zapatistas, collecting money and even offering "military training" - which the real Zapatistas do not do and have not done.

"*And so, members of civil society will now know with whom they must reach agreement for projects, peace camps, visits, donations and etc. Human rights defenders will now know to whom they should turn over the denuncias they receive and from whom they should expect a response. The army and the police now know whom to attack (just bearing in mind that we, meaning the EZLN, have already gotten involved there). The media, which say what they're paid to say, now know whom to slander and/or ignore. Honest media now know where they can go in order to request interviews or stories on the communities. The federal government and its 'commissioner' now know what they have to do to not exist. And the Power of Money now knows who else they should fear.*"

This "self government" for indigenous regions was part of the San Andres Accords signed by the EZLN and the Federal Government back in 1996. Immediately after taking office in December of 2000 Fox sent the long delayed accords to the legislature for ratification, but the intended law was changed by members of the PRI and even Fox's own PAN, stripping away many of the indigenous rights reforms included in the original agreement. With the formation of the Good Government Juntas, the Zapatistas have announced that they are going ahead with the letter and spirit of the Indigenous Rights Law, without waiting for permission from what they call the "Bad Government".

The objects of history suddenly became main subjects of social change. Those who have been oppressed are now standing up against the oppressors, waging war against the wealthiest, the strongest. They surely had to bare in mind a moral that Old Antonio tells us in one of his stories:

> "If you cannot have both reason and strength, always choose reason, and leave strength to the enemy. In many battles, it is force that makes it possible to win a victory, but the struggle as whole can only be won by reason. The strong man will never be able to draw reason from his strength, whereas we can always draw strength from our reason..."

Ten years later everything had changed, yet nothing had changed... Technically, the war is still going on in the state of Chiapas. The demands of the indigenous people are still not fulfilled. "*The beast*" is still governing, and "*the greys*" still hope to win. Therefore, "*the rainbow*" is still needed urgently. You could say that things are depressing. True, you could say so, if you are just sitting at home with your hands crossed, still seeing things falling before your eyes, pretending that you are blind, cold, indifferent, although the sights are tearing your soul and make you sick. I know there is a tendency to think that what we see in the present moment, we will continue to see. But don't forget how often in the past centuries people have been astonished by the sudden crumbling of institutions, by extraordinary changes in people's thoughts, by unexpected eruptions of rebellion against tyrannies, by the quick collapse of systems of power that seemed invincible! Therefore always remember: No building is too tall for even the smallest dog to lift its leg on... Considering this, people in Chiapas have already won. Now it's up to you... to follow...

If you find this book a depressing one and its story sad, at least what you can do is to close the book immediately, find your nearest politician, corporate manager, or stockbroker, and then suggest him to do something for people in Chiapas - to raise his ("influential") voice or money... If he is not willing, you can use this book with its few hundred pages to smack him, thus forcing him to do that. One time will probably suffice, but I must admit that they are very headstrong, so you will maybe have to hit him one more time...

Otherwise, you can read the rest of the book and arm yourself with something more lethal - with knowledge, optimism, words... *Nuestras fuerzas, nuestra palabra!* Armed with a new weapon, you will find out that things are not so depressing after all. You will find out that things can change sooner or later - it's up to you and your choice of life - to stay at home and hide or stand up and fight. But remember that you don't have to engage in "grand", heroic actions to participate in this process of change. Small acts, when multiplied by thousands of people, can change the world. And if you do participate, in however small way, you should not expect too much. To live in this present moment as we think all human beings should live, in defiance of all bad around us, is itself already a great victory...

So, you can still join our struggle for bringing democracy alive. And as long as possibility of real democracy is still alive, one basic truth can give you hope: that in "our" democracy every politician, corporate manager, or stockbroker has the same number of votes as you or I - one. And there are more of us than there are of them...

> "...Rise like lions after slumber
> In unvanquishable number!
> Shake your chains to earth, like dew
> Which in sleep had fallen on you -
> Ye are many; they are few!"
> - Percy B. Shelley

TO BE CONTINUED...

Chapter I: 1994-1996 – Spreading the Word

— Subcomandante Marcos

1. THERE WILL BE A STORM

October 8, 1994

To the national magazine Proceso

To the national newspaper La Jornada

To the national newspaper El Financiero

To the local newspaper in San Cristobal de las Casas, Tiempo

Sirs,

I don't know why they say that Mexico has changed, that now nothing is the same, that a new democratic era has begun for the country. I don't know about there, but here everything is the same. The PRI perjures itself and swears (after the disgraceful fraud) that it won fairly. Ranchers and businessmen join in, saying that they "respect the will of the people" - in other words they are saying that they only respect their own will. The Catholic Church is an accomplice (to the fraud). The indigenous peasants know that the PRI didn't win fairly. They aren't going to endure another PRI governor. They know that a traitor to his own blood can't be allowed to govern.

Little by little the Chiapaneco world is beginning to divide. The wind from above assumes its old forms of arrogance and haughtiness. The police and the Federal Army close ranks around money and corruption. The wind from below once again travels the ravines and valleys; it is beginning to blow strongly. There will be a storm...

We are in the same situation that existed in December of 1993; the country is living in euphoria of high economic indicators, political stability, promises of better times for ordinary citizens, and promises of continued stability for powerful citizens. In Chiapas there is a PRI government that is said to have "popular support." The country is calm. Everyone is calm... and then the first hour of January First... Enough already! No?

OK. I wish you health and hope you have a little understanding for what's coming.

From the mountains of Southeastern Mexico,
Insurgent Subcomandante Marcos.
Mexico, October 1994.

P.S. Ana Maria tells me that "the water is rising in the mountain streams." I look worriedly at the greyness that is stretched across the horizon. She adds: "If it doesn't stop raining, those streams are going to run as they have never before." She goes off to check the guards. "As they have never before," I mutter. I light my pipe. The elder

Antonio approaches me and asks for a light for his cigarette. I shelter the lighter's flame with my hands. I can just see, in that brief light, that Antonio is crying. Ana Maria returns. She comes to attention and reports. Then she asks: "The troops are ready. What are we going to do?" I look once again at the greyness that is spreading across the sky and dominating the night. I answer her with a sigh: "We wait. We wait..."

P.S. One of the mysteries of Ezeelen is uncovered. A lively and violent wind, sweet and bitter, blows a paper to the feet of an indigenous peasant. On the paper one can read: "Declaration of Principles of the EZLN"

"A certain dose of tenderness is necessary in order to walk when there is so much against you in order to awaken when you're so exhausted. A certain dose of tenderness is necessary in order to see, in this darkness, a small ray of light in order to make order from shame and obligations. A certain dose of tenderness is necessary in order to get rid of all of the sons of bitches that exist. But sometimes a certain dose of tenderness is not enough and it's necessary to add... a certain dose of bullets."

2. The Long Journey from Despair to Hope

September 22, 1994
For Mr. Ik, Tzeltal prince,
founder of the CCRI-CC of the EZLN, helped in the battles of Ocosingo
Chiapas, in January of 1994
(Wherever he is...)

> "When He arrives we are living, and from the depths of the Castle of the poor, where we had so many just like us, so many accomplices, so many friends, the sail of courage is raised. We must raise it without vacillation. Tomorrow we will know why when we triumph. A long chain of passion was unimprisoned. The ration of injustice and the ration of shame are truly too bitter to bear. Everything is not necessary to make a world. Happiness is necessary and nothing more. To be happy it is only necessary to see clearly and fight. We must not wait even an instant: Let us raise our heads. Let us take the land by force."
> - Paul Eluard

"Mexico: between dreams, nightmares and awakenings"

Chapter 1.

Which speaks of neoliberal chants of 24 mermaids, of reefs of gold, of grounding on sandbars of depression and of other dangers that threaten the pirates on high seas.

To this country one may arrive through the Penthouse or through the basement. To Lower Mexico one arrives on foot and crying... in mud. In 1993 we conversed, close to San Quintin, in the town of Ocosingo, with a Guatemalan who was beginning the long and improbable journey, across Mexican lands, to the American Union. To achieve this he had to risk his money, his health, his life and his dignity. He and his family had to traipse from Chiapas all the way to Northern Baja California, navigating through a nightmare of misery and death. We asked him why he was risking everything to go to the United States, and why he didn't just stay and work in one of the Mexican states that he would be crossing in his journey. He answered, laughing facetiously: "I'd have to be crazy to do that. If Guatemala translates to 'bad toilet', you Mexicans are in a 'worse toilet' then." And he told us the story that was told by those who had made it clear to the northern border of Mexico and had been deported by the Border Patrol: A Mexico quite distant from tourism promotions - murderous police, corrupt government functionaries, panhandlers, prices from North America and salaries from Central America, death squads, population living in poverty, despair. A story we already knew. The nightmare that lives in the basement of this country, the nightmare that brought us to our awakening in January of...

1994: To Penthouse Mexico...

One arrives by plane.

An airport in Mexico City, Monterrey, Guadalajara or Acapulco, is the entrance to an elevator which neither rises nor falls, but rides horizontally across the country of the 24 richest men in the country, the scenes of Mexico of modern times: the government offices where neoliberalism is administered, the business clubs where the national flag becomes more diffused every day, the vacation resorts whose true vocation is to be a mirror of a social class that does not want to see what is below their feet: a long stairway, spiral and labyrinthed, which leads all the way down to the Lower Mexico, Mexico on foot, mud Mexico.

Above the blood and clay that live in the basement of this country, the 24 omnipotent are busy counting $44.1 billion, a gift from the Presidential term of these modern times. Penthouse Mexico simply has no time to look down, it is too busy with complicated macroeconomic calculations, exchange of promises, praises and indexes of inflation, interest rates and the percentage, of foreign investment, import-export concessions, lists of assets and resources, scales where the country and dignity have no weight: the public debt guaranteed, long range, has gone from $3.196 billion in 1970, to $76.257 billion in 1989. The private, non-guaranteed U.S. debt was $2.77 billion in 1970 and was up to $3.999 billion in 1989. In 1989 the short term public debt reached $10.295 billion.

By the beginning of the decade of the 90s Mexico owed $95.642 billion. Each year this country pays off more debt and, however, each year it owes more. The use of International Monetary Fund credits went from $0 in 1970 to $5.091 billion in 1989. The industrial and commercial economic growth takes its toll in the Mexican countryside: in agriculture, in the period of 1965 to 1980, production grew at an average national rate of 3 percent. In the period from 1980 to 1989, only by 1 percent. Meanwhile, in foreign trade, imports speak their complicated language of numbers: grain imports in 1974 were only 2.881 million metric tons, and they reached 7.054 million in 1984. Of the total, in 1965, only 5 percent of imports were foodstuffs; in 1989 the percent of food imports reached 16 percent. On the other hand in the same period, the percentage of importation of machinery and transportation equipment was reduced (50 percent in 1965, 34 percent in 1989).

The ratified exports: of the total, the sale of combustibles and minerals increased from 22 percent in 1965 to 41 percent in 1989. Foreign sales of machinery and transportation equipment increased from 1 percent in 1965 to 24 percent in 1989. The export of products of prime necessity were reduced from 62 percent in 1965 to 14 percent in 1989. (Data: International Bank for Reconstruction and Development The World Bank, July 1991).

Mr. Carlos Salinas de Gortari is, in Penthouse Mexico, The President... but of a stockholders board. These modern times in Mexican neopolitics make public functionaries into something like a species of retail salespeople, and the president of the republic, into the sales manager of a gigantic business: Mexico, Inc. To be a politician in the state party in Mexico, is the best business to be in. A paternal shadow protects the steps of the new generation of Mexican politicians; that of ex-president Miguel Aleman Valdes, "Mr. Amigo". The Neo-elect, Ernesto Zedillo, is repeating the fallacy of the American Dream (poor children who grow up to be rich, that is to say, to be politicians) and the modernistic economic program... which is 48 years old! The smokescreen about the lack of solvency, credit and markets, will again blind the heads of medium to large businesses. The "law of the jungle" from free trade will repeat the dosage: more monopolies, fewer jobs. "To grow", in neoliberal politics means simply "to sell". To practice politics one must practice marketing technology. The "citizen" of Penthouse Mexico will be, sooner or later, named MAN OF THE YEAR by some foreign institution. To achieve this he must follow...

"Instructions to be named Man of the Year"

1. Carefully place a technocratic functionary, a repentant opposer, a businessman for a front, a Union Cowboy, a property holder, a builder, an alchemist in computational arts, a "brilliant" intellectual, a

television, a radio, and an official party. Set this mixture aside in a jar and label it: "Modernity".

2. Take an agricultural worker, a peasant with no land, an unemployed person, an industrial worker, a teacher without a school, a dissatisfied housewife, an applicant for housing and services, a touch of honest press, a student, a homosexual, a member of the opposition to the regime. Divide these up as much as possible. Set them aside in a jar and label them: "Anti-Mexico".

3. Take a native Mexican. Separate the crafts and take a picture of her. Put her crafts and the photo in a jar and set aside, labeling it: "Tradition".

4. Put the native Mexican in another jar, set it aside and label it: "Dispensable". One must not forget to disinfect oneself after this last operation.

5. Well, now open a store and hang a huge sign that says: "Mexico 94-2000 Huge End of the Century Sale".

6. Smile for the camera. Make sure the makeup covers the bags and dark circles under the eyes caused by the nightmare the process has caused.

Note: Always have on hand a policeman, a soldier and an airplane ticket out of the country. These items may be necessary at any time.

Penthouse Mexico has no foreign vocation. In order to have a foreign vocation one must have a nationality and the only country spoken of, with sincerity, on that narrower and narrower top floor, is the country called money. And that country has no patriots, it has only profit and loss indexes. Historical events happen only within the stock markets and the modern heroes up there are only Good Salesmen. For some reason in the other history (the real one) that top floor, far from expanding, is quickly contracting. Every time there are fewer able to stay there. Sometimes with delicacy, other times with brutality, the incapable are obligated to descend... by the stairs. The Penthouse elevator of Mexico, whose door opens to the great international airports, neither rises nor falls. To leave the Penthouse one must descend, going further and further down until one gets to...

To Get to Middle Mexico...
One goes by car.
It is urban and its image is a carbon copy, which repeats itself in various parts of the country, of Mexico City. An image of concrete which can not deny the contradiction of the co-existence among the extremely rich and the extremely poor, Middle Mexico smells bad. Something is rotting there inside at the same time as that the feeling of collectivity is being diluted. Middle Mexico does have a foreign vocation. Something tells it that, to rise to Penthouse Mexico, the road passes through a country that is not this one. In order to 'triumph' in Mexico one must go abroad. It does not necessarily mean to go physically, but to go in history, in goals.

This vocation of exile as a synonym to triumph has nothing to do with the physical crossing of a border. There are those who, even in leaving, stay behind. And there are those who, even in staying, leave.

Only 3 states of the federation have indexes of margina(liza)tion which are VERY LOW: the Federal District (Mexico City), Nuevo Leon and North Baja California; 10 more are within the LOW margination index: Coahuila, Baja California South, Aguascalientes, Chihuahua, Sonora, Jalisco, Colima, Tamaulipas, Estado de Mexico and Morelos; another 4 have a MEDIUM index of margination: Quintana Roo, Sinaloa, Nayarit and Tlaxcala.

Middle Mexico survives in the worst possible way: thinking that it is alive. It has all of the disadvantages of Penthouse Mexico: historical ignorance, cynicism, opportunism and an emptiness that import products can only fill partially or not at all. It has all the disadvantages of Lower Mexico: economic instability, insecurity, bewilderment, sudden loss of hope and, furthermore, misery knocking, on every corner, upon the window of the automobile. Sooner or later, Middle Mexico must get out of the car and get into, if he still has enough left, a taxi, a collective taxi, a subway, a bus terminal, and start the journey down, all the way to...

Lower Mexico...

Where one may arrive almost immediately.

It coinhabits, in permanent conflict, with Middle Mexico.

The 17 Mexican states which are found in the indexes labeled MIDDLE, LOW and VERY LOW margination, have half of their inhabitants living in cramped conditions (with more than 2 people per room) and 50 percent of Mexicans who live in the 'middle' states earn less than 2 minimum wages daily, that is, in poverty (in Tlaxcala three quarters of the population lives in poverty).

Aguascalientes, Chihuahua, Jalisco, Colima, Tamaulipas, Morelos, Quintana Roo, Sinaloa, and Tlaxcala have a third of the population over 15 years old, not having completed primary school, in Nayarit the percentage is higher than 40 percent. Tlaxcala has a third of its population without sewers nor plumbing. Quintana Roo and Sinaloa has a fourth of its inhabitants living on dirt floors. The states of Durango, Queretaro, Guanajuato, Michoacan, Yucatan, Campeche, Tabasco, Zacatecas and San Luis Potosi have HIGH indexes of margination. Nearly half of their population above the age of 15 have not completed primary school, one third have no plumbing nor sewer, nearly two thirds live in crowded conditions and more than 60 percent earn less than two minimum wages per day.

Lower Mexico does not share, it disputes an urban and rural space, but still, it has its own internal divisionary lines, its borders. Estates, haciendas and grand agricultural firms impose their rural space upon Agrarian Reform parcels and peasant communities. Urban colonies, their names and locations, the services that they have, the manner of speaking of their people, the way they dress, their entertainment, education, everything limits and classifies, trying to put in order, to accommodate the chaos that rules in Mexican cities. It is not necessary to state the level of income, social position and political vocation, it is enough to say in what colony of what city one lives. Within one city there are thousands of cities, fighting, surviving, struggling.

Out in the countryside it is the transportation vehicle, the way one dresses and the attention one receives from the bank manager which indicate one's classification. One's position in the countryside of Mexico can be determined by how long it takes a person to be received in the reception areas of the financial or political world. In Lower Mexico the Big House of the Porfirian Hacienda has been replaced by the inner office of the bank, which is how modern times have penetrated rural Mexico.

Lower Mexico has a fighter's vocation, it is brave, it is solidary, it is a clan, it is the "hood", it is the gang, the race, the friend, it is the strike, the march and the meeting, it is taking back one's land, it is blocking highways, it is the "I don't believe you!", it is "I won't take it anymore!", it is "No more!".

Lower Mexico is the master tradesman, mason, plumber, factory worker, driver, employee, the subway-bus-shared cab student, the street cleaner, truck driver and dialectic, the housewife, small businessman, traveling salesman, farmer, mini and micro entrepreneur, miner, colonizer, peasant, tenant farmer, provincial although living in the Capital, peon, longshoreman in port cities, fisherman and sailor, used clothes dealers, butchers, artisans, it is all the etceteras that one finds on any bus, on any corner, in any given corner of any given place of any Mexico... Lower Mexico, that is.

Lower Mexico is the substance of the imprisoned, of the dispossessed, of garnishments, of liens, of layoffs, of evictions, of kidnappings, of torturing, of disappearance, of battle, of death. Lower Mexico has absolutely nothing... but it has not yet realized it. Lower Mexico already has overpopulation problems. Lower Mexico is a millionaire, counting its misery, its despair. Lower Mexico shares both urban and rural space, slips and falls, battles and downfalls.

Lower Mexico is really far down, so far down that it seems that there is no way to go further down, so far down that one can hardly see that little door that leads to...

Basement Mexico...
One arrives on foot, either barefoot, or with rubber soled huaraches.

To arrive one must descend through history and ascend through the indexes of margination. Basement Mexico was first. When Mexico was not yet Mexico, when it was all just beginning, the now Basement Mexico existed, it lived. Basement Mexico is "Indigenous" because Columbus thought, 502 years ago, that the land where he had arrived was India. "Indians" is what the natives of these lands have been called from that time on.

Basement Mexico is: Mazahuan, Amuzgan, Tlapanecan, Nahuatlan, Coran, Huichol, Yaqui, Mayan, Tarahumaran, Mixtec, Zapotecan, Chontal, Seri, Triquis, Kumiain, Cucapan, Paipain, Cochimian, Kiliwan, Tequistlatecan, Pame, Chichimecan, Otomi, Mazatecan, Matlatzincan, Ocuiltecan, Popolocan, Ixcatecan, Chocho-popolocan, Cuicatec, Chatino, Chinantec, Huave, Papagan, Pima, Repehuan, Guarijian, Huastec, Chuj, Jalaltec, Mixe, Zoquean, Totonacan, Kikapuan, Purepechan, Oodham, Tzotzil, Tzeltal, Tojolabal, Chol, Mam. Basement Mexico is indigenous... however, for the rest of the country it does not count, produce, sell or buy, that is, it does not exist...

Review the text of the Free Trade Agreement and you will find that, for this government, the indigenous do not exist. Furthermore, read Addendum 1001.a-1 to the Free Trade Agreement, from the 7th of October, 1992 (yes, just 5 days before the "festivities" of the 500th Anniversary of the "Discovery of America"), and you will find that Salinas' government has "forgotten" to mention, on the list of Federal Government Entities', The National Indigenous Institute.

We have been in the mountains a very long time, perhaps the National Indigenous Institute has been privatized, but it is not surprising that, listed as "government entities" appear such well known organizations as the "Patronage for Aid to Social Reintegration" or "Aid for the Commercialization of the Fishing Industry" and the "Institute for Human Communication Doctor. Andres Bustamante Gurria".

On the other hand, in Canada there is the Department of Indian Affairs and Northern Development. Basement Mexico amasses traditions and misery, it possesses the highest indexes of margination and the lowest in nutrition. Of the 32 states, 6 have VERY HIGH index of margination. The 6 have a HIGH percentage of indigenous population: Puebla, Veracruz, Hidalgo, Guerrero, Oaxaca, Chiapas.

The stratum in The Mexico's is repeated in the municipalities. On a national level there are 2,403 municipalities. Of these 1,153 have a level of margination considered HIGH or VERY HIGH. 1,118 have MEDIUM and LOW levels of marginality and only 132 municipalities have VERY LOW levels of margination. In the states with high indigenous population: Chiapas of 111 has 94 municipalities HIGH and VERY HIGH levels. Guerrero of 75 has 59. Oaxaca of 570 has 431. Puebla of 217 has 141. Queretaro of 18 has 10. San Luis Potosi of 56 has 33. Veracruz of 207 has 130. Yucatan of 106 has 70.

Between mud and blood one lives and dies in Basement Mexico. Hidden but in its foundation, the contempt that Mexico has for this will permit it to organize itself and shake up the entire system. Its charge will be the possibility of freeing itself from it. The line of democracy, liberty and justice for these Mexicans, will be organized and it will explode and shine on...

January of 1994...

When the entire country remembered the existence of the Basement.

Thousands of indigenous armed with truth and fire, with shame and dignity, shook the country awake from its sweet dream of modernity. "That is enough!" their voices scream, enough of dreams, enough of nightmares.

Ever since steel and evangelists dominated these lands, this voice is condemned to resisting a war of extermination that now incorporates all of the intergalactic technological advances. Satellites, communication equipment and infrared rays keep watch on their every move, locate their rebellions, point to, on military maps, places for the seeding of bombs and death. Tens of thousands of olive green masks are preparing a new and prosperous war. With indigenous blood they want to wash their dignity in serving the powerful... to be accomplices in the unjust delivery of poverty and pain.

The indigenous Zapatistas paid for their sins with their blood. What sins? The sin of not being satisfied with handouts, the sin of insisting on their demands for democracy, liberty and justice for all Mexico, the sin of their "everything for everyone, nothing for us".

Those who deny the indigenous Mexican peasant the possibility of understanding the concept of NATION and who obligate him to look to his past (which separates him from the rest of the country) and prohibit him from looking to the future (which unites the Nation and which is the ONLY possibility for survival of the indigenous people) reiterate the division, not of social classes, but (a disguised form of the aforementioned) the division of categories of citizens: The first (governing class), the second (the political parties of the opposition) and the third (all the rest of the citizens). The indigenous would be in the VERY inferior category of "citizens in formation", the basement of the Mexican nation, the waste pile where one goes every once in a while to look for something that could still be used on the upper floors, or to fix some imperfection that could endanger the stability or balance in the building.

Basement Mexico is the most dangerous for the Sale Season that is being organized by Penthouse Mexico. Basement Mexico is the one that has nothing to lose, and the one that has everything to win. Basement Mexico does not give up, has no price, resists... From Basement Mexico a voice arose in August of 1994, a voice that does not speak of war, that does not plan to turn back the clock of history by 502 years, that does not demand vanguard, that does not exclude tribulations. "Everything for everyone, nothing for us" speaks the language of the millennium. The faceless voice, of the unnamable, became common in the National Democratic Convention. This voice is precisely aimed. It calls Basement Mexico, and it calls Middle Mexico. "Do not let our blood be wasted. Do not let the death be in vane!" say the mountains. Let the word join the separate roads, let the rebellion also include...

Women: In Double Dream, Double Nightmare, Double Awakening;
If among men the division of The Mexico's to a point is evident, in women it produces new effects, which show potentials of submission and rebellion.

While in Penthouse Mexico women reiterate their position of being gold plated, like a trinket on the executive desk of the world, the wise and "efficient" administrator of familial well being (that is, dolling out dinners at McDonalds), and in Middle Mexico the ancient cycle of daughter-girlfriend-wife and/or lover-mother, in the Lower and Basement Mexico's the nightmare is doubled in the microcosms where the man dominates and determines.

For women in the Lower and Basement Mexico's everything is doubled (except for respect): referring to women the percentages of illiteracy, of subhuman living conditions, low salaries, of margination, are incremented into a nightmare that the system prefers to ignore or disguise within general indexes that do not show the exploitation of the gender that makes general exploitation possible. But something is beginning not to fit in this double submission, the double nightmare doubles the awakening.

Women from Lower and Basement Mexico awaken fighting against the present and against past that threatens to be their future. The conscience of humanity passes through female conscience, the knowledge of being human implies they know they're women and fight back. They no longer need anyone to speak for them, their word follows the double route of rebellion with its own motor, the double motor of rebel women in this...

Space for paradoxes...

3. We Know What We're Doing; It is Worth It

December 1994

Zapatista Army of National Liberation

Mexico

To Whom It May Concern

> "I am the escaped one, after I was born. They locked me up inside me but I left.
> My soul seeks me, through hills and valley, I hope my soul never finds me."
> - Fernando Pessoa

I write this, while reports from our companeros arrive about preparations for the advance of our units, and as I burn a last stack of unanswered letters. That is why I write to you now. I always told myself I would respond to each and every letter we received. It seemed to me that it was the least we could do, answer so many people who had bothered to write a few lines and risk putting their name and direction on in hoping for a response.

The war is imminent. I definitely cannot save these letters. I should destroy them because, if they fall into the hands of the government, they could cause many problems for many good people and a few bad people. Now the flames are high and their colors change. Sometimes they are an iridescent blue which never fails to surprise this night of crickets and far-away lightning which announces the cold December of prophecies and pending accounts. There were quite a few letters. I managed to answer a good part of them, but I would barely shrink a pile when another would arrive. "Sisyphus (who was doomed to roll a stone uphill forever)," I said to myself. "Or the vulture eating the entrails of Prometheus," my other adds, always opportune in its venomous sarcasm.

I should be sincere and confess that, lately, the little pile which arrives habitually was growing smaller. At first I attributed it to the nosy Government agents. Then I realized that good people get tired... and they stop writing... and sometimes, they stop fighting...

Yeah I know that writing a letter isn't exactly an assault on the Winter Palace. But the letters made us travel so far. One day we would be in Tijuana, the next in Merida, sometimes in Michoacan, or in Guerrero, Veracruz, or Guanajuato, Chihuahua, Nayarit, Queretaro or the Federal District (Mexico City). Sometimes we would travel farther to Chile, Paraguay, Spain, Italy, Japan. Well, so those trips that gave us more than one smile and warmed cold sleepless night or refreshed the heat of the days are over.

Anyway, I have told you I have decided to respond to all the letters, and we the walking gentlemen, know how to keep our promises (as long as they're not a romance). So I have thought your generosity would alleviate my heavy guilt if all of you accepted one solitary and overwhelming missive in which you each find yourselves as the solitary recipient.

Vale, since you cannot protest or express disagreement (you could do it but I won't learn about given the mail and etcetera will be useless), I will proceed then to give free reign to the insane dictatorship which takes over my agile hand when it comes to writing a letter. What better way to begin than a few verses from Pessoa, curse and prophesy, which say, I think...

"The gaze, which is looking where it cannot see, turns: Both of us are talking. What was not conserved. Does this begin or end?"

Such and Such a Month of the Ineffable Year of 1994,
To Whom It May Concern,

I want to say a few things about what has happened since January. Many of you wrote to say thank you. Imagine our surprise when we read in your letter that you are grateful that we exist. I, for example, whose most affectionate gesture from my troops has been one of resignation when I arrive at one of our positions, was surprisingly surprised. And when I am surprised by a surprise unusual things happen. For example, I will bite my pipe too much and the stem breaks. Then, for example, as I look for another pipe I find some candy and commit the grave error of crackling it, a sound which only cellophane-wrapped candy makes and which that plague called "children" can hear from dozens of meters away, kilometers, if the wind is in their favor. It so happens for example, that when I raise the volume on the little tape player to drown out the noise from the cellophane with a song which says...

> "The one who has a song
> will have a storm,
> company,
> solitude.
> The one who follows a good road
> will have dangerous points
> which will invite them to stop.
> But the song has worth,
> good storm
> and the company
> is worth the solitude.
> The agony of haste
> is always worth it
> though the points
> are filled with truth."

In the little room (all these things invariably happen in a little room with a roof of tin or cardboard or grass or nylon) appears Heriberto. He has a face of "I found you". I pretend not to see him and whistle a tune from a movie whose name I can't remember. Anyway, the hero had good results with his whistle, because a girl, who was [as good-looking] as Cejas said, smiled and came closer.

Then I realize that it is not a girl but Heriberto who comes near. Next to him comes Tonita with her corncob-doll. Tonita, she who gripes about a kiss because "it itches", the one with the cavities, who is between five and six, the favorite of the Sup. Heriberto, the fastest crier in the Lacandon jungle, the one who draws the Anti-SUP-marine ducks, the terror of the large red ants and the Christmas chocolate, the favorite of Ana Maria. Heriberto the punishment which some vengeful god sent to the Sup for being a transgressor of violence and professional of the law. What, wasn't that it? Well, don't worry about it...

Attention! Listen! Heriberto arrives and tells me that Eva is crying because she wants to see the singing horse and the Major does not let her because he is watching the BEDROOM OF PASSOLINI. Of course Heriberto does not say the title of the movie but I can guess by his description which is "...the Major is watching naked viejas..." For Heriberto all women who wear a skirt above their knees or higher is "naked," and any woman above the age of four like Eva, are "viejas". I know that this is one of Heriberto's sneaky schemes to take the cellophane-wrapped candy, which rang like the siren on the Titanic in the middle of the fog. Heriberto and his ducks are coming to the rescue, because there is nothing sadder in this world than a candy without a child to rescue it from its cellophane prison.

Tonita, on the other hand, discovers a "mud-proof" rabbit, in other words it's black. She decides to submerge it in a puddle which, in her estimation, has all the necessary characteristics to distinguish it as a quality test.

Before the invasion of the "general command of the ezetaelene" I play dumb and pretend like I'm very absorbed in my writing. Heriberto finds out and draws a duck. He titles it irreverently, the "Sup". I pretend to be offended because Heriberto argues that my nose is just like the duck's bill. Tonita meanwhile, puts the muddy bunny on a rock next to her corncob and looks and analyzes them with a critical eye. It occurs to me that the results don't satisfy her because she shakes her head with the same obstinacy she does when she refuses to give me a kiss. Heriberto, confronted by my indifference, seems to give up and I am satisfied with my complete victory. Then I learn that the candy is gone, and I remember that Heriberto made a strange movement as I gazed at the drawing. He took it from under my nose. And with this nose, that says a lot! I am depressed and more so when I learn that Salinas is beginning to pack to leave to the "World Trade Organization". It occurs to me that it was unjust when he called us "transgressors." If he knew Heriberto he would know that compared to Heriberto, we are much more law-abiding than even the PRI leadership.

Anyway I was talking about my surprise when I read those "thank yous" in your letters. Sometimes they were written to Ana Maria, Ramona, Tacho, Moy, Mario, Laura, or any of the men and women who cover their faces to show it to others and show it to others to hide from everyone.

I rehearse my most reverent thoughts to appreciate so many thank yous when Ana Maria appears in the doorway. Heriberto is crying and holding her hand. She asks me why I won't give Heriberto any candy. "Not give him candy?" and I look at his face. The tracks of the candy have been covered with snot and tears, which have won Ana Maria to his side. "That's right," says Ana Maria. "Heriberto says he gave you a drawing in exchange for candy, and you didn't keep your word." I feel like a victim of an unjust accusation, and I put on the look of an ex-president of the PRI who is preparing to take over a powerful government department and climbing to the podium to give his best speech. Ana Maria, without comment, takes the bag of candy where the original came from and gives it all to Heriberto. "Here," she says, "The Zapatistas always keep their word."

They both leave. I am reeeeaaally sad because that candy was for Eva's birthday. And I don't know how old she is because when I asked her mother she said six. "But the other day she told me she was going to be four," I complained. "Yes but she becomes four and begins to be five, in other words she's around six," she responded firmly. She leaves me counting with my fingers and doubting the entire educational system, which taught you that 1+1=2, 6x8=48 and other transcendent things, which, in the Southeast mountains of Mexico, obviously do not hold true. Another mathematical logic functions here.

"We Zapatistas are very other," declared Monarch once when he told me that when he ran out of brake fluid, he would urinate into the container and get the same effect.

The other day for example there was a birthday party. The "youth group" got together and organized "Zapatista Olympics". The master of ceremonies declared that the long jump competition was about to start, which really means who jumps highest. The high jump was next; which really means who jumps the farthest. I was counting on my fingers again when Lieutenant Ricardo arrived and told me that they had gone to sing happy birthday at dawn. "Where was the serenade?" I asked. I was happy that everything was returning to normal since it was logical that happy birthday be sung at dawn. "In the cemetery," answered Ricardo. "The cemetery?" I began to count my fingers again. "Yes, well, it was the birthday of a companion who died in combat in January," Ricardo says on his way out (the drag races were next).

"Good," I said to myself, "a birthday party for a dead person. Perfectly logical in the mountains of Southeast Mexico." I sighed.

I have been sighing with nostalgia, remembering the good old times when the bad guys were the bad guys and the good guys were the good guys. When Newton's apple followed its irresistible trajectory from the tree towards some childish hand. When the world smelled like a schoolroom on the first day of class: of fear, of mystery, of newness. I'm sighing with true emphasis when, without previous arrangement, Beto comes in to ask if there are any balloons. Without waiting for my answer, he starts to look among maps, operative orders, pieces of guns, ashes of pipe tobacco, dried tears, red flowers colored with pen, cartridge belts and a smelly ski-mask. Somewhere Beto finds a bag of balloons and picture of a playmate, pretty old (the picture, not the playmate). Beto stops for a minute to decide between the bag of balloons and the picture and he decides what all children do; he takes both of them.

I've always said that this is not a general headquarters but a kindergarten. Yesterday I told Moy he should install some anti-personnel mines. "You think the soldiers will come all the way here?" he asks me, worried. I answer trembling: "I don't know about them, but what about the children." Moy nods agreeably and begins to tell me about his complicated design for a booby trap, a fake hole, with stakes and poison. I like the idea, but none of the children are boobies so I recommend that we electrify everything and place machine guns at the entrance. Moy thinks a while and says he has a better idea and leaves me...

What was I saying? Oh yeah! About the candy for Eva which Heriberto took. There I am talking over the radio so they can look in every camp for a bag of candy for Eva. Eva appears with a little pot of tamales which "my mother sent me because today is my birthday" Eva says to me with that look that in ten years or so will provoke more than one war.

I thank her profusely and ask what else I can do for her, then say I have a present for her. "Whereizit?" she says-asks-demands and I begin to sweat because there is nothing more terrible than a look of "moreno" anger. Eva's face begins to transform itself like in that movie of "El Santo against the Wolfman", and all I can do is stutter. To make things worst, Heriberto arrives to see "if the Sup is still mad" at him. I begin to smile to give me time to calculate where I could place a good kick on Heriberto when Eva notices that Heriberto has an almost-empty bag of candy.

She asks him where he got it, and he says in a sugary and slurry voice the "Chup". I don't realize that he means the "Sup" until Eva turns and reminds me, "and my present?" Heriberto's eyes pop out when he hears the world "present". He drops the bag of candy, which by now was empty and gets near Eva to say with a sticky cynicism: "Yeah, what about our present?" "Our?" I repeat as I figure where to kick him when I notice that Ana Maria is hovering nearby, and I quash my intent. So then I say: "I'm hiding it." "Where?" asks Eva already tired of the mystery. Heriberto, meanwhile views this as a challenge and starts to open my backpack. He tosses out my blanket, altimeter, compass, tobacco, a box of bullets, a sock. Finally I stop him by screaming: "It's not there!" Heriberto then starts on Moy's backpack and he is about to open it when I say: "You have to answer a riddle to know where the present is".

By that time Heriberto was getting fed up with Moy's backpack and he comes to sit at my side. Eva does too. Beto and Tonita come near, and I light my pipe to give me time to measure the size of the problem of the riddle. Old Man Antonio comes near. He makes a gesture to point out a tiny statue of Zapata made of silver sent by sandal, and repeats...

4. THE STORY OF THE QUESTION

The cold is harsh in these mountains. Ana Maria and Mario are with me on this exploration, 10 years before the dawn of January.

The two have barely joined the guerrilla. I am an infantry lieutenant and it is my turn to teach them what others taught me: to live in the mountain. Yesterday I ran into Old Man Antonio for the first time. We both lied. He said he was on his way to see his field, I said I was hunting. We both knew we were lying and we knew we knew it. I left Ana Maria to follow the path and I went towards the river to try to find a very high mountain and Old Man Antonio. He must have thought the same thing because he appeared at the same place where I found him before.

Like yesterday, Old Man Antonio sat on the ground, and leans against a patch of dark-brown green and begins to roll a cigarette. I sit in front of him and light the pipe. Old Man Antonio begins.

"You're not hunting."

"You're not on the way to the field," I answer.

Something made me speak to him in the proper tense, with respect, that man of undetermined age and cedar skin who I was seeing for the second time in my life.

Old Man Antonio smiles and adds:

"I've heard of you. In the canyons they say you are bandits. In my village, they're upset because you are here."

"And you, do you think we're bandits?" I asked.

Old Man Antonio releases a huge puff of smoke, coughs, and shakes his head. I'm encouraged and ask him another question.

"So who do you think we are?"

"I would prefer if you told me," he says and looks into my eyes.

"It's a long story," I say.

So I begin to talk about the times of Zapata and Villa and the revolution and the land and the injustice and hunger and ignorance and sickness and repression and everything. And I finish by saying so "we are the Zapatista Army of National Liberation". I wait for some sign from Old Man Antonio who never took his eyes from my face.

"Tell me more about that Zapata," he says after smoke and a cough.

I start with Anenecuilco, then with the Plan de Ayala, the military campaign, the organization of the villages, the betrayal at Chinameca. Old Man Antonio continued to stare at me until I finished.

"It wasn't like that," he says.

I'm surprised and all I can do is babble.

"I'm going to tell you the real story of Zapata."

Taking out tobacco and rolling paper, Old Man Antonio begins his story, which unites and confuses modern times with old times, just like the smoke from my pipe and his cigarette which mingle and converge on one another.

"Many stories ago, in the time of the first gods, the ones who made the world there were two gods who were Ikal and Votan. Two were one single one. When one turns the other could be seen, when the other turns the one could be seen. They were opposites. One was like the light, like a May morning in the river. The other was dark, like a night of cold in a cave. They were the same. One was two, because one made the other. But they didn't walk they were always stationary these two gods who were one. 'So what do we do?' 'Life is sad like this,' they lamented the two who were one. 'The night won't go,' said Ikal. 'The day won't go,' said Votan. 'Let's walk,' said the one who were two. 'How?' said the other. 'Where?' said the one.

When they did this they saw they moved a little bit. First by asking why, and then by asking where. Happy was the one who was two. Then both of them decided to move and they couldn't. 'How do we do it then?' One would move from the other and then the other would move. So they agreed that in order to move they had to do so separately. And no one could remember who moved first, they were just happy that they moved and said 'What does it matter who is first as long as we move?' The two gods who were the same one said and they laughed and agreed to have a dance, and they danced, one little step behind the other. Then they tired of all the dancing and asked what else they could do and saw that the first question was 'how to move' and brought the response of 'together but separately and in agreement.' They didn't care much that it was so.

They were so happy they were moving until they came to two roads: one was very short and one could see the end of it. They were so happy they could move that they decided to choose the long road, which then brought them to another question. 'Where did the road go?' It took them a long time, but the two who were one finally decided that they would never know where that long road took them unless they moved. So they said to one another 'Let's walk it then'. And they began to walk first one and then the other. They found it was taking them a long time and asked 'how will we walk for such a long time?' Ikal declared he did not know how to walk by day and Votan declared that by night he was afraid.

So they cried for a long time, then finally agreed that Ikal would walk by night and Votan by day. Since then the gods walk with questions and they never stop, they never arrive and they never leave. So that is how the true men and women learned that questions serve to learn how to walk, and not to stand still. Since then true men and women walk by asking, to arrive they say good-bye and to leave they say hello. They are never still."

I chew on the now-short stem of the pipe waiting for Old Man Antonio to continue, but he never does. In fear that I will disrupt something very serious I ask: "And Zapata?" Old Man Antonio smiles: "You've learned now that in order to know and walk you have to ask questions." He coughs and lights another cigarette and out of his mouth come these words that fall like seeds on the ground.

"That Zapata appeared here in the mountains. He wasn't born, they say. He just appeared just like that. They say he is Ikal and Votan who came all the way over here in their long journey, and so as not to frighten good people, they became one. Because after being together for so long Ikal and Votan learned they were the same and could become Zapata. And Zapata said he had finally learned where the long road went and that at times it would be light and times darkness but that it was the same, Votan Zapata, and Ikal Zapata, the black Zapata and the white Zapata. They were both the same road for the true men and women."

Old Man Antonio took from his backpack a little bag of nylon. Inside there was a very old picture from 1910 of Emiliano Zapata. In his left hand Zapata had his sword raised to his waist. In his right hand he had a pistol, two cartridge belts of bullets crossed his chest, one from left to right, the other from right to left. His feet are positioned as though he's standing still or walking and in his gaze there is something like "here I am" or "there I go". There are two staircases. One comes out of the darkness, and there are dark-skinned Zapatistas as though they were coming out of something. The other staircase is lighted but there is no one and one can't see where it goes or where it comes from. I would be lying if I told you that I noticed all those details. It was Old Man Antonio who told me. Behind the picture, it said;

"Gral. Emiliano Zapata, Jefe del Ejercito Suriano.

Gen. Emiliano Zapata, Commander in Chief of the Southern Army.

Le General Emiliano Zapata, Chef de l'Armee du Sud.

C.1910. Photo by: Agustin V. Casasola."

Old Man Antonio says to me: "I have asked a lot of questions of this picture. That is how I came to be here." He coughs and tosses the cigarette butt. He gives me the picture. "Here," he says, "So that you learn how to ask questions... and to walk."

"It's better to say goodbye when you arrive. That way it's not so painful when you leave," he says giving me his hand as he leaves, while he tells me he is arriving. Since then, Old Man Antonio says hello by saying "goodbye" and leaves by saying "hello".

Old Man Antonio leaves. So do Beto, Tonita, Eva and Heriberto. I take out the photo of Zapata from my backpack and show it to them.

"Is he climbing up or down?" says Beto.

"Is he going or staying?" asks Eva.

"Is he taking out or putting away his sword?" asks Tonita.

"Has he finished firing his pistol or just started?" asks Heriberto.

I'm always surprised by how many questions that 84-year-old photograph provokes and that Old Man Antonio gave me in 1984. I look at it one last time and decide to give it to Ana Maria and the picture provokes one more question; Is it our yesterday or our tomorrow?

In this climate of curiosity and with a surprising coherence for her 4-years-almost-five-or-six, Eva asks: "What about my present?" The word "present" provokes identical reactions in Beto, Tonita and Heriberto. They all start yelling, "Where's my present?" I'm trapped and at the point of sacrifice. Ana Maria who saved my life in San Cristobal almost one year ago (in other circumstances) saves me again. Ana Maria has an enormous bag of candy with her. "Here's the present the Sup had for you," says Ana Maria while she gives me that I-don't-know-what-you-men-would-do-without-women look.

While the children decide, or fight over how they will divide the candy, Ana Maria salutes me and says:

"I report. The troops are ready to leave."

"Good," I say as I strap the pistol on. We will leave as always - at dawn. "Wait!" I tell her and give her the picture.

"What's this for?"

"We need it."

"For what?"

"So we'll know where we're going."

Above flies a military airplane...

In conclusion I will answer some questions you are surely asking;

Do we know where we're going?

Yes.

Do we know what awaits us?

Yes.

Is it worth it?

Yes.

Whomever has answered the previous questions with a yes can surely not sit and do nothing without feeling that something deep inside is tearing.

Vale. Health and a flower for this tender fury, I think it deserves one.

> *From the mountains of the Mexican Southeast,*
> *Subcomandante Insurgente Marcos.*
> *Zapatista Army of National Liberation.*
> *Mexico, December 1994.*

P.S. For writers, analysts and the general public. Brilliant pens have found some valuable parts in the Zapatista movement. Nevertheless they have denied us our fundamental essence: the national struggle. For them we continue to be provincial citizens, capable of a consciousness of our own origins and everything relative to it, but incapable without "external" help of understanding and making ours concepts like "nation", "homeland", and "Mexico". They will chime in during this grey hour with small letters. For them it is all right that we struggle for material needs, but to struggle for spiritual needs is an excess.

It is understandable that these pens now turn against us. It's too bad, someone has to be responsible, someone has to say "no", someone has to say "Ya Basta (Enough)!" Someone has to leave prudence to one side, and give higher value to dignity and shame, than to life, someone has to... Well, to these magnificent pens; we understand the condemnation which will flow from your hands. All I can argue in our defense is that nothing we ever did was for your pleasure, what we did and said was for our please, the joy of struggle, of life, of speech, of walking... Good people of all social classes, of all races and generations helped us. Some helped to relieve their conscience, others to be fashionable, the majority helped because of their convictions because of their certainty that they had found something good and new.

We are good people, that is why we are letting everyone know what we are about to do. You should prepare yourselves, you should not be taken by surprise. This warning is a disadvantage for us, but not as great a disadvantage as would be a surprise.

To those good people I want to say, I hope you continue to be good. That you continue to believe, that you do not allow skepticism to bind you to the sweet prison of conformity. That you continue to search, to seek out something in which to believe, something for which to fight.

We have had some brilliant enemies. Pens which have not been satisfied with the easy condemnation, pens which have sought out strong, firm coherent arguments with which to attack us. I've read some brilliant texts which attack the Zapatistas and defend a regime which must pay and dearly, for the sake of appearances for someone to defend it. It's a shame that in the long run, you wound up defending a vain and childish cause, which will be demolished along with that building which is crumbling...

P.S. On horseback and with mariachi, Pedro Infante sings that song called "They say I am a womanizer" and ends with...

> "Among my sweet loves
> One is worth more than others
> Which has loved me without rancor
> of my tarariraran...
> A sweet old woman
> Who I don't deserve
> Who with all her heart
> Has given me the most divine love.
> In front of a grandmother one is always a child,
> and it hurts to leave...
> Goodbye,
> Grandmother I am coming.
> I've finished,
> I'm beginning..."

5. LETTER TO ERNESTO ZEDILLO

December 3, 1994

Ejercito Zapatista de Liberacion Nacional Mexico

To: Ernesto Zedillo Ponce de Leon Mexico, D.F.

From: Subcomandante Insurgente Marcos

Indigenous Clandestine Revolutionary Committee

General Command of the Zapatista Army of National Liberation

General Quarters

> "I must conclude due to lack of time, but I will add one more observation. Someti-
> mes men are given to attack the rights of others, to take their assets, threaten the li-
> ves of those who defend their nationality, make the highest virtues appear to be cri-
> mes and give to his own vices the luster of true virtue. But there is one thing which
> neither falsity nor perfidy can reach, and that is the sentence of history."
> - Benito Juarez to Maximilian of Hapsburg in response to a confidential letter where
> Maximilian proposes a secret negotiation and a position in his government

Mr. Ernesto Zedillo Ponce de Leon,

Welcome to the nightmare.

Through this letter I direct myself to you in reference to your inauguration speech.

You should know that the political system which you represent (the one to which you owe your position of power, although not your legitimacy) has prostituted the language to such a degree, that today "politics" is synonymous to lies, crime, treachery. I only say to you what millions of Mexicans would like to say: we don't believe it.

And I add, what perhaps not all believe: enough with waiting for the day when things will change. Your words today are the same ones we have heard at the beginning of other administrations.

The distrust of the Nation towards electoral processes includes him, who took you to that deceitful transfer of powers. So I direct myself to you, as well as to your tutor, Mr. Salinas de Gortari, who, as evidenced by the cabinet which accompanies you in this new lie, refuses to retire from national political life.

How do you expect the Nation to believe you will secure justice in the assassinations, which have stained the modern history of Mexico, and demonstrated the true and criminal face of your Party-State? How can we believe you, if you award one of those who have been accused of the cover-up with the position of the management of the underground wealth of the Nation?

I see that you perpetuate that government office of alms, called Sedesol. What dignified relationship can you offer in exchange for a frank dialogue and respectful negotiation, when you appoint as your conscience-buying teller one of the links of the chain inherited to you by Salinismo and which, since May of 1993, instead of assigning economic assistance to those places which most need them, has been dedicated to buying indigenous dignity as if it was a trinket in a market?

Is this your counterinsurgency plan? The proliferation of social work in order to weaken our popular base of support? It is a good strategy, it comes in all the Northamerican manuals of anti-guerrilla strategy (and in all its history of failures). Don't you realize that money only winds up in the pockets of the corrupt leaders and municipal presidents of the PRI in the Chiapanecan countryside? Is this advice from military advisors of Argentina? Are you to be deceived once again? Like the time you were told that millions and millions of old and new pesos were invested in the region which, after January 1, suddenly became a "conflict zone"? How much more money, how much more blood is necessary for you to learn that corruption, which up to now has allowed you to survive as political system, will tomorrow be your grave?

Allow me to continue to comment upon your cabinet, it is the proof that your inauguration speech is only a bunch of words. It is more a storefront than a governmental team; in it you have a group inherited from your tutor and distinguished by their opportunism in anything which refers to national sovereignty and Mexican dignity. In External Relations you have someone who looks good to outsiders but not to Mexican nationals. Have External Relations simply become Commercial Relations? In Agriculture and Hydraulic Resources you have the guarantee that poverty and discontent will increase in the Mexican countryside.

In general, a foreign and French shadow can be seen in all your cabinet, under which Mexicans suffered this past administration. So many lies and so much make-up will be useless, this country will explode in your hands no matter how much you believe that you control all the resources necessary to maintain all the Mexicans in the category of "puts-up-with-everything".

I listened carefully to your speech on the radio. You are correct when you say that it is not our violence which the Nation fears. But your lesson is incomplete, you characterize the climate of insecurity which the country lives as something amorphous. The principal promoter of instability, insecurity and violence is the party system of the State. The political system which you cannot destroy, because, quite simply, you owe the power you now hold, to its existence. The cabinet, which you present today to the country, is a small demonstration of the pending invoices with which your administration is born. All of your speech will crumble when you confront the debts you owe to the different accomplices, which allowed you to assume the Presidency by covering up the crimes of the State. The crime began with the assassination of the one from whom you inherited your candidacy. It continued in the mockery of the electoral campaigns. It passed a self-test on the 21st of August and it culminates in this fateful December 1st.

Two first days now mark the history of this country in opposite ways; the first of January marks the increase of the volume of the cries of dignity and rebellion of Mexicans of all social origins but with the same disgrace. Since that day, with indigenous voices, men, women, children and the elderly of the city and the countryside, of different colors, of different races and languages, but of a common suffering. The first of December completes the burial of what began before the 21st of August; burial of a hope for the peaceful transition to democracy, liberty, and justice.

The indigenous communities do not just suffer, as you point out, "serious privations, injustices, and lack of opportunities." They have as well a serious illness, which begins, little by little, to affect the rest of the population; rebellion. You will bear witness to this while your government lasts.

You say that "against poverty we will all unite, the government, society, the affected communities". Nevertheless, you appoint a cabinet along the same lines as that man who buried the country in misery: Carlos Salinas de Gortari. We do not want that kind of unity of Mexico upon which you call. It is a call to unity, which will assure the permanence of the same system of oppression, now with the make-up of a new administration. It is not the unity which Mexico needs. The one, which our history reclaims, is the unity against the party system of government, the system which has the Nation submerged in a poverty of the body and the spirit.

You point out that "during this year the spirit of all Mexicans has been darkened by events in Chiapas, by violence, and more so, by the conditions of profound injustice, by the conditions of misery and negligence which fertilized that violence."

Neither the conditions of profound injustice, nor violence, belong exclusively to the state of Chiapas. The entire Nation suffers the high social cost imposed by neoliberalism. If there are not profound transformations, violence will darken all the national territory and not necessarily because we promote it.

You contradict yourself when you say, "there will not be violence on the government's part" because the white guards of the large cattleranchers and businessmen act without impunity, with government complicity. You are starting wrong if all you can offer is half-truths.

You say you are "indignant to learn that women suffer violence in public; that children and adolescents are victims of abuse outside their schools; that workers lose their salaries in muggings, and small businessmen in armed robberies. I am outraged to learn of cases that are the result of the abuse of authority, venality, and corruption." Yes, and it is also outrageous to learn that there are 24 billionaires at the expense of a paltry

4% increase in the minimum wage; it is also outrageous to learn that our national identity has been robbed within the "legal" process of a North American Free Trade Agreement which only means freedom for the powerful to rob and the freedom of misery for the dispossessed; it is outrageous now that the one who wears the Presidential sash does so not by popular will but by the will of money and fear.

"The brutal assassinations of outstanding political figures of the country have deeply wounded the citizenry, they have sowed discontent and doubt about certain institutions and, we should admit it, have divided the Mexicans." Yes, but not only those crimes, also that perpetrated, day and night, by all the members of the governmental apparatus, beginning with the previous leader of the Executive branch and ending with the last of the minor bureaucrats at the municipal level.

You ask for unity and point out that "the moment has arrived when we must gather our wills, without sacrificing our differences". But you are only looking for the endorsement and legitimacy not given you by the popular vote. Your offer of a "permanent dialogue" has manifest itself in the repression which has inaugurated December. Perhaps you are thinking of a kind of "Dialogue Commission" made up of grenadiers and policemen to deal with the press and the opposition.

It is not necessary to declare that, as president of the Republic you will not intervene, "under any form, in the processes and decisions which belong only to the party" to which you belong. That will be done by Mr. Carlos Salinas de Gortari. Your cabinet and the impunity enjoyed by the PRI leadership is proof enough.

We are clearly in agreement with you when you say that "in this historic moment, no one should run from responsibility, lessen our effort, give in to the temptation of letting our arms fall."

The Zapatistas will not run from our responsibility, lessen our efforts, or give in to the temptation of letting our arms fall. We will continue to struggle, with our arms in our hands, against the system of the Party-State, the same one which allows the figure of Salinismo to be perceived behind you.

Today, and since the 17th of November of 1994, I have been given the baton of the supreme command of the rebel forces, and consequently I assume the responsibility of responding to you in the name of all our Army.

In this your first speech as the President, you point out your desire to seek negotiations as a way of resolving the conflict and you offer us that road. Mister Zedillo, it is my duty to say to you that we do not believe you. You are part of a system which has arrived at the greatest aberration, resorted to assassination in order to settle its differences as if you were a group of criminals. You do not conduct yourself as a representative of the Nation, you speak with an enormous stain on your word: the stain of the blood of thousands of assassinations, including those which belong to your own political circle, stain which covers the Institutional Revolutionary Party. Why should we believe in the sincerity of a negotiated solution?

From the beginning of the presidential assessment, the amount of troops have increased and the reinforcement of a clear disposition to annihilation is evident. From the 14th day of November there are obvious and continuous intrusions of airplanes, of "Hercules" transports which move men and military supplies to the units used against insurgents on the Guatemalan border. The foreign military "advisors" (and I want to say clearly that they are not Argentinean, because these animals have no country) have their pupils prepared. You have now finished, I assume that you are ready. We know the number and location of your troops, your general strategy and a few tactical plans. Unfortunately we can do nothing on political and military terms. We are surrounded militarily and this prevents a military action of any breadth. Our repeated declarations against the increase of your belligerent preparations have only frustrated and bored the Nation.

You should know that I have circulated orders that the totality of the members of the CCRI remain in the rearguard in order to guarantee that the political direction of our just cause not be lost. Know as well that, as in January, the military leaders will be at the front of the different units. I will do the same. I have made the necessary preparations so that my successors in the military leadership can assume their responsibilities without major problems in case I should die.

Our major strength is also our major weakness. The support of the civilian population, which allowed us to grow and become strong, now obliges us to abandon all intents at retreat which does not include them. That is why, for us, there is no backward step. We will fight at the side of the peoples, who in the past have protected us, we will be the shields and guardians of their lives. I know that takes from us all possibility of survival. To confront as a regular army another regular army superior to us in weapons and personnel, although not in morality, nullifies the possibilities of success. Surrender has been prohibited; the Zapatista leaders who opt for surrender will be decommissioned. However, no matter the result of this war, sooner or later the sacrifice, which today appears to be useless and sterile, will be compensated in the thunderbolts which light up other skies. The light will come, it is sure, to the deep South and will sparkle in the Mar de Plata, in the Andes, the land of Artigas, Paraguay and all this inverted and absurd pyramid which is Latin America. Strength is not on our side; it has never been on the side of the dispossessed. But the historic logic, the shame and ardor which we feel in our chests and which we call dignity, makes us, the nameless, the true men and women of forever.

Through the dull exchange of a watch for a jacket, your offer to incorporate ourselves as "part of the solution" and to a secret and direct dialogue arrived. In reference to your offer to be "an active part of the execution of actions" I should say that
if you refer to the price of Zapatista dignity, know that there is not enough money
in the entire Nation capable of approximating its price. Don't deceive yourself into
thinking that our cry of "Everything for everyone, nothing for ourselves" is a passing style or deceit which covers up our ambition for power. The Zapatistas don't
have a price, because dignity does not have a price.

In reference to the direct and secret dialogue, in my role as supreme commander of the EZLN I solemnly reject your invitation to a secret negotiation, behind the
backs of the nation.

You say that after years of war and thousand of deaths and great destruction, you
and I will wind up negotiating. That it is best to do it now. That war should be
avoided. But, which war is to be avoided? The one which we began against your
system by making legitimate use of self-defense and rebellion? Or the one which
you have made against us, since you have been power and government in these
Mexican lands? The war, which we want to end, is the one waged by the political
system behind and above you against us. The war against any democratizing effort,
against any desire for justice, against any aspiration for liberty. This is the war
which all Mexicans suffer and which must come to an end. Once it ends, the other
war, our war, everyone's war will extinguish itself. Useless and sterile it will end by
leaving like a nightmare which is healed by the first light of day. This is the peace
we want. Any effort in another direction is a deceit.

To avoid the war of the dispossessed by maintaining or increasing the war which
follows the steps of the powerful is to postpone the execution of a historic sentence;
the triumph of democracy, liberty and justice in the earth and skies of Mexico.

If you are a man of honor and dignity I invite you to resign your title. You should
resign the shame of heading up that great lie, which has betrayed the hope of the
Mexican people of a peaceful transition to democracy. But before you do so, bring
Carlos Salinas de Gortari to a political trial and help the world avoid another lie,
the one behind the World Trade Organization, the one like the North American
Free Trade Agreement. And before that, as supreme chief of the federal army, liberate officials, ranks and troops, so they can choose the path dictated by their consciences and their patriotic sentiment. Don't humiliate them by obliging them to
accept foreign intervention, which advises them to kill Mexicans.

In my own case, I have done the same; I have liberated my troops of the commitment to continue and have allowed them to choose, to be able to give up, to choose

conformity. Not one of them has accepted. Nothing binds them to our ranks, not a salary nor threats, but shame and dignity form chains which are difficult to break. All of them have chosen the same path of yesterday; the one of patriotism and justice.

For my part, I recognize that I have been mistaken in regards to you. In February I believed that your patriotic interest would be superior to your arrogance, that your intelligence would allow you to see that you have constituted yourselves into the major obstacle to the development of the country, that you would step to one side and open the door to a peaceful transition to democracy. But it did not happen that way. You decided to slam the door on the 21st of August and repeat the arrogance of a land-slide victory. It so happens that, in history, the doors to peaceful change and violent change, of peace and of war, are inversely linked; when one is closed the other opens. Closing the door to a peaceful transition to democracy opened the heavy gate of war.

The stupidity, which has guided your conduct in Chiapas, has beaten me back to reality; the system of the party-state is not intelligent. Even more, I see today that this imbecility is inherent to your state of decomposition. Having had the opportunity to deactivate the political knot of the conflict, you not only main-tained it, you tightened it and incorporated sectors which were once on the mar-gin in the extremes of polarization. The deterioration is irreversible; the middle ground has disappeared and the extremes confront themselves demanding the extermination of the other. We have grown by tens of thousands. As I pointed out to you, the supreme government has always taken pertinent measures and taken us out of a problem and made us grow. Instead of risking extinction by political isola-tion, by a vacuum, the government, with its clumsy local and regional politics, oxy-genated a fire, which will ultimately consume it.

You must disappear, not just because you represent a historic aberration, a human negation and a cynical cruelty; you should disappear also because you represent an insult to intelligence. You made us possible, you made us grow. We are your other, your siamese opposite. In order for us to disappear you must disappear as well.

It is very difficult to try to listen to you. One supposes that one is speaking with rational beings and apparently not. Accustomed to buying, corrupting, imposing, breaking and assassinating all which is in front of you, when you confront dignity you assume the pose of the crafty businessman seeking the best price for his goods. This has been the attitude of your system in this 11-month unstable cease-fire. The "intelligent" attitude of he who, in front of a slot machine after depositing a coin, waits until the product which he has chosen and bought drops out: peace.

You should know that we have done all that is possible to keep the conflict within the political realm, avoiding at all costs the re-initiation of hostilities. We have called upon different national political personalities, inviting them to an initiative which can head, through political and civil means, the discontent which now overflows towards violent means. If these personalities refused to risk their political capital in what justice demands; the annulment of the elections, a transitional government and a new electoral process, there will be no remedy and the horror will be inevitable. Mexico will not have today, statesmen who are willing to pay the price of their public image in exchange for being responsible to the struggle for democracy. Nevertheless, though they may not exist today, this does not mean that tomorrow men and women will not appear for whom politics is not synonymous with cynicism and surrender disguised as "gradualism".

Mister Ernesto Zedillo,

Until today you were nothing more than a citizen to us. Today you are the official inheritor of a system, which sacrifices, without any vision at all, the future of the country and the national sovereignty. After today, in the unlikely case that you should try to make contact with us, I declare we will make public all communication which comes from your government, while it lasts.

I am sure that in your rise to power you have found men and women ready to sell themselves and compromise "under reasonable circumstances", which is nothing more than a rationalized surrender. The men and women, who have confronted the party system since the 1st of January 1994, are perhaps of a kind which you have not come upon before.

We are men and women to whom "Country", "Democracy", "Liberty" and "Justice" should be, besides grand and noble words, a reality for the Mexican nation. For us, to live without reaching that goal is a shame, and to die fighting for it, is an honor.

I want you to know that, since today, I take with me the seven elements of the Baton of the Zapatista command, the two original volumes of a 1917 edition of the Diary of the Constitutional Congress from November of 1916 to February of 1917. As long as a new Constitution is not created, the one from 1917 for us is the true one. For it, as a national norm, we will fight.

In historic terms, you and I are of little value; random luck has placed us one against the other. In you is personified all the reactionary, antidemocratic and contrary sentiments to the interests of the dispossessed. In us, only hope is personified. The hope to have, at last, the opportunity to decide our own destiny. The hope that democracy, liberty and justice become more than the subject of speeches and textbooks. The hope that they become reality for everyone, but above all, for those who have nothing. You have a face, a name, a past, a present, and a future. In our name we carry the curse of carrying weapons in our hands and the honor of rescuing a history of dignity; in our last name is our national and liberating vocation. We are barely candidates for the common grave and immediate oblivion.

But in "us" there are thousands of Mexicans in all the national territory, men and women, children and old people who have recuperated, together with the word dignity, the conviction that human beings should struggle to be free when they are slaves, and that, once free, should struggle so that other human beings can join them.

We know that our refusal for a dialogue in the conditions, which you propose, will make a military solution your first choice in future decisions. We do not fear death nor the judgement of history.

If in truth the entire country is willing to submit its desires for liberty and democracy, then the clamor for our annihilation will be gigantic and you will not have to worry. High military commanders say they will annihilate us all in a few hours, days if the weather is bad. Therefore, the stock market may suffer a few days of uncertainty.

If, on the other hand as we believe, the people of Mexico wish to listen to our rebel cry for dignity, then millions of voices will unite with our demands for the three conditions for a dignified peace: democracy, liberty and justice.

You are no longer you. You are the personification of an unjust system, anti-democratic and criminal. We, the "illegals", the "transgressors of the law", the "professionals of violence", the "nameless" ones, are today and always, the hope of everyone.

This is all, Mister Zedillo. I have spoken to you with sincerity, in a way in which I don't believe you have spoken to me. I repeat our demands for peace: democracy, liberty and justice for ALL Mexicans.

As long as these demands remain unresolved there will be war in Mexican territory.

Vale. Health and a parachute for that cliff which exists in your tomorrow.

From the mountains of Southeast Mexico,
Subcomandante Insurgente Marcos.
Mexico, November of 1994.

6. The Zapatistas Hike up the Price of the Indigenous Mexican Blood

February 9, 1995

To the national weekly Proceso

To the national newspaper El Financiero

To the national newspaper La Jornada

To the local paper of San Cristobal de Las Casas, Tiempo

Gentlemen,

Here goes a communiqué... the last one, as we see the events. The Zapatistas hike up the price of the Indigenous Mexican blood. Yesterday it was worth less than the backyard bird. Today its death is the condition of the loan of greatest infamy in the world's history. The price of the Zapatista heads is the only one that maintains a high value in the ups and downs of financial speculation. Mr. Zedillo is starting to pay the loan. His message is clear. Either you speak with submission and kneel down in front of the supreme government or with support of my accomplices in the Congress, I will annihilate you. Now he is making up a proof that we do not want the dialogue? What is his objective? To pay the loan. Somebody should tell this man who the Zapatistas are. He seems not to have ever talk to people with dignity. He is inexperience in relating to human beings. He knows how to deal with figures, macroeconomic plans, a lying media, and submissive opponents, but not with human beings. We will see if he learns before he breaks up everything.

The first and most enthusiastic applause to the ultimatum in Queretaro, and to the "spectacular coup" of February 9, comes from the great landowners and great merchants of the Southeast. They know that their private armies do not have the guts to confront the Zapatistas. Now they hope that the federal army will do the job that before they used to do themselves without so much media: massive assassinations.

The supreme government threatens us... The Zapatistas.

The Zapatistas and not the ones who are mainly responsible of the present and future misery of millions of Mexicans, of unemployment, the low level of incomes, of the lost confidence in the supreme government and its "institutions".

The Zapatistas and not those who, with funds from the Mexican people, travel to sell the economic fallacies in other countries.

The Zapatistas and not the high hierarchy of the church, who while we eat beans, hot peppers and tortilla, they sit at great banquets, and ask about the "dark" financing of the ezzee-el-aen (ezetaelene), EZLN.

The Zapatistas and not Hank Gonzalez, to whom the U.S. State Department is tracking down in the laundering of dollars and his ties to narco-drug trafficking. What Mexican justice should be doing it's being done by the U.S.

The Zapatistas and not those who knew of the December devaluation and celebrated with champagne the floating of the peso (elegant way of describing a sudden fall).

The Zapatistas and not those surrounding the great lie of the Salinista boom who embroider the complicated net of theoretic caravans and "brilliant" and "objective" addendum analysis to sing praises to the macro-lie.

The Zapatistas and not those in Chiapas, Tabasco, Veracruz, Tlaxcala, San Luis Potosi, Guanajuato, Jalisco, who perpetrated, and now prepare, a greater economic fraud, the fraud of the hopes to the peaceful transition to democracy.

The Zapatistas and not those who raped the Tzetzal Indigenous women in Altamirano.

The Zapatistas and not those who executed with a coup de grace the insurgent combatants detained in the market of Ocosingo.

The Zapatistas and not those who with elegant clarification that bombs were not use, and drop "rockets" on civilian populations in San Cristobal, Los Altos and the jungle.

The Zapatistas and not those who use hunting dogs to persecute the civilians.

The Zapatistas and not those who appraised the Indigenous blood, in the stock exchange of Chiapas to be worth less than the price of a chicken.

The Zapatistas and not those who remained with the money in their pockets of the "peace agreements" in San Cristobal.

The Zapatistas and not those who from the impunity of their fraudulent curule (senatorial seat) violated and violate the Constitution.

The Zapatistas and not those responsible of a crime and now retain the power over the energy wealth of Mexico.

The Zapatistas and not those who were active or passive accomplices of the greatest crime since Porfirio Diaz: Salinismo.

The Zapatistas and not those who live the "insecurity" of a salary of thousands of new pesos monthly in exchange of the "tiring" exercise of raising the finger to approve yesterday the sale of the homeland and today the extermination of the Indigenous people of the Southeast.

The Zapatistas and not the political arm of organized crime and narco-drug trafficking which in addition dares to boast as supreme insult, the colors of the national flag in its seal.

The Zapatistas and not the handful of U.S. capitalists who already paid, in advance, for the purchase of our wealth under ground.

The Zapatistas and not those who from the pulpit of mass media, lied, lie and will lie to the Nation.

The Zapatistas and not those who on January, 1995, introduced themselves in Switzerland, to the IMF, saying, "President Salinas has instructed me... Excuse me, President Zedillo..."

The Zapatistas and not those who from the IDB with a foreign race and vocation lead the destiny of our country.

The Zapatistas and not the white guards.

The Zapatistas, the men and women who rose up in arms so as not to live on their knees anymore and not those who for centuries have kept us down in ignorance, misery, death, and hopelessness.

The Zapatistas, the ones who decided to give their life as a guarantee so that they never again will talk under threats with anybody.

The Zapatistas, the littlest ones, always forgotten, the flesh destined yesterday to death by diarrhea, malnutrition, forgotten, in the coffee fields, in the landowners fields, the streets, the mountain.

The Zapatistas, the littlest ones, always forgotten, the flesh destined tomorrow to serve as polygon of exercise for the modern armament of an army which instead of defending national sovereignty and point their weapons against the traitors of the homeland, they point to their siblings in blood, soil and history.

The Zapatistas, the millionaires of undelivered promises, the ones who cover their face, so that their brothers and sisters in other lands can see them. The Zapatistas the ones of "for everybody everything, nothing for us."

The Zapatistas, the ones who taught to the present rulers what they did not learn in post graduate studies abroad, and what is not in textbooks of the ones who miseducate the Mexican children: that which is shame, dignity for human beings and love for homeland and history.

The Zapatistas, the ones who, in the middle of a country of fritters, foreign goods, "grate" macroeconomic achievements, fictitious first worlds, despairs of change, they drew up again, in the soil and sky of these lands, the six letters that had already been sold cheap in the international market: Mexico.

The Zapatistas, the men, women, children and old people who (long before those who today usurp the Mexican will, were a dream even in the blood of their last generation), reside, live and die in these lands. The ones who together with other Indigenous people gave to this country, as national seal, the image of the eagle devouring a serpent.

The Zapatistas, we, you, all the ones who are not themselves...

Anyway, whatever happens, thanks to everybody for everything. If we were to turn back the clock of history, not for a second we would doubt in doing again what we have done. One time, one thousand times we would say again "Ya Basta," "Enough."

Vale, a salute and a strong, strong embrace (for the cold and so that we do not allow forgetfulness to reign again).

From the mountains of Southeast Mexico,
Subcomandante Insurgente Marcos.
Mexico, February 1995.

P.S. That applauds furiously to the new "success" of the government police: I heard that they discover another Marcos and he is very (much from Tampico) tampiqueno. It does not sound bad, the port is beautiful. I remember when I was working as a bouncer in a brothel in Ciudad Madero during the times in which La Quina did to the regional economy what Salinas did to the stock exchange: to inject money to hide poverty. I left the port because humidity makes me sleepy, and seafood makes the sleepiness go away.

P.S. That does not go away, inspite of the circumstance, its narcissism: Well, and about all of this, this new Subcomandante Marcos, is he handsome? It's because lately they have thrown at me only ugly ones and it ruins all the correspondence from females.

P.S. That counts ammunition and time: I have 300 shots, so try to bring more than 299 soldiers and policemen to catch me. Legend has it that I don't miss. Do you want to find out? Why 299 if there are 300 bullets? Well, the last one is for "yours truly." It happens that one becomes fond of things like that, and a bullet seems the only consolation for a solitary chest.

Vale again. Would there be a little piece in her bosom for a memory?

The Sup retouching with macabre flirtation the ski-mask.

7. Death Has Visited us Dressed in Olive Green

February 20, 1995
To the national and international press
To the national weekly magazine Proceso
To the national daily newspaper La Jornada
To the national daily newspaper El Financiero
To the local daily newspaper in San Cristobal de las Casas, Tiempo

Sirs,
Diverse communications are going. Let's see when and how. Here the cold and the military blockade bear down. The tobacco now smells and hurts of death. What's going on outside? Are you happy with the $20 billion? And who's going to pay them back?
Goodbye.

Health and one of those piggy banks to guard hopes of the size of an old cent (one is as scarce as another).

From the mountains of Southeastern Mexico,
Subcomandante Insurgente Marcos.
Mexico, February 1995.

CONTINUING OUR FAVORITE SECTION "THE RECURRING POST-SCRIPT IN TRANSGRESSION AND ILLEGALITY"

P.S. Laughing and zigzagging to the destination.

I failed you this time, Esteban M. Guajardo. Guadalupe Tepeyac was not Chinameca. More luck, more soldiers, and more balls the next time. What is your next move? Go to Yeso in Jatate? Or the Break in Yuro in Montes Azules?

P.S. Telling what is in the notebook of the Sup on February 14, Day of love and friendship.

"Here I go, breaking myself into pieces, and patching body and spirit. Today I broke a piece of my shoulder. It broke just like that and sounded like a dry branch under a boot. Hardly a 'crack'. A little later a dry blow was heard and it fell to the floor. I picked it up, and I arranged it to the best of my knowledge of anatomy. I tied it up with a reed and continued walking. Yesterday it was a piece of my right thigh that broke and fell. I do not lose hope that a good piece of such an impertinent nose will fall off, and leave me, therefore, with a profile that is less aerodynamic but more manageable. I do not desire it because I want to contradict the bread-crumbed Attorney General and the history of the man from Tampique, but because it would deform the ski-masks less.

Yesterday, day 13, death, dressed in olive green, came within 10 or 15 meters of where we were. I told Camilo that it was 20 meters, but when the soldiers left, we went down and counted 10 meters to exactly where the patrol of federal soldiers had passed. Now, like a year ago, every second there is a flight between life and death. An eagle or sun. Life falls or death falls. Like in the Cantinflas movie with Medel, where he sings of 'how I miss you woman, how I miss you...', and Marcelo explains to Cantinflas that 'the woman, since our mother Eve... because in the first global conflagration...' and Cantinflas responds with 'a woman is like a flower and a flower has to be watered, when one waters it, [pos] waters it...'

And thinking of Cantinflas, the money makes circles in the air, and we, advancing slowing, pulling ourselves along, without water or food but with mud and thorns sufficient enough to pay the total sum of the Mexican external debt if a price is set on them in the stock market. 'But they don't have any value', Camilo says to me. 'Neither does our blood' added my other self, who, instead of a suitcase carries skepticism everywhere and does not appear to tire. I noticed that the senses begin to dull. On this day of death. At 10 meters I was against a rock. I was relaxing little by little. Without making a sound I took off the safety on the weapon, and pointed it towards the sound. I wasn't thinking; it seemed like time stood still at the end of my finger, on the trigger. Without fear but without courage. As if seeing everything from outside, as if I was tiring, as if in a movie that I had seen many times before, in history, in life, in death. Dulled, I say. 'Like a machine,' says my other self. Camilo doesn't say anything, only murmuring that it was 10 meters and 30 soldiers and us 3 and that, according to higher mathematics, each of us had to take on 10 to come out alive. Camilo said that he did that calculation. I didn't calculate anything, all I saw was me with my finger on the trigger, immobile, like a single snapshot repeated until one is sick from an endless movie. Camilo didn't study at Oxford nor in Massachusetts (is that how it's spelled?); he barely got through second grade in a village in the jungle, and he learned mathematics in the mountains. Myself, I was thinking about a wonderful risk with this finger on the trigger... but my other self told me that this wasn't the time for banter...

Did I say a year ago? I lie, it was more than a year ago. In January. A year ago, in February, we were in the Cathedral in San Cristobal de las Casas talking of peace. Today we are in the jungle and talking of war. Why? Has someone asked this man why? Why did he trick us? Why did he feign a commitment to coming to a just political agreement and then launch a terror that has now escaped from his hands?

Well then, I talked to him, or better, I talked with Camilo and on this page in the notebook about how the body parts are falling and I don't understand why, and Camilo is not going to answer because he has fallen asleep in the middle of this tall grass. The helicopters above, and the chac-chac-chac-chac of the blades are all around us, and I remember that 'chac' in Tzotzil means 'asshole', and from the 'asshole-asshole-asshole' of the helicopters I return again to my notebook. My other self says to me, biting my pipe, 'It doesn't matter, no one is going to read it,' and the notebook, for a change, doesn't say anything. I let it go, and I realize that a first small crack has appeared in my body, and then it deepens, and then a piece comes off and falls. I tried to put it back again, and I tied it with a reed, and it doesn't hurt. But I'm not worried, but I happened to put in on the wrong side... For example, if it goes on the right side and I put it on the left side or vice versa? What political implications would this error have? Clearly, until now it has not been a problem, because the two sides have not fallen off at the same time... My other self looks at the notebook to read the last lines and capitalizes 'No one is going to read it' and tries to nap when the helicopters give up their place to the crickets.

Today is the day of love and friendship. Here there is no better friend than death nor better love than her mortal kiss..."

P.S. Foreseeing a reproach.

Anyway, I prefer to die here, rather than have to confront Eva someday and try to explain why I couldn't evacuate her videocassettes of Bambi, Jungle Book, and The School of Vagabonds with (somebody doubts it?) Pedro Infante and Miroslava. Eva said that Bambi is a female, Heriberto said that it was male. Eva argued that you could tell it was a she by the eyes. Heriberto said that it was male because of the horns "and in addition, at the end he leaves with a girlfriend" responded Heriberto who, as one can see, is not a child but a dwarf.

P.S. With the heart broken, I remember a gesture of disfavor.

Tonita also left fleeing for the mountains. She had on some new white shoes, that some good person from somewhere had sent her. Tonita had her shoes in her hands. "Why don't you put them on?" I asked her after receiving a gesture of rejection to my nth request for a kiss. "Well, because they will get dirty," she responded to me with the inexplicable logic of a 6 year old girl in the Lacandon jungle. I have not seen her again...

P.S. The offer of help from the Supreme Government.

I, the recurring postscript, recommend to the government that it withdraw the arrest order against the Sup. The result has been that since he has known that he was pursued, the Sup has been insufferable. And I don't just refer to his obsession with death, with the result that now he believes that in truth he is John the Devil and he's always telling us not to worry, that the Twisted One is going to come to save us... But this isn't the worst. The worst is that he doesn't let us sleep, talking with us about such and such Monica or such and such Aimee. What do you think we should do? Nothing decorous, believe me. My discretion prevents me from putting down the details. I tried to dissuade him by telling him this soap opera had ended a long time ago, but he said that he was going to look for Marimar. I reminded him of the boycott against Televisa, and he responded that then he was going to go with the kittens of Poorcell. Arguing against that, telling him that TV Azteca also had asked for his head (the Sup's), he murmured something like this "Someday there will be objective television in this country." He left, sleepy and murmuring: "What are we going to do, here we may die, in the region with the clearest air..." I told him that it will be "to live" but he no longer was listening to me. Overhead the sound of a military plane, and Belt of Orion were the only cover for his restlessness...

Goodbye again. Health and a small remembrance for this song of J.M. Serrat that ends with:

"It is not that I haven't returned because I have forgotten, It is that I lost the road to return..."

The Sup delinquent, transgressor and hiding in the hills,
Subcomandante Marcos.

8. THE RETREAT IS MAKING US ALMOST SCRATCH AT THE SKY

February 20, 1995
To the national weekly magazine, Proceso
To the national newspaper El Financiero
To the national newspaper La Jornada
To the local newspaper in San Cristobal de las Casas, Chiapas, Tiempo
To the national and international press

Dear Sirs,

Here are the communiqués. As things are becoming black, it's almost night. The cynicism is amazed with the negation of what is evident: the decision to seek a military solution. Us? Well, but almost scratching at the sky. The first time that something falls the sky, it will fall on me.

Let's go. Health and a well-equipped boat to break through so much darkness.

From the mountains of Southeastern Mexico,
Subcomandante Insurgente Marcos.
Mexico, February 1995.

P.S. Writing on February 15, 1995, sixth day of the retreat (we recommend that it be read before each meal; it is an excellent diet aid).

"The morning of the 15th we were going to drink our urine. I say 'we were going to' because we didn't do it as we all began to vomit after the first swallow. Previously there had been a discussion. Although all of us had been in agreement that each person should drink his/her own urine, Camilo say that we should wait until night came so that the urine gets cold in the canteens, and we can drink it thinking that it is a soda.

In defense of his position, Camilio argued that he had heard on the radio that imagination made anything possible. I opposed the idea, suggesting that time would only make the odor stronger, as well as mentioning that the radio had not been recently known for its objectivity. My other self alleged that a time of rest could help the ammonia settle on the bottom. "It will be the adrenaline," I said, realizing strangely that the skepticism was my own and not my other self. Finally we decided to take a sip, all at the same time, to see what would happen. I don't know who began the 'concert', but almost immediately all of us began vomiting what we had ingested, and also what we hadn't. We were left even more dehydrated, lying on the ground. Like dunces, stinking of urine. I think that our image was hardly soldier-like. At these hours, before the sun comes up, a sudden rain pelted us and alleviated our thirst and our spirits. With the first light of the sixth day we continued walking. In the afternoon, we came upon the outskirts of a small village.

Camilo went near to ask for something to eat.

He returned with a little fried pork, hard and cold. We ate it right there without any modesty. In a few minutes the cramps began. The diarrhea was memorable. We were tied to the foot of a small wooded hill. A patrol of federal troops passed by about 500 meters away. They didn't find us because God is grand. The smell of shit and urine could be smelled kilometers away..."

P.S. Reiterating their rebellion.

They can bring more. To do in all of the villages what they did in Guadalupe Tepeyac, where, for each resident, child or adult, they brought in 10 soldiers, for each horse a war tank, for each chicken, an armored vehicle. In total 5,000 soldiers who patrol a deserted village and "protect" a whole slew of dogs, in all of the areas, in all of the ranches. The whole state of Chiapas full of soldiers...

On top of everything and everyone, the mountains of southeastern Mexico will continue to be rebel territory against the bad government. This will continue being Zapatista territory. It will be forever...

P.S. Clarifying and rectifying.

It was not the EZLN who broke off the dialogue and reinitiated the war. It was the government.

It was not the EZLN who feigned political willingness while preparing a military attack and betrayal. It was the government.

It was not the EZLN who detained and tortured civilians. It was the government.

It was not the EZLN who murdered. It was the government.

It was not the EZLN who bombed and strafed communities. It was the government.

It was not the EZLN who raped indigenous women. It was the government.

It was not the EZLN who robbed and plundered the campesinos. It was the government.

It was not the EZLN who betrayed the will of an entire nation to find a political solution to the conflict. It was the government.

P.S. Pointing out incongruencies in the investigations of the Attorney General.

If the "Sup" had received political and military training from the Sandinistas, he would have already organized a "pinata" with the recovered properties and he would have expelled those who have criticized from the organization. If the "Sup" had received training from the Salvadorans, he would have already given his weapon to Cristiani. If the "Sup" had received aid from the Russians, he would have already bombed Chechnya, excuse me, Guadalupe Tepeyac.

In addition, what other guerrilla army, "of the millennium", "fundamentalist", and directed by "white university people" has carried out the military actions that the EZLN has done in January 1994 and in breaking through the military blockade in

December 1994? What other guerrilla force has agreed to sit down and dialogue only 50 days after having taken up arms? What other guerrilla force has appealed, not to the proletariat as the historical vanguard, but to the civic society which struggles for democracy? What other guerrilla force has put itself aside in order not to interfere in the electoral process? What other guerrilla force has convened a national democratic movement, civic and peaceful, so that armed struggle becomes useless? What other guerrilla force asks its bases of support about what it should do before doing it? What other guerrilla force has struggled to achieve a democratic space and not for power? What other guerrilla force has relied more on words than on bullets?

Note: Please send the responses to the, supposedly disappeared, CISEN so that it can help think in a "modern" way. Yes, to the CISEN. The Attorney General is only the pimp paying the ruling class.

P.S. Calling myself the "special investigator on the case of the Sup" and inviting the national and international civic society to be the jury and pronounce the sentence.

"Being such and such hour on such and such day, of such and such month, in the current year, see before this P.S. a man of indefinite age, between 5 and 65 years old, with his face covered with one of those garments that appears to be a sock with holes in it (and which the gringos call "ski mask", and the Latin Americans call "pasamon-tanas-mountain passes"). Among the particular signs of a face, two enormous protu-berances emerge, one of which, which was supposedly deduced after several sneezes, is the nose. The other, judging by the emanations of smoke and the smell of tobacco, could be a pipe, like the ones used by sailors, intellectuals, pirates and fugitives from justice. Exhorted to say only the truth and nothing but the truth, the individual in question said that he was called "Marcos Montes de la Selva", son of Old Anthony and lady Juanita, brother to young Anthony, Ramona and Susana, uncle to Tonita, Beto, Eva and Heriberto. He of the voice declared himself to be in full control of his physi-cal and mental faculties, and, without any pressure (other than the 60,000 federal sol-diers who are looking for him dead or alive) declares and confesses the following:

First. That he was born in the guerrilla camp called "Agua Fria" in the Lacandon jungle, Chiapas, in the early morning one day in August 1984. The man with the voice says that he was reborn the first of January 1994, and born again, successively, the 10th of June 1994, the 8th of August 1994, the 19th of December 1994, the 10th of February 1995, and each day and each hour and each minute and each second since that day up to this moment in which I am making this declaration.

Second. That, in addition to his name, he has the following aliases: "Sub", "Subcomandante", "Sup", "Supco", "Marquitos", "Pinche Sup", "Sup son of a ...", and others that the power of this P.S. Agent prevents from writing.

Third. He of the voice confesses that, since having been born, he has conspired against the shadows which cover the Mexican sky.

Fourth. He of the voice confesses that, before being born, being able to possess everything in order to have nothing, he decided to possess nothing in order to have everything.

Fifth. He of the voice confesses that, in the company of other Mexicans, the majority Mayan Indians, they decided to make a paper live up its words, a paper that they teach about in school, which lists the rights of the Mexican citizens and which is called, "The Political Constitution of the United Mexican States". He of the voice pointed out that, in article 39 of this paper, it is said that the people have the right to change the government. Coming to this point, the P.S., jealous of his right, ordered the very subversive paper confiscated, and ordered that it be burned with giving it a glance, and having done this, continued to take the statement of the individual with the obvious nose and the contaminating pipe. He of the voice confessed that, not being able to exercise this right by peaceful and legal means, he decided, together with his accomplices, (these whom he of the voice calls "brothers"), to take up arms against the supreme government and to shout "Enough!" to the lie that, says he of the voice, rules our destinies. The P.S. could not help but be terrified in the face of such unusual blasphemy, and was fixated on the idea of leaving him without "a bone".

Sixth. He of the voice confessed that, put to choosing between comfortableness and responsibility, he of the voice always chooses responsibility. This statement merited the disapproval of the people present to this preparatory statement and the instinctive reflex of the P.S. to put his hand on his wallet.

Seventh. He of the voice confessed that he has been irreverent with all of the truths that are called supreme, except those that emanate from being a human being and that they are, to declare clearly, dignity, democracy, liberty and justice. A murmur of disagreement ran through the Holy Inquisition, excuse me, the office of the special investigator.

Eighth. He of the voice confessed that they had tried to threaten him, to buy him off, to corrupt him, to put him in jail, and to murder him, and that they had not intimidated him nor bought him off, nor jailed him, nor killed him (up until now, he added, threateningly, to the Investigating P.S.).

Ninth. He of the voice confessed that, since he was born, he decided that he preferred to die before turning over his dignity to those who have made lies and crime a modern religion. A thought that was so impractical earned a cynical look from the people present.

Tenth. He of the voice confessed that, since then, he had decided to be humble with the humble, and to be arrogant with the powerful. The P.S. added "irreverent" to the charges that were being made against him of the voice.

Eleventh. He of the voice confessed that he had believed and believes in human beings, in their capacity to try indefatigably to be a little better each day. He confessed that, among the human race, he has a special affection for the Mexican race, and that he had believed, believes and will believe that Mexico is something more than six letters and a underpriced product on the international market.

Twelfth. He of the voice confessed that he believes, firmly, that the bad government has to be brought down by all means and by all parts. He confessed that he believes that a new political, economic and social relation has to be created among all Mexicans, and later on, among all human beings. These promiscuous intentions gave shivers to the P.S. investigator.

Thirteenth. He of the voice confessed that he will dedicate himself to the absolute last second of his life, to struggling for what he believes.

Fourteenth. He of the voice confessed that, in a small and egotistical act, he will dedicate his last second of his life to killing himself.

Fifteenth. He of the voice confessed that he was completely bored with this interrogation. This earned him a severe reprimand from the P.S. Interrogator, who explained to him of the voice that the case will continue until the supreme government finds another tale to entertain itself.

After these confessions, he of the voice was exhorted to spontaneously declare himself innocent or guilty of the following series of accusations. To each accusation, he of the voice responded:

The whites accuse him of being dark. Guilty

The dark ones accuse him of being white. Guilty

The authentics accuse him of being indigenous. Guilty

The treasonous indigenous accuse him of being mestizo. Guilty

The machos accuse him of being feminine. Guilty

The feminists accuse him of being macho. Guilty

The communists accuse him of being anarchist. Guilty

The anarchists accuse him of being orthodox. Guilty

The Anglos accuse him of being Chicano. Guilty

The antisemetics accuse him of being in favor of the Jews. Guilty

The Jews accuse him of being pro-Arab. Guilty

The Europeans accuse him of being Asiatic. Guilty

The government officials accuse him of being oppositionist. Guilty

The reformists accuse him of being ultra. Guilty

The ultras accuse him of being reformist. Guilty

The "historical vanguard" accuse him of calling to the civic society and not to the proletariat. Guilty

The civic society accuses him of disturbing their tranquility. Guilty

The Stock Exchange accuses him of ruining their breakfast. Guilty

The government accuses him of increasing the consumption of antacids in the government's Departments. Guilty

The serious ones accuse of being a jokester. Guilty

The adults accuse him of being a child. Guilty

The children accuse him of being an adult. Guilty

The orthodox leftists accuse him of not condemning the homosexuals and lesbians. Guilty

The theoreticians accuse of being a practitioner. Guilty

The practitioners accuse of being a theorist. Guilty

Everyone accuses him of everything bad that has happened. Guilty

Not having anything else to declare in this first preparatory statement, the P.S. Investigator ended the session and smiled imagining the congratulations and check that he would receive from his bosses.

P.S. Talking about what was heard on February 16, 1995, on the afternoon of the seventh day of the retreat. "And why don't we attack instead of retreating?" Camilo threw at me in the middle of a hill, precisely when I was concentrating most heavily on breathing and on not falling into the ravine at our sides. I didn't respond immediately, I made signs that he should continue climbing. At the top of the hill we three sat down. Night comes to the mountain before it comes to the sky, and in the semi-darkness of this indecisive hour in which light isn't the same, and the shadows waver. "Something is heard, far away..." I say to Camilo who is listening with attention. "What do you hear?"

"Crickets, leaves, wind," responds my other self.

"No," I insist, "Pay attention."

Now it is Camilo who responds: "Some voices... very far away... a boom-boom-boom... like a drum... from over there..." Camilo points to the west.

"This exactly!" I tell him.

"And?" intervenes my other self.

"It is the civic society. Yelling that there can't be war, there has to be dialogue, that words should talk and not weapons..." I explained.

"And the boom-boom-boom?" insisted Camilo.

"That's their drums. They are calling for peace. There are many people, thousands, dozens of thousands, hundreds of thousands. The government is not listening to them and is confronting them. We, all the way over here, we have to listen to them. We have to respond to them. We can not turn a deaf ear like the government is doing. We have to listen to them, we have to avoid the war until there is no other choice..."

"And then?" muses my other self.

"Then we fight," I responded to Camilo.

"When?" he insisted.

"When they fall, when they tire. Then that will be the black hour in which we will have to talk..."

"Fight," says my other self. I insist: "We do everything for them. If we fight, it is for them. If we stop fighting, it is for them. In the end they will win. If they annihilate us, they will have the satisfaction of having done everything possible to avoid it, to avoid the war. For this reason they rose up, and now they are not being held back. In addition, they have in their hands a flag that they are responsible for. If we live, they will have the satisfaction of having saved us, of having avoided the war and having demonstrated to us that they are better and that they can handle the flag. Whether we die or live, they live and will become stronger. For them everything, for us nothing..."

Camilo said that he preferred his version: "For them nothing, for us everything".

P.S. Reigning his nocturnal delirium.

Forgetfulness, a faraway lark, is the cause for our going around without face. To kill forgetfulness with a little memory, we cover our chests with lead and hope. If, in some improbable flight, our stay in the wind coincides, you will take off so many clothes and mask of sweet trick, and with lips and skin make the memory better, that of tomorrow. For this reason, a message goes from the earth to the concrete. Listen well!

> *"As an unperfect actor on the stage,*
> *Who with his fear is put besides his part,*
> *Or some fierce thing replete with too much rage*
> *Whose strength's abundance weakens his own heart;*
> *So I, for fear of trust, forget to say*
> *The perfect ceremony of love's rite,*
> *And in my own love's strength seem to decay,*
> *O'ercharg'd with burden of mine own love's might.*
> *O, let my books be then the elocuence*
> *And dumb presagers of my speaking breast,*
> *Who plead for love, and look for recompense*
> *More than that tongue that more hath more express'd.*
> *O, learn to read what silent love hath writ;*
> *To hear with eyes belonge to love's fine wit."*
> - William Shakespeare, Sonnets, Sonnet XXIII

Goodbye, amber lark, don't look for us under your flight. Up above yes, where our pain takes us up, to the sun, where hope rains...

P.S. Not being able to give anything on this birthday.

Heriberto has a birthday on the March 5th. They say he will complete 4 years and start on his fifth. Heriberto walks the mountains, while in his home soldiers live and a tank is on his patio. The toys that a "Operation Toys" brought him for the Three Wise Men's Day, are now in the hands of some general or being analyzed by the Attorney General in search of some secret organization. Heriberto, as much as he prepared for what happened the 10th of February (the invasion of the federal soldiers), at the actual moment, he left behind his best toy: a little car that Heriberto, inside it, played at being a driver around the patio where the coffee was dried. They tell me that Heriberto consoles himself saying that in the mountain his little car couldn't go. Heriberto asked his mom if he ever was going to have his car again, and if the Sup was not going to give him chocolates. Heriberto asked his mom why the war from last year returned, why his car was left behind. "Why?" asks Heriberto. His mom does not respond, continuing to walk with the boy and the pain weighing on her shoulders...

P.S. Remembering and I recite from memory, verses from Antonio Machado, which refer to distinct things, but which are coming.

> I.
> *In the heart I have*
> *the thorn of a passion*
> *I was able to pull it out one day*
> *Now I don't feel my heart.*
> *Sharp golden thorn*
> *who will again feel you*
> *in the stopped heart...*
> II.
> *At night I dreamed that I heard*
> *God yelling to me: Watch out!*
> *later it was God who slept*
> *and I was yelling "Wake up"!*
> *P.S. Bleeding unstoppably*
> *An injury I carry in my chest*
> *Of bloody wheat*
> *and there is no bread*
> *to alleviate the desire...*
>
> *The Sup at the top of a hill, seeing how the sun goes down, in the west, a twinkle*
> *that is going out...*

9. WELCOME TO THE ECUADOR - PERU BORDER

March 11, 1995
To "Proceso," "El Financiero," "La Jornada," "Tiempo"
To the national and international press

Sirs,

The communiqué goes out which demonstrates that man is the only animal who takes the risk of falling twice in the same trap. It certainly would be good if they would send a copy of the much-mentioned law to the federal troops. They don't seem to have been informed, because they keep advancing. If we keep withdrawing we're going to hit a sign saying: "Welcome to the Ecuador - Peru border." It's not that we don't enjoy trips to South America, but being between three fires must not be very pleasant. We are well. Here in the forest one can appreciate, in all its rawness, the transformation of man into monkey (anthropologists, abstain).

Go on. Health, and one of those crystals that lets you see the present and the future.

> From the mountains of the Mexican Southeast,
> Insurgent Subcommander Marcos.
> Mexico, March 1995.

P.S. That asks just out of curiosity.

The name of the general of the Federal Army who, before retreating from the ejido Prado, ordered the destruction of everything useful in the houses of the indigenous people and the burning of several huts? In Prado they earn, on average, 200 new pesos a month per family; how much does the general earn for such a "brilliant" military action? Will they promote him in rank for "campaign merits"? Did the general know that one of the houses he ordered destroyed was the house of Tonita? Will this general have a chat with his children and grandchildren about this "luminous" page in his record of service?

What's the name of the officer who, days after having assaulted and destroyed houses in the ejido Champa San Agustin, came back with candy and had himself photographed when he gave it to the children? What is the name of the officer who, emulating the protagonist of the novel Pantaleon and the Visitors of Mario Vargas Llosa, brought dozens of prostitutes to "attend" to the garrison that occupies Guadalupe Tepeyac? How much do the prostitutes charge? How much does the general earn who's in charge of such a "risky" military operation? How much commission does the Mexican "Pantaleon" get? Are the same prostitutes for the officers and the troops? Does this "service" exist in all the garrisons of the campaign "in defense of the national sovereignty"? If the Mexican Federal Army exists to guarantee the national sovereignty, wouldn't it be better for them to accompany Ortiz to Washington, instead of persecuting Mexican indigenous dignity in Chiapas?

P.S. That armor-plates its heart again to tell what follows...

The 8th of March, the inhabitants of Prado finished coming down from the mountains. Tonita's family was part of the last contingent. When they come to what was left of their little house, the scene of all the Prado families is repeated in Tonita's family: the men, impotent and enraged, look over the little that is still standing; the women cry and tear their hair, pray, and repeat, "My God, my God," while they pick up the torn clothes, the few broken pieces of furniture, the food, spilled and with excrement on it, the broken images of the Virgin of Guadalupe, the crucified Christs thrown down with "fast food" wrappers from the U.S. Army. This scene is now almost a ceremony among the inhabitants of Prado. They have repeated it 108 times in the last few days, once for each family. 108 times the impotence, the rage, the tears, the cries, the "My God, My God..."

Nevertheless, this time there is something different. There is a little woman who doesn't cry. Tonita didn't say anything, she didn't cry, she didn't yell. She passed over the rubbish and went right to a corner of the house, like she was looking for something. There, in a forgotten corner, was the little teacup, broken, thrown away like a ruined hope. That little cup was a gift, someone sent it to her, so that some day, Tonita-Alice could drink tea with the Mad Hatter and the March Hare. But this time it isn't a hare that Tonita finds in March. It is her house destroyed by orders of he who is said to defend sovereignty and legality. Tonita doesn't cry, doesn't shout, doesn't say anything. She picks up the pieces of the little teacup and of the saucer that gave it a base. Tonita goes out, passes again among the torn and dirty clothes on the ground, through the corn and beans scattered among the wreckage, between her mother, her aunts, and her sisters who weep, and cry, and repeat "My God, My God." Outside, near a guava tree, Tonita sits on the ground and, with mud and a little spit, starts to stick the pieces of the teacup together again. Tonita doesn't cry, but there is a cold and hard brilliance in her gaze. Brutally, as the last 500 years have been for indigenous women, Tonita leaves girlhood and makes herself a woman. It is the 8th of March of 1995, International Women's Day, and Tonita is five years old, going on six. The cold and cutting brilliance in her eyes rescues, from the broken little teacup, sparkles that wound. Anyone would say that it is the sun that sharpens the bitterness sowed by treason in these lands... As if putting a broken heart back together, so Tonita reconstructs, with mud and saliva, her broken little teacup. Someone, far off, forgets for the moment that he is a man. The salty drops that fall from his face don't rust his chest of lead...

P.S. That risks "the most valuable thing I have.

(The account in dollars?) I read that now there is a "subcommander Elisa," a "subcommander German," a "subcommander Daniel," a "subcommander Eduardo." So I have decided to make the following resolution: I warn the PGR [Justice Department] that if they keep coming out with more "subs," I will go on a total fast. I demand, furthermore, that the PGR declare that there is only one "sub" (Fortunately, says my alter ego when reading these lines), and that they clear me of all blame in the weakness of the dollar against the Japanese yen and the German marks (note the narcissistic repetition). (Don't send me to Warman, please!)

P.S. That acknowledges receipt of promises caught by a sonnet and returns with...

> *"When, in disgrace with fortune and mens' eyes,*
> *I all alone beweep my outcast state,*
> *And trouble deaf heaven with my bootless cries,*
> *And look upon myself and curse my fate,*
> *Wishing me like to one more rich in hope,*
> *Featured like him, like him with friends possess'd,*
> *Desiring this man's art and that man's scope,*
> *With what I most enjoy contented least;*
> *Yet in these thoughts myself almost despising,*
> *Haply I think on thee, and then my state,*
> *Like to the lark at break of day arising*
> *From sullen earth, sings hymns at heaven's gate;*
> *For thy sweet love remember'd such wealth brings*
> *That then I scorn to change my state with kings."*
> - William Shakespeare, Sonnet XXIX.

P.S. That tells about what happened February 17 and 18 of 1995, eight and ninth day of the withdrawal.

"We were following the double point of the lunatic arrow."

"Waxing quarter, horns to the East," I remembered, and repeated to myself as we came out into some pastures. We had to wait. Above, a military airplane rained down its purr of death. My alter ego started to sing softly, "and they gave us the ten and eleven, the twelve, the one, the two and the three. And hidden when the dawn came to us, we were soaked by rain..." I make him a threatening sign to shut up. He defends himself: "My life is a song by Joaquin Sabina."

"It sure must not be a love song," I tell him, forgetting my own prohibition on talking.

Camilo lets me know the plane is gone. We go out in the meadow and keep walking in the middle of a pasture all damp from the rain. I was going ahead looking upward, seeking in its darkness some answer to old questions. "You're headed for the bull," I managed to hear Camilo warn me. But now it was too late - when I lowered my gaze after a trip through the Milky Way, I met the eyes of a stud who, I think, was as frightened as I was, because he ran the same as I did, but in the opposite direction. When I got to the fence, I threw my pack over the barbed wire.

I stretched out to drag myself under the fence. I did it with such good luck, that what I thought was mud, was bullshit. Camilo roared with laughter. My alter ego even got hiccups. The two sat down and I made signs for them to shut up.

"Sssshh, the soldiers are going to hear us!" but it's no good, they laugh and laugh. I cut a bunch of star grass to clean, as much as possible, the shit off my shirt and pants. I put on my pack and went on walking. Behind, Camilo and my alter ego followed. Now they weren't laughing. When they got up, they realized it was shit they had sat down in. Attracting cows with such a seductive odor, we finished crossing the wide pasture, which had a stream running through it. When we got to the wooded zone I looked at my watch. 02:00. "Southeastern time," Tacho would say. With luck and with no rain, we would arrive at the foot of the mountain before dawn. So it was. We went in by an old trail cutting among big and well-spaced trees that announced the closeness of the forest. The real forest, where only wild animals, the dead, and the guerrillas live. There wasn't much need for a light; the moon still tore itself among the branches, like a white streamer, and the crickets hushed with our step on the dry leaves. We came to the great ceiba tree [a majestic species of tree renowned in Mayan myth] that marked the gate of entry, rested a while and, now with the morning light, advanced still for a couple of hours up the mountain.

The trail was lost at times, but despite the years gone by, I remembered the general direction. "To the east, 'til you hit a wall," we said 11 years ago. We rested beside a little creek that surely wouldn't last in the dry season. We slept a while. I was woken by a cry from my alter ego. I took the safety off my weapon, aiming it where I heard the groan. Yes, it was my alter ego, grabbing his foot and complaining. I came near. He had tried to take off his sock without thinking and had pulled off a piece of skin.

"You fool," I said to him, "You have to soak it first."

It was the ninth day with our boots on. The fabric and the skin, with the dampness and the mud, become one, and to take off the sock is like skinning yourself. The disadvantages of sleeping with your boots on. I showed him how to do it. We stuck our feet in the water, and little by little, pulled back the fabric. The feet smelled like dead dogs and the skin was a deformed and off-white mass.

"You scared me. When I saw you grabbing your foot, I thought a snake had bitten you!" I reproached him.

My alter ego didn't pay me any mind, he kept on soaking his feet and closed his eyes. As if he were calling it. Camilo began to hit the ground with a stake.

"What now?" I asked him.

"Snake," said Camilo while he threw stones, sticks, boots and everything he found at hand. At last a blow with a stick on the head.

We approached fearfully.

"Mococh," says Camilo.

"Nauyaca," I say.

Limping, my alter ego approaches. He puts on a knowing look when he says: It's the famous Bac Ne' or Four Noses.

"Its bite is fatal and its venom very poisonous," he adds, imitating the tone of a merolico in a town fair. We skin her. Skinning the snake is like taking off her shirt. The belly is opened like a long zipper, the guts are emptied and the skin comes off in one piece. The meat is left, white and cartilaginous. It's pierced with a thin stick and put on the fire. It tastes like grilled fish, like macabil, that we caught in the "Sin Nombre" [nameless] river, 11 years ago. We ate that and a little pinole [toasted corn flour drink] with sugar that we had been given. After a little rest, we wiped out our tracks and continued the march. Just like 11 years ago, the forest welcomed us as it should: raining. The rain in the forest is like no other. It starts to rain but the trees act as a big umbrella, only a few drops escape from among the branches and leaves. Afterwards, the green roof begins to drip, and then, really, to get wet. Like a big showerhead, it keeps dripping, raining within, though above it has stopped raining. With the rain in the forest it's like war: one knows when it starts, but not when it ends.

On the way, I was recognizing old friends: the huapac with its modest coat of green moss, the capricious and hard rectitude of the cante; the hormiguillo, the mahogany, the cedar, the sharp and poisonous defense of the chapaya, the fan of the watapil, the disproportionate gigantism of the leaves of the pij, that seem like green elephants' ears, the vertical rise to the sky of the bayalte, the hard heart of the canolte, the threat of the chechem or "mala mujer" [evil woman] that, as its name indicates, causes a very high fever, delirium, and much pain. Trees and more trees. Nothing but brown and green filling the eyes, the hands, the steps, the soul again...

Like 11 years ago, when I arrived here the first time. And then I was climbing this damned hill and thinking that each step I took was the last one, and saying to myself, "one more step and I die," and I took a step and then another and I didn't die and I kept walking and felt that the load weighed 100 kilos, and it was a lie since I knew that I was carrying only 15 kilos and "it's just that you're very new," said the compas that went to get me and laughed with complicity, and I kept repeating to myself that now for real the next step would be the last and cursed the hour in which it occurred to me to become a guerrilla, as well as I had been doing as an organic intellectual, and the revolution has many tasks and all are important, and why did I have to get into this, and for sure the next rest I'll tell them here and no farther, and it would be better for me to help them there in the city, and I kept walking and kept falling and the next rest came and I didn't say a thing, in part for shame and in part because I couldn't even speak, gulping air like a fish in a puddle that's too small for him, and I said to myself, all right, at the next rest I'll tell them, really, and the same thing happened and so I got through the 10 hours of that first day of walking in the jungle, and now getting on towards evening, they said: we're going to stay here, and I let myself fall right there, and I said to myself "I made it here" and I repeated "I made it" and we put up the hammocks and then they made a fire and then they made rice with sugar and we ate and ate and they asked me how the hill had seemed and how I felt and whether I was tired and I only repeated "I made it" and they looked at each other and said he's only been here one day and he's already gone crazy.

The next day I found out that the trail I'd covered in 10 hours with a 15-kilo load, they did in four hours and with 20 kilos. I didn't say anything. "Let's go," they said. I followed them, and at each step I took I asked myself: "Am I there?" Today, 11 years later, history, tired of going forward, repeats itself. We make it there. Do we? The afternoon was a relief, a light like that wheat which relieved me many early mornings, it bathed the place we had decided to camp. We ate after Camilo ran into some Sac Jol ("old man's face" or "white head"). It turns out that there were seven. I told Camilo not to shoot; maybe they were running deer and I thought that we'd come across them. Nothing, neither "Sac Jol" nor deer. We put up the tarps and the hammocks. After a while, at night now, the martruchas came to bark at us, and afterward, the woyo or night monkey. I couldn't sleep. Everything hurt, even hope...

P.S. SELF-CRITIQUE THAT, SHAMEFULLY, DISGUISES ITSELF AS A STORY FOR WOMEN WHO, AT TIMES, ARE GIRLS, AND FOR GIRLS WHO, AT TIMES, ARE WOMEN. AND, AS HISTORY REPEATS ITSELF ONCE AS COMEDY AND AGAIN AS TRAGEDY, THE STORY IS CALLED...

10. DURITO II (NEOLIBERALISM SEEN FROM THE LACANDON JUNGLE)

It was the tenth day, with less pressure now. I went away a little to put up my tarp and move in. I was going along, looking up, searching for a good pair of trees that didn't have a dead hanging branch. So I was surprised when I heard, at my feet, a voice that shouted, "Hey, watch out!" I didn't see anything at first, but I stopped and waited. Almost immediately a little leaf began to move and, from under it, a beetle came out who began to demand: "Why don't you watch where you put your big boots? You were about to crush me!" he yelled.

This demand seemed familiar to me.

"Durito? [little hard guy]" I ventured.

"Nabucodonosor [Nebuchadnezzar] to you! Don't be a leveler!" answered the little beetle indignantly.

Now I had no room for doubt.

"Durito! Don't you remember me?" Durito, I mean, Nabucodonosor, just kept looking thoughtfully at me. He took our a little pipe from within his wings, filled it with tobacco, lit it, and after a big puff which brought on a cough that wasn't at all healthy, he said: "Mmmmh, mmmh."

And then he repeated: "Mmmmh, mmmh."

I knew that this was going to take a while, so I sat down. After several "mmmh, mmh," Nabucodonosor, or Durito, exclaimed: "Captain? The same!" I said, satisfied to see myself recognized.

Durito (I believe that after recognizing him, I could call him that again) began a series of movements of his feet and wings that, in the body language of the beetles, is a kind of dance of joy and to me has always seemed like an attack of epilepsy. After repeating several times, with different emphases, "Captain!," Durito finally stopped and fired the question I so feared: "Got any tobacco?"

"Well, I..." I drew out the answer to give myself time to calculate my reserves.

At that, Camilo arrived and asked me: "Did you call me, Sup?" "No, it's nothing... I was singing and... and don't worry, you can go," I responded nervously.

"Oh, good," said Camilo, and retired.

"Sup?" asked Durito, surprised.

"Yes," I told him. "Now I'm a subcommander."

"And is that better or worse than Captain?" Durito asked insistently.

"Worse," I told him and myself.

I changed the subject quickly and held the bag of tobacco out to him saying: "Here, I have a little."

To receive the tobacco, Durito performed his dance again, now repeating "thank you!" over and over.

The tobacco euphoria over, we started the complicated ceremony of lighting our pipes. I leaned back on my pack and just looked at Durito.

"You look the same as ever," I told him.

"You, on the other hand, look pretty beat up," he responded.

"It's life!" I said, playing it down.

Durito started with his "mmmh, mmh." After a while he said to me: "And what brings you here after so many years?" "Well, I was thinking, since I had nothing better to do, I said to myself, why not take a turn around the old places and get a chance to see old friends," I responded.

"Old mountains still get green!" Durito protested indignantly.

After that followed a long while of "mmmh, mmmh" and of his inquisitive looks.

I couldn't take it any longer and confessed to him: "The truth is that we are withdrawing because the government launched an offensive against us..."

"You ran!" said Durito.

I tried to explain to him what a strategic withdrawal is, a tactical retreat, and whatever occurred to me in that moment.

"You ran," said Durito, this time with a sigh.

"Well, yes, I ran - and what about it?" I said, annoyed, more with myself than with him.

Durito didn't press. He stayed quiet a good while. Only the smoke of the two pipes formed a bridge. Minutes later he said: "It seems like there's something more that's bothering you, not just the 'strategic retreat'."

"Withdrawal, 'strategic withdrawal'," I corrected him. Durito waited for me to go on: "The truth is that it bothers me that we weren't prepared. And it was my fault we weren't prepared. I believed the government did want dialogue and so had given the order that the consultations for the delegates should begin. When they attacked us we were discussing the conditions of the dialogue. They surprised us. They surprised me..." I said with shame and anger.

Durito went on smoking, waited for me to finish telling him everything that had happened in the last ten days. When I finished, Durito said: "Wait for me."

And he went under a little leaf. After a while he came out pushing his little desk. After that he went for a chair, sat down, took out some papers, and began to look through them with a worried air.

"Mmmh, mmh," he said with every few pages that he read. After a time he exclaimed: "Here it is!"

"Here's what?" I asked, intrigued.

"Don't interrupt me!" Durito said seriously and solemnly. And added: "Pay attention. Your problem is the same one many have. You refer to the economic and social doctrine known as 'neoliberalism'..."

"Just what I needed... now classes in political economy," I thought.

It seems like Durito heard what I was thinking because he chided me:

"Ssshh! This isn't just any class! It is the Chair [as in university] par excellence."

That about the "Chair par excellence" seemed exaggerated to me, but I got ready to listen to it. Durito continued after some "mmmh, mmmh"s.

"It is a metatheoretical problem! Yes, you start from the idea that 'neoliberalism' is a doctrine. And by 'you', I am referring to those who insist on frameworks that are rigid and square like your head. You think that 'neoliberalism' is a capitalist doctrine to confront the economic crises that capitalism itself attributes to 'populism'. Right?" Durito didn't let me answer.

"Of course right! Well, it turns out that 'neoliberalism' is not a theory to confront or explain the crisis. It is the crisis itself made theory and economic doctrine! That is, 'neoliberalism' hasn't the least coherence; it has no plans nor historic perspective. In the end, pure theoretical shit."

"How strange... I've never heard or read that interpretation," I said with surprise.

"Of course! How, if it just occurred to me in this moment!" says Durito with pride.

"And what has that got to do with our running away, excuse me, with our withdrawal?" I asked, doubting such a novel theory.

"Ah! Ah! Elementary, my dear Watson Sup! There are no plans, there are no perspectives, only i-m-p-r-o-v-i-s-a-t-i-o-n. The government has no consistency: one day we're rich, another day we're poor, one day they want peace, another day they want war, one day fasting, another day stuffed, and so on. Am I clear?" Durito inquires.

"Almost..." I hesitate, and scratch my head.

"And so?" I ask, seeing that Durito isn't continuing with his dissertation.

"It's going to explode. Boom! Like a balloon blown up too far. It has no future. We're going to win!" says Durito as he puts his papers away.

"We?" I ask maliciously.

"Of course, 'we'! It's clear that you won't be able to without my help. No, don't try to raise objections. You need a superadvisor. I'm already learning French, for continuity's sake."

I stayed quiet. I don't know what is worse: discovering that we're governed by improvisation, or imagining Durito as a supersecretary in the cabinet of an improbable transition government.

Durito attacks: "I surprised you, eh? Well, don't feel bad. As long as you don't crush me with your big boots I will always be able to clarify for you the road to follow in the course of history, which despite its ups and downs, will raise this country up, because united... because united... Now that I think of it, I haven't written to my old lady..." Durito lets out the big laugh.

"I thought you were serious!" I pretend to be annoyed and throw a little branch at him. Durito dodges it and keeps laughing.

Now calmed down, I ask him: "And where did you get those conclusions that neoliberalism is the crisis made economic doctrine?" "Ah! From this book that explains the 1988-1994 economic project of Carlos Salinas de Gortari," he answers and shows me a little book with the logo of Solidarity.

"But Salinas isn't president anymore... it seems," I say with a doubt that shakes me.

"I know that, but look who drew up the plan," says Durito and points out a name. I read: "Ernesto Zedillo Ponce de Leon." I say, surprised, and add: "So there isn't any break?" "What there is a cave of thieves?" says Durito, implacable.

"And so?" I ask with real interest.

"Nothing, just that the Mexican political system is like that dead tree branch hanging over your head," says Durito and I jump and look up and see that, sure enough, there is a dead branch that is hanging threateningly over my hammock. I change places while Durito keeps talking: "The Mexican political system is just barely attached to reality with pieces of very fragile branches. It will only take one good wind for it to come down. Of course, when it falls, it's going to take other branches with it, and watch out, anyone who's under its shade when it collapses!"

"And if there isn't a wind?" I ask while I check whether the hammock is well tied.

"There will be... there will be," says Durito and looks thoughtful, as if he were looking at the future.

We were both left thoughtful. We lit our pipes again. The day began to get underway. Durito kept looking at my boots. Fearful, he asked: "And how many are with you?" "Two more, so don't worry about being stomped," I said to calm him. Durito practices doubt methodically as a discipline, so he continued with his "mmmh, mmmh," until he let out: "But those coming after you, how many are they?" "Ah! Those? Like some sixty..."

Durito didn't let me finish: "Sixty! Sixty pairs of big boots on top of my head! 120 Sedena [Defense Department] boots trying to crush me!" he yelled hysterically.

"Wait, you didn't let me finish. They aren't sixty," I said.

Durito interrupted again: "Ah! I knew so much disaster wasn't possible. How many are they, then?" Laconically, I answered: "Sixty thousand."

"Sixty thousand!" Durito managed to say before choking on the smoke of his pipe.

"Sixty thousand!" he repeated several times, crossing his little hands and feet together with anguish.

"Sixty thousand!" he said to himself desperately.

I tried to console him. I told him that they weren't all coming together, that it was an offensive in stages, that they were coming in from different directions, that they hadn't found us, that we had rubbed out our tracks so that they wouldn't follow us, in short, I told him everything that occurred to me.

After a while, Durito calmed down and started with his "mmmh, mmmh." He took out some little papers that, as I started to realize, looked like maps, and began questioning me about the location of enemy troops. I answered the best I could. With each answer Durito made marks and notes on his little maps. He went on a good while, after the questioning, saying "mmmh, mmmh." After some minutes and after complicated calculations (I say this as he used all his little hands and feet to do the figuring) he sighed: "What's said: they're using 'the anvil and hammer', the 'sliding lasso', the 'rabbit hunt', and the vertical maneuver." "Elementary, it comes from the Rangers manual of the School of the Americas," he says to himself and to me. And adds: "But we have one chance to come out well from this."

"Ah, yes? And how?" I ask with skepticism.

"With a miracle!" says Durito as he puts his papers away and lies back down.

The silence settled down between us and we let the afternoon arrive between the branches and vines. Later, when night finished falling from the trees, and flying, covered the sky, Durito asked me: "Captain... Captain... Psst! Are you asleep?" "No."

"What is it?" I answered.

Durito asks with pity, as if afraid to hurt me. "And what do you intend to do?" I keep smoking, I look at the silver curls of the moon hung from the branches. I let out a spiral of smoke and I answer him and answer myself: "Win."

P.S. THAT TUNES IN TO NOSTALGIA IN THE QUADRANT.

On the little radio someone, to a blues rhythm, tears out the one that goes: "All its gonna right with a little help of my friends..." [sic]

P.S. THAT NOW, REALLY, SAYS GOODBYE, WAVING A HEART LIKE A HANDKERCHIEF.

So much rain and not a drop to sate the yearning...

Go on again.

Health, and be careful with that dry branch that hangs over your heads and that pretends, ingenuously, to shelter you with its shade.

The Sup, smoking... and hoping.

11. ZAPATISTAS GUADALUPANOS AND THE VIRGIN OF GUADALUPE

March 24, 1995

To the national weekly Proceso

To the national newspaper El Financiero

To the national newspaper La Jornada

To the local newspaper of SCLC, Chiapas, Tiempo

Sirs,

A communiqué-report going out, on the advances of the dialogue by letters. Please, realize how many days it takes for things to get here and to get out, and don't be anxious.

Here the spring is disguised as autumn and the leaves tend to don uniforms of brown. By day with horseflies and by night with cocuyos, the forest also changes clothes and surprises.

Go on. Health and a fresh wind that relieves the tedium of desperation.

> *From the mountains of the Mexican Southeast,*
> *Insurgent Subcommander Marcos.*
> *Mexico, March 1995.*

P.S. That shows how much the e-z-l-n has "imposed" itself on the uses and customs of the communities, and explains how "interests foreign" to the indigenous people camp out in the ranks of the "neocriminals."

A few days ago, in the now migratory town of "Guadalupe Tepeyac," there was an argument. A gift came to them from the city. Among the little humanitarian aid they received, the "Zapatistas Guadalupanos" (as they call themselves) found an image of the Virgin of Guadalupe. From what they tell me, the image measures some 30 centimeters, has some gold cords and some colored candles. ("It's pretty," says the one who's telling me.)

The whole thing has generated different opinions: first a controversy, then an argument, and finally, a general assembly of these people who, far from their homes, traveling uphill and down, don't surrender, and call themselves with pride, "Guadalupe Tepeyac." The yellow laces that adorn the image were the first topic. "They're painted," said a man when he looked at them from far off. "No, they're made of gold," said a lady. Rapidly the community began to choose sides.

The argument goes on next to the church, in a little field that serves as a playground, a dance floor, or as it is now, a debating salon. The inhabitants of the settlement today serving as a temporary refuge for the Guadalupanos keep out of it.

This is an affair of the people from Guadalupe Tepeyac, and no one else. Even the militia members, who guard the safety of their people, don't intervene. They smoke and keep quiet in a corner of the houses, their weapons resting on their legs and their packs ready.

At some point (he who tells me all this can't say how it happened, he describes the scene from different angles at the same time), the argument moves to the topic of whether the image will stay in the town sheltering them, or will go together with those of "Guadalupe Tepeyac" when they return (when?) to their homes. The sides become radicalized and a confrontation begins to emerge between the men and the women: some men are in favor of the image staying as a gift of thanks for the people that received them; the women, who begin to gather in greater numbers, say that the image is a gift, and that a gift should not be given again, because then it isn't a gift anymore because gifts, once given, aren't given again (he who tells me says everything at a run, I gather that the argument is more complicated and that he is sparing something that is hard to understand and even harder to explain).

Clearly some are thinking of the weight and bulkiness when their improbable moving comes, but the women don't give in. On each side, reasons and spontaneous orators arise. The one in charge of the town is found on one side of the playground, seated and silent, listening. At a certain point he gets up and proposes that the matter be resolved in a general assembly. In "Guadalupe Tepeyac" they have assemblies and votes even to see how long a dance should go on, so that the proposal is acclaimed. The agreement on this is unanimous, since after all, the gift is for the whole town, and there are still men burning cornfields and women washing clothes in the river.

The assembly will be in the evening, when the heat abates and the coolness caresses and relieves the dark skins of these men and women who were the headquarters, in August of 1994 and in January of 1995, of the Zapatistas' will for peace and who received, in response, dozens of tanks and helicopters, and thousands of soldiers who now occupy their lands. (Yes, I know I'm continually changing the tense of the verbs, but that's how they're telling me the story).

When the meeting starts, the day has already deposited its sun coin in the mountain's money chest, but there is still light so that the candles and lighters aren't needed. Over the past hours, each side has worked at convincing the others who weren't there. After this "conferring" (which between some couples sounds like threats), the assembly repeats the arguments: the image of the Guadalupana stays in the town that give them lodgings, or the Virgin goes where the people of "Guadalupe Tepeyac" go.

Dona Herminia (or "Ermina," as he says who's telling me) starts to speak, hoarsely. With the weight of a hundred years on her, dona Herminia begins to speak slowly and quietly. She obliges a special attention, out of respect and to be able to hear what she says. She says that the Virgin of Guadalupe came again from the city, came to find her sons and daughters, the Zapatistas Guadalupanas, and that as she didn't find them, she searched for them up in the mountains, and came to their hands after much traveling, from one place to another, uphill and down.

The dona says that the Virgin must be tired of so much going up and down hills, especially with this heat that dries up saints and sinners alike, and that a little rest would do her no harm at all, and now that she is with them, it is good that the Virgin rest a while with her own. But she didn't come from so far away, the mother Lupita, to stay here, she didn't travel from one place to another, seeking us, to end up staying in a place if the Guadalupanos go to another.

The dona thinks (and here all the women, and a man here and there, assent with their heads and join in the thought of the dona) that the Guadalupana will want to be with her sons and daughters wherever they are, and that her tiredness will be better if she rests together with her family, and the sadness will hurt her less if it hurts her together with them, and that the joy will shine more if it shines on her being in a group.

The dona says that she thinks (now there are more who agree), that the Virgin will want to go wherever the people of "Guadalupe Tepeyac" go, that if the war throws them into the mountains, to the mountains the Virgin will go, turned soldier like them, to defend her dark dignity; that if peace brings them back to their homes, the Guadalupana will go to the town to reconstruct what was destroyed.

"So I ask you, madrecita, if you agree to going wherever we go, all of us you gave yourself to," the dona asks, addressing the image that is in front of the assembly. The Virgin doesn't answer, her dark gaze keeps looking downward. After a moment of silence, the dona finishes: "That is all my word, brothers."

He who is leading the assembly asks if anyone else wants to speak. A unanimous silence is the answer. "There will be a vote," he says, and takes the vote. The women win. The Virgin of Guadalupe will go wherever the Guadalupanos go. After the assembly there will be a dance. A marimba and the dark-skinned image preside over the festivity. In some circles they continue arguing over whether the little cords are of gold or only painted yellow. A cumbia grabs the ones arguing by the feet and carries them what is now the dance floor.

"So the women won again?" I ask.

"Sure!" says he who is telling me the story. "You never contradict a woman, and much less when spring is already warming the nights in the mountains of the Mexican Southeast..."

P.S. That wanders on a moonstruck theme and wishes, ingenuously, to be given a place in the scientific columns of the main dailies and magazines.

Mounted on a curl of the smoke of my pipe, I rise to the highest curl of the ceiba tree. It is night and a sorrow is gaining on the moon, now darkening a good bit of her figure. The Sup reflects: "The Moon is a satellite of the Earth. That is, the Moon spends her life turning around the Earth, with the same tedium with which a merry-go-round turns, empty, in a town fair. The Moon says nothing in the face of this sentence. What is she going to say, if in any case there is a long and invisible chain that ties her to the Earth and keeps her from leaving to take a turn around so many other stars and planets."

Nevertheless, as far as one can see, the Moon is not bitter. It doesn't occur to her, for example, to let herself fall on the Earth with the same wavering spin as a coin coming down to elucidate the first mystery: heads or tails? No, the Moon doesn't let herself fall. That means nothing else than that the Moon has hope. And this fact is what has, until now, gone unnoticed by all the astronomers, astrophysicists, astrologers, astronauts, and by the Houston "Astros." Up until now, I say, because I intend to unveil this technical and scientific datum that will revolutionize all modern science and, above all, the daily and nightly approaches of amorous couples.

"The Moon has hope," I have said, and here lies the point of an epistemological break and the birth of a new scientific paradigm (by the way, speaking of T. Kuhn and of the Scientific Revolutions, once I wrote a letter to Gilly where I explained the uselessness, scientifically and for the police, of speculation over who was behind the criminal nose and the ski mask. Time and the pathetic PGR [Justice Department] proved me right (and with the arrest warrant).

Well - let's repeat it: "The Moon has hope." The simplistic will go ahead and ask: "What does the Moon hope for?" But the problem will have no solution unless we first answer the following question: "What makes it possible for the Moon to have hope?" Clearly it isn't the same, but the question is as momentous as if we referred to "The Moon is sleepy," something that of course, is nonsense, because being a nocturnal animal, the Moon obviously suffers from insomnia.

A statement such as, "The Moon is feverish" sounds hot and sensual, and perhaps, may help to melt the resistance of the other person to a closer contact, and thence to the inevitable contagion, but nothing more. The pragmatic will discard such a claim immediately, since, they will argue, there is no thermometer capable of taking the temperature nor antipyretic imaginable for such a space fever.

An utterance like "The Moon has desires" is as ambiguous as "The Moon has hope," and leads one to ask, "What does the Moon desire?" By the way, I'm getting there...

(The Sup approaches the edge of the top of the ceiba with admirable balance, and after the characteristic sound that betrays the way in which mammals evacuate the contents of their bladders, returns with a face saying "duty done") "All right, let's return to science, now that the prosaic reminder of the body is answered, with its ebbs and flows. Where were we? Oh yes! On, "The Moon has desires." No, that we had already discarded (in more than one sense).

We'll go back to the rash statement that "The Moon has hope." It's elementary. Can you imagine someone turning and turning around the same thing, seeing always the same landscape and repeating always the same routine? What? The special under-attorney for the murder cases of LDC [Luis Donaldo Colosio], JFRM [Jose Francisco Ruiz Massieu] and Cardinal Posadas? For God's sake! We're talking about science, not comic strips! Back we go.

All right, isn't it logical to suppose that this "someone" would be bored and wish to be freed of such a circular sentence? Yes, I know that, in the case of the Moon, there is that silly chain of the "force of gravity." But... why then not let yourself drop? You still doubt! Okay, it's not important... We geniuses have always been misunderstood... at first. All right, all right, be kind (remember that it's spring), grant me that it's like this, that the Moon is a prisoner, and that, nevertheless, she takes no vengeance on the one who makes her a prisoner.

Who is it that keeps her prisoner? The human being! If they hadn't invented that "law of gravity," the Moon would have been off romping about Jupiter or Saturn or even further...

Thus, the Moon undoubtedly has hope, hope of seeing herself free and able to go wherever she lunatically desires. What is one of the main consequences of this fact? Well, it's that if the Moon escapes, whether it's because the silly chain breaks or because her jailer forgets to tie her, people in love won't be able to use her as a reference anymore, to convince or to deny.

How could they say, "In the double moon of your breast, hands, kisses and gazes surrender," or that other one, "with the complicity of the moon I discovered the pleasure you had hidden in your womb," or, also, "Don't bring your breath any closer, the Moon will flee, frightened to see us as one"? So, these are only some examples, but you can see what kind of problems would arise the night the Moon abandons her usual route and just leaves, to ride off into the stars...

P.S. To the lunatic P.S.

One must also be careful with the Moon. Many years ago, one Knight of the White Moon defeated me on the beaches of Barcino and obliged me, ungrateful, to put away arms and warlike desires for a good while. Now I have freed myself, but that's another story I'll tell you... another moon.

P.S. That, understanding, offers an alternative.

All right, if you don't want to publish it in the science column, at least do me the favor of tying that postscript with a little string to the UNAMSAT-1 and tell them to let it go when they pass by the Moon. It will do her good to know that someone understands her...

Go on again.

Health, and may hands and moons find each other.

The Sup, little embarrassed, because now he doesn't know how to get down out of the ceiba. How about sliding down that silver rail that turns to the ground?

12. A Year of the Zapatista Government

March 17, 1995

To the men and women who, in different tongues and roads, believe in a more humane future and struggle to achieve it today

Brothers and sisters,

There exists on this planet called "Earth", and in the continent called "America" a country whose shape appears to have had a big bite taken out of its west side, and which threw out an arm deep into the Pacific Ocean so that the hurricanes don't blow it far away from its history. This country is known by both natives and foreigners by the name of "Mexico". Its history is a long battle between its desire to be itself and the foreign desires to have it exist under another flag. This country is ours.

We, our blood in the voices of our oldest grandparents, we walked this land when it was not yet known by this name. But later in this eternal struggle, between being and not being, between staying and leaving, between yesterday and tomorrow, came into the thinking of our ancestors, now with the blood of two branches, that this piece of land and water and sky and dreams, a land which we had because it had been a gift of our earlier ancestors, would be called "Mexico". Then we became others with more, and then the history of the way that we all got the name and thus we were born was complete. And we were called "Mexicans", and they called us "Mexicans".

Later history continued giving blows and pains. We were born between blood and gunpowder, between blood and gunpowder we were raised. Every so often the powerful from other lands came to rob us of tomorrow. For this reason it was written, in a war song that unites us: "If a foreigner ever dares, to profane with his foot your dream, think, Oh beloved motherland, that heaven gave you a soldier in each son." For this reason we fought yesterday. With flags and different languages the foreigner came to conquer us. He came and he went. We continued to be Mexicans because we weren't happy with any other name nor to walk under any other flag that does not have the eagle devouring a snake, on a white background, and with green and red to the sides. And that's what happened to us.

We, the first inhabitants of these lands, the indigenous, we were left forgotten in a corner, and the rest began to grow and become stronger. We only had our history with which to defend ourselves, and we seized it in order not to die. Later even this part of the history became practically a joke because a single country, the country of money, put itself in the middle of all of the flags. And they said "Globalization" and then we knew that this was how this absurd order was called, an order in which money is the only country which is served and the borders are erased, not out of brotherhood, but because of the impoverishment which fattens the powerful without nationality. The lie became the universal coin, and in our country, a dream, based on the nightmare of the majority, of wealth and prosperity was knitted for the few.

Corruption and falsehoods were the principal products that our Motherland exported to other countries. Being poor, dressed in the wealth of our scarcities, and because there were so many lies and they were so broad, that we ended up thinking they were the truth. We prepared for the great international forums, and poverty was declared, by the will of the government, as an invention that vanished before the development that the economic statistics shouted. Us? We became even more forgotten, and now our history wasn't enough to keep us from dying just like that, forgotten and humiliated. Because death does not hurt, what hurts is to be forgotten. We discovered then that we did not exist any more, that those who govern had forgotten about us in their euphoria of statistics and rates of growth.

A country that forgets itself is a sad country, a country that forgets its past can not have a future. And so we took up arms and we went into the cities where we were considered animals. We went and we told the powerful, "We are here!" and to all of the country we shouted, "We are here!" and to all of the world we yelled, "We are here!". And they saw how things were because, in order for them to see us, we covered our faces; so that they would call us by name, we gave up our names; we bet the present to have a future; and to live... we died. And then the planes came and the bombs and the bullets and the death and we went back to our mountains and even to there death pursued us, and many people from many parts said, "Talk", and the powerful said "Let's talk", and we said, "Okay, let's talk", and we talked and we told them what we wanted and they did not understand very well, and we repeated that we wanted democracy, liberty and justice, and they made a face like they didn't understand, and they reviewed their macroeconomic plans and all their neo-liberal points, and they could not find these words anywhere, and "we don't understand" they said to us, and they offered us a prettier corner in the history museum, and death with an extended timeline, and a chain of gold in order to tie up our dignity. And we, so that they would understand what we want, began to create in our lands what we wanted. We organized based on the agreement of the majority, and we demonstrated what it was like to live with democracy, with liberty, and with justice, and this is what happened:

For a year the law of the Zapatistas governed the mountains of Southeastern Mexico, and you all were not there to know about it, nor can I tell it, but the Zapatistas are we. In other words, those of us who do not have a face nor a name nor a past, and for the most part we are indigenous, but lately more brothers and sisters of other lands and races have been entering. All of us are Mexicans. When we governed these lands we did the following:

When we governed, we lowered to zero the rate of alcoholism, and the women here became very fierce and they said that drink only served to make the men beat their women and children, and to act barbaric, and therefore they gave the order that no drink was allowed, and that we could not allow drinking to go on, and the people who received the most benefit were the children and women, and the ones most damaged were the businessmen and the government. And, with the support of some of those groups called "Non-Governmental Organizations" both from within the country and foreigners, health campaigns were carried out, and the hope for life for the civilian population was raised, even though the lack of trust in the government reduced the hope for life of us the combatants. And the woman, or in other words the women, began to see that the laws which were imposed on the men were fulfilled, and a third of our combatant force is women and they are very fierce and they are armed, and so they "convinced" us to accept their laws and they also participate in the civilian and military direction of our struggle and we don't say anything, and besides what are we going to say.

The destruction of trees also was prohibited, and laws were made to protect the forests, and the hunting of wild animals was prohibited, even if they were from the government, and the cultivation, consumption and trafficking in drugs were prohibited, and these laws were upheld. The infant death rate went way down, and became very small, just like the children are. And the Zapatista laws were applied uniformly, without regard for social position or income level. And we made all of the major decisions, or the "strategic" ones, of our struggle, by means of a method that they call the "referendum" and the "plebiscite". And we got rid of prostitution and unemployment disappeared as well as begging. The children had sweets and toys. And we made many errors and had many failures. And we also accomplished what no other government in the world, regardless of its political affiliation, is capable of doing honestly, and that is to recognize its errors and to take steps to remedy them.

We were doing this, learning, when the tanks and the helicopters and the planes and the many thousands of soldiers arrived, and they said that they came to defend the national sovereignty, and we told them that that was being violated in the IUE-SEI and not in Chiapas and the national sovereignty can not be defended by trampling the rebel dignity of the Chiapas indigenous. And they did not listen because the noise of the their war machines made them deaf and they came in the name of the government, and for the government, betrayal is the ladder by which one climbs to power, and for us loyalty is the egalitarian plane that we desire for everyone. And the legality of the government came mounted on bayonets, and our legality was based on consensus and reason, and we wanted to convince, and the government wanted to conquer and we said that no law that had to resort to arms to be fulfilled by a people could be called a law, and it is only an arbitrariness regardless of how much legalist wrappings it is covered with, and he who orders the fulfillment of a law accompanied by the force of weapons is a dictator even if he says that the majority elected him. And we were run out of our lands. And with the war tanks came the law of the government, and the law of the Zapatistas left. And behind the war tanks of the government came again prostitution, drinking, theft, drugs, destruction, death, corruption, sickness, poverty.

And people from the government came and said that they had now restored law in the Chiapas lands, and they came with bullet-proof vests and with war tanks and they were there only a few minutes and they just had enough time to say their statements in front of the chickens and roosters and pigs and dogs and cows and horses and a cat that had gotten lost. And that's how the government did it, and maybe you all know this because it's true that a lot of reporters saw this and publicized it. And this is the legality that rules in our lands now. And this is how the government conducted the war for "legality" and for "national sovereignty" against the indigenous people of Chiapas. The government also waged war against the rest of the Mexicans, but instead of tanks and planes, they launched an economic program that is also going to kill them, just more slowly...

And now I remember, that I am writing on March 17th, St. Patrick's Day and when Mexico was fighting, in the last century, against the empire of the bars and crooked stars, there was a group of soldiers from different nationalities who fought on the side of the Mexicans and this group was called the "St. Patrick Battalion", and for this reason the companeros said to me: "Go on, take this opportunity to write to the brothers from other countries and thank them because they stopped the war!" And I believe that this is their way of getting to go dance, and so that I don't yell at them because the government plane is wandering around there and that all these companeros want to do is to dance, even with everything and the war they keep dancing and dancing the marimba. And so I am writing you in the name of all of my companeros and companeras, because just as with the "Saint Patrick's Battalion", we now see clearly that there are foreigners who love Mexico more than some natives who are now in the government and tomorrow will be in jail or in physical exile, because their heart now belongs to foreigners, because they love another flag which is not theirs and another thinking which is not of their equals. And we learned that there were marches and songs and movies and other things that were not war in Chiapas, which is the part of Mexico where we live and die. And we learned that these things happened, and that "NO TO WAR!" was said in Spain and in France and in Italy and in Germany and in Russia and in England and in Japan and in Korea and in Canada and in the United States and in Argentina and in Uruguay and in Chile and in Venezuela and in Brazil and in other parts where it wasn't said but it was thought. And so we saw that there are good people in many parts of the world and that these people live closer to Mexico than those who live in "los Pinos", which is how the house where the government lives is called.

Our law made books, medicines, laughs, sweets and toys flourish. Their law, the law of the powerful, came without any argument other than that of force, and destroyed libraries, clinics and hospitals, it brought sadness and a bitter road to our people. And we thought that a legality that destroys knowledge, heath and happiness is a very small legality for such big women and men, and that our law is better, infinitely better, than the law of these misters who, with foreign vocations, say that they govern us.

And we want to say to you, to everyone, thank you. And that if we had a flower we would give it to you and since we don't have enough flowers for each man or for each woman, then a "enough" so that each person can get and save a piece, and when they are old, then they can talk with the children and young people of their country that, "I struggled for Mexico at the end of the 20th century, and from over here I was there with them and I only know that they wanted what all human beings want, for it not to be forgotten that they are human beings and for it to be remembered what democracy, liberty and justice are, and I did not know their faces but I did know their hearts and it was the same as ours." And when Mexico is free (which is not to say happy or perfect, but only free, or in other words, free to choose its road and make its errors and its successes) then a piece of you all, this that is at the top of the chest and that, despite the political implications or precisely because of them, is a little tilted to the left, will also be Mexico, and these six letters will represent dignity and then the flower will be for everyone or it will not exist, and now it occurs to me that with this letter a paper flower could be made and could be put in the lapel or the hair, depending on the person, and you could go dancing with this enchanting adornment. And I'm going to go because the surveillance plane comes again, and I have to put out the candle, but not the hope. This... nor death.

Goodbye...

Health and a promised flower: a green stem, a white flower, red leaves, and don't worry about the serpent, this that flaps its wings is an eagle which is in charge of it, you will see...

From the mountains of Southeastern Mexico,
Subcomandante Insurgente Marcos.
Mexico, March 1995.

13. Far Inside of the Cave of Desire

March 17, 1995
To the national weekly Proceso
To the national newspaper El Financiero
To the national newspaper La Jornada
To the local newspaper of SCLC, Tiempo

Sirs,
Another thank-you letter going out, this time for those abroad. Let's see if it gets to Gurria, who's sending out pure lies all over Europe. We aren't hiding from soldiers anymore, now we're fleeing legislators. There are piles of them and they turn up where no one expects them. It looks like they took that part about "verification" seriously. It's not bad, it may be the first committee that doesn't limit itself to buying crafts in San Cristobal. How are we doing in the Panamerican games? Too bad I couldn't attend. I'm sure I would have done very well in the "cross-country race." You should see the training I've put in since February 10th! Go on.

Health and may the spring in the blood have an address.

From the mountains of the Mexican Southeast,
Insurgent Subcommander Marcos.
Mexico, March of 1995.

P.S. That, in mourning, cries. I was listening on the little tape-player to that one by Stephen Stills, from the album Four Way Street, that goes: "Find the cost of free-

dom, buried in the ground. Mother Earth will swallow you, lay your body down…"
when my alter ego comes running and tells me: It looks like you got your way…

"Could it be the PRI has already fallen?" I ask with hope.

"No way!… They killed you," says my alter ego.

"Me! When? Where?" I ask while I go through my memories of where I've been
and what I've done.

"Today, in a confrontation… but they don't say just where," he responds.

"Oh, good!… And did I end up badly hurt or really dead?" I insist.

"Completely dead… that's what the news says," says my alter ego and leaves.

A narcissistic sob competes with the crickets.

"Why are you crying?" asks Durito while he lights his pipe.

"Because I can't attend my burial. I, who loved me so much…"

P.S. That tells what happened to the Sup and Durito in the 12th day of the withdrawal, of the mysteries of the Cave of Desire, and of other unfortunate events that
today make us laugh, but at that time took away even our hunger.

"And if they bomb us?" asked Durito in the early morning of the 12th day of the
withdrawal. ("What kind of withdrawal, a pure run," says Durito.) It's cold. A grey
wind licks with its icy tongue the darkness of trees and earth.

I'm not sleeping, in solitude the cold hurts twice as much. Nevertheless I keep
quiet. Durito comes out from his sheltering leaf and climbs up on top of me. To
wake me up, he starts tickling my nose. I sneeze with such emphasis that Durito
ends up, tumbling over himself, on my boots. He recovers and gets back to my face.

"What's up?" I ask him before he tickles me again.

"And if they bomb us?" he insists.

"Yes… well… well… we'll look for a cave or something like that to hide ourselves
in… or we'll climb in a little hole… or we'll see what to do," I say with annoyance, and
look at my watch to insinuate that it isn't the hour to be worrying about bombings.

"I won't have any problems. I can go anywhere. But you, with those big boots
and that nose… I doubt that you'll find a safe place," says Durito as he covers himself again with a little huapac leaf.

"Psychology of terror," I think, about the apparent indifference of Durito regarding our fate…

"Our? He's right! He won't have problems, but me…" I think, I get up and speak
to Durito: "Psst… Psst… Durito!"

"I'm sleeping," he says from under his leaf.

I ignore his sleep and begin talking to him:

"Yesterday I heard Camilo and my alter ego saying that there are a lot of caves
around here. Camilo says he knows most of them. There are small ones, where an

armadillo would barely fit. And there are big ones like churches. But he says there is one no one dares to enter. He says there is a ugly story about that cave. The cave of desire, he says they call it."

Durito seems to get interested, his passion for detective novels is his ruin.

"And what is the story of that cave?"

"Well… It's a very long story. I've heard it myself, but that was years ago now… I don't remember it well," I said, making it interesting.

"Fine, go on, tell it," says Durito, more and more interested.

I light my pipe. From within the aromatic smoke comes the memory, and with it…

The Cave of Desire

"It happened many years ago. It is a story of a love that was not, that was left just like that. It is a sad story… and terrible," says the Sup sitting on one side, with his pipe in his lips. He lights it, and looking at the mountain, continues: "A man came from far away. He came, or he already was there. No one knows. It was back in other times long past and however that may be, in these lands people lived and died just the same, without hope and forgotten. No one knows if he was young or old, that man. Few are those who saw him the first times. It was like that because they say that this man was extremely ugly. Just to see him produced dread in men and revulsion in women. What was it that made him so unpleasant? I don't know, the concepts of beauty and ugliness change so much from one age to another and from one culture to another… In this case, the people native to these lands avoided him, as did the foreigners who were the owners of land, men, and destinies. The indigenous people called him the Jolmash or Monkey-face; the foreigners called him the Animal.

The man went into the mountains, far from the gaze of all, and set to work there. He made himself a little house, next to one of the many caves that were there. He made the land produce, planted corn and wheat, and hunting animals in the forest gave him enough to get by. Every so often he went down to a stream near the settlements. There he had arranged, with one of the older members of the community, to get salt, sugar, or whatever else the man, the Jolmash, didn't obtain in the mountains. The Jolmash exchanged corn and animal skins for what he needed. The Jolmash arrived at the stream at the time when the evening began to darken and the shadows of the trees advanced night onto the earth. The old man was sick in his eyes and couldn't see well, so that, with the dusk and his illness, he couldn't make out the face of the man who caused so much revulsion in the clear light.

One evening the old man didn't arrive. The Jolmash thought that maybe he had mistaken the hour and arrived when the old man had already gone home. To make no mistake, the next time he made sure to arrive earlier. The sun still had some fingers to go before it wrapped itself in the mountains, when the Jolmash came near the stream. A murmur of laughter and voices grew as he approached. The Jolmash slowed his steps and came silently nearer. Among the branches and vines he made out the pool formed by the waters of the stream. A group of women were bathing and washing clothes. They were laughing. The Jolmash looked and stayed quiet. His heart became only his gaze, his eyes his voice. It was a while since the women had gone and the Jolmash stayed on, looking... Now the stars rained down on the fields as he returned to the mountains.

I don't know if it came from what he saw, or from what he thought he saw, whether the image that was engraved on his retina corresponded to reality or if it existed only in his desire, but the Jolmash fell in love or thought that he fell in love. And his love was not something idealized or platonic, it was quite earthy, and the call of the feelings that he bore was like a war drum, like a lightning that becomes fierce rain. Passion took his hand and the Jolmash began to write letters, love letters, lettered delirium that filled his hands.

And he wrote, for example: 'Oh, lady of the wet glimmer! Desire becomes a proud leaping colt. Sword of a thousand mirrors is the yearning of my appetites for thy body, and in vain rips the double edge of the thousand pantings that fly on the wind. One grace, long sleeplessness! One grace I ask thee, lady, failed repose of my grey existence! Let me come to thy neck.

Allow that to thy ear climbs my clumsy longing. Let my desire tell thee, quiet, very quiet, that which my breast silences. Do not look, lady so not- mine, at the poor mess which adorns my face! Let thy ears become thy gaze; give up thy eyes to see the murmurs that walk within me, longing for thy within. Yes, I wish to enter. To walk thee, with sighs, the path that hands and lips and sex desire. Within the mouth, she wet and I thirsting, to enter with a kiss. On the double hill of thy breast to run lips and fingers, to awaken the cluster of moans that in it hide. To march to the south and to take prisoner thy waist in warm embrace, burning now the skin of the belly, brilliant sun announcing the night that below is born. To evade, diligent and skillful, the scissors on which thy grace goes and whose apex promises and denies. To give thee a tremor of cold heat and arrive, whole, to the moist stirring of desire. To secure the warmth of my palms in the double warmth of flesh and movement. One slow first step, a light trot next. After that the runaway ride of bodies and desire. To reach the sky, and then fall.

One grace, promised tiredness! One grace I ask thee, lady of the quiet sigh!

Let me come to thy neck! In it I am saved, far off I die...'

One night of storms, like his passion burning his hands, a bolt of lightning burnt down the little house of the Jolmash. Wet and shivering, he took refuge in the neighboring cave. With a torch he lit his way in and found there little figures of couples giving and receiving, the pleasure worked in stone and clay. There was a spring, and little boxes that when opened, spoke of terrors and marvels that had passed that and would come to be. The Jolmash now could not or would not leave the cave. There, he felt the desire fill his hands once more and wrote, weaving bridges to nowhere...

'A pirate am I now, lady of the longed-for port. Tomorrow, a soldier at war. Today, a pirate lost in trees and lands. The ship of desire unfolds its sails. A continual moaning, all tremor and wanting, leads the ship between monsters and storms. Lightning illuminates the flickering sea of desperation. A wet salt takes the command and the helm. Pure wind, word alone, I navigate seeking thee, among sighs and panting, seeking the precise place the body sends thee. Desire, lady of storms to come, is a knot hidden somewhere by thy skin. Find it I must, and muttering spells, untie it. Free then shall be thy longings, feminine swaying, and they will fill thy eyes and mouth, thy womb and innards. Free one moment only, as my hands already come to make them prisoners, to lead them out to sea in my embrace and with my body. A ship shall I be and restless sea, so that in thy body I enter. And there shall be no rest in so much storm, the bodies moved by so many capricious waves. One last and ferocious slap of salty desire hurls us to a beach where sleep arrives. A pirate am I now, lady of tender storm. Don't await my assault, come to it! Let the sea, the wind, and this stone become ship be witnesses! The cave of desire! The horizon clouds over with black wine, now we are arriving, now we go...'

So it happened, they say. And they say that the Jolmash never again left the cave. No one knows whether the woman to whom he wrote the letters existed in truth or was a product of the cave, the Cave of Desire. What they say is that the Jolmash still lives in it, and whoever comes close becomes sick with the same, with desire..."

Durito has followed the whole story attentively. When he sees I have finished, he says: "We have to go."

"Go?" I ask, surprised

"Of course!" says Durito. "I need literary advice to write to my old lady..."

"You're crazy!" I protest.

"Are you afraid?" asks Durito ironically.

I waver.

"Well... afraid, really afraid... no... but it's very cold... and it looks like it's going to rain... and... yes, I'm afraid."

"Bah! Don't worry. I'll go with you and I'll be telling you where. I think I know where the Cave of Desire is," says Durito with certainty.

"All right," I say, giving in. "You'll be in charge of the expedition."

"Great! My first order is that you march in the vanguard, in the center nobody, to disconcert the enemy, and I will go in the extreme rearguard," indicates Durito.

"I? In the vanguard? I protest!"

"Protest denied!" says Durito with firmness.

"O.K., soldier to the end, I'll go along."

"Good, that's what I like. Attention! This is the plan of attack:

First: if there are many, we run.

Second: If there are a few, we hide.

Third: If there isn't anyone, forward, for we were born to die!" dictates Durito while he prepares his little pack.

For a war plan it seemed too cautious for me, but Durito was the chief now, and given the circumstances, I had no reason to object to prudence marching in the vanguard.

Above the stars started to be smudged out...

"It looks like it's going to rain," I said to Durito, "excuse me, to the chief."

"Silence! Nothing will detain us!" shouts Durito with the voice of the sergeant in that Oliver Stone film called Platoon.

A gust of freezing wind and the first drops...

"Haaalt!" orders Durito.

The drops of rain start to multiply...

"I forgot to mention the fourth point of the plan of attack..." says Durito with doubt.

"Oh yeah? And what is it?" I ask insidiously.

"If it starts to rain... Strategic withdrawal!" The last words are said by Durito now in an open run back to camp.

I ran behind him. It was useless. We got soaked, and shivering, we reached the little plastic roof. It rained as if desire had, at last, been unleashed...

Go on again.

Health, and that the hunger for tomorrow be a desire to struggle... today.

The Sup, inside, far inside, of the Cave of Desire. It's March, it's early morning, and for being dead, I feel verrry well.

14. That Reason Wins Always and Never Force

March 25, 1995
To: The Dialogue of the Civic Society
Aguascalientes, Chiapas, Mexico
From: Insurgent Subcomandante Marcos
Zapatista National Liberation Army
Mountains of Southeastern Mexico
Chiapas, Mexico

Brothers and sisters,

Welcome to Zapatista territory, which is to say "territory in rebellion against evil government". That is how things are, even though these lands are filled with war. Even though they want to trample dignity with war tanks and even though they want to shut up reason with the noise of planes and helicopters.

We wanted to participate personally in this dialogue, but there are approximately 60,000 olive green reasons that prevent us from doing so. It doesn't matter, we hope that you accept this letter as the means by which our voice, our thinking and our hearts can reach all of you, who, after detaining the government's war, came to our lands to reaffirm the search for civic and peaceful ways to resolve the problems that we, both nationals and foreigners, suffer from in this last part of the 20th century.

We hope that this will not be the last time that you visit us, and that many of you will be able to stay in the "Peace Camps" that are located in various villages in the state of Chiapas, and which have made it possible for our civilian brothers and sisters to return to their homes.

We hope, also, that on another occasion we can be present to receive you as it is the custom to receive brothers and sisters: with flowers and the music of marimbas. We owe you those two things, in addition to everything that we owe you.

In continuation, we present to you our proposal for "Complementary Protocol" for being incorporated into the "Universal Social Convention" which will be approved by you. We are clear that our proposal is equivalent to all the others, that it is subject to discussion, and we will respect from here the decision that you make.

Complementary Protocol for the Universal Social Convention

We human beings present today in this place demand:
1. That reason always win and never force.
2. That the majority finds what the majority does, imposing its will on the minority, without the minority disappearing or having its right to become the majority restricted.

3. That any man can give any woman any flower in any part of any world, and that this woman give thanks for the flower not with just any smile, but with the best and only one.

4. That the morning no longer be a great question or a disaster waiting to happen; that the morning be just that: the morning.

5. That the night not be a cave of fear; that the night be a bed of desire.

6. That sadness be surprised with a simple look of disdain; and that happiness and laughter be free and never lacking.

7. That for everyone there be, always, bread to illuminate the table, education to feed ignorance, health to surprise death, land to harvest a future, a roof to shelter hope, and work to make hands dignified.

8. That the words and hearts of men and women no longer be prisoners of jails, tombs or threats.

9. That war be part of a long ago and foreign past, and that neither armies nor soldiers be any longer necessary.

10. That those who govern command obeying. That those who do not fulfill this, be changed for others.

11. That there always exists someone who is willing to struggle so that all that came before become not a demand, but a reality.

Respectfully,

From the mountains of Southeastern Mexico,
Insurgent Subcomandante Marcos.
Mexico, March 1995.

15. Durito III (Neo-liberalism and the Labor Movement)

April 15, 1995

Sirs,

Here is a communiqué for vespers. Over here April plays at disguising itself like March, and May begins to flap its wings on some stray flowers, red-colored, among so much green. I do not tire of hoping and un-hoping among so many crickets. Meanwhile, I plan to begin the Tired Lung Society. I'm sure it will be quite successful in the D.F. (Mexico City). By the time this arrives, Holy Week will be once again, ordinary week. How much longer will the lie prevail?

Vale. Health and a mouthful of that fresh air which they say is breathed in the mountains and which some dislocated people call "hope".

From the Mountains of Southeast Mexico,
Subcomandante Insurgente Marcos.
Mexico, April of 1995.

P.S. So he continues undoing offenses in the dawn, and offers to a far-away maiden a little bouquet of red carnations hidden in a story called...

...Durito III (Neo-liberalism and the labor movement...)

The moon is a pale almond. Silver sheets re-shape trees and plants. Dedicated crickets nail white leaves to the treetrunks as irregular as the shadows of the night below. Gusts of grey wind agitate the trees and the uneasiness. Durito makes a bed in my beard. The sneeze he provokes makes the armed gentleman roll on the floor. Durito gathers himself deliberately. To his already impotent body armor, Durito adds half a shell of COLOLTE (which is a species of hazelnut native to the Lacandon jungle) on his head in addition to holding a medicine cap like a shield. Excalibur is sheathed and a lance (which is suspiciously similar to a paper clip) completes his attire.

"Now what?" I say as I try to, somewhat pointlessly, help Durito with my finger.

Durito rearranges his body, I mean, his armor. He unsheathes Excalibur, clears his throat twice, and says in a deep-throated voice.

"It is dawn, my battered shield bearer! It is the hour to arrange our garments, and march and the day sharpens the spiny mane of Apollo as he peers at the world! It is the hour when nomadic knights ride in search of adventure which will increase their prestige before the absent eyes of the maiden, which prevent them from, even for an instant, close their eyes looking for oblivion or rest!"

I yawn and let my eyelids bring me oblivion and rest. This irritates Durito and he raises his voice: "We must go out to wrong maidens, straighten widows out, give refuge to bandits and jail the destitute."

"Sounds to me like a government program," I say to him with my eyes closed.

Durito appears to have no intention of leaving without waking me fully: "Wake up, scoundrel! You must remember to follow your Master where ever misfortune or adventure may take him!"

Finally, I open my eyes and stare at him. Durito looks more like a broken-up Army tank than an errant knight. I wanted to clear up my doubt so I asked him: "And who are you exactly?"

"Errant knight am I, and not like those whose names history forgot, but of those who in spite of all the envy, of the magicians who created Persia, Brahmans India, women sophists Ethiopia, will put his name in the temple of immortality so it may serve as an example in the coming centuries, where other errant knights may see what steps to follow, if they wish to reach the peak and high honor of arms," Durito answers, assuming his most, according to him, gallant pose.

"Sounds to me like... like..." I begin to say but Durito interrupts me.

"Silence, insensitive commoner! You pretend to slander me saying that the ingenious noble Don Quijote of La Mancha plagiarized my speeches. And certainly, since we are on this subject, I should say there are those say that you are wasting space in your epistles. Bibliographical notes, huh! If you continue you will end up like Galio citing six or seven authors in order to cover up his cynicism." I felt profoundly wounded by the annexed comments and I decided to change the subject.

"That on your head... it looks like a cololti shell."

"It is a helmet, ignorant one!" Durito says.

"Helmet? It looks like a shell with holes," I insist.

"Cololti. Helmet. Halo. That's the order, Sancho!" Durito says as he arranges the helmet.

"Sancho?" I stutter-say-ask-protest.

"Look leave this haggling and hurry so we can leave. My indefatigable sword has tolerated too many injustices and its blade is anxious to touch the necks of independent unions." As Durito says this, he bends his sword like a regent from a capital city.

"I think you've read too many papers recently. Be careful, or they will suicide you!" I say to him while I attempt to delay the moment in which I rise. Durito, for a moment abandons his XVI century language and explains, proudly, that he has secured a mount. He says it is as swift as lightning in August, silent as the wind in March, docile as the rain in September, and many more marvels, which I don't remember, but there was one quality for month. I appear incredulous, so Durito announces solemnly that he will do me the honor of showing me his mount. I sit, thinking that in this way I can sleep a little.

Durito leaves and is so long in returning, that in effect, I fall asleep...

A voice awakens me: "A-h-h-hem-m-m!"

It is Durito and he is mounted on the logical reason for his delay; a turtle! At a pace which Durito has called "elegant trot" and which, to me appears to be a very prudent and slow one, the turtle comes toward me. Mounted on his turtle (they call it "coc" in tzeltal), Durito turns to look at me and asks: "So how do I look?"

I gaze at this errant knight who unknown reason has brought to the solitude of the Lacandon jungle, and keep a respectful silence. His appearance is "peculiar".

Durito baptizes his turtle, excuse me, his horse with a name which seems hallucinatory: Pegasus. So that there is no doubt, Durito writes on the saddle cover of the turtle, with large and decisive letters "Pegasus. Copy Rights Reserved" and below "Please fasten your seat belts". I almost cannot resist the temptation of making a comparison with the economic recuperation program, when Durito turns his mount so I can see his other side. Pegasus takes his time, even when Durito announces a "vertiginous turn of his horse", which is only a slow turn. The turtle does it so carefully one might think he fears dizziness. After a few minutes, one can read on Pegasus' left flank "Smokers Section", "Company unions not allowed", "Free advertising space. For information call Durito's Publishing Company". I believe, I cannot see much free space because the ad covers all the left and rear flank of Pegasus.

After praising the ultra-mini-micro entrepreneurial vision of Durito, the only way to survive the failures of neoliberalism and TELECE (phonetic Spanish for NAFTA), I ask him: "So where does your future lead you?"

"Don't be a clown. That language only belongs to noblemen and lords and not to vagabonds and commoners who, were it not for my infinite compassion, would continue in their empty lives and never be able to dream about the secrets and marvels of errant knighthood," Durito answers while trying to hold Pegasus back, who for some strange reason, is impatient to leave.

"It seems to me that, for 2 a.m., I've had enough scoldings," I say to Durito. "Wherever you go, you'll go alone. I don't plan to go out tonight. Yesterday Camilo found tiger tracks, close by."

Apparently I found a vulnerable flank on our brave knight, because his voice shook when he asked, after swallowing saliva with great difficulty: "So what do those tigers eat?" "Everything. Guerrillas, soldiers, beetles... and turtles!" I watch Pegasus reaction, but it must really believe it is a horse, because it did not seem to be alarmed. Actually, I though I heard a soft whinny.

"Bah! You just want to frighten me, because you know this armed knight has defeated giants disguised as windmills, disguised as artillery helicopters, he has conquered the most impenetrable kingdoms, defeated the resistance of the most demure princesses, has..."

I interrupt Durito. It's evident he can spend pages and pages talking and I'm the one who gets criticized by the editors, especially when the communiqués arrive so late at night.

"Fine, fine. But tell me, where are you going?"

"To the Federal District (Mexico City)!" Durito says, bending his sword. The Final destination surprised Pegasus, because he kind of jumped, which, for a turtle is like a discreet sigh.

"Mexico?" I asked, incredulous.

"Sure! Do you think that just because Cocopa (government negotiating body) denied you passage, that would deter me?"

I wanted to warn Durito about speaking badly about Cocopa because the legislators are so sensitive and then they get mad during the TRIBUNA, but Durito continued:

"You should know I am an errant knight, and more Mexican than the failure of the neoliberal economy. I have a right, therefore to go to the 'city of palaces'. What do they want palaces for in the D.F., if they're not so that errant knights like myself, the most famous, gallant, most respected by men, loved by women and admired by children, should honor them with my footstep?"

"With your many feet, I remind you that besides beings an errant knight and a Mexican you are a beetle too..." I correct him.

"With foot or feet, but a palace without errant knights arriving, is like a child without a present on April 30th, with a pipe without tobacco, a book without words, a song without music, an errant knight without a shield..." and Durito gazes at me steadily and asks:

"Are you sure you won't come with me on this intriguing adventure?"

"It depends," I say, pretending to be very interested, "It depends what you mean by interesting adventure."

"I'm going to the May 1st Parade," Durito says, almost as though he were announcing a trip to the corner for cigarettes.

"To the May 1st parade! But there will be none! Fidel Velazquez, who has always cared about workers' economics, says there is no money for the parade. Some bad tongues are insinuating that he is afraid that the workers will get out of control, and instead of being grateful to the supreme one, they curse him with those words that cartoonists dislike. But it is a lie, the Labor Secretary said it was not because of fear, it was just a v-v-v-ery respectable decision of the worker's sector..."

"Stop, stop your parade float. I'm going to the May 1st parade, because I am going to propose a duel to Fidel Velazquez who, as everyone knows, is a fierce ogre who oppresses poor people. I will challenge him to fight in the Aztec stadium, in order to improve box office receipts, because ever since they let Beenhaker go (don't criticize me if I didn't spell it right, not even the directors of 'America' can spell it, even though they wrote the checks), not even the vultures will see the 'eagles'." Durito was silent for a moment and looked pensively at Pegasus, who had gone to sleep, because he hadn't moved in a while. Then Durito asked me.

"Do you think Fidel Velazquez has a horse?" I doubt a bit.

"Well he's a charro [literally cowboy, but company union in Mexican slang] ... so it's likely he has a horse."

"Magnificent!" says Durito, and digs his spurs into Pegasus. Pegasus may think he's a horse, but his body is still that of a turtle and his hard shell proves it, so he doesn't even notice Durito's whoops as he eggs him on. After struggling a bit,

Durito discovers that by hitting his clip, excuse me, his lance on his nose, he can make Pegasus go into a gallop. For a turtle, this is about 10 centimeters per hour, so Durito will take a while before he arrives in the D.F..

"At that rate, they'll arrive when Fidel Velasquez dies," I say as a parting thought.

I should never have said anything. Durito tossed the reins and pulled his horse back like when Pancho Villa took Torreon. Oh well, it's a good literary image. In reality Pegasus stopped, which, at his rate was almost imperceptible. In contrast to Pegasus' calm, Durito was furious:

"You are just like the advisors of the labor movement in the last decades! They recommend patience to the workers, and sit and wait for the charros to fall, and do nothing to make him fall."

"Well, not all of them have sat down to wait. Some have really struggled to make a truly independent labor movement."

"I'm going to see those folks. I'm going to join them so I can show them that workers have dignity too," Durito says, and I recall that once he told me he was a miner in the state of Hidalgo and an oil worker in Tabasco.

Durito leaves. He takes a few hours to disappear behind the bush that is a few meters from my plastic roof. I get up and notice that my right boot is loose. I turn on the flashlight and learn that... the lace is missing! No wonder Pegasus' reins looked familiar. Now I have to wait until Durito returns from Mexico. I look for a reed to tie my boot and remember that I forgot to recommend that Durito visit that restaurant with the tiles. I lie down and dawn comes...

Above me the sky clears, and with reddish blue eyes, is surprised to find that Mexico is still there, where it was yesterday. I light the pipe, look at the last slashes of night leave the trees, and say to myself that the struggle is long and it is worth it...

1. Chapter XLVII.

"About the strange way in which Don Quijote de la Mancha was enchanted, and other Events."

P.S. WITH THE FACE OF A FULL MOON, HE LOOKS TOWARD THE JUNGLE AND ASKS...

Who is that man who gallops over a squalid shadow? Why does he not seek relief? Why does he seek new pain? Why so many journeys when standing still? Who is he? Where is he going? Why does he say goodbye with such a noisy silence?

P.S. FOR A CND (Democratic National Convention) WHICH CANNOT DECI-DE WHETHER TO FIGHT AGAINST THE SYSTEM OR AGAINST ITSELF.

I read somewhere, that while the supreme government beats on both sides, the CND beats on itself. About this and other things, a few lines:

As the poet with the greying mustache who hides behind the piano writes:

MEXICO IS A FLOWER OF JACARANDA
WHO NEVER SEEKS A VASE
A WILD BOAR WHICH BRAGS
ABOUT ITS YOUNG PEOPLE
A JAVELIN AT THE HEART
OF JUSTICE
THE CAMOUFLAGED BULL'S EYE
OF A JIG

And so Manuel may be right when he says that the meetings of the "collective cen-ters of civilian support" are like meetings of "alcoholics anonymous" or "weight watch-ers". Maybe there is more to learn from these meetings than from party assemblies.

After all, the CND was born with the idea of unity, and not with the intention of entering the market of party clientele. It was and continues to be necessary a plan that includes the majority and best quality of civilian will. The CND had (has?) that plan. It was not to be the political arm of the ezetaelene (EZLN) or a new party or a new white elephant of the Mexican irregular left. It was to be the space of imaginative encounters and proposals for democratic change. And imagi-nations and proposals, the freshest, the most audacious, came (come) from civil society, not political society, not political organizations. Its flag is national, above parties and armies.

From this space of encounter should come proposals, which can be imposed, with imagination, on the government, on the parties, and on the ezeta (EZ), and on itself. That ship does not want to arrive at the port of power. In that sense it does not comply with the pragmatic and cynical premises of Galio-Machiavelli, but it does want to arrive at the port of a country with no return to the shadows, a country with democracy, liberty, and justice. Are there bindings? Throw them over-board! Will only a few remain? Imagination will replace quantity with quality! Civil society has much to learn from itself, and very little to learn from political society (with all its spectrum of colors, flavors, and cynicism). It is not a space for anti-party people, but it is a place for those with no party. Civil society will then, in the midst of the threats of a dirty war (although I do not believe, there is a war which can be called clean), make the angel of Independence rappel its way down the column and make conversation with Juarez, Columbus, and the old grandfather Cuahtemoc. The kind Diana will catch stars, and a stray palm drunk with smog. Civil society will make its un-proposals realities; civil dialogues in the midst of tanks, machine guns and cannons; campaigns of humanitarian aid, in the midst of a profound crisis and a more costly standard of living, for the benefit of its most vulnerable and impoverished flank, the indigenous. If the CND is not the ample space for this and other initiatives, the informal but effective irreverence of civil society will grow out of that straitjacket. Then what? It will find its own spaces. The CND will become another acronym, added to other inefficient acronyms. There is much to learn yet. This country has a great deal to learn from itself.

P.S. TO WHOM IT MAY CONCERN IN THE SUPREME GOVERNMENT.

There is a special kind of glass cut so that it has many surfaces, like a multi-faceted prism. This glass is mounted on a small wooden viewfinder, like an eyepiece. Through this glass, the light becomes many. When it is turned or moved, it offers many new configurations. Is it the same light broken up into many lights? Is it many lights imprisoned in the eyepiece? Is it just confirmation that there is no uniqueness even in the most apparent? Is it one light or many lights which one must be able to distinguish, recognize and appreciate? And, finally, thinking about the small eyepiece, is it a light with many marcos (frames) or a marco (frame) for many lights?

Vale. Once again. Health and only by arriving in hell will we know the answer.

The Sup with a red carnation in his lapel, playing at being a crystal and a mirror.

16. A History About Herons and Eagles in the Lacandon Jungle (Letter from Subcomandante Marcos to John Berger)

May 12, 1995
Heriberto, Eva and the image of an English Countryside
To: John Berger
High Savoy, France
From: Subcomandante Insurgente Marcos
CCRI-CG of the EZLN
Chiapas, Mexico

I.

"A reader could ask himself: What is the relationship between the writer and the place and peoples about whom he writes?"
- John Berger

Agreed, but he could also ask himself: What is the relationship between a letter written in the jungle of Chiapas, Mexico and the response that it receives from the French countryside? Or, even better, what is the relationship between the slow beating of the wings of the heron with the hovering of the eagle over a serpent?

For example, in Guadalupe Tepeyac (now an village empty of civilians and filled with soldiers), the herons took over the sky night of December. There were hundreds. "Thousands", says Lieutenant Ricardo, a Tzeltal insurgent who sometimes has a propensity to exaggerate. "Millions", said Gladys who, despite being 12 years old (or precisely because of it), does not want to be left out. "They come every year," says the grandfather while the small flashes of white hover above the village, and maybe disappear towards? The East?

Are they coming or going? Are they your herons, Mr. Berger? A winged reminder? Or a greeting filled with premonition? A fluttering of wings of something which resists death?

Because as a result, months later, I read in your letter (in a dog-eared clipping from a newspaper, with the date hidden under a mud stain), and in it (your letter) the wings of dawn are hovering once again in the sky and the people of Guadalupe Tepeyac now live in the mountain and not in the little valley whose lights, I imagine, are of some significance on the navigation maps of the herons.

Yes, I know now that the herons about which you wrote me fly during the winter from North Africa, and that it is improbable that they have anything to do with those that arrived in December 1994 in the Lacandon jungle. In addition the grandfather says that every year the disconcerting tour above Guadalupe Tepeyac is repeated. Perhaps southeastern Mexico is an obligatory layover, a necessity, a commitment. Perhaps they were not herons, but fragments of an exploded moon, pulverized in the December of the jungle. December, 1994.

Months later, the indigenous of southeastern Mexico again reiterated their rebellion, their resistance to genocide, to death... The reason? The supreme government decided to carry out organized crime, essence of neoliberalism, that money, the god of modernity, had planned. Dozens of thousands of soldiers, hundreds of tons of war materials, millions of lies. The objective? The destruction of libraries and hospitals, of homes and seeded fields of corn and beans, the annihilation of every sign of rebellion. The indigenous Zapatistas resisted, they retreated to the mountains and they began an exodus that today, even as I write these lines, has not ended. Neoliberalism disguises itself as the defense of a sovereignty, which has been sold in dollars on the international market.

Neoliberalism, this doctrine that makes it possible for stupidity and cynicism to govern in diverse parts of the earth, does not allow for inclusion other than that of subjection to genocide. "Die as a social group, as a culture, and above all as a resistance. Then you can be part of modernity," say the great capitalists, from the seats of government, to the indigenous campesinos. These indigenous people irritate the modernizing logic of neo-mercantilism. Their rebellion, their defiance, their resistance, irritates them. The anachronism of their existence within a project of glob-alization, an economic and political project that, soon, will decide that poor peo-ple, all the people in opposition, which is to say, the majority of the population, are obstacles. The armed character of "We are here!" of the Zapatista indigenous peo-ple does not matter much to them nor does it keep them awake (a little fire and lead will be enough to end such "imprudent" defiance). What matters to them, and bothers them, is that their very existence, in the moment that they [the indigenous Zapatistas] speak out and are heard, is converted into a reminder of an embarrass-ing omission of "neoliberal modernity": "These Indians should not exist today, we should have put an end to them BEFORE. Now annihilating them will be more dif-ficult, which is to say, more expensive." This is the burden which weighs upon neoliberalism made government in Mexico.

"Let's resolve the causes of the uprising," say the negotiators of the government (leftists of yesterday, the shamed of today) as if they were saying: "All of you should not exist, all of this is an unfortunate error of modern history." "Let's resolve the causes" is the elegant synonym of "we will eliminate them". For this system which concentrates wealth and power and distributes death and poverty, the campesinos, the indigenous, do not fit in the plans and projects. They have to be gotten rid of, just like the herons... and the eagles... have to be gotten rid of.

II.

"Mystery is not what can be hidden deliberately, but rather, as I have already shown, the fact that the gamut of the possible can always surprise us. And this, is hardly ever represented. The campesinos do not present papers as do urban per-sonalities. This is not because they are "simple" or more sincere or less astute; sim-ply the space between that which is unknown of a person and what all the world knows of him - and this is the space of all representation - it is extremely small."
- John Beger

December, 1994.

A cold dawn that drags itself between the fog and the thatched roofs of the vil-lage. It is morning. The dawn goes away, the cold remains. The little paths of mud begin to fill with people and animals. The cold and a little footpath accompany me in the reading of Boar Land. Heriberto and Eva (5 and 6 years old respectively) come and grab ("they snatched" I should say, but I don't know if the distinction is understood in English) the book. They look at the drawing on the front cover (it is a Madrid edition from 1989). It is a copy of a painting by John Constable, an image of an English countryside. The cover of your book, Mr. Berger, summons a rapid connection between image and reality. For Heriberto, for example, there is no doubt that the horse in the painting is La Muneca [The Doll] (a mare that accompanied us in the long year during which the indigenous rebellion governed southeastern Mexico), whom no one could mount except Manuel, a playmate who was twice the age, size and weight of Heriberto, who was Chelita's brother, and consequently, also his future brother-in-law. And what Constable called "a river" was really a riverbed, a riverbed that crossed through "La Realidad" ("La Realidad" is the name of a village, a reality of which is the limit of Heriberto's horizons. The farthest place that his trips and running around has taken him is "La Realidad").

Constable's painting did not remind Heriberto and Eva of the English country-side. It did not take them outside of the Lacandon jungle. It left them here, or it brought them back. It brought them back to their land, their place, to their being children, to their being campesinos, to their being indigenous, to their being Mexicans and rebels. For Heriberto and Eva Constable's painting is a colored draw-ing of "La Muneca" and the title, "Scene on a Navigable River" is not a valid argu-ment: the river is the riverbed of "La Realidad", the horse is the mare La Muneca, Manuel is riding, and his sombrero fell off, and that's it, on to another book. And we do that, this time it is about Van Gogh and for Eva and Heriberto, the paint-ings of Holland are scenes from their land, of their being indigenous and campesinos. After this Heriberto tells his mother that he spent the morning with the Sup. "Reading big books", says Heriberto, and I believed that this earned him a free hand with a box of chocolate cookies. Eva was more far sighted, and asked me if I didn't have a book about her doll with the little red bandanna.

III.

"The act of writing is nothing more than the act of approximating the experience of what is being written about; in the same manner, it is hoped that the act of reading the written text is another act of similar approximation."
- John Beger

Or of distancing, Mr. Berger. The writing, and above all, the reading of the writ-ten text could be an act of distancing. "The written word and the image," says my other, which to add problems paints himself, alone. I think that yes, that the "read-ing" of the written word and the image could approximate the experience or distant it. And so, the photographic image of Alvaro, one of the dead combatants in Ocosingo in January 1994, returns. Alvaro returns in the photo, Alvaro with his death speaks in the photo. He says, he writes, he shows: "I am Alvaro, I am an indige-nous, I am a soldier, I took up arms against being forgotten. Look. Listen. Something is happening in the closing of the 20th century that is forcing us to die in order to have a voice, to be seen, to live." And from the photo of Alvaro dead, a far-off reader from the distance could approximate the indigenous situation in modern Mexico, NAFTA, the international forums, the economic bonanza, the first world.

"Pay attention! Something is evil in the macroeconomic plans, something is not functioning in the complicated mathematical calculations that sings the successes of neoliberalism," says Alvaro with his death. His photo says more, his death speaks, his body on the soil of Chiapas takes voice, his head resting in a pool of blood: "Look! This is what the numbers and the speeches hide. Blood, cadavers, bones, lives and hopes, crushed, squeezed dry, eliminated in order to be incorporated into the 'indices of profit and economic growth'."

"Come!" says Alvaro, "Come close! Listen!"

But Alvaro's photo also can "be read" from a distance, as a vehicle which serves to create distance in order to stay on the other side of the photo, like "reading" it in a newspaper in another part of the world. "This did not happen here," says the reader of the photo, "this is Chiapas, Mexico, a historical accident, remedial, forgettable, and... far away." There are, in addition, other readers who confirm it: public announcements, economic figures, stability, peace. This is the use of the indigenous war at the end of the century, to revalue "peace". Like a stain stands out on the object that is stained. "I am here and this photo happened over there, far away, small," says the "reader" who distances himself.

And I imagine, Mr. Berger, that the final result of the relationship between the writer and the reader, through the text ("or from the image", insists my other self again), escapes both. Something is imposed on them, gives significance to the text, provokes one to come closer or go farther away. And this "something" is related to the new division of the world, with the democratization of death and misery, with the dictatorship of power and money, with the regionalization of pain and despair, with the internationalization of arrogance and the market. But it also has to do with the decision of Alvaro (and of thousands of indigenous along with him) to take up arms, to fight, to resist, to seize a voice that they were denied before, to not devalue the cost of the blood that this implies. And it also has to do with the ear and eye that are opened by Alvaro's message, whether they see and hear it, whether they understand it, whether they draw near to him, his death, his blood that flooded the streets of a city that has always ignored him, always... until this past January first. It also has to do with the eagle and heron, the European campesino who is resisting being absorbed and the Latin American indigena who is rebelling against genocide. It has to do with the panic of the powerful, as the trembling, that is growing in its guts, no matter how strong and powerful it appears, when, without knowing, it prepares to fall...

And it has to do with, I reiterate and salute it in this way, the letters that come from you to us, and those that, with these lines, bring you these words: the eagle received the message, he understood the approach of the hesitant flight of the heron. And there below, the serpent trembles and fears the morning...

Vale, Mr. Berger. Health and follow closely the heron up above until it appears as a small and passing flash of light, a flower that lifts itself up...

From the mountains of Southeastern Mexico,
Subcomandante Insurgente Marcos.
Mexico, May 1995.

17. WHY MARCOS IS NOT AT THE DIALOGUE

May 5, 1995
To the national and international civic society
To the non-governmental organizations
To the national and international press

Brothers and sisters,

The initial sessions of the dialogue with the supreme government were attended by delegates named by the Clandestine Revolutionary Indigenous Committee-General Command of the Zapatista Army for National Liberation. Due to a series of circumstances, emphasized by the olive green people whom the supreme government facilitated, it was impossible for me to attend these first sessions. I have obtained the authority of the Committee to talk with you all through this medium. In this manner I want to take advantage of your attention and patience to touch on some of the points that have been left up in the air, abandoned because of the rapid developments of events at the national level.

It will not be new to anyone that there are prices on our heads, that the government has not stopped trying to assassinate us, thinking that by this means, the EZLN would be left without leadership, and would be brought to its knees and therefore would be forced to surrender. Seeing that it was useless to try and buy us off, the government decided on assassination and only waited for the appropriate occasion to carry it out. It thought that the deception of February 9th would be that occasion, but it did not work out that way. It will continue looking for a new opportunity. It has the resources to do so. As this sentence could be carried out at whatever moment, I am taking advantage of this opportunity to say what they want to keep silent.

There exists stories that in the EZLN there is a profound division regarding the dialogue, that the absence of the "Sup" was due to his being punished, or that the "hard liners" and the "moderates" of the EZLN's leadership could not come to an agreement. Regarding this and other lies, I want to say some things:

As you have already noticed (I don't know if the government also has figured it out), the EZLN is not just Marcos. In the CCRI-CG we have many companeros equal to or more capable than Marcos at explaining our struggle, at leading our movement, and at leading by obeying. The Comandante companeros who represent the different ethnic groups in the Committee are great companeros and good leaders, in their words we all talk and their decisions are ours. The CCRI has named delegates to the dialogue with the criteria of representation of the ethnic groups which comprise it, and they, like me or any other member of the leadership, are subjected to the vigilance of the entire Committee body and of the Bases of Support of the EZLN.

The particular circumstances in January 1994 caused the attention to be concentrated on the impertinent nose that was hidden, uselessly, behind a black wool ski mask. The need for a translator between the indigenous Zapatista culture and the national and international culture caused the obvious nose, in addition to sneezing, to talk and to write. All of you would be in agreement that he did it and to an excess. I talked and talked, and at times, it seemed to many that the EZLN was only this very visible nose. It was this error which we were late in seeing, and that we recognized in the celebration of November 17th, 1994. But we did not recognize that this protagonist was, not infrequently, counter-productive to the just cause that motivates us. During all of these months, the companeros of the Committee have been preparing intensively to carry, in their own voices, the voices of everyone, and so that this voice be heard and understood by all of you. The real protagonists will now be the formal protagonists. The pronounced nose will return to more sneezing and to less speaking but it will continue to be indigenous and dignified like any other Zapatista.

There is an act that caught many people's attention in the past few days, and that made it so that more than just one person, including a Chiapas bishop and journalists, felt obligated to say stupid things. The act that I am referring to is that the EZLN retreated in the face of the governmental offensive in February 1995, without fighting. Entire villages and military units retreated into the mountains without resisting with arms. Those analysts made an evaluation that it was a sign of military weakness of the Zapatistas, and they applauded the occupation of indigenous villages as a means of forcing a dialogue that had existed prior to the ostentatious deployment of military masses and technology. Inside the government the thinking was the same: the use of force is necessary, they say, to obtain advantages in the political negotiations with the rebels. This is the argument that tried to justify the unjustifiable: armed aggression against the indigenous of Chiapas and the taking of civilian hostages in order to impose a line for negotiations.

The government can command its soldiers to murder and die with only the objective being to gain advantages in the dialogue and negotiations. It can do this because, for the government, their soldiers are not human beings, they are things that are to be used for political ends, they are disposable.

The government is the commander of the federal Mexican army. The Army does not command itself, from its birth it has been this way. It is a disciplined army. We, who are their rivals, are the first ones to recognize this. Everything that the federal army has done in Chiapas, it has done to obey orders from its commander the federal government. The government wants the federal Army to be the one vilified; it wants to hide the fact that the government is who ordered the entire operation. It was the government who ordered the destruction of Aguascalientes. It was the government who ordered the destruction and sacking of the communities. It was the government who ordered the arbitrary detentions, the disappearances, the assassinations. The government ordered all of this to obtain advantages in the dialogue, because for the government human life, including those of the people who serve and obey it, is something disposable, something that can be "spent" to gain political advantages.

The Zapatista Army for National Liberation is not like this. For us our soldiers are our brothers and sisters, they are human beings with hopes and with sufferings which obligated us to follow this road of war which could lead us to death. For the EZLN the more valuable thing is dignity and life and, paradoxically, for this reason we are willing to die.

We knew that we should sit down and dialogue to seek a political solution to the conflict. We knew that we should do it not because we trusted the government, not because we feared them, not because we were weak. We should do it because we had and we have a commitment with thousands of citizens who asked us and ask that we try the political road and not the road of war. Since January 1994 many people have approached us. We have received much help, more that we had hoped for or even that we had dreamed of. But it has always been help for peace. No one since January 1994 has ever approached us to offer us help in waging war. No one has approached us to offer weapons, ammunition, explosives, or military training. Everyone who has approached us did it to offer us help to bring about peace, a peace that would not be like before, for a new peace, like our Comandante David speaks of.

Since January 1994 we have not received neither weapons, nor ammunition, not anything else that would be useful in waging war. Since January 1994 the only thing that we have received has been voices and help to continue the road to a just and dignified peace.

We could not be deaf to this help. We could not avoid seeing and hearing this movement that asked us not to continue the war, but rather advised us and offered to support us on the road to a new peace. We made a commitment to all of these people. And when the Zapatistas make a commitment, they do everything possible, including dying, to fulfill it. Like our men, women and children died in the first blockade, later in the retreat in February, and in the more than 80 days of exodus by the villagers who refused to surrender. The government could make commitments and not keep them, it could make promises and then forget them. But not the Zapatistas. For this reason we knew that we had to dialogue.

But we could not shed the blood of our companeros just to gain tactical or strategic advantages in the dialogue. For this reason since January 1994, the EZLN has not waged war against the government's forces. We have fired, this is true, (and it is what hurts the government), thousands of words saying our truth. Our truth that we are the first to recognize, is not the truth of everyone. Words do not kill, but they can be more lethal than bombs. The words, and not the weapons of the Zapatistas, is what the government is afraid of.

For this reason we retreated without fighting in February. We preferred to sit down to dialogue with all of the military conditions against us, rather than to have to do it with military advantages gained with the blood of our brothers and sisters, spilt uselessly, staining our words. The government can sit down with the blood of its soldiers on its conscience, because for the government this blood does not count because it has no value.

Anyway, the "parts" (as the government calls itself and the Zapatistas) returned to sit down to dialogue just like they had done in January 1995. The differences, however, were not small things. Now there is a mistrust that will be difficult to... There also exists one thing clear: the government is willing to destroy libraries and rural hospitals in order to force a dialogue under the conditions that it imposes. Distinct from February 1994 and January 1995, now the dialogue is being held in a climate of tension and agony. The hopes that it will be a success do not yet overcome the fears that it will fail. However, for everyone it is clear that it is possible to return to the negotiating table, it is because of the will of the Zapatistas and despite the intentions, to the contrary, of the government.

More than a year ago, in February 1994, we came to San Cristobal de las Casas with a list of demands. Amongst the 36 demands, two were emphasized. One was the renunciation of the then usurper of the Federal Executive, Carlos Salinas de Gortari. The other was profound political reform that guaranteed liberty and democracy for all Mexicans. Both demands were classified, by the prominent thinkers of Salinism, as "the delirium of neo-Zapatistism". They stated to us that, although there were deficiencies in the political system, the regimen of Salinas de Gortari represented astonishing economic advances. We responded then that the country was living a lie, that economic bonanzas could not exist without political freedoms. Our voice was first lost in the soccer euphoria, and then later in the electoral hopes. We were the little army of crazy people who, armed with wooden guns, planned to bring down a "triumpher", a model of the "modern Mexico". With machetes and boards, surrounded militarily, the indigenous in southeastern Mexico persisted in their delirium: democracy, freedom, and justice for all.

We did not shoot. We waited. Patience is a virtue of the warrior. Before a year had passed since our small and crazy voice had asked, in San Cristobal de las Casas, for the renunciation of Carlos Salinas de Gortari, the entire country awoke from the stupefying dream of the economic bonanza. Awakened from a dream that for us was always a nightmare, the Mexican people found themselves in worse economic conditions that when "neo-liberalism", this chaotic doctrine of improvisation, took us by the neck to take us, by force, into the first world. Millions of Mexicans demanded, and demand, that the person who tricked for all these years be punished. The so-called "delirium of neo-Zapatistism" is now shared by millions of Mexicans.

Today we are demanding a dialogue with national themes. We are demanding a broad national dialogue in which a new social and political pact is discussed and agreed upon. To many people it appears to be a new example of the Zapatista propensity for delirium. It is absurd, they say, that a minimal military force under attack proposed a debate about broad national problems. This national dialogue could or could not happen. But the need for it, and its urgency, is something real. Sooner than later it will become clear that this new "delirium" of the Zapatistas was, and is, a unpostponable necessity.

This is a dialogue that is not equitable, it is not a dialogue among equals. But in this dialogue the EZLN is not the weak part, it is the strong part. On our side are the moral authority and historical reason. On the side of the government is only military force and the lies that some of the communication media spread. And force and lies never, never will be stronger that reason. They can impose themselves for a few days, months or years, but time will put each in its place. For this reason we understand that the government is weak in this dialogue; for this reason our delegates go with a understanding and conciliatory attitude. For this reason we have done everything possible so that the dialogue can continue developing, despite the government's efforts to make it fail.

Our demands, and not our form of struggle, wins day by day thousands of supporters; war could become a reality or disappear completely from the historical horizon of our country, but not the struggle for democracy, liberty and justice. In war or in peace, we the Zapatistas will continue struggling so that these three words become a reality, and that they, and not desperation and misery, become the heritage of all Mexicans. For this reason we do not have any problem sitting down to talk about peace, because peace does not mean withdrawal or surrender. Whatever is the result of this new process of dialogue and negotiation, whether it is successful in creating a just and dignified peace, or whether it fails, opening the door to war, we the Zapatistas will continue struggling.

At one time someone said, referring to the EZLN, that it was not possible to be without peace and without war, that it had to define itself. In reality this is not the dilemma of this country. This lie was already used by Ernesto Zedillo Ponce de Leon in his electoral campaign, now the voters are paying for having believed him. The truth is that, until now, the system of the party-state has kept Mexico without democracy and without a dictatorship. It is no longer possible to keep this unstable equilibrium, it has to be defined: dictatorship or democracy. The evil government is doing everything possible to maintain a system that no longer sustain itself, wanting to stay without change will lead to ungovernability and fascism. We, and I do not refer only to the Zapatistas, struggle for the democratization of the country. The defenders of the party-state system and we will pass into history: those of the PRI for having done everything to take the country into fascism, we for having pushed for democracy, liberty and justice. I do not know what the immediate result will be, but I do know what the final one will be: the triumph of democracy.

The peace that the government wants and the peace that we struggle for are not the same. That of the government is a lie, an eternal postponement of change and improvements; ours is a wager for a new life. The supreme government is willing to kill to achieve the peace it wants. We are willing to die for the new peace, for all of us. Do you see why we are not talking about the same thing? When they say "peace", they mean "death"; when we say "PEACE", we mean "life"... For this reason the dialogue is slow, we have to make the government understand that PEACE is what we want.

The government negotiates like a terrorist. It has taken thousands of indigenous people in Chiapas as hostages, and a handful of innocent civilians in the city. With a pistol at the temples of all these people, the government wants to talk and negotiate. We know that we are working with terrorists and that we should be prudent. We should make the government understand that it should change for the benefit of everyone. The government responds to our conciliatory and prudent position with mocking, racist and authoritarian attitudes. They try to provoke us thinking that there will be a winner and a loser in a war that, they do not understand, will not be won with bullets.

The obstacles are not few that this process of peace will have to overcome to arrive at its goal. But we repeat now and in front of you all, the obstacles will not come from the Zapatista Army for National Liberation.

Vale, salud and buena letre in this effort to write and make history.

> From the mountains of Southeastern Mexico,
> Subcomandante Insurgente Marcos.
> Mexico, May 1995.

P.S. THAT DEMANDS REPLY TO THE THREAT.

The supreme government sent word to us that IT DOES NOT WANT any type of mobilization in the next meeting in San Andres. "Neither organized nor disorganized," says the government that, as it is clear, has serious problems with Spanish. In addition it threatened to mobilize the "displaced" in support of the governmental delegation. They think that the cattle rancher in Ocosingo is the same as the one in Los Altos in Chiapas. They also sent word to us that the EZLN has now lost all of its capacity to convene people and no one cares about what happens to the Zapatistas and the dialogue. "The government has the initiative and it is not going to let it go," they told us. Doesn't it make you tremble?

18. Marcos Invites the Government's Delegates to a Community Consultation

May 24, 1995
To: National Commission of Mediation (CONAI)
Chiapas, Mexico
From: Subcomandante Insurgente Marcos
CCRI-CG of the EZLN
Chiapas, Mexico

Brothers,

By orders from my companeros of the Clandestine Revolutionary Indigenous Committee-General Command of the Zapatista Army for National Liberation, I am writing to you the following:

I want to report that we have finished the first phase of the consultation regarding the latest proposal from the government. All of the members of the CCRI-CG of the EZLN and the regional leaders have now been informed and consulted. Now we will consult with the local leaders and base communities.

At the time of the last meeting for dialogue between the EZLN and the federal government, our delegates argued that they needed time to consult with the Zapatista bases before coming to an agreement. The government representatives stated that 20 days was too much time for a consultation. That they (the government's delegates) were willing to go wherever necessary so that it could be shown that the Zapatistas exaggerate, and that we were only trying to buy time and avoid making commitments. Our delegates responded by inviting the government's delegates to attend a consultation in a Zapatista community so that they could see the truth for themselves. The Zapatista delegates invited the government, Comcopa, the national and international press, (and everyone else who has doubts about the consultations and the amount of time it takes for communication to get through to the Zapatista communities), to attend, WITHOUT HELICOPTERS and walk to a consultation.

To follow-up on this invitation, and by orders from the CCRI-CG of the EZLN, by means of this letter we formally invite the government's delegation to a consultation in a community in the Lacandon jungle in Chiapas.

The conditions for attending this consultation are the following:

First. No type of vehicle, other than feet (just like our delegates) can be used. They will arrive at one of the sites where our delegates are picked up for each meeting of the dialogue, and where they are returned at the end of each session. From this point, and until returning to this point, they will have to walk to get to the village where the consultation will be held.

Second. No one from the government except those people who are members of the government's delegation to the dialogue in San Andres can attend. Only the legislators who belong to Comcopa can attend. Only those members of the national and international press who are accredited by CONAI can attend.

Third. Each person has to carry his belongings. He can not be accompanied by porters, aides-de-camp, or assistants.

Fourth. The government's representatives should make a public commitment that there will be no military attacks against the community where the meeting will be held. That is to say, to make a commitment not to do what Esteban Moctezuma Barragan did to the people of Guadalupe Tepeyac.

Fifth. Once in the community, if they arrive, they will have to follow the rules that govern the community, and they only will be allowed to speak when the community's assembly gives them the floor.

So. These are the conditions. For those who want to attend, they will be awaited on May 31, 1995 in the communal farm of La Realidad, in the municipality of San Pedro de Michoacan, Chiapas. From there they will go on foot to the site of the consultation.

That's all. I ask that some representative of CONAI be present that day in order to certify that the participants have complied with the conditions.

Vale. Health and that as words go out, it is the true ones which go farthest.

Respectfully,

> From the mountains of Southeastern Mexico,
> Subcomandante Insurgente Marcos.
> Mexico, May 1995.

P.S. Oh! I forgot: the companeros calculate that it will take two days of walking (we have to get around the federal garrisons) just to get there, and another two days to get back. So that there isn't any problem, they will get back in time for the third meeting on June 7th in San Andres. The community is in the heart of the jungle; so, for those who arrive alive, I will be happy to greet them personally. I can even give them a guided tour of our headquarters. Now, that's all. I wait for you here...

19. Dignity Cannot be Studied, You Live it or it Dies

June 20, 1995
To: Eric Jauffret, France
From: Subcomandante Insurgente marcos, CCRI-CG of the EZLN
Mountains of the Mexican Southeast
Mexico

> "I have seen Siqueiros mask the children and incite the wall to rebellion, and Rivera free the accomplice, enigmatic and anonymous tenderness..."
> - Eric Jauffret

I, on the other hand, have seen our own cover their faces in order to show them to the world and take off their ski-masks in order to hide from the enemy. For example, during a recent arrival of fresh government troops, one of the officials said good-bye to the townspeople. He sent greetings to the Zapatistas. I will return, he said, in four months. During those five months he looked for the Zapatistas and did not find them. "They left the mountain and they are in the towns. We'll never find them like that", says the official, explaining in his own way, that he is involved in an absurd war where the enemy shows himself by hiding and hides as he shows himself.

I've also seen that Beto (10 years old going on 11 and a half, a quarter to 12) has turned the world on its head and, as proof, sends me a drawing made with worn-out colored pencils, where the ocean is the sky and the sky is the ocean. Beto is, in terms of work in the community, old now. He carries his share of firewood and has already complicated the life of one of the women in the peace camps. "How about that about the ocean?" Beto asks, because he's had to confront a pile of books full of photos, drawings and letters. The explanation begins with the clarification of a question, which, according to the volunteer teacher appears important: is it "el" [male denomination in Spanish grammar] mar or "la" [female denomination]? Beto's question only concerns itself with learning whether helicopters and planes can fly in the ocean.

No, they can't... the teacher answers and continues a complicated explanation about density, physical laws, aerodynamics, chemical composition of H2O and other rules of grammar.

Beto sends a message with his uncle so that among the demands of the EZLN there be one about raising the ocean to the sky and lowering the sky to the ocean. Beto thinks that, this way the ocean will be more democratic because everyone will be able to see it and he, Beto, will no longer have to suffer through a long explanation in order to learn that the ocean, like hope, is of the female gender. Beto also says that he has a friend called Nabor. Nabor's father died on February 10th of 1995 when the government sent its troops to recover the "national sovereignty". Mortally wounded, he was separated from his unit, which retreated in order not to confront the federal troops. Hovering vultures pointed out, days later, where he laid. Beto has adopted Nabor and has shown him all he needs to know to survive in the Lacandon Jungle. The prodigious student Nabor, brags about how he has already kissed a companera.

Mmmh, delicious! Nabor says as he brings his hand to his lips and gives it a mock kiss.

Nabor agrees with Beto that the sky should be below and the ocean above. A helicopter with artillery passes by in order to confirm it. Beto thinks the change will not be too complicated. They're both blue, right? Both big? Anyway, Nabor says it's simpler to change the world than for us to learn how to walk on our heads. For Beto and Nabor happiness would be stooping in order to see the sky.

Oh, I forgot. Nabor is three years old, and, as is obvious, over here each year is a decade and the classes for "responsible sex" should begin at age 2...

But Mister Jauffret, I am not writing to tell you about Beto's drawing or about his friend Nabor and his plans to turn the world upside down. I am writing to thank you for your letter and to tell you about our actual situation.

The indigenous peoples who support our just cause have decided to resist without surrender, without accepting the alms with which the supreme government hopes to buy them. And they have decided this because they have made theirs a word which is not understood with the head, which cannot be studied or memorized. It is a word which is lived with the heart, a word which is felt deep inside your chest and which makes men and women proud of belonging to the human race. This word is DIGNITY. Respect for ourselves, for our right to be better, or right to struggle for what we believe in, our right to live and die according to our ideals. Dignity cannot be studied, you live it or it dies, it aches inside you and teaches you how to walk. Dignity is that international homeland which we forget many times.

Our ideals are simple, and for that reason very large: we want, for all the men and women of this country, and of the entire world, three things which are fundamental for any human being: democracy, liberty, and justice. It can appear, and the powerful means of communication certainly help this appearance, that these three things are not the same thing for an indigenous person of the Mexican southeast as for a European. But it is about the same thing: the right to have a good government, the right to think and act with a freedom which does not imply the slavery of others, the right to give and receive what is just.

For these three values, for democracy, liberty and justice, we rose up in arms on January 1st of 1994. For these three values, we resist today without surrender. Both things, the war and resistance, means that these three values represent everything for us, represent a cause worth fighting for, worth dying for... so that living is worthy of us. Our cause we believe, is not only ours. It belongs to any honest man or woman in any part of the world. And this is why we aspire so that our voice can be heard in all the world and so that our struggle will be assumed by everyone in the world. Our cause is not the cause of war, or the cause of destruction, or the cause of death. Our cause is that of peace, but peace with justice; it is the cause of construction, but with equity and reason; it is the cause of life, but with dignity, and always new and better.

Today, we find ourselves in a very difficult situation. The war is dressed in its terrible suit of hunger and entire communities suffer in conditions below the minimum survival level. We willingly accept this not because we like martyrdom or sterile sacrifice. We accept it because we know that brothers and sisters the world over will know how to extend their hand to help us triumph in a cause which is theirs as well.

Like yesterday, we cover our faces in order to show the world the true face of the Mexico of the basement and after washing with our blood the mirror in which Mexicans can see their own dignity. Now we hide our face in order to escape the treachery and death which walks in the steps of those who say they govern the country. We are not fighting with our weapons. Our example and our dignity now fight for us.

In the peace talks the government delegates have confessed that they have studied in order to learn about dignity and that they have been unable to understand it.

They ask the Zapatista delegates to explain what is dignity. The Zapatistas laugh, after months of pain they laugh. Their laughter echoes and escapes unto the high wall behind which arrogance hides its fear. The Zapatista delegates laugh even when the dialogue ends, and they are giving their report. Everyone who hears them laughs, and the laughter re-arranges faces which have been hardened by hunger and betrayal. The Zapatistas laugh in the mountains of the Mexican southeast and the sky cannot avoid infection by that laughter and the peals of laughter emerge. The laughter is so great that tears arise and it begins to rain as though the laughter were a gift for the dry land...

With so much laughter raining, who can lose? Who deserves to lose?

Vale, Mister Jauffret.

Health and remember that about "The world is as blue as an orange."

From the mountains of the Mexican Southeast,
Subcomandante Insurgente Marcos.
Mexico, June 1995.

20. MEXICO: THE MOON BETWEEN THE MIRRORS OF THE NIGHT AND THE CRYSTAL OF THE DAY

"I want you for a crystal, never a mirror."
- Pedro Salinas

May of 1985. Dawn. The moon peers at the mirror of the lake and jealously, the moon wrinkles its face with its waves. In the middle of the trajectory between one and the other side, we venture in a canoe which has the same firmness as my decision to cross the lake. Old Man Antonio has invited me to test his canoe. For the past 28 nights, from the new to the full moon, old man Antonio has worked, with machete and ax, a large cedar trunk. The vessel is seven meters long. Old Man Antonio explains that canoes can be made of cedar, mahogany, huanacastle, bariy, and he points out the different trees he names. Old Man Antonio is determined to point them out, but I can't tell them apart; they are all large trees as far as I'm concerned. That was during the day; now it is dawn, and as usual we are here navigating in this little wooden cedar vessel which Old Man Antonio has baptized "The Troublemaker". "In honor of the moon," says Old Man Antonio while he rows with a large and thick stick. Now we are in the middle of the lake. The wind paints curls on the water and the canoe rises and falls. Old Man Antonio decides he should wait until the wind dies down, and he allows the vessel to float.

"These waves cannot turn the canoe over," he says, as his cigarette makes smoke spirals much as the wind makes waves. The moon is full, and in its light, it is possible to make out the large islets which dot the Miramar lake. Through a smoke spiral Old Man Antonio calls up an old story.

I'm more worried about sinking, which appears imminent (I can't decide whether to be nauseous or terrified), so I'm not ready for fables or stories. This, of course, is neither here nor there for Old Man Antonio because, reclined on the bottom of the canoe, he begins to weave his tale...

The Mirrors' Tale

The oldest of the elders say that the moon was born right here, in the jungle. They say that a long time ago, the gods had overslept, tired of playing and doing so much. The world was somewhat silent. Quiet it was. But a soft cry was heard up there in the mountain. Seems like the gods had forgotten a lake and left it in the middle of the mountain. When they divided up the things of the Earth, the little lake was left over, and since they did not know where else to put it, they just left it there, in the midst of so many hills that no one could find themselves there. So the little lake was crying because it was alone. And its cries were such that the heart of the Mother Cedar, who is the sustainer of the world, was saddened by the cries of the little lake. Gathering its large white petticoat the Cedar came near the little lake.

"What is wrong with you now?" The Cedar asked the water, which was becoming a puddle, because of its incessant crying.

"I don't want to be alone," said the little lake.

"Alright, then I will remain at your side," said the Cedar, the sustainer of the world.

"I don't want to be here," said the little lake.

"Alright, then you will come with me," said the Cedar.

"No, I want to be down there, close to the earth. I want to be tall. Like you," said the little lake.

"Alright, then I will lift you up to the level of my head. But only for a little while, because the wind is mischievous and I might drop you," said the Cedar.

As it could, the Mother Cedar gathered up its petticoat and bent over to take the little lake in its arms. Carefully, because it is the mother, the sustainer of the world, the Cedar, placed the little lake on the crown of its head. The Mother Cedar moved slowly, being careful not to spill one drop of water of the lake, because the Mother Cedar could see that the little lake was very thin.

From above the little lake exclaimed:

"It is such a joy being up here! Take me to see the world! I want to see all of it!"

"The world is very large, little girl, and you can fall from up there," said the Cedar.

"I don't care! Take me!" the little Lake insisted and it pretended to cry.

The Mother Cedar did not want the little lake to cry itself so much, so it began to walk, very straight, with her on its head. Since then the women have learned to walk with a pitcher full of water on the head, so that not a drop falls. Like the Mother Cedar walk the women of the jungle when they bring the water from the brook. With a straightened back, their head raised, their step like clouds in the summer. That is how the woman in the mountain walks when she is taking the water which heals.

The Mother Cedar was good at walking, because in those days the trees were not stationary. They walked from one place to another, making children and filling the world with trees. But the wind was around there, whistling with boredom. So it saw the Mother Cedar and wanted to play by lifting its petticoats with a slap. But the Cedar became angry and said:

"Be still, wind! Don't you see that I have upon my head a stubborn and weepy lake?"

Then the wind finally saw the little lake, who peered at it from the curly crown of the Cedar. The wind thought the little lake was pretty and decided to flirt with it. So the wind rose up to the head of the Cedar and began to speak pretty words in the ear of the little lake. The little lake quickly preened itself and said to the wind:

"If you take me around the world, then I will go with you!"

The wind didn't think twice. It made a horse of clouds and put the little lake on the rump and took the little lake away, so quickly that the Mother Cedar did not even notice when the little lake was taken from her head.

The little lake traveled for a good long time with the wind. And the wind told the little lake how pretty it was, how darned cute it was, that any thirst would be quenched with the water of the little lake, that anyone would love sinking inside her, and many other things were said by the wind in order to convince the little lake to make love in a corner of the dawn. And the little lake believed all that was said to her and each time they passed a puddle of water or a lake, the little lake took advantage of its reflection and fixed its wet hair and blinked her liquid eyes and made flirtatious features out of the little waves on her round face.

But the little lake only wanted to go from one end of the world to the other and nothing about making love in a corner of the dawn. The wind became bored and took her very high and shied away with a loud neigh and threw the little lake and the little lake began falling but since it was so high it took much time and surely it would have hurt itself if some stars had not caught sight of it and hooked it to their points. Seven stars took it by the sides, and like a sheet, raised it once again into the sky. The little lake was pale because it was so frightened of falling. And since she no longer wanted to return to the earth, she asked to stay with the stars.

"Alright," said the stars, "but you will have to come with us wherever we go."

"Yes," answered the little lake, "I will go with you."

But the little lake was saddened to always take the same route and she began to cry again. Her crying awoke the gods and they went to see what was happening or where the crying came from and they saw the little lake, being pulled by the seven stars, crossing the night. When they learned the story, the gods were angry because they had not made lakes so they could wander in the sky, but so that they stayed on earth. They went to see the little lake and said to it:

"You will no longer be a lake. Lakes do not live in the sky. But since we cannot take you down, then you will remain here. But we will call you 'moon' and your punishment, because you are vain and a flirt, will be to reflect the well where the light is put away on earth."

Apparently, the gods had put away the light inside the earth and had made a large round hole so that whenever the light and the spirit diminished in the stars they could come and drink there. So the moon has no light, it is only a mirror, and when it appears full, its front reflects the great hole filled with light where the stars drink. Mirror of light, that is what the moon is. So whenever the moon strolls in front of a lake, the mirror looks in a mirror. And even so the moon is never happy or angry, it is the troublemaker...

The gods also punished the Mother Cedar for being such a pamperer. They no longer allowed it to walk from one place to the other, and they gave it the world to carry, and doubled the thickness of its skin so it would not respond to any crying it might hear. Since then, the Cedar has skin of stone and stands without moving. If the Cedar moves even a little the world will fall.

"So it happened," said Old Man Antonio "Since then the moon reflects the light which is stored inside the Earth. That is why when it finds a lake, the moon stops to fix its hair and its face. That is why whenever women pass a mirror, they stop to look at themselves. That was a gift from the gods; to each woman was given a piece of moon, so they could fix their hair and their face and so they would not want to travel and climb to the sky."

Old Man Antonio stopped, but the wind did not, the waves continued to threaten the little boat. But I said nothing. Not because I was reflecting upon the words of Old Man Antonio, but because I was sure, that if I opened my mouth, I would expel even my liver onto the agitated mirror in which the moon rehearses its flirtatiousness...

WITHIN THE NIGHT OF RANCOR AND CONFUSION

In Mexico, sometimes the moon is painted in a resplendent red. Neither blush nor blood, it is rage and rancor which illuminates its pearly face. Upon its return from its long voyage through the Mexican night the moon ends its repeated path of mirrors and returns to its tired walk. Its look is red... because of its rancor... and confusion...

Why? What has it seen? Stammering, annoyed and with a thin, thready voice which seems like a spiral of wind in May, the moon tells the story of its last voyage. It says it walked the Mexican night, and that, as it tumbled in the giant labyrinth of mirrors which is our contemporary history it came to...

Subcomandante Marcos.

21. POWER AS A MIRROR AND AN IMAGE

June 1995

First Mirror

Power as the mirror and the image

Chapter I.- Demonstrated is the absurd coherence of the mirror placed in front of the mirror, of the double deceit of the image of Power, and the great truth, which, it is said, we should believe: the Power is and is necessary, sufficient and eternal.

First Deceit:

In the Power the mirror reflects a double image: what is said and what is done. The mirror hides nothing. The resources are gone, it is not the same as before. Its surface is mildewed and stained. It can no longer "reverse" reality. On the contrary, it shows the contradiction. But in making this evident, it controls it and puts it at its service. Now it simply attempts to make that contradictory image seem "natural", as "evidence", as "unquestionable".

If the first half of the year 1994 was filled with surprises and unprecedented events, the same period of 1995 demonstrates that the course of neoliberalism has no course. The contradiction of neoliberalism is that it has no direction. The contradiction is its improvisation which constitutes the spinal chord of the new national politics which are converted into the program of the government.

Where its says "The well-being of your family" it shows scarcity, unemployment, the fall of all economic indicators.

Where it says "peace through a political negotiation" it shows all the military paraphernalia of tanks, airplanes, helicopters, thousands of troops. Where it says "definitive political reform" it shows the justification for the imposition of governors, "democracies" which are maintained by an army which each time acquires more characteristics of an army of occupation... in its own land.

Where it says "the defense of the national sovereignty": it shows the sales tickets with the special prices on the wealth of the country.

Where it says "speak always with the truth" it shows the manipulations of the mass media, especially the electronic media where the lie is so crude that it surprises and provokes laughter instead of indignation.

Where it says "He knows how to do it" it modifies the punctuation and recites: "Does he know how to do it?"

The mirror of the Power speaks: "It is I or fascism", and it increases repression, persecution, the terrorism of the State. "I or anarchy", and the political system and the economy, hand in hand lurch to and for without direction or order. "I or chaos", and the officials say and retract themselves in deed and in word. "I or uncertainty", and the only certainty is that the future will be incognito when it lands.

Second Deceit:

The image offered by the mirror of Power is a double image. On one side the image is inward, one which the Power gives to itself.

Arrogance testifies, in front of itself, its splendor. The image returns these words:

"We are the same, the eternal ones. There are less of us, but we are richer. The uncertainty of the future was supplied by importing sufficient doses of the past. Yesterday can be made today, all that is necessary is a modest investment in dollars and an appropriate public relations campaign."

For the Power, the present is a mirror which faces backward and is rearranged. It prefers not to look forward, the precipice causes vertigo.

But the Power is, also, an outward image, an image offered by the power for external consumption, international consumption. And what image does it offer the people of Mexico?

After all is said and done, it is the government of Mexico, no?

Well, there is nothing to worry about, that image will reach the country... through the foreign mass media!

Reports about the economic situation, about government plans, about domestic politics, about the pending assassinations, all will reach the people of Mexico through the foreign news agencies. The ordinary Mexican who wishes to know about the state of the economy, should not notice his salary, his purchasing power, the stability in his employment or in his finances, or in his quality of life.

Instead of that he should depend upon the declaration of officials... of other countries or international organizations!

The Power, or better said, neoliberalism made Power in Mexico has ended its struggle to legitimize itself before its constituents.

Now the mirror has a new trick.

It no longer needs to "reverse" the image of illegitimacy and "convert" it to legitimacy.

Now it must "impose" another image which erases or puts in second place the original one, an image called Legality. No longer able to win legitimacy, incapable of struggling to achieve it, the Power dresses itself with "legality". The legal mantle can do everything... including the violation of the law. That is how the mirror of Power works, with a legal although illegitimate image.

The common everyday citizen, in Mexico, should not wait for the government which (supposedly) he elected, to represent him and secure his well-being.

He should rather, be satisfied with a government-which-represents-the-law-which-represents-the- government-which-represents-the-law, ad infinitum in that bouncing of images from one mirror to another.

This is the Power: the tautological mirror. In its image, in the reflection it obtains of itself, the Power says:

"I exist because I am necessary,
I am necessary because I exist,
therefore:
I exist and I am necessary."

As the image it receives of itself is enough to satisfy itself, the Power believes it is enough, and once again the mirror in front of the mirror, eternal.

Parenthesis: The details in the image of the mirror.

(The alternation of power: change of reflective angles, but the same mirror).

Between populism and neoliberalism, between dinosaurs and technocrats, between the PRI and the PAN, the image of the power plays at finding its best angle, its most attractive one, its most efficient one.

The system is no stronger or weaker than yesterday. It continues in its contradiction and prepares itself to continue its mutation in order to remain the same and produce the same effect, secure for the power the reproduction of its image.

The right has always been a part of the mirror. It does not aspire to power via legitimacy, for the simple reason that they are already in power. But they have discovered that the images, due to so many reflections, are becoming scarce and deteriorating, are wearing away and begin to irritate the respectable. They stop being effective, become useless... and criminal. A new figure (which is not a new image, but, the movement of an existing detail to the front) is necessary; the alternation of power which is proposed is, in reality, the alternation of the images in the same mirror, the exchange of first and second planes in the details of the same image, the same mirror, of power...

The Salinistas of yesterday are the Panistas of today, and the dinosaurs of yesterday are the technocrats of today, crocodiles with postgraduate degrees earned abroad. The year 2000 is not when the reflection is expected to change. Within the power is the whisper of voices that the actual image may not survive until the end of the century.

It is the image which is expiring. The mirror, that is, the Power, is eternal...

With nausea and terror, like someone who, upon awakening from a nightmare knows it will return, the Moon shakes its pale veil. Hollow-eyed and emaciated, it makes a gesture of disillusionment as it tells its tale of bouncing from one image to another, when, being a mirror herself, finally she managed to see herself in it...

Second Mirror

Chapter 2.- She chats about how there are many truths which are opposing forces, of how power contaminates with its cynical market-technology whomever opposes it, and of other deformed images in the modern mirror.

In the second mirror the opposition lives. In Mexico, to belong to the opposition is simple: it is enough not to belong to the PRI. But there is the opposition and then there is the opposition. The image, only two decades ago, of the legal political spectrum in Mexico was very simple: In the center was the PRI, to its right the PAN and to its left the PRI again, and sometimes the PPS. The PARM only played at being a party in some localities. To the extreme left was the rest of the opposition which remained unregistered and illegal. A decade later, various left organizations participated in the electoral struggle for power. The left place of the Mexican political geometry was fought over by various parties. At the center the PRI remained, fearless. In the center the PRI could move to the left or to the right, whatever was convenient for the mirror. But then the crisis arrives, and the crisis of the system is also that of the political parties. And there are no internal crises quite like those of the PRI, which, on the eve of the presidential elections of 1988, fractures. National Action [PAN] finds in the charismatic Maquio [Manuel Clouthier] the leader which it needs. The legal left is pulverized, and discovers that an internal alliance would not be bad. An ample front arises around a man whose surname is Cardenas, first name Cuahtemoc, and who possesses an austere face. The discontent, arising from the most diverse social sectors, bursts and is channeled into Neocardenism.

The social discontent becomes votes, and for the first time, the PRI is defeated in the electoral ballot boxes of the Presidency by an opposition force. But losing, and turning over power are two different things. Prodigious cybernetics produces fraud and the PRI wins by law and loses its legitimacy. The post-electoral protests are quieted as the new administration of the future candidate to Almoloya [Mexican prison], Carlos Salinas de Gortari, constructs around himself a giant mirror of lies. The electronic media helps him, as does the reactionary clergy, and great capital and the flag of the bars and muddled stars. "By a hair!" the power says, "It can't happen again! Let's get ready for 94!"

The front surrounding Cardenas Solorzano begins to receive the first blows and the satellites which are always there come loose. The ample opposition front rehearses to become a political party and is converted to the Party of the Democratic Revolution [PRD]. It is baptized by its own spilled blood; selective assassinations begin the fatal count which accompanies the Salinist campaign against Cuahtemoc Cardenas and the PRD.

Born in the midst of these attacks, the PRD at times appears to synthesize all the disadvantages of a front and all the disadvantages of a political party. The PRI past of some of its leaders become mirror once again in this effort to become an alternative to the system of the Party-state. Nevertheless, no one can deny that the PRD has achieved, at the cost of the lives of its own, to open an important space for political citizen participation. A good part of the small democratic space which now exists in Mexico is due to the PRD.

The best tribute to the character of the opposition force which is the PRD is constituted in the multiple attacks which it received from the power. The power fears it and attacks it always and by all means. Now the great thinking reactionary minds run over one another, to decree through their different analyses the death of this party which is the only registered party, that has value as an opposition party. In terms of Cardenas, not only the power pretends to declare him dead politically. His own party members try to get rid of him, but above all they try to do away with what he represents; intransigent opposition to authoritarianism.

Now the PRD is a prisoner in the most fashionable mirror: the struggle for the center. The legal left erases itself and tries to fight to conquer a space which everyone is grabbing. The PRI, the PAN, Manuel Camacho Solis, everyone wants the center. The center, they say, guarantees a transition with no pain, a stable alternation, a change... "without eruption". Within such an embattled space, the PRD does not have the best of chances. Nevertheless, the apparent purge between "dialogue-ists" and "intransigents" is in reality the struggle between those who aspire to conquer the center (and repeat the electoral "victories" of National Action [PAN], and those who prefer the left because of vocation... and history).

And the left? Nothing legal aspires to occupy the vacuum which the PRD wants to leave. Nevertheless, that left exists. Its illegal character (which doesn't mean "clandestine") does not annul its political work and influence in regional spaces and in what is called "the critical junctures".

Both the legal and the illegal left however share a cannibalistic mirror, one which engulfs all that is nearby, and nevertheless suffers serious digestive problems: it spits up what it eats. All the left which considers itself worthy of its name is the vanguard. This means that there are so many vanguards that no one knows where to walk and no "contingent" exists to follow these vanguards. "Political realism" and cynicism are more than common places, they are articles of prime necessity. The new left professes the old left and the marks are the tiny mirrors of the great mirror of the opposition in Mexico.

Fragmented, confronting itself, the left opposition has the irrefutable honor of not having surrendered, of rising once again after each blow, of continuing to struggle (in spite of everyone and in spite of itself, and of believing that the revolution is necessary... and possible...

With anger, and frustration, the Moon leaves this reflection. Between the two mirrors a flash is perceived. With a clever pirouette, acrobat of both clouds and storms, the Moon manages to catch a sharp edge, and fling itself towards the reflection of...

Third Mirror

Chapter 3.- To speak of the "people", those "without a party", of "civil society", of the "majorities", of the "waiting masses" who seek a "vanguard", of "society", and of all those names attributed to those who have no name, or voice, or face, and who are barely, a possible vote, a place in the contingency, a cry in the demonstration, a guard in the sit-in, a consumer, a television viewer, a radio listener, a reader, a number to add to the appropriate count...

The protagonists of the greatest mobilizations in the last years are those who have been most severely hurt by everything and everyone. The crisis and, above all, the "brilliant" administration of the crisis carried out by the neoliberal technocrats, is creating an unusual "politicizing" campaign which few revolutionary vanguards ever dreamed of. The stubborn economic reality which is ever more deteriorated plants in the minds and hearts the anxious desire for change. The electronic media shows inefficiencies: the illegitimacy of power has caught up with it and there are no television viewers who receive its Zabludovski, its Ferriz of Con, its Alatorre and radial equivalents without a certain dose of skepticism.

Something stinks up above, something is rotting. Its decomposition provokes everyday dramatic effects; the suicides increase. The economic crisis flows from the stock market, from the great banking centers and the specialty pages in the financial analysis publications. The economic crisis is lived on the tables of that majority which is called the "Mexican people". As they dress, as they eat, as they live, as they work, as they love, and even as they die, the crisis charges its quota. They must pay and in cash. The crisis achieves what any opposition front dreams about; it unites sectors and social classes which the "bonanza" separates, and often, confronts.

When May packs its things to leave and not return until next year, a note is lost in the newspapers.

The country lacks 19.2 million jobs. In 1995 1.2 million job seekers were added to the unemployed.

They add themselves to the 6 million unemployed and the 12 million sub-employed.

The PEA [Economically Active Population) ascends to 36 million (40 per cent of the total of Mexico). (SHCP)

At least 622,000 will lose their jobs in 1995. According to the SHCP, 436,191 were fired during the first trimester of the year.

According to the GEA (Associated Economists Group), the PIB [Gross Domestic Product] will grow at a rate less than 4.9 percent in 1995. In 1994, the minimum wage will lose 17.6 percent of its purchasing power in real terms. (La Jornada, May 1995).

But what the economy unites, politics separate. On the first of May of 1995 one of the greatest independent national mobilizations in the last decades takes place. It has two characteristics: One is that it was a protest against government politics, the other is · that it did not have unified political direction. A great mobilization, symptom of great discontent. An absence of a unified direction, symptomatic of a missing "something"...

The re-named "people of Mexico" generates new and creative ways to speak. The death sentence for Mexican hope, synthesized in the phrase "the Mexicans tolerate anything", begins to lose validity. Hope begins, babbling, to rehearse its own words, to construct a new language, to create a new mirror, a new image...

The Moon comes out of the new mirror with a hope barely clinging to its hair. She departs reluctantly. Tired and numb with cold by the subtle rejection of the dawn, the Moon clothes herself in the ocean of the west.

It looks in the mirror of the waves and cleans its face with the salty water. Sleep and the ocean spray do not allow her to see that, far away, opens the...

Fourth Mirror
Chapter 4.- Send, through the ocean of the east, a greeting to the men and women who, in Europe, discovered that they share with us, the same ailment: the illness of hope.

Instructions to see the fourth mirror:

Find any mirror, place it in front of you and assume a comfortable position. Breathe deeply. Close your eyes and say to yourself three times:

"I am what I am, a little bit, of what I could be. The mirror shows me what I am, the crystal what I could be."

Once this is done, open your eyes and look at the mirror. No, don't look at your reflection. Direct your look downward, to the left. Ready? Good, now pay attention and in a few moments another image will appear. Yes it is a march: men, women, children, and old people who come from the southeast. Yes, it is one of the highways which go to Mexico City. Can you see what is crawling on the left flank of the caravan? Where? There, on the ground! Yes, that tiny, black thing! What is it? A beetle! Now pay attention because that beetle is...

Subcomandante Marcos.

22. Durito IV: Neoliberalism and the Party-State System

June 1995

Durito walks the highways. These folks from Tabasco, in spite of the long days of walking and illness, do not appear tired. They walk as though they had only begun this Exodus for Dignity and National Sovereignty this morning. Once again, as before in the voice of the Zapatistas, a call to all the Nation marches from the Mexican southeast. In the heroic delirium of the Mexican Southeast, hope implies a name, Tachicam, the unity of the desire for a better future. The dream of a place in which the right to dance be guaranteed by the Constitution. Durito takes advantage of a stop. Hot, he seeks refuge under a small bush. After a while catching his breath, he takes out a paper and pencil. A rock serves as a replacement for the tiny desk he left in the jungle. Durito writes a letter. Go on! Don't be afraid!

Look over Durito's shoulder and read:

Zapatista Army of National Liberation. Mexico
To: Mister So and So
Professor and Investigator
National Autonomous University of Mexico
Mexico, D.F.
From: Don Durito of the Lacandon
Errant Knight for whom SupMarcos is shield-bearer
Zapatista Army of National Liberation Mexico

Sir,
It may appear strange to you, that I, a beetle of the noble profession of the errant

knights, write to you. Don't be perturbed and don't run to find a psychoanalyst, since I will explain to you quickly and promptly. It seems as though you made a proposal to the Sup to write an article for a book (or something like that) about the Transition to Democracy. The book (or whatever it is) would be edited by the UNAM [National University of Mexico] (which by the way is a clear guarantee that no one would read it). However, I am not aware whether or not you are accounting for the crisis of the publishing industry and the increase in the cost of paper. The deal includes the exorbitant payment of 100,000 new pesos which UNAM would donate, in its equivalent dollars or Italian liras to the workers of Fiat in Turin. We have learned as well that the Italian workers of COBAS have already received this amount from the Zapatistas to the cause of European workers.

You have complied, the Fiat workers have complied, but here the only one who has failed to do so is the Sup, because it seems clear to me that the deadline was in January of 1995. The Sup however was busy being disingenuous thinking the government was inclined to a dialogue, and that is why he did not meet his obligations. The betrayal of February brought his mind back and made him run (the Sup) until he arrived at my side. Once he recovered from the deceit he told me about his commitment for an article and asked me to get him out of this grave predicament. I, dear sir, am an errant knight, and we errant knights cannot refuse to help the needy, no matter how big his nose or how criminal the derelict is. So in good time I agreed to provide this help and that is why I am writing to you and not the Sup. You may of course ask why, if I accepted the request in February, I am writing in May. Just remember, as a journalist pointed out, this is the "rebellion of the 'stood up'"

I should also advise you that I write veeery seriously and veeeery formally, so don't expect to find my writing style full of jokes and irreverence like the Sup who so scandalizes the government delegates. That is why I am late. Don't be outraged, it could have been worse, you could have had to wait for the Sup to write to you one day. But such an improbable act is certainly not worth it, so here I send you this rap about the theme which you proposed, and which, if memory serves me is called...

The Transition To Democracy According To The Zapatistas

Someone may want to title it "According to the Neo-Zapatistas", however as Old Man Antonio explained in THE HISTORY OF THE QUESTIONS, here the Zapatistas of 1994 and those of 1910 are the same.

I will proceed to expose our concept of the meaning of the present-day political situation, democracy, and the transition from one to the other.

I. The Actual Political Situation; The System of the Party-State, Principal Obstacle To A Transition To Democracy.

The Mexico of today finds itself with a structural deformation which cuts across the spectrum of Mexican society, in that it affects all social classes, geographical urban and rural "organizations". This "deformation" is in reality a consequence of the savage capitalism of the end of the 20th Century, which masks itself in the word "NEOLIBERALISM" and constructs all its development on the permanence and worsening condition of such a deformation. Any effort to "balance" this deformation from the same Power is impossible and never goes beyond cheap demagoguery (Procampo) or the more polished intent at fascist control at the national level: The National Solidarity Program. We intend to say with this that the social "imbalance" in Mexico is not a product of excess or a problem of budgetary adjustment. It is the same essence of the system of domination which makes it possible. Without this imbalance, the entire system would fall.

We will not refer to these social "deformities", but only to the political ones in a hurried manner:

The political system of Mexico has its historic basis, its present crisis, and its mortal future, in this deformation called "System of the Party-State". This is not just about the marriage of the government and the State-Party (The Revolutionary Institutional Party) but of an entire system of political, economic and social relations which invade even those opposition political organizations and the so-called "Civil Society."

Any intent to balance these political forces, within this system, never stops being, even in the best of cases, a wish, which drives the democratizing sectors within the PRI and some members of the opposition. The only way in which this political system survives, until now, is by the maintenance of that brutal imbalance which places, on one side, all the strength of the government apparatus, the repressive system, the mass media, great capital and the reactionary clergy on the side of the PRI emblem, and on the other side a divided opposition which primarily confronts, itself. In the middle, or better yet, marginalized from these extremes of the complicated organizational balance of the Mexican political system are the vast majorities of the Mexican people. Both forces, the system of the Party-State and the organized opposition, bet upon that third actor which is the Mexican people, upon their absence or presence, their apathy or mobilization. In order to immobilize it all the system's mechanisms move, to mobilize it the political proposals of the opposition are moved (legal or illegal, open or clandestine).

Any attempt to balance this imbalance within this system is impossible. To balance it requires the death of the Mexican political system consolidated 60 years ago. Within the "rules of the game" of the system it is not possible to even arrive, not just to a new social model of organization which is more just, but also to a system of parties. Similar to that dream of the free play of supply and demand which cannot be realized in an economic system increasingly dominated by monopolies, the free political game of the parties cannot become reality in a system based on the monopoly of politics: the system of the Party-State.

Allow me to emphasize this point in this way (I point out a problem and not a solution. Allow me to postpone, for another improbable moon, the continuation of this explanation). As to a more profound characterization of the system of the Party-State you should refer to those brilliant and forceful analyses (I say this without sarcasm) written by excellent analysts. We point out one difference in reference to other positions, which in all likelihood will be presented in the book you are preparing: any intent to "reform" or "balance" this deformation is impossible FROM WITHIN THE SYSTEM OF THE PARTY-STATE. There can be no change without a rupture. A profound and radical change of all the social relations in today's Mexico is necessary. A REVOLUTION IS NECESSARY, a new revolution. This revolution is possible only from outside the system of the Party-State.

II. Democracy, Liberty, And Justice; Base For A New Political System In Mexico.

The triptych of democracy-liberty-justice is the base of demands of the EZLN, even within its primarily indigenous base. One of these is not possible without the others. It is not about which comes first (ideological trap which whispers at our ear: "Let's postpone democracy, and first get justice"). It is more about the emphasis, the hierarchy of expression, of the dominance of one of these elements in the different historical eras (precipitous in 1994 as well as 1995). In February, when the government forces tightened their grip on our troops and the leadership was "hunted" by commando units of the Federal Army we said:

"We believe that revolutionary change in Mexico will not be the product of action in a sole arena. In other words, it will not be, in a strict sense, an armed revolution or a peaceful revolution. It will be, primarily, a revolution which is the result of the struggle on different social fronts, with many methods, within different social forms, with different degrees of commitment and participation. And its results will be, not a party, organization or alliance of victorious organizations with its specific social proposal, but a chance for a democratic space in order to resolve the confrontation among diverse political proposals. This democratic space for resolution will have three fundamental premises which are inseparable historically: democracy, in order to decide upon the dominant social proposal, liberty in order to subscribe to one or the other proposal and justice in which all proposals should be enclosed (February 20 of 1994)."

Three points in a single paragraph, three dense points similar to bitter pozol [corn meal]. This is the style of the Sup: murky concepts, and difficult ideas to understand and more difficult to digest. However, I will allow myself to develop, what he has barely outlined. These three points all contain a conception about a revolution (in small letters, in order to avoid polemics with the multiple vanguards and protectors of "THE REVOLUTION"):

The first refers to the nature of the revolutionary change. It is about a process which incorporates different methods, different fronts, different and various levels of commitment and participation. This means that all methods have their place, that all the fronts of struggle are necessary, and that all levels of participation are important. This is about an inclusive process, which is anti-vanguard and collective. The problem with the revolution (pay attention to the small letters) is then no longer a problem of THE organization, THE method, THE caudillo [dictator, political boss]. It becomes rather a problem which concerns all those who see that revolution as necessary and possible, and whose achievement, is important for everyone.

The second point refers to the objective and the result of that revolution. This is not about the taking of Power or the imposition (by peaceful or violent means) of a new social system, but about something which precedes all this. It is about the construction of the ante-chamber of the new world, a space where, each of the different political forces, with equal responsibilities and rights can "fight for" the support of the majority of society. Does this confirm the hypothesis that we Zapatistas are "armed reformists"? We don't think so. We just point out that a revolution which is imposed, without the support of the majority, eventually turns against itself. I know this is a theme worthy of pages, but since this is only a letter, I am pointing out themes to be developed on other occasions and to provoke debate and discussion (which seems to be the "specialty" of the house of the Zapatistas).

The third point is not about the characteristics of the revolution, but of the results. The space which results, the new political relationships, should fulfill three conditions; democracy, liberty and justice.

In summary, we are not proposing an orthodox revolution, but something even more difficult: a revolution which will make a revolution possible...

III. A Broad Opposition Front?

The fragmentation of the opposition forces allows the system of the Party-State to, not only resist the attacks, but co-opts and weakens that opposition. The system of the Party-State does not worry about the radicalism of the forces which opposes it, it only worries about their eventual unity. By parceling out the political forces against the regime, this allows the Party-State System to negotiate or "fight" to conquer the political "islands" which form in the opposition. They apply a law of war, the "economy of forces": to a diffuse enemy in tiny nuclei which are beaten by concentrating forces against each nucleus, isolating one from the other. These opposition nuclei do not see that they confront ONE enemy but MANY enemies, in other words they emphasize what makes them different (their political proposals) and not what makes them similar (the enemy which they confront: the system of the Party-State). Of course, we are referring here to the real, honest opposition, not to the puppets. This dispersion of opposition forces allows the system to "besiege" and conquer (or annul) each "island".

The unity of these "islands" would be a serious problem for the system of the Party-State, but unity, in and of itself, is not enough to defeat the regime. The presence and action of the "third element": the Mexican people, would still be necessary. This is written in small letters in order to avoid definitions and invocations. Does this third element have a defining characteristic of social class? Yes, but that is not the most "striking" characteristic at first. The most striking is its skepticism and lack of trust towards politics, or political organizations. When we say "Mexican people" now, we point out a problem and not a solution. A problem and a reality which obstinately presents itself and overcomes all theoretical schemes on one side, and corporate controls, on the other.

The unity of the "islands" face many obstacles. One of them, not the only one, is the difference in the character of that unity. A unity or organization of exploited classes, versus a multi-class unity. It is from this that the subdivisions arise.

Is a parallel construction of both fronts possible or does one counter the other? We believe it is possible, that they do not contradict one another. Anyway, perhaps it is best to ask the third mirror, the one which is to be "liberated" or "redeemed". Ask, respond. Speak, listen. A dialogue, then. A national dialogue.

(End of the article, commitment fulfilled.)

This is all sir. I am sure my literary style deserves to be printed under the slogan "Through my raza, speaks the rock", and not that of my shield-bearer who, although he is loyal and honest, tends to view life as though it were a game of crystals and mirrors...

Vale. Health and Vitality! The crystal is somewhere. Just a matter of finding it.

From the who-knows-which kilometer on the who-knows-which highway, although we are indeed in Mexico.
DON DURITO OF THE LACANDON.
MEXICO, MAY OF 1995.

II. The Day To Come. The Crystal To Be Seen From The Other Side

Cut on the other side, a mirror stops being a mirror and becomes a crystal. And the mirrors are for seeing on this side and the crystals are for seeing on the other side.

Mirrors are for cutting. Crystals are for shattering... and crossing to the other side...

> From the Mountains of the Mexican Southeast,
> Subcomandante Insurgente Marcos.
> Mexico, February-May 1995.

P.S. That, image of the real and imaginary, they seek, among so many mirrors, a crystal to shatter.

Durito V

Dawn. City of Mexico. Durito wanders through the adjoining streets to the Zocalo. Sporting a small trench coat and a hat angled like Humphrey Bogart in CASABLANCA, Durito pretends to pass unnoticed. His outfit and slow crawl are unnecessary as he sticks to the shadows which escape the bright display windows. Shadow of the shadow, silent walk, inclined hat, dragging trench coat, Durito walks through the dawn of Mexico City. No one notices him. They do not see him, not because he is well- disguised or because of that tiny, quixotic detective outfit from the 50's, or because he is barely distinguishable from the mounds of garbage. Durito walks near the papers being dragged by whomever or by some whisk of unpredictable winds which populate the dawns of the Federal District. No one sees Durito for the simple reason, that in this city, no one sees no one.

"This city is sick," Durito writes to me, "it is sick of loneliness and fear. It is a great collective of solitudes. It is many cities, one for each resident. It's not about a sum of anguish (do you know of loneliness which is not anguish?), but about a potency; each loneliness is multiplied by the number of lonely people which surround it. It is as though each solitude was a mirror which reflects the others, and bounces off more solitudes."

Durito has begun to discover that he is in foreign territory, that the city is not his place. In his heart and in this dawn, Durito packs his bag. He walks this road as though it were an inventory, a last caress, as though he were leaving a lover who knows this is goodbye. At certain moments, the sound of footsteps diminishes and the cry of the sirens which frighten outsiders increase. And Durito is one of those outsiders, so he stops on the corner each time the red and blue blinkers cross the street. Durito takes advantage of the complicity of a doorway in order to light a pipe with guerrilla technique: a tiny spark, a deep breath, and the smoke engulfing his gaze and face. Durito stops. He looks and gazes. In front of him, a display window preserves his image. Durito comes near and looks at the great crystal and what exists behind it. Mirrors of all forms and all sizes, porcelain and glass figures, cut crystal, tiny music boxes. "There are no talking boxes!" Durito says to himself without forgetting the long years spent in the jungle of the Mexican southeast.

Durito has come to say goodbye to Mexico City and he has decided to give a gift to this city about which everyone complains and no one abandons. A gift. This is Durito, a beetle of the Lacandon Jungle in the center of Mexico City.

Durito says goodbye with a gift.

He makes an elegant magician's gesture. Everything stops, the lights go out like a candle does when a gentle wind licks its face. Another gesture and a light, like from a reflector, illuminates a music box in the display window. A ballet dancer with a fine lilac costume, keeps a perpetual position with its hands held high, its legs together as it balances on tip-toes. Durito tries to imitate the position, but promptly gets his many arms entangled. Another magical gesture and a piano the size of a cigarette box appears. Durito sits in front of the piano and puts a jug of beer on its cover, and who knows where he got it from, but it's already half-empty. Durito cracks and flexes his fingers like those digital gymnastics done by pianists in the movies. Durito turns toward the ballerina and moves his head. The ballerina begins to move and makes a bow. Durito hums an unknown tune, beats a rhythm with his little legs, closes his eyes and composes himself.

The first notes begin. Durito plays the piano with four hands. From the other side of the crystal, the ballerina begins a turn and slowly raises her right leg. Durito leans on the keyboard and plays furiously. The ballerina performs her best steps as allowed by the prison of the little music box. The city is erased. There is nothing but Durito on his piano and the ballerina in her music box. Durito plays and the ballerina dances. The city is surprised, its cheeks redden in the manner in which this happens when one receives an unexpected gift, a pleasant surprise, good news. Durito gives the best of his presents: an unbreakable and eternal mirror, a good-bye which doesn't hurt, which heals, which washes clean. The spectacle lasts only a few instants. The last notes end as the cities which populate this city take form. The Ballerina returns to her uncomfortable immobility, Durito turns up the collar of the trench coat and makes a smooth gesture towards the display window.

"Will you always be behind the crystal?" Durito asks and asks himself, "Will you always be on the other side of my over there and will I always be on the other side of your over there? Health and until eternity, my beloved troublemaker. Happiness is like a gift, it lasts for a moment but it is worth it."

Durito crosses the street, arranges his hat and continues to walk. Before turning the corner, he turns towards the display window. A hole like a star adorns the crystal. The alarms are ringing uselessly. Behind the window the ballerina in the music box is gone...

"This city is sick. When its illness becomes a crisis, it will be cured. This collective loneliness, multiplied by millions and potent, will end by finding itself and finding the reason for its impotence. Then, and only then, this city will lose the grey of its dress and will adorn itself with the brightly-colored ribbons which are abundant in the province.

This city lives a cruel game of mirrors, but the game of the mirrors is useless and sterile if there is not a crystal as a goal. It is enough to understand this, and as who-knows-who said, struggle and begin to be happy...

I'm coming back, prepare the tobacco and the insomnia. I have a lot to tell you, Sancho..." ends Durito.

It is morning. A few piano notes accompany the day which comes and Durito who is on the road. To the west, the Sun is like a rock shattering the crystal of the morning...

Vale once again. Health and leave surrender for the empty mirrors.

> *The Sup getting up from the piano and looking for, confused by so many mirrors, the exit door... or is it the entrance?*

23. THE TALE OF DURITO'S RETURN

June 30, 1995
To the national weekly "Proceso"
To the national newspaper "El Financiero"
To the local daily "El Tiempo" of S.C.L.C., Chiapas

Sirs,

Here go communiqués and letters to their respective destinations. June left after playing it would become May as it became July. In fact, according to the "efficient" PGR, supposedly June is the month of my birthday, and according to the complicated computers of the PGR, I should be 38 years old... I solemnly declare that I have not received (yet) not a single coin of gold of the 38 to which I am entitled. Camilo laughs and says what-38-you're-more-like-83. So, it should be 83 coins of gold or its equivalent in UDI's.

Vale. Health and about that jigsaw puzzle, it's my opinion, that its solution is a measure of... shame.

> *From the mountains of the Mexican Southeast,*
> *Subcomandante Insurgente Marcos.*
> *Mexico, June of 1995.*

P.S. HE TELLS THE TALE OF DURITO'S RETURN AND OF OTHER UNHAPPY (FOR ME) EVENTS.

"No, no and no!" I answer Durito who has begun the conversation with a brief description of an encounter with Merlin, with a skull's face and a skeleton's body, in order to reveal the secret of the bewitchment of Dulcinea of the Lacandon.

"Why do you say 'no' if you still don't know what I am going to ask?" says Durito.

"Because I know that story from Part 2 of the Ingenious Hidalgo Don Quijote de La Mancha, where Merlin tells Sancho that he should give himself 3,300 lashes on his buttocks."

And then I remember not Sancho's donkey or the winged "Clavileno Aligero..." whose name rhymes with wood, and with the peg he has on his head, and with the swiftness with which he walks; and so, in terms of the name, he could compete with the famous "Rocinante", the mount upon which the noble knight defeated the gigantic and bewitching Malambruno. I remember instead the mounts which he suffered with in previous adventures: El Salvaje, who, like his name loved to take off into the thickest bushes when he wanted to be free of his mount, or he would throw himself on the ground and get rid of saddle and cargo whenever both bothered him.

El Puma, that famished horse, as skinny as a hatrack which barely serves to keep others company, and who, so they tell, died of melancholy in a pasture. El Choco, who, if seniority were worth military rank, would be a comandante. Old and noble horse, with a blind right eye who maneuvered with his left in order to clear steep banks and mud heaps, which were abundant in the routes of those days. El Viajero, vivacious and high-stepping burro. El Tractor, a brilliant black male with an elegant and helpful step, a gentleman on the hills of smooth stones filled with the promise of missteps and falls.

P.S. SO HE TELLS HOW CRITICISM AND SELF-CRITICISM... IS FORMATIVE?

A heavy cloud rest among the trees and the moon pierces it with thousands of white pins. Some caterpillar, who forgets that it is June, makes his way dubiously between the campfire and the red-gray of the cigarettes. Any dawn, any mountain, any men somewhere and... a beetle?

"You have a beetle on your shoulder," Camilo tells me. I remain still and answer:

"And you have a tick on your neck and the other Me a spider on the ear, and I say nothing. At any rate it is not a beetle but a parrot which speaks in French..." Durito looks at me, surprised, but he is not intimidated and subsequently begins to recite:

"Me pauvre muse, helas! qu'as-tu done ce matin! Tes yeux creux son peuples de visions nocturnes, Et je vois tour a tour reflechies dut ton teint La folie et l'horreur, froids et taciturnes..." Then he adds, loudly:

"We are not ten, nor a hundred... There are about three of us, count us well!" The "cell" of three are meeting and Durito has decided to add his stubborn tendency to have nature imitate art so he joins the session.

"Weren't the three musketeers four?" Durito asks me when I protest his presence at the meeting.

I defer and Durito interprets that as approval so here we are... the three of us are four. The first point of order is to give the cell dedicated to political study and cultural activities a name. In honor of Etore Scola we call ourselves the "dirty, bad and the ugly". There were protests. Camilo says we may be dirty and ugly, but that about being bad is simplistic and Manichaeistic [a dualistic philosophy dividing the world between good and evil]. Camilo wants to change "bad" for "smartalecks" so now we are the "dirty, ugly, bad and smartalecks". Criticism and self-criticism always provoke a profound silence which reveals complicity.

But today there are too many mosquitos, and threats of rain, and no one wants to leave the fire and the smoke so my other Me begins a session which promises to be like a dialogue between the e-zee-el-en and the supreme government. "I make this self-criticism, because I went to gather firewood when it was the Sup's turn and so I have fomented his laziness and his lollygaging with his stories about beetles and gallant knights". I remain calm and answer with a conciliatory: "I make the self-criticism that I am always picking up after my other Me and I foment in this way his laziness, procrastination, and royal fuck-ups." Camilo makes no criticism or self-criticisms, he just amuses himself listening to my other Me and yours truly exchange criticisms disguised as self-criticisms. We would have been there all night had it not been that it began to rain. The wood got wet, the fire went out...

The secretary of the cell did not get named because Durito, or the parrot, alleged that the electoral registry should be purged.

P.S. He declares: I received a writing booklet (which they say was sent since April) with a reproduction on the cover of an oil painting by Pablo Picasso called Woman with Yellow Hair. On the first page it says: "For sonnets and other things. Take care of yourself." I inaugurated the booklet with the following: "If I knew how to write sonnets I would not have taken up arms, and if I took care of myself I would not be here. Signed, the Sup" and I've gone on to use the booklet for "other things".

Vale once again. Health, and if the eyes shine, what does it matter if the night drowns us?

> *The Sup blowing out the candles on the cake, just to show he can still blow... (Durito says you can't put out candles with sneezes. I told him you can't have cakes of mud in order to thicken the soup for the pee-gee-are [PGR, Mexican justice department].)*

1. Chapter XI. "Of things which concern and touch this adventure and memorable history".
2. "La Muse Malade", in Les Fleurs Du Mal. Charles Baudelaire.

24. DURITO: NEOLIBERALISM THE CHAOTIC THEORY OF ECONOMIC CHAOS

July 17, 1995

Stupid improvisation directs the Cabinet

To the national weekly Proceso

To the national newspaper El Financiero

Io the national newspaper La Jornada

To the local newspaper of San Cristobal de las Casas, Chiapas, Tiempo

Ladies and gentlemen,

This is Durito writing you, because el Sup isn't here right now. He climbed up the highest peak and is watching the horizon. He hopes that so many presents will arrive for his birthday that they'll need "the Grandmother of all Caravans" to reach the mountains of southeastern Mexico. He says that we'll be able to appreciate the long line of trucks from faraway. Poor guy! He doesn't realize that everybody already knows that his birthday is the 30th of February.

O.K. Here come the communiqué, and a postscript that I found thrown away here.

Finally we can breathe calmly! The government has now declared that within two years, we will all be ve-e-e-ery happy. Now the only thing left to do is wait and see who can weather the 730 days that separate us from Paradise.

Farewell, then. I wish you good heath, and hope that they don't put Mejma Barsn in the government team for the dialogue in San Andres.

From the mountains of the Mexican Southeast,
Don Durito of the Lacandon Jungle.
Mexico, July of 1995.

P.S. SAY "HELLO" TO THE WHEAT, WHICH WAVES LIKE A FLAG ON AN ORDINARY AFTERNOON.

Towards the West, the Moon lowers itself down between the parted legs of two mountains and rests its cheeks on their belly, where the river stirs up its sex, dripping a serpentine rumor. Some excited clouds stroke the trees with their moisture. In the East, there's lightening and tremors, the crickets piped up with their alarms, and now only a few scattered stars will be surprised by the storm that announces itself to the South. The watchful airplane purrs its threat and recedes into the distance.

Another daybreak of waiting and tobacco. Everything calm. An excellent occasion for the uninvited (as usual) appearance of...

Durito VI!

(Neoliberalism: the Catastrophic Political Management of Catastrophe)

A glow-worm is shining on Durito's shoulder. A stack of newspaper clippings serves as a bed-chair-desk-office for my master, the illustrious Don Durito of the Lacandon Jungle, maximal representative of the noblest profession that any human being has ever practiced: knight-errantry. Through the smoke of his pipe, I observe and guard the last and greatest righter of wrongs, the famous knight for whose security I pass a watchfulnight, and for whom I keep myself alert and ready in case... y-a-a-a-awn.

"Yawning again, knave!"

Durito's voice interrupts a blink which, he says, lasted for hours.

"I wasn't asleep!" I defend myself, "I was thinking..." I look at my watch and I notice that...

"It's three o'clock in the morning! Durito, can't we sleep?"

"Sleep! Thou thinkest only of sleep! How canst thou aspire to achieve the supreme station of knight-errantry if thou dost occupy the most opportune hours in sleep?"

"Right now, I only aspire to sleep," I say as I yawn and curl back up against the backpack that serves as my pillow.

"Do so, then. I, until Apollo scratches the skirt of the night with his golden knives, I will devote myself to thoughts of the highest and most dignified lady that any knight has ever chosen for his flag and desire, theone and only, the best, the one without equal, the... are you listening to me!?" I hear Durito shout.

"Mmmmfg," I respond, knowing that I don't need to open my eyes to notice that Durito must be standing on his stack of newspaper clippings, with Excalibur in his right hand and the left hand on his heart, and the other right on his belt, and the other fixing the armor of the other... Actually, I don't remember how many arms Durito has anymore, but he has enough, more than enough for the gestures he has to make.

"And what keeps thee up, my sluggardly shield-bearer?" Durito asks, with evident will to keep me awake.

"Me? Nothing, if it weren't for your midnight speeches and studies... Really, what is it you were studying?"

"The governmental cabinet," Durito responds, returning to his papers.

"The governmental cabinet?" I ask with surprise, doing what I didn't want to do - opening my eyes.

"Of course! I have discovered why the members of the cabinet contradict each other, why each one takes off in his own direction, apparently forgetting that the boss is..."

"Zedillo!" I say, losing interest in the talk.

"Error! It isn't Zedillo," says Durito with satisfaction.

"No?" I ask at the same time that I feel around in my backpack for the little radio that I use to listen to news. "Did he resign? Did they get rid of him?"

"Negative," says Durito, enjoying my sudden activity.

"There it is, just where we left it yesterday."

"So?" I ask, now completely awake.

"The boss of the governmental cabinet is a character who, for the sake of convenience and discretion, I will now call, 'Character X'."

"Character X?" I ask, remembering Durito's enjoyment of police novels, "and how did you find him out?"

"Elementary, my dear Watson."

"Watson?" I manage to stammer out, upon noticing that Durito has turned the cacati shell that he uses as a helmet, and I see that it looks like a rapper's cap (although he insists that it is a detective's deerstalker hat). With a magnifying glass, Durito examines his papers. If I didn't know him better, I'd say he isn't Durito, but...

"Sherlock Holmes was the Englishman who learned from me to assemble apparently unimportant details, to unify them into a hypothesis and to look for new details that would confirm or refute it. It's a simple exercise of deduction like those which my pupil Sherlock Holmes practiced when we were out drinking in the bad neighborhoods of London. He would have learned more from me, but he went off with some Conan Doyle who promised to make him famous. I never heard about him since."

"He got famous," I say lazily.

"I don't suppose he became a knight errant?" asks Durito with some interest.

"Negative, my dear Sherlock became a character in a novel and got famous."

"Thou dost err, my dear big-nosed Watson, fame only arises in knight-errantry."

"O.K. let's leave this and get back to all this about the governmental cabinet and this mysterious 'Character X.' What's going on with this?"

Durito begins to review his magazine and newspaper clippings.

"Mmmmh... Mmmmh... Mmmmh!" exclaims Durito.

"What? Did you find something?" I ask on account of the last admiring "mmmmh."

"Yes, a photo of Jane Fonda in Barbarella," says Durito with a look of ecstasy.

"Jane Fonda?" I ask-lift-myself-up-stir.

"Yes, and au naturel," he says with a prolonged sigh.

A photo of Jane Fonda "au naturel" is enough to wake anyone with a little self-respect up, and I have always respected myself, so I get up and ask Durito for the clipping, who refuses to give it to me until I swear that I will listen to him attentively. I swore and swore again. What else could I do?

"All right. Attention!" says Durito with the same emphasis with which he clamps down on his pipe. He puts one of his many pairs of hands behind his back and begins to pace up and down in a straight line as he speaks. "Suppose that we have some country whose name is accented on the antepenultimate syllable and which happens to be located, unfortunately enough, beneath the empire of the chaotic stars and stripes. And when I say, 'beneath,' I mean just that, 'beneath.'

Suppose that this country is struck by a terrible plague. Ebola? AIDS? Cholera? No! Something more lethal and more destructive... neoliberalism! All right now, I've talked to you before about this sickness, so I won't waste time in repeating myself. Suppose now that a young generation of 'junior politicians' has studied abroad how to 'save' this country in the only way in which that generation conceives of its salvation, that is to say, without knowing its history and annexing it to the tail of the fast train of brutality and human imbecility: capitalism. Suppose that we manage to get access to notebooks full of notes from these students without countries. What do we find? Nothing! Absolutely nothing! Does this mean they're bad students? By no means! They're good and quick students. But it so happens that they've learned one single lesson in each subject that they studied. That lesson is always the same: 'Act like you know what you're doing.'

'This is the fundamental axiom of power politics under neoliberalism,' their teacher has told them. And they asked her, 'and what is neoliberalism, dear teacher?' The teacher doesn't respond, but I can deduce from her perplexed expression, her red eyes, the drool that drips from her parted lips, and the evident wear on the sole of her right shoe, that the teacher doesn't dare to tell the truth to her students. And the truth is that, as I discovered, neoliberalism is the chaotic theory of economic chaos, the stupid exaltation of social stupidity, and the catastrophic political management of catastrophe."

As Durito stops to light his pipe, I seize the moment to ask:

"And how did you deduce all of this from the teacher's face, drool, eyes, and shoe-sole?" but Durito doesn't hear me. His eyes are glowing, and I don't know if it's from the lighter or from what he says as he continues.

"All right. Let's move on. The aforementioned students return to their country, or what remains of it. They arrive with a messianic message that nobody understands. While the respectable person deciphers it, they make off with their booty, that is to say, the power. Once they have that, they start to apply the only lesson they ever learned: 'act like you know what you're doing,' and they use the mass media to build that image. They obtain exquisite levels of simulation, to the point that they construct a virtual reality in which everything works perfectly. But the 'other' reality, the real reality, marched on, and something had to happen. Then, they started to do whatever occurred to them: this way one day, that way the next. And then..."

Durito stops, examines his pipe and looks at me in silence...

"And then what?" I urge him on.

"And then... the tobacco ran out. Have you got any more?" he responds. I don't want to take the time to warn him that the strategic reserve is about to run out, and I throw him the little bag I have in my hand. Durito refills his pipe, lights it, and continues.

"Then it happens that they lose their understanding of the real reality and start to believe that the virtual reality that they created with lies and simulation is the 'real' reality. But this schizophrenia isn't the only problem. It turns out that each student started to create his own virtual 'reality' and to live according to it. That's why each of one dictates measures that contradict those of the others."

"That explanation is pretty... mmh... let's say... bold."

Durito doesn't stop, but continues with his explanation.

"But there's something that gives coherency to all of this governmental incoherence. I've been analyzing several different clues. I read all of the cabinet's declarations, I classified all of its actions and omissions, I contrasted their political stories, I analyzed even their most minute acts, and I arrived at a very important conclusion."

Durito stops, sucks in air to give himself importance and lengthen the pause so I will ask: "And what is the conclusion?"

"Elementary, my dear Watson! There's an invisible element in the cabinet, a character which, without making itself evident, gives coherence and a systematic quality to all of the government team's braying. A boss under whose command all are subject. Zedillo included. That is to say, 'X' exists, the real governor of the country in question..."

"But who is this mysterious 'Mr. X'?" I ask, unable to hide the shiver that runs up my spine as I imagine that it might be...

"Salinas? Something worse...," says Durito, putting away his papers.

"Worse than Salinas? Who is he?"

"Negative. It's not a 'he', it's a 'she'," says Durito, blowing smokeout from his pipe.

"A 'she'?"

"Correct. Her first name is Stupid, and her last name is Improvisation, and note that I say, 'Stupid Improvisation.' Because you ought to know, my dear Watson, that there are intelligent improvisations, but this isn't the case here. 'Ms. X' is the Stupid Improvisation of neoliberalism in politics, neoliberalism made a political doctrine; that is to say, Stupid Improvisation administering the destinies of the country... and of others... Argentina and Peru, for example."

"So you're insinuating that Menem and Fujimori are the same as... ?"

"I'm not insinuating anything. I'm affirming it. It's enough to ask the Argentine and Peruvian workers. I was analyzing Yeltsin when my tobacco ran out."

"Yeltsin? but wasn't it the Mexican cabinet you were analyzing?"

"No, not only the Mexican one. Neoliberalism, as you should know, my dear Watson, is a pestilence that plagues all of humanity. Just like AIDS. Of course, the Mexican political system has an enchanting stupidity that is difficult to resist. But nevertheless, all of these governments that are depopulating the world have something in common: all of their success is based on lies, and therefore, it's base is only as solid as the bench you're sitting on."

I jump up instinctively and examine the bench of sticks and creepers we've constructed and make sure it's firm and solid. Relieved, I tell Durito: "But suppose, my dear Sherlock, that the bad guys are able to maintain their lie for an indefinite period of time, that this false base remains solid and they keep having successes." Durito doesn't let me finish. He interrupts me with a shout of...

"Impossible! The basis of neoliberalism is a contradiction: in order to maintain itself, it must devour itself and, therefore, destroy itself. That's where we get the political assassinations, the blows under the table, the contradictions between the statements and the actions of all levels of public functionaries, the squabbles between 'interest groups, 'and all of those things that keep the stockbrokers up at night..."

"It kept them up at night. I think they're getting used to it already, because the bolsa is going up," I say with some skepticism.

"It's a soap bubble. It will burst before too long. Remember me," says Durito as he smiles with an a know-it-all air and continues,

"What keeps the system going is what will bring it down. It's elementary. All you have to do is read Chesterton's three riders of the apocalypse to understand it. It's a police story, but as is well known, life ends up imitating art."

"Sounds to me like your theory is pure fantasy..."

"I wasn't finished talking."

As I sat down on the bench of sticks, it fell down with the muffled sound of my bones hitting the ground and my not so muffled cursing. Durito laughs as if he's about to smother. When he calms down a little bit, he says:

"You were going to say that my theory is pure fantasy? All right, as you can appreciate from your current low position, nature proves me right. History and the people will also give their help."

Durito ends his talk there and lies back against his newspaper clippings. I don't even try to get up. I pull my backpack over and lie down against it again. We fall silent, watching how in the East, a wheat and honey colored light pours through the space between the legs of the mountain. We sigh. What else could we do?

Farewell, good health, and may neither history nor the people wait long.

"El Sup" with a tender pain in his flank.

25. TODAY ENDS THE NATIONAL PLEBISCITE FOR PEACE AND DEMOCRACY

September 29, 1995
"La Realidad" Zapatista Center of Resistance
Rebel Municipality of San Pedro de Michoacan, Chiapas, Mexico

Through my voice speaks the voice of the Zapatista Army of National Liberation,

Today, September 29, 1995, ends a great social mobilization that included all of the Mexican territory and a good number of countries of the world. Today ends the National Plebiscite for Peace and Democracy, and a new stage in the national dialogue begins.

We want to thank the men and women of the CND who made up the Promotional Direction Committee, the brothers and sisters of the National Civic Alliance who made up the Organizational Direction Committee, the State Conventions, the State Civic Alliances and the dozens of thousands of Mexican men and women who promoted and organized this Plebiscite, whose main beneficiary was the process of peace.

Also we want to thank the men and women of the CND who participated in the International Linkages Commission, our brothers and sisters in North, Central and South America, in Europe, Asia and Australia, who organized the Plebiscite in their respective countries and who, being from distinct yet similar countries and histories, helped with their voice to speak the word of a new and better peace for the Mexicans.

The brothers and sisters of the Civic Alliance have made a great effort and given the country, and especially the government and the political parties, a beautiful lesson in honesty and organization. Through organizing the National Plebiscite, the Civic Alliance has proved to be a trustworthy channel for the dialogue of Mexican citizens amongst themselves. No one, not even the dullest members of the criminal bureaucracy that governs us, has dared to question the credibility of the Plebiscite.

This was possible because of the impeccable line taken by the Civic Alliance members.

Civilian Army

Good Health, brothers and sisters of the Civic Alliance. We give you our admiration and respect. You contribution to the cause of peace with justice and dignity is something that no one will ever doubt. We want to thank the men and women of the CND and those who, without being members of the CND, participated in the promotion of the Plebiscite. You represent the will of the civil society, the will of a new peace, a peace without hypocrisy, that is not an undercover war. Dozens of thousands of Mexicans mobilized knowing that the only reward would be the satisfaction of an accomplished duty; that not only did they not improve their economic situation with this work, which demanded effort, time and sacrifice, but they even had to spend money. These people are the same ones who have stopped the war every time the powerful required our blood and demanded our death: they stopped it in December 1994, February 1995 and now, in September 1995, the month of the motherland.

This civilian army has convinced us innumerable times, not with guns, lies, deceits or treason. They have convinced us countless times by showing us that the motherland, that strange sensation in our chest and that has not been buried by government cynicism and its devotion abroad, has other men and women who love this motherland in the same way we love it, who are willing to do everything in order to free this motherland. They have convinced us by talking with us and listening to us, because before, no one listened or talked to us. They have convinced us by forcing us to stop saying "us" and "you". They have convinced us, by forcing us to think about "us" in a way that goes beyond weapons and masks. They have convinced us by showing us that the motherland is not the property of organizations or groups in power, that the motherland lives and is ours.

The people in the national and international art world, who selflessly and with good will collaborated in the call for peace represented by the Plebiscite, deserve special mention. Distant in time, place and culture, those men and women build a bridge uniting with those for whom oblivion was a perpetual condemnation, silence an ominous future and death a daily companion. The men and women workers of culture and art put their work to serve a just cause: peace and democracy. Their face is now a reminder not of neglect, nor deceit, nor pointless dream, but an invitation to do something to improve the reality in which we find ourselves.

Also the national artistic community held activities which managed to win an important battle in the Lacandon Jungle, the battle against Leshmaniasis or Mountain Leprosy. Today the dark skin of indigenous men, women, children and elderly have begun to heal and renew itself, thanks to the men and women of other colors, but equally human, who remembered them and helped.

There are many who make their names with films, plays, soap operas, magazines, books, and everything that is the daily cultural duties in Mexico. Starting today, their names will also have a place, not only in the marquis or in the cultural cocktail hours or in television or movie credits, but also in the heart of the indigenous of Chiapas, and their image is a print on the dark skin that is now healing and cleaning itself.

We can't offer them prizes that are traded in the cultural market, we have nothing to give them , but we are sure that they can write with pride in the long paper that describes their artistic development, the following "in the mountains of southeast Mexico there is a human being whose wounds I healed; whom I healed from oblivion and whose solitude I alleviated."

Perhaps they won't find a better role with these notes, nor a raise in income, nor better opportunities in the artistic field, nor perhaps will the number of their fans increase. But what is certain, at least for us, is that their status as human beings grew. They are, for us, giants, that is, our equals.

We especially want to thank those social groups who, like the Indigenous, have suffered from marginality and unfair treatment. We want to thank the women, the young men and women, the homosexuals and lesbians, and the prisoners. In different ways, and in different manners, these human beings suffer intolerance, persecution, mistreatment and disdain... The voice of the always forgotten, of the eternally defeated, of the Mexican indigenous found an ear and support in them.

Thanks to the Mexican women, the always forced into submission, silence and conformity, those who broke free from the double prison enclosing them and went out into the streets, the fields and all the activities of social life and said: Here we are. We have come to bring the voice of others, who like us, refuse a senseless, sterile and silent death. The Mexican women, the single ones, the married ones, the widows, the divorced ones, all those who are always named according to their relationship to a man: the singles to possess, the married ones possessed, the widows and the divorced women who have lost their owner. The Mexican women, no longer just single, married, widowed or divorced, those who no longer are owned or to be owned. The Mexican women now speaking and making themselves heard. The Mexican women so uneasy, so upset, so not women, the Mexican women. And the other uneasy ones, the other upset ones, the Mexican indigenous thank them.

Thanks to the young Mexicans, the always postponed, the too immature to demand, the right age to be exploited. The young Mexicans, to whom all rationale is denied, who are accused of not having their own ideas, whose authentic aspirations are denied, who are assumed to be manipulated, always deceived, always confused. The young Mexicans always treated as a bothersome but passing illness, the current sin and future regret. Those condemned to shame themselves in tomorrow's submission of today's proud rebellion. The meat of the barrios, the drugs, prostitution, death, disenchantment. The young Mexicans filling all of what the cynicism of Power left empty, which is to say, everything. The young Mexicans carrying the voice and image of the other rebels, of the other eternal sub-citizens, the other sub-human, of the other "immature-manipulated-confused-tricked", of the others who thank them today: the indigenous Mexicans.

Thanks to the Mexican homosexuals and lesbians, the always persecuted, the always obliged to be shamed and to be hidden, the always sick, the undesirables, the target of the barrel of the gun of intolerance and hypocrisy, the identity as a synonym for insult and disqualification, the "you are a whore" as a judge, jury and execution-er. The Mexican homosexuals, the "whores" that are less "whores" than the valiant one who populate the national lie, the dignified struggle for equality in the difference. The Mexican homosexuals responding to the voice of the other persecuted, the others hidden by shame, the others synonymous with insult, the "you are an Indian" as a historic disqualification and cultural incapability, the others more Indian, is to say more intelligent than the wise men who populate the national lie, of the others of the dignified struggle for equality in differences, of the others who appreciate the listening, the voice and the ear, of the others: the Mexican indigenous.

Thanks to the Mexican prisoners, to the incarcerated for the historic crime of being poor, the put aside from the stupid normality that is sicker than those who are decreed to be abnormal, the prisoners for thinking what they think or simply for thinking in a country where intelligence is a crime, the prisoners for thinking that words follow thinking and that acting plants one's thinking, like a seed is planted, the prisoners for believing, for struggling, for trying to be better together with others and not alone, the prisoners for refusing to be criminals, which is to say, to be accomplices in the crime of not doing anything.

The Mexican prisoners breaking through with letters the walls of the penitentiaries, making a joke of the vigilance and stupid penal codes. The Mexican prisoners responding, speaking, saying "here we are, we are listening to you" to the other criminals for being poor, to the other transgressors of the law of oblivion and indifference, the other abnormals who combat the normality of racism and lies, to the other illegals for thinking, for speaking and for acting, to the other criminals of today and heroes of tomorrow, to the others who refuse to be accomplices of the crime of treason to the Motherland that those who are the government today commit, to the other prisoners of history: the Mexican indigenous.

First we should say that now that we have the complete results, now that the Plebiscite has ended, we declare the Promotional Direction Committee, the Organizing Committee for the Young People's Plebiscite, and the International

Linkages Commission dissolved. The men and women who participated in them are honorable men and women who fulfilled the commitment that we asked of them. Their work has ended. Thank you.

The Plebiscite Ended

For us there wasn't three Plebiscites, for us it was a great Plebiscite with three parts. For this reason, today as we receive the results of the Young People's Plebiscite and the International Plebiscite and along with those of the National Plebiscite, we say that the Plebiscite has ended and we are expressing our thanks to all of you. For us there isn't a first class, second class or third class Plebiscite. For us the word of a 12-year-old young person is valued as much as that of an 86 year old elderly person, the word of the Greeks, the Spaniards, the French, the Italians, the English, those from the United States, those from South America, those from Asia and those from Australia.

All of you were able to overcome many difficulties to get to this day and to provide good reports to those from whom we sought help and participation in this effort of the country. The initial derision of the government later became harassment and sabotage. Your effort and the actual nature of the National Plebiscite enabled the partial opening of the difficult terrain of the electronic communication media.

The Plebiscite was treated in two fundamental ways by the electronic media: on the one hand, it was ignored, and on the other it was ridiculed (such as in the case of TV Azteca). We should recognize that, however, there were other electronic media which reported with objectivity the nature of this exemplary citizenry effort and that some spaces were opened within the principal television monopoly. The reaction of the Powerful to the communication media, especially the electronic ones, was displayed again with regard to the National Plebiscite. Some demonstrated that they are controlled by the system by their lack of credibility and the scarcity of legitimacy, and they tried to keep their distance; others (like TV Azteca) bet that everything would be fixed, and they replaced the Pharisees of yesterday.

Special mention should go to those few media and some radio programs which did not hesitate in supporting an effort of peace in the middle of the war going on within the group governing that is difficult to ignore.

Independent of this incomplete hole in the larger communication media, the promoters of the Plebiscite developed ingenious and creative initiatives that deserve to be recorded in the history, in small letters, of this country, for the history that matters, that transforms and enriches. Young people and women principally achieved breaking through the fence which the government has had around the society and they began a dialogue whose real impact will be seen in the near future.

All of you, against everything, against everyone, lifted up a cause, the cause of peace and democracy. All of you, with all of the power and without anything to gain, lifted us up again, you took us out of oblivion again, you took us to you, you and yours felt together with us again, you heard us, you talked with us. You have earned the greatest things that we have. You have earned now and for ever that we will call you "brothers".

And this is the most important thing that we wanted to say today, that we wanted to show to you, that we wanted the others equal to all of you but who are not here to hear, that we wanted to have taken to all corners of the country and the globe. Only a pair of little words like us, forgotten like us, denigrated like us, butt of jokes like us.

Thanks, brothers and sisters!

The Search for Becoming Human

The National Consulta has spoken, it has answered and, in agreement with the definition of a dialogue, it now is our turn to speak. We would like, therefore, to talk a little about the results of the Consulta, both the National as well as the Young People's and the International.

More than 1,300,000 human beings, in Mexico and the world, took the time to respond to the questions that an armed group, clandestine, without face, and in a corner of the mountains of the Mexican Southeast, put forth. 1,300,000 men and women who responded not to the questions of the EZLN but to the effort of the dozens of thousands of organizers and promoters who invited them to dialogue and convinced them to do so. The quantity is a triumph, a triumph of all of you.

The biggest lesson, the most important teaching of this Consulta is that, yes, we can organize ourselves to talk and to listen, without being tutored or given permission by anyone we can construct the mechanisms for dialoguing. The results of the Consulta show that yes we can, that there are dozens of thousands of human beings willing to work and seek a way to a better world, a world that no one has promised us or given us, a world that we can construct ourselves as we want it and not as the Powers want it to be.

We have made the Power of Money tremble. It has noticed that there is something that it can not buy or sell, that dignity has begun to organize. The Power of Money is afraid because the meeting of dignities signifies its end, its rapid passage to becoming a nightmare that passes, the end of an historic stage ruled by arrogance and stupidity.

The Consulta was an exercise in the sovereignty of human beings over themselves. The Consulta was an act of affirmation in the face of the great Power. The Consulta was a warning to the powerful.: WE do not need you!

The Consulta was part of this never ending search: the search of becoming human.

The Six Questions

From the answers to the six questions of the Consulta we can also draw some conclusions: Questions 1, 2, 3, and 6 were answered, by the majority, affirmatively. This means that:

a. The base of a program for struggle is in the sixteen points. That these demands are the most important ones and it is not enough to enunciate them but rather we have to go further, to advance not only a plan of struggle that brandishes them, but that also provides an alternative program to solve them.

b. The necessity of a broad front regarding this program. The feeling of being the majority by this part of civil society that participated in the Consulta exists because the wills that are seeing something new and better are uniting and walking together even while respecting their differences.

c. The minimum conditions that would render the armed struggle useless and permit civilized and peaceful participation of the citizenry in politics.

d. The recognition of a fact: the growing and outstanding participation of women in the struggle for the solution of the great national problems. Nothing was authorized or given to women. Everything was what they earned or are earning of their own right.

We should reflect upon the results of questions 4 and 5 and give our response. This requires an effort of internal dialogue and a public response. That's the way we will do it...

In addition to these initial reflections about the results of the Plebiscite there are facts that come up immediately; a first response to the will for peace and democracy expressed in the National Consulta has been given already by the EZLN by means of their delegation to the dialogue in San Andres Sacamchen do Los Pobres. To a new government initiative whose objective was to break off the dialogue definitively, the delegation of the EZLN responded with a proposal that dismantled the theme of negotiation regarding the procedural rules and set the peace process on a new path. CONAI helped with these efforts and the sensibility of the legislators of the COCOPA helped. They were able to see in the Consulta that which the stupid blindness of Power kept the government from seeing: the nation's support for the demands of the EZLN and its will for a new peace, just and dignified.

The EZLN has now given an initial response to the more than one million men and women of Mexico and the world who participated in any of the three stages of the Consulta for Peace and Democracy: the National Consulta, the Young People's

Consulta, and the International Consulta. It was the position of the EZLN which succeeded in getting the dialogue out of the agony in which the government's delegation had gotten it.

With this first response to the national and International civil society, the EZLN succeeded in overcoming the foolishness of the gray and mediocre little men of the government, those bureaucrats of the negotiated death, of those renegades from dignity, those salaried traitors, made in the image and appearance of their boss, and whose only diversion is to humiliate the Indigenous, making fun of their way of speaking, their dress, their struggle, their being Indians. Set on having the peace process fail, and concerned only with keeping their paychecks and commissions, they were beaten by the great national and international mobilization which was the Consulta, which shook them and made the accept what they had said that they would never accept: a dialogue based on respect and seriousness.

The exhausted dialogue of San Andres, gained a new life not in the will of the government but in the voices of hundreds of thousands of men and women who demanded that the powerful and their subservient bureaucrats change their attitude at the negotiating table. The dawn of San Andres Secamchen de Los Pobres was made possible by the Consulta.

However, this first response is not enough. The question that more than one million three hundred thousand human beings who cast a ballot with their opinion on a street corner is still pending. The response to the 7th question is still pending...

And After the Consulta, What?

To begin to respond to this question we have to quickly recall what 1995 has meant for Zapatism, the national situation and the international situation.

In reference to Zapatism, we can say the following:

Stage 1: It was characterized by the political transition and the military offensive of the government. Putting aside the fact that they had already begun the dialogue with the EZLN, the supreme government concretized their betrayal on February 9 1995 with those stupid arguments about the supposed military preparations of the EZLN, the supposed unmasking of the supposed Zapatista leaders, and the supposed application of the supposed legality of the supposed government. Trying to cover the lack of legitimacy of their actions with the thin veil of legality, the evil government put the entire country at the edge of a civil war. Instead of what they assumed and expected, the government had to confront an immediate and massive social mobilization of repudiation. During the first days of the offensive they were able to carry forward their strategy of social mobilization of destruction and persecution of civilians accused of being Zapatista. For this they counted on the support of the electronic communication media, and with the people on their payroll in the print media. The so-called "Iruegas" doctrine, the strategy that replaces legitimacy with legality, failed. An illegitimate action can not gain agreement with an imposed legality. The popular protests, in Mexico and around the world, that far surpassed those of January 1994, were successful at stopping the machine of death that had begun to walk. A commission of legislators called COCOPA was able to realize that this idiotic action would take the nation toward an endless descent, and presented the Law of March 6, 1995 that provided a legal way out of the illegal stupidity that had overrun legitimacy.

Stage 2: Based on the law of March 6, 1995, the government tried again to take up the idea of dialogue and negotiation. The Legislative Branch, the Law of March 6, and COCOPA opened the hope that things could return to their line. But the "Iruegas Doctrine" continued to help the Executive and the lack of definition in the government's policy with regard to Chiapas ended up being displacement by EMB. An outstanding political person, opposed to the regime and committed to the peaceful struggle for democracy he put forth a good effort and achieved the so-called "Meeting in San Miguel" on April 9, 1995. Without the intervention of this person, the start of the dialogue and negotiations would have been impossible. Meanwhile, the civil society look up new initiatives to secure the fragile peace that the new law allowed.

The first Peace Camps were established, and the meeting in the San Miguel ejido, in the municipality of Francisco Gomez, Chiapas, took place.

Stage 3: The agreements achieved in San Miguel were quickly betrayed by the government, just 10 days after having been agreed to. The racist vocation of the Federal Executive was clearly demonstrated in the so-called "San Andres I". The indigenous mobilization which sought to protect their own from a new betrayal was denigrated by the government's delegation which refused to dialogue surrounded by Indians. One person representative of the government's stupidity distributed a video full of lies and ensnared the communication media in the lie. The lie didn't hold up long, but the stupidity of the government would have many more opportunities show itself in the gray delegation that was sent to the dialogue in San Andres. Full of traitors and hypocrites, the government delegation did not just try to humiliate the Zapatista delegates. The distinct ideas regarding ways to reduce tensions simply hid a fundamental difference regarding what the dialogue should be about: a humiliation as the government delegation tried to impose, or a negotiation as the EZLN proposed... Having put aside the ways to reduce tensions, the discussion regarding the Procedural Rules were a new opportunity for the government to cause the dialogue to fail.

Stage 4: The consulta for Peace and Democracy again found receptive ears in

COCOPA, and its initiative, along with the mature wisdom of the Zapatista delegation enabled the meeting of San Andres VI to end well, and the stage that we are in now to begin.

Analysis of the National and International Situation But the ineptitude of the government did not just show up in the dialogue of San Andres. The national situation reflects a deep crisis in all aspects of the country's life. The economic crisis can be summarized in the equation that, today, the rich are fewer but richer, and the poor are poorer and poorer. This is the final cry of the continuation of an economic policy whose only objective is to pay tribute to international financial capital. The social crisis is seen in the fact that crime is increasing at the same rate as the corruption of the public security forces, and the social fabric is being torn apart by the impact of the economic crisis and the lack of political solutions. The political crisis (moral and ethical) ties up the parties and births a lack of trust and skepticism. The cultural crisis (the communication media) within the group in power all rules were broken. There is a process of accommodation that searches, with futility, the means to survive.

The crimes that follow will be its undoing. Whatever might be the result, it does not include us, as we are not its victims. None of the factions in conflict are thinking about the nation; they are searching for their own well being, their own survival. The ordinary citizen does not exist in the best of cases, in the worst of cases he/she is expendable. For the Power and her internal struggles we are all dispensable, without regard for whether we're ordinary citizens, cardinals, candidates for President of the Republic, secretaries of political parties or magistrates. They continue imposing the politics of the loss of sovereign will, delivering the Nation to the international financial markets. Oil and sovereignty, once synonymous in the history of the country, today in the government's policies, are mutually exclusive.

With the popular struggles, nuclei of resistance are forming, isolated and in search of unity. Chiapas, Guerrero, Tabasco, Ruta-100, the excluded from UNAM, El Barzon, are only examples of a wider movement of popular resistance that persists, although dispersed but yet willing to coordinate together, even though it hasn't been accomplished yet.

The disorder, the lack of trust, the anger of the majority, known as the Mexican people, are the constants. The hope is still small, but it persists.

In the face of the chaos created by the government rise "alternatives" for power: the leadership of the PAN, whose apologists should be reminded of the declarations of their president in the sense that he was in favor of having a "multinational military force" intervene in Mexico; the impossible political "center" that the leadership of the PRD seeks, declaring without [embages] the replacement of the "legal fight" for the "struggle by agreement", which is nothing but an elegant form of saying "give up"; the reformed PRI that offers the politicians of yesterday as an option to the ineptitude of the technocrats; the efforts at self-government or of new forms of what is called "government of the people, for the people, by the people," which is to say, democracy: 1985, 1988, Alianza Civica, the boom of the NGOs, the EZLN, Tepotzlan, El Barzon, the union Ruta-100, the civil resistance in Tabasco, the movement of excluded students in UNAM.

In the international panorama, chaos is already the form that distinguishes the new world order.

World War IV is already being waged by the financial markets: the United Europe, Japan, North America, three great belligerent powers that are not national, but that represent only financial capital. The modern armies are being formed by information and economic specialists. The new battle camps are in the stock markets.

The process of globalization and her real antithesis, the pulverization of the nation states, is the future that is offered to the entire world. War continues its logical journey of resource distribution and possession, the division between countries is now replaced by the division between parts of a country. The nation state is confronting itself. The new enemy of this new war is ourselves.

Neoliberalism, as a theory of modern chaos, of the destruction of humanity, is the ideological inheritance of the Nazis and the founding theory of wars for "ethnic purity" and intolerance. Neoliberalism is the theory of modern war. Its objective is, as in all wars, the destruction of the enemy: humanity - physically and morally.

However, in the midst of all this, there is appreciation for the global left's finding again its original banner: the human being. Just barely glimmering lightly, but now with its own brilliance, those who believed they were defeated realize that their work had not ended, that there was still something to be done, that history had not ended...

What's Next?

It's simple to respond to this question. Nationally, what follows is to reconstruct the motherland that is now falling apart. Internationally, to reconstruct humanity that today is systematically destroyed. In summation, what follows is to fight and to win.

This is our answer to the question "And now what, after the Consulta?" We invite you to join us and we will respond together. No more asking you to work and then we wait here. Now, to make real the "we" that we offered you.

On the national level...

The next step is to organize a big table of national dialogue in which there are the principal political and social forces of opposition who are not political parties. They, those grand gentlemen of politics, the elite who decide or believe they decide the destinies of the nation, think that the rest of the Mexicans don't deserve a space next to them.

But the transition to democracy will not come from this non-existent table of dialogue, it will come from where it has to come, from the will of the Mexicans from below, from the people.

That is to say, we are going to leave the government and the political parties to make their dialogue and their political agreements for electoral reform and such things, but we are going to continue to insist in a dialogue with people, with the population, in search of new forms of organization which are not like the old kinds of political organizations.

This is what we think: a national table of dialogue amongst everyone who does not have a voice, a giant table of national dialogue which looks for a way to unite those who truly struggle for national liberation.

What we want is that the people of Mexico hear us and not the government. The people of Mexico is whom we want to hear from and not the government. We expect to reach an agreement with the Mexican people so that together we can make the transition to democracy. From the government we can only expect lies, treason and deceit. Liberty, democracy and justice can only be constructed by ourselves, no one is going to give it to us.

This is our response to the question "And after the Consulta, what?"

There is a new step that we have to take together: to create a giant table of national dialogue, without the government. Our idea of national dialogues is not one of sitting down with the grand gentlemen of the national politics, but rather sitting down with the civil society. This is what we want to tell COCOPA so that this will be the "format" of participation of the EZLN in the national dialogue... What we want is a "special forum" with our guests and our agenda... This great table of national dialogue between the EZLN and the civil society is what we ask the COCOPA to support, as part of their contribution to the peace process.

If the COCOPA asks the EZLN to participate in the national dialogue "for the reform of the State", and they are looking for a format, well then we will tell them that the format that we want is this one of dialoguing with the civil society, a table in which the EZLN and other independent forces such as the NGOs, Ruta Cien, Barzon, individual citizens, social organizations, unregistered political organizations, etceteras.

We want to propose to COCOPA that it be the link of this giant National Dialogue with the table "for the reform the state". We want them to be the ones who sit with the political parties and the government and present them the results of this National Dialogue. We also want to ask them to agree to present the proposals that result from this National Dialogue in the Congress of the Union. We want to propose that they participate more actively in the process for peace with democracy not only in Chiapas, but in all of Mexico. If citizens have a space where they can express themselves and be listened to, they will not have to resort to the argument of weapons to be heard. The COCOPA has the historic opportunity to become an important player in the transition to democracy. It is their turn to respond and affirm the independence of the Legislative Power with respect to the Executive power.

If the COCOPA accepts, then good, and if they don't, it doesn't really matter, since regardless, we will find a way to do it, a way to carry the voice of the civil society to the high forums of national politics. But this is not all, we invite you to begin now to work in this new stage of National Dialogue. We invite you to work in a new relation with EZLN and civil society. We invite you to:

1. Form local, municipal, regional and state Civil Committees of Dialogue.
2. The object is to lead into a Civil Table of National Dialogue.
3. The themes will be:
   a) The Nation program based on a program of struggle and the equitable participation of women: the 16 points
   b) The National opposition Front project
   c) New Political relationships among organizations, the government and the citizens and a new relationship between the Nation and the indigenous people
   d) The creation of a new independent political force based in the EZLN
4. Characteristics: no party affiliations, not conditional, not organically committed except to one cause: the reconstruction of the country. Open, civil, not clandestine, not illegal, protected by the Constitution.
5. Registry Offices: The central one in the EZLN and accredited affiliates throughout the country.
6. New Aguascalientes: We want to offer to the civil society that we the civilian indigenous Zapatistas and the civilians of the cities (NGOs, etc.) begin to work together. The Zapatista support bases have created "centers of Zapatista resistance" that is to say, villages or communities that continue with resistance, without accepting anything from the government. These populations are our flags, are our symbols of Zapatista resistance.

We invite you to make many Aguascalientes as a response to the destruction of the Aguascalientes of Guadelupe Tepayac, and that these Aguascalientes be in the centers of resistance. We want to say to civil society: let's go make many Aguascalientes and we need you to help us. We are going to have centers of resistance and there we want you (the civil society) and me (EZLN) to do something together for the well-being of the indigenous people: we'll put a good hospital that won't be from the government, with medicines, doctors, equipment, etc. with schools and classrooms, with children's toys, and studios and schools for women, with its own theater and cinema, sports and all that. But with nothing from the government. That way, together, we will make a place where the people are in charge, where it can be seen that we don't need the government, where it can be seen that the Mexican people can have dialogues and come to agreements. Where we can construct a peace with justice among ourselves, without the government and its armies and its police.

We want to demonstrate that the people can do for themselves without help from the government and we want you to help us to keep the flag of Zapatism standing firm, and to maintain the flag of Zapatista dignity in many places. If the government wants to attack us it will have to destroy not one Aguascalientes but many, it will have to destroy schools, libraries, hospitals, children's toys, theaters, cinemas, dance halls, and it will have to show the world its true face: that of murderers of all that signifies humanity.

These are our 6 proposals for work in response to your 6 answers to the 6 questions which we made...

On the international level...

Create an intercontinental meeting of all the forces that fight for humanity, that is to say, against neoliberalism.

Brothers and sisters,

From the first of January 1994 we have talked and we have listened. We have participated since then in a dialogue we were not ready for and which we never had dreamed of: the dialogue with women and men who, without arms but with faces, fight for the same flag that wraps us all: the flag of the eagle devouring the serpent, the flag of the white flanked by green and red, the flag which in its center shamelessly declares our indigenous roots, the flag which should always be rescued from the bandits that hold it hostage in the National Palace, the flag that makes us brothers, the Mexican flag.

We will not forget what made us be born, what has put in the place where we are now.

We the insurgents have a historic inheritance that was given to us by the transgressors of the law of yesterday, the criminals of the past, those persecuted of before, the Hidalgos, Morelos, Allendes, Pipilas, Ortiz de Dominguez, Narciso Mendozas, Guerreros, Minas, Galeanas, Guadelupes, Francisco Villas, Emiliano Zapatas. We the insurgents, the heirs of Madera, of Arturo Gamiz and of the generation of the dignity of the political-military movements of the seventies and eighties, we have the right to a future without hiding places and shames.

We the insurgents will receive our only pay by accomplishing our responsibilities.

We the insurgents are also all of you. You and we, the insurgents of today, need to recognize the giant subterranean river that communicates and links us in all this time: the Motherland.

You and we, the insurgents, have a cause, our movement is a movement which is legitimate because legitimate is the cause that in our hands becomes the flag: the cause of democracy, liberty and justice.

The cause of the insurgents, the cause of "for everyone everything, nothing for ourselves."

You and we, the insurgents, are persecuted like criminals by a false and hypocritical legality, the legality which imposes, with the force of stupidity, on those who with blood and mud stain the national dignity: those from the evil government.

The future that they offer us is that of the exiled, of the renegade, the eunuch, of the sterile repetition, of that without reason. They offer the democracy of oblivion, the liberty for money and crime, justice as impunity, as the exclusive possession of power.

The government lies so much that at times it seems to behave in agreement with the lies it spreads. But at times the government should remember that the Nation is not formed only by the serpent of power, but by some other things. And the result is that those other things, us, have had to learn to govern ourselves by ourselves.

Like 185 years ago in Dolores, like 85 years ago in the center of the country, like 30 years ago in Madera, like 27 years ago in the student movement, like 10 years ago in the earthquake which shook the city of Mexico, September is the time that the Country speaks, our country. In Tepotzlan, in Tabasco, in Ruta 100, in Chiapas, in the Ciudad Universitaria, in the movement of the Barzon against usury, in the awakening of the indigenous nation, in all the corners of the country, the Homeland lives.

Today, as always, the Power does not listen. Today the Power does not dialogue, it monologues. The Power does not negotiate, it compromises. The Power doesn't fulfill commitments, it cheats. The Power doesn't keep its word, it betrays. The Power doesn't live, it kills.

They are no longer a government. They can continue thinking that they are, and that they will recuperate from the political crisis and that all will return to the way it was before. But already they have been overthrown, the emptiness of power should be filled with a new alternative for its exercise.

The country has been destroyed, we should reconstruct it. Us. We can construct, us, the peace that the powerful refused to construct.

We need to disregard the government, we should construct that which was first taken from us, then destroyed, and whose rubble is now for sale. To reconstruct the motherland.

The dialogue needs to be between us. From confrontation with ourselves we can create a new proposal of Nationhood. A historic project for the country, the redemption and the reconstruction of the Motherland. No longer any more of that which they want to offer us, or impose upon us, now that which we want, which we need, the only thing possible, the only thing dignified, the Motherland where democracy, liberty and justice are communal and equitable.

This is what follows: the National Dialogue between all the political patriotic forces to discuss and carry out a new historic project of Nationhood, the dialogue to find, together, the road to democracy, liberty and justice, the road to the Motherland, the road to Mexico.

> *From the mountains of the Mexican Southeast,*
> *For the Indigenous Clandestine Revolutionary Committee*
> *-General Command of the Zapatista Army of National Liberation,*
> *Subcomandante Insurgente Marcos.*
> *Mexico, September 1995.*

P.S. That which gives tactical and strategic lessons.

A September dawn of mud and rain surprised us in that year in which another earthquake shook the apathy and the isolation within ourselves of a country then called Mexico. Old Antonio revived the campfire in which we took refuge. Old Antonio knew that trying to dry ourselves was useless. As the mud dried it returned to crusty earth that bruised our skin and memories. Old Antonio thought, as I did, not in the mud which plastered up to our hair, but in driving away the chasquistes and mosquitoes which feasted on our damp arrival. After the ceremony of the fire followed one of tobacco and, between the smoke of one and the other we began a talk about the war for independence.

Old Antonio listened and agreed with a glance as my words brought back Hidalgo, Morelos, Guerrero, Mina, Pipila, and Galeana. I did not repeat a learned history nor recite a lesson, I tried to reconstruct the solitude of these men and women and their pledge to continue onward despite the persecution and the slander which they suffered. I hadn't finished, but when I spoke of the long resistance of the guerrilla of Vincente Guerrero in the Mexican mountains Old Antonio interrupted me by clearing his throat in that way of his which announces that a new wonder had arrived at his lips, as the warmth of the smoke form his pipe reached his lips.

"That reminds me of something," said Old Antonio while he blew to revive the fire and his memories. Here, between insurgents past and present, between the meeting of smoke and fire, Old Antonio unloaded, like someone frees from a heavy but valuable load, words which I relate...

The Story of the Sword, the Tree, the Rock and The Water

Old Antonio chewed at the pipe. He chewed the words and gave then form and meaning. Old Antonio spoke, and the rain stopped to listen and the water and the darkness rested.

"Our oldest ancestors had to confront the stranger who came to conquer these lands. The strangers came to give us other ways, other words, other beliefs, other gods and another justice. It was his justice only so that he could have it and strip us of ours. Gold was his god. His superiority was his belief. Lies were his words. Cruelty was his way. Ours, the greatest fighters fought them, there were great battles between the aboriginal of these lands to defend the land from the foreigner's hand. But great also were the forces that the foreign hand brought. Great and good soldiers fell fighting and died. The battles continued; there were few warriors left, and the women and the children took up the arms of those who fell.

So, the wisest of the ancestors met and told the story of the sword, the tree, of the rock and the water. They told of the olden times and that far away in the mountains things that men need to work and defend themselves were brought together. The gods went around as it was their custom to do, which is to say that they were sleepy because the gods who were not the most powerful gods - those who birthed the world, the first ones - were very lazy. It was the man and the woman spending their physical energies and growing in heart in one corner of the dawn. The night was silent. It was quiet because it knew that it had little time left. And so the sword spoke."

"A sword like this," Old Antonio stopped and brandished a two-edged machete. The light of the fire created some sparks, just an instant, then the dark returned. Then Old Antonio continued:

"So the sword spoke and said:

'I am the strongest and I can destroy everything. My edge cuts and I give power to the person who takes me and death to those who confront me.'

'Liar!' said the tree. 'I am the strongest, I have resisted the wind and the most ferocious torment.'

The sword and the tree fought. The sword fought strong and hard, and confronted the tree. The sword struck and struck until it had chopped the trunk and felled the tree.

'I am the strongest!' the sword said again.

'Liar!' said the stone. 'I am stronger because I am hard and old, I am heavy and full.'

And so the sword and the stone fought. The stone fought hard and strong and confronted the sword. The sword beat and beat and could not destroy the stone but it broke it into many pieces. The sword was left without a sharp edge and the stone was in many small pieces.

'It is a tie!' the sword and the stone said and the two cried because of the futility of their battle.

Meanwhile, the water in the ditch only watched the battle and said nothing. The sword looked at it and said:

'You are the weakest of all! You can't do anything to anyone! I am stronger than you!' and the sword attacked the water in the ditch with great force. It made a great scandal and noise; it shocked the fish and the water did not resist the blow of the sword.

Little by little, without saying anything, the water returned to its original form, enveloping the sword. And it continued its path to the river that would take it to the great body of water that the gods made to heal their thirst.

Time passed and the sword in the water began to grow old and rust, losing its edge, and the fish came near it without being afraid and made fun of it. With shame the sword withdrew from the water in the ditch. Without an edge and defeated, it complained: 'I am stronger than it, but I couldn't hurt it, and it, without fighting, has beaten me!'

The dawn passed and the sun came to wake up the man and the woman who had slept together in order to renew themselves. The man and the woman found the sword in a dark corner, with the stone in pieces, the tree felled and the water in the ditch singing..."

The ancestors ended the telling of the history of the sword, the tree, the stone and the water and said:

"There are times when we have to fight like we were the sword in the face of the animal; there are times when we have to fight like the tree in the face of the torment; there are times when we have to fight like stones in the face of time. But there are times when we have to fight like the water in the face of the sword, the tree and the stone. This is the hour to make ourselves like the water and to continue our path to the river which will take us to the great water where the great gods soothe their thirst, those who birthed the world, the first ones."

"That's what our ancestors did," said old Antonio. They resisted like the water resisted the most fierce blows. The stranger came with his force, surprising all the weak ones, thinking that he had won and in time he started to become old and rusty. The stranger ended up in a dark corner full of shame and without understanding why, if he had won, he was losing.

The old Antonio again lit his pipe and the firewood and added: "That's how our oldest and wisest ancestors won the great war against the stranger. The stranger left. We are here, like the water in the ditch, we continue to go towards the river that has to take us to the great water that soothes the thirst of the greatest gods, those who birthed the world, the first ones..."

The dawn left and with it old Antonio. I continued in the path of the sun, to the west, crossing a ditch that snaked towards the river. In front of the mirror, between the sun of the dawn and the sun of the afternoon is the tender caress of the midnight sun. An alleviation that is hurting. A water that is thirst. A meeting that continues to be a search...

Like the sword in the tale of old Antonio, the government's offensive in February entered without any difficulty into the Zapatista territories. Powerful, lumbering, with a beautiful handle, the sword of Power beat the Zapatista territory. Like the sword of the tale of old Antonio, it made a lot of noise and scandal, like it, it surprised some fish. Like in the tale of old Antonio, its blow was great, strong... and useless. Like the sword in the tale of old Antonio, it stayed in the water, rusting and aging. The water? It continued its way, enveloping the sword, and without paying any attention to it, going to the river which will have to take it to the great water where the greatest gods soothe their thirst, those who birthed the world, the first ones...

Vale again. Health and that the water alleviate and quench.

The Sup sailing the lower ditch.

26. LETTER TO THE PEOPLE OF THE U.S.

September 13, 1995

The U.S. government has been wrong more than once in regards to its foreign policy. When this has occurred it is due to the fact it is making a mistake as to the man it ought to be backing up. History is not lacking in this type of examples. In the first half of this decade, the U.S. government made a mistake backing Carlos Salinas de Gortari. It made a mistake signing a NAFTA which lacked a majority support from the North American people and which meant an order of summary execution against the Mexican Indigenous people.

On the dawn of 1994 we rose up in arms. We rose up not seeking power, not responding to a foreign order. We rose up to say "here we are." The Mexican government, our government, had forgotten us and was ready to perpetrate a genocide without bullets or bombs, it was ready to annihilate us with the quiet death of sickness, of misery, of oblivion. The U.S. government became the accomplice of the Mexican government in this genocide.

With the signing of NAFTA, the U.S. government acted as guarantor of and gave its blessing to the murder of millions of Mexicans. Did the people of the U.S.

know this? Did it know that its government was signing accords of massive extermination in Mexico? Did the people of the U.S. know that his government was
backing a criminal? That man is gone. We remained. Our demands had not been
solved and our arms kept saying "here we are" to the new government, to the people of Mexico, to the people and governments of the world. We waited patiently
for the new government to listen to us and pay attention to us. But, within the dark
circles of U.S. power someone decided that we, the insurgent Indigenous people of
the Mexican South East, were the worst threat to the United States of America.
From the darkness came the order: Finish them up!

They put a price on our brown skin, on our culture, on our word, because, above
all they put a price on our uprising. The U.S. government decided, once more, to
back a man, someone who continues with the politics of deceit of his predecessor,
someone who denies the people of Mexico democracy, freedom and justice.
Millions of dollars were lent to that man and his government. Without the
approval of the American people, an enormous loan, without precedent in history,
was granted to the Mexican government. Not to improve the living conditions of
the people, not for the democratization of the country's political life, not for the
economic reactivation promoting factories and productive projects. This money is
for speculation, for corruption, for simulation, for the annihilation of a group of
rebels, Indians for the most part, poorly armed, poorly nourished, ill equipped, but
very dignified, very rebellious, and very human.

So much money to finance deceit can only be explained by fear. But, what does
the U.S. government fear? Truth? That the North American people realize that their
money is helping to back the oldest dictatorship in the modern world? That the
North American people realize that their taxes pay for the persecution and death of
the Mexican Indian population? What are the North American people afraid of?
Ought the people of North America fear our wooden rifles, our bare feet, our
exhausted bodies, our language, our culture? Ought the North American people fear
our scream in demand of democracy, liberty, and justice? Aren't these three truths
the foundation which brought forth the birth of the United States of America?
Aren't democracy, liberty, and justice rights that belong to all human beings?

How many millions of dollars justify that one may deny, to any human being, anywhere in the world, his right to be free in the thoughts that bring about words and
actions, free to give and receive that which he justly deserves, to freely elect those
who govern him and enforce the collective goals? Should the North American people on the other hand fear money, modern weapons, the sophisticated technology of
drug-trafficking? Should the North American people fear the complicity between
drug-trafficking and governments? Should the North American people fear the con-

sequences of the single party dictatorship in Mexico? Should it fear the violence that the lack of freedom, democracy and justice usually brings about irrevocably?

Today, the American government, which for decades prided itself in promoting democracy in the world is the main support of a dictatorship which, born at the beginning of the XXth Century, pretends to end this century with the same lie, governing against the will of the Mexican people. Sooner or later, in spite of the support of the U.S. government, in spite of the millions of dollars, in spite of the tons of lies, the dictatorship that darkens the Mexican sky will be erased. The people of Mexico will find the ways to achieve the democracy, liberty and justice that is their historical right.

Americans: The attacks against the Mexican nation brought about by political U.S. personalities have been big and numerous. In their analysis they point out the awkwardness and corruption of the Mexican government (an awkwardness and corruption which have increased and are maintained under the shadow of the U.S. government's support) and they identify them with an entire people who take shelter under the Mexican flag. They are wrong.

Mexico is not a government. Mexico is a nation which aspires to be sovereign and independent, and in order to be that must liberate itself from a dictatorship and raise on its soil the universal flag of democracy, liberty and justice. Fomenting racism, fear and insecurity, the great personalities of U.S. politics offer economic support to the Mexican government so that it controls by violent means the discontent against the economic situation. They offer to multiply the absurd walls with which they pretend to put a stop to the search for life which drives millions of Mexicans to cross the northern border.

The best wall against massive immigration to the U.S. is a free, just, and democratic regime in Mexico. If Mexicans could find in their own land what now is denied them, they would not be forced to look for work in other countries. By supporting the dictatorship of the state party system in Mexico, whatever the name of the man or the party, the North American people are supporting an uncertain and anguishing future. By supporting the people of Mexico in their aspirations for democracy, liberty and justice, the North American people honor their history... and their human condition.

Today, in 1995 and after 20 years and tens of thousands of dead and wounded, the American government recognizes that it made a mistake getting involved in the Vietnam war. Today, in 1995, the U.S. government has begun to get involved in the Mexican government's dirty war against the Zapatista population. War material support, military advisors, undercover actions, electronic espionage, financing, diplomatic support, activities of the CIA. Little by little, the U.S. government is beginning to get involved in an unequal war condemned to failure for those who are carrying it on, the Mexican government. Today, in 1995 and 20 years before 2015, it is possible to stop and not to repeat the error of other years. It is not necessary to wait until 2015 for the U.S. government to recognize that it was an error to get involved in the war against the Mexican people.

It is time for the people of the U.S. to keep its historical compromise with respect to its neighbor to the South. To no longer make a mistake as to which man to support. To support not a man but a people, the Mexican people in its struggle for democracy, liberty and justice. History will signal, implacable, on which side were the people and the government of the U.S. On the side of dictatorship, of a man, of reactionarism, or on the side of democracy, of a people, of progress.

Health and long life to the people of the United States of America.

> *From the Mexican Southeast,*
> *Subcommander Insurgent Marcos.*
> *Mexico, September 13, 1995.*
> *(20 years before…)*

27. The History of the Little Mouse and the Cat

August 27, 1995

To the men and women in solidarity with Chiapas, meeting in Brescia, Italy
To the peoples of the world
From: Don Durito de la Lacandona, Mexico

Brothers and Sisters,

Don Durito of The Lacandona, knight-errant, undoer of wrongs, restless dream of females, aspiration of males, last and greatest exemplary specimen of this race that made humanity great with such colossal and selfless feats, beetle and warrior of the moon, writes to you.

I have ordered my loyal squire, the one you call "SupMarcos," that he send you a greeting in writing with all the requirements deserved by today's diplomacy, excluding the rapid intervention forces, the economic programs and the capital flights. Nevertheless, I want to write to you some lines with the only end of contributing to enlarge your spirit to inundate in your minds the good and noble thoughts. That is why I send you the following story-tale that for sure is full of rich and various feats. The story forms part of the collection "Stories for a Night of Asphyxiation" (of improbable near publication) and it's called:

The History of the Little Mouse and the Cat

There once was a little mouse who was very hungry and wanted to eat a little cheese that was in the tiny kitchen of the small house. And then the little mouse went very decidedly to the tiny kitchen to grab the little cheese, but it happens that a little cat came across the path and the little mouse became very frightened and run away and was not able to get the little cheese from the tiny kitchen. Then the little mouse was thinking of what to do to get the little cheese from the tiny kitchen and he thought and he said:

"I know, I am going to put a small plate with a little milk and the little cat is going to start drinking the milk because little cats like very much the little milk. And then, when the little cat is drinking the milk and is not noticing, I am going to the tiny kitchen to grab the little cheese and I am going to eat it. Veeery good idea!" said the little mouse to himself. And then he went to look for the milk but it turns out that the milk was in the tiny kitchen and when the little mouse wanted to go to the kitchen the little cat came across his way and the little mouse was very frightened and ran and could not get the milk. Then the little mouse was thinking of what to do to get the milk in the tiny kitchen and he thought and he said:

"I know, I am going to throw a little fish very far away and then the little cat is going to run to go eat the little fish because little cats like very much the little fish. And then, when the little cat is eating the little fish and is not paying attention, I am going to go to the tiny kitchen to grab the little cheese and I am going to eat it. Veeery good idea!" said the little mouse.

Then, he went to look for the little fish but it happened that the little fish was in the tiny kitchen and when the little mouse wanted to go to the tiny kitchen, the little cat came across his way and the little mouse became very frightened, and ran away and could not go to get the little fish.

And then the little mouse saw that the little cheese, the milk, and the little fish, everything that he wanted were in the tiny kitchen and he could not get there because the little cat would not allow it. And then the little mouse said "Enough!" and he grabbed a machine gun and shot the little cat and he went to the tiny kitchen and he saw that the little fish, the milk, and the littlecheese were already rotten and could not be eaten. And then he returned where the little cat was and cut it in pieces and then he made a great roast and then invited all his friends and they made a party and ate the roasted little cat and they sang and danced and lived very happily. And history started...

This is the end of the story and the end of this letter. I remind you that the divisions between countries only serve to typify the crime of "contraband" and to give sense to wars. Clearly there exists at least two things that are above borders: the one is the crime which is disguised as modernity and distributes misery on a world scale; the other is the hope that shame exists only when one fumbles a dance step and not every time we look in the mirror. To end with the first and to make the second one flourish we only need to struggle and to be better. The rest follows on its own and is what usually fills libraries and museums. It is not necessary to conquer the world, it is sufficient to make it anew...

Vale. Health and know that for love, a bed is only a pretext, for dance, a tune is only an adornment. And for struggle, nationalism is merely a circumstantial accident.

From the mountains of the Mexican Southeast,
Don Durito of The Lacandona.
Mexico, August 1995.

P.S. Excuse the lack of abundance in these letters. It happens that I have to hurry up my expedition to invade Europe this winter. How do you feel about a landing for the next January 1st?

28. To Solidarity Groups Meeting in Brescia
"The Flowers, Like Hope, are Harvested"

To the men and women in solidarity with Chiapas, meeting in Brescia, Italy September 1995
To the peoples of the world

Brothers and sisters,

In the name of all the men, women, children, and old people of the Zapatista Army of National Liberation, I greet you and express our desire that the results of your encounter go well. We know we have brothers and sisters in other countries and continents. We are united by a world order that destroys nations and cultures.

The great international criminal, money, today has a name that reflects the incapacity of Power to create new things. We suffer a new world war today. It is a war against all of the peoples, of human beings, of culture, of history. It is a war headed by a handful of financial centers without homeland and without shame, an international war: money versus humanity. They call it Neoliberalism now, this Terror Intentional. The new international economic order has already provoked more death and destruction than the great world wars. More poor and more dead and we became brothers. We are united by dissatisfaction, rebellion, the desire to do something, unconformity.

History written by the Power taught us that we had lost, that cynicism and profit were virtues, that honesty and sacrifice were stupid, that individualism was the new god, and hope was devalued money, without value in the international markets, without buying power, without hope. We did not learn the lesson. We were bad pupils. We did not believe what the Power taught us. We skip school when in class they taught conformism and idiocy. We failed grades in modernity. Classmates in rebellion, we discovered and found ourselves brothers. We are united by the imagination, the creativity, the tomorrow. In the past we not only saw defeat but also we found desire for justice and dreams of being better. We left skepticism hanging on the clothes rack of big capital and we discovered that we could believe, that it was worth believing and that we should believe... in ourselves. We learn that solitude's that add to each other could be not a great solitude but a collective that is found and united above nationalities, languages, cultures races, genders.

We, the Zapatistas, continue being in the mountains of the Southeast of Mexico, we continue being surrounded, we continue being persecuted, we continue with death watching our every movement, each breath, each step. The government is still in the palace, still circling, still persecuting, still offering death and misery, still lying. More than a million Mexicans have manifested their agreement with our principal demands, in an unprecedented democratic exercise. Many brothers and sisters in foreign lands have ratified it. The government is still deaf. Tens of thousands of men and women mobilized themselves to support the CONSULTATION FOR PEACE AND DEMOCRACY.

The government is still blind. Hunger and illnesses drown our entire communities. The Federal Army increases their military actions and their preparations for assassination. The political parties deny recognition of citizenship to the Indigenous people. The media make themselves accomplices of the lie and the silence. The desperation and anger become the national heritage. We are ignored, despised, and forgotten. As is evident, the triumph is closer than ever. We are already preparing to form the Groups in Solidarity with the respective struggles of your countries. Be assured that we will support you to the end (which is not necessarily the triumph) and that we will not abandon you. You should not be discouraged by difficulties and you should resist. You should continue forward and know that in the mountains of Southeast Mexico there is a collective heart and that it is with you and supports you. Do not feel alone or isolated. We will keep attentive of you and will not forget you.

Vale. Health and don't forget that the flowers, like hope, are harvested.

From the mountains of the Mexican Southeast,
Subcomandante Insurgente Marcos.
Mexico, August 1995.

29. WHAT PRICE IS DIGNITY?

November 2, 1995
To: Cecilia Rodriguez
National Commission for Democracy, USA
From: Subcomandante Insurgente Marcos
CCRI-CG of the EZLN
Chiapas, Mexico

Cecilia,

I write these lines to you during this dawn in which the dead, our dead accept the bridge extended to them through thousands of offerings in the indigenous mountains of the Mexican Southeast.

The reason for it is not pleasant, it is not a salute, yet it is a salute.

We want you to know that we repudiate, together with all honest men and women, the criminal intent to which you were subjected. Yes, "subjected", because that kind of aggression consists of making a thing, an object of a human being and "using" that human being as things are used. Those responsible for the attempt will be hunted. Yes, hunted like animals, which is what they are.

But we also want you to know that we salute your determination, your refusal to be humiliated and converted into what the Powerful call a "normal woman", a conformist, a resigned, quiet and objectified woman. As you have well pointed out, the aggression against you is part of a "silent" war, a "discrete" war, a war beyond the reach of the headlines in the press and therefore, distant from the financial markets. We salute your wisdom in reminding everyone that here, in this country called Mexico, there is a war, a war by those who would preserve irrationality and eternal omnipotence against those who want a democratic change. We salute all that, this is true. But above all we salute you as a Zapatista woman, your "I will not surrender!" your "I am here!", your "enough is enough!". We salute the fact that being a Zapatista is not limited by borders or customs checkpoints, that it jumps walls and mocks the "border patrol", that it finds voice and a banner in the Latino blood upon which, among others, rests the power of the American Union.

The body of a woman is also a battle ground in this "new type" of war designed for extermination. They wound you as a woman, but above all as a Zapatista. And, more so because you are a North American citizen who sympathizes with the EZLN and its cause of peace with democracy, liberty and justice.

Some women, among which are those who say they are close to Zapatismo, take advantage of the dilemma of rape to denounce the Zapatista machos! They now demand that we take off our ski-masks, they say, in order to distance ourselves from the rapists and so that we will not promote, they say, crimes such as the one you suffered. We are not the enemy, and our ski-masks do not hide criminals. They remain indignant, they demand a denial, an explanation, a penance for the simple fact that we are men. This is the new crime of which we are accused; of being men. Because of it, they say, we are accomplices of the rapists. Because we have taken up arms, they say, we have created a climate of violence against women.

But this is not a position common to everyone. The great majority of women close to Zapatismo (in other words close to you) understand that this crime forms a part of a belligerent chain which has found in the body of a woman a battle ground. They and we understand that it is the political, economic, social and cultural system which holds up as its banners crime and impunity, which promotes, nurtures, protects and permits this and other aggressions. We understand, they and us, that we should fight to transform the entire world into something better: a world with democracy, liberty, and justice.

Before January 1st of 1994, in this land there were rapes of all kind. Not just of women, and also of women. The fact of being indigenous added a double silence to the fact of being women. Here, and I do not just refer to Chiapas but to the entire country, the human being is raped, dignity is raped, history is raped.

The indigenous Zapatista women, those women who do not belong to us but who march at our side, those women who are so far from the Peking Summit, those women who fight against everything and everyone (and this includes us Zapatista men), those Zapatista women, have decided to stop being women in order to win the right to be women. You know all this well. In the year or more that you have been our legal representative in the American Union, you have discovered us and have found thousands of those women (and men) who are your sisters and with whom you are united by something which is in your blood: human dignity.

The companera comandantes of the CCRI-CG of the EZLN will give you our communiqué in regards to this aggression which you have suffered and that all of us Zapatistas, suffer with you. They are the ones with the best ability for it. Personally, I feel incapable of putting in pen and paper the bridge of support, sympathy and admiration which you inspire in me. My clumsiness, or perhaps my fear at being clumsy tie up my words. They, our companeras, are not free because they are Zapatistas. But the fact that they are Zapatistas, as you are, makes them fighters who fight to change everything, including us. Rape is not solely the concern of women, it involves all men, not only because men are capable of its perpetration, but because we can be accomplices as well, by engaging in harmful ridicule and by our silence. But the struggle for respect for the specificity of gender, can also include us, by acknowledging what we are, what we are not, and above all, what we are capable of becoming.

So I do not write to you as though you were someone who sympathizes with Zapatismo and is wounded for that reason. I write to you as a companera, as a Zapatista. Perhaps this can explain the paucity of these thoughts and the hesitant lines which try to express it. I only write to you, in the name of my Zapatista companeras and companeros, to remind you and to remind all of us that we are one, we are the intuition that something new is possible and that the fight in order to win it, is worth it.

Vale. Health and a hope that humiliation not be the present or future of women, or of any human being.

> From the mountains of the Mexican Southeast,
> Subcomandante Insurgente Marcos.
> Mexico, November 1995.

30. OF TREES, CRIMINALS, AND ODONTOLOGY

September-November of 1995
To: Carlos Monsivais,
Mexico, D.F.
From: Subcomandante Insurgente Marcos
Mountains of the Mexican Southeast Chiapas
Mexico

Master [teacher],
I [throughout his text Marcos plays with the formal and informal pronoun, in his letter to Monsivais implying doubt as to his right to be informal with Monsivais] send you a greeting and claim receipt of the book THE RITUALS OF CHAOS. I read it while running from one of those impasses that the Supreme Government calls the Dialogues of San Andres.

Vale. Health and try finding out if Alice manages to find the Red Queen and resolve the enigma to which the last P.S. invites.

> From the mountains of the Mexican Southeast,
> Subcomandante Insurgente Marcos Mexico.
> Fall of 1995.

P.S. He recalls, a little late, the principal reason behind this chaotic epistle and titles it: EHT RORRIM DNA OTIRUD (OF POLITICS, DENTISTRY AND MORALITY)

> *"In that instant I saw the Apocalypse face to face. And I understood that the holy terror about the Final Judgement lies in a demonic intuition: one will not live to see it. And I looked into the eyeball of the Beast with seven heads and ten horns, and among its horns ten crowns, and on each head a blasphemous name. And the people applauded it and took pictures and videos, and recorded its exclusive declarations, while, with a clarity which would become a painful burden, I had the belated realization: the most horrible nightmare is that one which definitely excludes us."*
> - Carlos Monsivais, THE RITUALS OF CHAOS, page 250.

A point is the hinge which binds two mirrors, which face to face, spread out to the sides like wings for flying over a chaotic era. That's the POINT, a hinge.

"Look on page 250," Durito says, as he unpacks his bags.

And I look hurriedly and murmur, "Page... 250... mmh... yes, here it is!" I say with satisfaction. "Or the one which excludes us momentarily," I think, while Durito insists on hauling his tiny piano on top of what is already his tiny desk, to show me how it is that the small holds up the large, in history and in nature. The argument falls together with the piano and Durito who rolls under, after that rickety operation, with the piano and the desk on top of his shell. I finish reading that part of the book and search for the pipe, the tobacco and Durito (in that order). Durito has no intention of coming out from under the catastrophe which is on top of him, and a tiny column of smoke announces two things: the first is the location of my tobacco, and the second that Durito is alive.

I light the pipe and the memories which are one. Something about the text takes me back many years. That was a sweet and simple time. All we had to worry about was food. The books were few but they were good, and re-reading one meant finding new books inside them. And this is relevant because Durito has brought me this book as a gift, and has pointed out a text on page 250 to tell me that something is still pending, because there are more important things than pointing out for example, that books are made of pages, and pages, added to branches and roots, make trees and shrubbery. The trees, as everyone knows, are for guarding the night which, by day is idle. Among branches and leaves, the night distributes its roundness the same way in which a woman shares her curves inside moist and breathless embraces. In spite of this sensual mission, the trees take time for other things. For example, they tend to house many different kinds of animals, mammals, oviparous animals, arthropods and other rhyming syllables which serve only to show that children grow up. Sometimes, the trees also house masked men. These are, no doubt, of course delinquents and outlaws. The covered face and the fact that they live in trees no doubt means that they are persecuted characters. These type of people live in the night, even by day, in the trees. That is the reason for their passion and drive to love the trees. It is also true that in the trees rest beetles like...

Durito interrupts me from the depth of, now he says to me, the modern sculpture made by the piano and desk on top of his head.

"Do you have a lighter?"

"That sculpture should be called something like CHAOS ON A SMOKING BEETLE," I say as I throw the lighter to him.

"Don't offend me with your ridicule. All you show is your ignorance. It's clear you've never read Umberto Eco who writes about the open work of art. This lovely sculpture is the best demonstration of modern and revolutionary art, and it shows how the artist so commits himself to his work that he becomes a part of it."

"And what's it called?"

"That's the tricky part. It should have a name if it's to be respectable. That is why it is an 'open' work of art. As you know my dear 'Guatson', the 'open' work of art is not finished but becomes so within the process of circulation and consumption in the artistic market. Elementary. In this way the spectator stops being one and becomes a 'co-artist' of the work of art. Zedillo, for example could call his work something like MY GOVERNMENT PROGRAM and put it at Los Pinos [Mexican white house]; Salinas de Gortari could call his MY ECONOMIC AND POLITICAL LEGACY and house it at Almoloya [Mexican federal prison], and the neoliberals could call theirs OUR PROPOSAL FOR A NEW WORLD ORDER. And you... what would you call this work of art?" Durito asks me.

I stare with a critical eye and answer: "Mmmh... something like BEETLE BURIED UNDER A PIANO AND A DESK."

"Bah! That's just descriptive," Durito complains.

As we talk the rituals of the night go on slowly: the sound of the airplane, the smoke of the pipe, the loneliness, the discreet scandal of the crickets, the luminous and drawn-out blinking of the fireflies, the heaviness of the heart, and above, the stars made dust on the Milky Way. Maybe it'll rain. The past months have had inconsistent rain; even the seasons seem disoriented and cannot find themselves within so much coming and going. Durito asks me for the name of the author of the book.

"Monsivais," I answer.

"Oh, Carlos!" Durito says with a familiarity which surprises me.

I ask if he knows him.

"Of course! History is a subject we share... but you should keep writing. I have other things to do," Durito answers.

I delay because at the beginning of this letter I was unable to resolve the dilemma of whether to use the informal or formal pronoun in order to address you[sir]. Durito is a firm supporter of an axiom, which is a pillar of his global conception; there is no problem large enough which cannot be avoided. And so with that philosophic corpus, I've decided, once again, to leave the solution to this dilemma pending and continue with the soft pendulum which takes us from YOU to SIR.

So then I decide. I bite the pipe in determination. I take on a look of a Southeastern-governor-willing-to-defend-the-popular-will-at-all-costs-who-sees-how-things-are-and-provokes-them and undertake the rude task of writing to you [sir].

I must look like a real phenomenon, too bad I have no witnesses (Durito is already snoring underneath the ruins of his work of art), too bad I sent all the mirrors in that writing called something like MIRRORS: THE MEXICO FOUND AMONG THE NIGHTS OF DAY AND THE CRYSTAL OF THE MOON. What? That wasn't the title? Oh well, no matter. The thing is I now need a mirror to check myself for that delirious glow of genius getting ready to abort his own best idea. What? A self-imposed goal? Why? In order to abort? But no! You[sir] must agree with me that the best ideas are those which are never expressed. The moment they go inside the jail of language, they are materialized, they become letters, words, phrases, paragraphs, pages... even books if you're careless and give them free reign. And once there, ideas become tangible, they can be weighed, measured, compared. Then they are really boring, in addition to the fact that they become independent and do not obey orders of any kind. I understand that to you[sir] it matters little that orders go unobeyed, but for a military leader like myself it is a true pain in the molars. The molars, as all scientists with postgraduate degrees know, are pieces of bone which exist in order to give jobs to dentists, and in order to make the toothpaste industry flower, and in order that the profession of shameful torture exist; dentistry. The word "dentistry" is an idea made language and once so, becomes measurable and classifiable; it has nine letters, syllables, and is as heavy as the bill which must be paid after you leave the waiting room...

"Definitely," Durito says.

"What?" is all I can muster in response to Durito's interruption.

"There's no doubt that this plebiscite excludes beetles," Durito continues, who to all appearances was not asleep but reviewing papers even beneath the chaos on top of him.

"This plebiscite left out all beetles and is a form of racism and apartheid. I shall take my protests to all pertinent international organizations."

It's useless to try to explain things to Durito. He insists that the Seventh Question was missing, and whose wording was more or less something like; "Are you in agreement that gallant knighthood should be added to the National Professional Register?"

I explain to him that I sent various postscripts making discreet insinuations to the CND [National Democratic Convention] and the Civic Alliance, but no one noticed.

"It's insulting that that question is missing. It's a matter of aesthetics. Whose silly idea is it to have a plebiscite with six questions? Even numbers are anti-aesthetic. Uneven numbers, however have the charm of asymmetry. It's strange to me that someone as asymmetrical as you my big-nosed shieldbearer, should not have fixed a detail like that."

I pretend to be offended and keep silent. An atrocious noise is heard from the north. The lightning bolts tear the dark curtain which dilutes the distance between mountains and sky.

Durito tries to console me by telling me a story (which I can't understand too well from under the modern sculpture) about how he once had a practice which specialized in the big toe of the left foot. I appreciate the subtle insinuation which Durito offers in order to help me concentrate on the subject of this article, which is something like "Ethics and Political Parties" or "Politics and Morality" or "The new Left, New Morality and New Politics," or "We are all Prigione [a reactionary moralistic Vatican representative in Mexico City] or..." Just now a thunderbolt jolted me so that I even forgot about the Apocalypse, and Durito says that it serves me well for picking on members of the high clergy, and I tell him I'm not picking on him, I'm just looking for a g-o-o-o-o-d title for this article, so that it impresses some ambassador who will copy it.

"What about this one... The Lovely Lie and the Lost Cause..."

Durito says I've lost my mind, and he'd rather go to sleep, and that I should wake him once civil society arrives to save him from the ruins. Then I realize that I now have all the necessary elements for the article: title, characters (political parties, the ambassador, the papal nuncio, the political spectrum and civil society), a polemics (that one about the relationship between morality and politics) in which to stick my nose, and for which I have plenty of nose. Now I only need a subject to justify the paragraphs, the stamps, the request to Juan Villoro of The Weekly Jornada in order to have an audience for such a "beautiful" story, and the excuse to renew that amiable epistolar exchange which we began shortly before the Convention a year ago. Do you remember?

My other me comes near and says that if I'm going to get into polemics, I should be serious about it, because you can't play with the nuncios and the Machiavellians. "And if you don't believe me just ask Castillo Peraza, who demonstrated the efficiency of his political ethics in Yucatan," my other me says as he leaves to watch the beans cook.

All polemics are nightmares, not just for the polemicists, but, for the readers most of all. That's why it occurs to me that it's not worth it, especially when I remember that prophesy of a certain Salinista intellectual(who now has amnesia) in December of 1993, who foresaw great victories for Salinas in 1994, since he had all "the marbles" in his pocket.

It occurs to me that I cannot remain a spectator and that I should take sides. So I take sides, in this case, the side of those who do not have a party, and who, together with Durito create a "wave", and no small one either; being that Durito has so many feet and hands that it appears to be a "wave" of Mexican fans during the last games of the World Cup.

But Durito is dreaming with Brigitte Bardot, because he's let out a sigh which is more like a stray lament, so I can't count on him and I should concentrate on the discussion. And the most important part of the discussion is that about the relationship between morality and politics, even more so, between morality and political parties, and more so between politics and power.

However, there is reasoning beyond this, and the problem of the relationship between morality and politics is overcome or displaced by the relationship between politics and "success", and politics and "efficiency." Machiavelli revives the argument that, in politics, the "superior" morality is the "efficient" one, and efficiency is measured in quotas of power, or, in the exact amount of access to power. And from here comes the Machiavellian juggle which defines democratic change as the political opposition made government. The National Action Party is the example, they say, of this political "success", this political morality.

But then they correct and re-arrange themselves: the accumulation of power, they say, serves to contain the antagonism that pluralistic societies guard inside themselves. Power is exerted in order to defend society from itself!

O.K., so let's leave this new reference for measuring political efficiency pending, and return to the original. Not to polemicize with those who measure "success" and political "efficiency" in the number of governor's offices, mayor's offices, and congressional seats, but to reclaim the evidence of "success" which has so many followers in the actual government, in that government of Carlos Salinas De Gortari.

Is "success" in politics defined as efficiency? Are politics more successful in as much as the efficiency of its products? In such a case, Carlos Salinas de Gortari deserves a monument, and not a police investigation due to his alleged complicity in the murders of J.F. Ruiz Massieu and Luis D. Colosio. His politics were "efficient" in as far as it kept the entire country living in virtual reality, which was of course, torn up by real reality. The knowledge of this reality was acquired through the mass media. A great success, no doubt. The "efficient" politics and economics of Carlos Salinas de Gortari deserves applause from National Action and from those orphaned intellectuals; and not just from them but from powerful businessmen and high clergy members who now complain about having been deceived. Together they used to praise one another about having "all the marbles". The consequences of the Salinista "success" are suffered today by all Mexicans, and not just the poorest ones.

After all, isn't "political efficiency" as perennial in Mexico as an administration? Sometimes it is less. The government of Ernesto Zedillo is an excellent example of "successes" as durable as the pages of a calendar without pictures.

The other problem, the one about the quotas of power, points out that the efficiency of a democratic change lies in the alternation of power. The alternation of power is not synonymous with democratic change, or with "efficiency, but with indulgences and divorces in the form of projects. The politics followed by National Action in Baja California, Jalisco, and Chihuahua, are far from being another "way" of making politics, and are sufficiently authoritarian in order to adjust the length of the skirts (Guadalajara) and the un-covering of the human body (Monterrey).

The alternation of power is a separate problem, and perhaps a rebound to the polemics of the master Tomas Segovia with Matias Vegoso: "Well, the ideal of bi-partisan government is tied to this position, not just because bipartisanism is its only manifestation, but because until today it is the only concrete manifestation of a 'non-ideological' government, in other words, of a 'technical' government." The first thing I have to say (and surely not the most important) is that this position gives clear proof of the continuation of ideologies and not of their end. The conviction that a "technical" government is better than an "ideological" one is in itself an ideology, a conditioning and distorting belief towards reality, exactly the same way in which the conviction of a "positive" truth is better than the 'metaphysical' truth, which in itself is a metaphysical conviction.

(Sure, I interrupt, and now there is talk of "tripartisanship" but the problem remains). Tomas Segovia continues: "In the same way, I advise you as a friend to remember that to defend neoliberalism you must remember that it is only an ideology, and nothing more." Don't you understand that this is a most astute, and insidious ideology? There is nothing more ideological than to say: "Everyone else is ideological; I am the only one who is lucid."

Here I could deduce in my favor those arguments of the master Tomas Segovia with Matias Vegoso, but in addition to the fact that I do not have his authorization, this discussion would take me to my other problem: the morality of immorality (or should I say amorality?). Mutatis mutandis: the ideology of no ideology. And from here we can jump to the problem of the knowledge and the intellectuals who produce and distribute this truth.

The process followed by some intellectuals is typical: from criticism of the powerful they went on to criticize from the summit of the powerful.

With Salinas they showed that knowledge exists to serve the powerful. Then they collaborated to give theoretical substance to him. Their logic, no matter how you look at it, arrived at the same result: the powerful cannot be wrong when they analyze reality, and if they are wrong, it is reality's problem not theirs.

It is a painful but inevitable truth; the powerful have not only managed to gather around them a group of "brilliant" intellectuals; they have also produced a team of analysts capable of theorizing today, the future hardening of the powerful (regardless of whether the images in the mirror of the powerful belong to the PRI or PAN).

Machiavelli is today the head of a group of intellectuals who seek to give theoretical-ideological substance to the repression to come (in this line you can find Porfirio Diaz's grandson and his Rebellion of the Pipeline [here the book's title is changed from what was intended to be Ravine to what the Subcomandante believes to be the government's official line on their history]). This is the fundamental contribution of its elite; the evolution from the justification of a stupid system to the theorization of the imbecility yet to come. Oh well, these are the new kind of organic intellectuals in power. They are capable of seeing beyond power. They represent the image of what organic intellectuals of neoliberalism aspire to be. They will leave their books...

I stop here in order to re-stock the pipe and rest my back. Now, a grey weight adds a new layer to the heavy theater curtain of the night. There are noises which come from the "open" work of Durito, evidence that he is not asleep and is still working. A small column of smoke rises between the drawers of the desk and the keyboard of the piano. Somewhere, beneath that scribble which pretends to be a sculpture, Durito is reading or writing.

In the fire, the dance of the colors ends and little by little turns black. In the mountains the sounds and the colors change constantly. And what to say about the inevitable changing of the day into afternoon, of the afternoon into the night, of the night into the day...

I've got to get back to the article. Machiavelli is revisited and converted not into a guide but into an elegant garment which disguises cynicism as intellectuality. Now there is an ethic of "efficient politics" which justifies whatever means necessary to obtain "results" (or quotas of power). This political ethic should put distance between it and "private ethics" whose "efficiency" is zero, because it adheres to a loyalty to principles.

Once again efficiency and its results in addition to the theme of political morality is confined by "private ethics", to the ideology of the "salvation of the soul". In front of the moralists, Machiavelli and his contemporary equals propose their "science", their "technology": efficiency. One must hold to these.

This "non-ideological" doctrine has followers and adherents. I mean, in addition to the Salinista intellectuals and neo-panismo [doctrine of the PAN party]. Then the ambassador displays, in all its details, the doctrine of cynicism and efficiency before the applause of the intellectual who have no memory: If I assault it, it speaks; if it speaks, it assaults.

The ambassador does not represent just himself. He represents a political position, a form of making politics characterized by the undefined eleven months of the present Salinas administration without Salinas. The ambassador is a part of the neocorpus of presidential "counselors" who recommend that Zedillo assault in order to speak. The high cost of these assaults, they say, can be covered with the makeup of the mass media.

I don't remember the name of the movie (maybe the master Barbachano remembers) but I do remember that a main actor was Peter Fonda. I remember the plot clearly. It was about a group of brilliant Harvard students who raped a woman. She accused them in a public hearing and they responded that she was only a prostitute. Their lawyer defended them by using their grades and good families. They're found innocent. The woman commits suicide. As adults, the "juniors" look for stronger emotions and they dedicate themselves to hunting down vacationing couples on weekends. And "hunting" is no figurative term; after the standard rape, the "juniors" free the couple to run into the countryside, and they hunt them down with shotguns.

I don't remember the ending, but it's one of those where justice is done, where Hollywood resolves on the screen what in reality often goes unpunished.

Today, the modern "juniors" have found that they have a country to play with. One of them is at Los Pinos and the other in Bucareli, they get tired of the Nintendo and they play at hunting down "the bad guys" in a game of real war. They give their prey time to escape, and move their game pieces to surround them and make the game more interesting. But it appears that the country is in no mood for games and mobilizes and protests. The "juniors" find themselves in a quandary because the game grows longer and they can't catch the "bad guys". Then the ambassador appears to save them: "It was all planned," he says to us, "the dead are not dead, the war is not the war, the displaced are not displaced, we always wanted to talk and we only sent thousands of soldiers to tell the 'bad guy' that we wanted to talk." A pathetic argument for an idem government.

Meanwhile, reality approaches and the mass media tries to impose itself on reality. Forgetfulness begins to populate the government discourse; they forget the fall of the stock market, the devaluation, the "negotiations" of San Andres as a window dressing to hide the true indigenous politics of neoliberalism, instability, jealousy and distrust, ungovernability and uncertainty. They forget the principal objective, according to Machiavelli; they've had no results, they've not been "efficient".

They forget that they defend a lost cause, and the ambassador knows this but he forgets it when he's giving exclusive interviews. The last declarations of the government are clear; they forget reality, they forget that with each passing moment there are less of them who believe in the lovely lies and who support lost causes...

Meanwhile, the modern Machiavellians complain about our morality and their diagnosis is that in politics there is no good and bad, and therefore the affair cannot be settled by classifying factions.

And here they affirm, but only in reference to the relationship between ethics and politics, that it is not easy to resolve this with the classification of factions: bad vs. good. In other words "If the Machiavelli of the nostalgic Salinista intellectual is bad, then we, who do not agree with him, are good." It remains tempting to take this polemic further, but I think that when you [sir] pointed out that "If efficiency in the manner of neoliberalism has taken us to the present tragic situation, the cult for doctrinaire purity, which has not had such costly results, has also not taken us far" (Carlos Monsivais, Proceso, n.966). You pointed out a new problem which is worth examining.

From the left the alternative to Machiavelli is not more attractive, this is true. But "doctrinaire purity" is not the problem. It's also something else. The complicity of a mirror which offers itself as an alternative and simplifies all its political relationships (and human ones as well, but that is another subject) into an inversion. This is the fundamental ethic of "revolutionary science"; that scientific knowledge produce an inverse morality to that of capitalism. So, altruism is the response to egotism, collectivity to privatization, social context to individualism.

But this knowledge remains inside a mirror, like a fundamental morality, it does not contribute anything new. The inversion of the image is not a new one, but an inverted one. The alternative moral and political proposal is in a mirror: where the right dominates, now the left will do so; where the white dominates, now the black; where the one above, now the one below; where the bourgeoisie now the proletariat, and so on. The same, but inverted. And this ethic is what is recorded (or was) in all the spectrum of the left.

I agree. But the modern Machiavellians say, and say well, that we offer nothing better than they do: cynicism and efficiency. That we criticize them from a new "morality" as criminal as theirs (well, they don't say that theirs is a criminal morality, but that ours is) and that we want to reduce politics to a struggle between black and white, forgetting that there are many greys. It's true, but we do not only say that the morality of the resurrected Machiavelli is cynical and criminal, we also point out that it is inefficient...

Durito interrupts again to say I must be prudent when I talk about morality.

"Your immorality is public knowledge," Durito says, trying to overlook his failure to bring videos, those with a lot of X's that I asked him to bring from the capital.

"We're not talking about that kind of morality. And stop lecturing me like a Panista mayor," I say in my own defense.

"I'd never do that. But it's my responsibility to deter you from your perverted cinematic preferences. Instead of those I brought you something more constructive. They're the pictures of my trip to the D.F."

This said, Durito threw an envelope at me. In it there are pictures of different sizes and subjects. In one of them Durito is standing in Chapultepec.

"You don't look too happy in this picture at the zoo," I said.

Durito answers from under the desk, that the picture was taken after he was detained by a guard from the zoo. Seems the man mistook Durito with a dwarf rhinoceros and was determined to take him back to a cage. Durito argued using different lessons about botany, zoology, mammology, and anthropology, and even gallant knighthood, but he wound up penned up with the rhinos. He escaped somehow, in that moment when the guard took a break.

He was so happy to be free he decided to take a picture when he looked exactly like a white rhinoceros. He was that pale. He was that scared, he says.

And then there were other pictures with Durito in different poses and urban backgrounds.

There was one with Durito among many feet. He wanted me to notice that none of the feet wore boots, and that made Durito applaud. I told him not to be so enthusiastic, that Espinosa [Mexico City mayor] had not yet shown his claws.

There was a picture with a lot of people in it. Durito took that one so that I wouldn't feel so lonely.

There was another one of Durito and another beetle. In the background you could see the buildings of University City. I asked him who the other beetle was.

"It's not a he, it's a she..." he answered with a long sigh.

No more pictures. Durito was silent and all you could hear were sighs which emanated from the sculpture. I turned back to the indignation of Machiavelli at my criticism of efficiency.

In view of this morality and this criticism does this mean that we offer an alternative? Is this the blasphemy which knocks down the adopted Machiavellians? A new morality? A better morality? A more successful morality? More efficient? Is that what we offer? Negative. Insofar as the Zapatistas are concerned we believe it is necessary to construct a new political relationship, whose source will not only be neo-Zapatismo. We believe that that relationship should act upon itself. This relationship will be so new that it will not only be a new politics, but create new politicians. A new form of defining the arena of politics and of those who practice it.

I won't argue why a new political morality won't come solely from neo-Zapatismo; its enough to say that our existence is also, old. We have undertaken the argument of weapons (no matter how much J. Castaneda, in the hopes of salvaging his book from failure, denies them and claims that only in name are we an army), and together with them, we use the argument of force. Whether the weapons are old or new or have gone largely unused does not change the situation one way or another. The fact is that we were, and are willing to use them. We are willing to die for our ideals, yes. But we are also willing to kill. That is why, from an army, whether "lame" or revolutionary, heroic or etcetera, cannot come a new political morality, or better yet, a political morality superior to that which oppresses us a good part of the day and much of the night. She, the night, still keeps some surprises, and I'm sure that many hairs will be torn out trying to figure out what...

"Things are not that simple," Durito says, "It may be that I did not bring you the videos you wanted and that's why you want to lay on my noble shoulders a blame much heavier than this piano and desk. But I should tell you that, I brought some things for the Zapatistas: bracelets, headbands, earrings, hair-clasps... I worked ten nights straight to get these things..."

Speaking of nights, the one today shows the sharp horns of a bull-moon which, new, returns from the west. Her clouds are gone, and without a cape to help her, the night fights the bull solely and in silence. Her enthusiasm is not dampened by the storm announced in the east, and among her treasures are as many comets as rhinestones on the suit of the best bullfighter.

And there I was, trying to decide whether I would rise to her defense, when I was held back by the wide smile, painted inside the horns of the moon. Ten times I sought to avoid her, and ten times the stars demanded that I continue the passes of the bullfight.

Then I tossed the article aside and moved towards the center of the nightly stadium, asking Durito to play a pasodoble. He said I should go back to my writing because I'd taken too much time to finish it, and he, Durito, would not help me. Oh well, I left the round pending and returned to the article and the problem of political morality. The thousand heads thrust forward by the light barely peeked and shook the wall of the night gently...

What was I saying? Oh yes! Our criticism to Machiavelli does not mean that we are better, superior, or best. But we do say that it is necessary to try to be better. The problem is not what political morality is better or more efficient, but what is necessary for a new political morality.

In any case, it's not the diluted cynicism of those intellectuals, anxious to find a theoretical explanation for chaos, which will produce a new or more efficient political morality. In terms of the political parties, Machiavelli runs a complicated scale of rewards; once legalized as alternatives to power, all of their pettiness (secrets, negotiations, opportunisms, pragmatisms and betrayals) do not weigh enough in order to shift the balance in their favor.

However, the nature of that "pettiness" soon makes a historic payment. And the higher the position reached with those "small and great political wits", the larger the payment that history demands. Once again, Carlos Salinas de Gortari is an example made historic lesson (which, it seems, no one in the political class wants to learn).

Is it a better world that we offer? Negative: we do not offer a new world. Machiavelli does, and he says it is not possible to be better, to conform ourselves with the greys which populate Mexican politics and the necessity to keep them from being antagonistic, thus diluting them into greyer greys. We disagree, and not just because of the mediocrity of that sad view of "not one or the other", but because it is a lie, it has no future, and sooner or later, reality comes, with that pig-headedness that reality assumes, and with the tendency to decompose medium tones and sharpen even the most neutral grey...

"Seven questions. That was the correct thing to do!" Durito says, who obviously does not let go of his disagreement with the National Plebiscite.

I try to distract him and ask him about Pegasus. Durito's voice breaks as he answers.

"What happened to Pegasus is part of that daily tragedy which lives and dies in the D.F. Pegasus was an amiable and intelligent beast, but too patient for the traffic of Mexico City. I had just disguised him as a compact car, because he refused to be a Metro car being afraid of sliding in the rain. Things were going well, but as it turns out Pegasus was a she and she fell in love with a bus from Ruta 100. The last time I saw her she was collecting money in a can for the resistance fund. But I don't regret it, I'm sure she will learn good things. I told her to write but she didn't know where to send the letter."

A tremor shook the sky. I stare at the place where Durito is. A silence and a cloud of smoke surrounds the sculpture. I try to encourage Durito and ask him to tell me more about his trip to the capital.

"What else can I tell you? I saw what is to be seen in a large or small city; injustice and anger, arrogance and rebellion, great wealth in the hands of a few and a poverty which each day claims more people. It was worth seeing. For many, fear is no more; for others it disguises itself as prudence. Some say it could be worse; others will never have it so bad. There is no unanimity, except about the repudiation of everything which is government."

Durito lights the pipe and continues.

"One early morning I was about to go to sleep in one of the few remaining trees of the Alameda. And the city was another, different from the one that lives during the day. From high in the tree I saw a patrol car going by slowly. It stopped in front of a woman and one of the officers stepped out of the car. His demonic look gave him away. My intuition was correct: I knew instantly what was going to happen. The woman did not move, and waited for the officer as though she knew him. Silently, she gave him a roll of bills and he put it away as he looked to the sides. He said goodbye by trying to pinch the woman's cheeks but she brushed his hand aside brusquely. He returned to the vehicle, and then the patrol car left instantly..."

Durito is quiet for a long time. I suppose he has finished and returned to his paperwork, and I should return to mine: instead of discussing which political morality is better or more "efficient" we should talk and discuss the necessity of fighting for the creation of a space in which a new political morality may be born. And here the problem departs from the following:

Should political morality be defined always in relationship with the issue of power? Alright, but that is not the same as saying "in relationship to the taking of power". Perhaps, the new political morality is constructed in a new space which will not be the taking or retention of power, but the counterweight and opposition which contains and obliges the power to "rule by obeying", for example.

Sure, "rule by obedience" is not within the concepts of "political science" and it is devalued by the morality of "efficiency" which defines the political activity which we suffer. But in the end, confronted by the judgement of history, the "efficiency" and "success" of the morality of cynicism is naked unto itself. Once it looks at itself in the mirror of its accomplishments, the fear it inspires in its enemies (who will always be the majority) turns against it.

On the other side, the side of the "pure" ones, the saint learns he is a demon, and the inverse image of cynicism discovers that it has made intolerance into direction and religion, in the measuring cup of a political project. The puritanism of National Action for example, is a part of the sample which remains unexhausted in the Mexican right wing.

Well, the dawn is coming, and with it, time to say goodbye. Maybe I didn't understand the polemic of the resurrected Machiavelli to which I was invited, and I see now that I presented (and did not resolve) more polemical lines than the original ones. That's not bad; "inefficient" maybe, but not bad.

Surely the polemic can continue, but it's unlikely to happen face-to-face given the ski-mask, persecution and the military siege in the words of Munoz-Ledo: "I don't believe that [Marcos] is someone who will remain in the political scene of the country." What, does he already have a pact with Chuayffet? A disappearance, maybe of the kind ordered by that Justice Secretary of Chiapas, that other great PRD member, Eraclio Zepeda?

Meanwhile, the Powerful will continue to promise us the Apocalypse in exchange for change. It is His conclusion that it is better to avoid it and be comfortable. Others deduce, in silence that the Apocalypse is eternal and that chaos is not about to come, but is already a reality...

I don't know how to finish this so I ask Durito for help. The spectacle of his sculpture is erased by the bolts of lightning of the storm. The reluctant light makes the contrast of the shadows darker. Maybe that's why I never saw Durito come out from under the ruin, and for a moment I thought something extraordinary had happened. Durito was smoking and sitting on top of the piano.

"How did you get out from under there?"

"Simple. I was never down there. I moved to one side when the piano started tumbling. I decided instantly that no work of art deserved being on top of my body. Anyway, I am a gallant knight, and for that you need to be a soulful artist and there are few of those. Alright, what is your problem my dear 'Guatson'?"

"I don't know how to end this letter," I say, ashamed of myself.

"That's an easy problem to resolve. Finish the way you started."

"How did I start? With a point?"

"It's elementary my dear 'Guatson', it is in any book of mathematical logic."

"Mathematical logic? And what does that have to do with political morality?"

"More than you think. For example, in mathematical logic (not to be confused with algebra) the point represents a conjunction, an AND. The point is the same as an AND. To say A AND B or A plus B, you write A.B. The point is not final, it is a sign of unity, of something which is added. It is defined, between one point and another, by X number of paragraphs, where X is a number which the mirror does not alter and reflects faithfully," Durito says as he arranges his papers. To the west, the sun uncovers clouds and takes over the sky.

And things being like this, this postscript comes to an end with a point which, according to Durito, does not mean the end but a continuation. Vale then: Y

P.S. So I invite you to resolve the enigma which encloses the central theme: Instructions:

First. Through the Looking Glass, Lewis Carroll, Chapter II, "The garden of the living flowers"

Second. Each period means the end of a paragraph.

Third. Punctuation marks don't count.

Fourth. Numeric chaos in the logic of the numbers in the mirror:

1-111. 14-110. 9-109. 247-107.
11-104. 25-103. 47-97. 37-96. 3-95.
14-94. 3-89. 24-87. 22-86. 6-85.
10-84. 48-82. 21-81. 43-79. 55-78.
10-77. 49-76.83-72. 21-71. 42-64.
6-63. 27 62. 52-61. 63-59. 13-58.
11-57. 3-56. 6-54. 101-53. 141-51.
79-50. 35-49. 32-49. 51-46. 11-45.
88-44. 12-43. 12-42. 31-41. 3-40.
24-39. 15-38. 20-37. 18-37. 17-36.
27-35. 22-33. 111-32. 7-32. 115-31.
20-31. 12-31. 5-31. 68-30. 46-30.
31030. 12-30. 9-30. 54-29. 45-29.
12-29. 49-28. 20-28. 9-28. 40-27.
15-27. 42-22. 111-21. 91-21. 29-21.
3-21. 34-20. 6-20. 81-19. 66-19.
44-19. 36-19. 18-19. 11-19. 123-18.
90-18. 80-18. 76-18. 65-18. 43-17.
4-17. 51-15. 48-15. 28-15. 16-15.
47-14. 20-14. 8-14. 39-13. 12-13.
55-12. 54-12. 53-12. 18-11. 43-10.
25-10. 41-8. 9-6. 6-4. 1-1.

Fifth. In the mirror, chaos is a reflection of the logical order and the logical order a reflection of chaos.

Sixth. A.A=?

Seventh. There are seven mirrors: the first is the first. The second and third open the mystery of chaos which is ordered in the fourth. The fourth is constructed with the fifth and the sixth. The seventh is the last one.

Vale once again. Health, and it appears that (given trees, outlaws, and dentistry) it is not so easy to love the branch.

Subcomandante Insurgente Marcos,
Zapatista Army of National Liberation.
Mountains of the Mexican Southeast,
Chiapas, Mexico.

31. THE STORY OF THE COLD FOOT AND THE HOT FOOT

October 27,1995

To the National and International Press

Sirs,

Here goes a communiqué. We are not going to run away anymore. By custom we run once a year and we already did that in February, 1995. With regards to the judicial police, they deserve the national prize of agronomy for their ability to "plant" evidence. Any way you see it, the key question is: Who gave the orders for the arrest? And from this question comes others, for example: Who benefits by the failure of the dialogue process in Chiapas? Send the answers (if somebody has them) to the Secretary of State, where they already know them. They only need to corroborate it. By now they have already ruined the October classics for me, although in baseball (as in politics) the best does not always win. If you don't believe me, ask Castillo Peraza. No, it's better not to ask him anything. He is capable of thinking that it is a flirtatious compliment. What ignorance illiteracy is capable of!

Health to you and make yourselves always walk with a notary public at your side to certify that you don't carry any more "arms" than what God has given you.

> *From the mountains of the Mexican Southeast,*
> *Insurgent Subcommander Marcos.*
> *Mexico, October 1995.*

P.S. That accepts all the admonitions which don't come from the mediocre arrogance that leads in certain political parties.

The dawn barely begins to appear. The cold and darkness cover the wake of a gallant knight-errant and the sorrow of his wretched squire. As for the moon, nobody finds her and the lightening is followed by thunder. Mud renews itself with rain and wheat with a kiss. Durito reviews the newspaper, bites his pipe and looks at me with reproach.

"So you have caused an outrage like those that make history!" He says while putting down the newspaper.

"Me?" I say pretending that I am veeery busy with my torn boot.

"Definitely! Who else? You have demonstrated once more that by talking you have the same ability as a stampede of elephants inside a china shop. And not just that. Your clumsiness has allowed an avalanche of mediocre people to declare one and a half foolishness about the half foolishness which you said..."

"I... What happens is that they did not understand me! I did not want to say what I said, but to say what I did not say, and that is why I did not say what I wanted to say and said what I did not want to say..." I defend myself while hiding my shame in the hole in my - does anybody doubt it? - left boot.

"Rubbish! This reasoning has the same logic as that of a PRI congressman explaining their vote against the reduction of IVA."

I remain quiet and start to draw spirals and little circles on the ground with a short stick. Durito feels sorry for me and pats my shoulder. To do this, Durito must climb on my arm and loosen his chin strap. He sits on the side of my neck, and says "Oh my dear and clumsy squire, speaking is slippery and problematic. In reality, it's only worth the trouble to speak to a woman - the only being with which it is gratifying to be slippery and get into trouble. To talk to a woman, one must do it close to her ear. This way, it does not matter what one says, but the warm closeness to the neck. The words in politics, contain many traps and tangles, and it is not only the words spoken to us, but the words that we say. And now that we speak of politics, it reminds me of a story that could be helpful for the book that you are preparing, and which is titled, if I don't remember poorly, 'Stories for a Night that Asphyxiates'."

I sighed, resigned to tolerating another of Durito's stories, but he thinks that it is because of the sorrow of the declarations against Don Porfirio, so he continues. He clears his throat and orders me to take pen and pencil, and I write while he dictates the story that he calls...

The Story of the Cold Foot and the Hot Foot

The two feet were once together. They were together, but not united. One was cold and the other one was hot. And then the cold foot said to the hot foot, "You are very hot." And the hot foot said to the cold foot, "You are very cold." And they were both doing that, which means fighting each other, when Hernan Cortes arrived and burned both of them.

"Is it over?" I ask unbelieving.

"Of course! It is a story, not one of your press conferences." He answers me.

I look at him with reproach.

He says: "Enough. It's fine. Let me think... Mmmmh, Mmmmh, I know! At the end write: 'And Hernan Cortes lived very happy. And that's not the end of the story.'"

"It isn't?" I ask him while I put the paper in my pocket.

"Of course not! There are still many cold and hot feet, so Hernan Cortes would end up having a veeery disagreeable surprise."

"Speaking of disagreeable things," I interrupt, "they are complaining about you in some newspaper."

"About me? Who dares complain of the knight-errant for whom many damsels, of all ages, long for, of whom many big and small children dream of, and who is respected and admired by all the noble men who have existed in the world?"

"Well, they don't precisely complain about you. They only say that enough of Durito being everywhere. Anyway, they suggest that I leave you out of my epistles and that..."

Durito does not allow me to continue and shouts in my ear. "Shut up insolent evil! Only a ragamuffin like you could think that respectable people would not enjoy the stories of my great feats, of my undeniable sympathy, and the profound wisdom which is plentiful in my discourse."

"But Durito! It is not I who has thought of such absurdity! Consider that some person could exist, it's a hypothesis, who does not respond with the same enthusiasm as..."

Durito interrupts again. "Well, I concede that is possible that some being exists that could not be interested in me or my wonders. So we would do something to determine the rating you, insolent yokel, have and the one I have, high knight-errant."

"I agree with the 'errant', but allow me to doubt that of 'high'."

"I am talking of the high ideals, cretin."

"Well, what do you propose?"

"A consultation."

"A consultation? But Durito... They are going to say is a joke..."

"Not another word! A consultation will be. National, International, and Interplanetary. And these will be the questions: First. Should the Sup eliminate the Durito stories in his letters? Second. Should the despicable being who dares to demand the disappearance of the Durito stories die in the midst of an inferno that would make the one of Dante's look like a freezer? These are two questions to be answer 'yes', 'no', 'I don't know'."

"And where should the ones who want to respond they send their answers?" Skeptical, I ask.

"To my office: 'Don Durito of the Lacandona, Hoyito of Huapac number 69. Mountains of Southeast Mexico, Chiapas, Mexico.'"

I see that Durito is very determined, so it's better for him to clarify some matters. "What are the minimum and maximum ages to participate in this 'consultation'?"

"Minimum is six months old. Maximum is a minute before expiring the last sigh..."

"But Durito, do you think that at six months old somebody could answer these questions?"

"Of course! At the age of six months I was already composing those sonnets that make storms in a humid and feminine womb which paradoxically also brings calm."

"But you are a beetle!"

"Even more in my favor! No more discussion! Elaborate the convocation and add that all females could attach to their ballot their best sigh... Although, on second thought... No, it's better not the sighs... Because for sure with so many sighs that will arrive here that they will turn into a hurricane which will leave Roxana in the category of 'inopportune breezes'. It's better that they send red carnations. Maybe we can do business and exploit them... Well, what do you think?"

"I think you are delirious. You have gone mad." I say to him.

"My dear and wretched squire! The dawn can only rise up with a certain doses of delirium and craziness..." Durito says while he goes back to his place and he covers himself again with the little leaf of Huapac, not before drawing a great and resounding "69" on the top.

"Let me know when the answers start arriving. Hell! I won't be able to get to sleep because of this sweet wait..." Durito says seconds before starting to snore as if he were a motor saw with no exhaust valve.

I remain quiet. I light up the pipe and inhale slowly some memory. The dawn above me dilutes its last and dark grays, far away the day takes a bite of the horizon and the cold turns into lukewarmness here... in the mountains of the Mexican Southeast...

Vale again. Health and that the craziness and the delirium multiply.

The Sup yearning for the flower with which October decorated the Ceiba.

32. LIKE HERE IN CHIAPAS?

November 10, 1995
To the National and International Press
(Only the one that is read in the 14 municipalities where, according to Mart'in del Campo Iruegas, we have "some influence").

Ladies and Gentlemen,

Here goes a communiqué. We are doing more or less well. Yes, I know nobody asked, but I say it just in case anybody thought about it. Over here the increase of the military mobilization and the re initiation of the nocturnal military flights (perhaps now they "supply the troops" at night also) demonstrate that the climate is appropriate "for dialogue and negotiation."

Vale. Health to you and the rumor that it is possible to be better turns into reality.

> From the mountains of the Mexican Southeast,
> Insurgent Subcommander Marcos.
> Mexico, November 1995.

P.S. Which cannot resist the temptation to add oneself to the patriotic campaign to "adopt a rumor."

I was negotiating with Olivio the exchange of animal crackers for a can of a well known drink of cola when... But well, before that, I should frame the story for you. Olivio is a child who has the undefined age of all the indigenous children who are younger than five years old in the reality of Chiapas. He does not speak Tojolabal, Castillian even less, so the negotiation is more complicated than if we were talking with Bernal and Del Valle. Olivio declares firmly that blgb-aclug. I don't let myself to be intimidated and as if I were Secretary of Foreign Relations defending the right of asylum of the old Mexican foreign policy, I answer with a categorical splf-glgl (making sure that the "s" of splf prolongs itself sufficiently to shower Olivio with spit). I think I was able to make an impression because he answered me with a dubious mglu-aclug. With the accomplished success, I got excited like a stockbroker who perceives unmistaken times of political and economic stability, and I tried to accomplish more with a prepotent splf-slsl, inspired by the Ap Dow Jones. Olivio kept his eyes on me and twisted his eyebrow imitating the gesture of wheat as it moves away. He thought about it for a few seconds and repeated the original blgb-aclug, ending with a shrill note. Anyway, the negotiation, like the economic program of Apre, had all the appearances of failure, when she arrived at the time...

The Yeniper (I say that her name is Jenifer, but she corrects me all the time and makes me repeat Yeniper to the point of surrendering to my clumsy pronunciation) is...

"How old are you?" I ask her.

"Who knows," she said.

Such is, like in most women, that the age of Yeniper is a mystery. Perhaps a description helps to calculate her age. Her height is about 80 centimeters, pugged-nosed, olive-skinned, with a haircut like the protagonist of Azul, except that it is very uneven, stomach full of earthworms, knee-length blue dress, and bare feet. I calculate that she is four years old going on five, which means that it is that age where life is a toss-up in the air, when the night is for sleeping and the daytime to carry firewood. Yeniper came to interrupt the transaction Olivio and I were doing because she wants to know what is a "coup de tat". Her question still surprises but I start to clear my throat like a member of the Congress of the Union (who knows that, whatever he says, he is going to make a fool of himself, because he has a hangover and because they tell him that the rumor comes from New York and he doesn't know whether to start a long list of compliments or to praise the goodness of NAFTA), to allow myself time to respond.

"Weeell," I say prolonging the "e" sufficiently to search for the adequate answer so that it is not misunderstood as a flirtatious remark by some president of some political party of some right wing.

Yeniper understands that, because of the length of the "e," that this is going to be a long story and she sits and starts to eat the animal crackers which Olivio brought as proof of his economic solvency. I add on. A coup de tat is when the military go around with their arms, their planes, their helicopters and their tanks watching over the civilians...

"Like here in Chiapas?" Yeniper interrupts me spitting in my eye a little foot of an elephant cracker.

"No. Let me explain, It is when the main preoccupation and investment of the government are of military character and not social ones."

"Like here in Chiapas?" Yeniper interrupts me again.

"Not exactly. In reality it is when the political power is in the hands of somebody who was not elected but was instead imposed in a provisional manner..."

"Like here in Chiapas?" Yeniper repeats.

"No. It's when they harass foreigners who come to help the civilian population..."

"Like here in Chiapas?" Yeniper affirms with the mouth full of a little cow of flour, sugar and artificial color.

"I'm telling you not that. It's when the functioning law is the law of the strongest and not of reason and all the civilians are subjected to the abuse of the government and its repressive forces..."

"Like here in Chiapas?" Yeniper states with the sadness of seeing that the animal crackers are all gone.

"Well, a coup de tat is when there is no respect for individual guarantees, there is impunity for the powerful and there is a lot of poverty and hunger..." I say with the doubt of whether what I am saying is or is not part of reality.

"Oh, like here in Chiapas." Yeniper affirms as she walks away in search of somebody who has more crackers.

I am not able to tell her before she walks away. In Chiapas there is no coup de tat. There is... There is... I don't know what there is, but Laco says that peace and democracy and other tales...

Yeniper does not even turn around. I suspect that she is as much an unbeliever as we were when Bernal send us a message saying that the rumors of a coup de tat demonstrates that they (meaning Bernal, Irruegas, Del Valle) were the soft and negotiating position of the government! and therefore, we had to support them to have a "successful" negotiation and if they fail then the bogeyman was going to show up, etc. Amazing to live in virtual reality! I kept thinking about the questions of Yeniper until Olivio stands up in front of me demanding blgb-aclug-aguto. This means, if I'm not mistaken, that I should give the can of the known beverage of cola. I argue declining to turn it over in a way so that Olivio understands that Yeniper ate the crackers and therefore there is no exchange. Olivio does not go into a hunger strike and he does not promise to execute a criminal economic program. What he does is to start crying with some bellows which may cause, and they can cause, a coup de tat. I gave him the soda... What else could I do? A rumor of a coup de tat would worry anybody... or not?

P.S. Which is waiting for tons of ballots. The moon multiplies herself over the loops of the stream. The plane above us rumored times of stability. I asked Durito whether he was going to be in this missive. He flatly answered. Don't even think of it! I have to wait the results of the consultation...

Thus, if Bartlett does not help us, the absence of Durito is going to be as long as the fall of the peso against the dollar.

Vale. Health to you and remember that hope is like a cracker: It's worth nothing if you don't have it inside.

The Sup waiting under the ceiba...

33. 12 Women in the Twelfth Year

During the 12th year of the EZLN, many kilometers, and at a great distance from Peking, 12 women meet March 8th with their faces erased...

I. Yesterday...

A face wreathed in black still leaves the eyes free and a few hairs dangling from the head. In that gaze is the glitter of one who searches. An M-1 carbine held in front, in that position called "assault," and a pistol strapped to the waist. Over the left side of the chest, that place where hopes and convictions reside, she carries the rank of Infantry Major of an insurgent army which has called itself, this cold dawn of January 1, 1994, the Zapatista Army of National Liberation. Under her command is a rebel column which takes the former capital of that southeastern Mexican state Chiapas, San Cristobal de Las Casas. The central park of San Cristobal is deserted. Only the indigenous men and women under her command, are witness to the moment in which the Major, a rebel indigenous tzotzil woman, takes the national flag and gives it to the commanders of the rebellion, those called "The Indigenous Clandestine Revolutionary Committee". Over the radio, the Major says: "We have recovered the Flag. 10-23 over." At 0200 southeastern time, of January 1 of 1994. It is 0100 hours of the new year for the rest of the world, but she has waited 10 years to say those words. She came to the mountains of the Lacandon Jungle in December of 1984, not yet 20 years of age and yet carrying the marks of a whole history of indigenous humiliation on her body. In December of 1984, this brown woman says "Enough is Enough!", but she says it so softly that only she hears herself. In January of 1994, this woman and several thousand indigenous people not only say but yell "Enough is Enough!", so loudly that all the world hears them...

Outside of San Cristobal another rebel column commanded by a man, the only one with light skin and a large nose who belongs to the indigenous who attack the city, has just finished taking police headquarters. Freed from these clandestine jails are the indigenous who were spending the new year in jail for the most terrible crime in the Chiapanecan southeast; that of being poor. Eugenio Asparuk is the name of the insurgent Captain, indigenous rebel tzeltal, who together with the enormous nose is now overseeing the search and seizure at the headquarters. When the Major's message arrives, Insurgent Captain Pedro, indigenous rebel chol, has finished taking the headquarters of the Federal Highway Police and has secured the road which connects San Cristobal with Tuxtla Gutierrez; Insurgent Captain Ubilio, indigenous rebel tzeltal has taken the entryways to the north of the city and with it the symbol of the government handouts to the indigenous people, the National Indigenous Institute. Insurgent Captain Guillermo, indigenous rebel chol, has taken the highest point of the city. From there he commands with his sight the surprised silence which peers out the windows of the houses and the buildings. Insurgent Captains Gilberto and Noe, Indigenous tzotzil and tzeltal respectively, and equally rebellious, end their take-over of the state judicial police headquarters and set it on fire before marching on to secure the other side of the city which leads to the barracks of the 31st Military Zone in Rancho Nuevo.

At 0200 hours, southeastern time of January 1 of 1994, 5 insurgent officials, indigenous rebel men, hear over the radio the voice of their commander, an indigenous rebel woman saying "We have recovered the flag. 10-23 over." They repeat this to their troops, men and woman, all indigenous rebels in their totality and translate the words "We have begun...".

At the municipal palace, the Major organizes the defense of the positions which will protect the men and women who now govern the city, a city now under the rule of indigenous rebels. A woman who is armed protects them.

Among the indigenous commanders there is a tiny woman, even tinier than those around her. A face wreathed in black still leaves the eyes free and a few hairs dangling from the head. In that gaze is the glitter of one who searches. A 12 caliber sawed-off shotgun hangs from her back. With the traditional dress of the women from San Andres, Ramona walks down from the mountains, together with a hundred more women, towards the city of San Cristobal on that last night of 1993. Together with Susana and other indigenous men she is part of that Indian command of the war which birthed 1994, the Clandestine Indigenous Revolutionary Committee-General Command of the EZLN. Comandante Ramona will, with her size and her brilliance, surprise, the international press when she appears during the first Dialogues for Peace held in the Cathedral and pulls from her backpack the national flag re-taken by the Major on January 1st. Ramona does not know then, nor do we, but she already carries in her body an illness which eats her life away in huge bites and dims her voice and her gaze. Ramona and the Major, the only women in the Zapatista delegation who show themselves to the world for the first time declare: "For all intents and purposes we were already dead, we meant absolutely nothing" and with this they almost count the humiliation and abandonment. The Major translates to Ramona the questions of the reporters. Ramona nods and understands, as though the answers she is asked for had always been there, in that tiny figure which laughs at the Spanish language and at the ways of the city women. Ramona laughs when she does not know she is dying. And when she knows, she still laughs. Before she did not exist for anyone, now she exists, as a woman, as an indigenous woman, as a rebel woman. Now Ramona lives, a woman belonging to that race which must die in order to live...

The Major watches the light take the streets of San Cristobal. Her soldiers organize the defense of the old city of Jovel and the protection of the men and women who in those moments sleep, indigenous and mestizos, all equally surprised. The Major, this indigenous rebel woman has taken their city. Hundreds of armed indigenous people surround the old City. A woman who is armed commands them...

Minutes later the rebels will take the city of Las Margaritas, hours later the government forces which defend Ocosingo, Altamirano, and Chanal will surrender. Huixtan and Oxchuc are taken by a column which is heading towards the principal jail of San Cristobal. Seven cities are now in insurgent hands following the 7 words of the Major. The war for the word has begun...

In other places, other women, indigenous and rebellious have re-made that piece of history which they have been given and which until that day of January 1, had been carried in silence. They also have no name or face;

Irma. Insurgent Infantry Captain, the chol woman Irma leads one of the guerrilla columns which takes the plaza at Ocosingo that January 1 of 1994. From one of the edges of the central park, together with the soldiers under her command, she attacks the guarnicion inside the municipal palace until they surrender. Then Irma undoes her braid and her hair falls to her waist as though to say "here I am, free and new, Captain Irma's hair shines, and continues to shine even as the night falls over an Ocosingo in rebel hands...

Laura. Insurgent Infantry Captain. Tzotzil woman, fierce in battle and fiercely committed to learning and teaching, Laura becomes the Captain of a unit composed completely of men. Not only that, but they are all novices as well. With patience, in the way of the mountain which has watched her grow, Laura teaches and gives orders. When the men under her command have doubts, she shows them by doing. No one carries as much or walks as much as she does. After the attack on Ocosingo she orders the retreat of her unit. It is an orderly and complete one. This woman with light skin says little or nothing, but she carries in her hands a carbine which she took from a policeman who only saw someone to humiliate or rape when he gazed upon an indigenous woman. After surrendering, the policeman ran away in his shorts, the same one who until that day believed that women were only useful when pregnant or in the kitchen...

Elisa. Insurgent Infantry Captain. As a trophy of war she still carries in her body some mortar fragments which are planted forever on her body. She takes command of her column when the rebel line is broken and a circle of fire fills the Ocosingo market with blood. Captain Benito has been injured and has lost his eye. Before losing consciousness, he explains and orders: "I've had it, Captain Elisa is in command." Captain Elisa is already wounded when she manages to take a handful of soldiers out of the market. When Captain Elisa, indigenous tzeltal gives orders it is a soft murmur... but everyone obeys...

Silvia. Insurgent Infantry Captain. She was trapped for 10 days in the rathole which Ocosingo became after January 2nd. Dressed as a civilian she scuttled along the streets of a city filled with federal soldiers, tanks and cannons. At a military checkpoint she was stopped. They let her through almost immediately. "It isn't possible that such a young and fragile woman could possibly be a rebel," say the soldiers as they watch her depart. When she re-joins her unit in the mountain the indigenous chol rebel woman appears sad. Carefully, I ask her the reason that her laughter is less. "Over there in Ocosingo" she answers me, lowering her eyes. "In Ocosingo I left my backpack and with it all the cassettes of music I had collected, now we have nothing." Silence and her loss lies in her hands. I say nothing, I add my own regrets to hers and I see that in war each loses what he/she most loves...

Maribel. Insurgent Infantry Captain. She takes the radio station in Las Margaritas when her unit assaults the municipality on January 1, 1994. For nine years she lived in the mountain in order to be able to sit in front of that microphone and say:

"We are the product of 500 years of struggle; first we fought against slavery..."

The transmission does not go through because of technical reasons and Maribel takes another position in order to cover the backs of the unit which advances towards Comitan. Days later she will serve as guard for the prisoner of war, General Absalon Castellanos Dominguez. Maribel is tzeltal and was less than 15 years old when she came to the mountains of the Mexican Southeast. "The toughest moment in those 9 years was when I had to climb the first hill, called 'the hill from hell', after that everything else was easy," said the insurgent official. When General Castellanos Dominguez is returned to the government, Captain Maribel is the first rebel to have contact with the government. Commissioner Manuel Camacho Solis extends his hand to her and asks her age: "502" says Maribel who counts all the years since the rebellion began...

Isidora. Infantry Insurgent. Isidora goes into Ocosingo as a buck private on the first day of January. And as a buck private Isidora leaves Ocosingo in flames, after spending hours rescuing her unit, made up entirely of men 40 of whom were wounded. She also has mortar fragments on her arms and legs. When Isidora arrives at the nursing unit and hands over the wounded, she asks for a bit of water and gets up again. "Where are you going?" they ask her as they try to treat her wounds which bleed and paint her face as well as redden her uniform. "To get the others," answers Isidora as she re-loads. They try to stop her and cannot, the buck private Isidora has said she must return to Ocosingo to rescue other companeros from the music of death which the mortars and the grenades play. They have to take her prisoner in order to stop her. "The only good thing is that when I'm punished at least I can't be demoted," says Isidora as she waits in the room which, to her, appears to be a jail. Months later, when they give her a star which promotes her to an infantry official, Isidora, tzeltal and Zapatista looks first at the star and then at her commander and asks, as though she were being scolded "Why?"... But she does not wait for the answer...

Amalia. First lieutenant in the hospital unit. Amalia has the quickest laughter in the Mexican Southeast and when she finds Captain Benito lying in a pool of blood unconscious, she drags him to a more secure place. She carries him on her back and takes him out of the circle of death which surrounds the market. When someone mentions surrender, Amalia, honoring the chol blood which runs in her veins, gets angry and begins to argue. Everyone listens, even above the ruthless explosions and the flying bullets. No one surrenders...

Elena. Lieutenant in the hospital unit. When she joined the EZLN she was illiterate. There she learned to read, write, and that which is called medicine. From caring for diarrheas and giving vaccines, she went on to care for the wounded in a small hospital which is also house, warehouse and pharmacy. With difficulty she extracts the pieces of mortar carried by the Zapatistas on their bodies. "Some I can take out, some I can't" says Elenita, insurgent chol, as though she were speaking of memories and not of pieces of lead...

In San Cristobal, that morning of January 1, 1994, she communicates with the great white nose: "Someone just came here asking questions but I don't understand the language, I think it's English. I don't know if he's a photographer but he has a camera."

"I'll be there soon," answers the nose as it re-arranges the ski mask.

Into a vehicle go the weapons which have been taken from the police station and he travels to the center of the city. They take the weapons out and distribute them among the indigenous who are guarding the municipal palace. The foreigner was a tourist who asked if he could leave the city. "No," answered the ski-mask with the over-sized nose, "it's better that you return to your hotel. We don't know what will happen." The tourist leaves after asking permission to film with his video camera. Meanwhile the morning advances, the curious arrive, journalists and questions. The nose responds and explains to the locals, tourists and journalists. The Major is behind him. The ski- mask talks and makes jokes. A woman who is armed watches his back.

A journalist, from behind a television camera asks: "And who are you?" "Who am I?" says the ski-mask hesitantly as it fights off the sleepiness after the long night. "Yes!" insists the journalist, "Are you 'Commander Tiger' or 'Commander Lion'?" "No!" responds the ski-mask rubbing the eyes which are now filled with boredom. "So, what's your name?" says the journalist as he thrusts his camera and microphone forward. The big-nosed ski-mask answers "Marcos. Subcomandante Marcos..." Overhead the planes of Pontius Pilate begin to circle...

From that time on, the impeccable military action of the take-over of San Cristobal is blurred, and with it is erased the fact that it was a woman, a rebel indigenous woman, who commanded the entire operation. The participation of other women rebels in other actions of January 1 and during the long road of 10 years since the birth of the EZLN, become secondary. The faces covered with ski-masks become even more anonymous when the lights center on Marcos. The Major says nothing, she continues to watch the back of that enormous nose which now has a name for the rest of the world. No one asks her for her name...

At dawn on January 2 of 1994 the same woman directs the retreat from San Cristobal and the return to the mountains. She returns to San Cristobal 50 days later as part of the escort which guards the security of the delegates of the CCRI-CG of the EZLN to the Dialogue at the Cathedral. Some women journalists interview her and ask her name. "Ana Maria, Mayor Insurgente Ana Maria" she answers with her dark gaze. She leaves the Cathedral and disappears for the rest of the year of 1994. Like her other companeras, she must wait, she must be silent...

December of 1994, 10 years after becoming a soldier, Ana Maria receives the order to prepare to break out of the military blockade established by government forces around the Lacandon Jungle. At dawn on December 19th, the EZLN takes positions in 38 municipalities. Ana Maria commanded the action in the municipalities in the Altos of Chiapas. Twelve women officers were with her in the action: Monica, Isabela, Yuri, Patricia, Juana, Ofelia, Celina, Maria, Gabriela, Alicia, Zenaida and Maria Luisa. Ana Maria herself takes the municipality of Bochil.

After the Zapatista deployment, the high command of the federal army orders silence around the rupture of the blockade and it is represented by the mass media as a purely "propagandistic" action of the EZLN. The pride of the federales is deeply wounded: the Zapatistas escaped the blockade and to add insult to injury, a woman commands a unit which takes various municipalities. It is of course impossible to accept and so a great deal of money must be piled onto the event so that it will remain unknown.

Due to the involuntary actions of her armed companeros, and the deliberate actions of the government, Ana Maria and the Zapatista women at her side are dismissed and made invisible...

II. Today...

I have almost finished writing this when someone else arrives...

Dona Juanita. After Old Man Antonio dies, Dona Juanita allows her life to slow down in the same rhythm which she uses to prepare coffee. Physically strong, Dona Juanita has announced she will die. "Don't be silly, grandmother," I say to her, refusing to meet her eyes. "Look you..." she answers. "If it is to live that we must die, nothing will keep me from dying, much less a young brat like yourself," says and scolds Dona Juanita, the woman of Old Man Antonio, a rebel woman all her life, and apparently, a rebel even in response to her death...

Meanwhile on the other side of the blockade, appears.

She. She has no military rank, uniform, nor weapon. She is a Zapatista only she knows. She has no face or name, much like the Zapatistas. She struggles for democracy, liberty and justice, the same as the Zapatistas. She is part of what the EZLN calls "civil society", of a people without a party, of a people who do not belong to "political society" made up of rulers and leaders of political parties. She is a part of that diffuse, but real part of society which says, day after day, its own "Enough is Enough!"

At first she is surprised at her own words, but later, based on the strength of repeating them, and above all, living them, she stops being afraid of them, being afraid of herself. She is now a Zapatista, she has united her destiny to that of the Zapatistas in that new delirium which so terrorizes political parties and the intellectuals of the Power, the Zapatista Front of National Liberation. She has already fought against everyone, against her husband, her lover, her boyfriend, her children, her friend, her brother, her father, her grandfather. "You are insane" was the common judgement. She leaves a great deal behind. What she renounces is much larger than what is left behind by the rebels who already had nothing to lose. Her everything, her world, demands she forget "those crazy Zapatistas" and conformity calls her to sit down in the comfortable indifference which lives and worries only about itself. She leaves everything behind. She says nothing. Early one dawn she sharpens the tender point of hope and begins to emulate the first of January of her sister Zapatistas many times in one day, at least 364 times a year which have nothing to do with a January 1.

She smiles because she once admired the Zapatistas but no longer. She ended the admiration in the moment in which she learned that they were only a mirror of her rebellion, of her hope.

She discovers that she is born on the first of January of 1994. From then on she feels that her life and what was always said to be a dream and a utopia, might actually be a truth.

She begins to knit in silence and without pay, side by side with other men and women, that complex dream which some call hope: Everything for everyone, nothing for ourselves.

She meets March 8th with her face erased, and her name hidden. With her come thousands of women. More and more arrive. Dozens, hundreds, thousands, millions of women who remember all over the world that there is much to be done and remember that there is still much to fight for. It appears that that thing called dignity is contagious and it is women who are more likely to become infected with this uncomfortable ill...

This March 8th is a good time to remember and to give their rightful place to the insurgent Zapatistas, to the Zapatistas, to the women who are armed and unarmed.

To the rebels and uncomfortable Mexican women who are now bent over underling that history which, without them, is nothing more than a badly-made fable...

III. Tomorrow

If there is to be one, it will be made with the women, and above all, by them...

From the mountains of the Mexican Southeast,
Subcomandante Insurgente Marcos.
Mexico, March of 1996.

34. Support Letter for Leonard Peltier

The following letter was sent to US President Bill Clinton on April 7, 1996

Mr. President,

On June 25, 1975, two FBI agents were killed in Pine Ridge, South Dakota, without anyone ever finding out who was responsible for this crime. In a biased and fixed trial, Leonard Peltier, member of the Chippewa-Sioux Nation, was declared guilty for these acts as part of the permanent and systematic campaign against the indigenous men and women of North America who struggle for justice, democracy, and freedom. We know that this campaign is carried out by the government that you preside over.

Today, the participants in this American Encounter for Humanity and against Neo-liberalism reunited in the Lacandona Jungle, who come from every corner of the Americas, demand the immediate and unconditional freedom of Leonard Peltier, a representative of North America's indigenous resistance, and the absolute respect for the human rights of the indigenous peoples on the continent.

Sincerely,

Subcomandante Insurgente Marcos,
Comandante Tacho,
Mayor Insurgente Moises and more than 200 other signatures.

35. Our People Cannot Continue in This Dialogue

September 1, 1996
To: Mister Ernesto Zedillo Ponce de Leon
From: Zapatista Army of National Liberation

Mister Zedillo,

I have just finished listening to your second State of the Union address. We waited, uselessly, for some sign of your serious disposition to achieve peace. In fact, your speech was even further to what you declared on television on the 30th of august of 1996, and very close to the speech you made on February 5th of 1995, which preceded your betrayal of that year. Perhaps those advisors who approved the military solution of 1995 have returned to your side. Perhaps they never left. In any case, what they advised you to do in those days, and what they now repeat to you, does not contemplate the progress of this country, but its complete decomposition. Will you listen to them again?

We do not want power nor your position. What is more we do not care if you sit there, the PRI, the PAN, the PRD or the PT or the ERP-PRDP. We will nevertheless struggle for democracy, liberty and justice.

The delegation which you have sent to represent you at the dialogue of San Andres has treated our indigenous leaders with racism, discrimination and arrogance, it has done everything possible to regress the dialogue and to avoid any real solutions, it has not made any serious proposals to make agreements, and those which have been made have not been carried out. Its delegation has managed to achieve a new failure which is very likely definite at San Andres. Our people cannot continue in this dialogue which has been imposed by your messengers. We are willing to seek peace, but not the peace your delegation seeks. Our peace is another peace; one of which we and our children may be proud.

If you were unaware of this and if you really want a just and dignified solution, as we do, then do something. If you already knew this and in fact this was your strategy in order to wait for the opportune moment for the military solution, well, too bad. It seems you have achieved the climate of terror your were seeking, and surely, you believe that your have in your favor the national and international opinion necessary to attack the Zapatistas. If this is so, then we will see one another in hell.

Vale. Health and a good trip to Bolivia. They say there are still people who believe Che was killed there.

From the mountains of Numancia,
Subcomandante Insurgente Marcos.

P.S. If we are neither delinquents nor terrorists, then why are the alleged Zapatistas sentenced as though they were delinquents?

36. THE SEA SHELL OF THE END AND THE BEGINNING

October 23, 1996
To: International and National Civil society
From: Sup Marcos

Madam,

Yeah, it's us again. But please don't be perturbed. Not yet. Now we write to thank you for the perturbing joy which took Comandante Ramona, and with her all of us to the center of Power in Mexico. We've seen some of the images of those days during which all the Mexican political system trembled as our most powerful weapon passed. And we also learned about the National Indigenous Congress. And also about its slogan calling to the struggle under the subversive banner of "Never again a Mexico without us". Yes, that "us" is a difficult invitation to resist. And well, I think what's next is "Never again a world without us!" Don't you think? Of course, everything turned out fine. And you are right, it was like a party. Of course it ruined more than one person's breakfast, but those things are inevitable.

Know what? Something very strange is happening in this country. When you give no signs of life and wrap yourself up in problems you believe are individual ones, the Power smiles and leaves everything for later, but the moment you get determined to speak and go out to the street to dance, it gives the supreme government this strong urge to dialogue and to show it is serious about resolving the problems. I don't know why this happens, but it's so good that you go out and dance that little tune that goes... how? Yeah, that's it!

Well then, I also write to you to tell you that we continue in the dialogue and today (I write these lines at dawn) we finished the first encounter they call "tripartite" because one is supposed to split up into three in order not to forget the local, national and galactic perspective. Speaking of galaxies, I'm going back to the ceiba. No, it's not that I'm afraid that Heriberto has eaten all the candy in my absence, or that Eva has organized feminist seminars with that movie with Pedro Infante called WHAT HAS THAT WOMAN DONE TO YOU? No mam, she's done nothing to me, that's just the name of the movie. And I'm not returning to the ceiba because I want to avoid Olivio's soccer ball in my face or Yeniperr's questions, and believe me, they're both just as terrible. No, see... well... you know... Have you heard that song about the moons of October? Yes, well it seems the other dawn I escaped my security escort and... No... really, the only thing I caught was a cold so bad that everytime I sneeze... well, the tremors caused by January 1st are nothing in comparison. Anyway, the thing is I escaped because when I am here they keep me inside four white walls where my friends DON'T come to see me one by one, two by two, or six to seven. I got out, and before I was captured by my security escorts I managed to catch sight of a moon, which reminded me of a moon two years ago...

And on that dawn, like this one, the moon was a solitary breast wasting away on the night's hand of desire. But on this dawn I re-read Durito's last letter, and I should warn you Durito has a marked tendency for philosophical treatises so along with the letter, comes what follows and can only be explained by it's title called...

The Sea Shell of the End and the Beginning

(Neoliberalism and Architecture or The ethics of the Search versus the Ethics of Destruction)

In the Lacandon jungle, in the southeast Mexican state of Chiapas, there is a deserted village surrounded by well-armed military posts. The name of this abandoned village was Guadalupe Tepeyac. Its inhabitants, indigenous Tojolabales, were expelled by the Mexican government's army in February of 1995, as the federal troops attempted to assassinate the leadership of the Zapatista Army of National Liberation.

But it isn't the painful exile of these indigenous people who pay for their rebellion by living in the mountains, that I want to talk to you about. I want to talk to you about an architectural masterpiece which was born, on the skirts of the then-living Guadalupe Tepeyac, in July and August of 1994. Illiterate for the most part, or with a third grade education among the most "educated" of them, the Tojolabal architects raised in 28 days, a masterpiece capable of holding 10,000 members of what the Zapatistas called "The National Democratic Convention". In honor of Mexican history, the Zapatistas called the meeting place Aguascalientes. The giant meeting place would hold 10,000 seated participants, a stage which would hold 100, a library, a computer room, kitchens, hostels, parking lots. It included as well, they say "a staging area for assaults".

Anyway, all this is now anecdotal and you can see it through other means (books, reports, photos, videos and movies from that time). Now what matters is a detail which went unseen by most of those who were present at the Aguascalientes of Guadalupe Tepeyac that 1994 (Aguascalientes was destroyed in February of 1995). The detail I refer to was so large, that it was hard to see at first glance. This writing is about that gigantic and unseen detail.

It seems that the auditorium and the stage were in the middle of a giant sea shell going and coming, without end or beginning. Don't get frustrated, let me explain. The indigenous Zapatistas had raised a more or less conventional auditorium; the kind of construction which appeared to be the keel of a boat, a flat part in front, with chairs, and a gallery with wooden benches (using the side of a knoll). Anyway, nothing extraordinary. If anything was interesting it was the benches mounted on split wood and tied with vines. There was no metal in that gallery.

When they began to construct the hostels, the library and other facilities, the indigenous tojolobales of the Zapatista rebellion, now spontaneous architects, sprinkled the facilities in what appeared to be great disorder, anyway, so thought the Sup, who limited himself to sprinkling the immediate surroundings of the gigantic auditorium. It wasn't until, while counting the housing capacity of each building, that the Sup noticed that one of the houses was "crooked", it had an inexplicable break in one of its extremities. The Sup didn't pay much attention. Until the Tojolabal Comandante Tacho asked him:

"What do you think of the sea shell?"

"What sea shell?" the Sup answered, following the Zapatista tradition of answers which are questions, the eternal game of the question to the mirror.

"The one that surrounds the auditorium," answered Comandante Tacho in a voice which said "the day has light".

The Sup only looked at Tacho and Tacho understood that the Sup did not understand what he did, so he took him to the crooked house and pointed out how the roof made a capricious break.

"That's where the shell curves," he told him.

The Sup then put on a "So?" face (similar to the one you have now), so Comandante Tacho hurried to make a drawing in the mud with a stick. Tacho's drawing gave the location of all the buildings and yes, thanks to the break in that crooked house, the totality looked like a sea shell. The Sup agreed in silence after looking at the drawing. Then Comandante Tacho went to see about the tarp to cover the auditorium in case it rained.

The Sup was left standing there, in front of the crooked house, thinking that the crooked house was not really "crooked". It was only the curve which the sea shell needed in order to be complete. He was thinking on that when a journalist approached him and asked, looking for an answer with deep political meaning, what Aguascalientes meant to the Zapatistas.

"A sea shell," was the laconic answer of the Sup.

"A sea shell?" he asked wondering if he'd understood the question.

"Yes!" he told him. And the Sup pointed out the curve of the house as he was leaving.

Yes, I agree with you. The sea shell of AGUASCALIENTES could only be seen from a certain height. What's more, only from a certain altitude.

You have to fly high to discover the Zapatista sea shell which sketches itself on these poor rebel lands. In one of its extremities there was a library and in another the old "safe house". The history of that "safe house" is similar to the story of the EZLN in the Mayan indigenous communities. That little house was built far from anyone, so no one would see those first clandestine tojolabales who joined the EZLN. There they held meetings, they studied, and they gathered the tortillas and the beans they would send to the mountains where the insurgents were.

So there you have the Mayan sea shell. A spiral with no beginning or end. Where does sea shell begin and end? In its most inner part or in its outer part? Does a sea shell go in or out?

The sea shell of the Mayan rebel leaders began and ended in the "safe house", but it also began and ended in the library. The place of the encounter, of the dialogue, of the transition, of the search, that is what the Aguascalientes sea shell is.

From what "architectural" tradition did the indigenous Zapatistas borrow? I don't know, but surely that sea shell, that spiral, invites entry as well as exit, and really, I would not dare to say what part ends or begins a sea shell.

Months later, in October of 1994 a small group from civil society arrived at Aguascalientes to complete the installation of lighting in the library. They left after a few days of work. That morning, especially cold and foggy, the moon was a promise upon which to rest the cheek and desire, and a cello bled a few notes at midnight and in the mist. It was like a movie. The Sup watched from a corner, protected by the shadows and the ski-mask. A movie. The beginning or the end of a movie? After that group left, no one else returned to Aguascalientes until the party at year's end. Then they disappeared again. On February 10th of 1995, troops moved in by air and took Guadalupe Tepeyac. The first thing they did when they entered Aguascalientes was to destroy the library and the safe house, the beginning and end of the sea shell. Then they destroyed the rest.

For some strange reason, the breaking point of the crooked house remained standing for several months afterward. It is said that it fell in December of 1995, when other Aguascalientes were born in the mountains of the Mexican southeast.

All the past shows that the ethics of Power is the same as that of destruction, and the ethics of the sea shell is the same as the search. And that is very important for architecture and understanding neoliberalism. No?

Here Durito's thesis ends, which, as you can tell, is only for specialists...

So what is all this about beetles, sea shells and rouge moons? Well, the truth is that ten years ago on a morning in October, Old Man Antonio explained that a sea shell served to see inside and for jumping up, but I'll tell you about that later. Now I share Durito's thesis because he's very exacting and says that "humanity should benefit from my great wisdom".

Yes, you're right. I also think that, for a beetle, he's very pedantic, but he argues that errant knights are not pedantic, only knowledgeable about their own strength and great talent, especially when it comes to beating up scoundrels and picking on rogues.

And so madam, I say goodbye. I hope you don't forget that we're still here. Hope you don't forget often, anyway.

Vale. Health to you and the pending question is: If one is inside the sea shell, towards what direction should one walk? Towards the inside or outside?

> *From the mountains of the Mexican Southeast,*
> *Subcomandante Insurgente Marcos.*
> *Mexico, October 1996.*

P.S. THE ONE WHICH FULFILLS ITS EDITORIAL DUTY. Oh, I forgot, in Durito's letter there is a story which I guess I should add to his book STORIES FOR

A SLEEPLESS SOLITUDE, in the section called "STORIES FOR DECIDING".
Here goes then, the story is called:

> *The story of the live person and the dead person*
> Once there was a live person and a dead person.
> And the dead person said to the live person:
> My, I envy you, you and your restlessness.
> And then the live person said to the dead person:
> My, I envy you, you and your tranquility.
> And there they were, envying one another, when suddenly, at full gallop a bay horse
> at bay went by. End of story and moral: I repeat that all final options are a trap. It's
> imperative to find the bay horse at bay.

> *Don Durito of the Lacandon.*
> *(For love letters, interview requests, carnations, and signatures of support for the
> "Anti-Big-Boots Beetle Society" please write to "Huapac Leaf #69, Mountains of
> the Mexican Southeast (to the side of where the Sup lives)". Please note for phone
> calls: do not worry if the answering machine is not on. I don't have one.)*

Vale once again. Health and, since we're talking about the trap of final options
everyone will agree with me that when it comes to choosing whether to come or
go... it's always better to come...

The Sup with a bad cold, and obviously a little bit of fever.

37. URGENT TELEGRAM TO CIVIL SOCIETY

December 8, 1996
URGENT TELEGRAM
For: National and International civil Society
From: Subcomandante Insurgente Marcos
CCRI-CG of the EZLN

Madam,
Health, greetings. Stop. Bow to you many times. Stop. Supreme government with
amnesia. Stop. Forgotten agreements. Stop. Renewed excuses. Stop. Probable need for
more Indian blood in order to refresh memory. Stop. Your presence is urgent. Stop.

An intercontinental dance may serve to refresh memory. Stop. The grays hope to
win. Stop. Rainbow needed urgently. Stop. If there is dance I want one. Stop. Sigh. Stop.

After you. **Stop**. Sigh. **Stop**. Hand in hand and hand on waist. **Stop**. Sigh. **Stop**. 1. 2. 3. **Stop**. Sigh.

Vale. **Stop**. Health. **Stop**. May the dance paint floor-ceiling. **Stop** and End.

The Sup - thinking telegraphically and naively, that the periods and hyphens mark a tune for dancing and a path for walking.

From the mountains of the Mexican Southeast,
Subcomandante Insurgente Marcos.
Mexico, December of 1996.

P.S. WHICH ANNOUNCES THE REAPPEARANCE OF A BETTLE REMEMBERED AMONG SO MANY FORGOTTEN AGREEMENTS.

A letter from Durito arrived. He says he is returning in order to return the memory of the scoundrels who have come back for their jurisdictions. He says he may be a little late because "Pegasus" (his turtle, I mean, his mount) gets vertigo at high speeds (you know, those above 50 centimeters per hour), and because he has many gifts (among them a lock of hair which holds promise according to Durito). He also says someone should save him a dance, that with that "hand in hand and hand on waist" he has many hands left over and asks if he can put them (his hands, of course) where the sighs become stereophonic. He says other things which morality and good behavior do not permit to be repeated if the stocks of the Lilliputian vendor are to keep their value (I mean what if we are sued).

Ah! He also adds a story whose text says;

The Story of the Forever Never

"Once there was he who was all night. Shadow of shadows, solitary step, he walked many nights in order to find her.

Once there was a she who was all day. Twinkle of wheat, pure dance, she walked many days in order to find him.

They looked for each other much, he and she. The night pursued the day much. They both knew, he and she of the search which could not be found. It seemed it would never happen, it seemed impossible, it seemed never, ever...

And then the dawn came, for he and she. Forever, never..." Tan tan.

Durito's letter ended with this story. I, meanwhile, have already asked for sanctuary against being forgotten.

A vale made of nuts with nutmeg. Health and hope that the dawn will arrive soon and forever...

The Sup looking at a photo of Ché, which inexplicably, smiles (Ché does, of course).

CHAPTER II: **1997-1999 – Building the World**

— *Subcomandante Marcos*

38. THE STORY OF THE NOISE AND THE SILENCE

February 14, 1997

Ladies and Gentlemen,

Health and hellos (believe me that amongst so many airplanes, helicopters and tanks, one and the other is necessary). Here goes a letter attached to mark the betrayal of a year ago and the betrayal of two years ago. In spite of one and the other we are still here. You don't seem to be faring too well. Here the only games are the head games (because of the rocks from Beto's slingshot) and there are no potential candidates who fall ill. I'd like to take the opportunity to salute the people of Ecuador. Too bad someone doesn't teach those who govern Mexico to sing. Then maybe...

Vale. Health and remember that the flag celebrated this 24th belongs to us as well.

From the mountains of the Mexican Southeast,
Subcomandante Insurgente Marcos.
Mexico, February 1997.

P.S. WHICH ASKS (SPECIFICALLY IN REGARDS TO THE HYSTERICAL LITTLE SCREAMS OF THE YO-YO IN THE STATE OF HIDALGO).

That about "not validating the political interests of false redeemers" is a... self-criticism? That about the "fragmentation of the Mexican nation"... does it refer to the orders obeyed at Los Pinos which are issued from Dublin? That about "we cannot accept that demagogic positions be nurtured under the guise of the indigenous cause and illegitimate aspirations for power"... does it mean that the PRI will modify its electoral strategy? And, last of all, were the red bandannas awarded to the "vote carriers" (well, that way we may save...) (Remember Salinas and the "vote carriers" inaugurating the hospital at Guadalupe Tepeyac).

P.S. WHICH ACTUALIZES A STORY WHICH IS 174 YEARS OLD.

"Once there was a parrot which knew no other word except 'victory'. Yes sir, days came and went, and in one of them when our poor parrot was sitting carelessly on its perch, a hawk put its eye on it and carried it away through the airs of God. Looking at the sad green between its claws, it began to complain, but it could not say any other word except the one it knew by memory. Each peck the hawk took out of it would elicit a yell of 'victory'; another peck, another 'victory'; and in this way it was ripped apart as it said 'victory' all the while..." (The Victory of the Parrot. The Mexican Thinker. Jose Joaquin Fernandez de Lizardi, October 11, 1823). Today, "victory" is substituted by "democracy", "independence" or "justice". The role of the parrot can be played by any bureaucrat of your preference.

P.S. FOR LOCAL ACCOMPLICES.

Speaking of anniversaries and lies, Mister Ruiz Ferro marks two years since he usurped the Chiapanecan government. In exchange for not being sent to Almoloya (the prison), Ferro dictates editorials and news bulletins while the military govern. In Ecuador, the hypocrites and pretenders are expelled, in Chiapas they are appointed interim governors.

P.S. Which says what should be said. It rained a lot. The sea of rain rocked the tiredness which love had given it and on the little cassette player, Mercedes Sosa unthreaded that song which said: "My thanks to life which has given me so much…"

It was dawn and the airplane had already growled death over the dark mountains of the Mexican southeast. I was remembering Neftali Reyes, the self-named "Pablo Neruda" in that poem which says: "May the hour arrive at its time in that pure instant, and may the people fill the empty streets with their fresh and firm dimension. Here is my tenderness until then. You are familiar with it. I have no other banner." The clock of the war marked February 14th 1997. 10 years earlier in 1987 it rained the same. There was no sea of rain, nor tape recorder, nor airplane, only the dawn circled our guerrilla camp. Old Man Antonio came to chat. He arrived with the afternoon and a sack of tostadas. There was no one else in the kitchen of the camp besides he and I. The pipe and the rolled cigarette competed with the smoke which came out of the folds of the fire. We could not speak however, except by yelling. It seemed silent, but the rain shredded every corner of the night and there was not a sane part anywhere. The noise of rain hung on the roof of trees the mountain used to cloak itself, and another noisy rain was on the ground. Double was the noise of the rain below, and the one filtered by the trees above, and the one which already made the ground moan. In the middle, there was another sound, the one from the plastic sheets we used as cover which spoke the rain of February in the jungle. Noise above, below, in the middle. There was no corner for the word. That is why I was surprised when I clearly heard the voice of Old Man Antonio who, without losing the rolled cigarette from his lips, began to tell a story…

The Story of the Noise and the Silence

"Once there was a moment in time, when time did not measure itself. In that time, the greatest gods, the ones who birthed the world, were walking as gods do, dancing of course. There was much noise at that time, from every direction came voices and yells. There was much noise, and none could be understood. And it was that the noise there was, was not for understanding anything, but for NOT understanding anything. At first, the first gods believed that the noise was music and dance and quickly they chose a partner and began to dance like that," and Old Man Antonio stood up and tried a dance step which consisted of standing on one foot and then the other.

"But it seems as though the noise was not music or dance it was only noise, and so one could not be dancing and be happy. Then the great gods stopped to listen attentively because they wanted to know what it was the noise was saying, but they couldn't because it was only noise. And since one cannot dance to noise, the first gods, the ones who birthed the world could no longer walk because they could only do so by dancing so they were saddened by having to stop because the first gods were fervent walkers, the first ones. And one of the gods tried to walk or to dance himself with the noise but could not because the step would be lost and on the path one would run into the other, trip and fall with rocks and trees and hurt themselves."

Old Man Antonio stopped to re-light the cigarette the rain and the noise had extinguished. After the fire, the smoke came, after the smoke came the word.

"Then the gods searched for silence in order to re-orient themselves, but they could not find it anywhere, they did not know where it had gone. And the gods became desperate because they could not find the silence which held the path and so in an assembly of gods they came to an agreement which was very difficult because of all the noise. They finally agreed that each should seek a silence in order to find themselves and they began to look to the sides and could find nothing above and there was nothing below and since there was no other place to find the silence, they looked inside themselves and there they sought silence and found it there and found one another and found their path once again, those great gods who birthed the world, the first ones."

Old Man Antonio was silent, the rain was silent as well. The silence was short. Quickly the crickets came to tear apart the past pieces of that night of ten years ago.

The mountain had dawned when Old Man Antonio said good bye with a "I arrived". And I stayed smoking the little pieces of silence which the dawn had forgotten on the mountains of the Mexican southeast.

Vale once again. Health and may the noise lead you to find the silence once again, may the silence help you to find the path, and may the path help us to find one another...

The Sup sneezing because of the "demagogic positions and illegitimate aspirations for political power" being played out on a wet ceiba tree.

39. LETTER TO INDIGENOUS LEADERSHIP IN U.S.

March of 1997

To: The Leadership of the Indigenous Peoples of the United States of America

From: Subcomandante Insurgente Marcos, CCRI of the EZLN

Brother and Sisters,

I write these words to you in the name of the children, elders, men and women, all of them Indigenous Mexicans, of the Zapatista communities in the Mexican Southeast. We want you to receive our recognition of your stature as Indigenous peoples and human beings, and we want you to accept our salute sent by my hands from all the indigenous rebels of the Zapatista Army of National Liberation.

We have taken up arms against the bad Mexican government because the demands of the indigenous peoples have not been resolved. The Indian peoples, for the Mexican government and the great Power which sustains it, are nothing more than objects for tourism, producers of arts and crafts, an uncomfortable nuisance for neo-liberal modernization. For the powerful in Mexico, the indigenous are not human beings with rights and legitimate aspirations, they are only museum pieces and legends and past histories. But our indigenous communities want a life with dignity and justice, a life where they can continue to be indigenous without it signifying misery and death, a life with respect. This is why we declared our selves as rebels and why we have said "Enough is Enough" to the oblivion with which they want to annihilate us.

Today we await a response for peace from the government of Mexico which has not arrived. Not respect, or a life with dignity, or a new peace has been acknowledged by the Mexican government to the indigenous people of these lands. The powerful see us as small and weak and they believe they can conquer us and make us surrender with their great machines of war. The big North American government supports the government of Mexico. With money, machines of war and military advisors, the government of the USA supports the persecution and assassination of Mexican indigenous blood. The money, equipment, weapons, and the military advisors are not used by the government of Mexico to improve lives of its inhabitants, to combat drug trafficking and to bring peace to Mexican lands. No, that money, those people and those weapons are used to asphyxiate, to persecute, jail and assassinate an attempt at indigenous dignity.

But our struggle is not just that of the Zapatistas of the EZLN, our struggle is that of all the Indian peoples of America, the struggle to recognize our differences and our right to an inclusive autonomy, which makes us a part of, with full rights, the great human concert.

That is why we direct our small words to you. You, the Leaders of the dignified Indian peoples of North America, have the true word and the path of dignity. Your great wise men have shown you the path for understanding justice in the cries of the first peoples of Mexican lands. You will know how to understand our cries, and we are sure, you will know how to extend to us your hearts and your hands in order to achieve the peace which we desire and we deserve.

Your word is heard with attention and respect by the big government of the United States of America, that is why we ask you to support us with your mediation. We do not want the war, nor what does not belong to us, nor our destruction or enslavement. We want peace, we want to conquer our right to become better human beings, we want to create our world and be respected inside it, we want liberty.

We ask you, great leaders of the Indian peoples of North America, to intervene before the powerful who governs the United States of America and to tell him to stop his support for the war against our people and the persecution of our ideals. We serve no foreign interest, we serve only our history and our desires for dignity, democracy, liberty and justice.

We ask this of you, great Indian leaders. We ask for your support and your accompaniment in a struggle which is that of all human beings in any part of the world, the struggle for liberty.

Vale. Health to you and may the earth which is mother and root nurture tomorrow.

From the Mountains of the Mexican Southeast,
Subcomandante Insurgente Marcos.
Mexico, March of 1997.

40. To the Solidarity Committees of the Zapatista Struggle in All the World

March of 1997
(When the 20th Century hurries to go to sleep in the place where history, in other words, we have assigned it).
To: The solidarity committees of the Zapatista struggle in all the world
Planet Earth

Brothers and sisters,

Greetings and health to you. We are still here, we continue here. The night above is barely a gray reflection of the night below. For some reason, here the night below is always more night than the night above. I'm unaware whether the same thing happens in other parts or whether it is vice versa. Finally, the dawn. Perhaps because of the dark night or the "vice versa" of the reflection, the memory of the poem which Do-re-mi (or was it Mi-re-do?) recited to Alice in "The other side of the looking glass". The poem was called "The Walrus and the Carpenter" and it begins like this:

> *"THE SUN SHINES ABOVE THE SEA*
> *WITH ALL ITS STRENGTH*
> *SO THAT THE WAVES COULD APPEAR,*
> *SMOOTH AND BRILLIANT,*
> *A RARE THING THIS WAS*
> *BECAUSE IT WAS THE DARKEST NIGHT."*

And given that the sea with its strength and the sea with its insistence, a kind of urgent whim came upon me to write to you in order to chat, and say hello, or simple to have a pretext and attempt to build a multiple bridge, a walking octopus which arrives at the same time at the European continent as the Asian, which plants an arm on Australia and another in Africa, which rests one of its many arms on whatever American corner there is where rebellion is a banner. Here, in this fragmented piece of mirror of rebellion in the world, the March Hare awakens and stretches out among rains and suns which take turns at disordering the weather and the hours...

And speaking of hours, the hour arrives for us to sit down, together once again, those who are so similar in our differences who are us and all of you... But, well, this is not (not yet anyway) the purpose of this letter. What is it then? Well, strictly speaking, the object of this letter is the paper, the ink and the heart which dresses as one and covers itself with the other in order to extend a long bridge which can cross languages, colors, cultures, borders, armies, police and a considerable amount of kilometers by air-sea-land, which can arrive at that other heart which you (and us) carry in our left side.

And therefore, supposing that the bridge has been extended and the hearts have been found, from here goes a greeting for all of you, from the men, women, children, and elderly of the Zapatista Army of National Liberation.

From this side of the greeting and the bridge, in the national Power under which we Mexicans suffer, the hour becomes "showtime", time for the spectacle. Just like in a three ring circus, the Power in Mexico photographs itself in tragi-comedies, its corruption revealed and exposed, its demagoguery dressed in modernity, in a strident and brash supermarket of electoral political proposals. There is a lot of time for the spectacle, little time for democracy, much less for justice and nothing for liberty. The large and small trip over themselves in order to march to the rhythm marked by the Power. In the middle of the hurry to arrive, the question "Where are we going?" indefinitely postpones the solution.

Outside this time for lamentable spectacles, the time for the small ones reflects and looks inside in order to find themselves with the other small ones of Mexico and the world. great in the multiplication of hopes offered by your walk, we find within ours, in others, with you, the breath which dignity demands as nutrition, hope as direction, the patient and tender fury of he who knows that strength lies in the reason which moves it.

The dismissal of the San Andres agreements by the government has served for something positive. Now it is clear that the indigenous demands of the EZLN do not solely belong to Chiapas. They respond to the aspirations of all the Indian peoples of these lands and they reflect, with their specific particularities, the aspirations of the indigenous people of all the American continent.

A spokesperson for the Power in Mexico has said recently that the government does not need the Internet in order to demonstrate its disposition for a dialogue with the indigenous Zapatistas. It is obvious that, for the monologue which it simulates, it needs nothing... maybe only a mirror. But more than one demonstrated in the tone of the powerful bureaucrat a sensation of frustration and rancor due to the ruckus which circulated in cyberspace. Letters and manifestos, directed to who is supposed to be the president of Mexico, molest the government because one and the others demand the same; that the government of Mexico keep its word given in the dialogue of San Andres. Some of those letters reached the Mexican press, the majority do not. With an apparent national indifference they try to cover up the international restlessness with a government incapable of a political solution to a situation which it provokes with a military argument. The demands to comply with the agreements are received by the government, they arrive from all over the world. The government does not listen, or it appears not to listen. And if you could see, over here the Supreme only have ears for praise and gratitude... and of course, the orders of the financial Power.

This bothers the Mexican government. Not only those protests and demands in the Internet but the mobilizations in front of the embassies and consulates all over the world.

And since we are chatting, let me relate something which, well understood is only a timid homage to the efforts all of you make to help us and not to forget us again.

Over here they tell a story of the local agent of foreign sales (the real occupation of the self-named Mexican "Secretary of exterior relations") who prepared himself conscientiously on the eve of a visit to the exterior, to explain the problems of corruption, drug trafficking and elections in Mexico, and in order to pacify the so-called investors with great political and military plans of control, and of course, appetizing merchandise. But this was not much use to him because, after the "brilliant" speech of the traveling salesmen, the foreign spokesperson weighed him down with questions about the negotiation with the EZLN and the reasons why they remain suspended. The Mexican bureaucrat pulled out a map of Mexico in order to show the foreigner how the EZLN was only a tiny problem in a tiny corner of the tiny Mexican southeast, and that it was perfectly besieged and controlled by the powerful military forces of the federal government. As a response, the foreigner showed him a pile of papers with cyberspace messages and clippings of newspapers which told of the mobilizations in front of embassies and consulates in various parts of the world. The Mexican (who aspires to become a citizen of money) argued that subversion has many ramifications in the world, and that the attempts to destabilize would fail, that a few "HACKERS" (I think that's what they call cyberspace pirates) did not have a reason to impact the solid commercial exchange which the bountiful Mexican State etceteras...

The foreigner interrupted him and made it clear; "These mobilizations are not about subversion and the messages are not promoted instability. They are simply asking that the Mexican government keep its word. Whether they are a few, well, millions all over the world use the Internet and the mobilizations in Europe and the United States include dozens of thousands. They all say the same thing; keep your word."

There was a small respite and the foreigner added: "Tell me something in confidence, why don't you comply with what you signed? If the Mexican government is afraid of being fragmented, it should look at the example of other countries which recognized and legislated autonomies and did not fall apart. On the contrary, those who did not do this have broken up into many pieces. But, in any case, why did you sign something which you are not willing to fulfill? Are we to believe as well that the agreements signed with us will not be kept? No sir, is Gurria your name? No, there is more. Now tell me, what is the Mexican government afraid of?"

The businessman disguised as a Mexican bureaucrat shook, as did his foreign counterpart when he answered: "Tomorrow..."

"Bah! It's useless to speak of awakening him," said Do-re-mi, "since you are one of the things in his dreams. You know perfectly well that you are not real."

"I am real!" said Alice, and she began to cry.

Lewis Carroll, "The Other Side of the Looking Glass"

From this side of the bridge and the greeting, the medium and small struggles (the large ones are neither here nor there) demand of you your forces and attention. The Power rehearses magic acts and tricks, noises of all kind and origin, so that you will not look far. Nevertheless, you have taken the time and ingenuity to extend your support and your sympathy which refreshes us. While the Power has done all within its power to erase us from the map of actual history, you have taken the word and the streets (the asphalt ones and the media ones) in order to remind us, and in passing the Mexican government, that we are not alone.

We know little of your struggles. The bridge your generosity has extended to us in order to hear the world of the indigenous Zapatistas has only begun its return flight. With surprise and admiration we begin to recognize your collective histories of rebellion and resistance, your struggles against racism, against patriarchy, against religious intolerance, against xenophobia, against militarization, against ecological destruction, against fascism, against segregation, against moral hypocrisy, against exclusion, against the war, against hunger, against the lack of housing, against great capital, against authoritarianism, against dictatorship, against the politics of economic liberalization, against poverty, against robbery, against corruption, against discrimination, against stupidity, against the lie, against ignorance, against slavery, against injustice, against oblivion, against neoliberalism, for humanity...

And for humanity and against neoliberalism is what announces the new encounter of rebellions and resistance which appear this year. Then and there, we will have learned more from you and from all the pieces, disperse as yet, of the crystal which dignity preserves even within the best men and women of humanity.

So here, taking advantage of the trip, we want to send our thanks for turning to look at us and for the hand which you extend to us so we will not fall once again into oblivion. Some time ago we sent you a flower. Today we send you a little cloud of rain from here, so that you may water that flower, as you should, by dancing.

Vale. Health and may the joy of rebellion continue to fill the streets of all the continents.

> *From the mountains of the Mexican Southeast,*
> *Subcomandante Insurgente Marcos.*
> *Mexico, March of 1997.*

41. Marcos on May day, Tupac Amaru and Fidel Velazquez

To the National and International Press

Ladies and Gentlemen,

Here goes a letter for a powerful Priista politician. No, I'm not talking about Zedillo, but about Fidel Velazquez. We are well, some days ago we heard by radio the news of the military assault on the Japanese Embassy in Peru. The great international Power decided upon a new crime in Latin-American lands and ordered the assassination of the rebels of Tupac Amaru (who, let us not forget, was negotiating with the government of Fujimori a solution to the crisis) and one of the personages who had been detained. You will all recall that there was a search for a resolution to the problem without violence. But the military went in accompanied by gunfire. "Clean operation", said the news programs. And they described Fujimori as smiling and happy. And, way above him, the supranational powers, which had given the order for annihilation also, smiled. For months, the Peruvian government pretended to negotiate in order to find a peaceful solution. In reality it only searched for the precise moment to strike. That is how they are, the Power and its neoliberal governments, they pretend to dialogue and negotiate, when in reality they only seek the opportunity to exert their violence.

This new tragic episode for Latin America is an international blow to the path of dialogue and negotiation as a viable means of resolving conflicts.

Fujimori and his bosses hurry to smile. The consent for Zedillo was also hurried. But a lot of history remains to be written.

And to think they have told us we should wait, not for an attack, but for the compliance to the agreements that were signed by the government.

> *From the Japanese embassy, oops;*
> *from the mountains of the Mexican Southeast,*
> *The Sup who is so afraid he got diarrhea.*
> *Mexico, April 25th of 1997.*

42. Letter to "Commander in Chief Zapata"

April 10, 1997
To: General Emiliano Zapata
Top Commander in Chief of the Zapatista Army of National Liberation
Over there, where he usually lives

My General,

With the novelty that we are still here. Don Emiliano, here we are. You probably already know that I am writing to you in the name of all men, women, children, and the elderly of this your Zapatista Army of National Liberation.

Here we are, my General, here we remain. Here we are because these governments continue to display a lack memory towards the Indians and because the rich landowners, with different names, keep on stripping the farmers of their land. Like when you called to fight for land and liberty, today the Mexican lands are turned over to the wealthy foreigners. Like it happened then, today, governments make up laws to legitimize the theft of lands. Like then, those who refuse to accept injustices, are persecuted, jailed, killed. But just like then, my General, there are righteous men and women who do not keep silent and fight not to be victimized, they organize to demand land and liberty. That is why I write to you Don Emiliano, so that you know that we are here, that we continue to be here.

You already remember what you wrote to a Gringo president named Woodrow Wilson, because it is good that foreign governments know and understand the struggle of the Mexican people. And then you wrote him that part which said... "And it is that the large landowners, stripping by stripping, today with one pretext, tomorrow with another, have been absorbing all the properties which legitimately belong and have belonged from time immemorial to the Indigenous people, out of whose cultivation they used to get their sustenance and that of their families." And that was in 1914. Now, in 1997, the story hasn't changed.

There are now laws which attack the communal property and the "ejido", which favor the monopolizing of lands, which allow the sale of our riches to the foreigner's monies. And the laws were drafted by the bad Mexican governments, we call them "neoliberal", which rule this country, yours and ours, my General, as if it were an Hacienda in full decadence, a large property which must be advertised for sale with all of its peons, that is to say with all Mexicans, my General, included in the bargain. Yes, you are right Don Emiliano, it is a shame. And we could no longer live nor die with such a shame and then we remembered the word "dignity" and we remembered to live by it and die by it, and so we rose up in arms, and we tell everyone that it is enough, that this is as far as they get, that no more, that we demanded shelter, land, bread, health, education, independence, democracy, liberty and peace, and that we say that everything is included in democracy, liberty, and justice, and that everything for everyone and nothing for ourselves, and many ears and hearts listened to your words, my General, which were spoken through us.

As in your time, Don Emiliano, the governments have tried to deceive us. They talk and talk and no promises are kept, except for the killings of farmers. They sign and sign papers and nothing materializes, except for the evictions of Indigenous people and their persecution. And they have also betrayed us, my General, and Guajardos and Chinamecas (ref. to the town in the state of Morelos where Carranza had Zapata murdered) have not lacked, but it turns out that we don't allow ourselves to get killed that easily. It looks as if we learned something, Don Emiliano, as if we are still learning. So that I don't want to bore you, my General, what would be the sense of it if these are things you already know, since when all is said and done you are us. And you see, the farmers keep on being landless, the Indians keep on being forgotten, the bad governments continue, the rich keep on getting fatter, and, that's for sure, the peasant rebellions continue. And they will continue my General, because without land and liberty there is no peace.

Now the governments are saying that there is no war because the law says there is no war. But there is, my General, that is why we are your army, because before, the war was only from there to here, and now it will also be from here to there. And if they want to kill farmers then governments will have to die. Because just demands are not answered with death, because death will bounce back. If only the demands for democracy, liberty and justice were to be answered with truth, history would dance to a different tune. But not now, my General, now that dance they call history does so to a tune of sheer destruction...

But like in those days, my General, there are now people with great thoughts and a big heart. There is, for instance, a gentleman by the name of Fernando Benitez, who wrote a great work called "The Indians of Mexico" and in that work he explains that modern history, the one written by governments and by the powerful, was made to render the Indigenous population invisible. That's what bad governments usually do, Don Emiliano, you know that. They think that by forgetting or killing a problem they solve it. But this problem we Indians represent we will not let it be forgotten. We have to fight to have a place in this country and in its history, the true one, we have to make ourselves visible, to make them see us, to make them take us into account. And that can only happen with justice.

And yes, my General, just like you, we understood that land and liberty, that memory in other words, can only become true in justice. That is why we rose up in arms, like you taught us, Don Emiliano, for liberty and justice. And we also saw, like you did, that they could only be gotten through democracy. And we understand, like you, that we have to fight against the bad governments to obtain what is ours.

The landless farmers in Mexico are many, Don Emiliano, as many are the forgotten Indians. They are both obstacles for the bad governments and the very wealthy. They both are persecuted by the armies and the police forces, as criminal as those who give them orders. But the landless Indigenous people and farmers, the many that are not many are many also in the rebellion and the struggle. We are like you, my general, exactly like that, rebellious and struggling.

And I was only writing to you, my General, to tell you that here we are, here we remain, and here we will remain even if they persecute us with weapons and lies, even if they want to buy us, even if they want to deceive us, even if they want to forget us. Here we are going to remain because we listened with our innermost being and we made ours those words of yours which say: "Let us keep on fighting and let us vanquish those who have recently become powerful, who help those who take lands away from others, those who make a lot of money for themselves out of the work of those who are like us, those deceivers in the haciendas, that is our honorable duty, if we want to be called men of a good life and truly good inhabitants of the community".

As a final note I only want to tell you Don Emiliano so you get to laugh for a while, that these bad governments we have, still believe they were able to assassinate you that April afternoon in 1919. They don't know you didn't die, that you simply became us and that you thus went on hiding and reappearing in us and in all the landless peasants, in all the forgotten Indians. You see, my General, how short of memory these governments are. They forget the most important thing, what you and us know well, Don Emiliano, that is, that Zapata lives, that the struggle continues.

"Vale" my General Zapata. Health and plenty of heart, because there are still many accounts left to settle in the Mexican lands.

> From the mountains of the Mexican Southeast,
> For the Indigenous Revolutionary Clandestine Committee
> -General Command of the Zapatista Army of National Liberation.
> Mexico, April 10, 1997.

43. THE SEVEN LOOSE PIECES OF THE GLOBAL JIGSAW PUZZLE (NEOLIBERALISM AS A PUZZLE)

"War is a matter of vital importance for the State, it is the province of life and death, the path which leads to survival or annihilation. It is indispensable to study it at length."
- The Art of War, Sun Tzu.

Modern globalization, neoliberalism as a global system, should be understood as a new war of conquest for territories. The end of the World War III or "Cold War" does not mean that the world has overcome the polarity and finds its stability under the hegemony of the victor. At the end of this war there was, without doubt a loser (the socialist camp), but it is difficult to say who was the victor. Western Europe? The United States? Japan? All of them? The fact is that the defeat of the "evil empire" (Dixit Reagan and Thatcher) signified the opening of new markets without a new owner. Therefore a struggle was needed in order to possess them, to conquer them.

Not only that, but the end of the "Cold War" brought with it a new framework of international relations in which the new struggle for those new markets and territories produced a new world war, the IV. This required, as do all wars, a redefinition of the national states. And beyond the redefinition of the national states, the world order returned to the old epochs of the conquests of America, Africa and Oceania.

This is a strange modernity that moves forward by going backward. The dusk of the 20th century has more similarities with previous brutal centuries than with the placid and rational future of some science-fiction novel. In the world of the Post-Cold War vast territories, wealth, and above all, a skilled labor force, await a new owner.

But it is a position of owner of the world, and there are many who aspire to it. And in order to win it another war breaks out, but now among those who call themselves the "Good Empire".

If the World War III was between capitalism and socialism (lead by the United States and the USSR respectively) with different levels of intensity and alternating scenarios; the Fourth World War occurs now among the great financial centers, with complete scenarios and with a sharp and constant intensity.

Since the end of the Second World War until 1992, there have been 149 wars in all the world. The results are 23 million dead, and therefore there is no doubt about the intensity of this Third World War (Statistical source: UNICEF). From the catacombs of international espionage to the astral space of the so-called Strategic Defense Initiative (the "Star Wars" of the cowboy Ronald Reagan); from the sands of Playa Giron, in Cuba, to the Mekong Delta in Vietnam; from the unbridled nuclear arms war to the savage blows of the State in the tormented Latin America; from the ominous maneuvers of the armies of the North Atlantic Treaty Organization to the CIA agents in the Bolivia which oversaw the assassination of Che Guevara; the badly-named "Cold War" reached temperatures which, in spite of the continuous change of scenery and the incessant ups-and downs of the nuclear crisis (and precisely because of that) ended up sinking the socialist camp as a global system, and diluted it as a social alternative.

The Third World War showed the magnanimity of the "complete war" (in all places and in all forms) for the victor: capitalism. But the scenario of the post-war was profiled in fact, as a new theater of global operations. Great extensions of "No man's land" (because of the political, social and economic devastation of Eastern Europe and the USSR), world powers in expansion (The United States, Western Europe and Japan), a world economic crisis, and a new technological revolution: the revolution of information. "In the same way in which the industrial revolution had allowed the replacement of muscle by the machine, the information revolution replaced the brain (or at least a growing number of its important functions) by the computer." This "general cerebralization" of the means of production (the same as occurred in industry as in services) is accelerated by the explosion of new telecommunications research and the proliferation of the cyberworlds." (Ignacio Ramonet "La planete des desordres" in the "Geopolitique du Chaos" Maniere de Voir 3. Le Monde Diplomatique (LMD), April of 1997.)

The supreme kind of capital, financial capital, began then to develop its strategy of war towards the new world and over what was left of the old. Hand in hand with the technological revolution which placed the entire world, through a computer, on its desk and at its mercy, the financial markets imposed their laws and precepts on the entire planet. The "globalization" of the new war is nothing more than the globalization of the logic of the financial markets. The National States (and their leaders) went from being directors of the economy to those who were directed, better said tele-directed, by the basic premise of financial power: free commercial exchange. Not only that, but the logic of the market took advantage of the "porosity" which in all the social spectrum of the world, provoked the development of telecommunications and penetrated and appropriated all the aspects of social activity. Finally there was a global war which was total!

One of the first casualties of this new war was the national market. Like a flying bullet inside an armored room, the war begun by neoliberalism bounced from one side to the other and wounded the one who had fired it. One of the fundamental bases of power in the modern capitalist State, the national market, was liquidated by the shot fired by the new era of the financial global economy. International capital took some of its victims by dismantling national capitalism and wearing it out, until it disabled its public powers. The blow has been so brutal and definitive that the national States do not have the necessary strength to oppose the action of the international markets which transgress the interests of citizens and governments.

The careful and ordered escapade which the "Cold War" handed down, the "new world order" quickly became pieces due to the neoliberal explosion. World capitalism sacrificed without mercy that which gave it a future and a historic project; national capitalism. Companies and States fell apart in minutes, but not due to the torments of proletarian revolutions, but the stalemates of financial hurricanes. The child (neoliberalism) ate the father (national capitalism) and in passing destroyed all of the discursive fallacies of capitalist ideology: in the new world order there is no democracy, liberty, equality, nor fraternity.

In the global scenario which is a product of the end of the "Cold War" all which is perceptible is a new battleground and in this one, as in all battlegrounds, chaos reigns.

At the end of the "Cold war" capitalism created a new bellicose horror: the neutron bomb. The "virtue" of this weapon is that it only destroys life and leaves buildings intact. Entire cities could be destroyed (that is, their inhabitants) without the necessity of reconstructing them (and paying for them). The arms industry congratulated itself. The "irrationality" of nuclear bombs could be replaced by the new "rationality" of the neutron bomb. But a new bellicose "marvel" would be discovered at the same time as the birth of the Fourth World War: the financial bomb.

The new neoliberal bomb, different from its atomic predecessor in Hiroshima and Nagasaki, did not only destroy the polis (the Nation in this case) and imposed death, terror and misery to those who lived in it: or, different from the neutron bomb, did not solely destroy "selectively". The neoliberal bomb, reorganized and reordered what it attacked and remade it as a piece inside a jigsaw puzzle of economic globalization. After its destructive effect, the result is not a pile of smoking ruins, or tens of thousands of inert lives, but a neighborhood attached to one of the commercial megalopolis of the new world supermarket and a labor force rearranged in the new market of world labor.

The European union, one of the megalopolis produced by neoliberalism, is a result of the Fourth World War. Here, economic globalization erased the borders between rival States, long-time enemies, and forced them to converge and consider political unity. From the National States to the European federation, the economist path of the neoliberal war in the so-called "old continent" would be filled with destruction and ruins, one of which was European civilization.

The megalopolis reproduced themselves in all the planet. The integrated commercial zones were the territory where they were erected. So it was in North America, where the North American Free Trade Agreement between Canada, the United States and Mexico is no more than the prelude to the fulfillment of an old aspiration of U.S. manifest destiny: "America for Americans". In South America the path is the same in terms of Mercosur between Argentina, Brazil, Paraguay and Uruguay. In Northern Africa, with the Union of Arab States (UMA) between Morocco, Algeria, Tunis, Libya and Mauritania; in south Africa, in the Near East, in the Black Sea, in Pacific Asia, etc., all over the planet the financial bombs explode and territories are reconquered.

Do the megalopolis substitute the nations? No, or not only. They also include them and reassign their functions, limits and possibilities. Entire nations are converted into departments of the neoliberal megacompany. Neoliberalism thus operated DESTRUCTION/DEPOPULATION on the one hand, and RECONSTRUCTION/REORGANIZATION on the other, of regions and of nations in order to open new markets and renovate the existing ones.

If the nuclear bombs have a dissuasive, coercive, and intimidating character in World War III, in the IV global conflagration the financial hyperbombs play the same role. These weapons serve to attack territories (National States) DESTROYING the material bases of national sovereignty (all the ethical, judicial, political, cultural and historic obstacles against economic globalization) and producing a qualitative depopulation on their territories. This depopulation consists in detaching all those who are useless to the new market economy (as are the indigenous).

But, in addition to this, the financial centers operate, simultaneously a RECONSTRUCTION of the National States and they REORGANIZE them according to the new logic of the global market (the developed economic models are imposed upon weak or non-existing social relations).

The World War IV in rural areas, for example, produces this effect. Rural renovation, demanded by the financial markets, tries to increase agricultural productivity, but what it does is to destroy traditional economic and social relations. The results: a massive exodus from the countryside to the cities. Yes, just as in a war. Meanwhile, in the urban zones the market is saturated with labor and the unequal distribution of salaries is the "justice" which await those who seek better conditions of life.

Examples which illustrate this strategy fill the indigenous world. Ian Chambers, director of the Office for Central America of the ILO (of the United Nations), declared that the indigenous population of the world, estimated at 300 million, live in zones which have 60% of the natural resources of the planet.

Therefore the "MULTIPLE CONFLICTS DUE TO THE USE AND FINAL DESTINATION OF THEIR LANDS AS DETERMINED BY THE INTEREST OF GOVERNMENTS AND COMPANIES IS NOT SURPRISING(...)THE EXPLOITATION OF NATURAL RESOURCES (OIL AND MINERALS) AND TOURISM ARE THE PRINCIPAL INDUSTRIES WHICH THREATEN INDIGENOUS TERRITORIES IN AMERICA" (interview with Martha Garcia in "La Jornada". May 28, 1997). Behind the investment projects comes the pollution, prostitution and drugs. In other words, the reconstruction/reorganization of the destruction/depopulation of the zone.

In this new world war, modern politics as the organizer of National States no longer exists. Now politics is solely the economic organizer and politicians are the modern administrators of companies. The new owners of the world are not government, they don't need to be. The "national" governments are in charge of administering the businesses in the different regions of the world.

This is the "new world order", the unification of the entire world in one complete market. Nations are department stores with CEO's dressed as governments, and the new regional alliances, economic and political, come closer to being a modern commercial "mall" than a political federation. The "unification" produced by neoliberalism is economic, it is the unification of markets to facilitate the circulation of money and merchandise. In the gigantic global Hypermarket merchandise circulates freely, not people.

As in all business initiatives (and war), this economic globalization is accompanied by a general model of thought. Nevertheless, among so many new things, the ideological model which accompanies neoliberalism in its conquest of the planet is old and moss-covered. The "American way of life" which accompanied the Northamerican troops in Europe during World War II, and in Vietnam during the 60's and more recently, in the Persian Gulf War, now goes hand in hand (or hand in computers) with the financial markets.

This is not only about material destruction of the material bases of the National States, but also (and in a very important and rarely-studied manner) about historic and cultural destruction. The dignity of indigenous history of the countries of the American continent, the brilliance of European civilization, the historic wisdom of Asian nations, and the powerful and rich antiquity of Africa and Oceania, all the cultures and histories which forged nations are attacked by the model of Northamerican life. Neoliberalism in this way imposes a total war: the destruction of nations and groups of nations in order to homogenize them with the Northamerican capitalist model.

A war then, a world war, the IV. The worst and cruelest. The one which neoliberalism unleashes in all places and by all means against humanity.

But, as in all wars, there are combats, winners and losers, and torn pieces of that destroyed reality. In order to construct the absurd jigsaw puzzle of the neoliberal world many pieces are necessary. Some can be found among the ruins this world war has left on the planetary surface. At least 7 of these pieces can be reconstructed and can fan the hope that this world conflict not end with the death of the weakest rival: humanity.

Seven pieces to draw, color, cut, and arrange, next to others to form the global jigsaw puzzle.

The first is the double accumulation, of wealth and poverty, at the two poles of global society. The other is the total exploitation of the totality of the world. The third is the nightmare of the migrant part of humanity. The fourth is the nauseating relationship between crime and Power. The fifth is the violence of the State. The sixth is the mystery of megapolitics. The seventh is the multi-forms of pockets of resistance of humanity against neoliberalism.

First Piece

The Concentration of Wealth and the Distribution of Poverty.
The First Figure Can Be Constructed by Drawing a Dollar Sign.

In the history of humanity, different social models have fought to hoist the absurd as a distinctive world orders. Surely, neoliberalism will have a place of privilege at the time of the awards, because its "distribution" of social wealth does no more than distribute a double absurdity of accumulation: the accumulation of wealth in the hands of a few, and the accumulation of poverty in millions of human beings. In the actual world, injustice and inequality are distinctive characteristics. Planet earth, third of the solar planetary system, has 5 billion people. Of them, only 500 million live with comfort while 4 1/2 billion live in poverty and levels of subsistence.

Doubly absurd is the distribution among rich and poor: the rich are few and the poor are many. The quantitative difference is criminal, but the balance between the two extremes is secured with wealth: the rich supplement their small numbers with millions upon millions of dollars. The fortune of the 358 wealthiest people of the world (thousands of millions of dollars) is superior to the annual income of 45% of the poorest inhabitants, something like 2 1/2 billion people.

The gold chains of the financial watches are converted into a heavy chain for millions of beings. Meanwhile the "total number of transactions of General Motors is larger than the Gross National Product of Denmark, that of Ford is larger than the GNP of South Africa, and that of Toyota far surpasses the GNP of Norway" (Ignacio Ramonet, In LMD 1/1997 #15). For all workers real salaries have fallen, in addition to having to survive the personnel cuts in companies, the closing of factories and the relocation of workplaces. In the so-called "advanced capitalist economies" the number of unemployed has arrived at a total of 41 million workers.

Little by little, the concentration of wealth in the hands of a few and the distribution of poverty among many begins to trace the profile of modern global society: the fragile equilibrium of absurd inequalities.

The decadence of the neoliberal economic is a scandal: "The world debt (combining that of all companies, governments and administrations) has surpassed 33 trillion dollars, or 130% of the global GNP, and grows at a rate of 6 to 8% per year, more than 4 times the growth of the global GNP" (Frederic F. Clairmont. "Ces deux cents societes qui controlent le monde", in LMD, IV/1997).

The progress of the great transnationals does not imply the advancement of developed Nations. To the contrary, while the great financial giants earn more, poverty sharpens in the so-called "rich nations".

The chasm between the rich and poor is brutal and no tendency appears to the contrary, indeed it continues. Far from lessening, we won't say eliminating it, the social inequality is accentuated, above all in the developed capitalist nations: in the United States, 1% of the wealthiest Americans have conquered 61.6% of the total national wealth between 1983 and 1989. 80% of the poorest Northamericans share only 1.2% of the wealth. In Great Britain the number of homeless has grown; the number of children who survive on social welfare has gone from 7% in 1979 to 26% in 1994, the number of British who live in poverty (defined as less than half of minimum wage) has gone from 5 million to 13,700,000; 10% of the poorest have lost 13% of their purchasing power, while 10% of the richest have gained 65% and in a period of the past 5 years the number of millionaires has doubled (statistics from LMD,IV/97).

At the beginning of the decade of the 90's "...an estimated 37,000 transnational companies held, with their 170,000 subsidiaries, the international economy in its tentacles." Nevertheless, the center of power situates itself in the most restrictive circle of the first 200: since the beginnings of the 80's, they have had an uninterrupted expansion through mergers and "rescue" buy-outs of companies.

In this way, the part of transnational capital in the global GNP has gone from 17% in the middle of the 60's to 24% in 1982 and more than 30% in 1995. The first 200 are conglomerates whose planetary activities cover with distinction the primary, secondary, and tertiary sectors: great agricultural exploitation, manufacturing production, financial services, commercial, etc. Geographically, they are divided amongst 10 countries: Japan (62), the United States (53),Germany (23), France (19), United Kingdom (11), Switzerland (8), South Korea(6), Italy (5), and others (4)". (Frederic F. Clairmont, Op.Cit.).

THE "FIRST TWO HUNDRED" OF THE WORLD:

Country	Number of Companies	Businesses	Profits (billions)	% of Global Businesses	% of Global Profits
Japan	62	3,196	46.0	40.7%	18.3%
USA	53	1,198	98.0	25.4%	39.2%
Germany	23	786	24.5	10.0%	9.8%
France	19	572	16.0	7.3%	6.3%
U.K.	11	275	20.0	3.5%	8.0%
Switzerland	8	244	9.7	3.1%	3.9%
South Korea	6	183	3.5	2.3%	1.4%
Italy	5	171	6.0	2.2%	2.5%
UK/ *Lower Countries	2	159	9.0	2.0%	3.7%
*Lower Countries	4	118	5.0	1.5%	2.0%
Venezuela	1	26	3.0	0.3%	1.2%
Sweden	1	24	1.3	0.3%	0.5%
Belgium/ *Lower Countries	1	22	0.8	0.3%	0.3%
Mexico	1	22	1.5	0.3%	0.6%
China	1	19	0.8	0.2%	0.3%
Brazil	1	18	4.3	0.2%	1.7%
Canada	1	17	0.5	0.2%	0.2%
Totals	200	7,850	251.0	100%	100%
Global GNP			25,223.0		31.2%

(Frederic F. Clairmont. Op. Cit.)
  *LOWER COUNTRIES - loosely-translated as city-states, regions, autonomous zones

$$ Here you have the symbol of economic power. Now paint it the green of the dollar. Don't worry about the nauseating odor, the aroma of manure, mud, and blood which it carries since its birth...

Second Piece

The Globalization of Exploitation.

The Second Piece is Constructed by Drawing a Triangle.

One of the fallacies of neoliberalism is that economic growth of the companies brings with it a better distribution of wealth and a growth I employment. But this is not so. In the same way as the growth of political power of a king does not bring as a consequence a growth of political power of the subjects (to the contrary), the absolute power of financial capital does not better the distribution of wealth nor does it create major employment for society. Poverty, unemployment and instability of labor are its structural consequences.

During the years of the decades of 1960 and 70's, the population considered poor (with less than a dollar a day of income for their basic necessities, according to the World Bank) was about 200 million people. By the beginning of the decade of the 90's this number was about 2 billion. In addition to this the "mainstay of the 200 most important companies of the planet represent more than a quarter of the world's economic activity; and yet these 200 companies employ only 18.8 million employees, or less than 0.75% of the world's labor force" Ignacio Ramonet in LMD. January 1997, #15).

More poor human beings and an increase in the level of impoverishment, less rich and an increase in the level of wealth, these are the lessons of the outline of the First Piece of the neoliberal jigsaw puzzle. To achieve this absurdity, the world's capitalist system "modernizes" production, circulation and the consumption of merchandise. The new technological revolution (the information revolution) and the new political revolution (the emerging megalopolis on the ruins of the National States). This social "revolution" is no more than a readjustment, a reorganization of the social forces, principally the labor force.

The Economically Active Population on a global level went from 1,376 million in 1960 to 2,374 million workers in 1990. More human beings with the capacity to work, in other words, to generate wealth.

But the "new world order" not only rearranges this new labor force in geographic and productive spaces, it also reorders its place (or lack of a place, as in the case of the unemployed and subemployed) in the globalizing plan of the economy.

The World Population employed by sector was substantially changed in the last 20 years. In fishing and agriculture it went from 22% in 1970 to 12% I 1990; in manufacturing from 25% in 1970 to 22% in 1990; while in the tertiary sector (commerce, transport, banking and services) it grew from 42% in 1970 to 57% in 1990; while the population employed in the agricultural and fishing sector fell from 30% in 1970 to 15% in 1990 (Statistics from "The Labor Force in the World Market in Contemporary Capitalism". Ochoa Chi, Juanita del Pilar. UNAM. Economy. Mexico, 1997).

This means that each time more workers are channeled towards the necessary activities to increase production or to accelerate the elaboration of merchandise. The neoliberal system operates in this way like a mega-boss, conceiving the world market as a single company, administered with "modernizing" criteria.

But neoliberal modernity appears more like the beastly birth of capitalism as a world system, than like utopic "rationality". "Modern" capitalist production continues to base itself in the labor of children, women and migrant workers. Of the 1 billion, 148 million children in the world, at least 100 million of them live in the streets and almost 200 million of them work. It is expected that 400 million of them will be working by the year 2000. It is said as well that 146 million Asian children labor in the production of auto parts, toys, clothing, food, tools and chemicals. But this exploitation of child labor does not only exist in underdeveloped countries, 40% of English children and 20% of French children also work in order to complete the family income or to survive. In the "pleasure" industry there is also a place for children. The UN estimates that each year a million children enter sexual trafficking (Statistics in Ochoa Chi, J. Op. Cit.).

The neoliberal beast invades all the social world homogenizing even the lines of food production "in global terms if we observe particularities in the food consumption of each region (and its interior), the process of homogenization which is being imposed is evident, including over those physiological-cultural differences of the different zones" ("World Market of means of Subsistence. 1960-1990. Ocampo Figueroa, Nashelly, and Flores Mondragon, Gonzalo. UNAM. Economy.1994).

This beast imposes upon humanity a heavy burden. The unemployment and the instability of millions of workers all over the world is a cutting reality which has no horizons and no signs of lessening. Unemployment in the countries which make up the Organization for Cooperation and economic Development went from 3.8% in 1966 to 6.3% in 1990. In Europe alone it went from 2.2% in 1966 to 6.4% in 1990.

The imposition of the laws of the market all over the world, the global market, have done nothing but destroy small and medium-size businesses. Upon the disappearance of local and regional markets, the small and medium-size producers see themselves without protection and without any possibility of competing against gigantic transnationals.

The results: massive bankruptcy of companies.

The consequence; millions of unemployed workers.

The absurdity of neoliberalism repeats itself: growth in production does not generate employment, on the contrary, it destroys it. The UN calls this stage "Growth without employment."

But the nightmare does not end there. In addition to the threat of unemployment workers must confront precarious working conditions. Major on-the-job instability, longer working days and poor salaries, are consequences of globalization in general and the "tertiary" tendency of the economy (the growth of the "service" sector) in particular. "In the countries under domination, the labor force suffers a precarious reality: extreme mobility, jobs without contracts, irregular salaries and generally inferior to the vital minimum and regimes with emaciated retirement benefits, independent activities which are not declared and have hit-and-miss salaries, in other words, servitude or forced labor within populations which are supposedly protected such as children" (Alain Morice. "Foreign workers, advance sector of instability." LMD. January 1997).

The consequences of all this translates itself into a bottoming out of global reality. The reorganization of productive processes and the circulation of merchandise and readjustment of productive forces, produce a peculiar excess: left-over human beings, not necessary for the "new world order", who do not produce, or consume, who do not use credit, in sum, who are disposable.

Each day, the great financial centers impose their laws to nations and groups of nations in all the world They reorder and readjust their inhabitants. And, at the end of the operation, they find they have "left-over" people. "They fire upon the volume of the excess population, which is not only subjected to the brunt of the most cruel poverty, but which does not matter, which is loose and separate, and whose only end is to wander through the streets without a fixed direction, without housing or work, without family or social relations with a minimal stability, whose only company are its cardboard and plastic bags (Fernandez Duran, Ramon. "Against the Europe of capital and economic globalization". Talasa. Madrid, 1996).

Economic globalization "made necessary a decline in real salaries at the international level, which together with the reduction of social costs (health, education, housing and food) and an anti-union climate, came to constitute the fundamental part of the new neoliberal politics of capitalist reactivation (Ocampo F. and Flores M. Op. Cit.).

Third Piece

Migration, The Errant Nightmare.

The Third Figure is Constructed by Drawing a Circle.

We spoke beforehand of the existence of new territories, at the end of the Third World War, which awaited conquest (the old socialist countries), and of others which should have been re-conquered by the "new world order". In order to achieve it, the financial centers carried out a criminal and brutal third strategy; the proliferation of "regional wars" and "internal conflicts", which mobilized great masses of workers and allowed capital to follow routes of atypical accumulation.

The results of this world war of conquest was a great ring of millions of migrants in all the world. "Foreigners" in the world "without borders" which the victors of the Third World War promised. Millions of people suffered xenophobic persecution, precarious labor conditions, loss of cultural identity, police repression, hunger, prison, death.

"From the American Rio Grande to the "European" Schengen space, a double contradictory tendency is confirmed. On one side the borders are closed officially to the migration of labor, on the other side entire branches of the economy oscillate between instability and flexibility, which are the most secure means of attracting a foreign labor force" (Alain Morice, Op. Cit.).

With different names, under a judicial differentiation, sharing an equality of misery, the migrants or refugees or displaced of all the world are "foreigners" who are tolerated or rejected. The nightmare of migration, whatever its causes, continues to roll and grow over the planet's surface. The number of people who are accounted for in the statistics of the UN High Commission on Refugees has grown disproportionately from some 2 million in 1975 to 27 million in 1995.

With national borders destroyed (for merchandise) the globalized market organizes the global economy: research and design of goods and services, as well as their circulation and consumption are thought of in intercontinental terms. For each part of the capitalist process the "new world order" organizes the flow of the labor force, specialized or not, up to where it is necessary. Far from subjecting itself to the "free flow" so clucked-over by neoliberalism, the employment markets are each day determined more by migratory flows. Where skilled workers are concerned, whose numbers are not significance in the context of global migration, the "crossing of brains" represents a great deal in terms of economic power and knowledge. Nevertheless, whether skilled labor, or unskilled labor, the migratory politics of neoliberalism is oriented more towards destabilizing the global labor market than towards stopping immigration.

The Fourth World War, with its process of destruction/depopulation and reconstruction/reorganization provokes the displacement of millions of people. Their destiny is to continue to wander, with the nightmare at their side, and to offer to employed workers in different nations a threat to their employment stability, an enemy to hide the image of the boss, and a pretext for giving meaning to the racist nonsense promoted by neoliberalism.

This is the symbol of the errant nightmare of global migration, a ring of terror which roams all over the world.

Fourth Piece

Financial Globalization and the Globalization of Corruption and Crime.

The Fourth Figure is Constructed by Drawing a Rectangle.

The mass media reward us with an image of the directors of global delinquency: vulgar men and women, dressed outlandishly, living in ridiculous mansions or behind the bars of a jail. But that image hides more than it shows: the real bosses of the modern Mafiosi, or their organization, or their real influence in the political and economic regions are never divulged publicly.

If you think the world of delinquency is synonymous with the world beyond the grave and darkness, you are mistaken. During the period called the "Cold War", organized crime acquired a more respectable image and began to function like any other modern company. It also penetrated the political and economic systems of the national States. With the beginning of the Fourth World War, the implantation of the "new world order" and its accompanying opening of markets, privatization, deregulation of commerce and international finance, organized crime "globalized" its activities as well.

"According to the UN, the annual global income of transnational criminal organizations are about 1000 billion dollars, an amount equivalent to the combined GNP of countries with weak income (according to the categories of the global banks) and its 3 billion inhabitants. This estimate accounts for the product of drug trafficking, the illegal trafficking of arms, contraband of nuclear materials, etc., and the profits of activities controlled by the Mafiosi (prostitution, gambling, black market speculation...).

However, this does not measure the importance of investments which are continuously realized by criminal organizations within the sphere of control of legitimate businesses, nor the domination which they exert over the means of production within numerous sectors of the legal economy" (Michel Chossudovsky, "La Corruption mondialisee" in "Geopolitique du Chaos". Op. Cit.).

The criminal organizations of the 5 continents have made theirs the "spirit of global cooperation" and, associated, participate in the conquest and reorganization of the new markets. But they participate not only in criminal activities, but in legal businesses as well. Organized crime invests in legitimate businesses not only to "launder" dirty money, but to make capital for their illegal activities. The preferred business endeavors for this are luxury real estate, the vacation industry, mass media, industry, agriculture, public services and... banking!

Ali Baba and the 40 bankers? No, something worse. The dirty money of organized crime is utilized by the commercial banks for its activities: loans, investments in financial markets, purchase of bonds for foreign debt, buying and selling of gold and stocks. "In many countries, the criminal organizations have become the creditors of the States and they exert, because of their actions on the markets, an influence over the macroeconomic politics of the governments. Over the stock markets, they invest equally in the speculative markets of finished products and raw materials" (M. Chossudovsky, Op. Cit.)

As if this were not enough, organized crime can count on the so-called fiscal paradises. There are all over the world at least 55 fiscal paradises (One of these, the Cayman Islands, has fifth place in the world as a banking center and has more banks and registered companies than inhabitants). The Bahamas, the British Virgin Islands, the Bermudas, Saint Martin, Vanuatu, the Cook Islands, Luxembourg, Maurice Island, Switzerland, the Anglo-Normandy Islands, Dublin, Monaco, Gibraltar, Malta, are good places so that organized crime can relate with the great financial companies of the world.

In addition to the "laundering" of dirty money, the fiscal paradises are used to avoid taxes, so they area point of contact between those who govern, CEO's and capos of organized crime. High technology, applied to finances permits the rapid circulation of money and the disappearance of illegal profits. "The legal and illegal businesses overlap more and more, they introduce a fundamental change in the structures of capitalism of the post-war era. The Mafiosi invest in legal businesses, and inversely, they channel financial resources towards the criminal economy, through the control of banks and commercial companies implicated in the laundering of dirty money or which have relations with criminal organizations. The banks pretend that the transactions are carried out in good faith and their directors ignore the origin of the funds deposited. The rule is to ask no questions, the bank secretary and the anonymity of transactions, all this guarantee the interests of organized crime, they protect the banking institution from public investigations and from blame. Not only do the large banks accept laundered money, in view of their heavy commissions, but they also concede credits to at high interest rates to the Mafiosi, to the detriment of productive industrial or agricultural investments" (M. Chossudovsky, Op. City.).

The crisis of the world debt, in the 80's caused the price of prime materials to go down. This caused the underdeveloped countries to dramatically reduce their income. The economic measures dictated by the World Bank and the International Monetary Fund, supposedly to "recuperate" the economy of these countries, only sharpened the crisis of the legal businesses. As a consequence, the illegal economy has developed in order to fill the vacuum left by the fall of national markets.

In accordance with a report by the United Nations, "The intrusion of the crime syndicates has been facilitated by the structural adjustment programs with the indebted countries have been obliged to accept in order to access the loans of the International Monetary Fund" (United Nations. "La Globalization du Crime" New York, 1995).

So here you have the rectangular mirror where legality and illegality exchange reflections.

On which side of the mirror is the criminal? On which side of the mirror is the one who prosecutes the criminal?

Fifth Piece

The Legitimate Violence of an Illegitimate Power.

The Fifth Piece is Constructed by Drawing a Pentagon.

The State, in neoliberalism, tends to shrink to the "indispensable minimum". The so-called "Benefactor State" does not only become obsolete, it separates itself of all it was made up of as such, and it remains naked.

In the cabaret of globalization, the State shows itself as a table dancer that strips of everything until it is left with only the minimum indispensable garments: the repressive force. With its material base destroyed, its possibilities of sovereignty annulled, its political classes blurred, the Nation States become, more or less rapidly, a security apparatus of the megacorporations that neoliberalism builds in the development of this Fourth World War. Instead of directing public investment towards social spending, the Nation States, prefer to improve their equipment, armaments and training in order to fulfill with efficiency a duty that its politics could no longer carry out some years hence: control of society.

The "professionals of legitimate violence" as the repressive apparatus of the modern states call themselves. But, what is there to do if violence is already under the laws of the market? Where is the legitimate violence and where is the illegitimate? What monopoly of violence can the battered Nation States pretend if the free game of supply and demand defies that monopoly? Didn't the Fourth Piece demonstrate that organized crime, governments and financial centers are more than well related? Isn't it evident that organized crime counts on real armies which have no borders except the fire power of its rival? And so the "monopoly of violence" does not belong to the Nation States. The modern market has put it on sale...

This is taken into account because under the polemic between legitimate and illegitimate violence, there is also the dispute (false, I think) between "rational" and "irrational" violence.

A certain sector of the world's intellectuals (I insist that their duty is more complex than to simply be of the "left or right", "pro-government or opposition", "good etcetera or bad etcetera") pretends that violence can be exerted in a "rational" manner, administered in a selective way, (there are those, also, who to something like the "Market technology of violence"), and can be applied with the ability "of a surgeon" against the evils of society. Something like this inspired the last stage of

arms policy in the United States: precise "surgical" weapons, and military operations like the scalpel of the "new world order". This is how the new "smart bombs"
were born (which, as a reporter who covered Desert Storm told me, are not that
intelligent and have difficulty distinguishing between a hospital and a missile
depository. When in doubt, the smart bombs don't abstain, they destroy). Anyway,
as the compañeros of the Zapatista communities would say, the Persian Gulf is farther than the state capital of Chiapas (although the situation of the Kurds has horrifying similarities with the indigenous of a country who praises itself as "democratic and free"), and so let us not insist on "that" war when we have "ours".

And so the struggle between rational and irrational violence opens an interesting
and lamentable path of discussion, it is not useless in present times. We could take for
example what is understood as rational. If the response is that it is the "reason of the
State" (assuming that this exists, and that above all, one would be able to recognize
some reason in the actual neoliberal state) and then one can ask if this "reason of the
state" corresponds to the "reason of society" (always assuming that today's society
retains some reason and furthermore if the rational violence of the state is rational to
the society). Here there is no point in rambling (idly), the "rationale of the state" in
modern times is none other than the "rationale of the financial markets".

But, how does the modern state administer its "rational violence"? And, paying
attention to history, how much time does this rationality last? The time it takes
between one election and another or coup (depending on the case)? How many
acts of violence by the State, that were applauded as "rational" during that time,
are now irrational?

Lady Margaret Thatcher, of "acceptable" memory for the British people, took
the time to prologue the book "The Next War" of Caspar Weinberg and Peter
Schweizer (Regnery Publishing, Inc. Washington, D.C. 1996).

In this text Mrs. Margaret Thatcher, advances some reflections about the three
similarities between the world of the Cold War and that of the Post Cold War: The
first of these is that the "free world" will never lack potential aggressors. The second is the necessity of the military superiority of the "democratic" states above possible aggressors. The third similarity is that this military superiority should be,
above all, technological.

To end her prologue, the so-called "iron lady" defines this "rational violence" of
the modern state by stating: "A war can take place in different ways. But the worst
usually happens because one power believes it can reach its objectives without a war
or at least with a limited war that can be won rapidly, resulting in failed calculations."

For Misters Weinberg and Schweizer the scenes of the "Future Wars" are: North
Korea and China (April 6, 1998), Iran (April 4, 1999), Mexico (March 7, 2003),

Russia (February 7, 2006), and Arabs, Latinos and Europeans. Almost the entire world is considered a "possible aggressor of modern democracy".

Logic (at least in neoliberal logic): In modern times, the power (that is, financial power) knows that it can only reach its objectives with a war, and not with a limited war that can be won rapidly but with a total war, world wide in every sense. And if we believe the secretary of state Madeleine Albright, when she says: "One of the primary objectives of our government is to ensure that the economic interests of the United States can extend itself to a planetary scale" ("The Wall Street Journal". 1/21/1997), we need to understand that all the world (and I mean everything, everything) is the theater of operations of this war.

We should understand then that if the dispute for the "monopoly of violence" does not take place according to the laws of the market, but is rejected and defied from the bottom, the world power "discovers" in this challenge a "possible aggressor". This is one of the defiances (of the least studied and most condemned among the many it represents), launched by the armed indigenous rebels of the Zapatista National Liberation Army against neoliberalism and for humanity...

This is the symbol of North American military power, the pentagon. The new "world police" seeks that the "national" army and police only be the "security corps" that guarantee "order and progress" in the neoliberal magapolis.

Sixth Piece
Megapolitics and the Dwarfs.
The Sixth Piece is Constructed by Drawing a Scribble.

We said before that Nation States are attacked by the financial centers and "obligated" to dissolve within the megalopolis. But neoliberalism not only operates its war "unifying" nations and regions, its strategy of destruction/depopulation and reconstruction/reorganization produces one or various fractures in the Nation State. This is the paradox of the Fourth World War: it is made to eliminate borders and "unite" nations, yet what it leaves behind is multiplication of the borders and a pulverization of the nations that die in its claws. Beyond the pretexts, ideologies and banners, the current world dynamics of the breaking up of the unity of the Nation States responds to a policy; equally universal, that knows it can better exert its power, and create optimum conditions for its reproduction, on top of the ruins of the Nation States.

If someone had doubts about characterizing the process of globalization as a world war, they should discard it when adding up accounts of the conflicts that have been provoked by the collapse of some nation states. Czechoslovakia, Yugoslavia, USSR are examples of the depth of the crisis that leaves in shreds not only the political and economic foundations of the Nation States but also the social structures. Slovenia, Croatia and Bosnia in addition to the present war within the Russian federation with Chechnya as a backdrop, not only mark the outcome of the tragic downfall of the socialist camp in the forbidding arms of the "free world", all over the world this process of national fragmentation repeats itself in variable stages and intensity. There are separatist tendencies in the Spanish state (the Basques, Catalonia and Galicia), in Italy (Padua), in Belgium (Flanders), in France (Corsica), United Kingdom (Scotland, Galic peoples), Canada (Quebec). And there are more examples in the rest of the world.

We have also referred to the process of the construction of the megalopolis, now we talk of fragmentation of countries. Both processes are based upon the destruction of the Nation States. Is it about two parallel, independent processes? Two facets of the globalization process? Are they symptoms of a megacrisis about to explode? Are they merely isolated cases?

We think it is about an inherent contradiction to the process of globalization, one of the essences of the neoliberal model. The elimination of commercial borders, the universality of telecommunications, the information super highways, the omnipresence of the financial centers, the international agreements of economic unity, in short, the process of globalization as a whole produces, by liquidating the nation states, a pulverization of the internal markets. These do not disappear or are diluted in the international markets, but consolidate their fragmentation and multiply. It may sound contradictory, but globalization produces a fragmented world, full of isolated pieces (and often pieces which confront each other). A world full of stagnant compartments, communicating barely by fragile economic bridges (in any case as constant as the weathervane which is finance capital). A world of broken mirrors reflecting the useless world unity of the neoliberal puzzles.

But neoliberalism not only fragments the world it pretends to unite, it also produces the political economic center that conducts this war. And yes, as we referred to before, the financial centers impose their (laws of the market) to nations and grouping of nations, and so we should redefine the limits and reaches pursued by the policy, in other words, duties of political work. It is convenient than to speak of megapolitics. Here is where the "world order" would be decided.

And when we say "megapolitics" we don't refer to the number of those who move in them. There are a few, very few, who find themselves in this "megasphere". Megapolitics globalizes national politics, in other words, it subjects it to a direction that has global interests (that for the most part are contradictory to national interests) and whose logic is that of the market, which is to say, of economic profit. With this economist (and criminal) criteria, wars, credits, selling and buying of merchandise, diplomatic acknowledgements, commercial blocks, political supports, migration laws, coups, repressions, elections, international political unity, political ruptures and investments are decided upon. In short the survival of entire nations.

The global power of the financial centers is so great, that they can afford not to worry about the political tendency of those who hold power in a nation, if the economic program (in other words, the role that nation has in the global economic megaprogram) remains unaltered. The financial disciplines impose themselves upon the different colors of the world political spectrum in regards to the government of any nation. The great world power can tolerate a leftist government in any part of the world, as long as the government does not take measures that go against the needs of the world financial centers. But in no way will it tolerate that an alternative economic, political and social organization consolidate. For the megapolitics, the national politics are dwarfed and submit to the dictates of the financial centers. It will be this way until the dwarfs rebel...

You have here the figure that represents the megapolitics. You will understand that it is useless to try to find within it a rationality and even if you untangle it, nothing will be clear.

Seventh Piece
The Pockets of Resistance.
The Seventh Figure Can Be Constructed by Drawing a Pocket.

> *"To begin with, I beg you not to confuse Resistance with political opposition. The opposition does not oppose power but a government, and its achieved and complete form is that of a party of opposition: while resistance, by definition (now useful) cannot be a party: it is not made to govern at its time, but to... resist."*
> - Tomas Segovia, Allegations, Mexico, 1996.

The apparent infallibility of globalization clashes with the stubborn disobedience to reality. At the same time as neoliberalism carries out its world war, all over the world groups of those who will not conform take shape, nuclei of rebels. The empire of financial pockets confront the rebellion of the pockets of resistance.

Yes, pockets. Of all sizes, of all colors, of the most varied forms. Their only similarity is their resistance to the "new world order" and the crime against humanity that the neoliberal war carries out.

Upon its attempt to impose its economic, political, social and cultural model, neoliberalism pretends to subjugate millions of human beings, and do away with all those who do not have a place in its new distribution of the world. But as it turns out these "disposable" ones rebel and they resist against the power who wants to eliminate them. Women, children, the elderly, the indigenous, the ecologists, homosexuals, lesbians, HIV positives, workers and all those men and women who are not only "left over" but who "bother" the established order and world progress rebel, and organize and struggle. Knowing they are equal yet different, the excluded ones from "modernity" begin to weave their resistance against the process of destruction/depopulation and reconstruction/reorganization which is carried out as a world war, by neoliberalism.

In Mexico, for example, the so-called "Program of Integrated Development for the Isthmus of Tehuantepec" pretends to construct a modern international center of distribution and assembly for products. The development zone covered an industrial complex which would refine the third part of Mexican crude oil and elaborate 88% of petrochemical products. The routes of interoceanic transit will consist of highways, a water route following the natural curve of the zone (the river Coatzacoalcos) and as an articulating center, the trans-isthmus railroad line (in the hands of 5 companies, 4 from the United States and one from Canada). The project would be an assembly zone under the regime of twin plants.

Two million residents of the place will become stevedores, assembly line workers, or railway guards (Ana Esther Cecena. "El Istmo de Tehuantepec: frontera de la soberania nacional". "La Jornada del Campo", May 28, 1997). In Southeast Mexico as well, in the Lacandon Jungle the "Program for Sustainable Regional Development for the Lacandon Jungle" begins operations. Its final objective is to place at the feet of capital the indigenous lands which, in addition to being rich in dignity and history, are also rich in oil and uranium.

The visible results of all these projects will be, among others, the fragmentation of Mexico (separating the southeast from the rest of the country). In addition to this, and now we speak of war, the projects have counterinsurgency implications. They make up a part of a pincer to liquidate the antineoliberal rebellion which exploded in 1994. In the middle stand the indigenous rebels of the Zapatista Army of National Liberation (EZLN).

A parenthesis is now convenient in the theme of indigenous rebels: the Zapatistas think that, in Mexico (attention: in Mexico) the recuperation and defense of national sovereignty is part of an antineoliberal revolution. Paradoxically, the EZLN is accused of pretending to fragment the Mexican nation. The reality is that the only ones who have spoke of separatism are the businessmen of the state of Tabasco (rich in oil) and the federal deputies of Chiapas who belong to the PRI. The Zapatistas think that the defense of the national state is necessary I view of globalization, and that the attempts to slice Mexico to pieces comes from the governing group and not from the just demands for autonomy for the Indian Peoples. The EZLN, and the best of the national indigenous movement, does not want the Indian peoples to separate from Mexico, but to be recognized as part of the country with their differences.

Not only that, they want a Mexico with democracy, liberty and justice. The paradoxes continue because while the EZLN struggle for the defense of national sovereignty, the Mexican Federal Army struggles against that defense and defends a government who has destroyed the material bases of national sovereignty and given the country, not just to powerful foreign capital, but to the drug traffickers.

But resistance against neoliberalism does not exist only in the mountains of Southeast Mexico. In other parts of Mexico, in Latin America, in the United States and Canada, in the Europe which belongs to the Treaty of Maastricht, in Africa, in Asia, in Oceania, the pockets of resistance multiply. Each one of them has its own history its differences, its equalities, its demands, its struggles, its accomplishments.

If humanity still has hope of survival, of being better, that hope is in the pockets formed by the excluded ones, the left-overs, the ones who are disposable.

This is a model for a pocket of resistance, but don't pay too much attention to it. There are as many models as there are resistances, and as many worlds as in the world. So draw the model you prefer. As far as this things about the pockets is concerned, they are rich in diversity, as are the resistances.

There are, no doubt, more pieces of the neoliberal jigsaw puzzle. For example: the mass media, culture, pollution, pandemias. We only wanted to show you here the profiles of 7 of them.

These 7 are enough so that you, after you draw, color and cut them out, can see that it is impossible to put them together. And this is the problem of the world which globalization pretends to construct: the pieces don't fit.

For this and other reasons which do not fit into the space of this text, it is necessary to make a new world.

A world where many worlds fit, where all worlds fit...

From the mountains of the Mexican Southeast,
Subcomandante Insurgente Marcos.
Zapatista Army of National Liberation.
Mexico, June of 1997.

P.S. Which tells of dreams that nest in love. The sea rests at my side. It shares with me since some time ago anguish, doubts and many dreams, but now it sleeps with me in the hot night of the jungle. I look at its agitated wheat in sleep and I marvel once again at how I have found her as always; lukewarm, fresh and at my side. The asphyxia makes me get out of bed and takes my hand and the pen to bring back Old Man Antonio as was years ago...

I have asked that Old Man Antonio accompany me in an exploration to the river below. We have no more than a little bit of cornmeal to eat. For hours we follow those capricious channels and the hunger and the heat press on us. All afternoon we spend after a drove of wild boar. It is almost nightfall when we catch up with them, but a huge mountain pig breaks away from the group and attacks us. I quickly take out all my military knowledge by dropping my weapon and climbing up the nearest tree. Old Man Antonio remains defenseless before the attack, but instead of running, goes behind a grove of reeds. The giant pig runs frontally and with all its strength against the reeds, and becomes entangled in the thorns and the vines. Before it is able to free itself, Old Man Antonio picks up his old musket and shoots it in the head, settling supper for that day.

At dawn, after I have finished cleaning my modern automatic weapon (an M-16, 5.56 mm. Caliber, with cadence selector and effective reach of 460 meters, in addition to telescopic site, tripod and a 60 shot drum clip), I wrote in my military journal, omitting the above: "Ran into a pig and A. killed one. 350 m. above sea level. It didn't rain."

While we waited for the meat to cook I told Old Man Antonio that the part which I would get, would serve for the parties being prepared back at the camp. "Parties?" he asked as he tended the fire. "Yes," I said, "no matter the month, there's always something to celebrate." Afterwards I continue with what I supposed would be a brilliant dissertation about the historic calendar and the Zapatista celebrations. In silence I listened to Old Man Antonio, and assuming it did not interest him, I settled in to sleep.

Between dreams I saw Old Man Antonio take my notebook and write something. I the morning, we gave out the meat after breakfast and each one took to the road. In our camp, I report to my superior and show him the logbook so he'll know what happened. "That's not your writing," I'm told as he shows me a page from the notebook. There, at the end of what I had written that day, Old Man Antonio had written in large letters:

"If you cannot have both reason and strength, always choose to have reason and let the enemy have all the strength. In many battles strength can obtain the victory, but in all the struggle only reason can win. The powerful can never extract reason from his strength, but we can always obtain strength from reason." And below in smaller letters: "Happy parties."

It's obvious, I wasn't hungry anymore. The parties, as always, were very joyful. "The one with the red ribbon," was still, happily, very far from the hit parade of the Zapatistas...

44. BEADS AND ACCOUNTS OF NUMBERS

August 23, 1997

Ladies and gentlemen,

Recently we found out about the new dissonance of the ineffable office of the Governance Secretary. They say that the Zapatistas can march to Mexico City "if and when they present themselves without masks." Given that all we can say is:

Hijole!! If they only knew!!

Well then, I entrust the attached communiqué. The Zup (as pronounced by Yeniperr), always willing to cooperate in the work of the mass media, presents the following informative report about the new communiqué of the easyelen. The report follows the well-known technique of the "inverted pyramid" (which no one else seems to use) in order to facilitate the work and not cause problems, At the end, without extra cost, you will find the complete communiqué. You're welcome.

THE ZUP, SUPERSPECIAL REPORTER, LACANDON JUNGLE, 20-WHAT-EVER OF AUGUST OF 1997. In a communiqué dated on the 22nd of this month, the alleged Zup made public the route to be followed by the representatives of the 1,111 villages which form the ranks of the EZLN. According to the rebel communiqué, the march will leave the state of Chiapas on September 9th (which is still surprising, because everyone supposed that the 1,111 were already in Mexico City and the announcement of the march was solely so that Ruiz Ferro could look ridiculous by offering the protection of his police), and after a farewell ceremony in San Cristobal de Las Casas, would walk to the Federal District through the states of Oaxaca, Puebla, and Morelos.

The insurgents state the dates in which they expect to be in Oaxaca, Puebla and Morelos and they say that they will arrive at the Zocalo of the capital on September 12th.

The EZLN, as everyone knows, made its public appearance on January 1 of 1994, and since that date has dedicated itself to pestering the Supreme Government will all kinds of absurd ideas. A year ago, the easyelenists suspended the talks with the Supreme Government alleging they were unwilling to collaborate with the governmental farce. The Supreme Government protested vehemently, stating that all available theater space had already been rented.

The Zup, a handsome and enchanting guerrilla who says he is military chief of the Zapatistas, once again recurs to the mischievous and playful style which gives so much happiness and joy to the old and young, and inserts, without explanation, a few stories within the letter of presentation for the communiqué, etcetera. The jumbled tales are disconcerting to say the least and it is clear that the Zup uses the communiqués as a pretext to offend with impunity the history of universal literature. What is true is that; the ineffable government intelligence services (if any are left) who are usually terribly bored in San Cristobal, are now very busy trying to decipher the meaning of this collection of stories called...

Tales of the sea horse (for the sea)

Introduction - The sea horse, as indicated by the name is a walking (or swimming) contradiction. So it should not surprise use that without asking much less getting permission, it has inserted itself into the dreams of the sea. The sea, as usual, has insomnia. So in order to secure sleep, the sea horse tells tales, tales like this one...

Section "Beads and Accounts of Numbers"

Roman Numeral One Tale: "The 600"

"The numbers in the 600's are quite envious. For example, it so happened one afternoon I overheard a discussion between 609, 665 and 637. The subject was, as usual, 616.

'He is so spoiled!' 609 said angrily, who could not forgive 616 because he always followed him.

'He's hateful!' 637 almost screamed, who was jealous of 616 because he was always in front of him.

'Intolerable!' argued 665, who found the proportion of 616 hard to tolerate.

'We must get rid of him!' brayed the 687, who could not accept the fact that 616 added up to the mysterious "13" when you added up his digits.

They conspired these numbers 600's against the 616 (the rest of the 600's were too busy holding their place in the tale of the sea in order to participate in this tale), and they took the number 616 prisoner and banished him to the land of the 700 numbers.

That is why when the sea counts sea-horses in order to get to sleep, when it arrives at 615 it becomes confused and cannot continue. Therefore it goes quickly to sleep.

And the number 616? He was detected almost immediately by the repressive forces of the 700's. He was accused of being a destabilizing and incompatible force and condemned to dissolve 88 times until reaching his 7 of origin. Tan, tan" [The End]

Roman Numeral Two Tale: "The 100"

"No one would think it, but the 100's are much more complicated than the rest of the numbers. According to them they reflect good taste and exclusivity. 'To be within the 100's,' they say, 'is a sign of good taste and lineage'. This arrogance is reflected in the daily behavior of the 100's. Number 101, for example, believes he is unique and original, he sees himself as alpha and omega. The rest share this sentiment. 'After us, there is only the common folk,' says the slogan of the 'Club of the 100' which, as its number indicates only has 100 members. Tan, Tan" [The End]

Roman Numeral Three Tale: "The 1"

"The number one is well known for being the most elusive of the numbers. And rightly so, I mean it is enough to know that when one has 1, one wants two. Tan, Tan" [The End]

Roman Numeral Four Tale: "The 200"

"The 200's are frankly numbers which tend to be aquatic. They have the irrefutable shape of a duck which since their beginning makes them a common sight floating on the dreams of the sea. Tan, Tan" [The End]

End of Tales.

Indigenous Revolutionary Clandestine Committee General Command
Zapatista Army of National Liberation.
Mexico.

45. THE TALE OF THE LITTLE NEWSPAPER VENDOR

September 3, 1997

Ladies and Gentlemen,

Over here, we are continuing the preparations. We will go even though, after the State of the Nation address, it is quite clear to us where the indigenous problem fits into the government's agenda. Is there anyone truly listening up there?

Vale. Health, and may the homeland now be ours as well.

From the mountains of the Mexican Southeast,
The Sup, preparing his little flag.
Mexico, September of 1997.

Section "The Counting Postscript of Stories and of the Dead". (for when the sea awakes).

P.S. THAT GREETS ALL THE CLOSETS WHICH HAVE BEEN IN THE WORLD:

I. The Tale of the Little Seamstress

"Once upon a time, there was a little seamstress who sewed a lot and sewed very well on his sewing machine. The machines in his neighborhood laughed at him, and shouted 'Fairy', 'only old women are seamstresses', etcetera. So then the little seamstress sewed the mouths shut of everyone who made fun of him, and now we don't know how the story ended because no one could tell it. The end."

P.S. THAT WARNS:

II. The Tale of the Little Newspaper Vendor

"Once upon a time, there was a little newspaper vendor who was very, very poor, and only could sell old newspapers because he didn't have enough money to obtain new ones. The people didn't buy his newspapers, because they were all so old, and the people wanted new newspapers. So the little newspaper vendor didn't sell anything, and every day he accumulated more and more old newspapers. So then what the little newspaper vendor did was put up a paper recycling plant and he became a millionaire, bought out all the newspaper enterprises and the news agencies, prohibited the publication of current news, and thus obliged the people to read only the news of the past. In the papers which went out on sale today, for example, one could read that the Zapatistas were about to arrive in Mexico City and that there they would meet with the Villistas. The date can't quite be made out, but it seems to say either '1914' or '1997'. The End."

P.S. FOR THE CCN OF THE FAC-MLN.

That argument of "we are the organization with the most prisoners, the most dead, and most repression against us" was already thrown in our face by the PRD three years ago. It would be better for you to learn to add and, above all, to subtract. Indigenous Mexico has many schools in which to learn to the deadly mathematics of repression and oblivion. There, they teach that the legitimacy of an organization is not obtained with the number of dead, but with honest and consequent practices, those which allow the dead to live.

While you learn the arithmetic, add into the total that which some of your leaders receive from Ruiz Ferro, the trips to the United States and Europe which, dressed as "Zapatistas", two of the signers (one of whom didn't even put their name correctly) of the letter of "clarification" enjoyed during all this time, and add all of the support which they have spared to the rebel indigenous peoples, with the argument of the "reformism of the FZLN". If after totaling it all up, you still believe that it is not "clear opportunism", then you can use the term "political realism", which, yes, is the same thing, but doesn't sound quite as bad.

Anyway, you are now going to find real Zapatistas even in the soup. Your monopoly on the radical left is over. What's coming is coming, and then what follows will follow. As someone said whose name I can't remember, "let the bases decide".

The little letter of follow-up reinforcement by the Dynamic Duo of Miron and Botey is useless, and we are not losing any sleep over it. We are not worried by their threats, their "annoyance", and their governmental calls to "prudence".

In any case, we are going to Mexico City, now not only without the "support" of the leadership of the FAC-MLN. Now we are going in spite of it and, of course, in spite of the government. The end.

The Sup reading, in the late-edition newspapers, the letter that Villa writes to Zapata on January 8th, 1916.

46. THE TABLE AT SAN ANDRÉS

March 1998

Between the amnesia from above and the memory of below
For my Mariana, in other words, the sea of my insomnia.
(First Key)
> *"And all this happened to us.*
> *We saw it.*
> *We watched it.*
> *With this lamentable and sad luck.*
> *We were anguished.*
> *On the roads lay broken spines.*
> *Hair is scattered everywhere.*
> *The houses without roofs.*
> *The walls are reddened.*
> *Worms crawl through the streets and plazas,*
> *and brains are splattered on the walls.*
> *The waters are red, they are colored,*
> *and when we drink of them,*
> *it is as though we are drinking brine water.*
> *We beat, meanwhile, the adobe walls,*
> *and our inheritance was a web of holes.*
> *Swords were their defense,*
> *not even the swords could sustain their solitude."*
> - Anonymous, Tlatelolco, 1528
> In "Apparition of the Conquered", Miguel Leon-Portilla

I.- The Dispute in San Andres: Oblivion Against Memory.

On February 16th of 1996, the representatives of the federal government and the Zapatista Army of National Liberation signed the first agreements of the so-called "Table of San Andres", so named because it occurred in the municipality of San Andres Sacamchen of the Poor, in the Highlands of Chiapas. In those first agreements a large part of the rights and culture of the Indian peoples of Mexico are recognized. Two years have gone by and they have not been fulfilled. Two years during which the true nature of the Table of San Andres has been revealed.

The federal government, through its spokesmen (Zedillo, Labastida and Rabasa) have made it clear that in word and deed THEY WILL NOT fulfill the agreements of San Andres.

Why? At the present time there are three versions.

1. It is said that they intend to fulfill them, but they disagree with the "legal interpretation" contained in the initiative developed by the COCOPA.

2. It is said, that the government learned somewhat late, that those agreements constituted an act of "treachery to the Nation" since they implied the wounding of national sovereignty, the fragmentation of the country and the creation of a "State within a State".

3. It is said that the government did not sign those agreements in the belief it would fulfill them, but in the pretense of a disposition which is far from reality.

    It is not likely that the government's reluctance to honor the agreements it signed almost two years ago - and whose lack of fulfillment has done nothing but aggravate the war it has in the Mexican southeast-is due to a "legal interpretation". Since its rejection of the COCOPA initiative, almost 14 months ago, the government is presenting arguments which contradict one another and none of them contain "legal technicalities". Its refusal to fulfill them is not due to a sincere preoccupation with the dangers of "balkanization" or something which attacks national sovereignty. The San Andres Agreements contain nothing which impact the first or contradict the second, and the government knows it.

Is it the third reason then? Yes, but it is not all. The signing of the agreements in themselves does not have major consequences, above all for an illegitimate government which has no credibility. To fulfill them presents a grave problem though. Because their fulfillment represents a defeat for the government at the table of San Andres.

Yes, because, while the table at San Andres was, for the Indian peoples, a table of dialogue and negotiation, for the government it was the site of a fight, the scenario for a struggle, a struggle between oblivion against memory.

On the side of oblivion are the multiple forces of the Market.

On the side of memory is the solitary reason of History.

This is the grand fight for the Mexican government, the fight of the 20th Century: the Market against History.

II.- A Fight of Many Rounds!

This fight at the end of the century which the Mexican government fights against itself San Andres is a small boxing ring. The boxers are the same ones which have fought, throughout the different eras of humanity.

On one side is the Market, the new sacred beast. Money and its conception of time which denies yesterday and tomorrow. On the other side is History (the one which Power always forgets). Memory and its trajectory is to ground and temper humanity in the past, the present and the future.

In the world of "modernity," the cult to the present is the weapon and the shield. Today is the new altar upon which principles, loyalties, convictions, shame, dignity, memory and truth are sacrificed. The past is no longer, for the technocrats whose rule our nation suffers, a guide to be learned from and upon which to grow. The future can be nothing more than a lengthening of the present for these professionals of amnesia.

In order to defeat History, it is denied a horizon which goes beyond the neoliberal "here and now." There is no "before" or "after" today. The search for eternity is finally satisfied: the world of money is not only the best of all possible worlds, it is the only one necessary.

For the "neo-politicians" the only acceptable attitude towards the past and history is a mix of nausea and regret. The past should be devalued, ignored, eliminated. The past and all it reminds us of, or which leads us to look at it another way. What better example of this phobia of history is there, than the attitude of the Mexican government towards Indian peoples? Are not the indigenous demands a worrisome stain which history puts out in order to dim the splendor of globalization? Is not the very existence of indigenous people an affront for the global dictatorship of the Market.

Fulfilling the San Andres agreements is equivalent to acknowledging that History has a place in the present. And this is unacceptable ("irrefutable" says Mister Labastida Ochoa, temporary Minister of Governance). To fulfill the San Andres Agreements is to admit that the end of the century is not the end of history. And this is intolerable ("not negotiable" says the up and coming ex-coordinator of the governmental dialogue, Mister Emilio Rabasa). The present (in other words "Me", translates the actual vice-president Ernesto Zedillo) is the only acceptable guide.

The Mexican federal government will not fulfill the San Andres Agreements. It thus believes that the present will defeat history and can proceed to the future. But History, that stubborn and rude teacher of life, will return to pummel a truncated reality, faked by the masks of power and money. History will return for a rematch in the time in which the present is most vulnerable, in other words, the future. Meanwhile, on the clock of San Andres, the hands mark a quarter to twelve. Attention! The fight is about to begin...

Come on, it is pointless for you to look for a seat so you can watch the fight as a spectator. There are no seats in the place. The Supreme One, upon making the space for a peace dialogue into a boxing ring, has forced everyone to climb up to the ring... in order to box everyone. So, oh well, there is only space inside the ring. Silence now, here comes the announcer to announce the boxers.

III.- In This Cornerrrrrr! The Federal Government!
(The Strategy of Amnesia Induced by a Knock-out Blow)

> "They put a price on us.
> Price of the young man, the priest,
> the child and the lady.
> Enough: for a poor man the price was
> only two handfuls of corn,
> only ten loaves filled with flies;
> our only price was
> twenty loaves of nitrous dog-grass."
> Ibid.

The beast of Power has made Chiapas into a war for the Nation, and in this fight it plays the role of boxer, judge, and often adversary. The Hydra of the State-Party system tries to completely fill the small boxing ring at the table of San Andres. Not only to capture the front stage and display all its trappings, but to keep any rival from stealing the show or winning. In this way Power forces the "others" to come into the Fight, but they are admitted only as losers...

"I am waiting for them to get tired," Zedillo informed his true teachers (the North Americans), referring to the more than 10 million indigenous people who are waiting for him to keep his word. Zedillo thus declares that he will wait for the past to get tired of presenting past due accounts to modernity. The head of the executive branch waits for the Indian peoples of Mexico to get tired, the ones who already inhabited these lands before it became nation or a nation of History, the ones who, with their blood, fought for independence, the ones who, with their bodies confronted the successive aggressions of foreign invasions, the ones who, with their bones, gave a spine to the Mexican revolution, the ones who shook and awoke the Nation from the false dream of modernity.

Mister Zedillo, who came to Power through a murder, who stays in power through the good graces of money and indolence of the Hydra, who stains his hands with the blood of Acteal, has informed his superiors in the United States that he will wait until the Indian peoples, who have been waiting for 500 years, get tired.

The Market feels powerful and omnipotent, it thinks it can dominate history and rewrite it. The result of the proposition is evident: a terminal crisis of the society. Without a foundation (since history has been erased) the social structure and its pinnacle, the State, crumble away.

In the unstable government of Zedillo, San Andres is only a sample of the crisis and the "style" for dealing with it. When he says he is going to wait for those who ask for justice to "get tired," the government is refusing to fulfill its word and resorts instead to two fundamental pillars to justify itself; some of the mass media and the army. For one and the other it has money, privileges and lies.

The "patient wait" of Zedillo is nothing more than another name for his strategy: he waits for the opportune moment to strike the resounding blow which will impose amnesia in Mexican society. He denies he will strike this blow, over and over again. This boxing "technique" has three fundamental parts: Violence, Lie and Intrigue.

Violence. The use of force in slowly increasing dosages. "Dodge, fake, attack" are the instructions Zedillo receives from his teachers. The extermination of the opponent can be achieved through a variety of means. Deception, treachery and crime are the preferred means of this man who has stamped his administration with these three "virtues" as his personal style of government.

Through his soon to be ex-minister of Governance, Francisco Labastida Ochoa and his still "dialogue coordinator", Emilio Rabasa Gamboa, Mister Zedillo attempts once and again, uselessly, to trap the Zapatista leadership in ambushes disguised as "meetings."

The first attempt is a letter without an addressee, address, or signature. Anonymous. The date? January 23, 1998. With the letter comes a verbal message: "We propose a secret meeting between Subcomandante Marcos and the Ministry of Governance for January 26th of 1998. The meeting will be private, there will be no witnesses, and will be made public (if it is agreed) after its conclusion. It is important that this be kept absolutely secret because the army knows nothing."

But the message, like everything the government does, arrives late. The General Command of the EZLN receives the proposal on January 26th of 1998, in the midst of an intense land and aerial military mobilization. The ambush fails and the Minister of Governance is offended by the answer he receives ("No!") from the Zapatistas. There are several reproaches, but one remains unsaid: "Why didn't they fall into the trap?"

Why was Mister Emilio Rabasa so afraid that the federal army would capture the document of January 23rd of 1998 which, without a signature, addressee or sender, was sent through CONAI?

The second is a document in the same style of the "letter" of January 23rd. Without return address, or signature or concrete proposal we receive a document which contains the "4 observations which used to be 27". The so-called "4 observations ("irrefutable", Labastida adds later, as a sample of his negotiating nature) which are not 4 but 15, and are not addressed to the EZLN nor to anyone.

But we will speak about this later on. For now, we only ask: Why does the army increase its pressure during the days in which the EZLN receives the "4-observations-which-are-15-but-at-least-not-27" anymore?

The answers may vary, but basic things do not change: force attempts to replace reason. And the Federal Army is here to exert force. In exchange for its services it is offered the opportunity to charge a high price for the challenge of the Zapatista rebellion. It doesn't matter that its "supreme commander" obliges the armed forces to walk against history. In order to assist this end, arises...

The Lie. Overdose of slander. The attempts, failed until now, of an annihilation of the Zapatista leadership is accompanied by a "media campaign" for public opinion. In order to hide the governmental plan of re-negotiation (or lack of fulfillment) of the San Andres Agreements and to justify the military and police persecution, the debate is centered no longer on the rights of Indians and the failure to fulfill what has been signed, but upon who doesn't want to sit at the negotiating table.

But negotiation for what? Haven't we already dialogued? Didn't we come to some agreements which have not been carried out? Was there an attempt to resolve the conflict or a pretense of dialogues and negotiations that have no results?

The fundamental questions are buried underneath the tomb of declarations of the government and its goals. "No to intransigence. We do want to negotiate," declares the Ministry of Governance, and with the noise they try to confuse. But Zedillo has spoken clearly in the nation which really owns him, North America. "No to San Andres. We are going to wait for the moment of payment." The failed action is amended in Mexico by the neo-pretender Emilio Rabasa with one more declaration, just as hollow and noisy as all the ones before.

In some mass media there continue to be symptoms of stupidity which have not been relegated and which work so that everything will continue to be as before. In them the government finds echo and mirror for its words and deeds. The slander is recycled: indigenous who are manipulated, foreigners who manipulate, strange forces which use the conflict to favor their perverse interests, occult intentions, intransigence. They are the same accusations they made 4 years ago, 3, 2, even one year ago: the indigenous are good, the perverse ones are the mestizos and the foreigners who manipulate them. These governmental "media campaigns" always accompany a military campaign.

And it is not that the government and "modern" journalism are betting that they will be believed, but they do believe that they can plant confusion and mete out the illegitimacy that they enjoy. "You must believe in no one," says the actual governmental campaign. "We are all equal," in other words, "we are all the worst."

Remembering that crimes attract reflectors, the crime of Acteal in Chiapas has attracted different personalities of the "Zedillo mob." There you have the Minister of Health exploiting his own sickening image near an indigenous child. The child does not know if her most terrible stigma is having lost her parents at Acteal, or being used by the assassins in order to wash their hands. The photo and the lie is accompanied by Lady Roccatti of the CNDH [Mexican Commission on Human Rights].

In another corner up above, in the so-called "Ministry of Governance" "alternatives" are offered, which accompany the couple violence-lie which confront the indigenous rebellion. Blows and slander accompany them...

Intrigue. The price tag of the dialogue. But in spite of all its barbarity, the government offers, out of its bounty, an alternative to annihilation: another kind of negotiation: the one specialty of the political class, the agreement which is secret and made among a select few.

In Zedillo's government no one really believes that the indigenous demands really matter to the EZLN. They think the Zapatistas have a price and that they are using the Indian demands only to sell themselves at a higher price. So they ponder and they try to figure the price and let their "opponent" know that they are willing to pay it.

With its effort to think of the EZLN as though it were a "normal" political organization, it offers to negotiate the indigenous theme, again and again, in exchange for "other" things: the retreat of the federal army, participation in local organizations, the reorganizing of the municipalities to the convenience of the Zapatistas, the management of money in governmental projects, credits and even... a pardon for what the EZLN did!

The last "offer" of Mister Labastida (the "review of the positions of the army in exchange for the re-negotiation of the indigenous theme") is only an example of the lures which, just like Mister Rabasa, are thrown out in order to deceive the Zapatistas and confuse public opinion. So the government increases the military presence and the persecution. Then it says it will return the Army to its previous position if, in exchange, the EZLN forgets its demand that the San Andres Agreements be fulfilled. It attacks the autonomous municipalities and offers to reorganize them in order to "erase" their indigenous essence; it proposes that the commanders of the CCRI-CG of the EZLN receive money directly from the government and administer it; it offers to "forget" the rebellion which shook Mexico and ruined the end of the year and the century party.

Consequently, the threats of the government increase in tone and volume. "Accept my conditions or we will kill you" is the message repeated once and again by the voices of Power. Replace the dialogue through gangster-style intimidation. The threats provoke worry in minds which are honest and enthusiasm in the cynics. The first see how easy it will be to go from words (ultimatums of different kinds) to deeds (the war), and the second unleash their bravado and call for extermination. Each step of the government brings the war closer and can bring on amnesia. It will be forgotten that peace should come with justice and dignity and not as a simulation.

They want the threats to make public opinion choose re-negotiation over annihilation. And behind the re-negotiation that the government pretends to hold about the indigenous theme, is the negation of San Andres, the negation of "another politics," of the politics which grew and deepened when the table of San Andres stopped being a boxing ring and became a wide and deep table of encounter and birth...

IV.- In the Other Corners!...

The COCOPA and the CONAI! (the Mediation and the Coadjutation in the trap: Will they be effective and endure the beating, or will they be accomplices and be dishonest?).

The government insists upon its plan to make the COCOPA and the CONAI into messengers who deliver anonymous mail, cowardly threats and invitations to failed ambushes. Both know that the document "27 pretend observations in 15 and hidden in 4" have nothing to say to the Zapatistas. The real object of the mail is the COCOPA, which is the entity which wrote the legal initiative. The government document points out that the COCOPA doesn't want to carry out the San Andres Agreements!

The Cocopa can become mired once again. Under the leadership of the Bernal-Del Valle duo it has already suffered a strategy of reduction and mockery. The "cocopos" said then "never more". But now the new dynamic duo Labastida-Rabasa wants to reassign them to the role of governmental spokesmen, replacements for the mediation, saviors of a regime without credibility, and legislative sanction of state violence.

The new trap which has been laid out by the government consists of making the Cocopa believe that the ice breaker would be the total re-negotiation of the San Andres Agreements or at least that the legislators accept the observations made to their legal initiative. The cocopos resist entering a situation which would take them to break their word (and with that lose all credibility with the Indian peoples and make the illegitimacy of the government their own): they responded that they would sustain their legal initiative on indigenous rights but they would accept transmitting the observations of the government to the Conai so that it, would send them to the Zapatistas. This is how they created an equally grave situation for the conflict.

As has been stated before, the governmental observations are not intended for the EZLN (if someone possesses enough "Zedillista" patience to read them, they are an attachment to this document), but for the legislative commission. The government has stated publicly that they are expecting a response from the EZLN, and some members of the Cocopa have echoed this wait. Why fall into the trap? Why the complicit silence about the true content and significance of the document from Governance? Why add legislators to the snapping of fingers with which the government demands the surrender while it shows the ostensible club of repression?

There can be several answers. One is that the legislative commission has decided to participate actively or passively in the new belligerent strategy of the government (it seems unlikely, there are still honest and responsible people in the Cocopa). Another is that the Cocopa has decided that it is preferable to re-negotiate the agreements rather than return to war (an understandable position... yet erroneous: to re-negotiate the agreements means - for us - that no agreement will be fulfilled and the dialogue will be destroyed as a means for a solution. This will give the government the excuse to return to the war). Another possibility is that the Cocopa is still absorbing what is happening and is trying to clarify its role in the midst of the confusion which reigns.

In addition to the pressure and the governmental traps, some of the "cocopos" suffer the traps of their own party leadership. Chiapas has become, in addition to a prelude which prepares the presentation of pre-candidates for the year 2000, into "negotiable" currency in exchange for other things (Governor's seats? The Bartlett law? Definitive enrollments? Municipal presidencies? Cabinet posts? Etcetera?).

The CONAI meanwhile suffers continual persecution from the networks of Power and its good faith in the search for peace is used to reinforce the governmental strategy. The reluctance of the mediators to convert themselves into instruments of war is responded to with a governmental campaign which tries to destroy the Conai, or at least, reduce its profile to a piece of scenery. If the Conai shows optimism towards the dialogue, the government salutes it and uses its declarations in its favor; but when the mediation expresses worry about the militarization and the lack of peace gestures from the government, the attack on the members of the mediating body is immediate.

If the tactic of making the Conai and the Cocopa go into the "ring" is successful, the result will help the government in two ways: on one hand it will recuperate (together with the mediation and the adjutant) the legitimacy it lost with the massacre of Acteal, with the failure of the politics of omission and diminishment, and the war of attrition against the Zapatistas and the Indian peoples; on the other hand using them (in the worst meaning of the word) to isolate and fence in the EZLN, it will make the Conai and the Cocopa as well, lose all legitimacy and trust of the source of their legitimacy and support, national and international civil society.

By beating the COCOPA on one side and the CONAI on the other, and by seeding xenophobia in order to avoid international mediation, the government does not seek a direct "dialogue", but the elimination of obstacles and uncomfortable witnesses of the crime whose commission was nurtured since the day Zedillo entered Los Pinos [presidential palace].

We do not gloat about this. We Zapatistas are not enthused about the "blue helmets" (which so enthuse the National Action Party). We do not celebrate the blows to the COCOPA and the CONAI. On the contrary, history shows that a weak mediation and an adjutant which has no independence and legitimacy, not only distance the proximity of a dignified and peaceful solution, but they also contribute to the deterioration of a situation which, day by day, adds deaths and impunities.

The Legislative Power and the Political Parties! (the Congress wavers between independence and servility; the political parties between pragmatism and principles).

With war knocking on the doors of the Nation, the Legislative Power has a role which can be defining and definitive. The military has convinced the executive branch and the legislators from the PRI, that the blow in Chiapas will be "surgical" and shed only the necessary blood. But the "sterility" of the necessary crime requires that inconvenient legal obstacles disappear, and there is a law (the one for dialogue) which is an obstacle. It requires then, the destruction of that law so that the military (or police) can act "legally."

The PRI line-up has a new opportunity to "serve the president" untying his hands (if there is one part which is reaping benefits from the conflict in Chiapas it is the Institutional Revolutionary Party, not for winning points, but for wiping out opponents - with the disinterested help of the paramilitaries), by annulling the law which prohibits the persecution of the Zapatistas. The other parties (PRD, PAN, PT and PVEM) works with these variable in order to win the elimination of the law for dialogue passed nearly 3 years ago (March 11 of 1995).

It appears to be an inconceivable horror to have a Congress and some political parties which give support to the genocide which Zedillo prepares for the Mexican southeast (the "surgical strike" is only possible on paper, in the mountains of Chiapas it will be only the first and last step into the abyss of war). Deputies and senators will have to choose between independence and servility, the political parties will have to choose between pragmatism and principles. Everyone will have to choose peace or war.

Not because this writer says so, but because the History of this country erupted in Indian lands. The arena of struggle which the government has made into a boxing ring, San Andres, does not leave space for spectators and forces everyone to take a side. If before Chiapas could be seen as a state of the Mexican southeast, after the State crime perpetrated in Acteal the "Chiapas" affair blew up in Tijuana and Merida, in Queretaro and Veracruz, in the Federal District and in the mountains of the Tarahumara, in Jalisco and in the mountains of Oaxaca, in Nayarit and Tlaxcala, in all the national territory.

Not only that, it also exploded in the cubicles, laboratories and departments of the Universities, in the theaters, the cafes, the movie theaters, the rock concerts, the art, the sculpture, the literature and journalism, in the unions and popular neighborhoods, in the living rooms, bedrooms and kitchen of the Mexican homes, in Europe and Asia, in Canada, the United States, Latin America, Africa and Oceania.

Everywhere it exploded and divided people between those who ratify cynicism and selfishness as a route, and those who walk with a commitment to hope as a guide and those who are obliged by the responsibility of being human beings to be accountable and to refuse to remain paralyzed before the mirror offered them by the mountains of the Mexican Southeast.

V.- Intermission: Chocolates and Swiss Airplanes, the Neoliberal Alternative for the Indian Peoples.

The Mexican government has continually referred to the situation of the Indian peoples as the product of "left-over" economic inequities which can be resolved through private investments and social programs. But, says Zedillo, these backward economic and social zones are insignificant. The rest of the nation moves through a macroeconomic bonanza and all that is needed is to accelerate the "modernization" of the indigenous Mexico so that it shares the well-being which all Mexicans share? A lie. "Neoliberal integration of Mexico in NAFTA, will deepen the regional inequalities, by prioritizing areas with a competitive edge, neglecting less favorable regions and thereby the gap between marginal and prosperous regions" (Jose Luis Calva. "El Universal". February 20, 1998).

In the eternal present polished by neoliberalism, the past is erased completely and redefined by defining a better future. The indigenous should stop being and convert themselves to the new religion of the market as "coupiers" of casinos or workers in the twin-plant industry. This last is the only branch of the economy (besides financial speculation and drug trafficking, of course) which has had the growth which the technocrats promised for all of Mexico with NAFTA. From 1974 to 1982 the number of twin plants grew by 28%, but in the period from 1983 to 1997 the percentage grew to 455%; the number of workers increased by 67% during the period of 1974-82 and by 747% from 1983 to 1997. (Jose Luis Calva. Ibid.)

Mister Zedillo, who likes to talk correctly in front of his teachers and mislead his subjects, defines in Davos, Switzerland, the alternative offered to Mexican indigenous people by his social model.

As a response to the international uproar about the massacre of Acteal, Ernesto Zedillo announced the signing of an agreement to build a Swiss chocolate factory in Chiapas!

Airplanes and chocolates are the only governmental proposals for "economic development" used to resolve the serious "historic residue" suffered by the Indian peoples.

There is no future with respect and dignity for the indigenous in the Mexico of Zedillo. He has only one alternative: surrender and turn into the employees of a Swiss chocolate factory, or continue to be rebels and be attacked by Swiss airplanes.

This is consistent globalization...

VI.- "Kill That Rock!"
(Resistance, a Prehistoric Weapon in Modernity).

Mister Zedillo cannot tolerate the fact that women and children confront the soldiers to defend their few belongings. The "supreme chief" of the Federal Army prefers that the children and women wait, with humility and resignation, for the shot which the Mexican government saves for them as a ticket to modernity. "Mister President" cannot tolerate the serious dignity with which men, women, children and elderly indigenous people reject food, medicine, government money and projects. He wants the Indians to be submissive, humiliated, servile, sitting in a corner with their hands out in order to receive the charity, which they should appreciate with enthusiasm.

In order to explain to himself something which to him is nonsense, Zedillo figures the brave resistance is due to those "perverse provocateurs", who, instead of promoting surrender, support and nurture the firm dignity of those who are opposed to neoliberal arrogance.

With great care, and for more than 12 years the technocrats who administer the seasonal liquidation sale of national sovereignty - in other words, the destruction of Mexico - have been constructing a gigantic dome of protection over financial capital. The objective is to isolate definitively (definitive is one of the favorite words of Mister Zedillo) the blows of social reality. In order to make this dome more resistant to the nightmare, which assails the doors of history ever stronger, the Mexican government has made "intermediaries" of the Army and the electronic media.

But the indigenous rebellion is now a rock which hits once and again the great dome of power of money.

With that brutal and bloody pragmatism which characterizes it, the Mexican government has prescribed the antidote: "KILL THAT ROCK".

That is what they are doing. There is only one problem: the rocks do not die. At most they become smaller rocks...

VII.- What's Next?

On behalf of the government the same continues except on a higher scale. It tries to win advantages before the electoral process. And it bets, after the elections, it will recompose itself in order to "regulate" the process of presidential selection which is out of control, and "de-Chiapanize" the national agenda, obtain a breathing space in order to recompose its international image and alleviate the weariness of the military. For this it needs for the law for dialogue of March 11, 1995 to be set aside, and the reactivation of the arrest orders and the pursuant renewal of the persecution.

In addition it carries out the media campaign about the "perverse provocateurs" and "manipulators" of the "poor" indigenous, the mining of the moral authority of the Zapatista leadership, etc. Meanwhile the Army refurbishes its role and redefines it as a container. Enter now the "special commandos" but perhaps under another name, and they apply to the EZLN leadership the so-called "rabbit hunt." The commanders pursue and the government waits for the prey to fall... in whatever way possible.

As far as the EZLN is concerned it will continue to resist and continue firm in its struggle for the recognition of the rights of the Indian peoples. It will continue to seek out the paths to extend new bridges of dialogue with national and international civil society and the political and social organizations of Mexico.

On behalf of the Cocopa, the Conai, the Congress of the Union and the Political parties, what follows is that they choose one of the alternatives which confront them.

On behalf of you, man, woman, child, youth, elderly, homosexual, lesbian, housewife, squatter, worker, farmer, employee, artist, intellectual, scientist, student, teacher, in whatever part of Mexico or the World, what's next is, is, well, you tell us what's next. Perhaps it is possible to refuse to sit in that absurd ring in which the Hydra lies and assassinates, and construct a dialogue which is no longer a fight in disguise. Yes, why not? Let the Hydra destroy itself. Construct in its place not a battleground, but a table where all that we are can sit down, a table which is very other, wide and deep such as the one all of you and us constructed in San Andres more than two years ago, a table which has yesterday as a foundation, the present as a cover, and the future as food, a table which lasts a long time and does not crumble, a table made of rocks, many little rocks, many resistances (this is the disguise of hope when times are difficult).

Vale. Health, and if memory continues, do not forget to pick up in your hand one of those rocks so feared by the neoliberal Goliath which, like all rocks, never dies...

From the (rocks) of the mountains of the Mexican Southeast,
Subcomandante Insurgente Marcos.
Indigenous Mexico, February of 1998.

47. THREE TABLES FOR THE END OF THE CENTURY DINNER

March 1998

> "Mariana, what is mankind without liberty?
> Without that harmonious and steady light which glows inside?
> How can I love you while I am not free, tell me?
> How can I give you this firm heart if it is not mine?
> Do not fear: I have escaped the foundling in the countryside,
> and so I think I will continue until I conquer you,
> who offer me your love, your home, and your fingers."
> - Federico Garcia Lorca
> (Fifth Key.)

The moon is a badly-cut pill, tossed on the table which the dawn serves over the mountains of the Mexican Southeast (below the river is a silvery streamer, forgotten and torn after a party).

There are barely a few stars inserting their lances of blue salt into the nocturnal table-cloth which February, grimy with clouds and winds, lays out to cover the shadows of the hills and the gullies.

This is the table for those tossed from modernity. It is a long and dark shadow, wounded by the piercing light of straight pins with bristly heads. A shadow, a table of shadows, whose accessibility is selective inversely: all who can avoid it do. The only ones who sit there are those who had only their memory as food and dignity as fork and spoon.

Seated in front of the splendor of this moon, the shadows do not dissipate or pretend. This light defines more than the darkness, it heightens blacks, proposes grays and reveals the few white hairs the mountain has. All of this, in effect, is like a table. A great and solitary table. The embattled table of those below. But I will not speak of this dark table at the beginning. I will speak of it at the end, the end of this century, and it and its guests will speak for themselves. For today we will begin by speaking of another table. Well, maybe just a photo of another table...

The place?

Mexico.

The time?

Somewhat after the beginning of 1998, and somewhat before the end of the 20th Century.

The Table of Above...

The still picture of horror and decadence. "They will awaken, those who are without awakening still in this time of seven days of ephemeral kingdom, of passing kingdom, of the seven suns of the kingdom. The faces of their men will be that of Holil Och, Zarigueyas-mice, uselessly they will govern disguised with jaguar skin."

The book of the books of Chilam Balam.

My-Other-Me says he was not present, he only got a still picture. A full-color photo. A photo which carries a double message: the hidden image of Power in Mexico, and the brittle future which the image announces. Under the light of a recently-lit candle, and while the Sea navigates through a restless dream, I look at the photo. I should confess that the sight shook me, so the reader cannot blame me if I cannot transmit this sensation. I will try to be objective and describe what I see in the printed image. If there is some raving which escapes me, blame it on the weak light which I must use (and make a little roof for it so it won't die out) and blame the permanent problem of putting a visual image into words.

The photo is take from an angle that those who know call "long shot" and it makes it clear that the photographer observes from outside the scene, as though it makes him sick to be a part of the object in front of the lens. The photographer trusts that he who is looking at the photo notices the fact that the people in the photograph do not know they are being watched (and fixed, I say) by the camera. There is in all of them that air of nonchalance which exists only when there are no witnesses. But then, how to believe that the photographer was not present as a part of the event which was photographed?

My-Other-Me intervenes to explain that a current theory of photographic art supposes that the image is a way of "going to the place in the visual representation". Therefore, the photographer-videographer-film producer-painter-cartoonist-etcetera sees himself as the one who provides the vehicle for the visual trip.

"He doesn't even offer to drive," says My-Other-Me seriously, "given that the 'trip' can 'go' wherever he wants. So the producer of the image sees himself as something distant from the pictured act, no matter how close he is. What is happening is that your encyclopedic ignorance includes the unfamiliarity with photographic art, that is why we photographers get pissed with that diatribe you wrote for I-don't-know-what photographic event on the Internet."

My-Other-Me is quiet so that I can appreciate how he includes himself among the photographers. He leaves with my bag of tobacco. I had not heard that theory before (it's suspicious that My-Other-Me just finished inventing it), but even so, the "liberty" to use the image has its limitations and there are always some "readings" which are possible and others which are not.

But this thing is not the one which impacts the still picture, so I will continue to describe what I see, in other words (following the lead of My-Other-Me), I will read the image.

First of all, it seems to be the scene of a meal. There is a great table (with what I imagine is food, diners and a few servants), which fills the center of the picture. There is a bit of a fog in the air, but you can distinguish perfectly on the front wall (the wall in front of the photographer anyway), a clock which marks the 11 hours and 45 minutes.

Morning or night? There is nothing which allows us to resolve this enigma, but suppose ("read") that it is 11 hours 45 minutes to midnight. "Quarter to twelve," I say, surprising myself. Yes it is a quarter to midnight. So this is a dinner. You can see, sole wall as backdrop, of a gray color, a great window with the windows drawn, and a clock which says it is a quarter to midnight. Beyond that nothing. Now, let me describe the table. It is oval and big (there are seven diners seated there). The chairs are high-backed with complicated gargoyles as decoration.

There are seven diners (I said that already?) by unfortunate coincide ("opportunity" says the photographer) all are visible. The 2 who have their backs to the "reader" of the picture are looking to the sides. Therefore their faces, although just the profile are perfectly visible. In front of them and in front of the reader, there are another 3. At the sharpest points of the oval you see the other two. Total: seven.

One can imagine there is some music livening this dinner, and some troubadour singing some verses, like those of Quevedo and Villegas which say:

> "Mother, I humble myself to gold;
> it is my lover and my beloved,
> well, out of pure love
> he is continuously yellow;
> double or single,
> he does all I want,
> powerful gentleman
> that Mister Money."

What? You are right. There's nothing in the picture to suggest music, a troubadour, or the satiric verses of Quevedo and Villegas made prayer and psalm. But the reader has already accepted (given that he reads this document, and therefore, becomes accomplice) the "driving" of the narrator in this "reading" of the picture, so this is due to the whims of this "chauffeur" who now is determined to add to the image what is not evident, but which, nevertheless is there, in what the picture keeps quiet and does not show.

We will continue with the description of the central image. A great bloody tablecloth covers the table of the seven diners. In reality, you could say that the table with the bloody tablecloth summons these 7 symbols of the beast of Power in Mexico. There are seven beasts here, in this picture of the end of the century, and they represent the horror and decadence of the Mexican political system.

At the head of one is the Hydra. A monster with 7 heads. I mean, apart from the 7 beasts which are gathered there. The Hydra does not seem to need the others, not to eat them, not to chat with them, not to fight with them (which is what appears in the picture). Yes, the Hydra fights with itself, the 7 heads swinging on long necks, with powerful fangs and forked tongues, they argue and bite one another...

A Hydra, whose heads, bite one another, is a small image to describe the size of the actual situation of the State-Party System in Mexico. This system capable of holding together a Nation during decades, is now torn and confronting itself. Like a jumbled jigsaw puzzle, you cannot distinguish the positions and the forces, the directors or the direction. The political system, the director, the conductor, the point of convergence of the fundamental parts of the Mexican State during almost a century, is now diluted as such and can not hide the internal crisis which afflicts it.

The Mexican political system is found in a war with three elements of combat: the one presented by the process of neoliberal globalization, the one which develops in its interior where the "old" and the "new" politicians fight, and the one which fights society.

The homogenization of the global economy runs parallel to the fragmenting and pulverizing tendencies of the old Mexican political class, the formation of "new" politicians, and the surrender (under global norms - in other words, North American - of social and cultural standardization) of Mexican society.

Prisoner of the frenetic and effective labor which the logic (economic, political, cultural and social) of globalization imposes, the Mexican State threatens to disintegrate with the same haste with which the power of the "old" Mexican political system fragments; the State-Party System. To confront the "new politics" demanded by the "new" global economy, the Mexican political system should remake itself, reconstruct itself according to the dominant logic, in other words, the market. The neoliberal model does not need "politicians", but "administrators." Now more than ever the economy possesses every one of the aspects of national life, markedly the political one, but organized crime as well.

At its side, looking at it steadily, is the Medusa of Organized Crime. Yes the image shows a head with serpents instead of hairs, a face of undefined gender and not eyes, but the glitter of eyes which are dollar-green. What? Is that why I call it organized crime? Well, if you observe with attention, in each hair-serpent you will read the name of a crime: drug trafficking; white slavery, black market of stocks, merchandise, organs, and human beings; militarism; genocide; contamination and destruction of the environment; and other names which are not legible. Ah! Pay attention to something under the table, between the Hydra and the Medusa! Yes, they are holding hands.

So there are the Hydra and the Medusa. Together they reside over a chaotic and disorderly table.

The Table of Above...

The ones who accompany them are personages of a different dimension. Each one of the tiny beasts carry on their chest a small tag which names it.

There is a "Politician," a "Thinker," a "Banker," a "Clergyman," and a "Military man." These two are found in the first row, their faces towards the photographer.

In this way, the "old" political class is not only displaced by the "new" politicians (those technocrats who give a macroeconomic indicator as a response to each social and political problem), but it is necessary to liquidate them completely. This process of "elimination of the adversary" is like "elimination of the competition" in savage capitalism, but in the Mexican political class - which grew very tied to organized crime - this reaches bloody levels.

The Mexican political system is willing to do anything to become echo and loyal interpreter of the neoliberal project. It is hell-bent on disposing of the Institutional Revolutionary Party as the State party, and its replacement stretches its cadaverous hand to the other parties looking for another face. The initials do not matter, it can lead (or "administer") the neoliberal affair regardless of its logos, initials and colors.

But doing away with the PRI is not easy. In addition to erasing its ideological profile and turning its program to the right, the Mexican political system operates against the PRI through "other" means: the embarrassing resignations, the "exportation" of candidates, the physical elimination (Colosio, Ruiz Massieu, who is the next, Mister Ernest?).

The modern Mexico of the neoliberals not only does not need the PRI in order to carry out its project of the no-Nation, but it sees it as an annoying nuisance, in bad taste and foul-smelling, old and rotting.

The beast marked with the name tag "politician" is something like a misshapen mass, with impeccable suit and tie, capable of changing form, size and color. Its face, surprisingly like that of a zarigüeya, only attempts to smile and barely eats. It is very busy, noting all the acts and gestures of the two principal figures. Its undefined figure suggests a propensity to permutation rather than a firm vagueness. I mean to say that this small beast is willing to change itself according to convenience.

Thus, the "neo kids" of modernity conduct a war. Not only against an emerging society and what is left of the Nation, but against the political class which gave them birth and gave them Power. The best analyst of the modern Mexican political system (unjustly called a poet, playwright and novelist), the British writer William Shakespeare, warned thus: "it is a rule that modesty is the ladder used by young ambition, the eyes turn towards it of those who wish to ascend it; but once the last step is climbed the back is turned towards the ladder, and the look turns towards the clouds dismissing the steps by which it climbed" (Brutus I "Julius Caesar" Translation: Ma. Enriqueta Gonzalez Padilla).

The struggle in the interior of Power in Mexico is to the death (and not just in a figurative sense). One part (the old) struggles to survive, the other (the technocratic) struggles to replace it. The result is a fragmentation of the Mexican political class which changes day to day. As in the old Kaleidoscopes, the bloody pieces of the political system permutes its combinations under a constant method: division and confrontation.

For those who resist "modernization" of the Mexican political system there are various options: the tomb (Colosio and Ruiz Massieu), jail (Dante Delgado), kidnapping (Gutierrez Barrios), "voluntary" exile (Silva Herzog), public stoning (Camacho Solis), political sacrifice in coordinated resignations (Ramon Aguirre, Ortiz Arana, etcetera), the withdrawal to the provincial estate (Bartlett).

The major political scandals of the last 12 years are exclusive monopoly of the Institutional Revolutionary Party. Divisions, assassinations, ties which are like chains with drug trafficking, frauds, jail, buried skulls, unburied skulls, reburied and new unburied skulls, historic amnesia, new divisions, more assassinations? In sum, all that is called a "political crisis" by some.

The beast named "Thinker" looks like a combination of a mousy face (with glasses, of course) and the body of an elephant. In the picture he appears to be reading very seriously a huge stack of paper, in front of a microphone decorated by the logo of some television network.

The crisis of the Mexican political system is not a crisis of the Nation. The politicians and intellectuals of the system want to present this crisis as a "crisis of the country." From here come their hysterical calls for prudence, for "slow" changes, for "stabilization", for "staying still." The political system cries "help me!" And some respond. But these politicians-intellectuals-clergy-bankers-military are willing to help the system fall, so warns the political analyst Shakespeare in the mouth of Anthony.

"It is that I have lived more years than you, Octavio, and even though we deposit some honors on that man to free ourselves of several slanderous charges, I will carry them as the ass carries gold, panting and sweating because of the labor, pulling or dragging, according to the road : and once I have transported our treasure where it is convenient, I will take off the load and throw him out, like a loose burro is allowed to shake its ears and graze on public land." (Ibid.)

"Banker" is the name tag for a beast with the body of a serpent and the face of a ravenous pig. In the picture it holds another serpent in its arms, as it offers it a spoonful of coins.

What is caving in, what is shredding everywhere, is a project of the country. Neoliberalism has tried to impose itself from the new phase of the rule of money, and works to homogenize ("globalize" it is said in modern terms) patterns of economic, social, political and cultural relations. In Mexico, since the administration of Miguel de la Madrid Hurtado, this crisis runs in the interior of the ruling political class.

But the new Mexican politicians have shown that they don't know how to do it. As if they were in a three-ring circus which scatters blood on the spectators the new "global" model presents different facets of the same tragedy: the destruction of the National State.

But far from the pantomime routine of old clowns, the circus acts offered to the respectable public spew mud and blood. The political note, as the reporters call the news which come from political actors, spew scandal and terror and gossip. The "experts" in political analysis now should know criminal science... and demonology.

"Cleric" the figure with the body of a gargoyle and the head of a dragon is called. It is dressed in deep purple and raises its hand, blessing the pair which presides at the table.

Incapable of homogenizing and leading, political power in Mexico seeks to support itself through other institutions even if, in the case of the Church, that support brings it near the gates of hell and is not free. If the high clergy of the Catholic Church offers its "disinterested" arm to accompany the crooked walk of the Mexican political system it does so, not betting on continuity, but seeking a good place for observation (and accommodation) when it all falls.

The beast called the "Military" has the body of an armadillo with cleft feet and the face of a hyena, it remains with its head lowered, its gaze fixed on its bloody claws. Upon seeing it the Hydra exclaims:

"Octavio - Good, you can do what you wish; but he is a brave soldier with experience.

Antonio - So is my horse, Octavio, which is why I give it a generous ration of feed. It is a creature which I have taught to fight, to turn away, to stand or run in a straight line, guiding always with my intelligence the movements of its body. And to a certain point Lepido is nothing else. He must be taught, trained and directed; he is a subject devoid of his own ideas, fed by artifices, curiosities and imitations, which, used and vulgarized by others, begin to be the style for him. Don't refer to him as anything else but an instrument."

William Shakespeare, Julius Caesar.

On the other hand, the State-Party System tries to "administer" its internal purges and distribute quotas and profits (it forgets that it also distributes costs and rebellions). While the "new" political class tries to keep itself in the national pinnacle grabbing the key posts, that is, the ones which make economic decisions: the "old" politicians withdraw to the regions.

"For national purges, regional resistance" is the new response with which the old political class tries to annul the curse of "modernity", and the displacement they suffer because of globalization, the leadership of the technocrats, and the rise of popular struggles. Examples? The Tabasco of Madrazo and the Puebla of Bartlett.

There are three national struggles which are evident: the one carried out to reject an economic model which is nothing but a slow death: the one played out in the capital for the possibility of another Mexico with major social participation and which demands a solution for indigenous demands and peace in Chiapas. The most regional of the struggles is the most national: Chiapas. The 4 municipalities in conflict or the demands of about 150 people (according to Labastida Ochoa) continue to shake once and again all the national territory and all the social sectors.

The heretofore improbable national struggle against national Power turns now, possibly. In order to free itself of it, the Power does not respond frontally, it changes arena and erases the national panorama and goes to the regional spaces. The national struggles do not have in front of them a political class. They clash (without any shock absorber) with the Army and the electronic mass media. There is no governmental interlocutor for national demands or dialogues.

The Sea ("With a waist fit for amorous gestures/ sweet, reddish, pleasant, lovely,/kind and measured, graceful and loving in all things" - "The book of Good Love", Arcipreste de Hita. Seventh Key), peeks at the picture over my shoulder and says: "It is a collage. The figures can be cut out of any national newspaper of recent days. It doesn't matter if it is out of the political section, the gossip columns or the financial section."

To the governmental technocrats the only thing which worries them are the macroeconomic indicators and their international image. They can (and in effect, they do) dismiss the society they are supposedly governing, and dedicate themselves completely to serve the "new voter": financial capital.

While nearly half of Mexicans lost their quality of life in 1997 as compared to 1996, 40% stayed the same and only 13% were better off, while the number of people living under the poverty level slowly increased (1994 - 11.3%, 1996 - 17.2%, 1997 - 16.3%). While jobs grow with salaries at less than minimum and only in the maquila industry; in sum, while the country crumbles at his feet, Ernesto Zedillo declares in Davos, Switzerland, without any embarrassment: "The challenge we confronted is not recuperation, that has already happened, it is in fact a thing of the past..." (Economic data from Jose Luis Calva, in "El Universal", 6-11-98).

At any rate, there is no attempt to brake the national crisis and seek political solutions, the objective is to do away with the old political class and make the markets impermeable in order to immunize them against the crisis and make them operational, productive, independent of political vicissitudes.

A collage? Vale. So here you have the seven beasts of the horror of Power in Mexico. A great table is presided by the Hydra of a State-Party system and the medusa of Organized Crime, and with them is the politician-zarigueya, the intellectual-mouse, the banker-serpent, the clergyman-demon, and the military man-hyena.

If the "old" politicians try to "govern" the country, the "new" politicians will only dedicate themselves to "administering" the destruction of the Nation. For years, De la Madrid-Salinas-Zedillo have not governed Mexico. They have dedicated themselves to constructing an impenetrable "dome" over the financial market. A "dome" which resists the earthquake of 1985, the Cardenista insurrection of 1988, the Zapatista rebellion of 1994, the Zedillista betrayal of 1995, the appearance of the EPR in 1996, the scandalous defeat of the PRI in July and the massacre of Acteal in December of 1997. It doesn't matter that the Nation is crumbling, the true obsession of Zedillo and his little men is the stability of the stock market.

Together they participate in this table at a quarter to twelve, at this dinner at the end of the century.

The food? I doubt you can call it that. But on the table you can see seven cups running over with a red liquid from a large bottle with a label which says "Acteal. Harvest 1997." Yes, the blood of Acteal is for this modern beast the appetizer for the main course yet to come: the destruction of the Mexican nation...

But if the technocrats can lie, forget and make themselves impermeable to the blood and the mud which they promoted in Acteal, they cannot control, for example, the ups and downs of Asia. So for Zedillo and his gang, the Tokyo stock market is closer to the National Palace than the Zocalo in Mexico City. With his mind concentrated on the international financial fluctuations, there is little for the government to do in regards to the Nation: only armed force and simulation.

In order to fulfill is government program (which is nothing more than waiting for the problems to become biodegradable in popular memory), Zedillo rehearses numerous training exercises with "government teams", and designs his "new" political class according to his own mediocrity (Liebano Saenz, Jose Angel Gurria and Juan Ramon de la Fuente); he remakes his ties and commitments with National Action; he mixes it up with the Minister of governance who is nothing more than the cherry on top of the political cocktail.

But the problems do not resolve themselves, they grow worse. Upon "revealing" his new potentate (the minister of health and the head doctor for the first lady, Juan Ramon de la Fuente) in the pastoral scene which the political system has made of Chiapas, Zedillo has added another factor to the unleashed forces which eye the year 2000.

The recomposition of his relationships with the PAN has the problem that there is now as many parties of National Action as pre-candidates to the presidency of the republic. With the molotov cocktail which Labastida has in Governance, the supreme one seems to make a decisive turn in his media politics: he will no longer pretend he doesn't have the foggiest idea about how and where to lead the country, he will now show it openly.

The old alliances are torn, there are no "government teams". The blender of the crisis mixes and concocts incredible cocktails: Shameful, confessing Salinistas, reluctant leftists, wild rightists, living cadavers of the old system, recycled mediocres, co-opted dissidents, fraudulent technocrats, diarrheatics of lies, deaf and deafening demagogues.

But the national chaos is not like that in the regional fiefdoms. The Mexico of yesterday actualizes itself in the province. Ineffective and inefficient, the "Mister President" isn't even taken seriously by his co-believers. For them, he is nothing but a bothersome parenthesis, a so-and-so part-time spectacle, a merchant with bad taste who sells a non-existent product: the Mexico of the macroeconomic bonanza. The internal purges of the PRI do not provoke a maladjustment of the political system, they are more the result of the disorder.

Here is the picture of the last dinner of Power. Treachery and dishonor in word and deed is the common denominator of the diners. Decrepit and broken-down, this image is sold to us on a daily basis as the most modern, the most new.

The new political class is not new, it is not a class, it is not political. It is a taste of what the Mexican political system never imagined would end. So it did not prepare its replacement, and now it improvises, prematurely and stupidly, "teams" which have nothing in common beyond the desire for Power and wealth.

The Mexican political system intends to celebrate not its end and the end of the century, but the birth of a new millennium and its rebirth.

This is not a final picture in this picture, it is a repetition. It is not the end of the nightmare, it is its eternal repetition. To do so it must feed on blood, on the lives of those who wait to sit at...

The Table Below...

The picture to be made.

"Happy will be the men of the world and the people of all the earth will prosper: the Bears, Honey Gatherers, Cabcoh, the Foxes, Chamacob, the Weasels who suck blood of the vassals are finished. There will not be miserable governors, miserable governments; there will not be lackeys of princes nor those who ask for their substitutes. This is the charge, the one manifest on this 12 Ahahu Katun... Just and obedient will be the orders of the legitimate Gentlemen for the happiness of the world."

The book of the books of Chilam Balam.

The table below is still disordered and unattended. There are only a few who come to it to eat and find one another. The new diners are scattered everywhere, in Civil Society, in the Non-governmental Organizations, in the Political Organizations and the Political-Military organizations, in the political parties, in the Churches, in the Means of Communication, even in the Army. For now each one seeks to satisfy his own hunger. Its collectivity is still, in despair. They are, we are, a fragmented hope, a rainbow of light to be made yet. Perhaps we are not "new" political actors in the modern national scene, perhaps we are the actors of always, the ones who must always be quiet while the "important" ones declare their parliaments and receive flowers, applause and whistles. In the new scene which we want to make reality, national sovereignty is sustained and wins.

Perhaps we are the same ones of always, but always other, new, better.

The table below is still not filled. They say that in order to sit at it only dignity is required and a... periscope?

Vale. Health and... what? A table is missing so there are three? Oh yes! The third was and is the first, a table for making love to the sea.

(Second Key).

From (the third table) of the mountains of the Mexican Southeast,
Subcomandante Insurgente Marcos.
Mexico, February of 1998.

48. An Inverted Periscope or Memory, a Buried Key

February 24, 1998

La Jornada

> "...so that this theory of the Hollow Earth gives body, so to speak, to the millenary hermetic intuition: what lies underground is the same as what lies above ground!"
> - Umberto Eco, Foucault's Pendulum

I. History: Learning to See Underground

In the midst of a beach of clouds so that the Sea may rest from her weariness (fourth key), the full moon is a pearly star, so fat that its edges seem filed down. Leaning back as we are, I tell the Sea the story Old Antonio told me on a dawn like this, but with tobacco smoke instead of clouds.

With a last spiral of smoke we completed the circle which, without saying so, we had been laying out around the moon to fix it in the sky. It was useless, she kept on going, vanquishing hours and clouds. We were quiet, stalking a "tepescuintle" (type of cava or large guinea pig). Old Antonio was set on demonstrating to me that one can also "shine" the "tepes" under a full moon.

"There it is! Do you see it?" Old Antonio shouted to me in a whisper.

"Yes," I lied, while I uselessly searched for the emerald color eyes that Old Antonio's flashlight's beam was supposed to draw up.

The cane shone with a dry sound which soon died down under the tenacious drum beat of the crickets. I ran towards the spot Old Antonio's flashlight had signaled. A "tepescuintle" of about one meter in length was shaking, with the blunt edge of the machete I completed the meal begun with Old Antonio's cane. I picked it up and carried it to where Old Antonio was rolling another cigarette.

"You didn't even see it," he says without looking at me.

I, to tell the truth, was "bird watching" waiting for the moon to fall down once and for all, but I firmly repeated the lie: "Yes, I saw it!"

The flash from a match lights up Old Antonio's smile and the cigarette on his lips.

"How did you know when to light the lamp and where to shine it?"

I ask him in order to change the conversation.

"I saw it down here," Old Antonio answers, and he points with a gesture and his hand towards the ground.

"Did you see it below the ground?" I ask-say mockingly.

Old Antonio does not respond. Well, not directly. Suddenly, leaning back, he begins to tell me...

The Story of the Buried Key

"They tell that the very first gods, those who gave birth to the world, had a very bad memory and they tended to easily forget what they were doing or saying. Some say that it was because the greatest gods had no obligation to remember anything, because they came from when time had no time, that is to say, that there was nothing before them, and if there was nothing, then there was nothing to have a memory of. Who knows, but the fact is that they used to forget everything. This ill they inherited to all those who govern the world, and have governed it in the past. But the greatest gods, the very first ones, learned that memory is the key to the future and that one should care for it like one cares for one's land, one's home, and one's history. So that, as an antidote for their amnesia, the very first gods, those who gave birth to the world, made a copy of everything they had created and of all they knew. That copy they hid underground so that there would be no confusion with what was above ground. So that under the world's ground there is another identical world to the one here above ground, with a parallel history to that of the surface. The first world is underground."

I asked Old Antonio whether the underground world was an identical copy of the world we know.

"It was," Old Antonio answered me, "no longer". An it's that-he explained-the outside world began to get messy and disorderly as time went by. "When the very first gods left, no one in the governments remembered to look down below in order to put in order what was getting out of place. So that each new generation of bosses thought that the world he inherited was simply that way and that another world was impossible. So that what is underground is identical to what is above ground, but it is so in a different way."

Old Antonio said that that's why it is a custom of the true men and women to bury the newborn's navel. They do it so the new human being may take a peek at the true history of the world and learn how to struggle so he/she may put it back in order, as it should be.

So that down below not only is the world, but also the possibility of a better world.

"And the two of us are also down there?" asks a sleepy Sea.

"Yes, and together," I answer.

"I don't believe you," says the Sea, but she discreetly turns on her side and peeks through a little hole left by a small pebble on the ground.

"Truly," I insist, "if we had a periscope we could take a look."

"A periscope?" she whispers.

"Yes," I tell her, "a periscope, an inverted periscope…"

II. The Chaotic Shell of Globalization

"Afterwards I understood that the image was being projected by another screen, located above my head, on which it appeared reversed, and that on that second screen it was the eyepiece of a rudimentary periscope, built, so to speak, with two boxes joined at an obtuse angle, the longest one extended like a pipe out of the box, above my head, and behind me, towards a window from which, clearly, thanks to an internal play of lenses which enabled it to cover a broad range of vision, it could catch the images from the outside."
- Umberto Eco, Ibid.

The world process of homogenization/fragmentation brought about by neoliberalism has swept away the old evidences of power and it has re-ordered them or replaced them with new ones. Among the victims of this new world war are the National State and the tryad upon which its survival used to rest, that is to say: the internal market, the national language and culture, and the local political class. In order to maintain, strengthen and make these three aspects grow, the National States relied upon the police force and the army, governments, institutions, and laws, the media, and the intellectuals, briefly upon all that WAS the essence of the Modern State. WAS, it no longer is.

The complex process of globalization seen as what it is, as a war of destruction/re-ordering, blows into pieces the internal markets, it tends to dilute within a brutal homogenization the national languages and cultures and insists upon displacing and destroying the local political classes.

With the crisis which have liquidated the three foundations of the National States, its supports: army, police, government, institutions, legislations, media, intellectuals, also come into crisis.

The gaps left behind by these annihilating crisis do not remain empty.

"The financial globalization has created, on the other hand, its own State. A Multinational State which has its own instruments, its networks and its action media. It is the constellation formed by the International Monetary Fund (IMF), the Organization for Cooperation and Economic Development (OCED) and the World Trade Organization (WTO)" (Ramonet, Ignacio. "Disarming the Markets". "Le Monde Diplomatique", December, 1997 # 525).

The financial hyperbombs, detonated at the convenience of the Global Power, have devastated the political, cultural and economic surface of the nations of the world. The recount of damages shows unemployed in the millions, multiple wars in microregions, irreversible destruction of the natural habitat, exploitation of child labor, countless deaths due to misery, millions of homeless in search of better life conditions, and massacres like the one in Acteal.

But also among the ancient "from above" there are losses. The agonizing National States drag with them the old political and economic powers. To the massive bankruptcies of companies are added the collapse of entire political classes.

The logic of the neoliberal globalization is not only economic, it is also political. The imposition of an across the borders' economy is not only a forced opening of the capillary of the national markets, it is also, (and above all) a fight against the one responsible for the emergence and protection of these markets, the National State. The homogenization of the economy runs parallel to the fragmentation and the pulverization of the "old" politics, and to its replacement by a "modern" political class.

There are disorderly remains left over from the complex puzzle which kept on top for decades the old dominant powers. A chaos of interests, and of personalities who represent those interests, strolls through the ever narrower hallways of the National Powers. The politicians of old are replaced with new models: politicians with a thousand faces...

III. The New Politics and Its Illegal Holders. The 7 Faces of Proffesional Politicians

> "'When I use a word,' Humpty Dumpty said, in rather a scornful tone, 'it means just what I choose it to mean - neither more nor less'.
> 'The question is,' said Alice, 'whether you can make words mean so many different things'.
> 'The question is,' said Humpty Dumpty, 'which is to be the master-that's all.'"
> - Lewis Carroll

At the same time that the National States are destroyed, the World State becomes consolidated. But the latter does not need any society, it can do away without one because the Power which it is made the repository of, is the one granted by the financial markets and the megacorporations. Instead of electing citizens, the stock exchanges grant the necessary and only legitimacy: that of economic power.

Things being as they are, the World State needs, and produces, new politicians to lead it. Politicians who are non-politicians (since the social founding stone of politics, the citizen, has been eliminated) who are a sort of cybernetic mutants capable of performing various functions (after being duly programmed according to the neoliberal software, of course). These non-politicians are "produced" in centers of "high" technocratic education (Oxford, Harvard, Yale), and are exported to the various countries to complete the destruction of the National States. To accomplish that, they must have...

Face One: The Manager-Politician- In the modern "National" State, politics are fundamentally market economy. The country must be conceived like a larger or smaller business enterprise and must be managed as such. The political plans resemble investment budgets and cost and benefits estimates. The so called "public administration" becomes each time more administrative and less public.

Like in a business enterprise, the most important factor is productivity, the largest benefit at a minimal cost. Social programs, political openings and closings, international alliances, national alliances and agreements, the ups and downs of political "success", governmental plans, and electoral processes are subordinated to this criteria.

For the Manager-Politician the citizens are nothing more than employees, and civil servants are foremen with a fluctuating decision making power. The Nation and its priorities are valued with "modern marketing" criteria: the only valued people are those who are worth as producers/consumers. And those who are not worth as such, can and should be discarded, eliminated.

Face Two: The Lawyer-Politician- For the economic globalization, the legislative structure of the former National State becomes a straight jacket and an obstacle to be overcome.

In general, the national legislations respond to a triple aspect. On the one hand, the historical aspect, which collects the Nation's past and which consists in a judicial assimilation of that past. On the other hand, the aspect which incorporates popular struggles and their demands, and regulates through judicial norms, the satisfaction of such demands and/or their redefinition. At a third level, it deals with the judicial forms with which the dominant political classes "legalize" their power and legitimacy.

But this judicial structure, the primary cohesive force of this National State, is a legal obstacle to the bringing about of the dissolution of the nations that globalization assumes and needs. So that neoliberalism breaks with that legal body and builds one to its own size. In the name of "free trade" "national" legislatures in education, labor law, the environment, public health, land tenure, the use of natural resources, migration, etc. are repealed/abrogated. To achieve this, transnational judicial instruments are created. An example? In the OCED the Multilateral Agreement on Investments (MAI) is being secretly negotiated since may 1995, to be signed by the member countries in 1998. This agreement gives investors a great deal of power before the governments, in matters related to investments, contracting, and benefits' management.

That is why the "modern" politician must also be a lawyer of the international monies, a devil's advocate.

Face Three: The Publicity Agent-Politician- The "markets' explosion" does not walk alone. It goes hand in hand with the "technological revolution" and with the resulting creation of the communication super-highways. By means of the first, and through the others, public space is invaded by the market and its key concepts, buy, sell. So that world politics is practiced as "global publicity".

The political leader is fabricated by means of publicity. Gray and mediocre men simulate to have a statesmen's stature (like Ernesto Zedillo in Mexico) thanks to the use of theatre and publicity techniques. The "legality" (not the legitimacy) of the government is more dependent each day on the publicity machine, which is a capricious as the market it serves. A well managed scandal can destroy a political career or elevate it, even in alternating times (see Clinton and the remiss of "Deep Throat" set up in the Oval Office of the White House). Once politics are reduced to a market issue, that is to say, to an exchange of merchandises, the politician must be proficient in publicity techniques.

Face Four: The General-Politician- Politics, from its start in the history of humanity, is above all the exercise of organized violence. That is why the modern politician is also a General. If yesterday the "Nation" was the pretext for wars, now it is the "ORDER-LY liberty" (with the clarifying "market" carefully simulated). Mass assassination and destruction are also marketing "publicity media". The United States are exemplary at this. In Mexico, Acteal, and the war that Zedillo is carrying on against the Indian populations, have won him the applause of television commentators, intellectual journals, corporations' managers, the high clergy, and decadent jurists.

The monsters that these generals provoke have little or nothing to do with "ORDER". Disorder is the rule, and chaos is carefully administered by a world economy that continues to have an important support in the war market. After the end of the third world war (or "cold war"), the weapons' expenditures are reduced all over the world. But they begin to peak again after 1994: In the Middle East it goes from 11.9 billion dollars to 15.3 billion in 1996. In Asia from 7.0 billion to 8.9. In Latin America from 0.8 to 1.6 billion. In South East Asia from 0.9 to 1.4 billion. In the former USSR from 0.1 billion to 0.3 billion. Only in Western Europe, OTAN decreases from 9.3 to 8.5 billion.

The International Institute of Strategic Studies (IISS) declared that in 1996 the world market of military hardware increased 8% and reached 39.9 billion dollars. In 1994 it had already increased 13%. All this after having fallen, from 1987 and 1994, at least 61.5% (International Courier #366. Nov., 1997). In relation to the main weapons' merchants in 1996: The U.S. have 42.6% of the world market, The United Kingdom 22.1%, France 14.1%, Russia 8.6%, Israel 3.3%, and China 1.5%. After 1990, The U.S., The United Kingdom, and France went up in weapon's sales. The former USSR fell back, and Israel and China remained in the same place (Ian Black and David Fairhall in "The Guardian", London, UK, 1997).

The Fifth Face: The Ambassador-Politician- Once the borders are broken for the capitals and the market is redefined as the supreme master, the internationalization of the political work forces modern politicians to perform more like travelling salesmen, flu-ent in foreign languages and drawing room diplomacy. The modern politician has no defined nationality and no other idiosyncrasy than that of the market. He is North American in the United States, and in Latin America, and in Europe, and in Asia, and in Africa, and in Oceania. His only fatherland is Wall Street, his color is dollar green, he thinks in English and lives according to the Dow Jones and Nikkei rhythm.

The Sixth Face: The Historian-Politician- In neoliberalim, History recycles itself in order to deny itself and provoke repentance. The globalized sacrifice of utopias includes the burning of the flags of rebellion and the banners of cynicism and conformity are embraced instead. Knowledge recycles itself and it recycles its "priests". The new truth, that of the financial markets, needs new prophets. The new politician is also a historian, but in the opposite sense. For him only the present has any value and the past has to be seen as responsible for everything bad that occurs. "The true history", the neo-politician tells himself and tells us, "begins with me".

The Seventh Face: The Generalist-Politician- As the markets logic invades everything social, and as the politician is transformed in the "conductor" of such an invasion, his "knowledge" must cover everything, that is why he feels he has the capacity to give opinions about everything. And if a part of that "general all encompassing knowledge" is not translatable in marketing terms, then that part does not deserve any attention whatsoever.

Those are the 7 faces of the modern politician. Are you interested in the job? No intelligence whatsoever is required (Menem in Argentina, Fujimori in Peru, Zedillo in Mexico prove that). It's enough to obey the markets.

IV. The Old Politician and Its Living Corpses.

> "No matter where we look, a substantial part of the silhouettes of what we used to know, of what we believed in, have disappeared, as if the memorized sky-line of ideas and social projects had vanished in smoke and we had been left without the fundamental imaginaries of a culture we, not too long ago, used to call progressive in opposition to reactionary culture."
> - Manuel Sanchez Montalban, Pamphlet from the simian's planet

The old politics, that of principles and programs, sacrifices itself on the altar of the global market. It is now the free interplay between supply and demand which determines the ideological orientation of the "modern" political parties. To have a good product to compete against others in the "consumer's choices" is what matters. The political proposal turns out to be a trivia item to be consumed, digested and disposable. Each day, less citizens know what the political organizations' history, principles and programs are all about. Increasingly, every day, the various offers are different in relation to the different characters (sometimes not even that, as the

Mexican PRD comes to show). The political proposals are not that, they are opinions and positions in regard to problems arising from a given situation. They have, therefore, the perseverance of a weather vane in the middle of a storm. As in a merry-go-round in a village carnival, the right wing becomes center and left, the left wing turns to the right and center. Mounted on top of the figure of his choice, the citizen goes through the entire ideological spectrum.

Modern politics are increasingly becoming an endeavor of the elite. And its supreme exercise in the work of an elite among elite's. Society goes from being an occasional actor to being a constant spectator.

Soon the citizen's "politics" will be practiced electronically. In front of a computer, the citizen will "vote", that is to say, act as a guarantor. No more closed streets, no more demonstrations, no more meetings, no more taking of buildings, no more disturbances, which as its name indicates only disturb the markets, that is to say the "Nation". The citizen will choose a political option like he chooses a product in a supermarket, but from home.

What exists overcomes and defeats that which is necessary. The polls and the statistics direct the political discourse, just like historical analysis and ideological convictions used to do previously. There is no longer the transformation of historical thought into political theory, and from it into principles and a program of struggle. Now "modern" politics are the translation of the market study into a marketing program, and of the latter into a publicity campaign.

The atrophy is vertiginous. The partisan machine becomes omnipotent and tramples over political philosophy, the proposal of transformation/conservation of social relations and definitions before the political specter. In that sense, the most "modern" politics can be found in the land of Mexico.

A chronic amnesia affects political organizations the world over. If anyone mentions the past, he must do so with a mixture of condemnation. shame, and repentance. The "I won't do it again" is the optimal and only axiom of modern historical thought.

But historical "oversights" will sooner than later present their bill. Exactly like in economics , in the political market there is no "fair play" as in free competition. Power "plays" on the side of its kindred and against its rivals. The basic cultural code contains fixed elements (for instance: left = revolution = violence = chaos = catastrophe...). The "good of the elite" transforms itself into "the common good". The conservation of power is equaled to the consolidation of progress, security and development. Once again Mexico demonstrates to be the brightest student in the mastery of the neoliberal lessons of "politics."

The so often mentioned (and so often violated) freedoms of the "modern democracies": freedom of speech, assembly, and association, are now redefined according to the world market's logic. But the only freedoms are those of the buying and selling (trade) which, as it is obvious, are rather selective, exclude the majority and make up the political endeavors (outside of the specifically electoral work, that is to say, most of the time) as something having to do with very few, the most powerful few ones.

V. The Underground Currents Of Critical Resistance.

"Now we had all modernity overrun by laborious moles that drilled the subsoil spying the planet from below".
- Umberto Eco, Ibid.

The Portuguese writer Jose Saramago says that "contrary to what they usually would like you to believe, there is nothing easier to understand than the History of the world, although many educated people are still adamant in affirming that it is too complicated for the limited understanding of the masses."

The neoliberal fear of history is not so much a fear of its existence (after all the poor also exist, and they can be ignored), but a fear that one may get to know it, and learn from it.

In order to avoid that, History is kidnapped by those "learned people" and adequately made up, so as to make it unrecognizable to those below.

The kidnapping of History by the elite's is meant to "remodel" its consumption in order to make the human being's fundamental patrimony: memory, disappear.

In the new "world history", the present defeats the past and takes hold of the future. Today is the new tyrant, it is to it that one swears allegiance and obedience.

But all over the world, moles of every color and size rummage in the hidden History and find, and understand. Every so often those moles emerge and open holes of underground light that illuminate the ground surface grays of neoliberal chaos.

Besides trying to kill them, globalizing power trains its "thinkers" to try and isolate those moles from History. The modern intellectuals determine, with dark judgements and juries, the banalization and disqualification of critical thought. "Poetry, utopia, mesianism", are the most common charges. The sentence? Persecution and slander.

It must be understood, that the constant emergence of these moles, scandalously coincides with the appearance of social mobilizations. And these defy the established order because they also defy the modern political endeavors. The "intruders" of politics stalk behind every corner of History.

Against modern politics, and with History as its flag, the world's civil society insists in reemerging once and again. It sparkles above ground, and it submerges itself again in order to reappear once more.

The She-Phoenix remakes herself in the nest of History...

VI. Noncomformity As a Road (Third Key).

"Que ella grito': !cuan verdadero par
Parece este uno concordante!
Amor tiene razon, razon ninguna,
Si asi pueden quedar las partes."
- El Tortolo y el Feniz, The Phoenix and the Dove
William Shakespeare
(SIXTH KEY)

Paraphrasing it freely it says something like:
"That she screamed: What a true pair
This one seems to be concordant!
Love is right, but reason is not,
If thus the parts may stay."

La Mariya (tojolabal, 4 years old and an IQ of 180 - which disqualifies her for modern politics) has come out a winner in the sling shot contest. She defeated three little boys (of the 6 of us who were present). The children, I imagine because of their age (Huber is 4, Andres 3, and Andulio 6), do not feel hurt in their "macho" feelings we Zapatistas are so proud of. The Sea places la Mariya on her shoulders and declares with solemnity the triumph of feminine power. I am the Sup, so I take the side of the "machitos" and I argue that it was sheer chivalry and not bad marksmanship what left "my little boys" out of the contest. "The prize!," the Sea and la Mariya shout in unison. I don't have any more candy so, instead, I offer...

The Tale of the Nonconformist Little Toad

Once upon a time there was a little toad who was not satisfied with being a little toad, and who wanted to be a crocodile. Then he went down to the swamp to look for the crocodile, and told him: "I want to be a crocodile." The crocodile answered him: "You can't be a crocodile, because, as things stand, you are a little toad." "Yes," said the little toad, "but I want to be a crocodile." What do I have to do to be a crocodile?" The crocodile said: "There is nothing to do, one is born a crocodile, and that's how things are, a crocodile is a crocodile." The little toad told him: "But I don't want to be a little toad, I want to be a crocodile." "Do you know where and with whom I can voice my nonconformity at being a little toad so they may let me be a crocodile?" "I don't know, maybe the owl knows," the crocodile answered. And then the little toad went into the woods in search of the toad. There he met another little toad and asked him where he could find the owl. "That one only works at night," the other little toad answered him, "but be careful when you talk to him, because the owl eats little toads." Then the little toad waited for night to fall and while he waited he built a fortification to protect himself from the owl's attacks. He piled one stone atop the other until he built himself a small cave and he went inside it. When night came, so did the owl, and the little toad asked him from inside his cave: "Mr. owl, do you know where and with whom I can voice my non-conformity at being a little toad so they may let me be a crocodile, which is what I want to be?" "Who is talking to me, and from where?," the owl asked in turn. "It's me, and I am here," answered the little toad, and the owl swooped on the little toad to grab him with its claws, but since the little toad was inside the cave, the owl could only grab a stone and he ate it thinking it was the little toad he was eating. Then the weight of the stone made the owl fall to the ground and it made his belly ache a lot. "Ouch!, ouch!" complained the owl, "help me get this stone out of my belly, otherwise I can't fly." The little toad told him that he would help him only if he answered his question. "First help me and then I'll answer you," the owl told him. "No way," said the little toad, "first tell me, because if I first help you get rid of the stone you are going to eat me, and you are no longer going to answer me."

"O.K." said the owl, "I am going to answer you, but the one you should show your unsatisfaction with being a little toad is the lion, he is the king and he knows why everyone is everyone. Now help me get rid of the stone." "No way, Jose," answered the little toad, "because if I get the stone out of your belly you are going to keep on eating little toads." "That's it," said the owl, "you want to be a nonconformist for nothing, you still worry about the other little toads, and you don't even want to be a little toad." But the little toad did not pay any attention to him and went on to look for the lion.

The lion lived in a cave, and the little toad thought that maybe the lion also ate little toads, and he had an idea. He soaked himself in a small puddle and he rolled himself on the dirt, and he came out disguised as a stone. When the lion came out of his cave, the little toad told him: "Mr. Lion, I come to show my non-conformity at being a little toad because I want to be a crocodile." "Who is talking to me?" asked the lion. And the little toad answered him: "It's me." "But you are a little pebble, what's all this about little toads and crocodiles?" the lion responded. "Well, I've come to show my nonconformity because one is not what one wants to be but what one already is," said the little toad. "That's the way it usually is," said the lion, "one is what one is and one cannot be something else." "All one can be is to be what one is well," said the lion yawning philosophically. At that point it started to rain, and the mud that covered the little toad was washed away and one could clearly see that it was a little toad and not a pebble. The little toad did not know if lions eat little toads and he left jumping along back to his pond.

The little toad was jumping along very sad, jumping, and jumping, because one is what one is and cannot be something else, and because all one can be is to be well what one is. Saddened by his thoughts the little toad arrived at his pond and he hurried to look for the crocodile. When he arrived at the swamp he didn't find the crocodile. He looked for him all over, and couldn't find him. He asked the other animals and they responded "Didn't you know? A hunter found the crocodile and now he is a purse, and a pair of crocodile shoes..." The little toad remained thinking, and when everyone thought he was going to say that he was very glad he wasn't a crocodile and that he was very glad to be a little toad, he exclaimed: "That's truly transcending being an animal and not fuck ups!" And he began to study and practice to become a good crocodile. It seems he did a fairly good job, and was able to deceive a hunter.

They say that the little toad is now a very expensive coin purse. "It is made with the skin of a very special crocodile," says the wealthy matron who bought it.

The lesson of this story is that the stone blow matches the size of the toad. Tan-tan.

La Mariya got bored and left when the little toad was only about to go see the owl. The Sea has stayed (she can't do otherwise) until the end of the story.

"Calm down, Aesop," she jokes.

I am a misunderstood man, no doubt about it.

VII. A Morning Gestating In The Depths?

> " It seems to me to be self evident! The one who plots, if he plots, does so below the surface, not in broad day light. That has been known since the beginning of time. The domination of the world means the domination of what lies below. Of the underground currents."
> - Umberto Eco, Ibid.

Finally I think that Old Antonio is right when he says that below us there is a better world than the one we suffer in, that memory is the key to the future, and that (I add) History is nothing but an inverted periscope...

From (under) the mountain of the Mexican Southeast,
Subcomandante Marcos.
Planet Earth, February 1998.

P.S. The fourth, third and sixth keys open doors only known to the Sea. More keys and more doors are upcoming.

49. ABOVE AND BELOW: MASKS AND SILENCES

Mexico, 1998

> *"For the public man, most especially for the political, we have to demand of him that he possess the public virtues, all of which can be summarized in: fidelity to his own mask (…), keep it in good repair, for there is no political mess which is not an exchange, a confusion of masks, a bad rehearsal for a play, in which no one knows their parts. Endeavor, however, those of you who go into politics, that your mask be, as much as possible, your own work, make it yours yourselves, in order to avoid that others might put it on - or take it off - your enemies or your fellow politicians; and do not make it so inflexible, so impervious or impermeable that it suffocates your face, because, sooner or later, you will have to show yourself."*
> - Antonio Machado, Juan de Mairena

I. Mexico, the Middle of 1998...

Leaning against my shoulder, the sea sighs when it sees the complex plans of this new construction, drawn up through long and silent dawns, thought up from behind the masks that we are. And suddenly a gust of wind arrives, whipping the trees which are our windows, and shaking the large sheets of paper, full of drawings, of staggered scales, incomprehensible logarithms, of illegible letters that look more like obscure formulas of alchemy than scientific calculations.

In the middle of the year 1998 in Mexico and a wind arrives to break silences and to pull off masks.

After a long and heavy dry period, the rains begin to appear on the horizon of this country whose leaders are striving to take it to catastrophe. Protected by a trail of cloud, damp and amazed, I see half of 1998 go by and the last death rattles of a century which refuses to leave without scandals and outrage.

Far from here the World Cup assembles and summons emotions. The spell that is cast each time the ball rolls has been well understood by the South Americans, one to describe it, and the other to practice it. Eduardo Galeano, collector of these daily showers which some call "the history from below," and Diego Armando Maradona, who uses the ball to sing and to demonstrate that magic does not necessarily have anything to do with potions and esoteric formulas.

But from up here I do not see either Don Galeano or Don Maradona. Neither do I manage to see Olivio exercising his vocation of breaking nets ("and heads," says the sea, while trying to hide, to no avail, the markswoman that Olivio abandoned in his flight, after splitting Marcelo's head open). I do see, though, millions of Mexicans in the role in which the powerful have always wanted to see them, as spectators.

With national history stopped each time the Mexican football team faces off, the leaders of this country win a respite which reality relentlessly denies them. Millions of eyes glued to French soil allow the Power a short rest. The pleasure is short-lived, defeat arrives and the impasse which the role of spectators has allowed them comes to an end.

On this side of the world, the tragicomedy of national political life is also converted into spectacle, and the disorderly charade which is displayed every day in the halls of Power in Mexico receives no applause at all. There is time for the majority of Mexicans to stop being spectators to the scandals with which the governing class plans to end the century... and the country. Millions of nationals are now the victims of mega crimes and jumbo frauds.

If the shameful acts of the Mexican political class are merchandise for the powerful communications media, and whose successful presentation is measured in "rating" points, for the immense majority of those who struggle and die between the Rio Bravo and the Suchiate, they are only a continuation of the State crime which spans almost the entire century.

Determined to alert the citizenry to the growth of delinquency and violence, some communications media (those tied to the government) conceal the essential: the bloodiest and most brutal delinquents hold government positions (or are closely tied to them), and violence finds the federal government to be its primary executor, its largest instigator and its apologist par excellence.

In the spectacle of "great" Mexican politics, the confusion of masks and speeches keeps one from knowing for certain who is the judge and who is the criminal, who is the fraudulent and who the defrauded.

But it becomes more and more clear that Mexico at the end of the 20th century has its most criminal mask in the State one party system. In this Mexico, the growing State criminality (that which is exercised by the political Power) sees itself only equaled by the impunity with which it gives money, influence and proximity (or professed or embarrassed membership) to the select circle hovering around what some people still call (not without blushing certainly) "Senor President."

The middle of Ernesto Zedillo Ponce de Leon's six-year term has indelible marks, but the bloodiest of those is the daily crime of an economic model imposed through the indisputable arguments of bayonets, jail and the cemeteries. Even so, this State crime finds somber marks. Aguas Blancas in Guerrero in June of 1995. Acteal in Chiapas in December of 1997. El Charco in Guerrero in June of 1998, and Union Progreso and Chavajeval in Chiapas in June of 1998.

This face, the most irrational which the Mexican state has had in all its history, conceals its terrifying image behind another mask. And the sound of the blood which it collects day after day, is quieted through silence.

It would seem evident that masks conceal and silence quiets.

But the truth is that masks also reveal and that silences speak.

To conceal and to quiet, to reveal and to speak, masks and silence. These are the signs that will help to understand the end of this century in Mexico.

Yes, this is a country of masks and silences. I tell this to the sea, and she answers me, from behind her ski mask, with a silent gesture of paradox, which is more than eloquent, as she rolls up and guards the great plans.

But I tell you, and I tell myself, that there are masks and masks, and silences and silences.

There are, for example:

II. Masks and the Silence from Above

"I have heard much of your cosmetics: God has given you one face, and you make another; you prance, you swing your hips, you mispronounce, you give nicknames to God's creature, and you make of your ignorance your lasciviousness."
- William Shakespeare, Hamlet

What is the government's role in society? What should its role be? These questions are asked by the political parties, the analysts and by society. There are many responses to one and the other question, but the Mexican government has their own and, despite the madness of the Four Horsemen of the Apocalypse - Zedillo, Labastida, Green, Madrazo, Gurria, Ortiz, Rabasa and Albores (yes, I know already that I gave 8, but 4 are horsemen and 4 are beasts, you choose) - they impose them with blood (contributed by those from below) and fire (from those above).

Lacking the legitimacy which can only be obtained by the governed, these characters from the Mexican tragedy at the end of the century, supplant it with a mask made "ex profeso", that of the State of Law. In the name of the "State of Law" they impose economic measures, they assassinate, they imprison, they rape, they destroy, they persecute, they make war.

Without rational arguments, without legitimacy, without morals, the government of Mexico seizes its only resource: violence. But the government does not direct this violence against organized crime or against delinquency (that is, it does not use it against itself), it is used against the most impoverished, that is, a now immense majority, but which continues growing at the same rhythm as the country is collapsing.

It could seem to us that a collapse could have a thunderous sound, but, in this case, a silence covers it and announces it, the silence of the forgetting.

In order to supplant its lack of legitimacy with legality, the Mexican State (and not just the government) must carry out a complex surgical operation on the entire social order. That is, to eradicate the historical memory from the governed. And they try to do this by substituting the true history (in lower case), with the Official History (in upper case). And this Official History is not learned in books, rather it was created in the mental laboratories of postgraduates in foreign universities. Harvard, Oxford, Yale, and the MIT are the modern "Founding Fathers" of the current Mexican leaders. And so the Official History comes from as far away as the indicators of economic growth, these have the constancy of a weather vane in the middle of a storm. And so the present is the only possible history for these "blackboard boys" (as Carlos Fuentes would name them), the "computer kids" (as who-knows-whom would name them), or the "Pines Cartel" (as their drug trafficking associates call them). If constancy and pain and hard work are characteristic of the history of those from below, the ephemeral is the preferred place for the Official History. The "Today" of the stock markets is the historical reference of these technocrats who, thanks to the criminal Carlos Salinas de Gortari, today find themselves in political power in Mexico. This Official History has its mask.

The Mask of "Modernity." Does it seem attractive? Functional? Aerodynamic? Biodegradable? Cool? Lite? It is nothing of that, but it is sold and consumed with similar arguments. The Modernity of the neoliberal leaders in Mexico reveals an empty and dry country. In spite of publicity and marketing techniques, and notwithstanding the millions spent in cosmetics and makeup, the mask of Mexican Modernity is being more and more chipped away. And it is more and more difficult to not see what it is hiding: the destruction of the nurturing bases of the Mexican State, that is, the bases of National Sovereignty.

With "modernity" as a spinal column, a series of arguments (mask beyond a doubt) are wielded to justify (in the double meaning of "making justice" and "giving a reason for being") the dramatic destruction of all that which allows a country to keep its "national sovereignty" from being a mere rhetorical device. Ownership of subsoil wealth, of the territorial waters and air, of the lines of communication, of the businesses with social functions (education, health, food, housing, security), social policy, effective control of financial and commercial markets, money, language, government, armed forces, history, these are some of the foundations necessary for a State. Through various means, and behind several masks, but always with the same urgency, these bases of national sovereignty are being weakened, when they are not outright destroyed, by the neoliberal governments of Miguel de la Madrid Hurtado, Carlos Salinas de Gortari and (the student surpasses his teachers) Ernesto Zedillo Ponce de Leon.

With the masks of "industrial restructuring," "adaptation to the modern era of globalization," the "streamlining of public spending," the "elimination of subsidies which hinder free trade and economic development," "the international fight against drug trafficking," and "the end of the populist State," the Mexican governments since 1982 until the present have operated a veritable extermination campaign against the fundamental supports of national sovereignty.

Selling off state enterprises for a song, giving in to the pressures of international markets, abandoning their social service functions (or changing their function into the buying of votes), ending supports for basic products and controlling salaries, leaving the future of the national currency to the discretion of large financial centers, yielding their governmental activities to the publicity campaigns which the sales market of countries demands, awarding the national armed forces the role of neighborhood policemen in the global village, rewriting (and erasing) national history, thinking in dollars, all in all, the last Mexican governments have managed, through various means, to make this country less and less ours, and less and less a country.

Pay attention. What remains of the Mexican State to allow it to claim that it is sovereign? Hundreds of state enterprises have been sold, the pompously named "Mexican Stock Exchange" looks like a branch of the Asian markets (and those who peddle the idea that it may be a branch indeed, but it's a branch of the North American Exchanges), the only consistency in the price of basic products is their upward mobility, the Mexican peso lacks a language in the international currency market, the Mexican governments think in English and only translate into Spanish when they are directing themselves to nationals (although not with any luck, as Chancellor Green demonstrated), the Mexican federal army carries out (under orders from North American advisors) in the national mountains the same work which General Custer did with the indigenous in the United States, and high officials in the Mexican government respond swiftly and with certainty to the question: "When is Independence Day?" with a conclusive, "the fourth of July." Scandalous? Right, but for this we reach for the Forgetting. Another silence...

Yes, forget what we were, what brought us to here. Forget all the past, not just that of Deception and pain, but also, and above all, that of struggle and rebellion. But the peculiarity of that forgetting is that it doesn't try to erase what came before, but rather to condemn it, being ashamed of it, regretting it. As is evident, all attempts to "bring" the past into the present is subversion of the "peace and tranquility," it is illegal, ultimately something to be combated. There you have, for example, those Indians who "bring" Zapata to these times of modern globalization and they have him speak and make history. And (what a scandal!) even on the Internet that terrorist cry of Zapata Vive! can be heard. Subversion, even to speak. How well off we were with that Zapata in his grave, in the museum, in the book that was never opened! Therefore, those who "bring" Zapata are illegal and subversive, that Zapata is illegal and subversive because of the nightmares he provokes, and, ergo, history is illegal and subversive - not just because it questions today, but also because it makes one believe (and struggle for!) that another today is possible. And to conceal this silence, another mask...

Ah, the macroeconomic achievements! But, where are they? In the fortunes of the richest men in Mexico who are on the Fortune 500 list? In wages? In prices? In employment? In social security? Look for them, look and you will find that, behind the macroeconomic mask, is hidden an economic model which has been imposed on this country since the beginning of the 80's, 16 years of economic policy, enough to evaluate it.

Results? In addition to the loss of National Sovereignty, we have an historical reversal of... 30 years! Yes, Mexico '98 and Mexico '68 have in common not only an assassin heading the government with the presidential sash across his chest, but also the growth of poverty and growth in the number of the poor, the concentration of wealth in fewer and fewer hands, and the deterioration of social services, which, at one time, eased the lives of Mexicans.

From 1968 to 1977 the percentage of the population living in poverty declined rapidly, between 1977 and 1981 this decline was accelerated. "In this way poverty was able to be reduced in 18 years, from more than three-quarters of the population to less than half. However, after 1981, there was an abrupt change in direction, in which poverty not only stopped declining, it started to grow at an accelerated rate." (Boltvinik, Julio. "Economy and Welfare. Mexico at the End of the Millennium," in Vientos del Sur, 12-13, 1998. Mexico; and Hernandez Laos, Enrique. "Economic Growth and Poverty in Mexico," cited in Boltvinik, J. Ibid).

Now, at the beginning of 1998, we are at the same poverty levels as in 1968, 30 lost years. In addition, today we have fewer possibilities for improving our economic situation, "(...) the opportunities for the Mexicans' well-being in 1996, after almost three 5-year periods of the neoliberal model, have not only not grown, but they are 30% lower than in 1981. This results in a two-fold incapacity in the model. One part is the incapacity to make investment increase as rapidly as is necessary. (...) The other part is the growing incapacity to equitably distribute the investment throughout the population (...) That is, the model was incapable of growth, but it also concentrated more and more investment in fewer hands, thus decreasing the possibilities for the wellbeing of the population." (Boltvinik, J. Ibid).

Certainly these macroeconomic facts will not be to the liking of Senores Gurria and Ortiz (and I doubt that they can refute them), but the real fact is that there is another "macroeconomy," that of those from below, lower salaries, less and worse education, less and worse housing, less and worse health, less and poor food. Yes, behind the mask there is a catastrophe.

On top of this, add a few abbreviations, Fobaproa, and you will have completed a nightmare cocktail, in addition to their poverty, millions of Mexicans will now have to take responsibility for the rescue of those other criminals, the bankers, who use the "State of Law" as an alibi, and who have an ever willing accomplice and procurer in the Government.

Outrageous, certainly. But. Silence! Nothing can be done, it is the fatalism of globalization, imposing on us an indisputable silence and a conformist religiosity. It should not concern us that this resignation has reached all the way to Havana, since the destruction of Nations (which the globalization, irretrievably, entails) is presented to us as something self-evident, that is, natural, unquestionable and without contradiction.

Certainly neoliberalism has constructed, with its great financial capital, a formidable enemy, capable of dictating wars, bankruptcies, "democracies," lives and, above all, deaths in every corner of the world. However, this process of total globalization (economic, political and cultural) does not involve inclusion of different societies, incorporating their own characteristics. On the contrary, it involves the true imposition of one, and only one, thought: that of financial capital. In this war of total conquest everything and everyone must be subordinated to the judgment of the marketplace, whatever opposes or impedes it will be eliminated. But, in addition, it implies the destruction of humanity as a sociocultural collective and its reconstruction as a market element. To oppose neoliberalism, to fight against it, is not just a political or ideological option, it is a question of the survival of humanity. Someone warned that to go against globalization would be like going against gravity. Then, in any way: Down with the law of gravity!

The destruction of Mexico as a Nation must be hidden. And so another mask is necessary, that of Chauvinism. Motivated by an eagerness for peace, and trying to stop the extermination of the indigenous which the Mexican government carries out on chiapaneco lands, hundreds of men and women from Mexico and from other parts of the world come to southeastern Mexico. There is nothing more uncomfortable for the criminals than to have witnesses of their extermination laboratory which they have set up on Indian grounds; and so the ineffable Department of Government brings the double recipe: for the nationals, jail, and for those from other countries, expulsion (with a prior xenophobic campaign in the press, radio and television). Suddenly, with equally stupid explanations, the primary peddler of the National Sovereignty has a fit of patriotism and to the cry of "a good foreigner is a dumb and blind foreigner!" he sets to persecuting, harassing and expelling all those born in other lands who join their hearts to the struggle for peace with justice and dignity. The hundreds of foreign observers are left with beatings, rapes, threats, insults. For the foreign "investors" servile bowing, flattery and adulation abound.

And, as a grotesque adornment on this mask, comes the silence of Treason. Yes, treason to the word given in San Andres. Treason to those who believe in the path of dialogue. Treason to those who fight for peace. Treason to those who thought that it was possible that the government would recognize the rights of the indigenous peoples. Treason to those who hoped that the war in southeastern Mexico would end. And the treason, the destruction, the forgetting, necessary to support an ideology, a "theory" that gives those crimes the reason that history so stubbornly denies them.

And so here comes the Mask of "Intellectual Objectivity." It is carried by a few characters in Mexico's cultural life who have free passage in the salons of the political, economic and religious power. Their first step was to begin criticizing the critics of the political system.

With the supposed "moral authority" which remorse confers, these intellectuals attack their colleagues who do not follow their frenetic path towards capitulation. "The operation to discredit critical reason was led by an intellectual 'beautiful people,' composed primarily of former young philosophers, former young sociologists and former young opinion leaders who knew the paths which would take them to the ancient teachings of the seated scribe." (Vazquez Montalban, Manuel. "Panfleto from the Planet of the Apes," Ed. Drakontos, Barcelona, P. 144). To that step is added others, and soon they are sharing the table with the high political, financial, religious, cultural hierarchies, that is, with the wills that drive the bloodthirsty vehicle of neoliberalism in Mexico. "The pragmatic power has relied not only on elegant teachers in order to move about with the old and new financial oligarchy, but it has also had at its disposal a chorus of organic intellectuals who have helped them to never write one line, nor have one idea of their own, at the same time providing them with the ideology indispensable for shooting and a complete collection of dithyrambs." Ibid.

At some moment these professionals of apostasy cease being court jesters with professional studies and/or published works, and become "advisors." Instead of sharing the crumbs from the table of Power (and making recommendations which will bring them significant economic advantages), these ideologues guide and advise our leaders. Certainly things don't always turn out the way the advisors and the advised might expect. And not just because of the continuous swings in their political positions and "serious" analysis (example: Jorge Alcocer, from the Salinas gang of intellectuals, who one day announced that he was forming a leftist party, and the next morning took a position as Under Secretary of Government), but also (and above all), because reality is not understood as it is, instead they counsel decisions based on the premise that reality should be what the Power wants it to be.

There is a long list of disasters, but by only mentioning "Chiapas," we have the one which represents all the others. The former independent intellectuals, and today devoted advisors, counseled "a strong hand," and "firmness" in the government treatment of the indigenous rebels of southeastern Mexico. "All the costs have already been paid, we have nothing to lose," they said to support their recommendation of using a military road to definitively solve the conflict. They also advised a "new media campaign" (the name by which the government, and their advisors, know the speeches during public activities, press conferences and interviews at receptions) that would be consistent with "the policy of action" (c'est a dire de war) that they were carrying forward in the indigenous communities in the country. Result: barking, slogans, scoldings, boasts, threats, words and contradictions ("Intergovernmental conflicts," the PGR would say, referring, not to Celosio's assassination, but to the statements by Zedillo, Labastida and Rabasa).

The consequences of these actions and words are not suffered only by the indigenous victims of the extermination campaign against them, not only by Zedillo who stains his hand more and more with dark blood, not just by Labastida who sees his political aspirations for the Presidency of the Republic going up in ruins, not just by Rabasa, who sees the necessity for demonstrating that there is no idiocy spoken which cannot be surpassed (by him, himself) with flying colors the next day, not just by "Marshall" Albores who now occupies a privileged position among the assassins and thieves of this century.

Not only by them, the consequences are also paid by the intellectuals who are not "on one side or the other." With its military and media campaign, the government has managed only to reduce even more the narrow space for intermediate opinions. And so the "neutrals" are caught in a false dilemma: support the government or support the rebels.

The courtesy of minds contributes to the spread of desperation and clamors for an end to the "chiapanization" of national life.

Chiapas is a problem of public opinion: the words of war and the violent actions are only on the government's side, and on the side of the rebels is a silence which, to them, appears enormous, the "neutral" intellectuals are uncomfortable, because if they applaud government speeches and practices, they put themselves on the side of irrationality and crime, and if they criticize them, they put themselves on the side of a few hooded persons who, in addition to being rebels, are indigenous.

Their desperation is comprehensible, the war which the government is carrying out in Chiapas and Guerrero is splattering all sides now, and it threatens to stain both pens and immaculate analysis.

But there are those who are not perturbed by the dilemma, and embrace with fervent and religious devotion the task of "giving reason" to the State crime which is taking place in indigenous Mexico.

However, nothing is ever perfect, and the mistakes follow each other at a dizzying pace, provoking unease in the officious advisors. The discomfort of these intellectuals in the face of governmental stupidity hides the dissatisfaction of unappreciated advisors. The intellectuals of the indigenous annihilation, "for reasons of State," are made uncomfortable by the governmental tardiness in putting "an end" to that stone in the shoe.

Fortunately, the intellectuals of criminal objectivity (as well as their advised) are fewer and fewer, and they are more alone. There are, on the other hand, news media who have the honor of relying, for their pages and microphones, on political analysts, journalists and artists, who refuse the juggling that the government wishes to impose on them, and who continue dissecting national problems (and taking positions on them), looking for solutions that are inclusive, peaceful and rational.

With reason, history, legitimacy and the Nation lost, there is little left to the Mexican political system. It thinks that there is only one mask now that could save it and take it alive (although not now healthy and whole) to the other side of this century: The Mask of War.

III. The Mexican Federal Army: Between Angeles and Huertas

(Audio can be used by any news media in the service of the Supreme. Images will be those of the attacks on the communities of Chavajeval and Union Progreso, in the autonomous municipality of San Juan de la Libertad, Rebel Chiapas, on June 10, 1998.)

Look at the federal soldiers: so young, so strong, so well fed, so well equipped, so well trained, so... Look at them fight so heroically from behind their tanks, their light artillery, their helicopters, their bomber planes. Look with what decisiveness and courage they shoot and confront the enemy. What dedication! What great heroism! What bravery! What contempt for danger! What commitment to the defense of national sovereignty! Aren't they admirable? Don't you feel like singing the National Hymn where it says: "Mexicans to the cry of war..."

This is patriotism. It doesn't matter that the other side, the "enemy's" side, only has machetes, stones, sticks, hands, fingernails, teeth. It doesn't matter that on the other side, the "enemy's" side, are Mexican indigenous, those who first populated these lands, those who resisted the war of conquest, those who gave birth to the Nation fighting with Miguel Hidalgo, Jose Maria Morelos, Vicente Guerrero, those who fought against the gringos in 1847, those who fought by Juarez' side against the French invasion, those who gave flesh, blood and cries for justice in the revolution of Villa and Zapata, those who refused to be liquidated by a model, the neoliberal model, which makes a war of extermination against them through all means and in all forms.

It is not important, look at the brave federal soldiers fighting.

Don't look at the rapes, the beatings, the executions, the extermination of men, women, children and old ones. Don't look at the exodus of tens of thousands of displaced.

Don't look. Don't listen.

Only listen to Comandante Zedillo, the chief of those soldiers whom he has ordered to save Mexico... from those who are more Mexican than anyone.

Look and listen to what we tell you to see and hear.

This is nationalism! This is being a patriot! This is the "State of Law!" This is the Federal Army! The armed guarantor of the defense of National Sovereignty!

So strong and not caring that those they are facing are so weak! So brave despite the fact that those they are fighting are unarmed! So bold even though those they are fighting are defenseless!

Do not look at or listen to your commander-in-chief lowering his head, embarrassed, in front of his North American equivalent. Do not see or hear the clumsy and grotesque "translation service" with which the Chancellor tries to hide the cowardice of Zedillo's government in front of the open faucets of the empire of the stripes and murky stars. Don't look at his army, the federal army, giving military honors to the Supreme Commander of the chief of the... North American Army. Don't look at the Mexican officials accounting to and following orders from their United States "advisors."

Do not see or hear the silence of those Mexican indigenous who are fighting for democracy, liberty and justice.

Do not see or hear that anachronistic "For everyone, everything, nothing for us." To whom would that occur during these times of "save yourself if you can"?

Do not see or hear reality.

These indigenous ("Zapatistas" I believe they call themselves) are the primary enemy, they sell the homeland; those who want to deliver national sovereignty to dark foreign interests; those who want to rebel against economic injustice; those who demand that he who governs, governs obeying; those who demand democracy for all; those who want a place in the Nation; those who struggle for justice; those who want a roof, land, work, bread, health, education; those who defend the independence of Mexico; those who want a new world, better...

What am I saying? Don't listen! Don't look! Applaud!

There are our brave soldiers killing the dark enemy (the color of their skin gives them away)!

Shout! Viva Mexico! Again! Viva Mexico!

Look at and listen to the part of the war which our selfless soldiers delivered to their chief, Comandante Ernesto Zedillo Ponce de Leon, and which we offer you exclusively on this channel:

Part of the War #1998/6.

TO: Ernesto Zedillo Ponce de Leon, Supreme Commander
FROM: Operational Command Group of the Federal Army
THEATRE OF OPERATIONS: Southeastern Mexico
MILITARY CAMPAIGN: "The State of Law via actions"
DATE: December 22, 1997 to June 10, 1998
NUMBER OF TROOPS OF THE FEDERAL GOVERNMENT: 60,000 (Note: not including the number of special forces, those which the opposition calls "paramilitaries")
MILITARY EQUIPMENT OF THE FORCES OF THE SUPREME GOVERN-MENT: War tanks, armed personnel carriers, Hummer vehicles, reconnaissance air-craft, combat and bomber airplanes, helicopters, howitzers, mortars, light artillery, machine guns, automatic rifles, grenades, electronic surveillance equipment
NUMBER OF TROOPS OF THE TRANSGRESSORS OF THE LAW: 300 (including the masked joker who commands them)
MILITARY EQUIPMENT OF THE REBEL FORCES: shotguns, the kind they call "chimbas," 22 caliber rifles, sticks, machetes, stones, hands, fingernails, words and (as discovered by our intelligent intelligence services)... silence
ACTIONS CARRIED OUT:

- Acteal, Chenalho, Chiapas: 45 enemy casualties (men, women and children included), carried out by our special troops, in a tactical action they call "undercover"
- Various indigenous communities, Chiapas: An undetermined number of decommissioned weapons (previously planted by us), subversive books such as "the gospel according to the masked joker"
- Navil, Tenejapa, Chiapas: Two sacks of beans (which shows that the transgressors were preparing for bacteriological warfare) and some weapons which we planted
- Chavajeval, El Bosque ("San Juan de la Libertad" for the transgressors of the law), Chiapas: 3 enemy casualties owing to our brave and bold light artillery fire, mortars and land and air machine guns
- Union Progreso, El Bosque, Chiapas: 5 enemies executed for the crime of having rebelled against sacrosanct institutions
- Amparo Agua Tinta and Taniperla, in the self-styled autonomous municipalities of "Tierra y Libertad" and "Ricardo Flores Magon," Chiapas: 2 wooden shacks burned, one mural destroyed, dozens arrested (alive, unfortunately)
- State of Chiapas in general: an undetermined number of dead, wounded and imprisoned, product of actions which are called "undercover," and the strict application of the law

Result: resounding triumph of the state of law which you honorably represent.
My dear sir: the national armed forces have covered themselves in glory.
Flourishes.

P.S. If they could!

P.S. To note the selfless labors and ample intelligence of Field Marshall Roberto Albores Guillen, under whose orders we had the honor of serving the Republic.

P.S. From Marshall Albores: grrrr, bow-wow, woof, grr.

Response:

TO: Operational Command Group of the Federal Army

FROM: Ernesto Zedillo Ponce de Leon

Congratulations. The federal Army will not be leaving Chiapas. Continue on with your enforcement of legality and the establishment of the state of law.

The only thing that is left for me to say: Guys, get tough on them!

"Everything with violence, nothing with politics."

EZPL

Flourishes

P.S. A big hug (and a few croquettes) for my faithful friend and servant, Camp Marshall Albores.

P.S. Never before have so few (me and those who support me) owed so much to so many (federales).

P.S. to the P.S. Didn't it go like that?

Look and listen to these courageous soldiers, applaud your eminent chiefs.

Don't see or hear the other soldiers, those who fight the fires and help the population with the natural disasters. Don't see or hear the soldiers who fight the national and international drug traffic. Don't see or hear the soldiers dead in the fight against organized crime, which means destruction, hunger and misery for hundreds of people.

Don't see or hear the soldiers who fall, those, yes, in the carrying out of their duties.

For these soldiers there is no applause, not even one word, nor one salute.

For these soldiers there is silence, the forgetting.

Don't see or hear the soldiers who fight fires in various states in the country.

Look at and listen to (and applaud!) the soldiers who set fires and worship the fire in the Mexican south and southeast.

Look at and applaud the Huertas soldiers. Do not see or hear the Angeles soldiers.

Don't look, don't listen. Take your mask and your silence. Don't look and don't listen. Don't choose...

General Felipe Angeles. Official of the Federal Army in times of the Mexican Revolution, he crossed over to rebel lines and put his ingenuity and his knowledge at the service of the cause of the oppressed. He fought under the orders of Francisco Villa in the Division of the North. His brothers in arms in the government army of that time branded him a traitor to his country. History remembers him as a military patriot.

General Victoriano Huerta. Official of the federal army during the times of the Mexican

Revolution, he put himself under orders of the ambassador from the United States of North America to the then President Francisco I. Madero. He headed the counter-revolution and organized massacres of indigenous and the destruction of villages in his military campaign against a transgressor of the law, the self-named "Emiliano Zapata." His brothers in arms of the then government army extolled him and praised him as a patriot. History remembers him as a traitor to his Homeland.

1998, the Mexican Federal Army: so close to the Huertas and so far from the Angeles. The mask of war, the silence of death always comes with it. And with death comes...

IV. The Masks and the Silences of Those From Below

"The night will pass,
The waters can spit,
They can shoot the sparrows,
They can burn the verses.
They can cut down the sweet iris,
They can break the song and throw it into a swamp.
But this night will pass."
- Manuel Scorza

The neoliberal model requires, for its maintenance and growth, the perpetration of a crime that is realized through millions of small and large crimes, and the State is in charge of collecting, in cash and efficiently, from the victims of those from below.

For this complicated (and useless) scheme, which serves as the stage for the death of the political system, to function, it is necessary to distribute large numbers of masks and silences for those from below. Anonymity, desperation, bitterness, apathy, impotence, resignation, skepticism, isolation and cynicism, are offered with full hands to be consumed by millions of Mexican men and women who barely survive in this country. Appearing to be free of charge, the silences and the masks which arrive from above to those from below tend to end up being very costly. The losses are exorbitant, but they are not measured in monetary terms, rather in human ones.

The masks of anonymity and isolation, which the frantic globalization tries to impose on men and women in all of Mexico, do not hide the singularity of every being, but rather the very real nightmare of the struggle of those from below. The daily injustice which the system inflicts on the Mexicans dilutes its impact precisely by the great multiplication of its crimes: a dismissal over here, a rape over there, an unjust imprisonment there, a robbery further over there, a political disappearance on that side, a fraud on this side, hunger and misery shut away between four walls of any over there. Victims anonymous and isolated by the system, millions of Mexicans lose (in the neoliberal alchemy that converts its exploitation by an exponential secret) the opportunity to rebel against the nightmare that isolates them in terror, because it is anonymous in the aggression which it perpetrates.

And the masks are accompanied by other masks, apathy and cynicism wants to multiply among those from below. It tries to unite "nothing matters to me" with "only I am important to me, and so what," and in this way the power will accomplish one of its primary objectives: impose immobility and hamper brotherhood.

Then the silences come. That of the bitterness against everyone or no one, which is unleashed against anything within its reach. That of the impotence of feeling oneself to be too small in front of an overwhelming, inaccessible and, nonetheless, omnipresent machine. That of the desperation of seeing oneself and knowing oneself to be alone, without the slightest suspicion that things could be better tomorrow. That of the resignation that assumes the inevitability of injustice and the role of victim while the murderer covers his face, becoming real in the boss, the police, the man, the mestizo, the thief, the neighbor, the other-always-the-other.

And the silence of fury explodes at any moment, a silence which accumulates and grows in situations that are absurd, unexpected, incomprehensible: the man with the woman, the gang with any passerby, the worker with the worker, the indigenous with the indigenous, the one with the other, the fury with the fury.

New forms of struggle are creating their own masks and are forging their silences. Little by little the honorable mask of resistance grows and multiplies, the "I will not leave," the "I will not surrender," the "I continue fighting," the "I will not give in," the "come on!" Behind the same mask of anonymity, the indigenous, workers, campesinos, housewives, neighbors, unionists, students, teachers, Christians, retired persons, disabled persons, drivers, shopkeepers, activists from political and social organizations, women, youth, children and old persons, all those who discover each other day by day, who resist...

And a terrible silence walks with and arises from the resistance: the silence which accuses and points.

V. The Seven Victims of the New Government Strategy in Chiapas

Comandante Zedillo's military campaign has been brilliant. Accompanying him in this bellicose enterprise have been Senor Labastida as chief of his Great State, Senor Rabasa as... as... what is it that Senor Rabasa does?, good, Senora Rosario Green in the service of not very simultaneous (nor very reliable) translation, and the senor? Albores Guillen as Field Marshall.

Besides filling the Chiapas jails (having been previously emptied of the paramilitaries) with Zapatista indigenous and members of civil society, besides promoting the use of the indigenous' huts as target practice for the federal Army, besides practicing summary executions which do not require envy from those practiced by military dictatorships around the world (an advantage of globalization?), besides having tied the name of "Mexico" to the blood-stained "Acteal", "Chavajeval," and "Union Progreso," besides having brought terror, misery and the lie to the Indian lands of Mexico, Comandante Zedillo and his team are wearing seven medals for the other victims they claimed.

Yes, there are seven victims of their war: peace, dialogue as the means for solution of the conflicts, the indigenous, national and international civil society, the movement towards democracy, the Commission of Concordance and Peace and the National Commission of Intermediation.

Continuing his personal fight against the Zapatista rebels, Zedillo doesn't just take peace prisoner of war, which was there for the taking, he also attacked the hope for any future peace.

The dialogue as the means for a solution to the conflicts is one of the most important losses of the war in southeastern Mexico. By failing to carry out the Accords which he signed, Zedillo shattered confidence in his government. Without confidence, it is impossible to reach accords. And if it is not possible to reach accords, why have dialogue?

For their part, the indigenous have been converted into the primary share of "triumphs" of Zedillo in Chiapas: no other regime has been responsible, directly and indirectly, for so many deaths, prisoners, tortures, expulsions, displacements and disappearances of chiapeneco indigenous as the current one.

Government warfare claimed another victim in national and international civil society, by ignoring its calls for dialogue and peace.

One more victim is the transition to democracy, which finds itself halted by a political system disposed for a bloodbath, so that it will not lose its privileges.

Only a nostalgic memory remains of national sovereignty. In its place are foreign military advisors, foreign arms, foreign combat tactics, foreign MRE's, foreign combat equipment. In the war in Chiapas the only thing that is national is the blood that is spilled.

Two other victims merit special mention: one was dragged away dying, the other lies irredeemably dead.

The first is the Commission of Concordance and Peace, formed by federal legislators of all the political parties with representation in the Congress of the Union. The Cocopa has been avoided, mocked, used, despised, humiliated and forgotten by the government. In his perverse and lethal game, Ernesto Zedillo feigned to the Cocopa his willingness to accept the legislators' offices to achieve, efficiently and rapidly, peace in southeastern Mexico. By withdrawing his acceptance of the initiative for the indigenous law, prepared by the Cocopa, the government made a fool of the legislators and robbed them of all moral authority to appear in front of the zapatista leadership. Afterwards, Zedillo set about battering the "cocopos" who did not align themselves with his war plans (that is, almost all of them), only to then ignore the commission for the long period during which he planned and executed the massive assassination of indigenous perpetrated in Acteal in December of 1997. In short, the government has treated the Cocopa with ridicule, traps, blows and sabotage. The EZLN will not do the same.

Simultaneous with the sabotages against the Cocopa, Government busied itself with assassinating and incarcerating more indigenous, and in fighting a total war against the National Commission of Intermediation (Conai) and, especially, against its President, the Bishop Samuel Ruiz Garcia. Ultimately, words and contradictions. Labastida says what Rabasa retracts, Zedillo corrects both of them. Rabasa clarifies Zedillo, Labastida scolds Rabasa, in short, a confusion of masks and roles which would make one laugh if it weren't that it hides a brutal and uneven war.

After suffering a long and intense campaign of attacks and lies, the National Commission of Intermediation (recognized by the parties, EZLN and the federal government, as the mechanism for mediation in the peace dialogue) was dissolved.

Take note of these names: Don Samuel Ruiz Garcia, Dona Concepcion Calvillo Viuda de Nava, Doctor Pablo Gonzalez Casanova, Doctor Raymundo Sanchez Barraza, poet Juan Banuelos, poet Oscar Oliva (these six as members), and Pedro Nava, Salvador Reyes, Gonzalo Ituarte and Miguel Alvarez as secretaries. The 10 formed the National Commission of Intermediation, one of the primary objectives for destruction by the government's war strategy.

Their crimes? All of them unpardonable: fight for peace with justice and dignity, represent national civil society as mediator in the conflict, believe firmly in dialogue as the solution to disputes, not submit to the government's orders, maintain autonomy and independence with respect to the parties, think that peace in Mexico must necessarily pass through the transition to democracy, commit oneself to the side of the Indians in their peaceful struggles and (the worst of all their crimes) make themselves into an obstacle to war.

For months these persons were the victims of attacks of all kinds, including attempts on their lives, property and liberty. For months they suffered the pressures of all the apparatus of the Mexican state; federal, state and municipal governments; the Army, police and paramilitaries; the two television monopolies and the local press; businesses; federal and local deputies; the high hierarchies of the Catholic and evangelical churches. Millions and millions of pesos wasted in smear campaigns against them.

All the political, economic, ecclesiastical and military power against these 10 persons and, particularly, against Don Samuel Ruiz Garcia, the bishop of the diocese of San Cristobal.

On June 7, 1998, the seventh victim fell in front of the advance of the Zedillo war machine. Don Samuel Ruiz Garcia resigned from the CONAI and it was dissolved. With the disappearance of the Conai, a fierce resistance against authoritarianism, crime and intolerance was ended, but the search for peace has not ended for them.

But the machine did not stop with the resignation of the president of the Conai. Senor Ernesto Zedillo was not satisfied with seeing Bishop Ruiz Garcia out of mediation in the conflict. No, he wanted to see him disappeared, erased, dead. With malice he nurtured the opportunity to get him completely out of his sight, if the attempt had failed once, there would still be other opportunities. After all, if a cardinal could be assassinated (Posadas Ocampo) with no punishment for the crime, it would be easy to take care of an inconvenient bishop and one could continue without problems. And this is not one of those bad jokes that Zedillo likes to torture his cabinet with, no, the bitterness had been converted in this man into a truly personal style of government. And as for personal revenge, "he knows how to do it."

Time and again, in each of his conjugal visits made to the next former interim Governor Albores Guillen, Senor Zedillo attacked, viciously and cowardly, the man who took peace and justice as flags, and who spared neither effort nor pain to complete his work with honesty, and which is, at the end of the day, the work of all human beings who respect themselves: to struggle for justice, respect and dignity.

This country owes these persons not a little. Although a chapter has ended in southeastern Mexico, national history reserves them a place alongside the best. Long afterwards, when Zedillo is forgotten or in jail for his innumerable crimes, the names of these persons will still hold a very special place in the hearts of all those Mexicans who are now from below, especially the indigenous.

Although outside this stage of the struggle, the "conaitas" have left it clear that they will continue struggling in different forms and in different places for the same thing: for justice for the Mexican indigenous, for the transition to democracy and for peace.

However, the seven victims of the government's war are multiplied in other combatants who are resisting. They remember yesterdays histories in the today, like that which speaks of...

IMPORTANT NOTICE, THAT IS, URGENT WARNING, OR HOWEVER YOU SAY IT: The section, Stories of the Little Horse of the Sea arbitrarily interrupts this veeery serious political analysis and, just like that, leaves us sea-sick like the tide which makes the sea dizzy ['mareados como la marea que marea a la mar'].

In the way of medicine, the seahorse tells us a story (what else could it do!).

Old Antonio tells that when he was young his father Don Antonio taught him how to kill the lion without a firearm. Old Antonio tells that when he was young Antonio and his father was the old Antonio he told him the story that he now tells me out loud so that the sea will learn my lips. Old Antonio tells it to me just like this, but I call it...

The History of the Lion and the Mirror

"The lion first skins its victim, afterwards he drinks the blood, eating the heart, and leaves the rest for the vultures. There is nothing that can go against the strength of the lion. There is not an animal which can confront him, nor a man who does not run away from him. Only a force which is equally brutal, bloodthirsty and powerful can defeat the lion."

The then old Antonio of the then young Antonio rolled his cigarette and, pretending to pay attention to the logs which were converging in the bright star of the flames from the bonfire, looked out of the corner of his eye at the young Antonio. He didn't wait long, because the young Antonio asked him:

"And what is this force great enough to defeat the lion?"

The old Antonio of then handed the young Antonio of then, a mirror.

"Me?" asked the then young Antonio, looking at himself in the round mirror.

The old Antonio of then smiled with good humor (that is what the young Antonio of then says) and took the mirror from him.

"By showing you the mirror I meant that the strength which could defeat the lion was the same as the lion. Only the lion himself can defeat the lion."

"Ah!" said the then young Antonio, who said that in order to say something.

The then old Antonio understood that the then young Antonio had not understood anything and he continued telling the history.

"When we understand that only the lion can defeat the lion we begin to think how to make the lion confront himself. The oldest of the old of the community said that you have to know the lion and name a boy in order to know him."

"You?" interrupted the then young Antonio.

The then old Antonio agreed through his silence and, after rearranging the logs on the fire, he continued:

"They took the boy up to the top of a ceiba tree and at the foot of it they left a tied-up calf. They went away. The boy was supposed to watch what the lion did with the calf, to wait for him to go away and then to return to his community and tell them what he had seen. And so he did, the lion arrived and killed and skinned the calf, and afterwards he drank his blood, eating his heart and he left when the buzzards were circling waiting for their turn."

"The boy went to his community and told what he had seen, the oldest of the old thought for a while and said: 'Let the death which the matador gives be his death,' and they gave the boy a mirror, some nails to shoe with and a calf."

"Tomorrow is the night of justice," said the old ones and they returned to their thoughts.

"The boy did not understand. He went to his hut and he stayed there for a good while watching the game. There he was and his father arrived and he asked him what was happening; the boy told him everything. The boy's father stayed silently next to him and, after a while, he spoke. The boy smiled while he listened to his father."

"The next day, when the afternoon had already made the gold, and the grey of the night had let itself fall over the treetops, the boy left the community and walked on foot to the ceiba tree carrying the calf. When he arrived at the foot of the mother tree, he killed the calf and took out its heart. Then he broke the mirror into many little pieces and stuck them into the heart with the same blood, then he opened the heart and put the nails inside. He put the heart back in the calf's chest and with stakes made a frame to keep it standing on its feet. As if it were alive. The boy went up to the top of the tree and waited there. Above, while the night let itself fall from the trees to the ground, he remembered his father's words: 'The same death with which the matador will die.'"

"Now the night was below all the time when the lion arrived. The animal came close and, with one leap, attacked the calf and skinned it. When he licked the heart, the lion became suspicious because the blood was dry, but the broken mirror hurt his tongue and made it bleed. And so the lion thought that the blood from his mouth was from the calf's heart and, excited, he chewed up the entire heart. The nails made it bleed more, but the lion continued to think that the blood he had in his mouth was the calf's. Chewing and chewing, the lion wounded himself more and more and bled more and chewed more and more."

"The lion was like that until it bled to death."

"The boy returned with the lion's claws as a collar and he showed it to the oldest of the old of the community."

"They smiled and told him: 'It is not the claws that you should keep as a trophy of the victory, but the mirror.'"

That is how old Antonio tells that the lion was killed.

But, besides the mirror, old Antonio always carries his old shotgun of chispa.

"It's in case the lion doesn't know history," he tells me smiling and winking an eye. From the side and here, the sea added: "In case the lion or the Orive."

And speaking of former Maoists and former radicals and former left, today brand-new advisors to the criminals of the right (who start out talking like cockatoos and now, in order to hide themselves, imitate the ostrich), old Antonio has his own version of that one about the revolutionary and the masses and the comparison with the fish in the water, and also the counterinsurgency strategy of "taking the water away from the fish" that the embarrassed government advisors are recommending today...

The Fish in the Water

Old Antonio tells a history that the oldest of the old of his community told him. He tells the history that there was once a very beautiful fish that lived in the river. He tells that the lion saw the fish and he had a craving to eat it. The lion went to the river but he saw that he could not swim in the river and attack the fish. The lion asked for advice from the opossum and he told him: "It is very simple, the fish cannot live without water. The only thing you have to do is to drink the water from the river and that way the fish will stay without moving and then you can attack it and eat it." The lion was pleased with the opossum's advice and he paid him with a position in his kingdom.

The lion went to the edge of the river and began to drink the liquid. He died bursting from the water.

The opossum remained unemployed. Tan tan.

NEW IMPORTANT NOTICE, BUT NOW NOT SO URGENT WARNING: the interruption by the little horse of the sea has ended, but not so the queasy nausea ['mareado mareo']. Perhaps its persistence is due to that which is shown and spoken of in...

VI. The Seventh Mask and the Seventh Silence

"It is clear that in the arena of political action,(…) only he who puts the candle where the wind is blowing will triumph; never the one who pretends the wind is blowing where he puts the candle."
-Juan de Mairena, Antonio Machado

1998. Mexico. While the supreme government stays on track towards war and tries desperately to join the winds from above, the growls of the beast and the spells in order to push the heavy sails of the ship of death, these Mexican indigenous, who add the name of Emiliano Zapata to their history, prepare in silence the justice and the dignity that will have to arrive in spite of their death (or perhaps because of it).

In silence, these indigenous watch the skies and the ground to predict the winds from below which run through the fields of Mexico and of the world, through the dusty streets of tiny villages and ranches, through the messy disorder of the popular neighborhoods, through the places of the honest unions, through the offices of the committed political parties, through the theatres-movies-auditoriums-salons-of shows-art galleries, through laboratories and centers of scientific investigation, through the university cubicles, classrooms and halls, through meetings and assemblies of political and social organizations, through the churches of the poor, through the international solidarity committees, through the national and foreign non-governmental organizations, through the highways, through the roads, through the neighborhood streets, through the breaches, navigating the rivers, in the lakes and in the seas of this country, today awash in wet, and of this world awakening, late certainly, but awakening.

In silence these indigenous see and are seen. In silence they feel where the wind from below is blowing. In silence these indigenous know. In silence they finish this new and absurd Noah's Ark and, knowing that the wind is blowing for democracy, liberty and justice, they set high the double sail of hope, motor and light for this ship, the boat of those of always, the ship of life.

With art and science they build the ark and choose from thousands of their own for the crew. The rest will wait in the port for it to arrive. If war and destruction arrive, they will resist as they have learned to do so in the hard school of the centuries, that is, with dignity. If democracy, liberty and justice arrive, they will know to share it, as they have known how to do through their history.

Mexico, the middle of 1998.

After a long silence these indigenous speak a boat and call on all to board it.

After such a silence, these indigenous speak a ship, a Noah's ark, a navigable Tower of Babel, an absurd and irreverent challenge.

In case there is any doubt as to who crews and directs it, the figurehead on the prow lights a ski mask! Yes, a ski mask, the mask which reveals, the silence that speaks. A "For everyone, everything, nothing for us" dresses the flag of the red star with five points over a black background which shines over the mainmast. In golden letters, to port, starboard and the stern, the "Votan Zapata" names the origin and the destination of this ship, so powerfully fragile, so resoundingly quiet, so visibly concealed.

"All on board!" the captain's voice is heard to shout-order-invite. The only ticket necessary is honesty. Several thousand oarsmen wait, are you ready to leave? No, we are missing...

With that strange and repeated tendency to complicate the life they have, these men and women of masks and silences built their boat... in the middle of the mountain!

"And now?" I ask them.

As if waiting, silence is the response. But behind their masks there is a smile when they bring me a message and a bottle.

I do what I always do in these cases: I put the message in the bottle, put the top on tightly with some chewing gum of chamoy which the sea gives me, I plant myself firmly by the side of the ceiba, with all my strength, I throw the bottle with the message very far. A trail of cloud gets it and, navigating, takes it to-wherever-it-knows-to-take-it. There goes the bottle. Whoever finds it can, by breaking it, break the silence and find some answers and many questions. Perhaps he will also be able to read...

VII. Declaration from the Selva Lacandona?

Right, that's all.

Vale. Salud and be ready. Prepare umbrellas, raincoats and life jackets. Who can deny now that the word can call up the damp?

> *From the mountains of the Mexican Southeast,*
> *Subcomandante Insurgente Marcos.*
> *In the name of the 300.*
> *Mexico, July 1998.*

50. THE HISTORY OF THE MEASURE OF MEMORY

To the national press

Ladies and gentlemen,

A few reflections on Fobaproa and a taking of a position.

From here nothing new, an abundance of planes and helicopters promising war, rains promising sowing, and dignities which are promising futures. The children continue being children, and little Pedrito has re-baptized me as "Up" (an easy abbreviation for "Sup" as I understand), while he tries to find out if my pipe is made of chocolate as were some cigarettes he had been given.

While the sea dreams with me in the womb, I remember that in the next few days (August 28?), the Ladies will be celebrating the twentieth anniversary of an act which, like everything that comes from below, began small and then grew. Twenty years ago a group of determined and inconvenient (for the Power) women and men began a hunger strike demanding the liberation of political prisoners and the presentation of the disappeared.

We, and others without memory, owe these women of foolish tenderness many things. One of these things, and not the only one, is that morning when they promised us, and promised those who, like the Ladies, know that memory does not rest nor yield, nor does it have age, nor does dignity have size. And then Old Antonio comes with one of the gifts for the sea, and he tells, just to tell...

The History of the Measure of Memory

The oldest of our old tell, that the first gods, those who created the world, shared out memory among the men and women who walked in the world.

"Memory is good," the greatest gods said and told, "because it is the mirror which helps to understand the present and promises the future."

The first gods measured out memory with a jicara in order to share it out and all the men and women came by to receive their measure of memory. But some of the men and women were larger than the others and then the measure of memory was not seen equally in all. It shone clearly in the smallest and in the largest it was made opaque. Because of that they say that they say memory is greatest and strongest in the smallest and it is harder to find in the powerful. That is why they also say that men and women become smaller and smaller when they grow old. They say it is so memory will shine more brightly. They say that it is the work of the oldest of the old: to make memory great. And they also say that dignity is no more than memory which lives. They say.

Vale. Salud and may memory carry out its mission, to make justice.

From the mountains of Southeastern Mexico,
Subcomandante Insurgente Marcos.
Mexico, August of 1998.

Here it is again!
The only!
The unequalled!
The feared (by the editors)!
The section of the recurring postscript! Yesss!!!

P.S. I applaud Zedillo's memory. In Ocosingo, speaking of the proposals for indigenous reform, Zedillo referred to the Cocopa's as "the one drawn up by a group of legislators along with the EZLN." He only missed saying "a group of dissident legislators."

P.S. Let the chips fall where they may. According to intelligence services it has become known that a new autonomous municipality has arisen in the territory today known as Tuxtla Gutierrez. The Autonomous Council in Rebellion is located close to the "Alvarez del Toro" Zoo and, with the clear intention of passing unnoticed, has hung a sign on the entrance which says "Cerro Hueco Jail." We demand that the State of Law be enforced with all vigor, that a thousand police officers and soldiers attack the rebel stronghold and destroy all the facilities, and those inside be immediately expelled.

P.S. Take notice (aside from the Fobaproa). The peso is being devalued, the stock market is plunging, white collar and no-collar crime is growing , narco-trafficking is making closer ties with the government, the San Andres Accords are continuing to not be carried out, the war is advancing in Chiapas, Guerrero and Oaxaca, international condemnations against the Mexican government for human rights violations are mounting, the Legislative branch is revealing itself, the PRI pre-candidates for the year 2000 are swarming, Fobaproa is being uncovered, and with it the illegality of the 1994 election,... (space for you to add anything that I missed), etcetera. All this is clear, but, what is Zedillo going to report on September 1 1/4? His successes in submarine diving?

Vale Nuez. Salud and best wishes! (If you are reading this, four years of "well-being for the family" has endured).

The Sup wrapped up as a gift.

51. IT CONTINUES RAINING HERE

September 8, 1998
Zapatista Army of National Liberation
Mexico
To whom it may concern

Ladies and gentlemen,

It continues raining here. The government only remembers Chiapas when it needs to make demagoguery and to improve its public image. Certainly Zedillo will come to the southeastern coast to hide the dead, to promise aid, to have photos taken, to repair croquettes and to cover up omissions and negligence. For the rest, the rains have been here several days now, but Albores is too busy in the boudoir to even think about an emergency plan. There the government knows how to kill indigenous, but never how to keep them from dying. Meanwhile the army's planes and helicopters are making their overflights of Zapatista communities, when they are freed up they will go to attend to the victims. The rivers seem to be angry, they are destroying weak bridges and roads with a ferocity, which the government report call "important infrastructure works" in the social spending in Chiapas. Why don't they go take a look at those works, whose inauguration they disseminated so widely?

Regardless, the rains do not watch television nor do they respect the set design for operettas. As always, not until the deaths reach national and international news, is there any sense of urgency to those forgetful ones whom we suffer as the government. This is how it is now with the indigenous in Mexico: they only exist and are named when they are dead.

Vale. Be well and, when will Chiapas no longer exist on government maps only when there are rebellions, deaths or catastrophes?

From the mountains of Southeastern Mexico,
Subcomandante Insurgente Marcos.
Mexico, September 1998.

P.S. Despite insignificant and irrelevant government reports, and as part of the great festivities, here is...

The recurring postscript section!

P.S. Where it rains and gets wet. Marshall 'Croquettes' Albores and his little soldiers are rubbing their hands together about the rain catastrophe which is battering the Chiapas coast. Millions of pesos will be sent to help the victims. Little or nothing will reach the hands of the needy. Much or all of it will go to fatten the back accounts of the substitute of the usurper of The Dogs gang. But, you can be sure, you will now see Zedillo on the main page in photos and reports, trying to look serious and announcing rescue plans and calm-everything-is-under-control-children. Ah, poor Chiapas! The government wanting to forget about you and the rains, which do not listen to government reports, come to batter paths and memories...

P.S. Which says what it says. I was with Pedrito one afternoon, both of us smoking (he, a chocolate cigarette, and I, a pipe), when I wanted to be like Old Antonio, and I began to lecture Pedrito (tojolabal and two years old) about life and painful treasures. And I began to tell him:

"Look, Pedrito, there are things you need to know about for when you grow up. Important things like tying your boots, doing up your shirt without missing any buttons, getting comfortable in the hammock, lighting the pipe with the pot mouth down, and other etceteras which you will be learning about. But now we are going to talk about when a man loves a woman."

Pedrito was looking at me seriously, and he continued sucking on his chocolate cigarette. I suppose that I had then, as they say, "captured" his attention, and I continued:

"Look, Pedrito, when a man loves a woman... because it's not the same as when a woman loves a man, or when a man loves another man, or when a woman loves another woman, because it is everything, and it's necessary to know and to understand it. But, good, when a man loves a woman... because it's not that easy to explain either as, for example, what you have to do in order to not miss buttons when you put a shirt on, a complicated thing if you don't pay the necessary attention and care. For example, I use the technique of 'from the bottom up' which, in addition to being a concept of political science, is very good for buttoning up. Look, you put on the shirt and look down below, seriously and with concentration..."

Pedrito frowned and looked at me seriously.

"Like that! Good, then continue lining up the lower edges of the shirt, the right at the same level as the left, and it's not as simple as the 'centrists' in politics make it appear, here, if you aren't careful, you can pass the left, which, in any case, wouldn't be consistent, but you could also pass the right, and then it would indeed be veeery regrettable. Then balance is very important, they must be even. Then you have to look for the bottom button on the shirt, and the bottom button isn't always the last one, but, you should know this Pedrito, there are some evil shirt manufacturers who put on an extra button (to put back on if you lose one, they say) for the obvious purpose of making this indispensable garment difficult to button. Good, now that you've found the last button, keep on looking for the corresponding button-hole (double entendre fanciers, refrain), something which is more difficult to find than any reference to Chiapas in Zedillo's report. As you will know much later on, you never lack a ripped seam for a hole. It could be, but what is certain is that there are more buttons than buttonholes, as you will see when you miss buttons. Certainly there are other techniques for not missing buttons. There is, for example, the method of the Sea, who puts on shirts as if they were T-shirts. That is, she does not undo them. Ergo, there are no missing buttons. However, I do not recommend that technique because... Good, but, given that the Sea, etcetera, I was explaining to you that when a man loves a woman... Good, you see now, Pedrito, that it is very difficult to explain how it is when a man loves a woman and, nonetheless, it's very important to understand it, because..."

While I was explaining, Pedrito ate his cigarette. "Cocate," he said to me, while stretching out his hand, asking me, in his dialect, for more chocolates. "There aren't any," I told him. He turned around and left. It's obvious that today's youth has no interest in important issues (sigh). Where was I? Ah, yes! When a man loves a woman...

P.S. "Sea-horse Stories" Section (the gifts follow)...

Rose-Colored Shoelaces

Once upon a time there was a pair of shoes which used, like all the other shoes, black or brown shoelaces. By day, this pair of shoes went about like all the other shoes, that is, dragging along the ground. But it so happened that this pair of shoes had hidden in its closet rose-colored shoelaces, and at night it put them on and cut loose. And so this pair of shoes went, until one day he got tired of hiding his happiness in the closet and he put on his rose-colored shoelaces and all the other shoes looked at him with serious disapproval and they made a circle around him with brown and black shoelaces in order to isolate him, so that he would not contaminate all the other shoes. The pair of shoes with rose-colored shoelaces dissented, and every day he marched with a sign which said, "Respect and dignity for rose-colored shoelaces," but the other shoes ignored him and they tied their black and brown knots even more tightly in order to leave the pair of shoes with rose-colored shoelaces by himself and they organized a counter-protest with signs reading "An end to the disease of the rose-colored shoelaces." And they were doing that when someone saw the pair of shoes with the rose-colored shoelaces and they put a big ugly hat on him and the hat had pastel blue feathers and they made him a song and the pair of shoes with rose-colored shoelaces became very famous and everyone danced to it and no one put a hat or feathers on the shoes with brown and black shoelaces and no one made them a song, what are they going to do! Tan, tan.

P.S. A gift of memories. Today, the 8th of September, is the birthday of Deni Prieto Stock (assassinated by the government on February 14, 1974, in San Miguel Nepantla, Mexico State). We all celebrate her.

Vale again. Be well and hopes that it stops raining in history.

The Archer Sup, leader of the Gorgonites.

52. The State Government is Stealing the Humanitarian Aid Intended for the Victims of the Flooding

September 12, 1998
Zapatista Army of National Liberation. Mexico
To Senor Mariano Palacios Alcocer
President of the Revolutionary Institutional Party (PRI), Mexico
From: Subcomandante Insurgente Marcos
CCRI-CG of the EZLN, Mexico

Senor Palacios Alcocer,
The political party which you say you lead is carrying out, on chiapaneco lands, one of the most outrageous crimes of recent times. It would seem difficult to equal

the cowardice, viciousness and treachery with which your organization (under orders from the federal government) perpetrated the Acteal massacre in December of 1997, but these days your political party, headed by Roberto Albores Guillen, is doing everything possible to achieve it. As you know, certainly from first hand, the chiapaneco PRI leadership and the state government are stealing the humanitarian aid intended for the victims of the Sierra and Coastal zones in Chiapas, and the little which does manage to arrive does so if, and only if, they belong to the PRI, or if their vote is committed in the next local elections. The primitive corruption of the chiapaneco PRI is now a treasonous crime against humanity, since it is one thing for Albores and his gang to spend the federal "social expenditures" on liquor and binges, but it is altogether different to appropriate humanitarian aid in the case of a disaster, or to use its distribution to buy votes. I hope, at the point at which you call on the citizens to vote for the PRI, you do so sincerely, and tell them that in Chiapas you possess the "medals" of Acteal, Union Progreso and Chavajeval, and to which can now be added the theft of thousands of millions of pesos in cash and material aid intended for the victims of the rains in the southeastern Sierra and Coast, and because of that, you are the "best" choice for the government. Yes, that, do not tell them that to govern they need, at the least, honesty, shame and dignity, nor should you confess that your leaders in Chiapas possess none of those three things, and that your only specialties are extortion, assassination and thievery (and it is with those that you have "governed" Chiapas).

That is all.

Vale. Salud and don't worry: there is no detergent capable of erasing that blood from your hands.

From the mountains of Southeast Mexico,
By the Clandestine Revolutionary Indigenous Committee
- General Command of the Zapatista Army of National Liberation,
Subcomandante Insurgente Marcos.
Mexico, September of 1998.

53. THE ALWAYS' AND THE NEVERS' IMPOSED BY THOSE FROM ABOVE

September 12, 1998
Beneath, the nuisances appear now and again
Zapatista Army of National Liberation Mexico
To the national and international press

Ladies and gentlemen,

The letter goes to the national PRI concerning the filth of the chiapaneco PRI, as does a communiqué concerning the atrocities which they are committing in the southeastern sierra and coast. Without comment.

Vale. Salud and, is there punishment for a crime of such immensity?

> *From the mountains of Southeast Mexico,*
> *Subcomandante Insurgente Marcos.*
> *Mexico, September of 1998.*

P.S. The great festivities continue! Now the gift is the story the Sailor-Sup calls...

Always and Never against Sometimes

Once upon a time there were two times. One was called One Time and the other was called Another Time. One Time and Another Time made up the family By Times, who lived and ate from time to time. The dominant empires were Always and Never which, as is clear, hated unto death the family By Times. Neither Always nor Never could tolerate the existence of By Times. They would never allow One Time to live in their kingdom because Always would then cease to be so, because if there is One Time now, then there is not Always. Nor could they permit Another Time to appear once more in their kingdom because Never cannot live with One Time, and even less if that One Time is Another Time. But One Time and Another Time were time and again bothering Always and Never. And so it went until they were always left in peace so that Always and Never again bothered them. And One Time and Another Time were play-ing time and again. "Do you see me?" One Time asked, and Another Time answered: "Don't you see?" And so they were very happy from time to time, you see. And they were always One Time and Another Time and they never stopped being By Times. Tan, tan.

Moral 1: By times it is very hard to distinguish between one time and another.

Moral 2: Never say always (well, sometimes, yes).

Moral 3: The "always'" and the "nevers'" are imposed from above, but below are "the nuisances" time and again which, by times, is another way of saying "the dif-ferent ones," or, from time to time, "the rebels."

Moral 4: I am never going to write a story like this again, and I always do what I say (well, sometimes, no).

Vale encore. Salud and, by times, the always and the nevers come from below (from the womb, for example).

The Sup once and again battling with his shirt buttons (long live t-shirts!). (From "beach," you understand). (And, "de trigo," which I prefer).

54. THE INVITATION FOR A DIALOGUE BETWEEN THE EZLN AND CIVIL SOCIETY

September 7, 1998
Zapatista Army of National Liberation
Mexico
To the persons and organizations who signed the invitation for a dialogue between the EZLN and civil society

My companeros,

Chiefs of the Clandestine Revolutionary Indigenous Committee - General Command of the EZLN, have told me to respond, in the name of all the zapatistas, to the invitation you made to us to have "a meeting of the signatory organizations and persons with the EZLN," and to "analyze proposals and to reach agreements on the carrying out of the consultation and, in addition, for an exchange of opinions, points of view and possible alternatives for a solution to the conflict."

The conflict (the one which does not exist in the government reports, the one which is so "insignificant" it requires more than half the federal troops just to "contain it," the one which is as equally "irrelevant" to the government as is the blood of the indigenous) continues to be painful and to signify. A year ago senor Zedillo was silent on the war in Chiapas in his Government Report. Weeks later, Acteal pointed out what the silence was concealing: the decision by the government to make crime a government policy. Today, "Chiapas" is again absent from the government's "priorities." What new nightmare does this omission portend?

Senor Zedillo bid farewell on September 1, and in doing so he has decreed that the year 2000 is now here. Those in his cabinet who want to succeed him repeat the lesson: apathy is another way to make war, and, as in the times of the conquest, assassinations of the indigenous are tools for lessons and for warnings.

We have to prevent the repetition of Acteal. And we also must seek the means for solving the unresolved which this pain points out: the recognition of the rights and culture of the indigenous. On this basis it will be possible to finally construct peace, the only peace possible; the peace with justice and dignity. This will not come from above (senor Zedillo has been very eloquent in his silence). It is good that you note you are not trying to be a bridge for the government (besides, the chair is still empty on the side above), but rather a dialogue between civil society and the zapatistas. And, in truth, we must construct the peace in the same way things which are solid and lasting are constructed: from below. Old Antonio says the very first gods created the world starting from below, and the greatest gods remained down there. They were making things from below, and from there they pushed them above. When they were finished, they saw that the world had become round, and they remained in the center, in the heart of the earth. That is why it endures and why the earth is hard, because it was created from below. Because of that, in order to understand what goes on above, one must know to look beneath...

We very much noted, in the invitation you made to us, the broad rainbow of thoughts who had signed it. Beneath every name and abbreviation there are men and women who are the center and the heart of an effort, of a hope and of a history. This demonstrates - in addition to the failure of the government strategy of offering forgetting at bargain prices - the place that memory still occupies among the many dignities who make this country.

And so we want to thank all of you for the invitation, but above all we want to thank you for giving memory the place that tomorrow needs, that place which, for the sake of physical geography, we generally locate between the chest and the back. Some call it heart, others call it soul, but, however it is named, it is what pains us when things such as liberty, democracy and justice... for all... are missing. And speaking of "all"... To everyone who invited and signed...

We inform you that we accept with much pleasure the invitation you made to us. It will be an honor for us to meet with all of you, and, together, to begin the consultation on the indigenous law, in addition to exchanging points of view on the current situation. We also inform you that at this time our companero chiefs have begun the selection of the CCRI-CG delegates who will attend, with the EZLN representation, the meeting to which you invited us. We will be waiting to hear more details on this dialogue from you.

Until soon, then, embraces for everyone as you will and, certainly, enough to fill the entire page.

Vale. Be well and I hope everyone fits at the meeting: those who signed, those who signed on and all the rest who neither signed nor signed on, but who also want to meet.

From the mountains of Southeastern Mexico,
Subcomandante Insurgente Marcos.
General Quarters "Playa de Trigo"
Mexico, September 1998.

P.S. And are all those who signed going to come? Don't be guerrillas, because then we would have to push 1111 (with everything and the buses).

55. These Bridges Which are Little Unarmed Paper Boats

October 12, 1998
Zapatista Army of National Liberation
Mexico
To national civil society and to the members of the working meeting for the preparation of the encounter between the EZLN and the signatories, those who signed on and those who are neither signatories nor have signed on, but who wish to meet with us.
(For your initials: AALRDTPTPDEEEEYLFLFYLQNSFNFPQE uf!!)

Brothers and sisters,

Greetings, bows, handshakes, hugs, respectful inclinations of the head.

From here, along with the pretense of aid to those affected by the rains, can now be added the grotesque operetta of some local elections which, despite the gifts and threats, did not manage to convoke even a fourth of the possible voters. So, mending the stage curtains and worn-out sets, the federal and state governments are not now counting on having their lies believed, but only that they do not cause scandals or indignation. They are counting on exhaustion, and that the pyrotechnics of an early presidential succession will distract you and us from the forgetting, from the postponements, from the legal victories of usury (ah, the state of law!! So far from justice and so close to crime!!), from the arbitrary acts and from the natural and the neoliberal catastrophes. We are waiting and we are preparing.

And, speaking of preparations, a few days ago we received a document with the main proposals and ideas which were made at your meeting on the... the... I do not know what day, but it's been some days since you met. Here we are sending you a response as to the place and date of the meeting. While we are meeting, we will continue to use these letters which some call "communiqués," and which are no more than bridges to solve distances and differences, and so we go.

And things are not easy. Here you have, for example, these sheets of paper with ink (or this screen with the Internet with little lights, because we do not want to forget that we are in the age of the information highways). You read the letters and, with a little luck, you are able to understand what they are saying. And it seems easy to you, there the letters are now, arranged in a way which may or may not please, but understandable and, in any case, the work is yours, because the letters have to be arranged and made into what some call words, and manage to have meaning. But do not believe it, gathering all those letters was quite difficult, getting them to remain quiet required seven-tailed whips, threats of all kinds, supplication, pleas and promises. Then the nightmare began, trying over and over to put the jigsaw puzzle together so that it would approximate, even moderately, the other jigsaw puzzle which we have in our head. Then, and only then, science and technological development came to our aid, and we opted then for the very efficient and effective mechanism of making a little paper boat, painting a little flag with a fierce skull supported by crossbones, putting inside it a little rubber monkey which the sea gave me, and which did not know (the little monkey) that its future would be that of being a sailor in such a fragile craft.

And then we continue to wait for the rain, which is not fussy or considerate these days, and here comes a little stream with twigs and mud and then the little stream becomes clear and it takes the little paper boat towards the West and down the mountain, and hours later (believe me it does not fail) the little paper boat appears unarmed now in the middle of your newspaper or on your computer screen and up top it reads: "Zapatista Army of National Liberation," and a little further down it says: "To civil society and etcetera," and you know these letters are directed to you and you start to read and you make your best effort to put the puzzle together and we-others are sad here not for putting the puzzle together, but because the little paper boat is unarmed and it is a shame, look how pretty, with what gallantry it dodged little branches, little rocks and not so "little" toads, and then we cure the sadness by making more little paper boats and Pedrito says horses would be better and I that seahorses would be better and soon I have a flotilla with all of them and their aircraft carriers and Pedrito plays with the horses, and meanwhile my stupendous flotilla is brought back to reality by the rains, or the mud, and it is for that I am writing to you, because hope is also a little paper boat, a 'no' which becomes a yes. And then I remember I read Benedetti the other day, who is a man who looks to the heavens, and he saw a fleeting star and he made many wishes which are one single wish and, for example, he asked the just "to take up all their no's in order to establish the one great affirmation," and I already know that Benedetti says he is from Uruguay, but I do not believe it, he only says that to disturb dictatorships and to bother, in those customs and borders places - with which those from above fragment the dream of those from below - and below, as ever, no's are dreaming, and that is what I am saying, if we meet together and join all the no's which, like the just, are the great majority in this country, then perhaps we can try to put together the puzzle of the morning, and we will find, with so many well-accompanied no's, that is, with justice and dignity, there will come a yes, which is not many yes's, but is worth as much as the no's which stop it, and now I remember that Old Antonio said that dialogue is like putting a puzzle together and perhaps Old Antonio did not say it, but he should have said it, and all the better then are these bridges which are little unarmed paper boats, or, because we say many no's and you say many no's and at the best you and we suspect that your no's and our no's are the same no's, I say, no?

And so here we are looking at and reading each other (which comes from the verb "mirolear," the action of jointly looking, in reciprocity, mutually). Bring your somewhat organized no's (because neither are we speaking of "no-ing" - the action of sharing no's - without thinking), we will carry ours in little paper boats, so if no one comes to meet with us we will be able to put them in the little streams which, most certainly, will not be lacking.

Vale. Salud and may the looks and the words be joined tomorrow.

From the mountains of the Mexican Southeast,
Subcomandante Insurgente Marcos.
Mexico, October of 1998.

56. I Will Deal With You Later

For: Roberto Albores Guillen and the Attorney General's Office of the State of Chiapas

I will deal with you later. Meanwhile, here I am ordering you to keep yourself entertained for the time being. Do not wear yourselves out and save something for when it's your turn to be guests in the jails you promise.

From the mountains of the Mexican Southeast,
Subcomandante Insurgente Marcos.
Mexico, October of 1998.

P.S. We share here ("Bobby," leave something for the others). And pardon us for being difficult, but the croquettes have not reached us.

57. THE DAY OF THE DEAD

November 4, 1998
To the national and international press

Ladies and gentlemen,

The military, that recurrent obstacle for the peace process, democracy and justice in Mexico for the last 30 years, returned to their old tactics of implementing new "operations", in order to then "negotiate" their temporary suspension. Now they are imposing more patrols, and they say they are prepared to "give demonstrations of detente," suspending what did not exist before. The dirty tricks they learned with the North Americans (they forget Vietnam?) are complemented by the open dispute between El Croquetas Albores and Rabasa, of seeing which makes the more stupid remarks.

Everything goes for the continuation of the war in the mountains of the Mexican southeast, everything as long as the 130% bonus is covered, which the soldiers receive for persecuting, harassing and threatening the indigenous (they do not charge for killing them, they do that for free).

Meanwhile, the man with "no cash" prepares banquets for Chirac and packs bags for Japan. There is no doubt that they are ominous signs. The assassination of nationals and the persecution of foreigners have an effect on the current government's accounts, as "when you see Pinochet judged, launder your bank accounts." In Mexico, Labastida rubs his hands: failed in Chiapas and in public security, he sees in the Fobaproa the trampoline to launch himself to 2000 (could someone let him know that the pool has no water?). Orive instructs his pupil in the Cocopa, Gurria practices in front of the mirror. And Ortiz? Well, damn, what else could he do? All of them remain silent about the truth: taxes go up, indicators of economic growth go down, prices go up, salaries go down, the number of unemployed goes up, the number of rich, down (but they will be richer). In the end, the country "is calm." Or not?

Vale. Salud and an embrace to reach to Nicaragua, El Salvador and Honduras. There is no doubt that death is enamoured with poverty.

From the mountains of the Mexican Southeast,
Subcomandante Insurgente Marcos.
Mexico, November of 1998.

P.S. Disguised as zapatista graffiti:
Death will die mortally dead. From death we shall kill, from life.
P.S. A story is told of...

The Day of the Dead...

It is the custom of our peoples to set out an offering for the dead every year in the celebrations from October 31 until the dawn of November 2. In addition to flowers and ornaments made of paper, between two candles, some food is gathered, whatever the deceased most liked, and, if he smoked, some tobacco. Some say this offering is to remind the dead person that he still has roots in life, that he walks in others, that he continues in others. Others say this offering is in case the dead person comes and is in need of food and rest, because he has not achieved what he wanted, and the deceased still goes about, seeking. The search can last for a long time, but the dead person is not saddened, because he knows he can return each year to his family to gain strength and to gather heart and so continue on his path.

To remind him that he still has roots on this side and that he walks in us and he continues, and in order to recover strength and hope in his search, each year the zapatistas put out an offering for Pedro (fallen in combat in 1974, raised up again fallen again in combat in 1994, raised up again, struggling always). At the dawn of each November 2, thousands of offerings in so many other indigenous homes shine for Pedro.

Each of the last four years, Don Jacinto offered to watch over the offering which we put out because of and for Pedro in the General Headquarters of the EZLN. Every year, with the arrival of the morning of November 2, the food and the tobacco which we had put out on the little table for this purpose, had disappeared. And early on we would find Don Jacinto leaving the little room with the offering, we would greet him and he would respond with a "the deceased came, he ate and drank, and he smoked the tobacco." We all knew it was Don Jacinto who had eaten the little plate with the bread and two oranges, who had drunk the coffee without sugar which Pedro worshipped, and who had smoked the little box of cigarettes (24 stubs were left scattered about). All of us knew. Not now.

Don Jacinto died a few weeks ago, after being brutally beaten in one of those attacks of the "State of Law" against the indigenous autonomous municipalities. Don Jacinto did not die, his son told me, they killed him. And he explains to me that it is not the same to die of death as to die of being killed.

Each year since 1994, Pedro's offering dawned empty on the morning of November 2. All of us knew that Don Jacinto had taken notice of it during the evening. All of us knew. On the day of October 31, 1998, we put out the offering as was our custom, but now with the added sadness of knowing that Don Jacinto would not be here to watch over it and to take notice of the bread, the oranges, the coffee and the tobacco, as we all knew. The morning of this November 2 we went to clean up the offering, and we found the plate with bread empty, the orange rinds, the little cup of coffee with grounds, and the stubs on the floor. It is curious, the rinds and the stubs were on both sides of the table, in equal parts: 12 stubs on one side and 12 on the other, the rind of one orange on one side, and the other on the other. We all looked at each other and we were silent, only the sea said: "The year which is coming, you will have to put out double."

All of us knew that Pedro's offering dawned empty because Don Jacinto took notice of it. All of us knew. Not now. All of this occurred at the dawn of the month of November of 1998, in the fifteenth year of the armed rebellion and the fifth of the war against forgetting, in the mountains of the Mexican southeast, dignified corner of the Patria, in the America they call "Latin," in the third planet of the solar system, just when, in the worn wheel of history, a century which some call "Twenty," is about to extinguish itself, all of which I bear witness to, and I affirm that it is destined to remain in the collective memory, which is another way of naming tomorrow.

P.S. For the February which is concealed in November: Now we are more and stronger. All of our dead will arrive. And so by nature are our dead: they make us great. Great to us, so small...

The Sup, asking for his little skull...

58. HISTORY OF THE ONE AND THE ALL

November 1998
To national and international civil society
To the participants in the civil society-EZLN encuentro of November 1998

Brothers and sisters,

Multiple and varied greetings. As agreed at the encuentro in San Cristobal, we zapatistas received the mandate to draw up - taking into account the presentations and participation there - the convocation for the Consultation for the Recognition of the Rights of the Indian Peoples and for the End to the War of Extermination.

This reminds me of what old Antonio once recounted to me... Do you remember old Antonio? Good, well, he told me something which has to do with the reasons for adding to and multiplying convocations, mobilizations, consultations and other irreverent acts.

It was a dawning in December. Dawnings in December in the mountains are cold and rainy. The fog binds itself to the trees and gives them new forms and shadows. And so there I was, watching the solitary column of smoke from my pipe, guessing, perhaps, that the fog would arrive later to give harbor to that cloud coming from my lips, when a form, half-fog, half-shadow, emerges from a nearby tree, and, with weary step, arrives next to me and tells me: "Wisdom is not in knowing many things or in knowing much about one thing." I tremble. A bit from the cold, another bit from the fog, very much from what I heard, and some more from the surprise of recognizing old Antonio behind the brief flash of the match lighting his rolled cigarette, I did what I always do under these circumstances: I rubbed my knees, chewed my pipe and pronounced a wise "Mmmmh". Old Antonio sat down at my side, arranged his cigar in the left corner of his mouth and, murmuring, gave form, color and warmth to the...

History of the One and the All

There was a time in which there was no time. It was the time of the beginning. It was like the dawn. It was not night nor was it day. The time was just like that, without going to either side nor coming from any part. There was no light but nor was there darkness. It was the time in which the greatest gods lived, those who gave birth to the world, the very first. The oldest of our old say that those first gods were seven and that each of them were two. The most ancient of our ancient ones say "seven" is how the most ancient number all, and that one is always two in order to walk. That is why they say that the very first gods were each two and they were seven times. And these most great gods were not created wise and great. They were small and knew little. But they did speak much and talk to each other much. These first gods were nothing but words. They all spoke much, at the same time, and none of them understood anything of the others.

Although these gods spoke much, they understood little. But, namely, the how and the why!, there came a moment in which all of them remained quiet at the same time. One of them spoke then and said and said to himself that it was good that when one would speak the others would not speak and thus the one who was speaking could be heard and the others who were not speaking could hear him and what they must do was to speak in turns. The seven who are two in one were in agreement. And the most old of our old say that was the first accord in history, that of not just speaking, but of also listening.

The gods looked about the corners of that dawn in which there was still no day nor night nor world nor men nor women nor animals nor things. They looked and they realized that all the little bits of that dawn were speaking truths and that one alone cannot listen to all the corners, and thus they divided the work of listening to the dawn and thus they could learn everything which the world at that time, which was not yet world, had to teach them.

And so the first gods saw that the one is necessary, that it is necessary in order to learn and to work and to live and to love. But they also saw that the one is not enough for setting the world in motion. And this is how the first gods, the most great, those who gave birth to the world, became great and knowing. These gods knew to speak and to listen. And they were wise. Not because they knew many things or because they knew much of one thing, but because they understood that the one and the all are necessary and sufficient.

Old Antonio goes. I remain waiting. Waiting as waiting for the sea and the wheat, that is, knowing they will arrive... because they have not gone.

Vale. Salud and do not forget Acteal. Memory is the root of wisdom.

From the mountains of the Mexican Southeast,
Subcomandante Insurgente Marcos.
Mexico, December 1998.

P.S. Of the super-showing: It's coming now! (Or has it come???) Don't miss it! The hit of the end of century! A jewel of the sixty-ninth art! What is it about? Nothing more and nothing less than... A video-hit! Yesss! Filmed in its totality in the mountains of the Mexican southeast! Special effects of the most abysmal quality! Wide distribution! Neither Sharon Stone is appearing, nor Leonardo Di Caprio, nor Gwyneth Paltrow nor Robert de Niro nor Meg Ryan nor Al Pacino nor Julia Roberts nor Brad Pitt nor Susan Sarandon nor Edward James Olmos nor Marisol Padilla nor Gene Hackman nor Demi Moore nor Bruce Willis nor Jennifer Lopez nor John Travolta nor etcetera! Nor the brothers Almohada and even less the Bichirs'. Brigitte Bardot and Alain Delon? No way! (Yes, I know I've missed many, but the post-script and the ink are running out). Not even one extra! Absolute stars! Unknowns, yes, but stars! No, none of them have won any prize whatsoever! Not even in the barrio lotteries! Not suitable for IQ's under 0.1! (Not a chance. Not Rabasa nor Orive nor Albores are going to be able to see it). Rated X to the Xth! Forbidden for the Supreme! (It would seem that none of them are suitable). Don't miss it! You'll never see it at the Festival! Jis and Trino recommend it before, after, or in place of! Oliver Stone refused to direct it! Fellini died of envy! Finally! The only! (Fortunately)

The video-hit which everyone is (not) waiting for!:

Sup-Speedy and the Consultation

First Part

Demands that the Fifth Declaration of the Selva Lacandona be included in the video (I don't know if we are going to include it, but if you want, you can demand it).

A super-production, sponsored by Pirates of the Sea Musical Productions, Carpenter of Paper Privateer Videos (Say yesss! to piracy) and Huaraches Yepa Yepa (the only glo-ba-lized huarache).

(Note: none of these businesses are on the Fobaproa list, or however it is now going to be called since Calderon's PAN is going to want to convince us that he did what he did because he was thinking of all Mexicans and of "the well-being of the family").

Ask for it from the pirate distributor closest to your heart!

P.S. Other: Anticipating that we will have tons of requests for this video, I'll tell you straight out that we haven't made anything yet. What's more, we don't even have any idea how to do it. But won't that be better?

P.S. For the 3000 from the encuentro: Do you remember about "Bombs, Firefighters and Lights"? Good, then that production would be, as they say, "pre-modern". This one which we haven't made is much better (Maybe because we haven't made it).

P.S. Another of the other: Don't be scared! We'll come up with something!

Vale of replay. Salud and no, I don't know when the video will be ready.

The Sup, thinking that the recording of the video camera is something like "remembering".

59. Are the Zapatista Indigenous Communities Worse off Than Before the Uprising?

January 1999
For: Guadalupe Loaeza
Reforma Newspaper
Mexico, D.F.
From: Subcomandante Insurgente Marcos

Madame,

I recently read your letter, published in the pages of the Reforma newspaper on December 31, 1998. I am grateful for your lines, as well as for the sincerity which inspires them and the honest interest which, from the beginning of our movement, you have had in Chiapas, and the Mexican indigenous in general.

I do not know Jean Marie Le Clezio's book, nor if Federal Express has service to the Selva Lacandona (but if it's gum and paste, the address is: Subcomandante Insurgente Marcos, EZLN, Playa de Trigo Headquarters, mountains of the Mexican Southeast, Chiapas, Mexico). It would also be good if you were to send a copy to

Senor Zedillo. In addition to avoiding being criticized for being biased that way, you would also be helping Zedillo read something which would open the narrow vistas of his political vision.

Good, let's get on to your letter. You ask if the zapatista indigenous communities are worse off than before the uprising. No. We continue without schools, teachers, hospitals, doctors, medicines, good prices for our products, land, technology in order to work it, fair salaries, food of sufficient quality and quantity, decent housing, exactly the same as before 1994. The communities which are not zapatista are in the same circumstances. We have not accepted the government's hand-outs. We have not accepted them, nor will we, because, as demonstrated by the living conditions of the indigenous who have accepted them, the problems are not resolved, and the quality of life does not improve on the most minimal level. But, above all, we do not accept them because we did not rise up for schools, credits and Conasupo stores for ourselves. We rose up for a better country, one where, among other things, our rights as Indian peoples are recognized, we are respected and we are considered to be citizens, and not beggars. Despite everything, we have tried to improve our conditions, and, in order to do that, in some places we have started schools, clinics and pharmacies with health workers. This little we have, we have built and re-built (because one of the "heroic" tasks of the federal Army in Chiapas is the destruction of schools, clinics, pharmacies and libraries) through our own efforts and with the help of good persons, organized and not, who come to these lands.

And, understand, Madame, that they have helped us very much (as never before in the long history of the indigenous peoples), but never to make war. No one has come to offer arms, bullets or military training.

All of them have come offering financial aid and knowledge, in order to improve the education, housing, food, health, work. These people live with us for a time, they see us as we are, with our defects (which are neither few nor small) and with our virtues (which we also have, but no more, nor greater, than people in other parts of the world, of other colors, cultures, races). Perhaps some day you can speak with some of these persons; any one of them would give you a more real and complete perspective than that which I am trying, ineffectively, to convey in these lines.

We have things now which we did not have before, and it is very little compared with all the needs. But the difference between what we lacked before and what we lack now, is that, before, it did not matter to anyone that we did not have the minimal necessities. What we did have before January 1, 1994, and what we have lost since then, is despair, is bitterness, is resignation.

We are poor, yes, but you will see that our poverty is richer than the poverty of others, and, above all, richer than that which we had before the uprising. And now our poverty has a tomorrow. Why? Well, because there is something more important, which we did not have prior to the uprising, and it has now become our most powerful and feared (by our enemies) weapon: the word. You will see how good this weapon is. It is good for fighting, for defending yourself, for resisting. And it has a great advantage over all the weapons which the government, its military and the paramilitaries have: it does not destroy, it does not kill.

I well know that Senor Labastida accuses us of being responsible for the deterioration in the standard of living in the zapatista communities. Labastida represents a government which has half its army in the indigenous communities, which keeps a substitute, interim, illegitimate and illegal governor in place with bayonets, which squanders thousands of millions of pesos, not in improving the standard of life of the non-zapatista communities, but rather in paying for costly press campaigns and for financing paramilitary groups, a government which orders its troops to thwart the working of the land, which rapes women, which promotes the cultivation and trafficking in drugs, which preaches the religion of alcohol and prostitution.

Tell me: is it not cynical to accuse us of what they classify in their manuals as "low-intensity warfare"? Is not a mockery of all of us that the same government which has promoted the deterioration in the standard of living of the Mexican people (let me cite information from the newspaper which has the honor of having you among their editorialists: In 1999, 4 million poor persons will no longer be receiving assistance for food or for their community development, 1,116,000 children no longer receive subsidized milk, the spending for UNAM, IPN and UAM fell 50%, the financing for scientific research loses 42%, the construction of health units is reduced by 20%, Conasupo reduces its spending by 75% and prepares for its disappearance, 34 million Mexicans who buy maize in Diconsa stores are confronting a price increase of 100%. Reforma, 1/2/99), accuses us of being those responsible for the low standard of living in the indigenous communities?

Now, Madame, suppose I were a fraud with amazing powers of manipulation. Suppose that I had managed to trick the most important media of the 5 continents, the Non-Governmental Organizations of various countries, the millions of Mexicans, and you. Suppose I had deceived them, and, in indigenous Mexico and in Chiapas, nothing is happening: the indigenous have not lived in conditions of the most outrageous misery, nor is it true that the life of an Indian in Ocosingo is worth less than that of a hen, nor is it the truth that in 1993, the finqueros exercised droit du seigneur in the families of their peons. Suppose that it is an invention that the best example of the application of the State of Law in Chiapas is the history (true, believe me) of the indigenous, imprisoned for some years, and condemned to 30 years in jail for having assassinated his father ("with malice aforethought", read the sentence, signed proudly by the judge in charge of the case), who paid his "debt to society" in the Cerro Hueco Jail, while the only thing he received from the outside was a package of tortillas that, without fail, was personally delivered by... his papa! Suppose that it is a lie that the army and the police participate, and participate with singular enthusiasm, in the attacks against the indigenous communities, that it is untrue and that it is a slander that Mexico is hurriedly rushing towards modernity while trying to forget the more than 10 million first inhabitants of these lands.

Anyway, Madame, suppose that everything is as I have written. Yes? Good, now I beg you to answer me the following:

1. If the EZLN had not risen up in arms on January 1, 1994, would the government, Mexico, the world, you, those columnists, what you pointed out, have turned around to look at the Indian peoples? Was it not, prior to '94, an insult to call someone an 'Indian'?

2. If the fundamental (and national) causes which caused the marginalization of the Indian peoples of Mexico, and which are the root causes of the zapatista uprising, have not been resolved, nor has the groundwork been laid for their solution (that is, could provoke another uprising): would it not be irresponsible to sign a peace agreement, knowing that the war could come again? Is it not more responsible to demand that the zapatista uprising end, but also everything which caused it, and which made it possible and necessary, to end?

3. If Marcos is the one responsible for the zapatista indigenous communities not having bettered their standard of living, because he 'induces' or 'obliges' (depending on the columnist) them to reject government aid: why are the indigenous communities which are not zapatista the same as, or worse off, than those who suffer 'the zapatista oppression'? Why, despite the thousands of millions that the government says it has invested in Chiapas, 'to resolve the cause of the conflict and the social backwardness', the more than one million indigenous persons have not raised their standard of living? Are they all zapatistas?

Good, now suppose that those columnists who keep you awake are telling the truth, and it is Marcos who is keeping the conflict from being resolved peacefully, and that he is only seeking to draw it out, just so he can correspond with the editorial page writers of the Reforma (something which would be impossible, they say, if the peace had already been signed), that the zapatistas say they want peace, but they do not return to the dialogue table with the government because, in reality, they are not interested in the Indian peoples, but rather in their political plans.

Suppose that Zedillo, Labastida, Rabasa, Albores, Green and the one you point out, are right, and the indigenous communities (except, of course, for the stupid zapatista peoples) are now living in the abundance which the government has had the goodness to provide them with. Suppose it is true that the government has given many demonstrations of its willingness to dialogue, and Zedillo's variously noted visits to Chiapas - in 1998 - were in order to support his will for peace, and not in order to threaten or to support the repressive strikes which Albores led throughout that year. Suppose it is true that the government does not see the EZLN as a military problem, but rather as a political one, and that it is true they want to resolve the problem politically.

Suppose all of that, Madame, and, then, answer these other questions:

4. If we zapatistas are not a military danger, and they could finish us off in a matter of minutes, why does the government have more than 60,000 troops in what they call the 'conflict zone'? So that the indigenous communities can learn the 'advantages of Western life', that is, the prostitution, drugs and alcohol which accompany the federal garrisons when they are set up within the communities?

5. If the government has 60,000 soldiers 'enforcing the Firearms and Explosives Law' in chiapaneco territory: where did the paramilitaries, Peace and Justice, Red Mask, MIRA, Chinchulines, Los Punales and Albores of Chiapas, obtain, and where do they obtain, their arms, ammunition, equipment and training? Where are the high-caliber arms used in the Acteal massacre?

6. If the objective of the dialogue and negotiations is to reach accords (such as those at San Andres, signed by the government and the EZLN on February 16, 1996), and the accords are not carried out: what are the dialogue and negotiations for?

7. If the government did not carry out the first peace accords which it signed, what guarantees the zapatistas that the government is going to carry out the final accords when the return to civil life is agreed?

No, Madame, it is neither task nor punishment. It is Old Antonio's old method: ask in order to walk.

If, despite all of this, confusion prevails, let me suggest something to you. Call your friend Sofia, and invite her to visit, along with you, the indigenous communities of Chiapas (the zapatista and the non-zapatista). Come incognito, that way we won't be able to set a stage in order to deceive you. If you want to experience directly the xenophobic atmosphere which the government has managed to create in Chiapas, remember not to speak Spanish at any of the military or immigration checkpoints (English or French is good, although, for Immigration, anything which is not Spanish, is English). Take the plane to Tuxtla, from there travel to San Cristobal de las Casas, and, making your base there, you can travel throughout the zapatista and non-zapatista communities in Los Altos, La Selva and the Northern zones of Chiapas. With the "look" of foreigners, you will be able to enjoy the humiliating treatment which the military and immigration agents give the people from other countries who dare to leave the tourist routes. Come. Come to the communities. See and listen to the people. Perhaps you will not find the absolute truth, but it is certain that you will discover where the lie is.

Almost at the end of your letter, you say, and say well, that we do not want another Acteal. No, neither you, nor we, want it. But they, those who say they are governing, are willing to repeat it as many times as might be necessary in order to destroy, not just the zapatistas, but the Indian peoples as a whole. They want to repeat it until the Indian peoples cease to be so and, or, disappear or are "westernized".

We would not think of allowing it, and we believe that many, such as you, would not allow this horror to be repeated either. That is why we are making a new effort for peace and dialogue with THE CONSULTATION FOR RESPECT FOR THE RIGHTS OF THE INDIAN PEOPLES AND FOR THE END TO THE WAR OF EXTERMINATION. Yes, I know the name is quite long, but what it aspires to is even greater.

I am not trying to recruit you, Madame (as some of your acquaintances are most certainly going to tell you), I am only inviting you to work for peace. That is why I am telling you something very simple and urgent: Acteal must not be repeated, and, in order for it not to be repeated, it is necessary to recognize the rights of the Indian peoples and to stop the war of extermination. Does that seem like a slogan? Believe me, Madame, it is not, it is something more definitive: it is a duty.

If, after all and everything, you are still confused, do not worry, Madame. Look at that bridge which joins the head with the heart, the thought with the emotion (the soul, some say). Look, and listen, I am certain that you will know what is good, which is not always the best, but which is never unnecessary. Finally, in order to increase your confusion, here goes a zapatuda anecdote: Around here, they set up a fashionable cooperative, it was called The Elegant Zapatista, and its motto was Against Reactionary Bad Taste, Revolutionary Elegance. How about that, eh? Isn't our perversity obvious?

Vale. Salud and, you will see, the only thing we are really guilty of is having let down the hem of hope.

> From the mountains of the Mexican Southeast,
> Subcomandante Insurgente Marcos.
> Mexico, January 1999.

P.S. We send you our best regards and we thank you for the reference to the little ski-masks. There are not any... yet, but we will keep you informed.

60. THE INTERNATIONAL CONSULTA AND THE INTERNATIONAL JORNADA FOR THE EXCLUDED OF THE WORLD

February 14, 1999

To: International and National Civil Society

From: Sup Marcos

Madame,

Here we are once again. I am reminded that, in the last letter, I had left open what I was going to tell you about the International Consulta and the International Jornada for the Excluded of the World. Sale y vale:

1. Good, first I'll tell you about the brigades that have been accredited on the five continents, and that have sent us their ideas, reports and concerns.

   There are now persons interested and working in Asia, specifically in Japan, South Korea (they tell us there that they do not believe the lies of the Mexican government), Hong Kong and Israel. They are similarly in Africa, specifically in South Africa. They are also mobilizing in Australia in Oceania.

   In Europe, they are in Germany, Belgium, Denmark, the State of Spain, the Basque Country, France, Holland, Italy, England, Portugal, Switzerland, Sweden, Norway and Ireland. For example, in Hamburg they have asked us how they can participate; in northern Norway they do not feel far from Mexico (despite the fact that they are very close to the North Pole), and they are organizing in order to be heard; in Ireland, the Irish Mexico Group will set up a voting table in... Dublin! Alright!

   In Latin American there are interested persons and groups in Argentina (in addition to Buenos Aires, Rosario, Bahia Blanca, Rio Cuarto and Bariloche, they are in Patagonia, close to the South Pole. Or, the Consulta is from Pole to Pole, no?), Brazil (Sao Paulo, Rio and Rio Grande del Norte, for starters), Chile (greetings to "Plomo," which is also close to the ends of the earth), Costa Rica, Panama, Puerto Rico, Uruguay and Venezuela.

   In Canada the Zapatista Support Group is already working in Victoria, British Columbia. There are also groups in Toronto (Peace Action for Chiapas), Montreal and Quebec.

   The American Union deserves special mention. Not just because millions of Mexican men and women are living there. Also because there are many persons and groups who are already mobilizing in order to organize the Consulta and to express their opinions.

   Some of the places where this is happening are: Alaska, San Diego, New York, Washington, Los Angeles, Santa Cruz (California), Philadelphia, Chicago, Michigan, Rochester (NY), Albuquerque (New Mexico), Columbia (in South Carolina), Seattle, Dallas, Oregon, Denver (Colorado), Mount Vernon (Washington), San Francisco, Tarzana (California), El Paso, Madison (Wisconsin), Lancaster (Pennsylvania),

Providence (Rhode Island), Bakersfield (California), Maywood (California), Richmond (California) and Minnesota.

More details? Take a look: in San Diego there is the Dignity and Liberty 99 brigade; the Aztlan Information Center tells us: "Here in Frisco, California, we are in the Consulta, we've already printed up the materials and they're being distributed all over..."; also there is the "Aztlan Chicana and Chicano Student Movement (MECHA)," and they send their greetings to the indigenous "buds" in Mexico; in New York, the color blue has become a brigade with the United Zapatista Dawn in the struggle; in Santa Cruz, it's the Bi-national Oaxacan Indigenous Front; in Michigan, the Group for Peace and Resistance; in other places there are the Coalition for Rights for the Raza, Harmony Keepers of Aztlan Nation, Tonantzin Land Institute, Coalition for the Rights of the Indigenous, Committee for Solidarity in the Americas, Vote Online Polling, Mexican National Front Abroad, Committee of the Chicano Minority, Renewal Center, Barrio Warriors of Aztlan, Emiliano Zapata Committee, Danza Mexica Cuauhtemoc, Chiapas Coalition, El Bracero, Zapatista Support Committee and the Parish of San Pascual Bailon.

It is here, in North America, where the excitement and energy being provoked by this Consulta can most readily be seen. The Mexican men and women who are living and working in the United States are mobilizing, and in a big way. They receive many insults and suffer many humiliations, but they also have their Ya Basta! And they see in the Consulta an opportunity to be heard and respected.

They all know that the struggle going on here is also theirs, and that is how we understand it. That is why we welcome them.

Wacha Bato! This is great. Join the consulta!

2. Now let me tell you that two great activities are being prepared on the five continents for this March.

One is the International Consulta. Since, for us (and for many others like us), the Mexican men and women living abroad have rights which should be recognized, we have thought that the Consulta for the Recognition of the Rights of the Indian Peoples and for an End to the War of Extermination should be open to the participation of all Mexicans, without regard to the country they are in. Then, what we did was call for the International Consulta, so that Mexican men and women who are living in other nations, and who are more than 12 years old, can also express their opinions on the 4 questions which will be answered on March 21, 1999.

And not only that, we have also decided to add a fifth question to the International Consulta, which says:

"Are you in agreement that Mexican men and women residing abroad should have an active part in the building of a new Mexico, and should have the right to vote in elektions?"

"Response: Yes. No. I don't know."

In this way, Mexicans living outside the country will also have the opportunity to express their opinions on the recognition of their rights (which are denied them by the government).

3. Certainly at this point one might ask what those who are not Mexicans - but who are interested and committed to peace and to the recognition of the rights of everyone - can do, or how they can participate.

Good, one way then is to participate in the International Action for the excluded of the world (which we'll talk about later), and another is by promoting and publicizing the Consulta in their countries, organizing the setting up of the voting tables in the different nations of the world, and organizing and carrying out the counting and the communication with Mexico in order to announce the results. All men, women, children and old ones of the world may participate in this task, without regard to their nationality, race, color, flavor, creed, size, weight, sexual preference or any of those kinds of classifications which the powers use to exclude those who are different. Nationality is of no importance here, the International Consulta has many spaces for participating beyond the voting.

4. Yes, I understand that you are asking how Mexicans abroad will give their opinions on the 5 questions, and how they will let us know their answers.

Good, we have thought to offer the following options:

a. So that Mexicans living abroad can express their opinions, everyone within a nation who is interested in this can get in touch with each other, and, by common agreement, organize the setting up of the Consulta tables and the counting centers. We call this "National Coordination," and it can be done in the countries where it's possible.

For example: all persons and organizations interested in the Consulta in the United States can get in touch with each other and agree to form the "US National Coordination." Through this coordination, they will organize the setting up of the Consulta tables in the places that are possible and convenient, so that the Mexican population residing in the US can express their opinions on the 5 questions. We should imagine that tables can be set up in Chicago, Los Angeles, Phoenix, San Diego, San Francisco, New York, El Paso, Albuquerque, San Antonio (to mention a few of the cities where there are people already interested in participating in the Consulta). Good, then the people and organizations in these cities should get in touch with each other, and with the other places in the American Union, form their National Coordination and organize the setting up of the tables in those and other cities, as well as the counting of the votes. This example also has the advantage that the National Commission for Democracy in Mexico-USA (NCDM) (email: moonlight@igc.apc.org) is already organizing the Consulta there, and they can be gotten in touch with, or they may organize themselves separately. We propose that the NCDM function as US National Coordination. The people and organizations who do not have contact with the NCDM can link directly with the EZLN Contact Office for the Consulta (whose address appears further on).

In this way, then, there can be several National Coordinations in the same country, because the term "national" here does not mean that it's the only one, but rather that it covers all or various parts of the nation where it is located.

b.   These National Coordinations should be accredited with the EZLN Contact Office for the Consulta, so that we can know in what countries and how the International Consulta is being organized.

c.   The National Coordinations' vote count results should be sent to the EZLN Contact Office for the Consulta.

d.   There is no problem if any group of persons, organizations or group of organizations in a particular country, want to organize themselves other than through the National Coordinations. We just ask that they accredit themselves in the same way with the EZLN Contact Office for the Consulta.

e.   In addition to going to the Consulta tables, opinions can be expressed on the 5 questions by sending your responses to the Consulta questions by telephone, fax, internet, email, satellite, paper ships or planes, intercontinental rocket, carrier pigeon, or by land, sea or air mail.

Good, now I'm going to talk to you a bit about the International Action for the Excluded of the World.

This international mobilization which we are calling is not just for March 21, 1999, but we are inviting actions to be carried out centered around this day in which the Consulta for the Recognition of the Rights of the Indian Peoples and for an End to the War of Extermination is being held. Certainly one form of mobilization for this International Action is through participating in the promotion and publicity for the Consulta, by forming National Coordinations, by setting up tables, by the counting and communication of the results (which are not tasks exclusively for Mexicans), but it is not the only one. One can organize, for example, demonstrations, public and private letters, displays, peaceful mobilizations, music concerts (absolutely, following the example of the honorable Mexican rock musicians - who are beat for beat for the Consulta, all the rock groups in the world echoing the zapatista Ya Basta!), recitals, assemblies, conferences, multimedia and/or cyber events, etcetera. Nothing that is civil and peaceful is excluded, and imagination and creativity will most certainly exceed anything we could propose here. We are talking about, then, an action for all the excluded, not just for the indigenous or for the zapatistas.

An act in Strasbourg is being planned, demanding a change in immigration policies by the European countries, and the organizers have decided to include the demands for the recognition of the rights of the Indian peoples and for an end to the war of extermination in Mexico. There is also, in France, the Feu Faux Lait. This is a theatre company which is preparing for their participation in the action for the excluded with a production in and around Paris.

Now you see that you can participate in many ways. You just have to come to agree among yourselves, organize yourselves and act.

Good, I'll say goodbye now. When I know more, I'll write you again.

Vale, salud, and we must not allow neo-liberalism to exclude humanity.

From the mountains of the Mexican Southeast,
Subcomandante Insurgente Marcos.
Mexico, February 1999.

61. THE LITTLE TREE AND THE OTHERS

February 20, 1999
To: National and International Civil Society

Madame,

It's us again. Yes, again. What? It was better when we were staying quiet? Voooy! A lo macho? What? It was a joke? Ah, good! Then it was in very bad taste. Now, just for punishment, I'm not going to tell you anything about how the brigades are doing in Mexico. That way you won't know that by February 16 (two days after we'd told you there were 600), more than 800 brigades had been accredited, and there are more than 10,000 volunteers working in them. And you won't know that Coordinators are being accredited in various states, and that some of them have made so much progress in their work that they already have their plan and methods in place for covering all their municipalities. What? You're sorry? Then we're even.

Look, I'm writing you to let you know that there is now a bank account so that you can make financial donations to the Consulta. The number of the account is CUENTA MAESTRA BANCOMER, No. 5001060-5, Plaza 437, San Cristobal de Las Casas, Chiapas, Mexico, and it's in the name of Dona Rosario Ibarra de Piedra. Let me clarify that this bank account is separate from the finances for each state. And so we ask everyone, in Mexico and in all the countries who want to help, to send your donation to this account. There are going to be many expenses, and, despite the fact that we've dipped into our war funds (which are, in truth, for peace, because we only use them for peace initiatives), it's not enough. We ask that you confirm your deposits with the Contact Office for the EZLN Consulta (email: contacto@laneta.apc.org. Telephone and Fax: 967-8-10-13 and 8-21-59).

I'll take advantage of this outing to accept the invitation that we received from the Metropolitan Autonomous University-Unidad Xochimilco, for zapatista delegates to visit that college during the days that they will be in Mexico City (hopefully March 14 to 21). Since we've accepted, we'll most certainly be there (of course, always and when the cafeteria menu changes). There are more requests from Institutions of Higher Learning, which we'll be responding to.

I'd also like to tell you (see, I don't have any hard feelings) that the zapatista video on the Consulta is now for sale, it's 20 minutes long, it costs 20 pence, and it can be gotten (I think) at the Contact Office for the Consulta. Hurry before they run out! (I hope!).

Vale. Salud and we've almost finished a video (a different one than the other), we're not kidding, and we're hoping, in all modesty, for a Grammy for best video or for an Oscar nomination in micro-short films (of less than 4 minutes). Don't miss it!

> From the mountains of the Mexican Southeast,
> Subcomandante Insurgente Marcos.
> Mexico, February of 1999.

P.S. WHICH CALLS FOR UNITY - During a recent dawn, the Sea was also tired. So I lit my pipe and turned to my Tales of the Seahorse and I read her the story of...

The Little Tree and the Others

Once upon a time there was a little tree who was very much alone but who was very willing to adorn and to sing in another's orchard. And so there was the little tree, and then the other came to look at it and to take it away. But it turned out that the other was not an other, but others. The others wanted to take the little tree to their respective orchards, but there was only one little tree, and the others were several others. And so the little tree was willing then to be planted in all the orchards, but there was just one little tree, and the others were several others.

Then the others began to discuss who was going to keep the little tree and take it to their orchard. And one of the others decided that he would take it, because he was a greater other than the other others. And another other of the others said no, he would take the little tree because he had a more beautiful orchard, etcetera, and another other said he would be better, because he was a simple gardener and he would be able to take care of the little tree and so they were fighting for a bit and they did not come to any agreement, because, although they were others, they did not respect the other who was among them but who was other. And then they stopped fighting and they said that each of them would take a piece of the little tree.

Then the little tree spoke and said: I do not agree, because, in addition to the fact that one should not go about cutting down trees because it disturbs the balance of nature, no one is going to win. If one of you takes my branches, and another takes my trunk, and another my roots and each one of you takes your piece then it's not going to turn out well. The one who takes the branches and plants them is not going to have anything because he will not have the trunk to sustain it nor the roots to feed it. The one who takes the trunk will not have anything either, because, without branches or roots, the trunk is not going to be able to breathe or to be fed. It is the same for the one who takes the roots, because without the trunk or the branches, the roots will not be able to grow or breathe. But if, on the other hand, we come to a good agreement amongst ourselves, I can be planted for a time in the orchard of the one and then for another time in the orchard of another and so on. In this way everyone will have fruits and seeds in each and every one of the orchards. The others were thinking. Tan-tan.

"That's how it ends?" the Sea asks.

"Well, yes," I said, closing the book. The Sea insisted.

"I don't know, we have to wait," I said, dodging the pen the Sea was throwing me.

Vale once more.

> The Sup, murmuring the one that goes "My father and I planted it, at the edge of the patio where the house ends, etcetera."

62. TO MUSICIANS ALL OVER THE WORLD

February 20, 1999
To: Musicians all over the world
From: Sup Marcos

Ladies and Gentlemen,

Old Antonio used to say (who, if he had been a musician, would have played the blues) that music opens paths that only the wise know how to walk, and which, along with dance, builds bridges which bring you close to a world which cannot even be dreamt.

This all comes to mind because we have received news of concerts and shows by musicians in Mexico and in other parts of the world. Their purpose? To promote the Consulta and to be in solidarity with the Mexican indigenous and their dignified struggle.

We want to express our appreciation to all of them, and to those who have had to do with those paths to peace, which criss-cross the planet from end to end, most especially, but not only, to the rhythms of rock.

Nothing pleases us more than those who compose, sing and play. As well as the producers, the sound people (is that how you say it?), the lighting people, the stage-hands, the drivers, the ticket people, the loaders, the artists' reps, the local owners and administrators, and all the men and women who have to do (and who, nonetheless, are not seen) with a concert or musical show (often doubly volunteering, receiving neither money nor credit). Thanks to everyone.

And now that we're into the "one, two, three, four," we want to salute all those who musicians who, over the last five years, have played, are playing, will be playing, for the peace with justice and dignity.

Everyone has called for an end to the war. Some have cut records, others have participated in concerts, or visited the indigenous communities, or spoken out in favor of the peace with justice and dignity, or protested against the Acteal killing, or given us their instruments or dedicated one or more tours to the struggle of the Mexican indigenous. Here are some of the names (some of them escape me, but you already know how space tyrannizes the written word). Sale and vale:

In Mexico: La Bola, Santa Sabina, Panteon Rococo, Maldita Vecindad, Sekta Core, Makina, El Mastuerzo, Tijuana No, Jambo, Los de Abajo, La Nao, Trolebus, La Dosis, Resorte, Guillotina, Estramboticos, Mana, Julieta Venegas, Petroleo, Juguete Rabioso, Rotor, Funkswagen, Cafe Tacuba, Salario Minimo, El TRI, Fratta, Botellita de Jerez, Serpiente sobre Ruedas, Los Hermanos Rincon, Los Nakos, Ana de Alba, Leones de la Sierra de Xichu, Jose de Molina (QEPD), Lidia Tamayo, Arturo Marquez, Nina Galindo, Nayeli Nesme, Eugenia Leon, Hebe Rossel, the men and women from the National Music and Conservatory Schools, the raza of the CLETA, and the not few singer-songwriters who, in vans and buses, delight their audiences in exchange for only "lo que sea su voluntad joven, senito, caballero."

In France, Germany, the State of Spain, the Basque Country, Italy, Canada, the United States, Brazil, Argentina, Uruguay, Chile, and in other parts of the world:

Negu Gorriak, Mano Negra, Hechos contra el Decoro, Color Humano, Sook and the Guay, Joaquin Sabina, Joan Manuel Serrat, Juan Perro, Ismael Serrano, Dut, Manu Chao, Hubert Cesarion, Ruben and Babakar, DKP, Ethnicians, Pushy!, La Huanda, Sree, Denise, P18, Ghetto 84, Radio Bemba, Banda Bassotti, Arpioni, Gang, Tupamaros, Klaxon, Radici Nel Cemento, R.D.E., Swoons, Another Fine Mess, Maltschicks, Dady Longleg, Jelly Gruel, Mundmachine, Lunchbox, Caution Sreams, Kommerzinfarkt, KJB, Deh-kadenz, Nervous, Ate Hands for Brains, The Evil Bad, Provisorium, Novotny Tv, Down The Stairs, Rubabs, Daisies, Plattrock, King Prawn, Steven Brown, Nine Rain y Tuxedo Moon, Tuxedo Moon, Paralamas, Xenreira, Planet Hemp, Fito Pez, Charly Garcia, Todos tus Muertos, Los Guarros, Divididos, Ilya Kuryaki anda The Valderramas, Andres Calamaro, Lumumba, Los Tres, Mercedes Sosa, Leon Gieco, Daniel Viglietti, Vicente Feli, Rhytm Activism, Rage Against The Machine, Aztln Underground, Indigo Girls, Quetzal, Ozomatli, Jackson Browne, Los Skarnales, King Chango, Sepultura.

We also know of groups and performers in Ireland, Greece, Nicaragua, Cuba, Canada, and many others in Italy, the United States, the State of Spain, France, Brazil, Germany and Mexico, whom we have heard about in the mountains of the Mexican southeast, but whose music has not reached us. There are many others who have spoken about us, have sung for us and who have made themselves heard for us.

Thanks to all those musicians, men and women, who, in Mexico and all over the world, have echoed the zapatista "Ya Basta!"

Once we have won, we are going to organize a super-mega-magna-hyper concert for everyone, with no time limits... and free! (You're kidding! You're going to end up playing only the San Jose marimba).

Vale. Salud and, doesn't the morning also arrive through song?

From the mountains of the Mexican Southeast,
Subcomandante Insurgente Marcos.
Mexico, February of 1999.

63. WE WANT TO GO WITH EVERYONE

March 1, 1999

To whom it may concern,

A communiqué and letter are off, both about the Consulta. I don't know right now how many brigades are coming or going, but I do know that they are all over the place, now in all 32 states.

We received an invitation for an act-rally at the UNAM. We'll certainly accept, we only ask them that the organization of the act be plural and inclusive. We're not going with any particular group, we want to go with everyone. For that reason we are asking them to send us the invitation with the names of the organizations, groups and individuals who are participating in the organization of this act. Ah, another thing; we're proposing that the date for the act be March 19. Sale?

We will take advantage of the moment to inform you that we are sending a special group of 12 zapatista delegates who will be visiting universities, teachers' schools and other middle and senior high schools. We are asking those who have sent us invitations (such as UNAM-Xochimilco, UNAM-Iztapalapa, UAM-Azapotzalco, UNAM, ENEP's, CCH's, ENAH and others), and those who are going to be doing so, to organize themselves for this, independently of the delegation coordinators, because it will affect the visits by the "university" delegates. We zapatistas have most certainly always wanted to study.

From the mountains of the Mexican Southeast,
Subcomandante Insurgente Marcos.
Mexico, March of 1999.

P.S. Concerning cafeteria self-criticism. I have been inundated with criticisms and gestures for the tasteless joke about the UNAM-X cafeteria. Of course the menu is the envy of the finest chefs, it is lovely, it is inexpensive and it is delicious. There, then! Do you forgive me? By the way, the yes we answered is to all those who invited us.

P.S. Yes, I left out many groups in the letter in which I recognized and thanked the peace efforts by musicians all over the world. For example? Here are a few (with our thanks and our apologies for not having been included in the other letter) from Mexico: Los Vantrol, Revuelta, Marcos Laneta, Restos Humanos, Antidoping, Atico, Tortura Social, Skaleros Inocentes, Tolos Famus, Cruel Decepcion, Estados de Control, Engrudo, Neoplasma, Cresta en Boga, Masacre 9, Rabia Proletaria, Skarbame, Dolor y Odio, Sonora Skandalera, Rompiendo Cadenas. From other places: Doctor Calypso and Los Discipulos de Otilia (both from Cataluna), Brujeria and A.N.I.M.A.L. (both Chicanos), Dios Elefante (US), Wemean (Switzerland). Once I remember more, I'll let you know (it would be worthwhile sending cassettes, CD's, LP's, demos and even 45's and 78's).

64. People in the Most Unexpected Places are Participating

March 17, 1999
To National and International Civil Society

Brothers and sisters,
Since I've been into soccer lately, I'd forgotten to talk to you about how the International Consulta and the International Action for the Excluded of the World are going.

It now turns out that there are people in the most unexpected places who are interested in participating, so that they may have their voices heard. They are, for example, in Jordan, Singapore, Hong Kong, Australia, the Canaries, Indonesia, Pakistan, India, Nepal, Zambia and the Fiji Islands. But not just there, there are also brigades in Scotland, Argentina, Bolivia, Chile, Cuba, Nicaragua, Panama, Puerto Rico, Uruguay, Paraguay, the United States, Canada, Japan, Germany, Belgium, Denmark, the State of Spain, France, Holland, England, Ireland, Italy, Norway, Sweden and Switzerland.

In Jakarta, which is an island of Java, in Indonesia, more than 2 dozen people, including Munir, Tatma and Dwi, signed a manifesto in support of the Consulta. And in the Sanin region (which means, they tell me, "the shadow of the mountains"), in Japan, they registered "The Ninjas" brigade, and they invited us to visit them, because the children there want to meet us (they think we are Mexican Ninjas!). In Chile, very close to the South Pole, the "Sherlock" brigade honors their name and solves mysteries in order to spread the Consulta. In Belgium, the "Manuel Alvarez Bravo" brigade is explaining the importance of the San Andres Accords. In Nicaragua, they are rising up from the rubble left by Hurricane Mitch, and they are preparing for the Consulta and the action for the excluded.

In Germany, the "Zapata Lebt Noch" brigade was created (which means, they say, "Zapata Lives"). Also in Germany, "The Incomplete Dadaists" are joining forces with an old dog from Paraguay and are preparing a 7 hour vigil on the Consulta, on the night of March 20. In Catalonia - which could well be an Autonomous Municipality of Chiapas (given the number of zapatistas there), except that it's in the State of Spain - and more precisely, in Vic, the capital of Osana - they have prepared a huge book with information on the Consulta. In Montreal, Canda, the Acteal brigade was giving out information on the Consulta outside a show with the tigers of the North. In Toronto, also in Canada, they sent their wishes on the departure of the zapatista delegates.

And in Norway, "La Cucaracha" brigade advises us that they can coordinate with all of those further north of Uruapan, yes, Michoacan!. In Strasbourg, France, there's a brigade called "CIA," that, most certainly, is not the gringo CIA, but the "Cercle de Idealistes Associes" (something like "Society of Associate Idealists"). In Barcelona, there's a brigade called "El Quijote Aguamielero," and in Rio Cuarto, Cordoba, Argentina, another that's called "La Mera Petatera."

In Albuquerque, New Mexico, USA, the Navajo/Dineh, Apache, Paiute, Lakota, Jemez, Cherokee, Pawnee, Comanche, Tewa, Tiwa, Towa, Acoma, Zuni, Hopi, Sac and Fox nations claimed their right to participate in the Consulta in accordance with the Mexican Constitution of 1821, and they formed the "First Nations North and South" brigade.

There are also brigades proliferating in the United States, promoted by the Chicano Student Movement of Aztlan (MECHA), the National Campaign for the Absentee Vote 2000, the Bi-national Oaxacan Indigenous Front, the Democratic Platform, Mexican Brotherhood and many others. For example, the ALAS brigade, in Glendale, California, has mounted a photographic exhibit; in Denver, Colorado, a woman demands that we register her husband (done, Madame); in New York, the AZUL brigade is covering the Bronx, Harlem, Manhattan, Queens, Staten Island and New Jersey.

In Sacramento, California, there is a radio program where they are explaining what's going on here, and, so, we send our greetings from here to the radio listeners of "Tiro Directo" in Sacramento, and we invite them to participate in the Consulta, which is for the recognition of the rights of the Indian peoples, that is, of the peoples who gave life and culture to many of those who are listening to that program. In Storrs, Connecticut, "El Solitario" brigade has only one member, but it is as if it were 1111. In New York, "La Realidad" brigade demonstrates that it's a small world, and we may go wherever we wish. The "Villista Anti-Imperialist Remember Columbus" brigade is in San Diego, and... needs no comment.

But the most significant thing in the last few days has been the formation of the Pro Derechos de La Raza - San Diego brigade, which has let us know that the Project of Chicano Mexican Prisoners is carrying out the Consulta in various jails in the United States, where there are thousands of Mexican men and women in prison. The Brigade does not have any money, and so they could only send 500 ballots to the main jails in the US. And from here we say to them: "No le aunque, raza! A darle ese!"

Continuing with this, we are letting you know that all the National Coordinators who have requested their registration with the Contact Office have been accredited. Ideas for the vote counting and for the sending of the results? Here's one for you: the brigades and coordinators send the Consulta results by email, and then, later, by regular mail, the actual ballots. I'm just saying it's an idea, but there can be others, and, I suppose better ones. Mutatis mudandi, which would be something like "a Consulta where many Consultas fit." No?

But you'll see that not everything is Consulta and brigades. They are also preparing, and preparing well, various acts for the International Action for the Excluded of the World. According to what they are telling us, there are activities planned now in: France, Germany, England, Puerto Rico, Canada, Nicaragua, Argentina, Denmark, the Iberian Peninsula and the Canary Islands. In Nicaragua they are planning a carnival meeting for the afternoon of the 21st. In Catalonia, Valencia and Zaragoza they are each planning fiestas of the imagination; in the Canary islands, they are holding a meeting in Guayadeque (Grand Canary Island). In Denmark, in Copenhagen, the Mexico Gruppen and Tinku have already prepared various activities.

In Argentina, in Bariloche, Bahia Blanca, Arequito, Chabas, San Jose de la Esquina, Buenos Aires and Rosario, they are linking the action of the 21st with the day of MEMORY, March 24, in which the Argentine fighters join together to march and to demand that the memory live. They wrote to us and warned us: "The explosion is coming!" How? Well, with posters, music, murals, radio transmissions, videos, seminars, batucada (Leon Gieco, they say, goes there), dance, in sum, dignity in many forms and colors.

These good persons (because they are good and they are persons) have committed themselves so much to the Consulta that they have taken upon themselves the task of seeking out Mexican men and women all over Argentina. And each one who finds one makes a fiesta whose noise can be heard even here. Just today, the Internet came out with some news that was going from one end to the other of that heroic network of the cyber-excluded. The reason? The net in Argentina had found, in a tiny village of less than 5000 residents... a Mexican! Fiesta! But, in addition, this Mexican woman was very interested in participating in the Consulta. Double fiesta! Things like this are what those from above will never understand: why so much fiesta and excitement when someone meets the other guy (other woman, in this case).

There are many other activities, and all of them good. We congratulate all of them, and we wish them our best (which, nonetheless, will always be but little, compared to what they deserve). As soon as we get more information, we'll be sending it to you.

That's how we are, then. As the date draws closer, the initiatives are increasing. And, with them, all of those who embrace the world from all the forgotten corners of the planet, and who, embracing, will meet each other.

Vale. Salud and may the fiesta of finding the other never be over.

From the mountains of the Mexican Southeast,
Subcomandante Insurgente Marcos.
Mexico, March of 1999.

65. WE ASK THAT YOU PROVIDE ECONOMIC HELP

To National and International Civil Society

Brothers and sisters,
As you know, the EZLN is currently engaged in developing a peace initiative at the national and international level, with the objective of demanding recognition of the rights of the indigenous peoples and an end to the war of extermination.

As part of this initiative, 5000 delegates from the civil support communities ['bases de apoyo'] of the EZLN - 2500 men and 2500 women - will come out of the mountains of Southeast Mexico and will visit the most remote corners of the national territory. In every state of the Mexican republic, there are men, women, children, and elderly people who have already organized, and who await the visit of the Zapatistas and the chance to join voices with their appeal for peace and justice.

In order to reach these people and dialogue with them, the Zapatista delegates will have to cover many kilometers, sometimes by car, sometimes on foot, sometimes on muleback, sometimes by bicycle, sometimes by plane, sometimes by boat. It's not easy to get those 5000 indigenous Zapatistas on the road, or to obtain the necessary funds for their transport. This is why we ask that you provide economic help, both for us and for those who will receive the delegates, to make it possible for the greatest number of people to make their voices and their opinions heard in Mexico.

The money that you donate to this mobilization will be used - do not doubt it - to win a peace with justice and dignity. Isn't it worth it? Please forward donations to the 'Bancomer' bank, account number 5001060-5, Plaza 437, San Cristobal de las Casas, Chiapas Mexico. The account is in the name of Rosario Ibarra de Piedra.

Get a move on! Don't be shy!

Pst! Pst! Hey you! Yes, you who are working in a brigade of the International Consultation! It doesn't matter that you're living way over there, in that other country which isn't Mexico but which, when you take a look this way, well it's almost as if you were. Neither does is matter whether you're Mexican or not, whether you're fat, skinny, or 'slender', whether you're heterosexual, homosexual, or bisexual, whether you're tall, stubby, or 'medium', whether you're black, white, yellow, coffee, red, blue, or yellow. Well, to make it brief, none of that matters - only whether or not you want to help build peace. If you do, then help us.

Alright. Salud [To your health]. Just imagine if we'd gotten the idea of going all over the world! How much does it cost to go to the North Pole or to Patagonia? A lot? Well, we'll need less than that.

> *From the mountains of Southeast Mexico,*
> *Subcomandante Insurgente Marcos.*

66. The Consulta, the Victories and the Questions of the Moment

April 1, 1999
To: The Zapatista Brigades, individuals and organizations in solidarity, new and old companeras and companeros

We responded. Over three million strong, our voice will not be silenced.

Your vision, solidarity, generosity and most importantly, your work, has once again forced the Mexican government to publicly and internationally answer for the violence it calls 'justice', the repression it calls 'democracy', and the war it calls 'liberty'. The small thoughtful acts of organization which have been multiplied millions of times over the past few months, weeks, and days through the International Consulta for the Recognition of Indigenous Rights & Against the War of Extermination have together won a great victory.

Through the commitment of each one of you, through the dozens of Zapatista Brigades and through the NCDM's Coordination, over 30,000 Mexican men and women joined their voice in a practice of popular democracy in the U.S. alone.

In Los Angeles, over twenty Brigades won the participation of over 15,000 people. Throughout the United States tens of thousands of Mexicans and non-Mexicans supported the Consulta. In Mexico, through over 15,000 voting tables across our land, over 3 MILLION Mexicans voted on March 21, 1999.

But the true victory is not about the quantity of votes. It is about hope. Hope is the reason which motivated these thousands to work hundreds of uncompensated hours under dangerous, difficult conditions. Hope is the weapon which annuls the physical force of the Mexican Army and begins to chart a new course for humanity.

The true victory lies in the individual and collective contributions each of us made towards building a new Mexico and a new World in which civil society exerts its strength in an organized way. The true victory lies in the fact that we are beginning to establish a new way of making politics.

Concretely, the Consulta succeeded in:

- Placing the demands for the constitutional recognition of Indigenous rights at the forefront of the national dialogue in Mexico once again,

- Organizing an international dialogue on Mexican Indigenous rights, the Accords of San Andres Saca'amchen, and the legal Initiative on Indigenous Rights developed by the Mexican congressional Commission on Concordance and Pacification (COCOPA),

- Breaking the military and informational blockade which the PRI-controlled government of Mexico maintains,

- Organizing the massive and international mobilization of civil society,

- Promoting a new practice of democracy from the ground up in Mexico and internationally,

- Uniting people with different agendas but a common aspiration: the desire to completely alter the paradigm of power which has kept us from establishing a more just society.

We believe that allowing the network we strengthened through the Consulta to fade would be a serious error. We would like to continue a dialogue with everyone who participated in the Consulta, in whatever capacity. Yet, we must first ask, IS IT NECESSARY TO CONTINUE TO BUILD UPON THIS WORK? HOW WOULD WE RE-DEFINE AND REGENERATE IT?

The following themes could serve as guides for our dialogue:

1. THE NEED for the organization of a local and national relationship that understands the importance of our voice in the struggle for justice, democracy and liberty in Mexico, while also understanding the demand for struggle here.

2. THE NEED for a process that identifies principles that unite us.

3. THE NEED to develop struggles that engage us as members of a civil society conscious of its role nationally and internationally.

4. THE NEED for the organization of people, a movement, which like the wind, spreads the seeds and pollinates the flowers of struggles locally, nationally and internationally.

5. THE NEED for the organization of a web that binds us to a practice that aspires to reclaim self-governance, in the establishment and defense of social norms and relationships while building an international political norm that demands that those who govern, 'govern by obedience'.

6. THE NEED to ask, dialogue and answer the following question: What is resistance to us?

Our wind, the wind from below, must be what some people call a network - a functional, practical and dynamic relationship of relationships among human beings and organizations capable of protracted and instant organization, dialogue and mobilization. Our wind, the wind from below, must continue to build these relationships, whispering hope to all who will listen, seeking other winds from other struggles and other parts of the world. Our wind, must move through the fields, the cities, the jungles, the mountains, the valleys and the plains, seeking the energies of human hands and hearts struggling to live life with dignity.

The wind from the south blows strong, may our wind find such strength.

67. SUBCOMANDANTE MARCOS TO MUMIA ABU-JAMAL

April of 1999
For: Mumia Abu-Jamal American Union
From: Subcomandante Insurgente Marcos
Mexico

Mister Mumia,

I am writing to you in the name of the men, women, children and elderly of the Zapatista Army of National Liberation in order to congratulate you on April 24, which is your birthday.

Perhaps you have heard of us. We are Mexican, mostly indigenous, and we took up arms on January 1 of 1994 demanding a voice, face and name for the forgotten of the earth.

Since then, the Mexican government has made war on us and pursues us and harasses us seeking our death, our disappearance and our definitive silence. The reason? These lands are rich with oil, uranium and precious lumber. The government wants them for the great transnational companies. We want them for all the Mexicans. The government sees our lands as a business. We see our history written in these lands. In order to defend our right (and that of all Mexicans) to live with liberty, democracy, justice and dignity we became an army and undertook a name, voice and face that way.

Perhaps you wonder how we know of you, about your birthday, and why it is that we extend this long bridge which goes from the mountains of the Mexican southeast to the prison of Pennsylvania which has imprisoned you unjustly. Many good people from many parts of the world have spoken of you, through them we have learned how you were ambushed by the North American police in December of 1981, of the lies which they constructed in the procedures against you, and of the death sentence in 1982. We learned about your birthday through the international mobilizations which, under the name of "Millions for Mumia", are being prepared this April 24th.

It is harder to explain this bridge which this letter extends, it is more complicated. I could tell you that, for the powerful of Mexico and the government, to be indigenous, or to look indigenous, is reason for disdain, abhorrence, distrust and hatred. The racism which now floods the palaces of Power in Mexico goes to the extreme of carrying out a war of extermination, genocide, against millions of indigenous. I am sure that you will find similarities with what the Power in the United States does with the so-called "people of color" (African-American, Chicanos, Puerto Ricans, Asians, Northamerican Indians and any other peoples who do not have the insipid color of money).

We are also "people of color" (the same color of our brothers who have Mexican blood and live and struggle in the American Union). We are of the color "brown", the color of the earth, the color from which we take our history, our strength, our wisdom and our hope. But in order to struggle we add another color to the brown: black. We use black ski-masks to show our faces. Only in this way can we be seen and heard. We chose this color as a result of the counsel of an indigenous Mayan elder who explained to us what the color black meant.

The name of this wise elder was Old Man Antonio. He died in these rebel Zapatista lands in March of 1994, victim of tuberculosis which ate his lungs and his breath. Old Man Antonio used to tell us that from black came the light and from there came the stars which light up the sky around the world. He told us a story which said that a long time ago (in those times when no one measured it), the first gods were given the task of giving birth to the world. In one of their meetings they saw it was necessary that the world have life and movement, and for this light was necessary. Then they thought of making the sun in order that the days move and so there would be day and night and time for struggling and time for making love, walking with the days and nights the world would go. The gods had their meeting and made this agreement in front of a large fire, and they knew it was necessary that one of them be sacrificed by throwing himself into the fire in order to become fire himself and fly into the sky. The gods thought that the work of the sun was the most important, so they chose the most beautiful god so that he would fly into the fire and become the sun. But he was afraid. Then the smallest god, the one who was black, said he was not afraid and he threw himself into the fire and became sun. Then the world had light and movement, and there was time for struggle and time for love, and in the day the bodies worked to make the world and in the night the bodies made love and sparkles filled the darkness. This is what Old Man Antonio told us and that is why we use a black ski mask. So we are of the color brown and of the color black. But we are also of the color yellow, because the first people who walked these lands were made of corn so they would be true. And we are also red because this is the call of blood which has dignity and we are also blue because we are the sky in which we fly, and green for the mountain which is our house and our strength. And we are white because we are paper so that tomorrow can write its story.

So we are 7 colors because there were 7 first gods who birthed the world.

This is what Old Man Antonio said long ago and now I tell you this story so that you may understand the reason for this bridge of paper and ink which I send to you all the way from the mountains of the Mexican Southeast.

And also so that you may understand that with this bridge goes pieces of salutes and hugs for Leonard Peltier (who is in the prison at Leavenworth, Kansas), and for the more than 100 political prisoners in the USA who are the victims of injustice, stupidity and authoritarianism.

And with this letter-bridge walks as well a salute to the Dine (the Navajo), who, in Big Mountain, Arizona, fight against the violations of their traditional Dine religious practices. They struggle against those who prefer the large businesses instead of respect for the religious freedom of Indian peoples, and those who want to destroy sacred grounds and ceremonial sites (as is the case of Peabody Western Coal Company which wants to take lands without reason, history or rights-lands which belong to the Dine and their future generations).

But there are not only stories of resistance against North American injustice in this letter-bridge. There are the indigenous, from the extreme south of our continent, in Chile, the Mapuche women in the Pewenche Center of Alto Bio-Bio who resist against stupidity. Two indigenous women, Bertha and Nicolasa Quintreman are accused of "mistreating" members of the armed forces of the Chilean government. So there it is. An armed military unit with rifles, sticks, and tear-gas, protected by bulletproof vests, helmets and shields, accuse two indigenous women of "mistreatment". But Bertha is 74 years old and Nicolasa is 60. How is it possible that two elderly people confronted a "heroic" group of heavily-armed military? Because they are Mapuche. The story is the same as that of the brothers and sisters Dine of Arizona, and the same which repeats itself in all America: a company (ENDESA) wants the lands of the Mapuches, and in spite of the law which protects the indigenous, the government is on the side of the companies. The Mapuche students have pointed out that the government and the company made a "study" of military intelligence about the indigenous Mapuche communities and they came to the conclusion that the Mapuche could not think, defend themselves, resist, or construct a better future. The study was wrong apparently.

Now it occurs to me that, perhaps the powerful in North America carried out a "military intelligence" study (this is frankly a contradiction, because those of us who are military are not intelligent, if we were we would not be military) about the case of the Dine in Arizona, about Leonard Peltier, about other political prisoners, about yourself, mister Mumia.

Perhaps they made this study and came to the conclusion that they might be able to violate justice and reason, to assault history and lose the truth. They thought they could do this and no one would say anything. The Dine Indians would stand by and watch the destruction of the most sacred of their history, Leonard Peltier would be alone, and you, Mister Mumia, would be silenced (and I remember your own words: "They not only want my death, they want my silence").

But the studies were wrong. Happy mistake? The Dine resist against those who would kill their memory, Leonard Peltier is accompanied by all those who demand his liberty, and you sir, speak and yell today with all the voices which celebrate your birthday as all birthdays should be celebrated, by struggling.

Mister Mumia,

We have nothing big to give you as a gift for your birthday, it is poor and little, but all of us send you an embrace.

We hope that when you gain your freedom you will come to visit us. Then we will give you a birthday party, even if it isn't April 24th, it will be an unbirthday party. There will be musicians, dancing and speaking, which are the means by which men and women of all colors understand and know one another, and build bridges over which they walk together, towards history, towards tomorrow.

Happy Birthday!

Vale. We salute you and may justice and truth find their place.

From the mountains of the Mexican Southeast,
Subcomandante Insurgente Marcos.

P.S. I read somewhere that you are a father and a grandfather. So I am sending you a gift for your children and grandchildren. It is a little wooden car with Zapatistas dressed in black ski-masks.

Tell your children and grandchildren that it is a gift that we send you, the Zapatistas. Explain to them places that there are people of all colors everywhere, just like you, who want justice, liberty and democracy for people of all colors.

68. Demand Justice in the Case of Mister Mumia Abu-Jamal

April of 1999
Zapatista Army of National Liberation
For: The Supreme Court of Pennsylvania, USA
Mister Tom Ridge, governor of Pennsylvania
United States of North America
From: Subcomandante Insurgente Marcos

Gentlemen Magistrate and Governor,

I write to you in the name of the men, women, children and elderly of the EZLN. Most of us are indigenous Mexicans and we struggle for liberty, democracy and justice.

The purpose of the following letter is to demand justice in the case of Mister Mumia Abu-Jamal, condemned unjustly to the death penalty in 1982. As you know, the judicial process against Mister Mumia Abu-Jamal was plagued with lies and irregularities: the police who accuse him lied about a supposed confession of his, one of the witnesses has changed testimony and declared that he was forced to lie or face prison, the ballistic evidence has proved it was impossible that Mister Mumia Abu-Jamal fired the weapon which killed the policeman. This should be enough evidence for a new trial, but even this recourse has been denied to Mister Mumia Abu-Jamal. If the Judicial system of Pennsylvania and the governor are certain of the guilt of Mister Mumia Abu-Jamal, they should not fear a new trial which adheres to the truth.

I do not ask clemency, pardon, nor mercy of you for Mister Mumia Abu-Jamal. I demand justice, something which I believe is within your powers. No one within the Supreme Court of Pennsylvania or governor Tom Ridge has anything to lose. A new trial can bring the truth forward, and justice, supposedly, is all that should matter.

That is all.

From the mountains of the Mexican Southeast,
Subcomandante Insurgente Marcos.

69. THE DAWN IS HERALDING HEAT AND FLUSHES

May 10, 1999
Dawn!

Brothers and sisters,

It is May and the dawn is heralding heat and flushes. But it is not this May, nor this dawn, no. Or, yes, it is this May and this dawn, but it is ten years earlier. The light from the campfire is painting shadows and lights on the walls of Old Antonio's hut. Old Antonio has been silent for some time, just looking at Dona Juanita who is looking at her hands. I am to one side, sitting in front of a cup of coffee. It has been some time since I arrived. I came to bring Old Antonio a deerskin, to see if he knew how, and could, tan it. Old Antonio had scarcely looked at the skin, he continued looking at Dona Juanita looking at her hands. They were waiting for something. I mean, Old Antonio was waiting for something from looking so long at Dona Juanita and Dona Juanita was waiting for something from looking so long at her hands. I chewed on my pipe and waited as well, but, of all of us who were here, I was the only one who didn't know what we were waiting for. Suddenly Dona Juanita sighed deeply and raised her face and gaze to Old Antonio, saying: "The water is coming on time." "It is coming," Old Antonio said, and right then he took out his roller and began rolling a cigarette. I knew what that meant, and so I quickly filled my pipe, lit it, and made myself comfortable in order to listen to and to remember, as and how I am now telling you...

The History of the Calendar

The oldest of the old of our peoples tell that during the first times, time was completely disorganized and it stumbled about like a drunk at the Santa Cruz fiesta. Men and women lost very much and they got lost, because time did not pass evenly, but, rather, sometimes hurried up and sometimes it went by slowly, dragging along almost like an old lame person, and by times the sun was a great skin that covered everything, and by times it was just water, water above, water below and water in-between. Or, everything was absolute chaos and one could barely plant, hunt or fix the straw on the roofs or the sticks and mud on the walls of the huts.

And the gods looked at everything and they looked, because these gods, who were the very first, those who gave birth to the world, were just strolling about and catching macabiles in the river and chewing sugarcane and sometimes they also helped separate the kernels from the maize for the tortillas. And so they looked at everything, these gods, those that gave birth to the world, the very first. And they thought, but they did not think quickly, rather they took a long time, because these gods were not hasty, and so they spent a long time just watching time go staggering about the land, and so, after putting it off like that, then they did indeed think.

After they had thought then, because they also took their time in thinking, the gods called on the Mama they called Ixmucane, and they just said to her:

"Mama Ixmucane, this time that goes about the lands is not doing well and it just skips about and runs and drags, sometimes ahead and sometimes backwards, and so one can absolutely not plant, and you will see that neither can they harvest when they want to and the men and women are growing sad and now many of us battle with each other in order to find the maxcabil and the sugarcane is not where we left it and so we are telling you, we do not know what you thought, Mama Ixmucane, but it is not good that time just goes about like this, without anyone being able to orient themselves as to when and where they must go and what is going on. This is what we are thinking, Mama Ixmucane, we do not know what you are going to tell us about this problem that we are telling you about."

Mama Ixmucane sighed for a good bit and then she said:

"It is not good that time is just out of control like that, wreaking havoc and ruining things for all these good people."

"Yes, that is right, it is not good," said the gods.

And they waiting a bit, because they well knew that Mama Ixmucane had not finished speaking, she had barely begun. That is why, ever since then, it seems that Mamas have already finished when they have barely begun talking to us.

Mama Ixmucane was sighing for another while and then she continued speaking:

"Up there, in the sky, is the tale that time should follow, and time will pay attention if someone is reading it to it and telling it what comes next and how and when and where."

"If it is there and if it does pay attention," said the gods.

Mama Ixmucane sighed more and at last she said:

"I am willing to read time the tale so that it learns how to run straight, but my eyes are not good now and I can scarcely look at the sky, I cannot."

"You cannot," said the gods.

"See, if I can," Mama Ixmucane said. "Then I would straighten out time, but I cannot look at and read the sky, because my eyes are not good."

"Mmmh," said the gods.

"Mmmh," said Mama Ixmucane.

And so they remained, the ones and the other, just saying "mmmh," until the gods finally began thinking again and they said:

"Look, Mama Ixmucane, I do not know what you are thinking, but we think it would be good if we brought you the sky down here below and then you could see it up close very well and read and put aright the passing of time."

And Mama Ixmucane sighed heavily when she said:

"Perhaps I have someplace to put the sky? No, no, no. Can you not see how small my hut is? No, no, no."

"No, no, no," said the gods.

And they remained a good bit longer with their "mmmh," "mmmh." And then the gods thought once more and they said:

"Look, Mama Ixmucane, I do not know what you are thinking, but we think it would be good if we copy what is written in the sky and we bring it and you copy it and then you will be able to read it and so you will set right the passing of time."

"That's good," said Mama Ixmucane.

And the gods went up and they copied the tale that the sky tells in a notebook and they came down once again and they went to see Mama Ixmucane with the notebook and they said to her:

"Look, Mama Ixmucane, here then is the tale that the sky tells, we wrote it down here in this notebook, but it is not going to last, so you will have to copy it someplace else where the tale that will set right the passage of time will last forever."

"Yes, yes, yes," said Mama Ixmucane. "Copy the tale on my hands and I will set the passing of time right so that it goes straight and does not go about like an old drunk."

And on the palms and the backs of Mama Ixmucane's hands, the gods wrote the tale that is told in the sky in order to set right the passage of time, and that is why knowing Mamas have many lines on their hands and they read the calendar on them and that way they see that time runs straight and the harvest that history plants in memory is not forgotten.

Old Antonio was silent and Dona Juanita repeats, seeing her hands, "the water is coming on time."

This that I am telling you happened ten years ago, a dawn in May. Today, on this dawn of May 10, we want to greet a group of persons who were with us in this meeting, and who have been with us even when they were not. I am speaking of the mothers of the political prisoners and disappeared, to whom we, their new children, send best wishes for this 10th of May. Through them, Mama Ixmucane returns to give us dignified memory and to remind us of the tale in order to harvest the dawn that history plants.

Salud, then, to these knowing mothers, salud to these women who assure us that there will always be someone who does not lose the memory.

Brothers and sisters: We want to thank all of you for having come here to meet with us.

During these days we have been able to put back together the puzzle that is the Consulta for the Recognition of the Rights of the Indian Peoples and For an End to the War of Extermination.

With all the pieces that you have brought, and with those we already had, we now all - you and we - have an approximate idea of the form of this movement - which, it needs to be repeated - has not ended.

But then you will see that, behind the puzzle of the Consulta, we have found other pieces that are helping us to imagine another form, a larger and more powerful one, although it continues hidden, although the solution to the enigma remains to be found.

The sacred book of Popul Vuh tells that the most ancient gods had to resist the attacks and deceptions of the great masters who governed people and lands. After an attempted deception, the gods sent three gifts to the great masters so they would learn of the strength and power of the gods. The three gifts were three lovely skins, beautifully painted. One had a powerful tiger painted on it, the other a valiant eagle and on the third there were many pictures of bumblebees and wasps. The great masters were made happy by those gifts and they set about seeing whether or not the power of the gods whom they wished to subjugate was great, and so then they fearfully put on the skin with the painted tiger and they saw that nothing happened and the skin with the painted tiger was in truth beautiful. The hearts of the masters were greatly gladdened when they saw that the painted tiger did nothing to them and they thought the power of the gods they wished to subjugate was not great, and they then put the second skin on their bodies, that of the painted eagle, and they saw the eagle did them no harm and the skin with the eagle shone brightly and their hearts became more happy, and now they took joy that they could soon subjugate those gods who were not powerful because their painted skins did not harm them. Now without any fear at all, the masters put on the third skin, the one that was decorated with thousands of wasps and bumblebees of many and varied colors. And at that very moment it happened that the bumblebees and the wasps came to life and they attacked the great masters most fiercely and their stings brought them much pain and the great masters surrendered before the wisdom and the power of the gods.

With what has been agreed to at this second meeting, we will be able - this we all hope - to finish painting the great skin that this country needs.

Vale. Salud and bon voyage.

From the mountains of the Mexican Southeast,
Subcomandante Insurgente Marcos.
Mexico, May of 1999.

70. "No!" To the War in the Balkans

June of 1999
To the peoples in struggle against the war
To Social Europe
To the men and women who are saying "No!"

Brothers and Sisters,

Greetings to all from the zapatistas of Mexico. All over the world different mobilizations and activities are being carried out at this time against the war that money has sown in the heart of Europe: the war in Kosovo.

In this war, the great Power has set itself to making all of us take part: either we support Milosevic's "ethnic cleansing" war or we support NATO's "humanitarian" war. This is the great alchemy of money, to offer us the option of choosing between two wars, not between peace and war.

On the shelves of the globalized market, the Powers are offering humanity only different versions of the same war: they come in all colors, flavors, sizes and shapes. They are for all tastes and all pocket books. There is only one thing that makes them the same, the results. Always destruction, always anguish, always death. And death, anguish and destruction are always for the other, for the different, for that which is unnecessary, for that which is in the way, for that which is below.

And, even within the mercantile logic of the merchants of death, neo-liberalism wants to offer us a fraud: the war that is supposedly going to avoid more deaths, has done nothing but multiply them; the war that should be holding back the possibility of the conflict expanding to other regions, has assured that the conflagration will now spread beyond its original geographical limit; the "intelligent" war has done nothing but demonstrate the great destructive capacity of stupidity; the war of "good faith" has re-defined human life: its loss is now counted as "collateral damage."

It is a lie.

It is not true that we have to take part in this lethal market.

It is not true that there are only options between different kinds of war.

It is not true that we must take part on the side of one or another stupidity.

It is not true that we must renounce intelligence and humanity.

Nothing can legitimize Milosevic's ethnic war. Nothing can legitimize NATO's "humanitarian" war.

The trap is there, but there are more and more who are refusing to fall into it and who are saying "No!" to the war in the Balkans.

In Kosovo, it is not just the existence and resistance of Social Europe that is at stake in the face of the Europe of Money; at stake is not just accepting or not the de facto power of the new global police, the new clothing with which the Pentagon is dressing their troops.

Also at stake is the possibility of recognizing the other, the different, in a way that he is not dead, imprisoned, humiliated, subjugated, persecuted, forgotten.

We will not fall into the trap, we will not allow the loss of humanity to pass into history in the category of "collateral damages," and to allow cynicism and conformity to be the triumphant generals of the European war.

Despite all the power of money, despite all the arms, despite all the arbitrary acts, despite all the attempts at hegemony and homogenization, despite all the traps, we still have the right to say "NO!"

And that is what we raise today. A world-wide "NO!" to the lie that feigns truths in the skies and the grounds of Kosovo. NO to the destruction of the different.

NO to the death of intelligence. NO to cynicism. NO to indifference. NO to having to choose between criminals who are more or less bloodthirsty, more or less perverse, more or less powerful.

If we do not say "NO!" to Kosovo today, tomorrow we will be saying "YES!" to the horrors that money is now concocting all over the world.

Another, different world is possible than this violent supermarket that neo-liberalism is selling us. Another world is possible, where the option is between war and peace, between memory and forgetting, between hope and resignation, between the gray and the rainbow. A world where many worlds fit is possible. It is possible for an imperfect "Yes!", unfinished and incomplete, to be born from a "NO!", a "Yes!" that gives humanity back the hope of rebuilding, every day, the complex bridge that joins thought and feeling.

This is what we zapatistas are saying: "NO!"

Viva life! Death to death!

From the mountains of the Mexican Southeast,
Subcomandante Insurgente Marcos.
Mexico, June of 1999.

71. WE DO INDEED SUPPORT THE UNAM STRIKE MOVEMENT

To the national and international press

Ladies and gentlemen,

The text is off concerning our position on the latest events. In case they get dumped on the Internet or you leave them in your house, we are at least letting you know here that something went out. Thanks, then.

We do not have automobiles, nor do we travel around the beltway, but we are lighting candles here to say that that we do indeed support the UNAM strike movement. And it does not matter to us if they continue attacking us with police and soldiers, and if they occupy more towns, or continue arbitrarily detaining indigenous accused of being zapatistas: we are going to continue supporting the university students simply because they have right on their side.

Vale. Salud and, before you throw the communiqué in a corner, happy two thousand! Or what?

> *From the mountains of the Mexican Southeast,*
> *Subcomandante Insurgente Marcos.*
> *Mexico, June of 1999.*

P.S. Now I don't understand anything. Is it that, for the government, the "New York Times" is the most important and influential newspaper in the world if it applauds Zedillo's economic policies, and, when it mentions the names of Mexican politicians tied to drug trafficking (Liévano, Hank), then it's a pamphlet at the service of obscure interests seeking to harm Mexico? Whatever, and, as consolation, the Secretary of Government went to have his picture taken in the football stands with one of the "alleged," Hank Gonzalez.

P.S. THAT POKES ABOUT. Completely buried under the "eliminate an ultra" (or a university striker), the earthquake, the execution of Paco Stanley, the visit by the country's greatest criminal (Carlos Salinas de Gortari - I say, if the issue is public security, one has to recognize that there are criminals and criminals), Zedillo's little jaunt to hide out in Guadalajara and the financial "armor plate," was the issue of Cabal Peniche's financial support of Zedillo's campaign.

P.S. THAT LOOKS FOR A LIFE PRESERVER. As is known, those ships that are "armor plated" sink.

P.S. CURIOUS. What PRI candidate just stated that he should not be considered as a neo-liberal, and, at the Department of Energy, Mines and Para-State Industries, during the period from 1982 - 1986, took part in the sales of more than

300 state bodies?

> *"But there is a ray of sun in the struggle*
> *that always leaves the shadow vanquished."*
> - Miguel Hernandez

Now the night of San Juan reigns in the mountains of the Mexican Southeast. And it reigns by law, that is, raining. The sea winds bring a little box of memories to the top of this ceiba. Out of one of the corners of the open mouth of the little jewel case, a streamer of light protrudes, and, with it, a history. Old Antonio suddenly appears, like nocturnal rain, and, as if nothing were going on, asks me for a light to fire his cigar and memory. Above the rough drumming of the rain on the nylon roof, Old Antonio's words are raised, given memories and luminous streamers, to recount...

The History of the Milky Way

"Before the rain undresses the mountain, a long path of dusty light is seen up above. It comes from there and it goes to there," Old Antonio says, with a slight gesture from one side to the other. "They say it is called the 'Milky Way,' or they also name it 'Santiago's Road.' They say there are many stars, and they have joined together, so tiny, making themselves opening and little path in the already riddled sky. They say, but they also say it is not like that. The oldest of our old say that which is seen above is a wounded animal."

Old Antonio pauses, as if waiting for the question I do not ask: a wounded animal?

Much time ago, when the very first gods had already created the world and they were laying around, men and women lived on the earth, working it and throwing it and so they went. But they say that one day there appeared in a town a serpent who fed on men. Or, rather, he only ate males, he did not eat women. And then when he had eaten all the men in a town, he went to another and did the same thing. The towns quickly let each other know of this great horror that was coming to them and they spoke fearfully of that great snake, that was so fat and long that it managed to surround an entire town, like a wall, not allowing anyone to enter or to leave, and he said that if they did not give him all the males, he would not let anyone leave, and so some of them surrendered and others fought, but the snake's strength was great and he always won. The towns lived in fear, merely waiting for the day that it would be their turn for the great snake to come and to eat all the men, as the serpent swallowed them whole. They say that there was a man who managed to escape from the serpent and he went to take refuge in a community that had already been attacked. There, in front of only women, the man spoke of the snake and that they must struggle to defeat it because it was doing much damage in these lands. The women said: what are we going to do if we are women? How are we going to fight him without men? How are we going to attack him if it does not come here now because there are no longer any men, he ate them all?

The women left, very discouraged and sad. But one remained and approached the man and asked him how he thought they could fight the snake. The man said he did not know but that he would have to think. And together, the man and the woman set to thinking and they made a plan and they went to call the women to tell them of the plan and everyone was in agreement.

And then it came to pass that the man began to show himself freely about the town and the serpent saw him from afar, because that snake that saw him from afar had very good eyes. And then the serpent came and surrounded the town with his large body and told the women to bring him that man who was walking about, or otherwise he would not let anyone enter or leave. The women said they would bring him, but they would have to meet in order to make an agreement. That is fine, said the snake. And then the women made a circle around the man and, since there were many of them, the circle was growing larger and larger, until the circle touched the very circle that the serpent's body had made around the town. Then the man said, that is good, deliver me. And he walked to the serpent's head, and when the snake was occupied in eating the man, all the women picked up sharp sticks and began jabbing the snake all over his body, and, since there were many and all over the place, and his mouth was full with the man he was eating, the serpent could not defend himself. And he had never thought that the weak would attack him in such a way and all over, and he was quickly weakened and defeated. And then he said: forgive me, do not kill me. No, said the women, we are going to kill you anyway, because you do much evil and you ate up all of our men. Let's make a deal, said the snake, if you do not kill me once and for all, I will return your men to you because I have them in my belly anyway. And then the women thought that was good, they would not kill him, but that the great serpent would not be living in those lands any longer and he would be expelled. Then the snake said: but where am I going to live and what am I going to eat, there is no deal. And then they were there with this problem when the first woman said they would have to ask the man who had come, to see what he thought and she said to the snake: release the man you have just eaten and we will see if he has an idea of what we can do. The serpent released the man who was already half dead and half alive and the man spoke with difficulty and he said he would have to ask the first gods to see what could be done, and he could go to look for them because now he was half alive and half dead. And the man went and he found the first gods sleeping under a ceiba and he awoke them and he told them of the problem and the gods met together in order to think and to reach a good accord and then they went to see the serpent and the victorious women and they listened and they said the serpent was to blame and he should be punished, that he should then give back the men he had swallowed and he would not die, and the snake brought up all the men from all the towns. And then the gods said the serpent would have to go and live on the highest mountain and, since he would not fit on just one mountain, he would then have to use two mountains, the highest of the world, and he would have his tail on one and his head on the other, and he would have sunlight for food, and the thousands of wounds the warrior women had given him would never close, and then the gods went, and the snake, the great serpent, went sadly to the highest mountains, and on one he put his head and on the other his tail and his large body reached from one side of the sky to the other, and, from then on, by day he feeds on sunlight, and by night that light spills out through all the little holes of his wounds.

The serpent is pale, that is why he is not seen by day, and that is why by night the light can be seen that falls from him and leaves him empty until, the next day, the sun feeds him once again. That is why they say that the large line that shines by night up above, is nothing but a wounded animal

That is what Old Antonio recounted to me and then I understood that the Milky Way is nothing more than a long serpent of light, that feeds by day and bleeds by night.

It has stopped raining on this night of San Juan. The sky quickly turns dark and clear and clearly one can see that a serpent of light hangs from the thick figure of a thousand wounds, from end to end, from one to the other horizon. The silver teardrops fall softly on the top of that ceiba, and another rain drizzles from there further downwards. From the faceless mirror there, the brightness bounces and goes further, to there, to that corner where, behind a shadow, can be seen...

72. THE UN's COMPLICITY IN THE WAR IN EUROPE WAS OBVIOUS

July 19, 1999

Communiqué from the EZLN to Asma Jahangir

For Maurice Najman, who continues feigning death

To: Asma Jahangir, UN Special Relator for Extrajudicial, Summary And Arbitrary Executions

From: Subcomandante Insurgente Marcos

CCRI-CG of the EZLN

Madame Asma Jahangir,

I am writing to you in the name of the women, men, children and old ones of the Zapatista Army of National Liberation.

We know that we will be receiving not a few criticisms for what I am going to say, and for having wasted a good opportunity to reveal the Mexican government in their genocidal policy against the Indian peoples. But, for us, "political opportunity" has little bearing in the face of political ethics. And it would not be ethical, given our confrontation with the Mexican government, for us to turn to an international body that has lost all credibility and legitimacy, and whose death certificate was signed with the NATO bombings in Kosovo.

With their war in the Balkans, the North American government - disguised as NATO, and with the regimes of England, Italy and France as grotesque pawns - managed to destroy their primary objective: the United Nations (UN). The "intelligent" mega-police actions of the global gendarme, the US, made a fool of the once highest international forum. Violating the precepts that gave rise to the UN, NATO carried out a war of cynical aggression, attacked civilians indiscriminately and tried to delegate intellectual authority to the satellites, who, more than ever, demonstrated that they are useless to those who already have the visions and who have made the decisions. NATO's bellicose cynicism was superceded only by the "brilliant" statements of their chiefs and spokespersons. The "humanitarian war," "the error in good faith" and the "collateral damage" were not the only pearls of war they were selling (because they were already counting on passing the bill) in Kosovar lands.

"A NATO military person with a good number of stars on his chest made two statements in Brussels on Tuesday that caused chills: Out of a total of 35,000 air operations, more than 10,000 were directed at concrete targets. And the other 25,000? Could they have been carried out in error? If concrete targets exist, do non-concrete ones exist? What kind of target is a person? The second statement raised as many questions as the previous: NATO's objective was never to completely destroy the Yugoslav army, nor was it to reduce the country to ashes. Thank goodness, although one cannot help but think that, before ashes come embers, and before those, bits, and before those, pieces: to what size of material had they been thinking of reducing the country and its army? The postwar banquet is served, the news sent by Roger Waters' satellite fills the media all day long. When more is being said, that which cannot be said can be concealed all the better." (Jordi Soler, in La Jornada, June 19, 1999).

The UN's complicity in the war in Europe was obvious, and, given our position regarding this war, the minimum of consistency leads us to distance ourselves from an organization that for years, it is true, did indeed carry out a dignified and independent role in the international arena. It is not so today. On one side and the other of the planet, the UN has turned into a predictable legal support for the wars of aggression that the great power of money repeats, without becoming glutted of blood or of destruction.

But, if the UN's silence was the accomplice of crime and destruction in Kosovo, in Mexico it has taken a more active role in the war the Mexican government is carrying out against the indigenous: in May 1998, at the request of the UNHCR [United Nations High Commissioner for Refugees], the government attacked the community of Amparo Aguatinta, beat up children, imprisoned men and women and militarily occupied the seat, then, of the Tierra y Libertad Autonomous Municipality. The results of the UN's "humanitarian work" in Chiapas are in the Cerro Hueco Jail in Tuxtla Gutierrez. More recently, today, July 19, 1999, Kofi Annan, the Secretary General of the UN, is delivering the United Nations Vienna Civil Society Prize to the self-styled Aztec Foundation. The Foundation, under the auspices of the native Milosevic, Ricardo Salinas Pliego, spends its time carrying out campaigns against drugs using cocaine addicts, promoting coup attempts and destroying indigenous schools with helicopters. For that: for its ties with drug trafficking and for its calls for coups, the Aztec Foundation will receive a medal and a certificate for 25,000 dollars from Mr. Annan.

And so we cannot have any confidence at all in the UN. And it is not out of chauvinism or in rejection of all things foreign. There have been here, risking their lives, liberty, belongings and prestige - men and women from the five continents, as international observers (we shall leave the term "foreigners" for those, like Zedillo and the members of his cabinet, who have no patria other than money). To go no further back, the International Civil Commission for Human Rights Observation (CCIODH) was here in February 1998. Not only are their initials larger than the UN's, so is their moral authority, their honesty, their commitment to the truth and the authenticity of their struggle for a peace with justice and dignity. Men and women from Germany, Argentina, Canada, Denmark, France,

Greece, Italy, Nicaragua, Switzerland, Andalucia, Aragon, Cantabria, Catalunya, the Basque Country, Galicia, Madrid, Murcia and Alicante: all defied the Mexican government's most ferocious xenophobic campaign so far this century. They documented everything in a report (that they dedicated to the indigenous Jose Tila Lopez Garcia, assassinated after having presented his community's denunciations to the CCIODH). Consult this report, it is inspired not only by the desire for a dignified peace, but also by veracity and honesty.

After the CCIODH, another group of Italian observers came, also in 1998. Things were worse for them than for the CCIODH, because they were summarily expelled by the current aspirant for the Mexican presidency, Francisco Labastida, and by the person who is now in charge of international public relations for his campaign team, and who was responsible at that time for hundreds of illegal expulsions, Fernando Solis Camara.

Thousands of men and women from all over the world have come here, all honorable and of good will, the majority of them young persons of the kind called "earringed," and who so bother the institutionalized left all over the world. They came here, and they saw what the government denies, a genocidal war. They left, many of them expelled, and they related, and they are relating, what they saw: an unequal war between those who have all the military power (the government), and those who only have reason, history, truth and tomorrow on their side (us). It is obvious who is going to win: we are.

And, not just alone, international organizations as well, such as Amnesty International, Americas Watch, Global Exchange, Mexico Solidarity Network, the National Commission for Democracy in Mexico-USA, Pastors for Peace, Humanitarian Law Project, Doctors of the World, Bread for the World, Doctors without Borders, and many others whose names escape me now, but not their histories or their commitment to peace.

For us, any of them, individuals or groups, have more moral authority and more international legitimacy then the United Nations, converted today into a cocktail party for the end-of-century neoliberal wars.

With good reason the government representatives (the pathetic Ms. Green, the similar Rabasa, El Croquetas Albores, etcetera) say they have nothing to fear from your visit. They do not fear it because they know the UN has been an accomplice to, and, in the case of the Tierra y Libertad Autonomous Municipality, part of, the war of extermination against the Indian peoples of Mexico.

According to what we have read and heard, you are an honest person. You probably entered the service of the UN during the time when that organization was preventing wars, supporting different groups who were victims of government injustices and promoting the development of the most needy. But now the UN promotes and supports wars, and it helps and awards those who are killing and humiliating the excluded of the world.

It has not escaped our attention that various international powers are nurturing the idea of using for their own benefit the rich oil and uranium deposits that exist under zapatista soil. Those, up above, are making complicated accounts and calculations and entertaining the hope that the zapatistas will make separatist proposals. It would be easier and cheaper to negotiate the purchase of the subsoil with the Banana Republic (Mayan Nation, they call it). After all, it is well known that the indigenous are satisfied with little mirrors and glass beads. Because of that, they are not giving up on their intent to involve themselves in the conflict and to manipulate it according to their interests. They have certainly not been able to, not on our side. Because it happens that the zapatistas take "National Liberation," the names of the EZLN, very much to heart and sword. And, anachronistic as we are, we still believe in "outmoded" concepts, such as "national sovereignty" and "national independence." We have not accepted, nor will we accept, any foreign interference in our movement. We have not accepted, nor will we accept, any international force being a part of the conflict, we will fight it with the same or more decisiveness that we have fought against those who decreed death through forgetting for 10 million Mexican indigenous. Those with moral authority and legitimacy will be welcomed, those who are not appendages of armed forces (such as NATO), or who have military forces at their service (such as the unhappily celebrated Blue Helmets of the UN), those who want to be part of the PEACEFUL solution of the conflict.

We do not need any help to make war, we can manage on our own. For the peace, we do, many are needed, but honest, and there are not many of those.

Do not be very unhappy, the UN is not the only official international body that collaborates with the Mexican government's counterinsurgency campaign. There you have the International Committee of the Red Cross, whose delegation in San Cristobal bordered on the sublime when speaking of servility and stupidity. At a meeting with displaced from Polhó, the CICR delegates stated, without even blushing, that the displaced are not in their homes because they are lazy and because they want to be supported by the Red Cross. To those imbeciles, who wander around under the CICR's purported flags of neutrality and humanitarian aid, the paramilitaries are an invention, the product of the collective hysteria of more than 7000 displaced indigenous; the 45 executed at Acteal in reality died of infections, and peace and tranquility reign in Los Altos of Chiapas. One can assume that Albores has already congratulated them (and has offered them some of his bones, because he is not very sharing we are told), and they are continuing to go about in their modern vehicles, fattening the curriculum vitae of that "distinguished" institution. Que tal? The CICR will surely be the next to receive an award from the UN in their "civil society" competitions.

This dawn in which I am writing these lines, the moon is a scythe of cold light. It is the hour of the dead, of our dead. And you should know that the zapatista dead are very restless and talkative. They still speak, despite the fact that they are dead, and they are shouting history. They are shouting it so it does not sleep, so that memory does not die, so that our dead will live shouting...

Ocosingo, the 3rd and 4th of January, 1994. Federal Army troops take the municipal seat of Ocosingo - in zapatista hands since the dawn of January 1 - by assault. Following orders from the then Brigadier General Luis Humberto Portillo Leal - who had been chief of the 30th Military Zone - Infantry major Adalberto Perez Nava executed 5 members of the EZLN. General Portillo Leal had ordered the execution of the zapatistas, whether or not they were armed. The instructions were to take no prisoners, all of them should be dead (they should only avoid doing so if the press were present, because that would damage the Army's image). The Second Infantry Captain, Lodegario Salvador Estrada, executed other zapatista indigenous. Days later, in the offices of the Department of National Defense, an Infantry Second Lieutenant, Jimenez Morales, was executed by military personnel in order to have him take the blame for the assassination of 8 indigenous in the IMSS hospital in Ocosingo. We did not invent any of this information, you can corroborate it in the act by the Department of Justice of the United States, Executive Office for Immigration Review, Immigration Court of El Paso, Texas, signed by Bertha A. Zuniga, Immigration Judge of the United States, dated March 19, 1999. Case Jesus Valles Bahena, A76-804-703. In this file, the officer Jesus Valles Bahena narrates why he had to desert from the Army, after having been threatened with death by Colonel Bocarundo Benavidez for his refusal to carry out orders for summary executions. Along with Valles, other officers refused to carry out instructions for assassination. Their fate is unknown.

Where, in addition to execution, there was brazen torture, it was in Morelia, then the municipality of Altamirano. On January 7, 1994, the Army entered the community and kidnapped Severiano Santiz Gomez (60 years old), Hermelindo Santiz Gomez (65 years old) and Sebastian Lopez Santiz (45 years old). A little later, their remains - with signs of fractures and with clear evidence of having been executed - were found. The analyses of the remains was carried out by specialists from the Physicians for Human Rights NGO.

Torture and execution were the methods also used by the "glorious" federal Army in the municipal seat of Las Margaritas, Chiapas. There, during the first days of combat, Major Teran (who had been previously tied to drug trafficking in the region) kidnapped, tortured and executed Eduardo Gomez Hernandez and Jorge

Mariano Solis Lopez in the neighborhood of Plan de Agua Prieta. Those executed had their ears and tongues cut off.

These deaths, our deaths, do not find rest. The butchers of Ocosingo and the assassins and torturers of Morelia and Las Margaritas continue to be free and to enjoy health and prosperity. Thousands of shadows are pursuing them now, and they are competing for the honor of seeing justice done.

Last year, contrary to what their propaganda for international consumption says, the government renewed its armed clashes with zapatista forces. On June 10, 1998, a military column, heavy with infantry, tanks, planes and helicopters, attacked the community of Chavajeval, in the municipality of San Juan de la Libertad (to the zapatistas) or El Bosque (to the government). The zapatista troops repelled the attack, and a heavy exchange of fire began, that was broadcast by a national television channel. Our troops brought down a helicopter, and, frustrated and angry, the soldiers repeated themselves, but they attacked the community of Union Progreso that same day of June 10, 1998. There they took 7 zapatista militia prisoners and summarily executed them.

(The television reporter who covered the military attack on Chavajeval received the national journalism prize. Over indigenous and rebel blood, his employers rewarded him, sending him to cover the campaign of one of the two intellectual assassins of Union Progreso - the other is Zedillo - the then Secretary of Government and now presidential aspirant, Francisco Labastida Ochoa).

This is the Mexican federal Army, the one that now wants to present an innocent image, announcing the dispatch of almost 7000 more troops to the Selva Lacandona, with the story that they are going to plant little trees. Everyone is silent. The military chief says that the 7000 are going unarmed, and the 7000 arrive armed. Everyone is silent.

This is the "new" government strategy that has been promised you by the pathetic character named Rabasa Gamboa (who is paid, and paid well, for coordinating emptiness). And since we are on this subject, a new bray by Rabasa clarifies that Acteal was not an execution.

This time he is right: Acteal, and all the policies followed by his boss Ernesto Zedillo, is GENOCIDE.

This is the history. With Ernesto Zedillo's gaining of power - through assassination - the federal Army gained cover and money in order to bring up their longing for blood and death. Seeking to improve the Army's depleted public image, paramilitary squadrons were activated, organized by active duty soldiers, trained by soldiers, equipped by soldiers, protected by soldiers, directed by soldiers, and, in not a few cases, created by soldiers, as well as by Institutional Revolutionary Party members. The objective was, and is, clear, it was, and is, about turning the conflict around and presenting it to the international public (the national public does not even minimally matter to them) as an inter-ethnic war, or, as the corrupt PGR tries to present it, as an inter-family war. The names chosen by the soldiers to baptize their new paramilitary units reflect their great imagination: Red Mask (their greatest "military" success: the Acteal massacre). Peace and Justice (responsible for the assassinations of dozens of indigenous in the north of the state). Chinchulines (they act in the North and in the Selva). Anti-Zapatista Indigenous Revolutionary Movement (they have training camps in military barracks in the Canadas, and are financed by the state PRI delegation). Los Punales (they are active in Comitan and Las Margaritas). Albores of Chiapas (they are directly dependent on El Croquetas Albores Guillen, they wear green caps and their war cry is "Albores carries through!").

The "new" government strategy for Chiapas is in plain view: in the ejido of El Portal, in Frontera Comalapa, a group of zapatista families demand that water service be restored, which was taken away from them by PRI soldiers in complicity with the municipal president there. Zapatista indigenous demanding anything is something the government cannot tolerate, given that, for them, the only thing the zapatistas should be receiving is blows and bullets. In response to the zapatista civil demonstration, the government mobilized the police. The PRI's, emboldened by the presence of the police, charged the zapatistas with sticks and shots, two zapatistas are seriously wounded. The police act rapidly and detain the zapatistas! accusing them of criminal association for having been found with ski-masks. With the alacrity afforded by the "State of Law" in Chiapas, a state government helicopter transfers the prisoners, in order to be tried "for breaching the peace" (because, in Chiapas, demanding potable water is an attack against the peace). The two wounded are fighting for their lives in the hospital, those who fired are free and healthy, and, in Government Palace, the new "victory" is being celebrated in the war against the EZLN. You will see none of this in the written or electronic press, too concerned with giving the front pages or the news headlines to Albores' barking dogs or to the PRI aspirants' fair of hypocrisy and fallacies. Zapatista indigenous imprisoned, beaten, wounded or assassinated are no longer news in Mexico. They are part of daily life.

This is the "new" federal government strategy for Chiapas, of Zedillo's government. There is nothing new about it, nor is it a strategy, it is the same stupid pounding that assumes that those who have known how to resist for 500 years, will not be able to do so for a year and a half.

Concerning Ernesto Zedillo Ponce de Leon, one must say now what everyone will be saying tomorrow: he is a man of no word, a liar and an assassin. This is what we are saying today. When he leaves Los Pinos, everyone (even those who are treating him with respect today) will be repeating it, and all his corruption and crimes will come to public light. Persecution, exile, jail: these are the probable stations for his future. It does not make us unhappy, our dead do not make us unhappy.

I read in the press that you have had meetings with some non-governmental organizations in Mexico City, and you will have others during your visit to Chiapas, these days. I congratulate you, may you have the good fortune and the honor to personally know men and women who - without official and/or institutional paraphernalia - have confronted every kind of threats and persecutions for their work in defense of human rights in Mexico.

I will not put any names here, because, in Mexico, and especially in Chiapas, the NGO's that are fighting for human rights are military objectives for the federal Army. But any of these NGO's, whether the smallest or the most newly created, have more moral authority in the Mexico of below than the UN does. Regardless, perhaps you are not to blame, and it is only the great leaders of the UN who have accepted, without even protesting, the sporadic role of spokespersons for NATO, and being accomplices in the Mexican government's war of extermination against the Indian peoples.

Nonetheless, we are not pessimists regarding the future of the international community. The UN's failure is not humanity's failure. A new international order is possible, a better one, more just, more human. In it, there will have to be a dominant place for all those international and national NGO's (who, unlike the UN, do not have at their service - or are at the service - of military forces), and for all those men, women, children and old ones who understand that the future of the world is being debated between the exclusionary difference (the war in Kosovo) and the world where many worlds fit (of which, zapatismo in Chiapas is, almost, a suggestion).

With them, and especially for them, the world will some day be a place where war will be a disgrace and peace a reality, and the relators for the various human rights violations, specimens whose only arena of action will be researching the prehistory of humanity.

Excuse the tone, Madame Asma Jahangir, it is not that this is a personal matter against you, it is just that the organization you represent no longer represents anything. That, and also that we do not forget Kosovo, nor Amparo Aguatinta, nor Ocosingo, nor Morelia, nor Las Margaritas, nor Union Progress, nor anything. Whatever, that is what is happening, that we do not forget.

We do not forget.

Vale. Salud and may dignity never forget memory, if it were to lose it, it would die.

From the mountains of the Mexican Southeast,
Subcomandante Insurgente Marcos.
Mexico.

73. THE PARROT AND THE MACAW

Previously 'unpublished' story by Marcos concerning an impossible love.
(This story was considered by Subcomandante Marcos to be an ad hoc response for getting out of writing a prologue to the book "From the heart of the Mexican southeast," since, according to him, his "scattered" circumstances were added to the claims of urgent tasks.)

It was the year of 1986. I left with a column of combatants on reconnaissance, a days' journey from our base camp. All my guys were very young, the majority of them had not even been there for a month, and they were still wavering between the diarrhea and nostalgia that generally accompany the new ones during the first days of their adjustment. The "oldest" of the group had barely completed two and three months, respectively. And so, then, there I was, dragging them by times, and, by times, pushing them, through their political and military training. Our mission consisted in opening up a new route for our movements and training them in the work of reconnaissance, marches and camps. The work was made even more difficult because there was no water, and we had to ration the use of what we had carried with us from the base. And so, the survival practice was added to the training, given that the meager ration of water prevented us from cooking. The reconnaissance would last a total of four days, with approximately one liter of water per person each day, with only cornmeal with sugar to eat. One hour after leaving the base, we discovered that our route was crossed by some tough hills. The hours passed, and we went up and down hills along paths that would have frightened even the most seasoned goats.

Finally, after seven hours of constant ups and downs, we reached the top of a hill where we decided to set up camp, since the afternoon had already begun giving way to twilight. The ration of water was distributed, and almost everyone - despite my warnings to save a little liquid for the cornmeal - "burned their bridges behind them," and finished off all their water, since they were very thirsty, and the psychological effect of knowing it was rationed increased their anxiety. When it was time to eat the cornmeal, they discovered the consequences of their imprudence. They chewed and chewed their mouthfuls of cornmeal with sugar, without being able to get it down, and without any water now to help it get past the barrier of their throats. There were, ultimately, two hours of such silence that one could clearly hear the grinding jaws and the sounds of their throats when they managed to swallow a bit of the sugared dust. The following day - and having now learned their lessons - everyone saved a bit of their liquid ration for the morning cornmeal. We left for the reconnaissance at 9:00 and we returned at 4:00, and so it was seven hours of walking and using our machetes, going up and down hills, with no water other than what we were so abundantly sweating.

And so three days passed; on the fourth, the fatigue was obvious throughout the column, and, during the meals, signs of the sadomasochism that seems to characterize the insurgents appeared: Between bites of cornmeal and sips of water there began to be talk of taquitos, tamales, steaks, drinks, and other things that made us laugh, because the lack of water prevented us from crying. The last straw was when, on the day we were going to return to the base, we found a stream, and, during the night, the mountain mocked us by presenting us with a strong downpour, drenching us before we managed to reach cover. We did not lose our good humor, and we freely cursed the rain, the selva, the roofs, and all their respective, damp tribe. But fine, this was all part of the training, and it didn't surprise us. The work was done, the people responded well generally, although one had seriously threatened to faint while we were loaded down, going up an especially obstinate hill.

All of this is no more than "setting the stage" for the history I wanted to recount to you: During one of those days of reconnaissance, we returned, exhausted as always, to the camp. While the rations of water and cornmeal were being distributed, I turned on the short-wave radio receiver in order to look for the evening news, but, when I switched on the radio, only the shrill song of parrots and macaws came out. I remembered something by Cortazar then (Last Round? The Book of Manuel? Historia de cronopios y famas?), that spoke of what would happen if things were-not-in-their-place. But I did not allow myself to be daunted by such a small thing, accustomed as I was to seeing such apparently absurd things in these mountains, like a little deer with a red carnation in her mouth (probably in love, otherwise, why a red carnation?), a tapir with lavender dance shoes, and a herd of wild boars playing in a circle, carrying the tune of "we will break down a column to see Dona Blanca..." with their teeth and hooves. As I told you, I was not surprised, and I turned the dial, looking for another channel, but nothing, everything was the song of parrots and macaws. I changed to mid-wave with the same results. Without becoming discouraged, I set about taking the receiver apart in order to discover the scientific reason for such an off-key song. When I took the cover off the back, the logical and dialectical reason for the irregular transmission was revealed: A flock of parrots and macaws escaped, flying and crying, pleased to have regained their freedom. I ended up counting 17 parrots, eight female macaws and three male, all rushing out. In a bout of belated self-criticism for not having cleaned the receiver, I set about giving it the maintenance it required. While I was taking out feathers and dung (and even the skeleton of a parrot whom the others had taken the care to give a Christian burial, since a carefully constructed cross glowed from his coffin, located in a corner of the little receiver, and a tombstone with an inscription in Latin? - Requiescat in pace), I encountered a little nest with a tiny grey egg mottled with green and blue. There was a small envelope to one side, which I began opening with ill-concealed anxiety. It was a letter directed "To whom it may concern." A parrot, in very tiny letters, recounted her sad and heartbreaking history.

She had fallen deeply in love with a handsome (so said the letter) young macaw, and her feelings were returned (so said the letter), but the parrots who were jealous of the purity of their race did not approve of such a scandalous romance, and they strictly forbade the parrot from seeing the handsome young macaw (so said the letter), causing them to meet clandestinely behind one of the transistors in the radio.

Since "the macaw is fire, the parrot burlap, the devil comes... and blows" (so said the letter), they soon came of age, and that little egg that I then had in my hands was the forbidden fruit of their irregular relationship. The parrot asked (so said the letter) whoever found it to give shelter and sustenance to the little being until it could look after itself (so said the letter), and it ended with a series of maternal recommendations, in addition to a heartrending lamentation over its cruel fate, etcetera (so said the letter).

Overwhelmed by the great responsibility of having become an adoptive father, and cursing my crazy notion to clean the radio, I tried to find moral and material support from some of my combatants, but they were all already asleep, probably dreaming of springs of café au lait, of rivers of Coca-Cola and lemonade. Following the oft-cited precept of "There is no problem so large that it should be agonized over," I abandoned the egg on one side of my hammock, and I set myself to enjoying a much deserved rest. It was useless, remorse would not allow me to sleep, and soon (deep down, very deep down, I have a good and noble heart) I picked up the little egg and settled it on top of my stomach. At midnight, that unhappy hour, it began moving. At first I thought it was my stomach protesting over the lack of food, but no, it was the little egg that was beginning to break open. With an inexplicable maternal instinct, I prepared to attend the sacred moment in which I would become a mother... what am I saying, a father. When, to my surprise I saw that it was not a macaw or a parrot coming out of the shell, truly, not even a chick or a little pigeon. No, what came out of the egg was... a little tapir! Seriously, it was a little tapir with green and blue feathers. In a fit of lucidity (something which is, of course, becoming more and more rare for me) I understood the true subtext of the horrifying history, the crux-of-the-question-like-I-don't-know-who-said. "Eureka!" I yelled, like I-also-don't-remember-who-said-either.

What happened was that the parrot "doublecrossed," that is, she "made out" with a male tapir, they sinned, and she wanted to pin the little "blame" on the macaw, but everything fell apart, given that the radio, etcetera. "Everyone is the same," I sighed. Deciphering the mystery, it only remained to be seen what the hell I was going to do with the bastard tapir... And I am still dealing with that. For one thing, I am carrying her hidden in my backpack and I'm offering her a little of my food. I do not deny that we get along well, and my maternal, excuse me, paternal, instinct has been giving way to an insane passion towards the tapir, who bestows ardent glances on me that have little to do with gratitude and much with contained passion. My problem is serious, since, if I were to give way to temptation, I would be committing, in addition to a crime against nature, incest, because I am her adoptive father. I have thought of abandoning her, but I cannot, I do not have the strength. Anyway, I don't know what the hell to do...

As you can see, I have too many problems to be able to deal with yours. I hope that you now understand my repeated silence regarding the questions you insist on positing to me.

Vale, it's no use, and, as whomever-you-guys-look-up-who-said, "books are friends who never betray you." Salud and send me some veterinary manual for wild animals of the tropics (look under "D" for "Danta" [tapir] and "Desperation").

74. DUALITY AND REMEMBRANCE

August-September of 1999
7 times 2
For Alberto Gironella,
Who painted so well that it seemed
As if he were writing.

> "The dovecote of letters
> opens its impossible flight
> from the trembling tables
> where remembrance is supported,
> the gravity of absence, the heart, silence."
> - Miguel Hernandez

The moon is my button of gilded silver, dented and poorly sewn onto the black shirt of the mountain. In the grand house of the calendar, May appears as a conjunction of the double and humid page of August and September. Perhaps that is why the sun travels the day spreading sweat and suffocating heat, while during the night, the moon fills its pages with the sleeping wind.

Down below, life is war, daily combat in the multiple dark alleys that people the Mexican night. Fighting at birth, fighting while growing up, loving and dying fighting, and, yes, even writing is combat.

See if it is not so: in that corner of the world they call the "mountains of the Mexican southeast," the last of a century's flickering death throes, words like stab wounds appear above the high and soft cushion of the Ceiba.

And that Ceiba seems more like a General Post Office than a tree: letters come and go, almost as frequent as the rains that lash deep ravines into the skin of the day or into the heart of the night. Look, there goes another, which is others. Yes, that letter is many letters, it is a letter-hedgehog. Seven double spines making out of skin what hurts on paper. Many are written by one hand, and they are destined for many others who are others, distinct and different. Sharp epistles that point out and warn, they do not threaten, just advising that the night continues without opening, and, nonetheless, one must still traverse it.

And so, seeming to write, the hand hones words that wound but do not injure, that point out, that mark, that are sharp spines, marks that hurt. If one letter is many letters, it is not out of a numerical whim, it is because the world is many worlds, and many also are the forgettings that conceal them. The One is a trap, out of which will come the reckoning, which is also called history.

Sshh! Attention! Look! The first wound is being opened there!

Letter One
  "The Indian, as master of the land, is a utopia of university students."
  - Tirano Banderas, Ramon Del Valle-Inclan

On the rickety table, leveled up with stones and cardboard boxes, two books are resting, their pages closed, their words mute. The candle is waving its fragile light like a flag and a hand lights the chewed up pipe for the umpteenth time. From here, his figure is just a seated and stooped shadow. But the candle brushes against the covers of the two books. "Ramon Del Valle-Inclan. Tirano Banderas. Illustrations by Alberto Gironella, Galaxia Gutemberg. Circulo de Lectores" can be read on one of the covers. The other shows "Julio Scherer Garcia, Carlos Monsivais. War Report. Nuevo Siglo Aguilar."

Suddenly the flame of the candle reclines, bound by the wind, scraping, more than illuminating, some loose, hastily scribbled, disordered pages. Slowly and deliberately, the luminous tongue laps the first words.

August-September of 1999

(...)

This book by Ramon del Valle-Inclan, "Tirano Banderas," comes in an extraordinarily well prepared edition, with the much-missed discernment (ever more distant from "postmodern" editors) of respect for the author, the illustrator and the reader. This book reached this desk twice, as if everything had conspired for this

August to be defined by the duality suggested by the mirror. One of the copies comes with the words "For a writer. MGG." The other has a laconic dedication, written in a trembling hand, "To Marcos, from Gironella."

Two copies, yes, but also two books in one book: the one that paints the letters of Ramon Del Valle-Inclan, the other that writes the - drawings? - of Alberto Gironella.

I met Gironella in that August of 1994, during the National Democratic Convention, in the Aguascalientes in the now former town of Guadalupe Tepeyac. Barely a greeting, and he gave us a magnificent painting of Emiliano Zapata, spattered with bullet holes and bottle caps. Tacho, or someone else, I don't remember, took the painting and hung it on the small podium of the Aguascalientes. Gironella's Zapata was presiding over the session when it survived the storm of the 8th. During the shipwreck of men and women that night, the painting disappeared.

Gironella left. Before his death, a lie sent an apocryphal letter to Don Alberto. Rebel and true, Gironella did not deserve the pathetic alms of the lie to the deceased. Because of that, because he never, neither in life nor in death, deserved pity, to wherever he may be found, I am writing these lines in order to tell him:

For: Don Alberto Gironella
From: Sup. Marcos

Teacher,

I did not write that letter. Someone thought that, by doing bad, they would do good, and they falsified the text and signature, believing that would give consolation and relief. I did indeed send the books, Don Alberto, and there were two because it was two that you had sent me (the Tirano Banderas and Potlatch), and because those two brought you or your painting (which are now the same) to mind. I put that about nature imitating art in those books for you, and, in one of them, The Revolt of Memory (CLACH editors), the picture of the zapatista guerrillas eating at Samborns of Los Azulejos, repeated your work in Tirano Banderas. On one of the jacket covers, you explain: "I had wanted to capture distinct real elements that Valle could have learned about during his visits to Mexico. If Valle used Huerta as a reference to tyrants, then I worked starting with an image of his, which incorporated characteristics attributed to him in the novel, such as the green color of his saliva... In order to depict Zacarias el Cruzado, I have used the image of a zapatista guerrilla... For the criollo Roque Cepeda, I started with a photo of Vasconcelos, who more than paralleled him... The frame takes its inspiration from the belt of an assassinated worker photographed by Alvarez Bravo: a belt made from the skin of the maguey..."

Yes, "parallel" you have said (the spectacles you painted on Huerta are repeated now in those Zedillo wears only to make his gaze even more baleful). And the Vasconcelos of "The spirit will speak through my race," painted anew in order to share the struggle with the indigenous risen up against Tirano Banderas, brings up other parallels: the UNAM and Chiapas, the university movement and the zapatista indigenous uprising.

In the nightmare that August and September are defining today for our country, the powerful are religiously repeating the arguments of Tirano Banderas' clique. Yes, for them "the Indian, as master of the land, is a utopia of university students. But revolutionary ideas are something more serious, because they alter the sacred foundations of ownership. The Indian, as master of the land, is a demagogic aberration, that cannot prevail in well ordered minds (Ramon Del Valle-Inclan, op. cit.).

And, in order to cure Indians and university students of this illness, Tirano Banderas' "postmodern" remedy dispatches tens of thousands of soldiers to the lands of the Mexican southeast. In February of 1995, Zedillo said, in a national broadcast to more than 90 million Mexicans: "They are not indigenous, they are not chiapanecos, they are white university students (I believe he said it like that) with radical ideas who are manipulating the chiapaneco indigenous."

Since then, this is the definition that has ruled the government "strategy" in the face of the conflict in Chiapas. In order to accomplish this, they count on the acquiescence of caciques who would make Tirano Banderas look like a sorcerer's apprentice. These are the ones who are governing, destroying and killing in Indian lands. Along with Banderas' brotherhood, they complain: "The Indian is contemptible by nature, he never takes advantage of his employer's benefits, he appears humble and he is sharpening his knife. He only stays on the straight and narrow with a riding crop. He is lazier, works less and gets drunk even more than the West Indian negro." (Ibid.). In order to execute such a great philosophy, hounds of diverse size are paraded through the government palace in Chiapas. The latest of them, with a particular taste for indigenous blood and croquettes, has made it clear: indigenous and students are not wanted in these lands. And the pack of hounds has already been enlisted for Zedillo's lapdog's clean-up campaign: "A good Indian is a dead Indian, and a good student is an absent student." Killing Indians and persecuting students is the fashionable sport in Chiapas. At the pinnacle of his alcohol and canine delirium, Albores declaims that he does indeed have his pants well hitched up (and he mistakes for a belt what is nothing more than a flea collar).

Yes, teacher, nature imitates art, and your words painted to illustrate Valle-Inclan's written images erupt in these times of Tiranos and arrogance, of university students and zapatista guerrillas.

And, to prove me right, a walnut ice cream did not turn up on my desk (which is what I would have wanted, and which, in that instance, nature does indeed surpass art), but rather a book which is also two books, War Report, by Julio Scherer Garcia and Carlos Monsivais.

A book times two evidenced by the fact that there are two authors, it is also double in what it rebels and reveals, in what it says about the past and in what both authors remain silent about concerning the future. Both, Scherer and Monsivais, are now a reference point in the history of Mexican culture in general, and of journalism in particular. Cutting in both word and pen, they arouse, by times, respect, and, not infrequently, fear.

Soldiers are paraded through Julio Scherer Garcia's text, their "toughness" and short-sightedness. Less and less frequent among civilians, the admiration for the military "forgets," after the mute epoch, that armies are the most absurd structures in existence. Absolute negation of reason, the crushing of the individual and the cult of destruction are some of their characteristics (and doors through which organized crime extends its reach).

I know that it sounds more than paradoxical that this is being said by a military commander of the EZLN, which is, also, an army. But that is precisely why we hope to disappear. But I have already explained this in other places, and I do not wish to bore you. What this book is about now is an army, the federal one, as a source of destabilization.

In my passage through the Heroic Military College and the Higher Education of War, I could see that it is neither a source of pride nor an honor to be what the federal Army turns into a closed, untouchable and unpredictable being. No, it is another world, and its internal logic allows injustices that would embarrass even the most corrupt of judges (of which there are many) of the Mexican judicial system: an article in a magazine, touching on the issue of human rights in the military (unthinkable, since we are speaking of "cold killing machines"), which rewarded General Gallardo with prison, disparagement and the daily harassment of his family. Those who refused to carry out assassination orders given by top military commanders in January of 1994, in response to the zapatista uprising, were given death and forced exile. Those who disapproved of the activation of paramilitary gangs in Chiapas, arguing that carrying weapons required discipline and responsibility, were disappeared. Those who enlisted dreaming of defending the Patria, "if a foreign enemy dares to profane by setting foot on your soil" - and who immediately found themselves confronted by civilians, children, old ones, women and men, all Mexicans, all poor - had to flee into hiding, imploring those same persons they had been attacking to lend them "civilian clothing" and a guide in order to leave the "conflict zone."

If 1968 had to wait 30 years for the illogical military logic to demonstrate its destabilizing injustice, in 1999 honest publications (which do exist) report daily on unpunished outrages and crimes, perpetrated with the sole arguments of an olive green uniform and a weapon. In a few words, a state of siege originally intended for the Mexican southeast, later extended to indigenous towns throughout the country, and now invading the streets of the cities.

While the government argues that the purpose of the massive military presence in Chiapas is to prevent destabilization, a quick recounting of events of the last two years demonstrate that it is the federal Army that is the primary cause of destabilization and deterioration in the Mexican southeast. Where the federales arrive, tensions go up and conflicts break out.

Since Señor Zedillo arrived at Los Pinos, by the hand of Colosio's assassins, the federal Army has broken the cease-fire on at least three occasions: in February of 1995 (leaving 5 zapatista deaths and a federal Army Colonel and 10 troops dead in combat); in June of 1998 in El Bosque (results: 8 zapatistas executed after having been taken prisoner by soldiers), and in August of 1999 in San Jose La Esperanza (results: 2 zapatistas wounded by gunfire and 8 soldiers "struck with sticks and stones"). The Secretaries of Government Moctezuma Barragan (alias "Guajardo") in 1995, Francisco Labastida (alias "El Suavecito") in 1998, and Diodoro Carrasco (still without alias) in 1999. With Chuayffet the confrontation continued along the path of the paramilitaries and "awarded Mexican history with one of its most shameful and humiliating pages: the Acteal killings in December of 1997."

In addition to military attacks by the federales, all of these destabilizing actions have one common denominator: Ernesto Zedillo Ponce de Leon.

Yes, Don Alberto, far from guaranteeing domestic order, the federal Army has been an important cause of disorder and ungovernability.

But, returning to War Report, it is impossible to read this book without the shadow of this August-September of 99. Impossible to do so "forgetting" about zapatista Chiapas. Impossible to read it without the presence of, not just the existence of the current student movement at the National Autonomous University of Mexico, and also the obvious and great differences, but, above all, of the not so obvious similarities. This is one of those books, of which there are few, which should be read many times, discovering in them new words and new silences (something which shall not be easy, since the binding is of the "use and throw away" type), according to the Augusts and Septembers that are using up calendars.

But, in addition to the University Movement of today and the Chiapas rebellion, this book converges with Tirano Banderas in many pages. Look, Don Alberto, the following dialogue between two "journalists" in service to the tyrant:

"Who would have independent writing! The boss wants a ruthless critique."

Fray Mocho pulled a bottle of beer out from his chest and bent over it, kissing the bottleneck:

"Very eloquent!"

"It's a dishonor to sell one's conscience."

"What do you mean? You do not sell your consciences. You're selling your writing, which is not the same thing."

"For thirty bloody pesos!"

"It's a living. You don't have to be a poet."

Now compare this with Monsivais' text: "The government unleashed a press, radio and television campaign against the 'subversives,' and the Patriotic Explanations began to flow." (op. cit. p. 148). "In 1968, Mexican journalism went through the mortifying experience of denying modernity out of 'respect for institutions,' which now have little or nothing to say to young people, and which, as a rule, are translated into the language of cynicism... The journalist, as a rule, is at the service of the politicians, the only readers who take them into account, and the more rhetoric they demonstrate, the more corruption results. (...) That explains the cry of 'Sold out Press!' in the marches, and the grotesquerie of disinformation." (p. 174) And, further along: "In 1968, private television refused to broadcast the Movement's positions. The slander proliferated, and the calls for moral lynchings, the news shows denounced the insignificant number of the marches." (p. 183).

The university movement of 1999 has suffered, as few have over the last years, a true media war. Private television (where Televisa and Television Azteca are fighting among themselves for the "honor" of being the backbone of the ultra-right in Mexico) and radio, in particular, have made efforts that have gone much further than the obvious complacency of the government. With singular enthusiasm, they have been handing out epithets as if they were free samples for a new product; "Agitators," "subversives," "assailants," "kidnappers," "criminals," "pseudo-students," "strikers" (to put them in counterpoint to "the students who want to study"), and, markedly, the former PRI-ism that some PRD intellectual provided them with: "ultras."

And, in the Mexican southeast, the powerful and their hounds do not want to be left behind. Large amounts of money, originally intended for the indigenous communities, are flowing to the media in Chiapas. If the demagogic tone of some "journalists" can be used as a standard for the amount of money they have received, it can then be understood how, in spite of everything the government has invested in the state, little or nothing is reaching the communities. A large part of it remains on the editorial desks and in the wallets of the "journalists" who have a particular fascination with travelling by Army helicopters to cover, "with complete objectivity," what is happening.

With the zapatista "desertions" out of fashion, there is a new issue: the wicked student strikers from the UNAM have come to sow discord amongst the placid indigenous communities, that were so calm, ergo, these young persons cannot be allowed to "violate" Chiapas' sovereignty (and what is paradoxical is that it is the zapatistas they accuse of separatism). "Or they're going to jail," says the totally drunk Croquetas, while the soldiers at the San Quintin barracks applaud him.

In the Chiapas of Zedillo-Albores, the echoes of '68 are reborn and the boss's barking dogs shout at the students who arrive in the town of Amador Hernandez. The "Get out, damn foreigners!" (because in Albores' Chiapas, everything that is not a PRI is a "damn foreigner") has its precedent in "We want dead Che's!" they shouted, and, like an enormous echo, the crowds responded: "We want dead Che's! Let all the expatriated guerrillas die!" they shouted again, and the crowds passionately responded: "Die!" (in El Heraldo de Mexico, September 9, 1968. Op. cit. 178).

If Scherer and Monsivais discovered that hysterical fear was the driving force behind the government response to the '68 movement, August and September are revealing something equally terrible: Zedillo and Albores, and the press that accompanies them, are convinced that a new ghost is moving about the university classrooms and the mountains of the Mexican southeast: the anti-Mexico. Hysteria leading the federal and state governments.

The book says more, and still more the August of this end of century. This book War Report is "almost" as good as The Night of Tlatelolco, that broken mirror that the princess' daughter gifted us with some years ago.

Then yes, Don Alberto, August is gone now, and September has already arrived, UNAM and Chiapas are sensitive to the pain of this country called Mexico. The university student movement and the zapatista rebellion are struggling against these pains. Perhaps they may not be able to relieve them, and they may only serve to feel them as they truly are: the pain of all.

I read here that the books did arrive on time and, perhaps, you were able to pack them in your suitcase, thinking that later you would be able to paint a few letters on those painted words.

Vale Don Alberto. Salud, and - who knows? - what hurts about death is that, by times, it embraces the one it should not.

Sup.

P.S. If you need anything, let me know, so that I can bring it when I go. Yes, I'll bring you War Report.

The writing is interrupted here. Holding, waiting for its place, a quotation from War Report stands alone: "The united rage of politicians, businessmen, bishops and news media did not dissuade the strikers, nor did the fear by the parents sap the movement's vitality." (p. 178).

The candle lends its last flicker above the last sentence, and it closes its sole eye. Barely an instant. A new flame momentarily illuminates the pipe and the face of the seated shadow. Impossible to see his face since his back is turned. And, even if he were facing, this man is without face, one more of those who abound in this corner of history.

From the mountains of the Mexican Southeast,
Subcomandante Insurgente Marcos.
Mexico, August-September of 1999.

75. Fifteen Years Ago

September of 1999
To: Everyone working at La Jornada
From: Sup Marcos
Zapatista Army of National Liberation Mexico

> "I am proposing to you, then, with the gravity of the final words of life, that we embrace each other in a commitment: we shall go out to the wide open spaces, we shall take risks for the other, we shall hope, with the one who extends their arms, that a new wave of history will raise us up. Perhaps it is already doing so, in a silent and subterranean manner, like the shoots that move beneath the winter ground."
> - Ernesto Sabato, Before the End

Ladies and gentlemen,

I was going to put "brothers and sisters," but journalists cannot be treated like that, because then Rodriguez Alcaine would ask for 'dittos,' and neither would one want to become related to criminals, no?

Where was I? Ah, yes! At "Ladies and gentlemen," I'll continue then:

I am writing to you in the name of the men, women, children and old ones of the Zapatista Army of National Liberation, in order to wish you all a very happy 15th anniversary, and that you may have many more for ever and ever.

I shall not add to what I must already have said concerning the importance of the work of journalism, merely perhaps to remember, and to remind those many people with a poor and selective memory (like those jumping on the tops of cars; by the way, the idea of Monsivais having a position in the next cabinet does not bother us, it would be the first time that someone with a sense of humor occupied such a position, although one might suppose that he would lose it - the sense of humor or the position - staying awake in that way), that La Jornada has always been sensitive to social movements and to what is bubbling and babbling below.

When those from below are given "coverage," it is not just because their movement shakes the Mexican system, but also because there is someone who is concerned about taking notice of the event, and contributing, in that way, to that daily memory which today appears chaotic, disorganized and distressing, but which will then have to be fit into that which is called history. Not just La Jornada, certainly, but La Jornada has also become an important page in paying attention to our country's contemporary history for the sake of memory.

We should imagine that it has not been easy to reach 15 years being what you are, with so much against you, in the midst of so much jealousy, suspicion, ambitionand absences such as that of Don Rodolfo F. Pena. Because of that, in addition to congratulating those who are making La Jornada today, we would like to congratulate those who have made it and, from wherever they may be, in their way and their time, accompany the pride of "the jornaleros."

But, fine, we need not be dramatic, and we must remember that we are speaking of a celebration. And so, just this once (given 15 double, as shall be seen further along), we shall reveal a few of the special prizes that, year after year, the "zapatones" award.

It must be clarified that, in order to decide who receives the prizes, we are verrry scientific and "postmodern," since (you're right) we carried out apoll! Conducted by the serious firm of "Marcos' Very Very Cheap Publishing Company," the 298 remaining zapatistas (well, 300 remain, but two of them were in bed) were surveyed, as well as the 4,265,312 former zapatistas who deserted...

The prizes, for this 1999, are as follows:

The best political analysis column in 1999: Trino, for Cops and Robbers and the Little King.

The most read section in 1999 (and for the last 15 years): Socorro Valadez, for "El Correo Ilustrado."

The best cartoon in 1999: Hector Aguilar Camin, for himself.

The most hated section in 1999: (and for the last 15 years, truly): The one with the announcements and listings.

The greatest injustice in 1999: Sending the supplements only to subscribers.

The best union at La Jornada in 1999: Sitrajor.

The best editor at La Jornada in 1999: It is not a "He," but a "She," Carmen Lira.

The most thankless work in 1999 (and for the last five years): "Capturing" the Sup's communiqués at a quarter to twelve (even though here, raza, we applaud them and we do not join in the demand that the pay should go up so that they don't say that we're increasing the size of our sheets of paper each time).

The best tribute to La Jornada in 1999: The seizure of the papers in Chiapas that

El Croquetas ordered for several days.

The most regrettable of 1999: Not having invited us to the 15 year blow-out (you'll have a chamberlain in our category shortly?).

The rest of the awards cannot be revealed for obvious reasons (rather, there is no space).

Good, dear jornaleros and jornaleras, congratulations, and do not fill up too much on sandwiches and drinks, because then you are going to need an "errata" supplement equally as tedious as the "debate" between the four puppets.

Best wishes to those who, like you, take risks for the other.

Vale. Salud and may many, always better, calendars follow the 15.

> From the mountains of the Mexican Southeast,
> Subcomandante Insurgente Marcos.
> Mexico, September of 1999.

15 Years

For Rodolfo Pena, Another mistaken embrace by death.

> "When I go to write you the ink becomes moved; the cold black ink becomes red and trembling, and clear human heat arises from the black depths. When I go to write you My bones are going to write you; I write you with the indelible ink of my emotion."
> - Miguel Hernandez

The moon is a mother-of-pearl pick now, and her strumming on the strings of the night produces a storm of all manner. The moon, frightened, hides herself, darkening light who tucks herself in among the dark storm clouds. The lady of the night is now the storm, and the lightening sketches, in short and hurried strokes, trees and foolish shadows.

Down below it rains many times, as many as war brings pain. Pain and remembrance, because it is memory which turns pain fertile. Without her, one would just hurt painfully the painful hurt and nothing would be born and nothing, therefore, would grow, accumulating calendars, each one of which is a life.

The shadow writes or paints. There is a double 15, second of the seven, which is anniversary and fiesta and remembrance and pain and joy and memory.

Letter One, dove of death, has barely left, when the shadow that concerns us is already sharpening the point of the second. If the One was for the person who left, the Two is for the one who is following the path of the absent one. The long and humid movement of August until it reaches September and reaches dates of celebrations and remembrances.

Like dissatisfied memory, the rain taps its impatience above the little roof, and, more than once, the mocking wind turns out lights and sends papers and ink into the mud. The shadow toils between lighting candles and picking up papers, as if it were about winds for one who is sailing. A sheet of paper remains in a corner of the little hut, and, beneath the blinking of the lightning bolts, it can be read. One moment. I will try to draw near. Right, the mud. And this fog that just fell like this. It is difficult. Good, there it is. This is what I managed to read:

Letter Two

P.S. As you will see below, explains the why of the 15 double, as this is the second of the seven.

Fifteen Years Ago

Every August, year after year, the mountains of the Mexican southeast arrange themselves so as to give birth to a particularly luminous dawn. I know nothing of the scientific causes, but during this dawn, a single one throughout the disconcerting August, the moon is a hammock of swaying iridescence, the stars arrange themselves so as to be background and object, and the Milky Way proudly illuminates its thousand wounds of clotted light. This August of the end of the millennium, the calendar was announcing the sixth day when this dawn appeared. And so, with the swaying moon, the memory returned of another August and another 6, when, 15 years ago, I began my entrance into these mountains that were and are, without wanting it or willing it, house, school, road and door. I began to enter in August and I did not finish doing so until September.

I should confess something to you, when I laboriously climbed the first of the steep hills that abound in these lands, I felt that it would be the last. I was not thinking of revolution, of the high ideals of humans, or of a shining future for the dispossessed and forgotten of always.

No, I was thinking that I had made the worst decision of my life, that the pain that was increasingly squeezing my chest would end up definitively closing off the ever more skimpy entrance of air, that the best thing would be for me to return and to let the revolution arrange itself without me, along with other similar reasonings. If I did not go back, it was simply because I did not know the return path, and I only knew that I should follow the companero who preceded me, and who - to judge by the cigarette he was smoking while crossing the mud without difficulty - seemed to be merely out for a stroll. I did not think that one day I would be able to climb a hill smoking and not feeling that I was dying with each step, nor that a time would come when I would be able to negotiate the mud that abounded below as much as the stars did above. No, I was not thinking then, I was concentrating on every breath I was trying to take.

Finally, what happened is that at some point we reached the highest point of the hill, and the one who was in charge of the meager column (we were 3) said that we would rest there. I let myself fall into the mud that appeared the closest, and I told myself that perhaps it would not be so difficult to find the return path, that it would be enough to walk down another eternity, and that some day I would reach the point where the truck had dropped us off. I was making my calculations, including the excuses I would give, and that I would give to myself, for having abandoned the beginning of my career as a guerrilla, when the companero approached me and offered me a cigarette. I refused with a shake of my head, not because I didn't want to talk, but because I had tried to say "no thanks" but only a groan came out.

After a bit, taking advantage of the fact that the person in charge had retired some distance in order to satisfy biological needs referred to as basic, I got up as best I could above the 20 caliber shotgun I was carrying, more as a walking stick than as a combat weapon. In that way I could see from the top of that mountain something which had a profound impact on me.

No, I did not look down, not towards the twisted scribble of the river, nor at the weak lights of the bonfires that were dimly illuminating a distant hamlet, nor at the neighboring mountains that painted the Canada, sprinkled with small villages, fields and pastures.

I looked upwards. I saw a sky that was gift and relief, no, more of a promise. The moon was like a smiling nocturnal hammock, the stars sprinkling blue lights and the ancient serpent of luminous wounds that you call the "Milky Way" seemed to be resting its head there, very far away.

I remained looking for a time, knowing I would have to climb up that wretched hill in order to see this dawn, that the mud, the slips, the stones that hurt the skin on the outside and the inside, the tired lungs, incapable of pulling in the necessary air, the cramped legs, the anguished clinging to the shotgun-walking stick in order to free my boots from the prison of mud, the feeling of aloneness and desolation, the weight I was carrying on my back (which, I knew this later, was only symbolic, since, in reality, there was always three times that or more; finally, that "symbol" weighed tons to me), that all of that - and much more that would come later - is what had made it possible for that moon, those stars, and that Milky Way to be there and in no other place.

When I heard behind me the orders to renew the march, up in the sky a star, certainly fed up with being subjugated by the black roof, managed to break away, and, falling, left on the nocturnal blackboard a brief and fugitive tracing. "That's what we are," I said to myself. "Fallen stars that barely scratched the sky of history with a scrawl." As far as I knew, I had only thought this, but it seems I had thought it out loud, because the compañero asked: "What did he say?" "I don't know," replied the one in charge. "It could be he's already come down with a fever. We have to hurry."

This that I am recounting to you happened 15 years ago. Thirty years ago, some scribbled history, and, knowing it, they began calling to many others so that, by force of scribbles, scratches and scrawls, they would end up breaking the veil of history, and the light would finally be seen, that, and nothing else, is the struggle we are making. And so if you ask us what we want, we will unashamedly respond: "To open up a crack in history."

Perhaps you are asking what happened to my intentions of returning and of abandoning the guerrilla life, and you might suppose that the vision of that first dawn in the mountain had made me abandon my ideas of fleeing, had lifted my morale and solidified my revolutionary conscious. You are wrong. I put my plan into operation and went down the mud. What happened is I made a mistake about the side, instead of going down the slope that would take me back to the road, and from there to "civilization," I went down the side that took me deeper into the Selva and that led me to another hill, and to another, and to another.

That was 15 years ago, since then I have continued climbing hills and I have continued making a mistake about which side to go down, August continues birthing a special dawn every 6th, and all of us continue to be fallen stars barely scratching history.

Vale de nuez, salud, andone minute! Wait. What is that shining brightly in the distance? It looks like a crack.

The Sup, on top of the hill, tossing a coin in order to see which side of the hill leads down.

76. THE HOUR OF THE LITTLE ONES, I

First Part: THE RETURN OF...

For Don Emilio Krieger, who was with the little ones of forever

For the children of "El Molino" (Francisco Villa Popular Front) who lost their homes in a fire

> "In the letter box of time there are joys that no one shall call for/that no one will ever claim/and they will end up faded, yearning for the taste of the elements and nonetheless/from time's letter box loose epistles will suddenly depart, ready to settle in to some dream where chance fears are waiting."
> - Mario Benedetti

It is raining a slight humid and cold breeze. There has been, however, such, and such fierce, beating of the rain against the mountain over the last few days that it has left not a few dents, and there are scars that have raked the entire side of the mountain. But, never mind, after such a storm, this drizzle is welcome. It is the time of the rains. The time of the little ones.

A good man has died. What can be said when a good man dies? Some children, who fearlessly opened their homes to receive one thousand one hundred and eleven faceless ones, have lost their homes. What can be said when a child loses her home? One says nothing, one is only silent. Because one often remains silent with sorrows. Nonetheless, in an attempt to make them feel better, the little ones from this side of the siege are extending their bridges, like hands, to where the good man is missing, and to where doors and windows are missing, in order to be opened to the other forgotten and little one, the other dignified and rebel. They are extended in order to accompany, in order to be close, in order to not forget. It is perhaps for that that the shadow, unhurriedly, is tenderly honing the first two of the fourth epistle, hoping to coax a smile amidst so much pain that is being suffered there.

Down there, the candle is repeating its vocation as lighthouse for that sailor in the mountain who, lost, is navigating the shadows of the dawn. Yes, let's go, but be careful with the mud and those puddles. You're going slowly? Good, I'll go ahead and let you know from in there. Good, here I am. Yes. The shadow is alone once more. No... Just a minute... There seems to be someone else. That candle won't stop sputtering! No, I can't manage to see who else is there, but it's obvious that there's someone, because the shadow is speaking. No, he's more refusing, because he's doing nothing other than repeating "no, no and no." I'll go over to that corner in order to see better. There it is. Mmhh. I believe our favorite shadow has gone crazy. No one can be seen hereabouts. And he, with his: "No, no and no." Ah well, it was to be expected, so much rain and so many dawns would end up driving anyone crazy. What? But I already told you no one was there! I should move closer? And if he sees me? Alright then, slowly and discreetly. No, I tell you, there's no one. Just a minute! Yes, something different now... There, in a corner! Yes! What a relief! He has not gone crazy, no. What happened is that he was so small I didn't notice him... What? Who is he speaking with? OK, then... you'll see. Do you really want to know? Then... then, with a beetle!

¡Durito! Letter 4

"No, no and no!" I tell Durito for the umpteenth time.

Yes, Durito has returned. But before explaining my repeated "no," I should recount the complete history to you.

When the rain formed a river the other dawn right in the middle of the hut, Durito arrived on board a can of sardines that had a pen stuck in its middle, and, on it, a handkerchief or something like that, which would later be discovered to be a sail. On the highest part of the mainstaff, excuse me, of the pen, a black flag was flying, with a fierce skull resting on a pair of crossbones. It was not a proper ship, landing right at the edge of the table, and it did so with such a tumult that Durito came flying through the air, and he landed right on my boot. Durito gathered himself up as best he could and exclaimed:

"Today... today..." he turns around to look at me and says: "Ah, you, carrot nose! Tell me the date promptly!"

I hesitate, a bit out of wanting to embrace Durito since he'd returned, another little bit out of wanting to kick him for the "carrot nose" thing, and another bit more for... for... the date?...

I look at my watch and say: "October 12, 1999."

"October 12? By my faith, nature imitates art! Good. Today, October 12, 1999, I declare discovered, conquered and liberated this beautiful Caribbean isle that answers to the name of... of... Quick, the name of the isle!"

"What isle?" I ask, still taken aback.

"What do you mean, what isle, fool? This one! And what else would it be? There is no pirate worth being so who has not an island for hiding treasure and sorrows..."

"Island? I always thought it was a tree, a ceiba to be more precise," I say, leaning over the edge of the dense branches.

"Then you are deceived, it is an island. When has it ever been heard of a pirate landing in a ceiba? So, either tell me the name of this island, or your fate will be to serve as lunch for the sharks," Durito says threateningly.

"Sharks?" I say, swallowing. And I hesitatingly venture: "It has no name..."

"'It Has No Name,' Mmh. By my faith, it is a right dignified name for a pirate's island. Good, today, October 12, 1999, I declare the island of 'It Has No Name' to be discovered, conquered and liberated, and I name this man with the obvious nose to be my boatswain, first mate, cabin boy and lookout."

I try to ignore the insult, as well as the multitude of positions conferred, and I say: "So... Now you are a pirate!"

"'A pirate,' hell no! I am THE PIRATE!"

Up to now I had been noticing Durito's figure. A black patch adorns his right eye, a red handkerchief covers his head, on one of his many arms a twisted wire is made into a hook, and in another is that shining wand that once was Excalibur. I am not sure now, but it must be some kind of sword, saber, or whatever pirates use.

And, in addition, there is a little branch tied to one of his little feet as if it were... as if it were... a wooden leg!

"And, so: what do you think?" asks Durito, making a half turn in order to show off all his finery concocted for his pirate's clothes.

I carefully ask him: "And so now you're called...?"

"'Black Shield'!" Durito says pompously, and he adds: "But you can put 'Escudo Negro' for those who aren't globalized."

"'Black Shield?' But..."

"Certainly! Was there not a 'Redbeard' and a 'Blackbeard'?"

"Well, yes, but..."

"There is no 'but'! I am 'Black Shield'! Compared with me, 'Blackbeard' would be but gray, and then with effort, and 'Redbeard' would be more faded than your old scarf!"

Durito had said this while simultaneously brandishing both his sword and his hook. Stopped now, in the bow of his can of sardines - excuse me, of his vessel, he begins reciting the "Pirate's Song"...

"'With ten cannons on each side'..."

"Durito," I try to bring him to his senses.

"'Wind at the stern, full sail'..."

"Durito..."

"'It does not cross the sea, it flies'..."

"Durito!"

"What? A royal galleon is within our reach? Quickly! Unfurl the sails! Prepare to board!"

"Duritooo!" I shout, desperate now.

"Calm down, don't yell or you'll look like an unemployed buccaneer. What's going on?"

"Could you tell me where you've been, where you came from, and what brought you to these lands, excuse me, these islands?" I asked, more calmly now.

"I have been in Italy, in England, in Denmark, in Germany, in France, in Greece, in Holland, in Belgium, in Sweden, in the Iberian Peninsula, in the Canary Islands, in all of Europe." Durito has said all this while taking bows to the right and to the left.

"In Venice I ate one of those 'postas' with Dario that the Italians are so keen on, and which leave me i-m-m-o-b-i-l-e."

"Just a minute! Which Dario? You didn't mean that you were eating with Dario...?"

"Yes, Dario Fo. Right. Eating, eating not. He was eating, I was watching him eat. Because, look, that spaghetti gives me a stomach ache, and even more so when they put 'pasto' [grass] on it."

"'Pesto'," I correct him.

"'Pasto' or 'Pesto,' it's all grass. As I was telling you, I arrived in Venice from Rome, after having escaped from one of those Temporary Detention Centers (for Immigrants), that are a kind of concentration camp where Italian officials isolate - before expelling from the country - everyone coming from other countries, and who are, therefore, 'different.' Leaving wasn't easy, I had to lead a sit-in. Obviously the support from those men and women in Italy who are against institutionalized racism was fundamental. The fact is that Dario wanted me to help him with some ideas for a theatrical work, and I didn't have the heart to say no."

"Durito..."

"Afterwards I went on the march against the UN for the war in Kosovo."

"That should be 'against NATO'..."

"It's the same, and then, after a series of adventures, I set off to the Island of Lanzarote."

"Just a minute! The island of Lanzarote? Isn't that where Jose Saramago lives?"

"Yes, right, I call him 'Pepe'. What happened is that Pepe invited me for coffee so that I could discuss my experiences in the Europe of the Euro. It was magnificent..."

"Yes, I'd imagine that it would have been magnificent to chat with Saramago..."

"No, I'm referring to the coffee that the Pilarica prepared for us. She makes a truly magnificent cup of coffee."

"You're referring to Pilar del Rio?"

"The same."

"So, one day you're eating with Dario Fo, and the next you're taking coffee with Jose Saramago."

"Yes, those days I was hanging out with nothing but Nobel prize winners. But I tell you I had a fierce discussion with Pepe."

"And the reason?"

"The prologue, that one he wrote for my book. It seemed to me in bad taste that I, the great and even-tempered Don Durito of La Lacandona should be reduced to the world of Coleopterous Lamellicorn." (Durito is referring to Jose Saramago's prologue to the book "Don Durito de La Lacandona." Ed. CIACH, A.C.).

"And what was the discussion about?"

"Well, I challenged him to a duel, as and how demanded by the laws of knight errantry."

"And...?"

"And nothing, I saw that the Pilarica's heart was breaking, since it was obvious that I would win, and I forgave him..."

"You forgave Jose Saramago?"

"Well, not completely. For me to forget the affront, he shall have to come to these lands and declare, at the top of his voice, the following speech: "Listen all. Tyrants, tremble. Damsels, sigh. Children, be of good cheer. The sad and needy, rejoice. Listen all. Once more across these lands walks the ever grand, the magnificent, the incomparable, the well loved, the eagerly awaited, the onomatopoetic, the greatest of the knights errant, Don Durito of La Lacandona.""

"You forced Jose Saramago to come here to say those... those... those things?"

"Yes, it seemed like a light punishment to me as well. But after all, he is a Nobel prizewinner, and I may, perhaps, need someone to do the prologue for my next book."

"Durito!" I chided him, and added, "Fine, but how did you happen to turn into a pirate, excuse me, into THE PIRATE?"

"It was Sabina's fault..." Durito says, as if he were talking about a partying compañero.

"You visited Joaquin Sabina also?"

"Of course! He wanted me to help him with the musical arrangements for his next record. But don't interrupt me. It happened that Sabina and I were chasing down bars and women in Madrid, when we reached La Ramblas."

"But that's in Barcelona!"

"Yes, there's the mystery. Because a few minutes before we had been in a pub in Madrid, captivated by an olive-skinned beauty, an Andalucian from Jaen, to be more precise, and then I had to go and satisfy one of those biological needs called 'primary.' That's when I made a mistake about the door, and, instead of the 'water' one, I opened the one to the street. And it happened that it was in La Ramblas. Yes, there was no longer any Madrid, nor Sabina, nor pub, nor olive skin, but I still needed a 'water,' because a knight cannot go about doing those things in just any corner. Ergo, I looked for a bar, trying to remember from when I had been hanging out with Manolo..."

"I imagine that you are referring to Manuel Vazquez Montalban," I asked, no longer capable of being astonished by anything.

"Yes, but it's too long a name, so I just call him 'Manolo.' Then I was anxiously, restlessly and meticulously looking for someplace with a 'water' when there appeared in front of me, in a dark alley, 3 gigantic shadows..."

"Bandits!" I interrupted, startled.

"Negative. They were three trash dumpsters, under whose shadow I calculated that I would be able, intimately and discreetly, to do what I had planned on doing in the 'water.' And so I did. And, with the satisfaction of a duty accomplished, I lit my pipe and heard, with absolute clarity, two chimes from 'Big Ben'."

"But, Durito, that's in London, England..."

"Yes, it seemed strange to me as well, but what wasn't that night? I walked until I came to a sign that read 'Pirates. Wanted. No previous experience required. Preference to Beetles and Knights Errant. Information at 'The Black Speck' bar." Durito lights his pipe and continues.

"I continued walking, looking for the sign for 'The Black Speck'. I was feeling my way, barely making out corners and walls, so thick was the fog that was falling over the alleys of Copenhagen that night..."

"Copenhagen? But weren't you in London?"

"Look, if you keep interrupting me with the obvious, I'm going to send you to the plank and from there to the sharks. I already told you that everything was quite strange, and if I had read the sign soliciting pirates in London, I was then looking for 'The Black Speck' bar in Copenhagen, Denmark. I got lost for a few minutes in the Tivoli Gardens, but I kept on looking. Suddenly I found it, on a corner. A weak light was emanating from a solitary street lamp, barely scratching through the fog, illuminating a sign that read: 'The Black Speck. Bar and Table Dance. Special Discount for Beetles and Knights Errant.' I had not previously realized the high regard and sympathy they hold in Europe for beetles and knights errant..."

"It could be because they do not suffer from them..." I barely breathed.

"Do not think that the irony of your murmurs escapes me," Durito says. "But, for the good of your readers, I will continue with my narrative. There will be time enough to settle accounts with you."

"I was saying that, after noting the great intelligence of the Europeans in recognizing and admiring the greatness that some of us beings possess, I went in to that bar in Montmartre, close to 'Sacre Coeur'..."

Durito stays silent for a moment, waiting for me to interrupt him and to say that that was in Paris France, but I say nothing. Durito nods with satisfaction and continues:

"Once inside - an amethyst mist was encroaching on the atmosphere - I sat down at a table in the darkest corner. Not even a second had gone by when a waiter, in perfect German, said to me: 'Welcome to East Berlin,' and, without saying anything else, left me what I took to be a carta or menu. I opened it, and it consisted of just one sentence: 'Potential pirates, second floor.' I went up by a staircase that was just behind me. I reached a long corridor flanked by windows. Through one of them the canals and 400 bridges that raise Amsterdam above the 90 islands could be seen. In the distance the 'White Tower' could be seen, which reminds the Greeks of Salonica of the extremes of intolerance. Still along the corridor, further ahead, through another window, the curved peak of the Swiss Matterhorn came into view. Further along could be made out the miraculous stones of the Irish Blarney Castle, that give the gift of words to those who kiss them. To the left, rose up the bell tower of the main Square in Bruges, Belgium. Following the passageway, before coming to a dilapidated door, a window looked out on the Plaza del Miracoli, and, by stretching one's hand a bit, one could touch the weak incline of the Tower of Pisa."

"Yes, that corridor looked out on half of Europe, and I would not have been surprised if there had been a sign on the door reading 'Welcome to the Maastricht Treaty'. But, no, the door did not have even one word on it. What's more, it didn't have a knob. I knocked, and nothing. I pushed the heavy piece of wood, and it gave way without difficulty. A mournful creaking accompanied the opening of the door..."

"I then entered a room that was partially obscured. Inside, on a table full of papers, an oil lamp was poorly illuminating the face of a man of indefinite age, with a patch covering his right eye and a hand-made hook that was pulling at his long beard. The man's gaze was fixed on the table. Nothing was heard, and the silence was so heavy that it clung like dust to the skin..." Durito brushed the dust off his Pirate clothes.

"'I have here a Pirate,' I said to myself, and I moved towards the table. The man did not turn a hair. I coughed a bit, which is what we educated knights do in order to attract attention. The pirate did not lift his gaze. Instead, the parrot (who I had seen on his left shoulder) began reciting - with such excellent intonation that even Don Jose de Espronceda would have applauded - the one that goes: 'With ten cannons on each side, wind at the stern, full sail, it does not cross the sea, it flies'..."

"'Sit down,' he said. I don't know if it was the man or the parrot, but the pirate, or what I surmised to be a pirate, handed me a piece of paper without saying a word. I read it. I will not bore your readers or you, I will tell you, in summation, that it was an application to join the 'Great Cofraternity of Pirates, Buccaneers and Terrors of the Sea A.C. of C.V. of R.L.' I filled it out without hesitation, not without previously underlining my status as beetle and knight errant. I handed the paper to the man and he read it in silence."

"When he finished, he looked at me slowly with his only eye and said to me: 'I was waiting for you Don Durito. Know that you are one of the last true pirates existing in the world. And I say 'true' because there is now an infinity of 'pirates' who are stealing, killing, destroying and looting from the financial centers and the great government palaces, without ever touching any water other than that in their baths. Here is your mission (he hands me a dossier of old parchments). Find the treasure, and put it in a safe place. And now, pardon me, but I must die.' And, as he said those words, he let his head fall to the table. Yes, he was dead. The parrot lifted up in flight and went out through a window, saying: 'I am going to the exile of Mitilene, I am going to the bastard son of Lesbos, I am going to the pride of the Aegean Sea. Open your 9 doors, fearsome hell, the great Redbeard is going to rest there. He has found the one who will follow in his footsteps, and the one who rendered the ocean into but a tear is now sleeping. The pride of the true Pirates will now be sailing with the Black Shield.' Underneath the window, the Swedish port of Goteborg was spread out, and, in the distance, a nyckelharpa was weeping."

"And what did you do?" I asked, now completely immersed in the history (although a bit seasick from so many names of places and locales).

"Without even opening the dossier of parchments, I retraced my steps. I went back down the corridor and down to the Table Dance-Bar, I opened the door and I went out into the night, right onto the Paseo de Pereda, in Santander, in the Cantabrian Sea. I put to towards Bilbao, entering Euskal Herria. I saw young people dancing Eurresku and Ezpatadantza to the rhythm of the txistu and the tabor, close to Donostia-San Sebastian. I climbed the Pyrenees and picked the Ebro River back up between Huesca and Zaragoza. There they managed to make me a vessel, and I continued on to the delta where the Mediterranean receives the Ebro, in the midst of the roar of the Vent de Dalt. I climbed Tarragonia by foot, and from there to Barcelona, passing by where the famous Battle of Montjuic took place." Durito paused, as if to gather speed.

"In Barcelona, I set off in a freighter that carried me to Palma de Mallorca. We headed southwest, skirting Valencia and, further south, Alicante. We sighted Almeria, and, further along, Granada. Throughout Andalucia, a flamenco song spread palms, guitars and heels. A huge gypsy fiesta accompanied us until, after doubling back by way of Algeciras, we crossed Cadiz, and at the mouth of the Guadalquivir, 'voices of death sounded,' coming from Cordoba and Seville. A flamenco song called out: 'Sleep now Durito, beloved son of the world, cease your aimless wandering, and may your path be beautiful.' We had just managed to sight Huelva, and then we headed to the 7 main islands of the Canaries. We put in there, and joined up with a bit of sap from the tree they call the 'Dragon,' good, they say, for the ills of the body and soul. That is how I arrived at the island of Lanzarote and had the altercation with Don Pepe, which I have already mentioned."

"Uff! You have traveled far," I said, weary from just the telling of Durito's long journey.

"And what I have left out!" he said, proudly.

I asked: "Then, you are no longer a knight errant?"

"Of course! The 'pirate' thing is temporary. Only as long as I am carrying out the mission entrusted to me by the deceased Redbeard."

Durito was staring at me.

I was thinking: Whenever Durito stares at me like that it's because... because...

"No!" I told him.

"'No' what? I haven't said anything to you," says Durito, feigning surprise.

"No, you haven't said anything to me, but that look doesn't augur well. Whatever you were going to say to me, my answer is 'no'. I have enough problems as a guerrilla to get involved now as a buccaneer. And I'm not crazy enough to set sail in a sardine can!"

"'Pirate', not 'buccaneer'. It's not the same, my dear and large-nosed cabin boy. And it's not a sardine can, it's a frigate and it's called 'Learn From Mistakes'."

I ignored the insult and replied:

"'Learn From Mistakes'? Mmh, strange name. But, in the end, 'Buccaneer' or 'Pirate', or whatever, means trouble."

"As you wish, but, before anything else, you should carry out your duty," Durito says solemnly.

"My duty?" I ask, letting down my guard.

"Yes, you should communicate the good news to the entire world."

"What 'good news'?"

"Why, that I have returned. And it doesn't have to be one of those long, dense, boring communiqués with which you torture your readers. Also, in order not to run any risks, I have the text written out here." Having said that, Durito takes a paper out from one of his bags.

I read and re-read. I turn around to look at Durito and begin with the 'no, no and no' that began this tale.

In order not to bore you more, I will tell you that Durito was trying to get me to release a letter or communiqué, with national and international civil society as the recipients, announcing that Durito had now returned.

Of course I refused, since I had to respond to the letter sent to us by those who are participating in the International Civil Commission for Human Rights Observation (CCIDOPLDH), asking us to grant them the same trust which we gave them in 1998, to receive them and to give them our word, and they would then shortly be coming for a new visit. And so it goes:

ZAPATISTA ARMY OF NATIONAL LIBERATION
October of 1999
To the International Civil Commission of Human Rights Observation

Brothers and Sisters,

In the name of the children, women, men and old ones of the Zapatista Army of National Liberation and of the Indigenous Communities in Resistance, I am communicating to you that it would be an honor for us for you to visit our lands. You have our trust; you will be treated with the respect you deserve as international observers, and you will not have, on our part, any impediments to your humanitarian work. It would also be our great pleasure to talk with you. We await you.

Vale. Salud and remember that here, in addition to dignity, mud also abounds.

From the Island that 'Has No Name', excuse me,
From the Mountains of the Mexican Southeast,
Subcomandante Insurgente Marcos.
Mexico, "Learn From Mistakes" Frigate, October of 1999.

Look out: Postscripts follow.

P.S. WHICH EXTENDS ITS ARM FOR TWISTING - It so happens that, following my repeated negatives, Durito convinced me, offering me part of the treasure. Yes, we have reviewed the parchments, and there is a treasure map. Of course, we still must decipher it, but the prospect of an adventure is irresistible.

P.S. FOR NATIONAL AND INTERNATIONAL CIVIL SOCIETY -

"Madame,

It is a great honor for me to be able to communicate to you the super duper (so says Durito's text) good news, the gift that will cause the small and great to rejoice. Let the great financial centers tremble! Let panic reach the palaces of the grand and false gentlemen! Let those from below celebrate! Let all hopes be reborn, and the most terrible nightmares prepare for their departure! May the most beautiful damsels prepare their best galas and may the spring of their hearts sigh! May good men take off their hats! May the children dance with joy! The best and greatest of pirates (crossed out in the original), excuse me, of the knights errant, that the world has ever seen, has returned! Don Durito of La Lacandona! (copyrights) (so says Durito's text). Hooray for humanity! Our most heartfelt condolences for neoliberalism. He is here, the great, I say 'grand', gigantic, marvelous, superlative, hyper-mega-plus, supercalifragilisticespialidoso (so says Durito's text), the only, the incomparable, himself, HIMSELF, Don Durito of La Lacandona! Yessssss! (so says Durito's text)."

End of Durito's text (from which I totally distance myself).

Okay then.

Durito is back now. (Sigh).

I don't know why I'm starting to get a headache.

Vale. Salud, and does anyone have an aspirin?

The SupPirate (looking extraordinarily handsome with the patch over his right eye).

77. THE HOUR OF THE LITTLE ONES, II

Second Part: THOSE OF BELOW
For all those little and different

> "*Soon will come those crazed with power refined/disloyal/a bit cannibalistic owners of the mountains and the valleys of the floods and the earthquakes those standard-bearers sans standard charitable and mean clothing letters favors demands sheathed in the letter box of time.*"
> - Mario Benedetti

The storm is letting up a bit now. The crickets are taking advantage of the clearing and they are going back to chirping the dawn. A great black cowl covers the sky. Another rain is being readied, although the puddles down below report they are already full. The night has its own words now, and it takes out apparently forgotten histories. This is the hour of the history of those of below, the hour of the little ones.

Down below, the long wail of a snail is calling, shadows answer it in silence, the snug iron and the hurried black covering their faces. The guards exchange passwords, and, to the "Who goes there?" hope invariably responds, "The Patria!" Night watches over the world of the forgotten. To do that she has made soldiers of their remembrances, and she has armed them with memory, in order to relieve the pain of the smallest ones.

Raining or not, down below the shadow without face continues his vigil. Most certainly he continues writing, or reading, but, always, smoking that increasingly foreshortened pipe. Good, there is nothing to do up here, so let's visit the little house again. That way, if it rains again, we'll be under cover. Here we are. Vaya! The mess is even more widespread now. Papers, books, pens, old lighters. The shadow toils away at his writing. He is filling pages and pages. He goes back to them. He takes some away, adds some. On the little tape player, a very otherly sound, like music from a far off land, in an equally different language.

"Very other," I said. Yes, at the hour of the small ones, the other, the different, also has its place. And that is what our visited shadow must be thinking of, because I have managed to read that "The Other" heads one of the pages.

But give us time for him to finish or to more completely define the bridge between what he is thinking and feeling and that elusive coquette that is the word. Good, he seems to have finished. He rises slowly and slowly goes over to the corner that serves as his bed. We are in luck, he has left the candle on guard. Yes, a few pages have been conveniently left on the table. It is in the first, which reads...

ANOTHER LETTER, ANOTHER BROKEN SILENCE. Letter 4B.

For the victims of earthquakes and floods.

I did not write the letter which now follows, I received it. Jolting about in a little paper boat, a river of rainwater brought the wet pages and damp letters to my hut.

October 8, 1999. 04.45 a.m.

Sup,

Here it is for you to distribute among your nets. Aside from the natural tragedy, what most pains is the criminal violence which - from the heights of Power - rains over a bleak, crippled, ignorant, exhausted population full of pain. We must do something for the more than 500,000 victims. These torrential rains have left children, old ones, men and women WITH NOTHING, especially the indigenous and campesinos, those condemned by this ruthless and genocidal, merciless and demagogic system. I am sharing with you a letter given to me by a young woman with whom I was speaking yesterday morning; in it one can feel the harsh reality that is battering us:

Or, as took place in the Town called _____ (put in any name of any affected community, the history is the same), visited by Zedillo and Governor _____ (put in the name of any governor, they are the same), along with their entire news machinery, with many trucks of food and aid, and - as soon as the helicopters carrying them took off - the trucks with the aid also started up, leaving just some of it, which moves us to something more than indignation. They are informing each Town that they are not giving us aid because they are aiding and attending to others who are more needy, not knowing that there is communication between all the Towns (the communication, which functions effectively, at least for learning about the situations in the Communities, is Civil Band), and that is how we found out that there is not effective aid for any of the towns (only some of them are reporting a minimal and scant aid that is consumed as soon as it is received). In the particular case of _____ (name of an indigenous community) (and it would appear to be the case everywhere), the only thing that is needed is for the road to be restored, since the civil organizations will be in charge of taking care of everything from the food to the housing needs. The concentration of the best and only means of communication (helicopters) causes the Government to become arrogant and to think that they are the only ones who understand and who are handling the situation. But the government machinery is insufficient for the opening and restoration of the roads: nonetheless, the officials in charge of that are not going to the Towns and Organizations that have the capability and the willingness to help, either.

_____ (name of state) most likely to be the last state in the unfair and inequitable distribution of federal funds.

At the beginning of his administration, Zedillo said that that his social policies would be put to the test in this state: he failed; because not only did he not manage to grant the state the resources necessary and sufficient for us to rise above marginalization and the thousand year backwardness to which we have been subjected (it is no use mentioning that the primary problem of _____ (name of state) is impoverishment, and that everything else is the effects of that), but, in addition, nor did he do enough to safeguard that the little that does come is administered well, and, finally, nor was there a satisfactory response in the cases of disasters (although within the Media, they have dressed it up and shown off).

The tragedy continues: the torrential rains are added to the earthquake. Just last night our promoters reported through Civil Band radio on an extremely serious situation that I'll sketch here: In _____ (indigenous community), 100 homes des-troyed by the EARTHQUAKE and 80 swept away by the river, a helicopter took them a minimal delivery of food, there are close to 250 sick children; in _____ (name of municipality) the Communities of _____ and _____ (names of indigenous communities) are abandoned, nothing has been taken to them, a helicopter just landed in order to greet them and it left; in _____ (municipality) they only took a minimal amount of aid to the community of _____ (indigenous community) (a third of the Community was buried under a mountain), while the other nine communities are still incommunicado; in _____ (municipality), in addition to 70% of the houses having been destroyed, the river swept away fields, coffee plantations and cut off roads, they have already been visited and they left them food (25 packets of meal), 3 boxes of water and 12 boxes of oil). The situation is dramatic: not only has the emergency not been overcome, but it is worsening: they lack medicines, clothing, covers, non-perishable food, sheets... In response, we have joined 4 Organizations together in order to stock-pile resources and to pool donations. We are not going to leave them. Not now."

The letter ends there. I mean, what can be read. The rest is smudged by water and with mud.

"What do you think?" I asked him.

"It's not the government's criminal irresponsibility that is surprising. Certainly they are not responsible for earthquakes and rains, but it is disgusting how they have confronted the situation. The misfortune of those of below only serves them to appear on the front pages and in the headlines of the electronic media. But that is not what strikes one, it was to be expected. The really great and impressive thing is that 'We are not going to leave them. Not now.'"

"Yes," I said, "as if another silence has been broken."

"There will be more..." says Durito, dropping to my boot.

Outside, the morning is breaking through the dawn.

Vale. Salud and, in agreement, "not now."

Subcomandante Insurgente Marcos.
The Sup, remaining respectfully silent.

78. THE HOUR OF THE LITTLE ONES, III

Third Part: THE UNDOCUMENTED OTHERS
For the "café" men and women in the United States

> *"We are the emigrants/the pale anonymous ones with the heathen and carnal century/on our backs where we accumulate the legacy of questions and perplexities."*
> - Mario Benedetti

Durito recounts that, once over the border, a wave of terror struck out at him and pursued him. It is not just the threat from "immigration" and the "kukluxk-lanes." It is also the racism that fills each and every one of the corners of the reality of the country of the clouded stars and stripes. In fields, on the street, in businesses, in school, in cultural centers, on television and in publications, even in bathrooms, everything pursues you to renounce your color, which is the best way of renouncing one's culture, land, history, that is, surrendering the dignity which, being other, is in the café color of the Latinos in North America.

"Those brownies," say those who hide behind the classification of human beings according to the color of their skin, the crime of a system that classifies according to purchasing power, always directly proportional to the sales price (the more you sell, the more you can buy). If the "brownies" have survived the campaign of bleach and detergent by the Powers of the American Union, it has been because the "café" Latin community (not just Mexican, but also Mexican and Puerto Rican, and Salvadoran, and Honduran, and Nicaraguan, and Guatemalan, and Panamanian, and Cuban, and Dominican, to mention some of the shades in which the Latin American café color paints North America) has known how to build a network of resistance without name and without hegemonic organization or as a product that is sponsored. Without ceasing to be "the others" in a white nation, Latinos carry one of the most heroic and unknown histories of this dying 20th century: that of their color, hurt and worked until it is made hope. Hope that café will be one more color in the rainbow of the races of the world, and it will no longer be the color of humiliation, of contempt and of forgetting.

And it is not just the "café" that suffers and is persecuted. Durito recounts that, in addition to his status as Mexican, must be added the black color of his shell. This courageous beetle was, thus, "brown and black," and he was doubly persecuted. And he was doubly helped and supported, since the best of the Latino and black communities protected him. In that way he was able to travel through the main North American cities, as those urban nightmares are also called. He did not walk the tourist's route, the glamour and the marquees. Durito walked the streets of below, where blacks and Latinos are building the resistance that will allow them to be, without ceasing to be the other. But, Durito says, that is a history for other pages.

And now "Black Shield" Durito, or "Escudo Negro" Durito (if you are not globalized) has begun insisting on the importance of my announcing, with great fanfare, his new book, which he has called "Cuentos de Vela en Vela." He has now given me a story which, he says, he wrote in remembrance of those days when he was a "wetback" or "mojado" in the United States.

"Above and Below are Relative... Relative to the Struggle that is Waged to Subvert Them" Letter 4C. (included in the story).

"It's a very long title," I tell Durito.

"Don't complain and put the story in or there'll be no treasure," Durito threatens with his hook. Vale, then:

"Once upon a time there was a little floor that was very sad because everything was happening above him. Why do you complain? the other floors asked him. What else could happen to a floor? And the little floor remained silent about his dream of flying lightly and having the little cloud fall in love with him, the one that appeared from time to time and paid him no mind. The little floor became more and more unhappy, and his sorrow was such that he began to weep. To weep and weep and weep and weep."

"How many times are you going to put 'and he wept'? Two or three would be enough," I interrupted Durito.

"No one is going to censure the great 'Black Shield' Durito, much less a big-nosed cabin boy, and, even worse, one who has the flu," Durito threatened me, while pointing out the fearsome plank over which the wretched walked to the bellies of the sharks. I gave in silently. Not because the sharks are frightening, but because a dip would prove fatal to my perennial flu.

"And he wept and he wept and he wept. The little floor wept so much that all and everyone began slipping if they were above, or walking above, him. And now he had nothing and no one above him. And the little floor wept so much that he was becoming very thin and light. And, since he no longer had anything or anyone above him, the little floor began to float and he flew very high. And he got his own way and he is now called sky. And the cloud in question turned into rain and now she is on the floor and she writes him futile letters saying: 'cielito lindo.' Moral: Do not look down on what is beneath you, because, on the day you least expect it, it can fall on your head. And tan-tan."

"'Tan-tan'? Is the story over?" I futilely asked. Durito was no longer listening to me. Remembering his old days, when he worked as a mariachi in the East End of Los Angeles, California, he had put on a cowboy hat and was singing, off-key, the one that goes: "Ay, ay, ay, ay, sing and do not weep, because when you sing, cielito lindo, you bring joy to hearts." And afterwards, an out of tune shout of "Ay Jalisco, no te rajes!"

Vale. Salud and I believe we will be late in setting sail. Durito has become determined to make modifications to the can of sardines... excuse me, to the frigate, so that it will look like a "low raider."

El Sup rale ...sssse.

P.S. OF WACHA BATO - Can anyone help? Durito is determined that the menu on board will include "chilli hot dogs" and "burritos." A qué carnal ésssse!

79. THE HOUR OF THE LITTLE ONES, IV

Fourth Part: THE OTHER...

> *"So they loved as love in twaine,*
> *Had the essence but in one,*
> *Two distincts, Division none,*
> *Number there in love was slaine."*
> -William Shakespeare, The Tortoise and the Phoenix

THE TRUE HISTORY OF MARY READ AND ANNE BONNY.

For lesbians, homosexuals, transsexuals and transvestites, with admiration and respect.

While reviewing the parchments, I discovered a history that Durito asked me to include in his new book, "Cuentos de Vela en Vela." It is about a letter whose sender is unknown (the signature is illegible). The addressee is also an enigma, although it is clearly noted, it is not clear whether it is a he or a she. Better that you see it yourselves. Upon my soul, if the lack of definition between the masculine and feminine is not quite explained in the epistle itself. The date is smudged, and we do not have the technology here to verify when it was written. But it also seems to me that it could have been as easily written centuries ago as weeks ago.

You will understand me.

Sale pues.

Letter 4D.

"You,

The histories of the pirates recount that there were two women, Mary Read and Anne Bonny, who dressed up as men, and, as such, sailed the seas in the company of other buccaneers, taking towns and vessels, hoisting the standard of the skull and crossbones. It was the year of 1720 and different histories have the one and the other living and fighting the eventful navigation of those times. In a pirate ship, commanded by Captain John Rackam, they met each other. They recount that, the one thinking the other was a man, love blossomed and, upon learning the truth, everything returned to normal, and each went their own way.

It was not like that. This, which I am writing you, is the true history of Mary Read and Ann Bonny. I was confided the other history, the one that will not appear in books, because they still persist in spinning only the normality and good sense they all have, and the normality of the 'other' goes no further than disapproving silence, condemnation or neglect. This is part of the history that walks the underground bridges that the 'others' extend, in order to be, and to be known.

The history of Mary Read and Anne Bonny is a history of love, and, as such, it has its visible parts, but the greatest is always hidden, in the depths. In the visible part, there is a ship (a sloop, to be more precise), and a pirate, Captain John Rackam. Both, ship and pirate, were protectors and accomplices of that love that was so very 'otherly' and 'different' that the history of above had to cover it up in order for it to be heard by later generations.

Mary Read and Anne Bonny loved each other knowing they shared the same essence. Some histories relate that the two were women, who, dressed as men, met each other knowing they were women, and, as such, loved each other under the affectionate gaze of Lesbos. Others say that the two were men who concealed themselves behind pirates' clothes, that they were attracted to the same sex, and that they hid their homosexual love and their passionate meetings behind the complicated story of women pirates disguised as men.

In either case, their bodies met in the mirror that discovers that which, by being obvious, is forgotten: those corners of the skin that have knots which, when undone, inspire sighs and torments; places sometimes known only to those who are the same. With lips, skin and hands, they extended the bridges that joined those who were the same, making them different.

Yes, in whichever case, Mary Read and Anne Bonny were transvestites who, in the masquerade, discovered each other and met. In both cases, being the same, they revealed themselves as being different, and the two lost all separateness and became one. To the unconventionality of their being pirates, Mary Read and Anne Bonny added that of their 'abnormal' and marvelous love.

Homosexuals or lesbians, transvestites always, Mary and Anne overcame with courage and cast out those whom 'normality' would put in chains. While the men surrendered without putting up any resistance, Mary and Anne fought to the end, before being taken prisoners. In this way they honored the words of Mary Read. To the question of whether she feared dying, 'She replied that, as to dying on the gallows, she did not think it so cruel, because, if it were not for that, all the cowards would become pirates and they would infest the seas to such an extent that the men of courage would die of hunger; that if the punishment were left up to the pirates, they would have none other than death, because their fear of that keep some cowardly criminals honorable; that many of those who today were swindling widows and orphans and oppressing their poor neighbors who have no money in order to obtain justice would go out onto the seas to rob, and the ocean would be full of thieves in the same way that the land is...' ("General History of the Thefts and Assassinations of the Most Famous Pirates" Daniel Defoe. Ed. Valdemar. Madrid, 1999. Translation by Francisco Torres Oliver).

Homosexuals or lesbians? I do not know, the truth that comes down: John Rackam, to his grave when he was hung in Port Royal (November 17, 1720); and the sloop that served them as bed and accomplice, to the shipwreck that rent it asunder. Whatever, their love was very 'other' and great for being different. Because it so happens that love follows its own paths and is, always, a transgressor of the law...

I do my duty by telling you this story.

Adios"

(an illegible signature follows)

There ends the story... or does it continue?

Durito says that those who are different in their sexual preferences are doubly "other," since they are "other" within those who are in themselves other.

I, a bit seasick from so much "other," ask him: "Can't you explain that a bit more?"

"Yes," says Durito. "When we are struggling to change things, we often forget that that also includes changing ourselves."

Above, the dawn is changing itself and making itself "other" and different. The rain followed, as well as the struggle...

Vale once more, with pleasure. Salud, and do not tell anyone, but I have not been able to figure out how in the hell I'm going to fit into the sardine can (sigh).

Subcomandante Insurgente Marcos.
The Sup, bailing water out of the frigate because, as you can imagine, it has begun raining again and Durito says that bailing water out is one of my "privileges."

80. THE HOUR OF THE LITTLE ONES, X

PART X: THE STUDENT OTHERS
To the young university students on strike.

"Sorrow takes hold of us, brother men, from behind, from the side, and it crazes us in the cinema, it batters us in gramophones, it thrashes us in beds, it falls straight down onto ourtickets, onto our letters..."
- Cesar Vallejo

All night long, raining. Dawn arrives and still the rain is there, washing roads, hills, fields, paths, huts. It is like a pounding of urgent drops, and completely without order, falling on roofs, on trees, on puddles that are already full, and, finally, onto the ground. Because that is how the hour of the little goes, disorderly, desperate, manifold.

Down below... We will have to wait to know what is going on down below, because now one cannot take a step without the mud seducing you and you end up kissing it with your entire body. Yes, it is rather complicated to define a fall this way, but it is raining so much that there is time for that and more. A fall... There are times that one falls and there are times that one is fallen on. I mean, there are falls and there are falls.

What? Yes? The rain is slowing down? Yes, but the mud is not. Good, let's go, but slowly. It is dark. Perhaps there will not be anyone, or perhaps the shadow that concerns us has finally gone to sleep. Shall we have a look? Do you have a lamp? Fine. Mmh. No, there is no one.

There is the usual disorder on the table. But today there is a different sheet on it. At one side, a copy of "La Jornada" newspaper, dated October 15, 1999. The headlines say "Riot Police and Strikers Clash on Beltway." A photograph takes up half the page. What? Do you want it described to you? Good, bring the light closer... There... Fine. It's in black and white. In the foreground there is a girl knocked down in the street, with her face bloody. Next to her, someone is being kicked by 3 riot police (two in the foreground and a third, between those two, half hidden by his shield and using his right hand to support himself while he's kicking). There are more details below: the photograph is by Rosaura Pozos, the girl on the ground is called Alejandra Pineda, and the person next to her, under the boots of the riot police, is her brother, Argel Pineda, one of the representatives of the General Strike Council, the scene is the South Beltway. In the photograph, the rest of the riot police (at least 6 more, if one carefully observes the number of helmets) are looking to the right of the photograph, only the last one in the scene is turned towards the pair of students, hesitating between continuing on ahead or joining the ones who are thrashing the young person on the ground.

More details? Good, at the back of the action of the blows against Angel and Alejandra, 5 men can be perfectly made out. Three of them are pointing their lenses (two are carrying still cameras and one a video camera) toward the right of the photograph. The other two are looking towards the scene of the kicking, one of them, with a checked shirt, is scratching his ear or holding something to his ear, the other is simply looking. Further back, in the far background, two vehicles can barely be made out: an automobile whose driver is blocked by the legs of the man who is just looking, and the front of another vehicle (probably a van), whose driver is looking in front of him, that is, to the left of the photograph. In the very far background, to the right, three "entertainment guides," whose texts cannot be read (that on the extreme right seems to be announcing a news program). In the same perspective, to the left, there is something that looks like a tower, of the type that has lamps or entertainment guides in its topmost part.

Good, I think that's all then. What did you say? The written sheet? What does it say? Yes, I'll read it...

LETTER TO A PHOTOGRAPH Letter 4

Ms. Photograph,

You will excuse me, but I was not able to see you until the dawn of the 17th day of October. No, do not think that I am reproaching you. I understand that, with so much rain, you have been delayed. Besides, the weight you carry is not at all light. You know? When I saw you, I felt a sadness here. Yes, I already know that there are photographs that hurt, I only wanted you to know that you are one of those.

If we go by the reporter's work (Roberto Garduño), we will have more means with which to read you. The girl, Alejandra Pineda, is a student at Preparatory 5, and her brother Argel is from the Faculty of Political Science, both from the UNAM. After the photograph (so we assume from the narrative), that is, after the blows from the riot police, Argel tries to help and to calm Alejandra, "who asked about her compañeros: How are they? They aren't hitting them more? My head hurts a lot, we don't want any more repression, we want free education." (La Jornada. October 15, 1999, p. 66). According to that reporter, and to some statements gathered by the same newspaper, the students were already withdrawing towards City University when they were attacked by the riot police.

What you speak with your image, and what the chronicles, reportage and statements describe, say some things to me. But - do you know? - there are other questions that are not answered by your image or in the inside pages. Then I would like you, Madame photograph, to allow me to ask you a few questions. Alright?

1. How old was Alejandra before the beating? 17, 18? And Argel? How old are they now?

2. If my eyes do not deceive me: the riot police are beating up Alejandra and Argel on the Beltway access road and not on the main lanes (which are the ones they were going to "dislocate")?

3. The riot police who are looking to the right in the photograph: are they looking that way in order to not see what their compañeros are doing? Or are they protecting the 3 who are beating up Alejandra and Argel, in order to prevent someone from coming and rescuing them? Further over there (to the right of the photograph), is another beating taking place? Are the students withdrawing?

4. The Mexico City government: is it beating up Alejandra for the crime of being Argel's sister? Is it beating up Argel for the crime of coming to Alejandra's aid? Is it beating up both of them for the crime of being "ultras"? Is it beating them because the cars are demanding free transit? Is it beating them because the polls demand it? Is it beating them to attract applause on Televisa and TV Azteca? Is it beating them for being young persons? Is it beating them for being students? Is it beating them for being university students? Is it beating them so that it can demonstrate in that way that they govern with firmness? Pardon me, Madame photograph, but I do not understand. Why are they beating Alejandra and Argel?

5. The women who congratulated Rosario Robles for having become head of the Mexico City government: did they also congratulate her for ordering the beating of Alejandra? She: did she send Alejandra a kind word? Were they silent? Or did they say to themselves: "she deserved it for being rebellious"? What? Yes, excuse me, you would have no way of knowing that...

6. You, Madame photograph, show at least 3 riot police hitting the student: why were only two brought before the authorities?

7. That billy club the riot policeman on the extreme right is carrying: is it an appeal to dialogue? A demonstration that the current government in Mexico City is "different" from the previous ones? Or is it merely the measure of the distance that separates words from actions?

8. Who is the man in the checked shirt talking to, if it's a cell phone that he has at his left ear?

9. The driver of the car that is moving, and who is not visible in the photograph: would he applaud the beatings the police are giving Alejandra and Argel?

10. What is it that Alejandra has under her body, other than blood, I mean? A poncho? A sweater? A cloth? A jacket?

11. The driver furthest back. is he inviting us to do the same? To pass by in front of the photograph of bloody Alejandra and fallen Argel, without looking at them, without looking at her?

12. On page 69 of the newspaper in which you are the headline, there is another photograph (also by Rosaura Pozos, with the caption: "Scene prior to the police dislocation on South Beltway"). In it can be seen, in the foreground, a young man, in a checked shirt, on his knees in front of a line of riot police. The young man has his backpack in front of his knees, and he is showing the riot police a book. On the police shields clearly can be read: "Public Security. Riot Police. Federal District." In the mid-ground, a woman with a hat. Further back, a cameraman. At the rear, trees and buildings. The questions...

12a. What is the title of the book the young man is showing the riot police?

12b. Is the young man on his knees saying something to the riot police?

12c. Was not Point 3 of the list of demands from the National Strike Committee of the 1968 movement, I cite it verbatim: "Abolition of the Riot Police Force, direct instrument of repression, and no establishment of similar forces" ("War Report." Julio Scherer and Carlos Monsivais, p. 161)?

12d. Is the existence and operation of the Riot Police Force constitutional?

What do you say? That is something that should be asked of the other photograph? Good, you are right. Allow me some questions:

Do you remember that the reason for the march by the students was to protest the news coverage by TV AZTECA and TELEVISA of the university conflict?

If you, Madame photograph, had not spoken: would we have remained with only the version that the electronic media and the Mexico City government gave out on the night of October 14 of 1999, in which the students were the aggressors, the police who intervened were all women, and only one student was injured ("nothing serious") by a "vehicle that ran over her"?

Do we have the right to expect that a government headed by the PRD would act differently? Should we remain silent and not ask anything?

You know, Madame photograph, that you give reason to the "Letter 3A." But you will see how much I would have wished that you had not given reason to that letter, but rather to those who, in front of a hollow mirror, boast of being "proud officials of a democratic government like Mexico City's."

And you know what? Every time I look at you, Madame, I do not know why, but I am taken by an irresistible urge to pick up a rock and to hurl it far and to break forever that silence that there, above, accomplice, remains quiet.

What? Yes, go on, Madame photograph, continue on your way and continue asking. So inconvenient you are, Madame photograph, such a busybody.

Vale. Salud and I believe that what Alejandra had under her body is a flag. And I also believe that it was raised up, along with her.

The Sup, accumulating questions as if they were rain.

81. SUBCOMANDANTE INSURGENTE MARCOS TO LEONARD PELTIER

October of 1999
Ejército Zapatista de Liberación Nacional Mexico
For: Leonard Peltier
From: Subcomandante Insurgente Marcos

Leonard,

Through the NCDM and Cecilia Rodriguez we extend greetings from the men, women, children and elders of the Zapatista Army of National Liberation.

Cecilia has told us about the grave injustice the North American judicial system has committed against you. We understand that the powerful are punishing your spirit of rebellion and your strong fight for the rights of indigenous people in North America.

Stupid as it is, the powerful believe that through humiliation, arrogance and isolation it can break the dignity of those who give thoughts, feelings, life and guidance to the struggle for recognition and respect for the first inhabitants of the land over whom, the vain United States has risen. The heroic resistance that you have maintained in prison, as well as the broad movement of solidarity, that your case and your cause have motivated in the U.S. and the world reveal their mistake.

Knowing of your existence and history, no woman or man if they are honest and conscious can remain silent before such a great injustice. Nor can they remain still in front of a struggle, which like all that is born and grows from below, is necessary, possible, and true.

The Lakota, a people who have the honor and fortune to have you among their blood, have an ethic that recognizes and respects the place of all people and things, respects the relations that mother earth has with herself and other living things that live and die within her and outside of her. An ethic that recognizes generosity as a measure of human worth, the walk of our ancestors and our dead along the paths of today and tomorrow, women and men as part of the universe that have the power of free will to choose paths and seasons, the search for harmony and the struggle against that which breaks and disorders it. All of this, and more that escapes because we are so far away, has a lot to teach the "western" culture which steers, in North America and in the rest of the world, against humanity and against nature.

Probably the determined resistance of Leonard Peltier is incomprehensible to the Powerful in North America, and the world. To never give up, to resist, the powerful call this "foolishness". But the foolish are in every corner of the world, and in all of them, resistance flourishes in the fertile ground of the most ancient history.

In sum, what the powerful fail to understand is not only Peltier's resistance, but also the entire worlds, and so they intend to mold the planet into the coffin the system represents, with wars, jails and police officers.

Probably, the powerful in North America think that in jailing and torturing Leonard Peltier, they are jailing and torturing one man.

And so they don't understand how a prisoner can continue to be free, while in prison.

And they don't understand how, being imprisoned, he speaks with so many, and so many listen.

And they don't understand how, in trying to kill him, he has more life.

And they don't understand how one man, alone, is able to resist so much, to represent so much, to be so large.

"Why?" the powerful ask themselves and the answer never reaches their ears:

Because Leonard Peltier is a people, the Lakota, and it is impossible to keep a people imprisoned.

Because Leonard Peltier speaks through the Lakota men and women who are in themselves and in their nature the best of mother earth.

Because the strength that this man and this people have does not come from modern weapons, rather it comes from their history, their roots, their dead.

Because the Lakota know that no one is more alive than the dead.

Because the Lakota, and many other North American Indian people, know that resisting without surrender not only defends their lives and their liberty, but also their history and the nature that gives them origin, home, and destiny.

Because the great ones always seem so small to those who can not see the history that each one keeps inside.

Because the racism that now governs can only imagine the other and the different in jail - or in the trashcan, where two Lakota natives were found last month, murdered, in the community of Pine Ridge. This is justice in North America: those who fight for their people are in jail, those who despise and murder walk unpunished.

What is Leonard Peltier accused of?

Not of a crime he didn't commit. No. He is accused of being other, of being different, of being proud to be other and different.

But for the Powerful, Leonard Peltier's most serious "crime" is that he seeks to rescue in the past, in his culture, in his roots, the history of his people, the Lakota. And for the powerful, this is a crime, because knowing oneself with history impedes one from being tossed around by this absurd machine that is the system.

If Leonard Peltier is guilty, than we are all guilty because we seek out history, and on its shoulders we fight to have a place in the world, a place of dignity and respect, a place for ourselves exactly as we are, which is also, very much as we were.

If the Indian people of the North and Indian people of Mexico, as well as the indigenous people of the entire continent, know that we have our own place (being who we are, not pretending to be another skin color, another tongue, another culture), what is left is that other colors that populate the entire world know it. And what is left is for the powerful to know it. So that they know it, and learn the lesson so well that they won't forget, many more paths and bridges are needed that are walked from below.

On these paths and bridges, you, Leonard Peltier, have a special place, the best, next to us who are like you.

Salud, Leonard Peltier, receive a hug from one who admires and respects you, and who hopes that one day you will call him "brother".

Vale, and health to you and I hope that injustice disappears tomorrow, with yesterday as a weapon and today as a road.

From the mountains of the Mexican Southeast,
Subcomandante Insurgente Marcos.
Mexico, October 1999.

82. BETWEEN THE SATELLITE AND THE MICROSCOPE

November 20, 1999

(The following are some notes for the talk our CCRI-CG of the EZLN delegation will be having with a group of international observers from the CCIODH (International Civil Commission of Human Rights Observation). This talk was originally envisioned as a letter, anticipating that a personal meeting might not be possible. And now it remains as a letter, to be read out loud and face to face with the recipient, or rather, face to face with one of the recipients, because it is directed to national and international civil society.)

I chose the date of the anniversary of the Mexican revolution, in addition to its being a prank, in order to have two images of this century here: one is the face of Emilio Zapata, the other is the face of an indigenous girl, with her face partially covered with a red scarf. Further on I will speak of these two images again.

This is not about demonstrating that there is a war on the Indian lands of the Mexican southeast (the Mexican government is doing everything they can to deny something so obvious), but to understand why this war is continuing.

Yes, this war that began in January of 1994 should have ended almost four years ago, when the first San Andres Accords were signed and the dialogue process appeared to be progressing definitively towards the attainment of peace. There are reasons that the war continues, despite the fact that it could have been ended in a dignified and exemplary manner. Why war in Chiapas?

I ask for your patience and understanding. Given that I am not now restricted by the number of pages and considerations regarding the cost of paper and ink, I am thus able to expand on matters that would be dry if dealt with between the talks of Don Durito of the Lacandona and Old Antonio.

Sale, then, general theses, developed during the oral statement:

1. World Wars

- Constants: conquest and reorganization of territories, destruction of the enemy, administration of the conquest.
- Variables: military strategy. Actors involved. Weapons, tactics.
- World War III, the "Cold War" period. Two large superpowers, two nearby peripheries (Europe and part of Asia) and the rest as spectator and victims (Latin America, Oceania, Africa and the other part of Asia). The global arms race and local and regional wars.
- World War IV, the unipolar world to globalization. Neoliberalism. The double pair of destruction/depopulation and reconstruction/reordering, financial bombs. Destruction of

nation states and what is inherent in them (language, culture, politics, economics, social fabric). Homogenization and hegemony began producing and encouraging the growth of their opposites: fragmentation and the increase in differences.

From the vast unified world to the archipelago, controlled and linked by computers and bombs (financial and otherwise). The war against humanity, that is, against the essentially human: dignity, respect, difference.

2. Military War. Projection in Concepts and Action. Stages:

a. World War III or Cold War.

Conventional war on European lands, localized nuclear war (Europe, Cuba, the east), total nuclear war. Strategy of advance positions, permanent logistical lines, stable rearguard. The large pacts. NATO, Warsaw, SEATO. Local wars: local armies and support of the metropolis. The dictatorships in Latin America, the wars in Africa, the Middle East conflict. The concept of total war is constructed, here incorporating economic, ideological, social, political and diplomatic arenas. Local wars within the concept of the "domino theory." The justification: the defense of democracy, aid and the prevention of world threats (according to the logic of World War II).

b. World War IV.

Development and consolidation of the concept of total war. War anywhere and at anytime, under any circumstances. Evolution of military strategy. Strategy of rapid deployment (the invasion of Panama, the Persian Gulf war). Later, strategy of show of force rejected almost immediately, anticipating protests, "remember Vietnam." New readjustment: "international" and "local" soldiers for world wars and the use of supranational bodies (Kosovo and NATO-UN). The justification: the defense of human rights (humanitarian war), in globalization, the entire world is the powers' backyard, ergo, anything that happens in any part of the world can be considered a direct threat to domestic security.

3. The World Military War

Doctrines and Compartments.

a. Theatre of operations. From certainty to uncertainty, from systematic responses to versatility.

b. From the strategy of containment to that of extension. War is not limited to the military, but is extended to "non-war" actions, (the media and human rights). Therefore the "enemy" to be defeated is not just the opposing army or opposing armed force, but the entire social, political, economic and ideological framework within which the conflict develops. There are no longer "civilians" nor "neutrals," everyone is a "belligerent."

c. The readjustment of national armies in the new world strategy. The "super-police" and their local helpers. Like in Hollywood, the main star and the "extras." The destruction of nation states forces national armies to restructure and to redefine their functions.

d. The budget. War as business. World military restructuring will be expensive. The budget Clinton presented for fiscal year 2000, and until 2005, could reach close to 1.9 trillion dollars, distributed among several accounts. The US' defense plan for the "future" is that of considering the enemy to be... the human species. The budget includes 12.6 billion for the Pentagon, 112 billion for military personnel, 280.8 billion for the military budget and 274.1 for other defense matters. The budget includes 555 billion for discretionary spending (281 for military personnel). In 2005, the United States will be spending more than the annual average during the Cold War (All figures from "The Defense Monitor," Center for Defense Information, Washington, D.C. #1, 1999. <www.cdi.org>. Each one of the 6900 soldiers in Bosnia cost the United States $261,000, $1.8 billion for the year).

4. The War on the American Continent

a. The Cheney Doctrine. Drug trafficking as America's enemy. Replacement of the National Security doctrine with that of National Stability (limited sovereignty). Local and international police.
b. The role of NATO... the OAS! The hemispheric defense system.
c. The testing of "versatility." Colombia and Chiapas. The objectives: redefine the archipelago according to the logic of the market. Business centers throughout the world, but disguised as old or "new" countries.

5. The War in Chiapas

Total war and total enemy. Everyone is the enemy. The objective is to destroy: the Indian peoples. The hindrance: the EZLN.

6. The War in Chiapas: The Conquest of the Land and the Plunder of War

a. Occupation Army: Behaviors: control of local political power (extension of the war), ad hoc creation of the media, distrust of the civilians, war plunder (children, drug trafficking, trafficking in precious woods, trade in blancas, alcohol, promotions, business, wages, benefits and desertions). The Military Police (insubordination, desertion versus civilians).
b. The surgical strike and the total strike. Not very propitious political environment. All options available for the right moment.
c. For the surgical strike: the GAFE (Air Transport Group of Special Forces).
d. For the total strike: Forces deployed in order to "block" the area. Underground cells, tunnels and crypts in the large barracks (San Quintin).

7. The Mexican Army

It is an Army moving towards its restructuring. Its current nature is that of a pawn to be sacrificed in the warlike game called "Chiapas." Its tests in the role of "local" police: drug trafficking, organized crime, subversion.

a. Restructuring of the general command. The interests of the military zones and regions (quota of the generals' powers).

b. Movement in quantity: from 170,000 in 1996. The budget grew by 44% between 1995 and 1996.

c. Fights between arms and between the Army, Air Force and Navy.

d. North American interference: The USADO (United States Attache Defense Office) had two special teams in Chiapas in 1995, with the SEDENA's [Department of National Defense] blessing.

8. Individual Human Rights and Human Rights of the Peoples

Life, Culture, Difference, Future.

9. The Images

Emiliano Zapata, yesterday, common and different face facing the Power. The zapatista indigenous girl, the future, common and different face facing the powers. Between the one and the other, the indigenous rebels of the EZLN, without face, and questioning everything, even their own steps.

From the mountains of the Mexican Southeast,
By the Comandancia General
- Clandestine Revolutionary Indigenous Committee of the Zapatista Army of National Liberation,
Subcomandante Insurgente Marcos.
La Realidad at War.
November of 1999.

83. THE MACHINERY OF ETHNOCIDE

November, 1999

> "Night had fallen now and Ramon Balam and Domingo Canche reached the village by way of a shortcut. They had escaped from the massacre the whites had perpetuated against the Indians. Balam had received a machete wound in his back and he was bleeding. Jacinto Canek told them:
>
> The prophecies of Nahua Pech are now being fulfilled, one of the five prophecies of olden times. The whites could not be content with what was theirs, nor with what they had won in war. They also wanted our food to be scarce and our houses to be meager. They raised their hate against us and forced us to take refuge in the mountains and in the isolated places. We shall go then like the ants, after vermin and we shall eat bad things: roots, rooks, crows, rats and locusts of the wind. And the poverty of this food shall fill our hearts with bitterness and war shall come.
>
> The whites shall shout. The Indians have risen up!"
>
> - Ermilo Abreu Gomez, Canek - History and Legend of a Mayan Hero

The Department of Foreign Relations launched a news campaign via the Internet, in order to publicize the work that the Mexican government is carrying out in order to end poverty in Chiapas. The text that is being distributed, written in Spanish, English, French, Italian and German, says that officials have made great progress in Chiapas, in education, health, agrarian distribution and agricultural development. The document, however, does not mention the armed conflict nor the displaced indigenous.

To: National and International Civil Society
From: SupMarcos

Madame,

A document will be circulating, prepared by the Department of Foreign Relations, concerning the Mexican state of Chiapas, where they will elaborate on government actions in the fields of education, health, agrarian distribution and agricultural development. For the purpose of completing what the Mexican government is "informing" about, the EZLN is launching the following pamphlet, titled "CHIAPAS: THE WAR," which may be fully or partially reproduced, and which may also be made into a paper airplane and thrown in the face of any Mexican ambassador or consul of your choice, or it can be classified in the "horror" category in the "H" of "History." It may also be delivered to any UN high commissioner for human rights to whom they want to show rabasa's face.

Sale y vale,

You have the pamphlet in your hands. On the cover you can see the image of a world map that, curiously, has the same geographical shape as the southeastern Mexican state of Chiapas. On top, in "bold" or "black" letters (or "negritas," as they're called), and in capital letters, "CHIAPAS: THE WAR" can be read.

Under the "chiapanized" world map, in smaller letters, it says: "Is this what the last wars of the 20th century are like? Or is this how the wars of the 21st century shall be?"

On the back part, or the back page, the image is a ski-mask, in the space where the eyes should be there is a mirror. Underneath it can be read: "The full or partial reproduction of this pamphlet is not only permitted, it is required, and above all, of that which is silent."

On the first cover, some facts:

Country: Mexico

Area: 1,967,183 square kilometers

Population: 91,800,000 (1994)

Indigenous population: 10 million (official figures speak of a little more than 5 million)

State: Chiapas

Area: 74,211 square kilometers

Population: 3,607,128

Indigenous population: More than 1 million persons (the government mentions only 706,000)

The first page begins without palliatives, stating:

If you wish to find "Mexico" on a modern map, you should make haste, because the current governments have set about to destroy it, and, if they are successful, it will soon not be appearing on world maps. First, locate the American continent. Good, now find the one that is called "North America." Now, what appears to the south of the North American states of Texas, Arizona, Colorado and California is not (yet) one more star in the United States flag. Carefully observe that piece of the continent whose west coast is caressed by the Pacific Ocean, an earlier cut that left Baja California like a solitary right arm, and whose belly slims down in order to give a privileged place to the Atlantic Ocean (protected by the thumb of the Yucatan peninsula). What does it look like to you? Yes, you are right, its figure is that of a waiting hand. Good, that is Mexico. Uff! It's good to know it's still there.

Now take note of the facts that appear on the front cover. As you will see as you read this pamphlet, the number of the indigenous population will be decreasing. The Mexican government is carrying out a war whose first step envisages the elimination of almost half a million indigenous (precisely those who were "missing" in their census, those indigenous who reside in the so-called "conflict zone"). Government sources estimate that the number of indigenous who are zapatistas or who sympathize with the EZLN cause, is at least 450,000, ergo, they are "potential zapatistas," that is, "expendable."

With bullets, bombs, grenades, paramilitaries, forced sterilization, kidnapping and trafficking in infants, deterioration of the environment, cultural obliteration, and, above all, with forgetting, the Mexican indigenous are being annihilated in a war whose intensity in the media rises and falls, but which is constant and inexorable in the quota of death and destruction it claims in the chiapaneco reality.

Good, now concentrate on the southeastern corner of the Mexican map. That dark region, full of mountains, is Chiapas. Yes, "Chiapas," and not "Chapas," as Zedillo pronounces it. Who? Zedillo? Ah! He's the one who's in front, or, better, behind. No, I mean to the side. No, it would be better to say he's under. In sum, some call him "the President of Mexico," but no one takes that statement seriously in this country. Good, let's not become distracted. Take a red pencil and color in that corner, the last one in Mexico. Why red? Well, it means several things: "struggle," "conflict," "alert," "danger," "emergency," "blood," "struggle," "resistance," "halt," "war." Chiapas means all of that, but now we shall only be considering the red as "war."

Yes, there is a war here. Yes, soldiers, planes, helicopters, tanks, machine guns, bombs, injuries, deaths, destruction. The opposing sides? Fine, on one side is the Mexican government; on the other side are the indigenous. Yes, the government against the Indian peoples. What? No, I'm not talking about something that has happened, it's something that is going on right now. Yes, at this end of the 20th century, and when the 21st century is already unpacking its baggage of uncertainty, the Mexican government is making war against the very first inhabitants of this country, the indigenous.

What did you say? That the Mexican government says that it's not a war, but a "conflict?" Fine, let's look at some facts that can be confirmed "on site," through the simple method of observation, looking and listening. The problem is that the Mexican government characterizes the actions indicated by the verbs "look" and "listen" as crimes. Every Mexican citizen, or citizen of the countries of the 5 continents, must be mute and blind, on pain of jail, expulsion, threats, disappearance or death.

But let us suppose that you do not wish to be imprisoned, threatened or disappeared, if you are Mexican, or, if you are of another nationality, to be threatened, harassed and expelled from our country by government officials who despise those who come to confirm the news stories "on site." What can you do? Fine, that's what this pamphlet is for, in it we will tell you only what can be confirmed by simply looking, and not anything that requires an in-depth investigation and "contacts" very high up in the government - the North American government. As moral backing for this information, we will tell you that we have never lied to you, and we have no reason to do so now. But, even so, you still have every right to doubt, and so you can turn to the international and national press, or take a risk by visiting the Indian lands of the Mexican southeast. You will see that there is no doubt that a war is being unleashed under these skies, and that this war is against the Indian peoples.

Good. First fact of the war: the presence of an extraordinarily high number of government armed forces.

According to official figures, there are 30,000 Mexican Army troops stationed in Chiapas. Unofficial calculations state that there are close to 70,000. In response to the uprising of the Zapatista Army of National Liberation on January 1, 1994, the federal government sent - during the first week of January - close to 10,000 soldiers from the Mexican Army to the conflict zone; as well as 200 vehicles (artillery jeeps and tanks, among others) and 40 helicopters. During ten days of conflict, however, the number of troops grew to 17,000. In that same year, the federal government restricted the armed conflict to four municipalities: San Cristobal de Las Casas, Las Margaritas, Ocosingo and Altamirano. And then it was extended. In 1999, the Mexican Army widened its radius of action to 66 of the 111 municipalities in Chiapas. Yes, more than half the chiapaneco municipalities are in a state of war. In those municipalities, the maximum authority is military.

For the war in the Mexican southeast, the federal army is organized into the 7th Military Region, which has 5 military zones: the 30th, with headquarters in Villahermosa, the 31st in Rancho Nuevo, the 36th in Tapachula, the 38th in Tenosique and the 39th in Ocosingo. It also has the following Military Air Bases: Tuxtla Gutierrez, PEMEX City and Copalar.

Officially, the federal army's first force, the so-called "Rainbow Task Force" has 11 groups: San Quintin, Nuevo Momon, Altamirano, Las Tacitas, El Limar, Guadalupe Tepeyac, Monte Libano, Ocosingo, Chanal, Bochil and Amatitla'n. But the perspective of a bird in flight would be enough to realize that this is false.

This just in the so-called "conflict zone." In order to meet the official figure of "30,000" soldiers in Chiapas, these garrisons would have to have an average of 300 soldiers each, something which is obviously not true. The large barracks exceed that number by ten times. The large barracks at Rancho Nuevo, Ocosingo, Comita'n, Guadalupe Tepeyac and San Quintin have between 3000 and 5000 troops each.

According to indigenous and social organizations (distinct and distant from the EZLN), the Mexican Army currently has 266 military positions in Chiapas, which signifies a substantial increase from the 76 positions it held in 1995. In a letter directed to Ernesto Zedillo and to the Secretary of National Defense, Enrique Cervantes Aguirre, those groups with a presence in the Canadas of the selva of

Chiapas said that 37,000 soldiers are stationed in the municipalities of Ocosingo, Altamirano, Las Margaritas, La Independencia and La Trinitaria alone. In these five municipalities - they added - the population does not reach 300,000, meaning that there is one soldier for every nine residents. Because of this, they note in their document that "the withdrawal of the Mexican Army from our communities is the primary demand of the indigenous peoples of Chiapas, and does not represent merely the interests of a few." In addition to the "regular" forces classified in the army and air force military forces in Chiapas, the government has:

- 51 Special Forces Air Mobile Groups (GAFE), of which at least 5 are in Chiapas: one in El Sabino, another in Copalar, others in Teran, Tapachula and Tonina. In order to train these GAFE's, the United States earmarked 28 million dollars in 1997 and 20 million in 1998. From 1997 to 1998, some 2500 military personnel were trained in Fort Bragg, North Carolina and in Fort Benning, Georgia, in the United States.
- Also in Chiapas, there is a Rural Defense infantry corps, 6 infantry battalions, 2 motorized cavalry regiments, 3 mortar groups and 3 unclassified companies. There are also 12 unclassified companies in Salto de Agua, Altamirano, Tenejapa and Boca Lacantun. There are an average of 145 to 160 soldiers per company, and approximately 500 to 600 per battalion.
- Paramilitaries - There are at least 7 paramilitary groups: Red Mask, Peace and Justice, MIRA, Chinchulines, Degolladores, Punales, Albores of Chiapas. The person responsible for their activation, in 1995, was General Mario Renan Castillo, trained at Fort Bragg, North Carolina, in the US, who was, at that time, military chief of the 7th Military Region.

The equipment for this war is surprising (we are only using figures that are public):

- Purchases in 1994: 4 S70A Black Hawk helicopters from the Sikorsky Company. Others from the Bell and McDonnell-Douglas companies. 7573 grenade launching rifles, 18 M203P1 40 mm. grenade launchers, 500 sniper rifles, 473,000 items for maneuvers, 14,000 sleeping bags, 660,000 rations, 120,000 pistol holsters, 608 laser pointers and 208 pieces of night vision equipment, 500 Belgian anti-tank weapons, 856 HK19 automatic grenade launchers, 192 M2HB machine guns. They are also using RPG-7's and weapons similar to the B-300.
- In 1996, the North American Congress authorized $146,617,738 in sales to Mexico. Ten million in replacement parts for aircraft, 6 million in cartridges. One and a half million dollars in herbicides, 378 grenade launchers, 3 MD-500 helicopters, gas masks, more than 61 million dollars in anti-personnel chemical products.
- In 1997, 10,000 pistols, 1080 AR-15 rifles, 3193 M-16's and replacement parts for tanks and artillery vehicles.
- In 1998, sales of at least 62 million dollars are being forecast.
   (The figures are taken from "Mexican Armed Forces at the End of the Millennium. The Military in the Current Climate." Lopez y Rivas, Gilberto, Sierra Guzman, Jorge Luis, Enrique del Valle, Alberto. PRD Parliamentary Group. Chamber of Deputies. LVII Legislature).

The Mexican Air Force, according to a National Defense Department report, has, over the last 5 years of Ernesto Zedillo's 6-year administration, increased their aerial operations by 37% in comparison with the previous 6-year term. They are now carrying out up to 110 operations a day (versus 87 in the previous 6-year term). The allocation of planes and helicopters grew by 62%. At the beginning of Zedillo's administration, there were 246 aircraft; now there are 398 (without counting the 74 Huey helicopters that were returned to the US). (Figures from the Mexican Air Force Bulletin and "El Universal").

There is an accident every 29 days, a fatal accident every 105 days and a military aircraft is lost every 86 days. Every 26 days there are "incidents" that can be classified under what is known as "war stress." The "incidents" have increased by more than 43% since the previous 6-year term.

The providers of the aerial machines of death for Mexico are the United States, Switzerland and Russia (figures from the International Airpower Journal, from Lieutenant Colonel Luis F. Fuentes and from the United States Air Force). With their support, 5 counterinsurgency squadrons have been armed. One of the counterinsurgency squadrons (which has 5 Bell 205A-1, five Bell 206 JeRanger and 15 Bell 212 helicopters) is being sent to Chiapas, and its 25 helicopters are artillery.

In the arena of reconnaissance aircraft, of the two aerial photography squadrons (for the drawing up of plans) with 10 Rockwell 500S Commanders that exist, at least 4 of them are operating in the "conflict zone," and the search and rescue unit - which has nine Ial-201 Arava aircraft - at least 2 of which are slated for aerial surveillance of the rebel territory.

Regarding helicopters, the new acquisitions of Russian made craft should be noted, as well as the total equipment: 12 Mi-8's, 4 Mi-17's, four Bell 206's, 15 Bell 212's, three Sa-330 Puma aerospace and two Bell UH-60 Black Hawks. The FAM (Mexican Air Force) uses the Lockheed AT-33 as a combat ship, because they are equipped with a variety of armaments, such as Browning M 3 caliber machine guns, as well as two points under the wings to support bomb loads of 500 pounds and/or grenade launchers. According to the official report, the FAM has not used them in the Chiapas conflict (La Jornada).

The reality is otherwise. There are videos taken on the 5th and 6th of January of 1994, in which Lockheed AT-33 planes were bombing the outskirts of San Cristobal de Las Casas, Chiapas. These videos were taken by Amnesty International, and they include photographs of shrapnel and pieces of bombs or "rockets" ("Chiapas 1994", Steven Czitrom, 1999).

As if that were not enough, a group of 17 foreign observers, headed by the United States organization Global Exchange, denounced the existence of pitfall traps built by the military as part of a low intensity war against the EZLN. They explained that these traps consisted of holes dug in the ground, which were covered over with leaves and which had 40 centimeter long stakes at the bottom. They added that the traps were discovered near the community of Amador Hernandez. Meanwhile, the observers said that the armaments being provided by the United States to Mexico were not being used to fight drug trafficking, but rather for the war against the indigenous peoples.

After reading, in a little box, that: Mexico refused US aid from 1993-1995, but in 1996-1997 it accepted 7 million dollars from the Pentagon for training and equipment (Nacla Vol. XXXII . #3 November-December, 1998), you will turn the page and find the following subtitle:

The Other Business Of War

All of this gigantic military apparatus has its raison d'etre. Although the government ineffectively insists that it is a "containment" force facing the zapatista rebels, the truth is that it is a war contingent. A war whose objective is the destruction of the rebel Indian peoples first, and, above all, the rest of the indigenous. It is not just about physical elimination, but rather an elimination of a different culture. What is being pursued is the destruction, the annihilation, of all indigenous references of these peoples. The crime is four-fold: they exist (and, for neoliberalism, the existence of difference is a crime), they do not respond to the laws of the market (they do not have credit cards, they do not consider land as merchandise), they live on lands full of natural wealth (See Letter 5.1: "Chiapas: The War. Between the Satellite and the Microscope, the Look of the Other," a presentation by the CCRI-CG of the EZLN to the CCIODH - the International Civil Commission of Human Rights Observers - on November 22, 1999. Soon to be published internationally), and they are rebels.

We shall not expand on this point, given that this pamphlet is only trying to demonstrate the evidence of a warlike military presence and of an active war in the indigenous mountains of the Mexican southeast.

We have mentioned previously that there at least 266 military positions in Chiapas. And now you can count, for each barracks or garrison, a brothel and at least 3 liquor stores. 266 new brothels and at least 798 cantinas. The "administrators" of these brothels and cantinas are generals. They are in collusion with the "polleros" in the trafficking in women from Central America, whose illegal status prevents them from having the most minimal defense against their military "bosses."

In addition to the proliferation of venereal diseases, the arrival of "imported" prostitution has led to the flourishing of the "local." In indigenous communities affiliated with the PRI, it is common for the women to become prostitutes who "work" in the barracks that are occupying their lands. The entrance of alcohol has increased family violence, and the number of women and children being beaten by drunken men has increased.

In addition to the fact that, in locating their units, the army is invading ejidal lands (and violating the law it says it is defending), and that the soldiers' de facto power finds docile accomplices in the municipal presidencies, in the state government and in the local press - the trafficking in human beings reaches its maximum horror: trafficking in infants.

In the hospital in old Guadalupe Tepeyac, Dr. Maria de la Luz Cisneros provides the General in command of the local garrison with the newborns she steals. Together they collaborate in a network of trafficking in children. The procedure is very simple: an indigenous woman comes to this "hospital" to give birth. She does so, and the above noted doctor demands that the woman present her identification, because, without it, she cannot give her the child. She terrorizes the woman and gets her to leave without the child. Other times the doctor "communicates" to the woman that the child was born dead, and they are not going to give her the corpse because "she doesn't have papers." The stolen children, with the collaboration of the general in command of the old Guadalupe Tepeyac barracks, are sent to an unknown location. How much is a probably zapatista, indigenous girl or boy worth? How much are their organs worth if they are sold "for parts?" Only Dr. Cisneros and the accomplice with the rank of general can answer these questions.

In addition to trafficking in women and in children (or in parts of children), top military commanders stationed to "contain" the zapatistas, also do a large business in drug trafficking. Up until February 1995, when the zapatistas had complete control of the "conflict zone," drug traffickers found themselves prevented from using the Selva Lacandona as a "springboard" to the United States. And the planting, trafficking and use of narcotics in that area was reduced to zero. But when the army "recovered national sovereignty," the great drug lords of Mexico and South America reached an "understanding" with the generals. In addition, the planting of marijuana and opium have proliferated since then, with the landing strips operating at their maximum under military control. International drug trafficking, thus, has a territory where only their partners, the military, are able to enter. The cut the generals get from this operation is not small.

It is not just the military that is doing business thanks to this shameful war. The federal and state governments are also enriching themselves through the militarization. The large investments in housing for soldiers and in barracks has a hidden beneficiary, the brother of Ernesto Zedillo Ponce de Leon (Name: Rodolfo Zedillo

Ponce de Leon) (Figures from "Debate. South-Southeast" #2 March, 1999), who is the owner of the building company that is constructing the complex housing, torture centers, warehouses and command posts for the federal army in Chiapas. Ernesto Zedillo's father is in charge of the electrical facilities for these barracks through his "Electric Systems S.A. of C.V." company.

How can the militarization be stopped if this will mean that Zedillo's family would lose an important source of income? The "wellbeing" of Ernesto Zedillo Ponce de Leon's "family" is being nurtured with indigenous blood.

The "Croquetas" Albores is not being left behind. According to a denunciation by State PAN Deputy Cal y Mayor, the product ("school breakfasts" they call them) that the Chiapas DIF is distributing to 675,000 children is made with "soy fodder pasta," and it needs additives such as "sodium metabisulfite and sulfur for texturizing." The "Abasto Global S.A. of C .V." company is the one distributing them, and it is the property of Albores Guillen through false names. The State government paid 1.56 pesos for each breakfast to this company, which was created on February 17, 1998 for "the purchase, sale and commercial representation of agricultural, agro-livestock and industrial products."

If you have not become fed up yet, then turn the page and learn about...

The Paramilitares

In the Chamber of Deputies, Attorney General Jorge Madrazo Cuellar admitted that there are 15 "probably armed" civil organizations operating in Chiapas: The Chinchulines, Peace and Justice, Abu-Xu, My Brother's Keeper, Tomas Munzer, MIRA, Tzaes, Guaches, Pates, Botes, Xoxepes, Xiles and Los Mecos, all of them from the municipality of Polho, in addition to the Bartolome de Los Llanos, Armed Forces of the Peoples, House of the People, OCEZ-CNPA, First Force and Red Mask. "Except for references in the press, there is no other kind of proof or evidence regarding the groups called MIRA, Tomas Munzer, First Force and Red Mask."

The history of paramilitaries in Chiapas goes back to 1995. When the federal government offensive of February of that year failed - and seeing the loss of prestige it brought to the government forces - Zedillo opted for activating various paramilitary groups. The person in charge was General Mario Renan Castillo, who had already translated into English the North American manual that recommends the use of civilians for fighting insurgent forces. A noted alumnus of the United States school for counterinsurgency, Renan Castillo set about selecting a group of military personnel for training, direction and equipping. The Department of Social Development (SEDESOL) put up the money, and the "soldiers" were chiapaneco PRI's.

"Peace and Justice" was the name thought up by these military men for the first of these groups. Their area of operation is the northern part of the state of Chiapas, and their legal impunity is such that they control all movement in that area. Nothing nor anyone enters or leaves that region without the "authorization" of "Peace and Justice." These paramilitaries have not a few "combat trophies": nothing less than the attempted killing of the Bishops Samuel Ruiz Garcia and Raul Vera Lopez, dozens of assassinated indigenous, dozens of women raped and thousands of displaced.

But the "achievements" of "Peace and Justice" pale in comparison with those of their younger brother: "Red Mask." Prepared and trained to operate in Los Altos of Chiapas, Red Mask has the trophy of the Acteal killings, on December 22, 1997. The paramilitaries outdid the Guatemalan Kaibils in that "action." "Red Mask's" operations have led to the existence of almost 8000 war displaced in Chenalho alone.

The success of "Peace and Justice" and "Red Mask" encouraged the army to arm another group, now assigned to the Selva Lacandona: the "Anti-Zapatista Indigenous Revolutionary Movement" (MIRA). The MIRA has had no military successes other than the killing of some indigenous, and their primary function is to lend themselves to the "zapatista deserters" theater mounted by the "Croquetas" Albores Guillen. The "Croquetas" did not want to be left behind, and he founded the paramilitary group, "Albores of Chiapas," which has very versatile functions: the very rounding up of indigenous for demonstrations in "support of Governor Albores," dislocating campesinos or summarily executing those pointed out by the pezuna who resides in the government palace in Tuxtla Gutierrez.

The actions by the military and paramilitaries requires the "accompaniment" of other forces. And so, go on to the next section and read...

The Other Persecuted

The work of the military and paramilitaries is complemented by the local caciques. In Tuxtla Gutierrez, chiapaneco PRI businesspersons presented the substitute Albores with the so-called Social Foundation for Chiapas, A.C. Gasoline businessman Constantino Narvaez Rincon is the President of the Foundation, and the collection campaign coordinator is Maria Elena Noriega Malo. This foundation is trying to collect 200 million pesos, between the government of the state of Chiapas and businesspersons in the state and in the country, in order to deal comprehensively with nutrition, education and health of the residents of the 134 highly marginalized communities belonging to the seven newly created municipalities. The businesspersons added that they have experience in similar campaigns in other countries. The allegedly independent organization's program supports the official Redistricting program and the Law for Indigenous Rights and Culture proposed by the substitute, the "Croquetas" Albores Guillen.

Nonetheless, in an article by Lourdes Galaz, titled "Netwar Against the EZLN," published in La Jornada newspaper, it indicates that the Foundation's objectives derive from "The Advent of Netwar" project (1996), created by analysts from the Institute of Research for National Defense in Santa Monica, California in the United States, John Arquilla and David Rondfeldt.

The article notes that, in some political and academic circles, they are warning that the Zedillo government had already defined a position for confronting the problem of the zapatista guerrillas in Chiapas. The strategy of the netwar is focused on analyzing, containing, isolating, destroying and immobilizing social networks, as well as those of drug traffickers, terrorists and criminal groups. According to this, the strategy should focus, not just on the EZLN, but on all the organizations, fronts and individuals who form part of zapatismo's broad net of support. The analysts recommended that all kinds of actions and tactics should be imposed, from the classical ones of counterinsurgency (harassment, threats, psychological actions, kidnappings, attacks by paramilitary groups, individual executions, etcetera) to campaigns of disinformation, espionage and the creation of NGO's financed by the government in order to counterbalance the independent ones (tied to the net), among others.

Consequently, the ones who are being most closely watched, in this war which refuses to say its name, are not the criminals who swarm about, most especially in the government palace. Those who are being watched most carefully, and whom they are lying in wait for, are human rights defenders. People who are working in the chiapaneco NGO's, in the Mexican Academy of Human Rights, in the Mexican Commission for the Defense and Promotion of Human Rights, A.C., in the Miguel Agustin Pro Human Rights Center, and, in general, those who form part of the "All Rights for Everyone" network, are the targets of surveillance, harassment and death threats.

The fact that human rights defenders are considered as a military objective in this war is not an accident. To the Mexican government, the risk in this war is not the death and destruction it causes, but that it be known. And this is the problem with human rights defenders: they do not remain silent in front of injustices and arbitrary acts.

But, if there are threats, persecution and harassment for Mexican human rights defenders, there are lies for international observers.

The Mexican federal army, whose war machinery in Chiapas is obvious, tries, ineffectively, to appear to the public as "social workers." The following are "pearls" captured by an excellent alternative news service:

"VII MILITARY REGION Tuxtla Gutierrez, Chiapas, September 11, 1999.

WITHIN THE FRAMEWORK OF COADVISEMENT WITH THE STATE OF CHIAPAS, TROOPS STATIONED IN THE VII MILITARY REGION CARRIED OUT THE FOLLOWING ACTIVITIES YESTERDAY... 8 HAIRCUTS..."

[Department of National Defense Communiqué]

"VII MILITARY REGION Tuxtla Gutierrez, Chiapas, September 12, 1999. AS PART OF THE ACTIVITIES CARRIED OUT BY TROOPS IN THE VII MILITARY REGION, IN ORDER TO GUARANTEE WELLBEING AND SECURITY IN DIFFERENT COMMUNITIES IN THE STATE OF CHIAPAS, THE FOLLOWING ACTIVITIES WERE CARRIED OUT YESTERDAY... 6 HAIRCUTS..."

[Department of National Defense Communiqué]

"VII MILITARY REGION Tuxtla Gutierrez, Chiapas, September 22, 1999. CONTINUING WITH ACTIVITIES CARRIED OUT IN ORDER TO GUARANTEE SECURITY AND PROVIDE WELLBEING FOR THE COMMUNITIES OF THE STATE OF CHIAPAS, THE FOLLOWING ACTIONS WERE TAKEN YESTERDAY... 6 HAIRCUTS..."

[Department of National Defense Communiqué]

"VII MILITARY REGION Tuxtla Gutierrez, Chiapas, September 23, 1999. TROOPS STATIONED IN THE VII MILITARY REGION CONTINUED SUPORTING THE GOVERNMENT OF THE STATE OF CHIAPAS AND CARRYING OUT SOCIAL WORK ACTIVITIES IN AID TO THE CIVIL POPULATION IN VARIOUS REGIONS OF THE STATE, CARRYING OUT THE FOLLOWING ACTIVITIES YESTERDAY... 5 HAIRCUTS..."

[Department of National Defense Communiqué]

"VII MILITARY REGION Tuxtla Gutierrez, Chiapas, September 24, 1999. WITHIN THE FRAMEWORK OF AID TO THE CIVIL POPULATION AND THE SUPPORT IT LENDS TO THE GOVERNMENT OF THE STATE OF CHIAPAS, TROOPS OF THE VII MILITARY REGION YESTERDAY CARRIED OUT, IN DIFFERENT REGIONS IN THE STATE, THE FOLLOWING ACTIVITIES... 7 HAIRCUTS..."

[Department of National Defense Communiqué]

Yes, you read correctly, in five days, more than 60,000 soldiers quartered in Chiapas carried out the social work... haircuts! Yes, you are right, they are the most expensive and the bloodiest haircuts in the history of humanity.

This pamphlet ends with this "humanitarian" image of the army in Chiapas. If you are a high commissioner of the UN, and you are visiting our country, do not be surprised that none of this coincides with the deplorable artifice the Mexican government has staged. It so happens that the lie is also a weapon. It remains to be seen whether or not you shall surrender, or, as the indigenous here teach, you will resist the lie.

Everything I have related here is true. It can be confirmed directly or by consulting news reports. Even so, it does not reflect the totality of the horror that this war means.

But what is surprising is not this gigantic war machine destroying, assassinating and persecuting more than a million indigenous. No, what is really extraordinary and marvelous is that it is, and it will be, in vain. Despite of it, the zapatistas not only do not surrender nor are defeated, they even grow and become stronger. As they say in these mountains, the zapatistas have a very powerful and indestructible weapon: the word.

Good, I shall say goodbye now, Madame. That is how things are here. It does not matter what the evil characters swarming about the state departments, embassies and consulates say to you, tell you or show you. This is the truth. But, if you do not believe me, come and confirm it personally. You will know you have arrived if you look towards those of above and you realize that what abounds are tanks, military checkpoints, police interrogation by immigration agents, barracks, liquor stores, the lie.

Do not forget to also look towards those of below, there you will realize that light can also be dark and very short, that there are those who must conceal their faces in order to be seen and who must hide themselves in order to show themselves.

But if any of these facts do not confirm that you have arrived - because there are certainly many corners of history that are painted like that, above and below - we have thought to facilitate your visit. At the entrance you will see a not very large sign, with colored and clumsily written letters, that says: "Welcome to Zapatista Territory, the last corner of rebel dignity." And do not think that the "last corner" is meant historically, or in terms of constancy, because certainly the world guards many corners for their rebel dignity, and they are all constant. When we say we are the "last corner," we only mean that we are the smallest...

Vale. Salud and, if you come, we will be waiting for you, even when we are no longer here. Travel with caution, because it is very easy to come to these lands, what is difficult is leaving.

From the Mountains of the Mexican Southeast,

For the Clandestine Revolutionary Indigenous Committee
- General Command of the Zapatista Army of National Liberation,
Subcomandante Insurgente Marcos.
La Realidad at War.
Mexico, November of 1999.

P.S. THAT WARNS. - Ah! I forgot. Be very careful when you come to rebel lands. It so happens that, since January 1, 1994, the law of gravity was abolished here, and it often happens that, at some daybreaks, the moon disrobes and shows herself as she really is, that is, one of the apples that defied Newton...

CHAPTER III: 2000-2003 – (R)evolution Continues...

— *Subcomandante Marcos*

84. EVERY TIME ZEDILLO COMES TO CHIAPAS

February of 2000
To the national and international press

Ladies and gentlemen,

Several letters are off which are not self-explanatory, and which I do not think I shall explain here.

Every time Zedillo comes to Chiapas, the army steps up their air and land patrols. That is logical since that gentleman is not, nor will he be, welcome in these lands. On February 20, we had the pleasure of an intensive coming and going of planes, helicopters, tanks, trucks and troops, throughout the entirety of what the gray whale calf Rabasa calls "the conflict zone." We thought it was another of Zedillo's conjugal visits to the Croquetas, but no. What happened is that day it was Labastida, and not Zedillo, who came to repeat the grays which characterize them.

One question: the mobilization of the federales, is it because they already consider Labastida to be their "supreme commander?" Is it because Labastida is the official candidate? Or is it because the military couldn't find anywhere to hide themselves in order to not hear the speeches of a campaign that is going like the Mexican Air Force planes over the indigenous communities, that is, at ground level?

Vale. Salud and may that flag always live where the eagle devours the neoliberal serpent (Because, if you have forgotten, February 24 is flag day. You are welcome).

From the mountains of the Mexican Southeast,
Subcomandante Insurgente Marcos.
Mexico, February 2000.

85. ONE DAY THINGS WILL GO STRAIGHT

February 21, 2000
To: Don Fernando Benitez
From: Subcomandante Insurgente Marcos

"Death is called as one, when it arrives, and there is no way for you to escape. I had a very strange dream like devils and animals I had never seen. But do not think that was bad There were iron horses that plowed the fields. Then some large vats, of stone, filled up with water inside them, to irrigate an infinity of fields beyond imagining some vats as large as hills, which seemed to me as if they were made for

giants to bathe in And I saw that the land was for everyone and that everyone looked happy I said to myself: then, where could I be? Could this be Mexico? And it was Mexico, it was Mexico, it was Mexico! It was then that I remembered…"
- "Zapata" Screenplay by Jose Revueltas

Don Fernando,

It was with bitter sorrow that we learned of your death. It was just a few days ago that I had written you a letter congratulating you on your birthday. January was barely underway when the Sea called my attention to the article in the newspaper where they were congratulating you on your birthday, and, together, we recalled that letter from your last anniversary. In this one which I am now writing, I could reiterate what those who are closest to you (and not so close) should already have told you, but I shall not wear out your eyes with things you knew and understood. Originally thought to congratulate you, these lines are also now to wish you a bon voyage.

I hardly dare to remember, to remind you, that my parents taught us to read (I am not speaking of literacy, but of reading) with that "always!" of Don Jose Pages Llergo, and, specifically, with that supplement you directed and that is called "Culture in Mexico." There we learned to read Poniatowska, Jose Emilio Pacheco, the philosopher Monsivais, and many others. We learned there. Afterwards, years later, we found your pages of "The Indians in Mexico," and your advance through other cultural supplements. I do not know if there is still time, but I wanted to tell you "thanks" for having taught us to read. Did you set out once upon a time to teach someone to read? Well, so it goes then, sometimes one does things without setting out to do so.

Don Fernando, we would like to give you something, something simple but very much ours. We do not have many things. Don Fernando. In fact, we have very little. The only thing we possess in abundance is memory, and, with that, we are sending you this gift which has the virtue of not taking up much space in your luggage, and it will serve you for laughing about that which some call "death."

In order to bring you close to ours, this story comes, with which we are also trying to remember those who are no longer with us, but who were before, and who made it possible for us to be here today. With that, Don Fernando, you are also ours.

Sale and vale,

That Day

To Pedro, 6 years later, 26 years later.

I remember that day. The sun did not travel straight, but went sideways. I mean, yes it went from here to there, but it went sideways, just that, without climbing up to that which I do not remember right now what it is called, but which the sup once told us. The sun was as if cold. Well, everything was cold that day. Well, not everything. We were hot. As if the blood, or whatever we have within our bodies, was with fever. I do not remember about what the sup said, "the zenith," or something like that, or when the sun reaches the highest point. But that day, no. More as if it were going from side to side. We were moving forward in the same way. I was already dead, lying down, belly up, and I could easily see that the sun was not traveling straight, but going from side to side. That day we were all already dead, wherever we advanced. That is why the sup wrote "we are the dead of forever, dying once again, but now in order to live." When did we all actually die? In truth, I do not remember, but that day in which the sun was traveling from side to side, we were all already dead. All of us, because there were women as well. That day, in the morning, there were people running about. I do not know if it was because the war had begun, or because they saw so many dead advancing, walking as always, without face, without name. Well, at first the people were running, then they were no longer running. Then they stopped, and they came close in order to hear what we were saying. What craziness! If I were alive, I would hardly have come close in order to hear what a dead person was saying! Since one would think the dead had nothing to say. They are dead, after all. Since it was the work of the dead to go around spooking, and not speaking. I remember that in my land it is said that if the dead still walk, it is because they have left something undone, and that is why they are not quiet. So it is said in my land. I believe my land is called Michoacan, but I do not really remember. I also do not remember well, but I believe I am called Pedro or Manuel or I do not know, I believe that it is not, in fact, important, what the dead are called, because they are already dead. Perhaps when one is alive, it is indeed important how one is called, but, once dead, for what?

Good, the fact is that these people, after their running around, were coming close in order to see what we, the dead that we were, were saying to them. And then, to talk, as we, the dead, do, in fact, talk, chatting as it were, without a lot of racket, as if one person were chatting to another and were not dead, but alive. Well, a bit like that. It had something to do with the fact that we were dead and at war.

We had taken the city at dawn. At noon we were already preparing everything to go for another. I was already lying down at noon, but I clearly saw the sun was not traveling straight, and I saw it was cold. I saw, but I did not feel, because the dead do not feel, but they do see. I saw that it was cold because it was as if the sun had gone out. Very pale, as if it were cold. Everyone was going from one side to the other. Not I, I remained lying down, belly up, seeing the sun and trying to remember what the sup said they say when the sun is just straight up, when it has already finished climbing and it begins letting itself fall to the other side. As if the sun were becoming embarrassed and it goes and hides itself behind that hill. I did not notice then when the sun went to hide itself behind that. The way I was I could not turn my head, I could only look straight up and, without turning, at the little that reached from one side and the other. That is why I saw that the sun did not go straight, but it was going from side to side, as if embarrassed, as if in fear of climbing up to that which I do not remember right now how the sup said it was said, but perhaps I shall remember in a while.

Just at that moment I remembered, because the stone cracked a bit and made a gash like a knife wound, and then I could see the sky and the sun traveling sideways like that once again, like that day. Nothing else could be seen. Lying down as I am, the sky barely reaches. There are not many clouds and the sun is as if pale, or becoming cold. And then I remembered that day when the dead who we are began this war in order to speak. Yes, in order to speak. For what other thing would the dead make war?

I told them the sky could be seen through this gash. Helicopters and planes pass through there. They come and they go, daily, sometimes until night. They do not know it, but I see them, I see them and I watch them. I also laugh. Yes, because, after all, those planes and helicopters come here because they are afraid of us. Yes, I already know that the dead themselves cause fear, but what those planes and helicopters are afraid of is that the dead who we are will start walking once more. And I do not know what the fuss is all about, if they can, in fact, do nothing, since we are already dead. They are hardly going to kill us. Maybe it is because they want to know and to let those in charge know in time. I do not know. But I do know that fear smells, and the odor of the fear of the powerful is like that of a machine, like that of gasoline and oil and metal and dust and noise and, and, and of fear. Yes, fear smells of fear, and those planes and helicopters smell of fear. The air that comes from above smells of fear. That from below does not. The air from below smells nice, as if things were changing, as if everything were improving and becoming better. Hope, that is what the air from below smells of. We are from below. We, and many like us. Yes, that is it, then: in this country, the dead smell of hope.

I see and hear all that through the gash. I think and my neighbors are in agreement (I know so because they have told me so) that it is not good that the sun travels from side to side and that it must be put right. Because that traveling sideways like that, all pale and cold making, no. Since the work of the sun is to give heat, not to be cold.

And, if you press me, I would even give you a political analysis. Look, I say that this country's problem is that it is has absolute contradictions. There, then, a sun that carries cold, and the living people see and let it do so as if they were dead, and the criminal is judge, and the victim is in jail, and the lying one is the government, and truth is persecuted like illness, and students are imprisoned and thieves run loose, and the ignorant deliver lectures, and the wise are ignored, and the idle have riches, and the one who works has nothing, and the least rules, and the greater obey, and the one who has much has more, and the one who has little has nothing, and bad is rewarded, and good punished.

And not just that, in addition, here the dead speak and walk and do rare things, like setting right a sun that is cold and, just look, it goes from side to side, without reaching that point that I do not remember how it is called but the sup told us once. I believe that one day I shall remember.

There, Don Fernando, may you have a very happy birthday and many more. Love from all of us, especially from this anonymous disciple of the window that you were and which is culture in Mexico. Be well and do not forget about us. There will always be an opening in our memory for you.

Vale. Salud and one day things will go straight, the dead will surely set them right.

From the mountains of the Mexican Southeast,
Subcomandante Insurgente Marcos.
Mexico, February of 2000.

86. A University Filled With Soldiers and a Jail Filled With Students

February of 2000
To: Don Pablo Gonzalez Casanova
From: Subcomandante Insurgente Marcos

"I, who have a youth full of voices, of lightning bolts, of living arteries, moored to my muscles, alert to how my blood runs and weeps, to how my anxieties crowd each other like bitter seas or like dense tombs of sleeplessness, I hear all cries joining together a forest of close cramped hearts; I hear what we are still saying today, all that we shall yet be saying, point first above our grave throbbing, from the mouths of the trees, from the mouth of the land."
- Jose Revueltas, Canto Irrevocable

Don Pablo,

We all send you our greetings. Not only for your courageous stance recently, but also for that. The firm distance you have taken from the violent and authoritarian attitude of those who head the government and the UNAM is worth much, especially during these times when consistency is a sarcasm and dignity a misunderstanding.

Know that our having been close to you fills us with pride. Your today is but the confirmation of what your life has been. Even before the time when you acted as a member of the National Intermediation Commission, your words helped us understand this sorrow we call "Mexico." Then, in the CONAI, at the side of those great men and women who made it up, your commitment to the search for a peaceful, just and dignified solution to the war was firm and for all times. I have read here that the former secretary of government and current official candidate for president, Francisco Labastida Ochoa, complained that the CONAI had been "unconditionally supportive" of one of the sides. If the "sides" were war and peace, it is obvious that those who made up the CONAI were "unconditionally supportive" of the side of peace. Bishop Samuel Ruiz Garcia, as well as Dona Concepcion Calvillo, widow of Nava, the poets Oscar Oliva and Juan Banuelos, and you, all strove to achieve peace in the Mexican southeast in the only way it is possible to achieve it: with respect, with justice, with dignity, with truth. It is clear that Senor Labastida will have to confront many Mexicans who, like you, "unconditionally support" the side of peaceful solutions and are against the use of violence.

Your explicit and forceful condemnation of the use of violence in confronting the demands of the UNAM student movement is nothing more than the logical consequence of one who is for all times. We are certain that your example will be followed by other intellectuals who, in their own means and ways, will let those who use violence as a government argument know that they shall not do so with impunity. And those students who now find themselves in jail or persecuted, who are suffering injustice, that they are not alone now. One and another will have to hear the voices and the steps which, "from the mouths of the trees, from the mouth of the land," are saying and will say: liberty and dialogue.

Today, despite the electronic media, a wave of popular indignation is being raised in order to demand the release of the imprisoned university students and the renewal of dialogue. Headed by courageous parents, this movement incorporates the best of the social organizations, of the political parties of the left, of artists and intellectuals, of religious men and women, of people, of university students. Their common objective, that which unites them, is the demand for justice. And this, justice, cannot be achieved while even one university student remains behind bars. The best of the party left have not only understood exactly that, but they have also been one of the primary driving forces.

Running counter to this feeling which is translated into mobilization, the electronic media become pompous with the funds they receive from political parties for their political campaigns, and they believe they have the moral authority and legitimacy to turn themselves into - simultaneously - prosecutor, judge, jury and executor of everyone who has not paid for program time. You experienced that firsthand, Don Pablo, and millions of Mexicans are experiencing it with their own eyes and ears. At the entrance to the 21st century, television is applauding Mexico's current "democratic" double image: a university filled with soldiers and a jail filled with students (the intensity of a country's democratic life is measured by the number of publicity spots, not by the number of political prisoners). In the country of television, the Magna Carta is not the Constitution, but the program guide (which bills the cacophony out on a triple A schedule) and there are no IFE directors any more effective than the news directors.

Regardless, beyond the TV movie schedule, the people (who do not count if they do not have a publicity advisor and another for marketing) were moved to protest, like you, Don Pablo, against repression. As we were able to read in the written press, the February 9 march was the largest in recent times. The cry was one: liberty for the political prisoners. Six years ago, in 1994 and on January 12, there was a similar great mobilization. As they are doing today for the university movement and yesterday for the zapatista uprising, the people are taking to the streets in order to make themselves heard.

Then, during that January of blood and gunpowder, we had to decide how we were going to "read" that great mobilization. We could have "read" it as a demonstration in support of our war, as a backing for the path of armed struggle we had chosen. Or we could have read it as a mobilization, not in support of our method (war), but indeed in support of our demands, and which was expressing itself against government repression.

We were isolated, falling back to the mountains, caring for our dead and wounded, preparing for the next fight. In that way, far away, very far away and under those conditions, we had to choose. And we chose to "read" that those people who took to the streets were against injustice, against authoritarianism, against racism, against war, that they were for dialogue, for peace, for justice, for the peaceful solution to our demands. We read that, and that marked our subsequent conduct.

Today the university student movement (and the CGH) are confronting a similar situation. Those who make it up can "read" the February 9 mobilization as a demonstration of support for the strike, or as a demand for justice (releasing the prisoners) and for dialogue. It is not the same.

Through the "reading" it chooses, the university student movement will have to decide its subsequent steps. They will choose, and they will do so well. They are not isolated, and they have the intelligence and the resources to achieve a good reading.

We? As always, Don Pablo: to all those who make up the university student movement, to their fathers and mothers, to their teachers, to those who support them and who are close to them, we love them, we admire them, they are going to win.

It is for all of this that, today, Don Pablo, we applaud you. You and all those who, like you, have expressed their repudiation of the soldiers disguised as police ("paramilitaries" in the strictest sense) entering the university campus.

We know that your voice and your step will also be joined with all of us who are demanding what is urgent and necessary: the release of the imprisoned university students.

Vale. Salud and may we never relinquish hope.

> *From the mountains of the Mexican Southeast,*
> *Subcomandante Insurgente Marcos.*
> *Mexico, February of 2000.*

P.S. We read here that the student prisoners are asking for books to be sent to them. Send them that one that is entitled "Democracy in Mexico." It is as valuable today as yesterday, and it is one of those books that produce fertile sorrows.

87. Chocolates Yes, Injections No!

February of 2000
To: Rene Villlanueva
From: Subcomandante Insurgente Marcos

Rene, brother,

We have learned here that you are sick. In these lands, when one has a relative (because you are a relative to all of us, the zapatistas) who is sick, it is the custom to foist every possible (and impossible, as well) remedy upon him in order to cure him. Since being sick is something common and frequent in these mountains, prescriptions come and go on all sides, abounding in syrups, tea, potions, pills, vapors and - horror! - injections (Lucha, big sister to all of us, has a varied and effective medicinal repertoire that would make the pharmaceutical monopolies tremble you are welcome, Lucha, but don't forget to cough up when you patent all that).

As you are our brother, we cannot give you just anything. Even less if that "thing" is an injection, that sophisticated instrument of torture which - despite the fact that we are entering the third millennium - has not been prohibited by any world organization in existence. Here, for example, Olivio has proposed that a slogan for the march of zapatista women this March 8 should be: "Chocolates yes, injections no!" I told him it didn't rhyme, and he answered me that injections itself doesn't rhyme with anything, and, on the other hand, "chocolates" rhymes with "juguetes" [toys] (Olivio is going to try to convince the Sea to use his slogan in the zapatistas' march).

No, senor, we cannot give injections. Certainly not chocolates either. Not just because Olivio has already wolfed them down, but also because they would most certainly arrive made into atole. And so we have consulted in our special medical book which is called "Remedies and Recuentos," and we found something that, although it will not cure you, is certain not to make you worse (which is, during these times of "modern medicine," already an advantage): an embrace! All of us are sending you an embrace. It can be applied as often as you like, but do not abuse it, because it can lead to addiction, and there are few embraces like the one we are sending you.

Sale then. Do not ignore it, take the medicine without making a face, and you will get better, because your and Beatriz' absence in "Correo Ilustrado" has caused that section's "ratings" to bottom out (I confess, I did a verrrrrrry scientific survey).

Vale. Salud and don't forget that embraces should be like gazes: wide and clear.

From the Mountains of the Mexican Southeast,
Subcomandante Insurgente Marcos.
Mexico, February of 2000.

88. MARCOS ON WINDOWS AND REALITY

March 21, 2000
To: German Dehesa, Mexico, D.F.

Don German,

I have been wanting to write to you for some time. I have been reading you for quite a while (always, of course, assuming the Reforma reaches the Selva Lacandona), attentively and with amused seriousness (there is such a thing, no?). Now, reading your column of Thursday, March 16, I see that you have generously turned an attentive ear to our words. I shall try to not go on too long. Sale y vale.

You ask first: "What has the Zapatista Army of National Liberation done to preserve the Selva Lacandona?"

I answer: pass laws and see that they are carried out. As you could not know (because the government has presented the autonomous municipalities as secessionist), the autonomous authorities of the zapatista indigenous communities in the Selva Lacandona have passed a law prohibiting "the grazing, cutting down and burning of the high mountain" (the companeros use the word "high mountain" to refer to the wooded areas, differentiating them from fields - planted lands - and from "acahuales," lands with low growth, invariably thorns, thistles, lianas and other parasitic plants).

The communities have not been content with establishing and promulgating this law. They have, in addition, taken charge of seeing to its compliance and to punishing its lack of observance. The penalties for these crimes are extra community work and fines. And, it's carried out. In this manner they have not only halted the destruction of the wooded areas of the Selva Lacandona, but they have also managed to partly modify the patterns of planting in the communities. In order to confront the fires which proliferate at this time of the year, the villages have a system of communication and signals so that they can come to each others aid if a fire spreads. The result? There are tens of thousands of expert "firefighters" in the zapatista areas. This, and more, is what the indigenous are doing, Senor Dehesa, in order to protect the land that is, for them, not just a means of survival, but also the place of memory, of culture, of history. This is what those indigenous are doing, who are rebels against a government that refuses to honor its word and which - in response to their demands for justice - has sent tens of thousands of soldiers who - believe me, Senor Dehesa - do not come to Chiapas to plant the little trees you saw in San Miguel de los Jagueyes, but rather to plant the terror that you will only see in the faces of the men, women, children and old ones who have the misfortune of having, on their lands, a soldiers' barracks, several bars, at least one brothel and no respect for civil authority.

I am telling you this, Senor Dehesa, not because I want to "convert" you into a zapatista or to recruit you. I am doing so because you are as intelligent as your words reflect (and, more, there is brilliance that cannot even be revealed by words). It is obvious that their inviting you to San Miguel de los Jagu:eyes (and not to Acteal, or Amador Hernandez, or Amparo Aguatinta, or Tani Perla, or Roberto Barrios, or to other sites of military "reforesting") was not done innocently, and that you understand that.

Since, I am sure, you are broadminded and eager to learn of the different images of the same reality, I am inviting you to come to Chiapas incognito. Go to Comitan and take an air taxi there to the community of Amador Hernandez. From the air, just as you arrive, you will be able to appreciate the brutal felling of trees by the soldiers stationed there for their heliports, as well as the amount of woods deforested in order to clear the "firing fields" for their machine guns. If you land and manage to penetrate the military fortification, you will be able to se the drums of defoliants in their warehouses and the flame-throwers which, along with mortars and light machine guns, form part of their arsenal.

Go to Amador Hernandez, you will not be received by any Secretary of State or by any "high command" of the zapatista guerrilla, nor will you be attended to by any public relations director. Indigenous Tzeltal men and women will receive you, they will show you their destroyed fields of crops, their contaminated water sources, the pitfall traps with sharpened stakes inside, the walls of branches and cut trees, behind which the soldiers hide so that they do not have to see the words the indigenous men and women show them every day demanding their withdrawal. Come, Senor Dehesa, you have nothing to lose and, perhaps, much to understand. You could (it is a suggestion) bring Madame Loaeza (who also wants to make the trip) along with you. I am certain that she could come up with a good disguise that would allow both of you to pass unrecognized, and you could, in that way, confirm the "other" reality of the federal soldiers in the Selva Lacandona.

Because those soldiers whom Senor Aguilar Zinser sees (and applauds), "caring for" the forests of the Selva Lacandona, are the accomplices of the talamontes (the large trucks with clandestine wood have free passage at the military checkpoints in the Canadas). They are the same ones who raped indigenous women in the community of Morelia. The same ones who summarily executed indigenous in Ocosingo. The same ones who are training paramilitaries (whose greatest "forest" task is the massacre of children, women, men and old ones at Acteal), who convert schools and churches into barracks (visit the north of Chiapas), who prostitute the indigenous women (talk with the PRI women of San Quintin), who steal newborns in the "brand new" hospital of old Guadalupe Tepeyac in order to sell them (completely or in parts) on the black market in the United States. Who plant, traffic in and consume drugs (let them show you the areas around the barracks at Guadalupe Tepeyac, San Quintin, TaniPerla, Ibarra or La Soledad, to mention a few). Who protect drug traffickers on their routes to the American Union (after 1995, the year of the "recovery of national sovereignty," the South American cartels recovered the springboard they had lost with the EZLN uprising). Who have introduced alcohol into the communities (you can observe the military convoys escorting trucks with alcoholic beverages). The same ones who are persecuting, threatening, beating, jailing, raping and killing Mexican indigenous (in any community which has the misfortune to have a barracks close by) who, as far as I understand, are worth the same (or less) than any little tree.

Come, Senor Dehesa, come and see and talk and ask that they show you what they have inside the army barracks in the community of San Quintin (at the door of the Montes Azules biosphere). There you will be able to see the efficient modern dungeons designed to torture indigenous, the tunnels for "disappearing" persons without leaving any traces for human rights observers. Come, look and listen.

Come, and you will see that there are two programs for the future: the government's and the indigenous'. Ours seeks "to create the conditions for our good people of the countryside to recover their strength: their history, their ways of thinking, their dignity, their respectability, their initiative" (Dehesa, G. Reforma, Friday, March 17, 2000), and that which is not present in the election campaign.

Do not believe me, Senor Dehesa, believe what your eyes see and your ears hear. If your trip is not possible, pay no attention to what that I am writing here. Look, instead, at the hundreds of reports from non-governmental organizations, from scientists and researchers, from the UN High Commissioner for Human Rights. All of them recommend the army's withdrawal from Chiapas. And it is not because they want to see the forests destroyed. It is because they do not see the soldiers planting little trees, but, rather, violating human rights.

Good, Senor Dehesa, I hope I have limited myself to the number of pages that I imagine your column takes up. As to the rest, do not believe that about email. The only effective means of communicating with the EZLN General Command is still provided by a pair of boots, somewhat worn-out, for sure, but still serviceable. I do not know if you will publish this, or what the tone of your response will be. Whatever it may be, know that you have, at the least, two readers (including La Mar) in the mountains of the Mexican Southeast who, despite their not sharing many of your opinions and values, laugh quite happily at your wit, your incisiveness and your joy.

Vale. Salud, and the tree that matters is the one of the morning.

> From the mountains of the Mexican Southeast,
> Subcomandante Insurgente Marcos.
> Mexico, March of 2000.

Cheeky P.S. I forgot, you also asked: "How many trees has Marcos planted?" I answer you: Without counting the little orange tree that graces the doors of the EZLN General Command, one could say that I have only planted one other tree. It is a very odd tree. Not just because its planting has required the support of thousands of men and women for several generations. Not just because its nurture involves much pain and, it is only fair to say, many smiles. No, Senor Dehesa, the tree we are planting here is odd because it is a tree for everyone, for those who have not yet been born, for those whom we do not know, for those who will be when we have been lost behind the corner of any calendar. When our tree grows, under its shade will sit the great and small, whites and darks and red and the red and the blue, indigenous and mestizo, men and women, the tall and the short, without those differences mattering, and, above all, without any of them feeling less or worse or ashamed for being as they are. Under that tree there will be respect for the other, dignity (which does not mean arrogance), justice and liberty. If I were pushed to define that tree briefly, I would tell you that it is a tree of hope. If, some morning on the map of Chiapas, instead of an immense green area broken up by the blue lines of rivers and streams, signs of oil wells are seen, and uranium mines, casinos, exclusive residential areas and military bases, then that will mean that those soldiers, who you say are caring for the Selva Lacandona, will have won. It will not mean that we have lost, just that we are taking longer to win than we had thought...

P.S. Proposing Another Window

(Off the record: La Realidad) (Postscript to Letter 6c)

March of 2000

To: Don Pablo Gonzalez Casanova.

UNAM, Mexico

> *"Windows are like cookies:*
> *they are tasty and nourishing."*
> *- Don Durito of the Lacandona.*

Don Pablo,

I am sure that the epigram at the top of this letter will seem strange to you, and its author even more so. It is not easy to explain, but I will try to do so. Everything began when;

Above, the sky stretches from horizon to horizon. It is stretched so much that its skin rips, and light can be seen through the tatters. There is very little wind. Even so, a fleeting breeze brings me the echoes of some voices. I climb down from the Ceiba and walk towards a little light covered by trees. It appears to be a small gathering or some such. I approach and "in order to distinguish between the voices of the echoes, I stopped and listened, among the voices, to just one." The Mad Hatter and the March Hare are sharing tea while discussing a poll with La Mar which says that 90% of human beings prefer to celebrate their non-birthdays and to give up birthday parties. These things only happen in the mountains of the Mexican southeast. I am of the 10% who prefer to celebrate their birthdays, and so I was left without tea and without discussion.

However it may be, it is now getting to be the 21st on all the calendars, and for lack of tea there will be coffee and animal cookies. And, speaking of little animals, Zedillo's expanded cabinet (that is, his own and the one called ostentatiously - Labastida's "campaign team") is abounding in their increasingly less respectable statements. And it is not that the respectable has lost respectability, what is happening is that the number of Mexican men and women who are paying attention to what the Supreme One is saying is dwindling rapidly.

Durito, who, charges like a politician trying to get nominated when cookies are spoken of, appears at one of the edges of the table. I was writing a response to Don Pablo Gonzalez Casanova (more of a postscript), when Durito, throwing eye patch, wooden leg and hook aside, exclaims-asks-demands:

"Did someone say cookies?"

"I didn't say them, I wrote them. And don't get excited because they're animal ones, and, as far as I'm aware, they aren't among your favorites."

"Why do you always mix politics up with things as noble as cookies. Besides, I know where there are some 'Pancremas' put away."

I immediately stopped writing.

"'Pancremas?' Where?"

"Nothing, nothing. If there's no tea, there's no cookies."

"But Durito; Okay, let's negotiate: I'll help you to work on the sardine cannier, excuse me, the galley, and you tell me where the 'Pancremas' are."

Durito thinks about it for a minute. Then he asks:

"Does that include washing the deck and bailing out the water in storms?"

"It includes it," I say, seeing that right now the sky has no room for clouds, and so I don't have to worry about any storms.

"Follow me," says Durito, and, getting down from the table, he embarks on the march in the mountains.

I took the lamp, although the moon made it unnecessary. We did not walk far. Durito stopped in front of a Huapac and pointed to one of its branches. "There," he said. I looked towards where he was pointing and I saw a little bag hanging. It must have been an old "mailbox," left some time ago by one of our units... Durito sat down at the base of the tree and began to smoke. I interpreted his silence and climbed the tree, undid the bag and climbed down with it. Upon opening it I saw that there indeed was a package of "Pancrema" cookies, and a pair of "AA" batteries, a lamp that was already oxidized, an old worn book by Lewis Carroll (Through the Looking Glass), a zapatista song book and a book of political theory whose author is Subcomandante Insurgente Marcos!

I do not remember having written any book on political theory. In fact, I don't remember having written any book, period. Certainly the idea of a long work, expounding on what the zapatistas think about politics, has been going round my head, but nothing has been decided. I began leafing through the book while Durito did a good job of polishing off the cookies. When I turned around, there were no longer even any crumbs left of the "Pancremas."

"You finished them all off?" I reproached him.

"You should be grateful to me. They were more rancid than the 'new' PRI." Durito looked at me and added: "I can see that something is bothering you. You can confide in me, my dear disconcerted nose."

"It's that I've found this book in the mailbox. How is it possible to find, in an old mailbox in the mountain, a book that hasn't been written yet?"

"The solution to your problem is in the other book."

"Which? The Lewis Carroll one?"

"Obviously! Take a look at Chapter 5."

And so I did. I'm not very sure, but I believe the answer would be in the following dialogue between Alice and the White Queen:

"That is the result of living backwards," the White Queen said kindly. "At the beginning it always makes one feel a little confused."

"Live backwards!" replied Alice, greatly surprised. "I have never heard of such a thing!"

"But there is a great advantage in that: our memory works in both directions."

"I'm sure that mine only works one way," Alice observed. "I cannot remember things before they happen."

"That is a sad memory that can only work backwards," the Queen answered.

"What kinds of things do you remember best?" Alice dared to ask.

"Oh, the things that happened within two weeks," the White Queen responded negligibly.

Lewis Carroll, Through the Looking Glass. Chapter 5

"So I have in my hands a book that hasn't been written yet?" I said.

"That is so. We are in one of those areas called a window."

I looked at him in surprise.

"Yes," Durito says. "Windows. Or, in those places where one can look at the other side, whether at what has happened, or at what is going to happen. Here, for example, you can see what Zedillo's administration has been, and also see the chaos which it is leading to. Now the only stable thing is instability. There will be all kinds of problems."

"Well it seems they are already happening. You can already see the stock market is sky high, and, I don't understand very well, economic indices assure there will be no 'December error'."

"That's because it will happen in another month." Durito seems to take notice of my perplexity, because he almost immediately adds: "You should understand." Durito looks at me doubtfully and corrects himself: "Okay, you should try to understand that look, better that you read what I'm writing." Durito hands me some written pages where it says:

Points Which Try to Explain What is Just Going To Happen When They are Just Going to Happen.

Macro-economic indices: Cosmetic Cover-up

In an election year, in addition to candidates, lies abound. One of the biggest is the one that sings the praises of an economic growth that is not to be seen anywhere. Blind to what the common people are suffering, government officials exhibit figures which say more in what they don't say. The high macro-economic indices are nothing but a cosmetic cover-up for concealing the reality: the growth in poverty and in the number of poor in the country. In response to the evidence that no one believes them, the government puts the achievements and the applause for the rapid and tumultuous sale of Mexico into the mouths of the large financial centers. While at business and government meetings (the most powerful club of the nation's criminals), they congratulate each other for the increased profits, in Mexico's streets and countryside survival becomes an everyday battle, and the price increases of basic products and services are reflected in the tables (less food and of poorer quality), in the streets (unemployed and under-employed are growing), in the small businesses (misery and closing), and in the countryside (emigration to the cities and to the American Union increases).

And, even so, the macro cosmetics present serious shortcomings. At the 13th Congress of the National College of Economists, the Zedillisto Secretary of Commerce (Herminio Blanco) encountered criticism of his publicity campaign. Enrique Dussel, UNAM researcher, told him: "The 3100 maquiladoras and 300 largest national and foreign companies are 0.12 of the country's businesses, and they create only 5.6% of the jobs." (El Universal, February 9, 2000, Financial Section, reportage by Lilia Gonzalez and Alberto Bello). Noting that large corporations had not created a productive chain with small and mid size industries (which are the primary source of employment in Mexico), the researcher had the sense of humor to point out to Senor Blanco: "These are facts, not globalphobia." (Ibid.).

In the great fraud called the "North American Free Trade Act" (product of the great Salinas lie), the future is now being projected with the signing of a free trade agreement with the European Union. With a liking for modern cover-ups, the European governments are extending their hands to Zedillo without caring that his is covered with indigenous blood, without noticing that his government is the one that has the most ties with drug trafficking, and closing their eyes to the lack of democracy in our country. The European Union's flexibility can be understood, what is at stake is a slice of the pie that is called, still, "Mexico." Due to the marvels of globalization, a country is measured by its macro-economic indices. The people? They do not exist, there are only buyers and sellers. And, within those, there are classifications: the small, the large and the macro. These latter ones buy or sell countries. At one time they were governments of Nation States, today they are only merchants in search of good prices and lucrative profits. The political class and their recruits: the army, the media, intellectuals, international bodies.

If we have said before that the political class is increasingly less political and increasingly more business oriented, in an election year cynicism achieves levels of a publicity "boom." The ones that "matter" are not the governed, rather those who contribute to, or make difficult, the exercise of power. Called upon by the Mexican political class, the high clergy, the army, the electronic media, the intellectuals and international bodies become "the great electors." Their respective parcels receive the regime's benefits, more conspicuously during an election. Citizens remain at the margins, and their demands are reduced to surveys of electoral preferences. The statements, counter-statements and comments among themselves belong to the so-called "leaders" of an opinion that is increasingly closer to an agreement among cronies, and increasingly removed from a serious debate about ideas and programs.

The high clergy advances, with purported divine backing, on terrestrial intrigues. Teaming up with those in power and/or those who aspire to power, the Catholic hierarchy sees with satisfaction that its words have influence and bearing on government policies. While the lay State is nothing more than a shameful date on the calendar, the clergy and politicians break bread and salt and share complicity and shame in public and private meetings. It is not a mutual respect between different arenas, no. It is a symbiosis that allows some bishops and cardinals to be closer to the Mexico of power than to the common, everyday Catholics (the great majority of Mexicans). The Reform Laws? Excuse me, my eminence: isn't that the name of a street?

In another space, other "bishops" and "cardinals" - but from the intellectual right - are fighting to occupy the space left by the supreme pontiff, Octavio Paz. If one could, in some way, measure Paz' stature as an effective intellectual with and for the power, it is measuring it by the dwarves who are fighting over his legacy. The last great intellectual of the right died with Paz, those who followed him might be of the right, but they are far from being intellectuals. Even so, the hierarchies of the intellectual right in Mexico have their acolytes and, if it were to become necessary, their soldiers. In recent days, the intellectual front against the university movement suffered a serious setback. The blow came from a university professor - an intellectual and from the left - called Pablo Gonzalez Casanova. The UNAM researcher demonstrated something fundamental: legality cannot replace legitimacy, and, in the case of the UNAM conflict, "legality" (since other intellectuals have demonstrated that the entrance by the Federal Preventative Police into UNAM was illegal, as the legal complaints against the imprisoned students are illegal) was converted into a means by which the senselessness of the violence received an honorary doctorate from the largest university in Latin America.

If being a leftist was already something unforgivable in Gonzalez Casanova, the fact of his working in congruence with his ideas was now too much. The "cardinals" of intelligentsia sent their pawns (it seems that some of them even have first and last names) to go after Don Pablo. Even though they had lost the battle, the intelligentsia of the right did not do their utmost for that failed skirmish. Their decisive battles are not in the arena of ideas (they would most certainly lose), nor against progressive intellectuals. No, the ground to be conquered, the one they want, the one which some of them are already enjoying, is at the side of the "prince," at the edge of his table, whispering praise into the ears of the great gentlemen of politics and of money. Nonetheless, they have to do something to differentiate themselves from the buffoons swarming around the government palace. That is why they do their magazines and their television programs. The dead letters they etch, their intellectual connections and their open areas are not targeted at anyone but themselves. In these places they make comments to themselves, they read themselves, they "critique" among themselves, they greet themselves, and, in so doing, they say to each other: "We are the conscience of the new power, we are necessary because we say we are necessary, the Power needs someone to set their economic interests and its costs to prose, what makes us different from the buffoons is that we do not tell jokes, we explain them."

In this dwarf-like world of dwarves, the surface is a chessboard where bishops, kings, queens, pawns, knights and rooks conspire at the tops of their voices. Everyone knows who is going to win, that is not what is important, but rather which square they occupy and for how long. The uproar deafens each of them, but the machine works. There are seven decades of a political system that is now being called the "new PRI." The noise of the machine does not resemble that of gears grinding, it is more and more like a publicity "spot."

The problems begin when pieces enter that do not belong on that chessboard, when some strange object jams the gears, or when some interference obstructs the omnipotent "buying and selling"

The National Agenda to the Entertainment Section?

The fundamental soundbox of this Mexico of the powerful is in the electronic media. However, far from being merely an echo of what the political class says, television and radio take on their own voice, and, without anyone questioning them, they become the primary voice. The great problems of the country do not define the national agenda, for that matter neither do the political leaders. No, election campaigns and government agendas go along with radio and television programs. The electronic media does not broadcast news, it creates it, feeds it, makes it grow, annihilates it. The differences among the partisan choices during elections are not based on the programs for the nation which they are proposing, but in the time slots they manage to secure in the media.

The "ratings" which matter are not the viewing public, but rather in what they can reach in the political class. The greatest part of the statements and declarations by the main political actors is not addressed to real situations, but rather to lead news stories. Thus the "up to the minute" issues covered by the media are those that they have selected to be such. In the great theater of Mexican politics, the politicians are the actors and, simultaneously, the spectators. Radio and television carry out the roles of screenwriter, producer, lighting, stage setting and box office.

If it is increasingly difficult to speak of a single Mexico, it is impossible during an election period. The existence of two countries is palpable: the one that exists in the headlines and the one that takes place "off the record," outside the news stories and the exclusives.

Off the Record: Reality

While radio and television try hard, ineffectively, to present an image of "normalcy" at the Autonomous National University of Mexico, the enthusiasts for the "Rule of Law" being exercised against social fighters find themselves surprised that the entrance into the CU by Wilfredo Robledo's paramilitaries and the detention of hundreds of university students did not "solve" the conflict in the seat of higher learning. The university movement is not over, nor is the pretender, De La Fuente, the rector. The selective and piecemeal release of the student prisoners (at great pains to leave a few still in jail) has not discouraged the struggle for the demand for free education and for a truly democratic and decision-making university congress. At times disconcerted, the university movement remains firm in its demand for freedom for the political prisoners, free education and the congress. Radio and television, irritated, try to make sure that the headlines belong solely to those have paid for air time. The rest should be relegated to the police blotter or used as "filler." Who cares about the parents who are bleeding to death in order to demand the release of their children, if Esteban (Guajardo) Moctezuma and Emilio Gamboa are fighting on Labastida's team? The same media which were horrified over the CGH's vocabulary, get excited about the "crap-drunk-hush" of the election campaigns and about the abundant exchange of digital signals among the candidates.

But, if Reality takes place mostly outside the programming, every once in a while it takes a bite out of the Mexico of above, and it ruins economic macro-indices, news programs and candidates' agendas. In a corner of the other Mexico, a community decides to do without tele-novels and news shows, it confronts the police and defends a rural teachers school. In El Mexe, Hidalgo, the protagonists are not education students, nor the police who went to crush them. They are the people. People who had no space allotted them in the news other than in the police blotter, a point in the candidate's rally, a number in the amount of tortillas and drinks to be given out during the campaign swing. As they appear, they disappear. An avalanche of statements bury the fundamental fact (the "Ya Basta!" firmly exercised) and one other thing.

Chiapas? It might be on the agenda of the UN or of other national and international non-governmental organizations, but not on the national one. In order to avoid that, the Croquetas Albores spares no expense. In one year, the Croquetas Albores has spent 28 million pesos in order to avoid Chiapas being the bad note on the news (Proceso Sur, Number 1, March 4, 2000). The man with the checkbook is the much loved son of TV Azteca: Manuel de la Torre, who just yesterday was destroying rural schools with his "helicopter buzzes." And today he is trying to round up journalists as if they were cattle.

While the governor insists he has made great economic investments in Chiapas, he "forgets" to say that that the greatest expense was made on publicity, paid journalistic notes, hush money in order to silence "disagreeable" news and in order to improve the federal army's battered image.

Between Albores' barking and Rabasa's braying, the army is taking up new attack positions, its garrisons are being ostentatiously reinforced, planes and helicopters are increasing their overflights, and the war continues, now keeping a prudent distance from press headlines.

The zapatista indigenous insist on the value of the word: the women in San Cristobal on March 8, the March 21 coordinadoras, the residents of Amador Hernandez, those from Amparo Agua Tinta, the Tzotzils of Los Altos, the Tzeltales of Las Canadas, the Chols and Zoques of the North, the Mames of the Sierra, all of them remembering once again that there is a word that the government did not honor, the San Andres Accords, and that there is no peace, nor justice, nor dignity for the Mexican indigenous.

Far from the front pages, from the electronic news programs, the Mexico of the people takes place in resistance, in patient waiting, in hope...

What are they waiting for?

I return the pages to Durito, asking him:

"That 'what are they waiting for?', Is it a question, a demand or a prophecy?"

"Go to the window," Durito tells me. I do so and I look and I do not believe it.

"So? Who would have thought?"

"That is how it is. Windows are like cookies: they are tasty and nourishing," says Durito, while beginning the return

With those words, Durito ended his talk of that dawn, Don Pablo. When I returned to the hut, I re-read your letter and began writing these lines. I should try to explain to you that we zapatistas see ourselves not just in the window of the left that you note in your text. We believe we have opened another window, a window within the window of the left, that our political proposal is more radical than those which appear at your window and that it is different, very "other" (note: I did not write "better," just "different"). And I suppose that this letter was in order to explain to you (and to others) what it consists of, according to us, that other window that we zapatistas have opened.

But it so happens that everything will be in that book that I have not yet written, but which can be read in one of the "window" areas that are in the mountains of the Mexican southeast. And so you will have to wait until that book is written (which is nothing if not optimistic) and has been published (which borders on ingenuousness). Meanwhile, Don Pablo, you have all of our best wishes and, if possible, may your next letter be accompanied by some "Pancrema" cookies (better if they are not rancid). Perhaps then I can convince Durito to take me to the damned "window" again. Because, as for the book which I have not yet written (but which, I suppose, I shall write), I only managed to read the dedication, and I didn't get any further because a damp tenderness prevented it.

Vale, Don Pablo. Salud and, when seen well, a window is nothing more than a broken mirror.

> *From the mountains of the Mexican Southeast,*
> *Subcomandante Insurgente Marcos.*
> *Mexico, March of 2000.*

89. MARCOS TO THE INSURGENTAS

> Insurgentas!
> To those who have fallen
> To those who are following
> To those who shall come

> *"There goes my heated letter,*
> *dove forged in fire,*
> *with two folded wings and the address in the middle.*
> *Bird who pursues only nest, air and sky, flesh, hands, your eyes,*
> *and the space of your breath."*
> - Miguel Hernandez

> *"The letters are late and they are not enough to say what one wants."*
> - Jaime Gil de Biedma

Performing a balancing act with its nocturnal hat, the March hare is indecisive. It still does not know whether to rain, or to be content with letting the sky be stained with black ink. It is now the women's March, from the 8th to the 21st, that of the zapatista women, of the insurgentas.

I have spoken before of the rebel women, the insurgentas, of our being beside them, of their small and large heroism. Every March 8, we insurgents face them and give them the military salute. A small fiesta usually follows, with the meager resources of our camps in the mountains. The women have been in the mountains of the Mexican southeast from the beginnings of the EZLN. As time passed, more were to join that small delirious group, which the world would later know as the "Zapatista Army of National Liberation."

There are things, small, daily, that form part of the guerrilla life, and which are like small dues that the mountain imposes on those who dare to be part of it. I know each and every one of these difficulties, and I well know that, for the women, they are double. Not because we impose them like that, but rather because of things that come from other parts and other times. If someone were to admire the fact that someone would abandon their history and, as we say, "join up with the guerrillas" - joining the profession of insurgent soldier - they should stop and look at those who make that choice while being women. Their admiration would be double. In addition to confronting a particularly harsh environment, the insurgentas must also confront a cultural code which, beyond the mestizo-indigenous division, determines "spaces" (I mean attitudes, places, duties, work, responsibilities and the multiple etceteras added by a society built on exclusion) which are not for women. If an insurgenta thinks she has too much work with carrying, walking, training, fighting, studying and working along with the men, she is wrong. It could always be worse. And, in our case, what is "worse" is to be in command.

Primarily indigenous, the EZLN carries with it, not just the hope of something better for everyone, but it also drags along the world's troubles and blindness, which we want to leave aside. If, in the indigenous communities and in the cities, women must confront a world where being male is a privilege that excludes those different (women and homosexuals), in the mountain and as troop commanders, they must confront the resistance by the majority of the insurgents to take orders from a woman. If this resistance saw itself substantially diminished during the 1994 combat, this does not mean that it has completely disappeared. The male will invariably think that he can do it better than his commander, if it is a she, a woman. Something similar takes place in the villages, but I am specifically speaking now of the regular troops, of the insurgents and the insurgentas.

Over the last few days, there has been just one merit promotion in the EZLN, that is, a raise in military rank. An insurgenta, Maribel, rose from First Captain to Infantry Major. The now Major Maribel is still small and dark, she is still a woman, the only thing that has changed is that now she commands an entire regiment. To those problems which she confronts in her new status as commander of a zone, must be added those that correspond to her for being a woman. Like her, other compañeras, with or without command, in arms and services, rigorously carry on, paying their dues of dedication and sacrifice, the same as all the combatants. But, if the part least exposed now to the glare of outside spotlights is the insurgent troops, the insurgentas add one more shadow to that of the ski-masks they wear: they are women. And, I should say, they also add a superior level of heroism to ours, the men. We might not understand it (in spite of regulations and statutes, of the revolutionary law of women, of talks and statements), but we shall not let it go unrecognized.

And alongside Maribel are other officers in what we call "Health Services," there are the Insurgent Captains Oli-Ale (the woman with the most active years within the EZLN) and Monica, and Insurgent Lieutenant Aurora. There are more, officers and troops, some of whom I have already mentioned, years ago, on an occasion like this one. I shall not name some others because there has already been an occasion to do so. Before them, there was Alicia, from the first group that founded the EZLN in 1983, and the first woman with troop command (and so the first in the mountains; in confronting the problem of, being a woman and commanding men): a little later Lucia arrived, who is the insurgent author of the words to the Zapatista Hymn (and of many of the songs that are heard today in the nights of the mountains of the Mexican southeast). And still earlier there were Murcia (the first woman in the zapatista guerrilla to fall in combat in 1974), Deni Prieto S. (fallen in combat in 1974), Soledad (fallen in combat in 1974), Julieta Glockner (fallen in combat in 1975) and Ruth (fallen in combat in 1983, who taught me how to shoot).

Through all of them, and with them, is Lucha, whom we call "the stainless steel insurgenta." More than 30 clandestine years cause Lucha's ski mask to shine among us in a special way. Today, in spite of the cancer that she hardly lets bother her, Lucha continues to be the first among our guerrilla women, the best memory.

This March 8, saluting our current insurgentas, we are saluting all those who preceded them and us, and who, in more than one sense, transcend us.

I shall tell you something about the name "insurgentas." The anecdote could have taken place at any time and in any place in that neglected dailiness of the life of the mountains. I found myself leading a military training. Between exercise and tactical exercise, the guerrilla column was trotting to the rhythm of more or less obvious chants: I would, for example, shout "Who lives?" and the troops would respond in unison "The Patria!" That is how it was done and how it is done. One of the chants of combat march is when the commander asks "What are we?" and everyone responds "Insurgents!" On that day that I am now recounting to you, half the column was made up of women, and, when I shouted "What are we?" the response was a disorderly clamor. I thought they were tired and I gave the order to halt. Deployed in what is called a "firing line," the troops remained in position, at attention and in silence. I put myself in front of them and again shouted "What are we?" and then I could clearly hear that, while the males were responding "Insurgents!" the women were overcoming the men's voices, and they were imposing their shout of "Insurgentas!" I remained silent. I gave the men the order to "fall out." Then, facing just the women, I repeated "What are we?" They responded, without any interference now, strongly and firmly, "Insurgentas!" I kept looking at them, disconcerted, and I noted a slight smile on their faces. I went back to the "What are we?" and they repeated "Insurgentas!" I lit my pipe and smoked slowly, not looking at anything. I called them all to formation and told them, in so many words, "Today we learned that we are going to win. Are there any questions?" Silence. In a strong voice I ordered "Attention! Insurgents!" I turned around to look at the companeras, and I added: "And Insurgentas! Fall out! Now!" The sound of the boots was, indeed, uniform. Thank goodness, I muttered to myself. Everyone went to the quartermasters'. I remained smoking, seeing how the afternoon, feminine as it is, was covered in sea and lilacs, in insurgentas.

The zapatista insurgentas! Now, this time, I want to speak more about one of them. Concerning this woman I could say that she is one more of us, but for me she is not one more, she is unique. The Sea is not a literary character, she is a woman, she is a zapatista. She was the architect of last year's national and international consulta (and an important part of each and every one of the peace initiatives during these 6 years), and, as frequently happens with the zapatistas, her anonymity is double for the fact of her being a woman. Now, given that it is March 8, I wish to make it clear that, although most of the time the public figure belongs to me, many initiatives belong, in their design and realization, to other companeros and companeras. In the case of the consulta, it was a zapatista woman: The Sea. As soon as March 21 was over, she picked up her pack and joined the unit.

One must also remember that the mobilization of women (in Mexico and in the world) in that consulta formed the backbone, in the contact office (national and international), in the brigades, in the actions: women (of all sizes, origins, status, colors, ages) were the majority. And so, in order to salute the women who are fighting and, above all, those who are fighting and who are not seen, in several senses, the insurgentas appear in these lines. In order to celebrate them I have asked for the accompaniment of an old indigenous wise man: Old Antonio, and also of the most intrepid and gallant knight these worlds have ever seen: Durito, alias Nebuchadnezzar, alias Don Durito of the Lacandona, alias Black Shield, alias Sherlock Holmes, alias Durito Heavy Metal, alias whatever occurs to him. Sale pues, best wishes to the rebel women, to those without face, to the insurgentas!

Down below, March is once again repeating its three first letters in the eyes which, wheat in the light, it reads. Fito Pae'z accompanies me to give a gift of dress and love, and I went ahead, on the little tape player, with "everything you tell me is too much." I take advantage of a gust of wind, and I reach Don Durito, who is painstakingly sawing and nailing I know not what on his sardine can. I already know that I have said before that it is a pirate ship. Durito has, in fact, turned around to look at me with eyes like sharpened daggers when I have written "sardine can," but I have done so only so that the reader might remember that Durito is now Black Shield (Escudo Negro), the famous pirate who shall inherit a truly difficult trust from the dead Barbarroja [Redbeard]. The vessel on which Durito, excuse me, I meant Black Shield, arrived here is called "learn from the mistakes of others," for reasons still unknown to me. Durito has proposed to me that I accompany him in the search for a treasure. I have already recounted all of this in a previous letter, and so I shall not go on about it. The fact is, in this March of the sea, I have come to where Durito is working in order to see what he is doing and in order to ask for guidance and advice.

Durito is giving the last blows to what I surmise to be a topmast with velacho, when I clear my throat in order to let my presence be known. Durito says:

"Good, there it is. Now, with you in the bow, no adversary shall be capable of opposing us."

I smile melancholically and look at the vessel with indifference.

Durito scolds me: "It is not just any 'ship'. It is a galley, a classic vessel, destined for the war in the 16th century. The galley can be propelled by sails or by the oars used by the so-called 'galley slaves'." He pauses and continues:

"And, speaking of sails [velas], might one know why the sadness is veiling your face?"

I make an "it's not important" gesture.

Durito interprets it and says: "Ah! Love sickness!" He slowly puts the hammer and saw aside, disembarks and, taking out his little pipe, he sits down next to me.

"I assume, my future run prow, that what has you sad and heavyhearted is nothing other than a she, a female, a woman, in fact." I sigh. Durito continues:

"Look, my dear bathtub sailor, if the one keeping you up is a woman, but a unique one, then the illness is serious, but the remedy possible."

"I confess! It so happens that, yes, it is a woman, a unique one, she who is sea for many more reasons than the 'Mariana' which names her. One unlucky day I drifted away from her, and now I cannot find the means or manner of taking refuge in her damp, of having bad storms forgotten, of her forgiving me."

Durito takes a long puff and sententiously declares:

"Your lacks and losses are great and serious, but I can give you some counsel if you promise to follow my directions to the letter."

I said "yes" with an enthusiasm that made Durito jump with surprise. He readjusts his eye patch as best he can and says:

"It is necessary to resort to a spell. In love, the world is, as always, a puzzle, but it so happens that, if a unique one finds a unique one, the pieces make sense and take form, and the puzzle is put off and breaks faces, arms and legs."

"And hearts I say, rubbing the anguish I am feeling in mine."

"Good, where I'm going is that the spell will only have an effect if she, the Sea in your case, is willing to submit to it, because, otherwise, all will be useless. I mean that the spell will not work if the person on whom the spell is cast is not aware that she is being charmed."

"A strange spell," this I say.

Durito continues without paying me any mind: "Bring her a good memory, one of those which serve for seeing ahead and far away, one that shall make her lift her gaze and take it long and deep. Tell her to look ahead, not to the following day, not to the next week, nor to the coming year. Further ahead, further away. Do not ask her what she sees. Only look at her looking ahead. If you see that her gaze smiles with tenderness, then you will be forgiven, and there shall be wheat and beach and sea and wind, and you will be able to sail once again, and that, and nothing else, is what love is."

Durito picks up his things once again and continues fixing the galley. The destination of the trip is still unknown to me, but Durito remains silent, letting me know that I should go and carry out what he has told me.

I wander about through the dawn a bit more. I seek to find The Sea in bed. I know that you are thinking that I am speaking of just bed, but here bed is any bed or table or ground or chair or air, as long as our shadow is doubled in the other, never one, always two, but so close together. I think that, if The Sea is sleeping, it will be a problem to wake her up with this absurd story of the spell. Then it occurs to me that I should address the issue indirectly, approaching while whistling some tune, commenting on the weather or trying to write a love poem.

But the problem, I sense, is that the poem of love holds a lock, an ultimate secret, which only a few, a very few, almost no one, is able to open, to discover, to free. One is left with the impression that what one feels for someone has already found its perfect, brilliant, complete formulation in someone else's words. And one crumples up the paper (or, in cybernetic times, decrees the file in question "deleted") with the commonplaces in which feeling is made word. I do not know much of love poetry, but I do know it enough that, when my fingers resort to something like that, I sense that it seems more like a strawberry malted than a love sonnet. In short, poetry, and more specifically, love poetry, is for anyone, but not everyone has the key that opens its highest flight. Because of that, when I am able to, I call on the poets, friends and enemies, and, to the ear of The Sea, I bring back the plagiarisms which, barely stammered, appear to be mine. I suspect that she knows, in any case, she does not let me know, and she closes her eyes and lets my fingers stroke her hair and her dreams.

I draw close and I think and I feel and I say to myself such desires to return to the beginning, to start again, to go back to the first stroke of the first letter, the "A" of the long alphabet of the company, to return to the first sketch that the two of us made together and to begin to grow once more, and, once more, to hone the point of hope. There she is. She sleeps. I draw close and...

...And all of this comes to mind, or to the story, because, in this sea of March, everything seems to smell of desolation, of impasse, of irretrievable fall, of frustration. Because I am sure that it would seem strange to all of you that I would dare, today, to prophesy the return of the flags of all colors, peopling, from below, fields, streets and windows. And I dare to do so because I am looking at this zapatista woman, her tender determination, her dream. I look at her and, through her and, above all, with her, I am promising and promising myself, new airs for those sister flags, banners, volanderos, that disturb and make the rich and poor anxious, although for different reasons the one and the other. I promise, and I promise myself, right in the midst of the most tedious night, another tomorrow, not the best, but better. For this woman who, in the mornings and in front of me, pricks up her ears and puts on her pistol while telling me "there comes the helicopter" as if she were saying "they are knocking at the door." For this zapatista, for this woman, and for many like her who, two and three times behind, carry the weight so that the little good that remains does not fall, and in order, with that material, to begin now to build that which today seems so far away: the morning.

Vale. Salud to all, and, for her, a flower.

> From the mountains of the Mexican Southeast,
> Subcomandante Insurgente Marcos.
> Mexico, March of 2000.

P.S. THAT FULFILS THE DUPLICITY - I am attaching here the memory that I gave to the Sea. This is how this Letter 6e. achieves its double wing and takes the flight necessary for the entire letter. Sale y vale,

Story for a Night of Anguish

I tell the Sea that, for some reason that I cannot manage to understand, Old Antonio might have read the German philosopher Immanuel Kant in part. Instead of becoming impassioned with xenophobia, Old Antonio took everything that was good from the entire world, without regard for the land that birthed them.

Referring to good persons from other nations, Old Antonio used the term "internationals," and he used the word "foreigners" only for those indifferent to the heart, not caring whether they were of his color, language and race. "Sometimes there are foreigners in the same blood," Old Antonio said, in order to explain to me the absurd stupidity of passports.

But I tell the Sea that the history of nationalities is another history. What I am remembering now concerns the night and its paths.

It was one of those dawns with which March affirms its delirious vocation. A day with a sun like a six-tailed whip was followed by an afternoon of grey storm clouds. For the night, a cold wind was already gathering black clouds above a faded and timid moon.

Old Antonio had passed the morning and afternoon with the same calmness with which he was now lighting his cigarette. A bat flew about us for an instant, most certainly disturbed by the light with which Old Antonio gave life to his cigarette. And, like the tzotz, it appeared suddenly, in the middle of the night.

The History of the Air of the Night

When the greatest gods, those who birthed the world, the very first, were thinking about how and for what they were going to do what they were going to do, they made an assembly in which each one brought forth his word in order to know it and so that the others would know of it. And so each one of the very first gods were bringing forth a word and they were throwing it into the center of the assembly and there it bounced and it reached other gods who grabbed it and threw it once more, and so the word went like a ball from one side to the other until everyone then understood it and then they made their agreement, the most great gods who were those who birthed all things we call worlds. One of the agreements they found when they brought forth their words was that each path has its traveler and each traveler his path. And then they went about making things complete, or, rather, each with his partner.

That is how the air and the birds were born. Or, rather, that there was not air first and then birds to travel it, nor were birds made first either, and then air, so that they could fly it. They did the same with water and the fish who swim it, the land and animals who walk it, the path and the feet which travel it.

But, speaking of birds, there was one that protested very much about the air. This bird said that it would fly better and more quickly if the air did not oppose it. This bird grumbled very much, because, even though its flight was agile and swift, it always wanted to be more and better, and, if it could not be so, it was, it said, because the air had become an obstacle. The gods became annoyed at how much bad this bird was speaking, who flew in the air and complained of the air.

And so, as punishment, the first gods took away its feathers and the light in its eyes. They sent him naked out into the cold of the night and blindly he would have to fly. Then his flight, once graceful and light, become disordered and clumsy.

But once found and after many blows and setbacks this bird was given the ability to see with its ears. By speaking to things, this bird, or the Tzotz, guides its path and knows the world, which answers him in a language only he knows how to listen to. Without feathers to dress him, blind and with a nervous and hurried flight, the bat rules the night of the mountain and no animal travels the dark air better than he.

From this bird, the Tzotz, the bat, the true men and women learned to grant great and powerful value to the spoken word, to the sound of thought. They also learned that the night contains many worlds and one must know how to listen to them in order for them to come forth and to flourish. The worlds of the night are born with words. Through sounds, they are made light, and they are so many they do not fit in the land and many end up adapting themselves to the sky. That is why they say that stars are made on the ground.

The most great gods also birthed men and women, not so that one would be the path of the other, but so that they would be, at the same time, the other's path and traveler. They were made different in order to be together. The most great gods made men and women so that they would love each other. That is why the air of the night is the best for flying, for thinking, for speaking and for loving.

Old Antonio ends his history of that March. In this March, here, the sea is sailing a dream where the word and bodies disrobe, they travel the worlds without colliding, and love can take flight without anguish. Up there a star discovers an empty space on the ground and quickly lowers itself, leaving a momentary rent in the window of this dawn. On the little tape player, Mario Benedetti, a Uruguayan of the entire world, is saying "You can go, I am staying."

ANOTHER P.S. Did the Sea accept the spell? It is, as I do not know who said, a mystery.

Vale de nuez. Salud and March is, as always, coming in very crazily.

The Sup, waiting as by law, that is, smoking.

90. TO THE RELATIVES OF THE POLITICALLY DISAPPEARED

To the relatives of the politically disappeared

"I dream in marble cloisters
where, in divine silence,
the heroes stand, at rest;
At night, by the light of the soul,
I speak with them: by night!
They are in line: I pass
among the lines: I kiss
the hands of stone: the eyes
of stone open: the beards
of stone tremble: the stone swords
are brandished: they weep:
the sword shudders in the sheath!
Mute, I kiss their hands."
- Jose Marti

April falls with stone hand over the Mexico of below. Sun and shadows abound during the day, and at night the moon negotiates a path mined with stars. This country now walks the path of uncertainty, that ravine, one of whose sides is threatened by oblivion and forgetting. On the other side, memory is made mountain and stone.

The dawn is plucking petals from lost lights when, in any city, in any house, in any room, in front of any typewriter, a mother (the heart of the flower of stone, hope) is writing a letter. Curious, the dawn leans over her shoulder and barely manages to steal a few lines: "and then you will imagine the sorrow that grieves me so...", "... for us, the mothers, who have lived as if with a dagger plunged into our chest for so very long...". The shadow brings the bowl of the pipe to the candle and lights the tobacco and the words which have already taken over the hands and which are, now, writing:

I did not know Jesus Piedra Ibarra, or Cesar German Yanez Munoz. Not personally. From other photographs I can recognize them now in the poster, in front of me, that shines a "EUREKA!" on the upper part. In the center, a group of men and women are carrying a large banner that reads "PRESENTATION OF THE POLIT-ICALLY DISAPPEARED," and it is filled with photographs of men and women, all young, all Mexicans. Among the images, I lightly mark with a pen that of Jesus Piedra Ibarra and that of Cesar German Yanez Munoz.

I examine the faces of those holding up the banner: mostly women, and it can be seen from their faces that they are forever mothers. Are? Forever? They are, and they are forever, that is for certain. The poster could be from 25 years ago, from 15, from 5 years ago, from this very day. It tells me nothing other than the firmness of those gazes, their determination, their hope.

The "White Brigade," the paramilitary group with which the government operated the dirty war against the Mexican guerrillas of the 70's and 80's kidnapped Jesus Piedra Ibarra on April 18, 1975, 25 years ago. Since then, nothing has been learned of him. The Mexican Federal Army detained Cesar German Yanez Munoz in February-March of 1974, 26 years ago. Since then, nothing has been learned of him. Thirty years ago, 20 years ago, 10 years ago, 5 years ago, right now in Mexico political opponents are being "disappeared."

I did not know Jesus Piedra Ibarra or Cesar German Yanez Munoz, nor any of the politically disappeared men and women. Or, yes, I did know them. They had other faces and wore different bodies, but it was their same gaze. I knew them in the streets and in the mountains. I saw them raising their fists, flags, weapons. I saw them saying "NO!," shouting "NO!" until they were left without voice in their throats but still in their hearts. I saw them. I knew them. Then they were confederates, companeros, brothers, they were us. I knew them. I know them. Their feet and arms are other, but their steps are the same, their embraces are the same. I know them. I know us. Those faces are ours. Just take a black tipped pen and paint a ski-mask on the faces of those men and women.

Jesu's Piedra Ibarra, Cesar German Yanez Munoz. I knew their mothers. I knew Rosa, mother of Cesar German, and, some time later, Rosario, mother of Jesus. I knew Rosa and Rosario, both mothers of fighters, both fighters, both seekers. Some years ago Rosa made as if she had died and went to look for Cesar German under the earth. Rosario continues above, looking for Jesus. Mamas of stone, Rosa and Rosario look above and beneath the stones. They are looking for a disappeared, two, three, dozens, hundreds...

Yes, there are hundreds of politically disappeared in Mexico. What were these and other men and women guilty of to deserve from their enemies, we are not now saying life and liberty, but neither jail nor grave? At times a photograph is the only material thing remaining of them. But in the mothers' hands of stone, that photograph is made flag. And the flags are made to wave in the heavens. And the heavens is where they are raised by men and women who know that memory is not a date that marks the beginning of an absence, but rather a tree which, planted yesterday, rises up tomorrow.

Of what material can the homage be made to those anonymous heroes who have no other corner than the memory of those who share their blood and their ideals? Of stone, but not of just any stone. Perhaps of the stone of memory that their mothers were and are. Because there are mothers that are stone, stone of refuge, of strength, of home, of wall that sustains the word "JUSTICE" in their hearts.

The mothers of the disappeared are of stone. What can those ladies fear who have confronted so much, who have struggled so much? Not absence, because they have carried that for many years. Not pain, because they live with that each and every day. Not exhaustion, because they have traveled all paths time and again. No, the only thing the ladies fear is the silence with which oblivion, forgetting and amnesia covers itself, staining history.

The ladies have no weapon against that fear other than memory. But where is memory safeguarded when a frenzied cynicism reigns in the world of politics? Where can those little pieces of history take refuge, which now appear to be only photographs, and which were men and women with faces, names, ideals? Why does the left of today seem to be so overwhelmed by the present and to forget its absent ones? How many of those fallen in the long night of the dirty war in Mexico are nothing other than stepping stones in the rise of the left as alternative politics? How many of those that we are owe much to those who are not here?

Is it over? Has the nightmare that was called the "White Brigade" ended now? What is the government body now called that is in charge of disappearing those who are opposed to the system? Mexico: Has it done better with political disappearances since it has been "modern"? Can one speak of justice while political disappearances exist?

Those who are relatives (through blood, through ideas, through both) of the politically disappeared: do they have company today in their anguish, in their pain, in the absences? Where are the hands and shoulders for them? Where is the ear for their rebellion? What dictionary contains their determined search that will banish forever the words "irremediable", "irretrievable", "impossible", "oblivion", "resignation", "conformity", "surrender"? The politically disappeared: where are their executioners?

Those who disappeared them appear at the old and beleaguered house of the current politics in Mexico. They see that no one is turning around, that no eye is even turning to the forgotten chest of those who have fought so that there may no longer be a below to which one's gaze might fall. The executioners congratulate themselves then, they have been successful, they raise their cups and toast with blood the death of memory.

This country is called Mexico, and it is the year 2000. The century and millennium are ending, and the belief continues that silence makes things disappear: if we do not speak of prisoners and the politically disappeared, they will then be erased from our present and from our past.

But it is not so. With silence not only will our history vanish, but, most certainly, the nightmare will be repeated, and other mothers will be made of stone, and they will travel to all corners, above and below, saying, shouting, demanding justice.

The executioners are celebrating their impunity (and their impunity is not just they have no punishment, it is also that the disappeared continue to be disappeared), but also the silence. Nonetheless, not everyone forgets.

Because, further below, where the roots of the Patria take life from subterranean rivers, the defeat of the executioners is brewing. The images that memory raises in this heart from below are of stone, and those men and women who, barely touching the strong skin of history, are rising up and speaking, have some part of stone. And there is also a bit of stone in that modest school which, in the midst of the zapatista Realidad, where the name shines like a flag: "Jesus Piedra Ibarra School."

The shadow crumples the written pages and sets fire to them with the same light with which he relights his pipe. He takes another clean page and, with concise tenderness, writes:

> "April 18, 2000
> Mama Stone,
> I do not know about the others, But we do not forget.
> With affection, Your zapatista daughters and sons.
> P.S. Best wishes to all the ladies."

Below, the dawn continues its hot embrace, while the sea arranges the breezes of her hair. Above the moon, partial, reminds us that nothing will be complete if memory is missing. And "memory" is how call justice is called here.

> From the mountains of the Mexican Southeast,
> Subcomandante Insurgente Marcos.
> Mexico, April of 2000.

91. THE ALONE-AND-ABANDONED POLL

June 19, 2000
To the National and International Press

Ladies and gentlemen,
A communiqué is off, with our position on the upcoming elections. It says what it says, which is enough. We ask for clemency for the editorial staff.

Meanwhile, here we are shivering. And not because the "croqueta" Albores has contracted with Alasraki to "improve" his image (Albores is probably already looking for work promoting dog food), nor over the six hundred thousand dollars he's going to pay them (with money originally earmarked for "resolving the conditions of poverty and marginalization of the chiapaneco indigenous"). Nor because of the barking by the puppy Montoya Lievano (he's more nervous than ever because he's already discovering that it was his "boys" - his paramilitaries, that is - who were the ones responsible for the attack on Public Security in El Bosque on June 12). No, we are shivering because we are getting drenched by the rain. And, between the helicopters and the rain, we can't find good cover. The sea says, whatever, there are storms and storms and we still haven't made it to July 3. I sigh and curse the lack of umbrellas. What else can I do?

Vale. Salud, and look and see if there are any birth control pills around here. There is more than one ballot box in urgent need of them.

> From the Promotional Committee for the Useless Vote, excuse me,
> from the mountains of the Mexican Southeast,
> SupMarcos Mexico, June of 2000.

P.S. That Tells an Ad Hoc Tale of the Current Times...

Once upon a time there was a poll that was very alone and abandoned. It went here and there and no one paid it any attention. In desperation, the alone-and-abandoned poll went to see a specialist in marketing and image. The publicist cost the alone-and-abandoned poll very dearly, not just because of the check he had to pay him, but also for what the taxi cost which was waiting outside the offices for him. And the image consultant was much in demand by candidates of some official party. The alone-and-abandoned poll followed the consultant's directions to the letter, and he completely changed his "look" (check out how the P.D. is using a new vocabulary now). With this done, he went back to the party offices. Everyone received him with enthusiasm, and he became very famous and much sought after. While he was walking through the city streets, a child saw him and he asked his mother: Why is that mirror walking? Tan, tan.

92. WHY DO WE ALL AGREE THE GLOBAL MARKET IS INEVITABLE?

"Do not forget ideas are also weapons"

The purpose of this text is to fuel the debate between right and leftwing intellectuals. It does not attempt to explain the relation of either with governments or changes in society.

I. Pay-per-view Global Domination

The world is not square, or so we learn at school, but on the brink of the third millennium it is not round either. I do not know which geometrical figure best represents the world in its present state but, in an era of digital communication, we could see it as a gigantic screen - one of those screens you can program to display several pictures at the same time, one inside the other. In our global world the pictures come from all over the planet - but some are missing. Not because there is not enough room on the screen but because someone up there selected these pictures rather than others.

What do the pictures show? On the American continent, we see a paramilitary group occupying the Autonomous National University of Mexico (UNAM); but the men in grey uniforms are not there to study. Another frame shows an armored column thundering through a native community in Chiapas. Beside this, we see United States police using violence to arrest a youth in a city that could be Seattle or Washington. The pictures in Europe are just as grey.

II. A Memorable Omission

Intellectuals have been part of society since the dawn of humanity. Their work is analytical and critical. They look at social facts and analyze the evidence, for and against, looking for anything ambiguous, that is neither one thing nor the other, revealing anything that is not obvious - sometimes even the opposite of what seems obvious.

These professional critics act as a sort of impertinent consciousness for society. They are non-conformists, disagreeing with everything - social and political forces, the state, government, media, arts, religion and so on. Activists will just say "we've had enough", but skeptical intellectuals will cautiously murmur "too much" or "not enough". Intellectuals criticize immobility, demand change and progress. They are, nevertheless, part of a society, which is the scene of endless confrontation and is split between those who use power to maintain the status quo and those who fight for change.

Intellectuals must choose between their function as intellectuals and the role that activists offer them. It is also here that we see the split between progressive and reactionary intellectuals. They all continue their work of critical analysis, but whereas the more progressive persist in criticizing immobility, permanence, hegemony and homogeneity, the reactionaries focus their attacks on change, movement, rebellion and diversity. So in fact, reactionary intellectuals "forget" their true function and give up critical thought. Their memory shrinks, excluding past and future to focus only on the immediate and present. No further discussion is possible.

III. Intellectual Pragmatism

Many leading rightwing intellectuals start life as progressives. But they soon attract the attention of the powerful, who deploy innumerable stratagems to buy or destroy them. Progressive intellectuals are "born" in the midst of a process of seduction and persecution. Some resist; others, convinced that the global economy is inevitable, look in their box of tricks and find reasons to legitimate the existing power structure. They are awarded with a comfortable armchair, on the right hand of the prince they once denounced.

They can find any number of excuses for this supposedly "inevitable" outcome: it is the end of history; money is everywhere and all-powerful; the police have taken the place of politics; the present is the only possible future; there is a rational explanation for social inequality; there are even "good reasons" for the unbridled exploitation of human beings and natural resources, racism, intolerance and war.

In an era marked by two new paradigms - communication and the market - rightwing intellectuals have realized that being "modern" means obeying one rule: "Adapt or go under". They are not required to be original, just to think like everyone else, taking their cue from international bodies like the World Bank, the International Monetary Fund or the World Trade Organization.

Far from indulging in original, critical thought, rightwing intellectuals become remarkably pragmatic, echoing the advertising slogans that flood the world's markets. In exchange for a place in the sun and the support of certain media and governments, they cast off their critical imagination and any form of self-criticism and espouse the new, free market creed.

IV. Blind Seers

The problem is not why the global economy is inevitable, but why almost everyone agrees that it is. Just as the economy is becoming increasingly global, so is culture and information. How are we to prevent vast media and communications companies like CNN or News Corporation, Microsoft or AT&T, from spinning their worldwide web?

In today's world economy the major corporations are essentially media enterprises, holding up a huge mirror to show us what society should be, not what it is. To paraphrase Regis Debray, what is visible is real and consequently true (1). That, by the way, is one of the tenets of rightwing dogma. Debray also explains that the center of gravity of news has shifted from the written word to visual effects, from recorded to live broadcasts, from signs to pictures.

To retain their legitimacy, today's rightwing intellectuals must fulfil their role in a visual era, opting for what is immediate and direct, switching from signs to images, from thought to TV commentary.

V. Future Past

In Mexico, leftwing intellectuals are very influential. Their crime is that they get in the way. Well, one of their crimes, because they also support the Zapatistas in their struggle: "The Zapatista uprising heralds the start of a new era in which native movements will emerge as players in the fight against the neoliberal global economy" (2). But we are neither unique nor perfect. Just look at the natives of Ecuador and Chile, and the demonstrations in Seattle, Washington, Prague - and those that will follow. We are just one of the pictures that deform the giant screen of the world economy.

The prince has consequently issued orders: "Attack them! I shall supply the army and media. You come up with the ideas". So rightwing intellectuals spend their time insulting their leftwing counterparts, and because of the Zapatista movement's international impact, they are now busy rewriting our story to suit the demands of the prince.

VI. Neoliberal Fascists

In one of his books Umberto Eco provides some pointers as to why fascism is still latent (3). He starts by warning us that fascism is a diffuse form of totalitarianism, then defines its characteristics: refusal of the advance of knowledge, disregard of rational principles, distrust of culture, fear of difference, racism, individual or social frustration, xenophobia, aristocratic elitism, machismo, individual sacrifice for the benefit of the cause, televised populism and use of Newspeak with its limited words and rudimentary syntax.

These are the values that rightwing intellectuals defend. Take another look at the giant screen. All that grey is a response to disorder, reflected in demands for law and order from all around us. But is Europe once more the prey of fascism? We may well see skinheads, with their swastikas, on the screen, but the commentator is quick to reassure us that they are only minority groups, already under control. But it may also take other, more sinister forms (see the articles by Christian Semler and Brigitte Patzold in this issue).

After the fall of the Berlin wall both sides of the political spectrum in Europe rushed to occupy the center. This was all too obvious with the traditional left, but it was also the case with the far right (4). It went out of its way to acquire a new image, well removed from its violent, authoritarian past, enthusiastically espousing neoliberal dogma.

VII. Skeptically Hopeful

The task of progressive thinkers - to remain skeptically hopeful - is not an easy one. They have understood how things work and, noblesse oblige, they must reveal what they know, dissect it, denounce it and pass it on to others. But to do this, they must also confront neoliberal dogma, backed by the media, banks, major corporations, army and police.

What is more, we live in a visual age - and so, to their considerable disadvantage, progressive thinkers must fight the power of the image with nothing but words. But their skepticism will get them out of that trap, and if they are equally skeptical in their critical analysis, they will be able to see through the virtual beauty to the real misery it conceals. So perhaps there is reason to hope.

There is a story that when Michelangelo sculpted his statue of David, he had to work on a "second-hand" piece of marble that already had holes in it. It is a mark of his talent that he was able to create a figure that took account of these limitations. The world we want to transform has already been worked on by history and is largely hollow. We must nevertheless be inventive enough to change it and build a new world.

Take care and do not forget that ideas are also weapons.

Subcomandante Insurgente Marcos.

93. Zedillo's Last Moments! (The Political Class)

November of 2000
Zapatista Army of National Liberation Mexico
To the National and International Press

Ladies and Gentlemen,
Here once again. The letters are off, for the one who is now leaving (fortunately), and an invitation for you to a press conference. We will do everything we can to not get hung up on the time.

Vale. Salud, and, no, you don't have to worry, Martha Sahagun is not going to be here.

From the Mountains of the Mexican Southeast,
Subcomandante Insurgente Marcos.
Mexico, November of 2000.

(Zedillo's last moments!)
Yepa! Yepa! Yepa! Andale! Andale! Andale!
Arriba! Arriba! Arriba!
PLAYWRIGHT's (ja!) PS WHICH SAYS WHAT IT SAYS. -
First Act - Characters: the political class, announcer, the headlines, the public.
Place: Mexico. Date: Prior to the elections of July 2, 2000.

(The curtain goes up. There are a television and a radio on the stage, turned up at full volume. In the background, the headlines of a national newspaper. The audio on the TV and the radio is the same: commercial jingles. The newspaper headlines are changing as they are signaled.)

The political class: "We are in the media, therefore we exist. We should now confront our greatness with the most difficult test in the supreme art of governing: the ratings. Call for the image consultants! (clapping of hands)."

The headlines: "THE IFE IS CREATED, THE FEDERAL INSTITUTE OF POLLS. The bother of going to the voting booths will be eliminated, says its boss."

The consultant (entering from the right): "Here I am (turning to the public). Modern political science consists not just of discovering which product will have the best acceptance in the marketplace, but - and here I have the science - in converting anything into something which resembles that product as far as possible (he takes a complete makeup kit out of his briefcase) (He painstakingly apples cosmetics to the face of the political class)."

The headlines: "CYBERNETIC CHALLENGE A DEMOCRATIC ADVANCE: EZPL"

The political class (sneezing): "Achoo! I think I'm allergic to this dust. What is it?"

Consultant (offering a handkerchief): "Bless you! It is the latest word in fashion, it is democratizing dust."

The political class (sighing in resignation): "Okay, anything to survive."

The headlines: "CANDIDATES' PRICES WILL BE GOING DOWN: SECOFI."

Announcer (entering hurriedly from the left): "Quickly! Hurry up! The sponsors are getting anxious! We have to tape the program."

Consultant: "The sponsors? I thought the members of the audience would be the ones who were anxious..."

Announcer: "No, no, no. The rhythm of politics is not set by clocks or calendars, but by program times. Hurry up! We don't have much time between the commercial breaks."

The political class (fixing itself up in front of a mirror being held by the consultant): "Good, how do I look?"

Consultant (smiling in satisfaction): "Magnificent! You are unrecognizable..."

The political class (to itself): "Commercial breaks! In the good old days there were no breaks other those produced by the happy sound of the rattles and slogans of 'You can see it, you can feel it, the PRI is omnipotent.'"

(The consultant moves to one side).

Announcer: "Lights! Camera! Action!"

Announcer (turning to the public): "Welcome to our program: 'The Modest

Truth'! Today, as a special guest, we have... the political class! (loud applause is heard, the public is still, but an audio tape is keeping them from the grueling task of having to applaud)."

The political class (turning to the announcer): "Is my tie okay?"

Announcer: "Tell us, political class, excuse me, can I call you 'tu'?"

The political class (fixing a decal which looks like a smile on its mouth): "Of course."

Announcer: "Good, tell us, what can the audience expect from the upcoming election?"

(The political class moves its lips, but no sounds at all come out).

Announcer: "Very interesting! Almost as interesting as these commercial messages from our sponsors!"

The political class (to the announcer): "Are we still taping?"

Announcer: "No. It went perfectly. Now we're waiting for the consultant to send us the audio of your response after he's done his marketing studies."

The political class: "Then can I leave now?"

Announcer: "Yes."

(The political class leaves. Someone comes and turns off the radio and television. The headlines disappear. The curtain falls. The audience yawns. An audio breaks into enthusiastic applause.)

Second Act - Characters: The political class; Senora X; a young man, Y; and Senor Z.

Place: Mexico.

Date: July 2, 2000.

(The curtain rises. There is only an empty street on the stage).

The political class (to itself): "We see faces, we do not know votes."

Senora X: "No."

The young man, Y: "No."

Senor Z: "No."

The political class (to the public): "We see faces, we do not know votes."

The public (breaking into the script, to everyone's shock): "No!"

This play is a problem. Those directing it are making a huge effort to convince the audience that it's already over. Not only is the public not leaving the premises, they're also insisting on getting up on the stage. The director and the actors are tearing their hair out. It is no longer possible to know where the stage is and where the seats are. Suddenly, apparently without an agreement having been reached, and with stern expressions on their faces, all the members of the public yell: "Third act! Third act! Third! Let's begin."

Does the curtain fall?

What? You didn't like it? Well, La Mar did. Okay, at least she smiled. What? Dari'o Fo, Carballido, Gurrola, Savariego and Lenero are going to reprove me? Let them do so. They reproved Einstein for his hygiene (or was it for his mathematics?).

The Sup in the box office.

94. TO SENOR ERNESTO ZEDILLO PONCE DE LEON

November of 2000
Zapatista Army of National Liberation.
Mexico
To Senor Ernesto Zedillo Ponce de Leon
Enroute to nowhere
Planet Earth

Senor Zedillo,

Six years ago I wrote to you in the name of all zapatistas, welcoming the nightmare. Many now think we were right. Throughout this administration, your term of office has been a long nightmare for millions of Mexican men and women: assassinations, economic crises, massive impoverishment, the illicit and brutal enrichment of a few, the selling off of the national sovereignty, public insecurity, the strengthening of ties between the government and organized crime, corruption, irresponsibility, war... and bad jokes badly told.

Throughout your administration you have striven to destroy the indigenous who rose up in defiance of everything that you represent. You strove to destroy them.

When you came to power you were free to choose how to confront the zapatista uprising. What you chose and what you did is now history. In your role as Commander-in-Chief of the federal army - and with all the power given to the head of the Executive - you could have chosen the path of dialogue and negotiation. You could have given signals of detente. You could have carried out what you signed in San Andres. You could have reached peace.

You did not do so.

You chose, rather, the double strategy of feigning a willingness to dialogue and of continuing the path of violence. In order to achieve that, you tried to repeat the history of the Chinameca betrayal (February 9, 1995), you squandered thousands of millions of pesos trying to buy the consciences of the rebels. You militarized the indigenous communities (and not just in Chiapas). You expelled international observers. You trained, equipped, armed and financed paramilitaries. You persecuted, jailed and summarily executed zapatistas (remember Union Progreso, June 10, 1998) and non-zapatistas. You destroyed the social fabric of the chiapaneco countryside. And, following the slogan of your putative child, the Red Mask paramilitary group ("We will kill the zapatista seed"), you ordered the massacre of children and pregnant women in Acteal on December 22, 1997.

We could understand why, being able to follow the path of dialogue, you opted to make war against us. It could have been because they sold you the idea that you could take us prisoners, that you could defeat us militarily, that you could achieve our surrender, that you could buy us, that you could deceive us, that you could make the Mexicans forget us and our struggle, that you could make people from other countries give up their solidarity with the indigenous cause. In short, that you could win the war against us. That we could understand. But, Senor Zedillo, why Acteal? Why did you order the assassination of children? Why did you order your henchmen to finish pregnant women off with machetes who, wounded or terrified, were unable to escape the massacre?

What, in fact, did you not do in order to finish off the zapatistas?

But were they finished off? They slipped through your ambush of February 9, 1995. They rebelled once more against your failure to fulfill the San Andres Accords. They escaped from your military siege as often as they wanted. They resisted your ferocious offensive, directed by the 'croquetas' Albores, against the Autonomous Municipalities. Over and over again they demonstrated with mobilizations that their demands had the support of millions of Mexicans. No, the zapatistas were not finished off.

And not only were they not finished off. In addition, they spread throughout the world. Do you remember the times that you had to leave, surreptitiously, through emergency exits, events being held in other countries, while zapatista solidarity committees were protesting your Chiapas policies? Is there any ambassador or consul who has not reported to you with desperation the actions carried out by international zapatistas at Mexican government events and buildings abroad? How often was your foreign affairs service estranged because of the failure to carry out the San Andres Accords, for the militarization of Chiapas and the lack of dialogue with the zapatistas? And, when you ordered the expulsion of hundreds of international observers, did solidarity actions throughout the world diminish?

And what do you have to say to me about Mexico? Instead of remaining "limited to 4 chiapaneco municipalities," zapatismo spread to the 32 states of the federation. It became worker, campesino, indigenous, teacher, student, employee, driver, fisherman, rocker, painter, actor, writer, nun, priest, sportsman, housewife, neighbor, independent unionist, homosexual, lesbian, transsexual, soldier, sailor, small and medium-sized business owner, street vendor, handicapped person, retiree, pensioner, people.

Such were these 6 years, Senor Zedillo. Being able to choose between peace and war, you opted for war. The results of this election are obvious: you lost the war.

You did everything you could to destroy us.

We simply resisted.

You are going into exile.

We will still be here.

Senor Zedillo,

You came to power through a crime which still continues unpunished. And your administration has been filled with unpunished crimes. In addition to carrying forward the privatization policies of your predecessor (and now open enemy), Salinas de Gortari, you disguised as law that other crime which is called FOBAPROA-IPAB, which involves not just poor Mexicans "rescuing" the rich and making them richer, but also causing that heavy burden to affect several future generations.

For more than 70 million Mexicans, the country's purported economic solidity has meant poverty and unemployment. While you have been scrupulously attending to the invasion of foreign capital, medium and small businesses were disappearing in the national market. During your term of office, the borders which divide government and organized crime were erased, and the continuous scandals caused serious problems in the press: it was impossible to deduce which news stories belonged in the political section and which in the crime blotter: "suicides," former governors on the run, prosperous businessmen who were "only" tortured, police officers "specialized" in fighting organized crime taking over universities.

Today, the same as your predecessor, you are leaving with those who worshipped you, served you, and who served themselves, having now become your worst enemies, prepared to pursue you. And so, Senor Zedillo, you will know, beginning tomorrow, what it is to be pursued day and night. And it will not last for only 6 years. Because, beginning tomorrow, the line will be very long of those who want to make you pay for what you owe them and for insults.

It is clear that we were right when, 6 years ago, the zapatistas told you welcome to the nightmare. But, now that you are going, is it over yet?

Yes and no.

Because, for us, the nightmare with you is ending today. Another could follow it, or the dawn could finally appear, we do not know, we shall do everything possible so that it will be the morning which flourishes. But for you, Senor Zedillo, the nightmare will only continue...

Vale. Salud, and it does not matter where you hide, there will be zapatistas there as well.

From the mountains of the Mexican Southeast,
Subcomandante Insurgente Marcos.
Mexico, November of 2000.

P.S. By the way, before I forget: a year ago, in September of 1999, you sent us an open letter thorough your Secretary of Government (and current candidate for the presidency of the PRI). I believe the letter was called "One More Step To the Abyss", "A More Ignominious Step", "A More Cynical Step," or something like that. In it, only 3 years late, your government was supposedly responding, with lies, to the conditions which we had set for the renewal of dialogue in September of 1996! The open letter was an attempt, more than deceiving us, of tricking national and international opinion. Something which it certainly did not achieve. Whatever it was, the lying letter told us we would be pleased with what was stated there, and it invited us to return to dialogue. It would be discourteous on our part to let it go without a response, especially now that you are leaving (finally!). Excuse the delay, but allow me to take advantage of these lines in order to respond. Our answer is: NO!

You are welcome...

95. 2 Years Without Vocho, TV's or Little Shops

December 8, 2000
Zapatista Army of National Liberation
Mexico
To the National and International Press

Ladies and gentlemen,

The letter for the travelers and the communiqué are off. It looks as if it's going to go on for a while yet. And I'm not saying that because of the abundance of commercials about a nonexistent peace in Chiapas, but because of what Dona Xo'chitl said: constitutional reform on indigenous rights and culture is going to take, at the least, some two years! (and then they say that the zapatistas want to drag out the resolution of the conflict). Fine, that's too bad. No less than 2 years without vocho, TV's or little shops.

Vale. Salud, and I'm not going to be starting a press conference on time any more. Don't think I wasn't aware of the sarcasm in your articles.

From the mountains of the Mexican Southeast,
Subcomandante Insurgente Marcos.
Mexico, December of 2000.

96. Withdrawing With a Great Public Show

December 22, 2000
Zapatista Army of National Liberation
Mexico
To the National and International Press

Ladies and Gentlemen,

The communiqué is off concerning the recent troop withdrawal.

While, when the soldiers arrived, they did so furtively, they are now withdrawing with a great public show. If peace does, in fact, arrive, it does not matter to us that that they present as zapatistas those who are not (the ones from Aric), and the ones who waged the dirty war (the military) as great promoters of peace. It is the syndrome of the chameleon, who navigates according to how the media winds are blowing.

Vale. Salud, and may the end of the year also be the end of despair.

> *From the mountains of the Mexican Southeast,*
> *Subcomandante Insurgente Marcos.*
> *Mexico, December of 2000.*

P.S. Durito says he is going to change his name. It will no longer be "Don Durito of the Lacandona," but "Durito dot com." He says he's riding the wave of "business excellence" now.

Dialectic (or Self-Contradictory)

P.S. Where Durito says always no, none of that "dot com," "nor excellence," nor "business." He said that during times of travel, what is needed is a sailor. La Mar agrees. I'm looking for seasickness pills.

97. The Zapatista Information Center

January 3, 2001
Zapatista Army of National Liberation
Mexico
To National and International Civil Society

Brothers and Sisters,

In order to be able to exchange information and to stay up to date on the zapatista mobilization for the fulfillment of the three signals (closure of the 7 military positions, release of the zapatista prisoners and constitutional recognition of indigenous rights and culture in accordance with the Cocopa legislative proposal), the EZLN has done the following:

First - Beginning today, the Zapatista Information Center will go into operation, with the help of Dona Rosario Ibarra de Piedra, a person who has generously put her time and work into the service of peace. The particular task of this Zapatista Information Center will be to serve as bridge between civil society and the EZLN.

Second - Through the Zapatista Information Center, national and international civil society will be able to be informed about the mobilization initiatives undertaken by the EZLN and others for the fulfillment of the three signals; about the precise date of the delegation's departure for the D.F.; about the delegation's itinerary; about the public acts it will hold; and about its agenda in Mexico City. It will also be able to learn about aspects related to the logistics of that mobilization: possible accommodations, possible means of transportation and their costs, etcetera.

Third - The EZLN will only receive national and international correspondence from all those persons and organizations who want to make contact with the delegation going to the Federal District through the Zapatista Information Center.

Fourth - Through the Zapatista Information Center, the EZLN will make known the different initiatives which civil society is organizing, in Mexico and the world, for the fulfillment of the three signals and for the accompaniment of the zapatista delegation to the D.F., whether through their physical presence or through public events in their areas.

Fifth - The Zapatista Information Center will NOT be a press office or spokesperson for the EZLN. It will be only a bridge for us to communicate with national and international civil society. There will be no need for any special accreditation for covering the EZLN's trip and stay in Mexico City. The media credentials they present will be sufficient. The Zapatista Information Center will not broadcast press bulletins, it will not provide news or photo materials, it will not organize transportation nor accommodations for the media, nor will it offer interviews or press conferences. As to the media, representatives of the press may have correspondence reach the EZLN, and vice versa, through this office.

Sixth - The EZLN, through the Zapatista Information Center, is calling on national and international solidarity to come to the financial aid of this peace initiative, by depositing any contribution in the following bank account:

Bancomer Branch 437 Number 5001060-5

Name: Senora Maria del Rosario Ibarra San Cristobal de Las Casas, Chiapas, Mexico.

Seventh - The information for communicating with the Zapatista Information Center is - Address: Avenida Ignacio Allende numero 22-A (between Hnos.

Dominguez and Alvaro Obregon) Barrio San Antonio San Cristobal de Las Casas, Chiapas, Mexico. Telephones: 67-82-159 and 67-81-013, Fax: 67-87-373.

Eighth - Regarding the Contact Office in San Cristobal de Las Casas, the EZLN announces that, beginning today, their work is temporarily suspended. Until further notice, it will not be providing the daily service to the different coordinators and the public in general.

Ninth - For the time being, the EZLN is calling on provincial contact coordinators who operated for the Consulta organization to make themselves open to all of civil society in their areas, and to incorporate all those persons who want to join in this peace effort, with the understanding that the Coordinadoras will only be a part of all the groups convened for this new initiative. It will not be necessary to participate in any Coordinadora in order to be part of the mobilization, since contact with the EZLN will be made directly through the Zapatista Information Center. The EZLN is calling on civil society to organize in accordance with their own initiative, without regard to religious faith, ideology, political activism, age, race, economic position, size, weight or sexual preference.

Tenth - The EZLN is calling on delegation Contact Coordinadoras in the D.F. to declare their activities suspended, and for all their members to organize in new ways in order to support this mobilization. The EZLN wants their stay in the D.F. to include the entire population, organized or not, and, in this way, to open new forms of dialogue.

Eleventh - At this stage, the EZLN is calling on national civil society for the following:

a) To publicize and disseminate in their towns the 3 signals which have been demanded.

b) To carry out acts of support in their towns for the three signals.

c) To organize in order to accompany the zapatista delegation in their towns, or to meet with them in the D.F.

d) To organize in order to carry out acts in their towns simultaneous with the zapatista delegates' actions.

We are also respectfully asking you to keep us informed about your activities through the Zapatista Information Center, and that you also let us know about your proposals, ideas, or how we can help you in those tasks.

Twelfth - The EZLN is making a special call to international civil society for the following:

a) To organize and carry out civil and peaceful acts in their towns, demanding the fulfillment of the 3 signals.

b) To organize in order to accompany the zapatista delegation, or in order to meet them in the D.F.

c) To organize and to carry out civil peaceful acts simultaneously with the zapatista delegation's activities, in their respective countries.

We are also respectfully asking them to keep us informed of that, through the international area of the Zapatista Information Center.

Brothers and sisters,

For dialogue, for the recognition of indigenous rights and culture, and so that war may be banished forever from the Indian lands of Mexico, let us support the demand for the fulfillment of the 3 signals, and let us walk beside the zapatistas to the D.F.

Vale. Salud and, with everyone, we shall secure peace with justice and dignity.

> From the mountains of the Mexican Southeast,
> Subcomandante Insurgente Marcos.
> Mexico, January of 2001.

98. 7 Years From What We Call "The Other Uprising"

January 1, 2001
Zapatista Army of National Liberation
Mexico
To National and International Civil Society

Madame,

As you know, this January 12, 2001 it will have been 7 years from what we call "the other uprising". On that date, but in 1994, hundreds of thousands of men and women of all colors and from all classes went out into the streets in order to demand, from the EZLN as well as from the federal government, a cease-fire.

Since then, this has marked the entrance of all those men and women who have your face, Madame, in the struggle for the path of dialogue and negotiation in order to resolve the conflicts. The EZLN has demanded that the federal government fulfill the 3 minimal signals as a requisite for the beginning of a true dialogue. That is how we will be able to reach a firm, just and dignified peace.

Those 3 signals are: the withdrawal of 7 federal army positions in the so-called "conflict zone" (two have already been withdrawn, but there are still five left remaining to be withdrawn), the release of all zapatista prisoners (only 17 have been released, and there are still almost 100 more), and the constitutional recognition of indigenous rights and culture in accordance with the Cocopa legislative proposal.

We are demanding the fulfillment of those 3 signals, which are nothing other than 3 responses to 3 other questions: Is the government going to commit itself to the path of dialogue and negotiation? If the answer is yes, then demilitarize those 7 places. Does the government recognize the zapatistas as a party in the dialogue and negotiation? If the answer is yes, then do not treat us as criminals. And, are they willing to recognize the indigenous as indigenous and as Mexicans? If the answer is yes, then the constitution should say so. That is why we are calling on you, Madame, to mobilize this January 12 under this flag: the fulfillment of the 3 signals.

Vale, salud and may every day be like January 12, 1994.

From the mountains of the Mexican Southeast,
Subcomandante Insurgente Marcos.
Mexico, January of 2001.

99. How Are We Going to Eat With Our Ski-masks On?

January 12, 2001
Zapatista Army of National Liberation
Mexico
To Civil Society

Madame,

I am writing to you while it is raining and we are waiting here for the return of the companeros and companeras who went to the march in San Cristobal de Las Casas. In a manner which is not customary for us, we are trying to keep you informed as to how things are going here through letters like this.

The Zapatista Information Center's mailbox has been quickly filling, being emptied, and filling up again. Greetings and mobilization proposals from various states in the Republic are arriving. In the D.F., for example, a very detailed proposal came from U.A.M. which, however, presents serious inconveniences. For example, they invite us to dine, but how are we going to eat with our ski-masks on? Ah, really? So the promises about improving the menu are of no use if, whenever they want, we're going to end up being fed intravenously. In Ciudad Juarez, Chihuahua, they were handing out flyers in the streets today, and in Tijuana, B.C., they held a rally. From Guanajuato, Morelos, Oaxaca, Puebla and Hidalgo, they are asking us for the dates and our itinerary in their states. Fine, we're going to make this public when we have it ready. Don't worry, and have the parties ready.

On the international level, the influx is no less: a delegation of Italians, between 200 and 300 persons, confirmed that they will be arriving in Mexico in February, and they'll be prepared for being expelled. From San Francisco, California, U.S., they are advising us they will be coming to accompany the delegation, and they will be informing the "Frisco" community of everything that happens along the route and during the stay in the D.F. From Switzerland, they have confirmed the attendance of a delegation. We are being advised of the same from Argentina and France. In the State of Spain, they don't stop. In addition to hanging from towers and mountains, they are going to set out (they don't say by what means, but I imagine it won't be walking) to throw themselves into the entire route.

Something verrry important: accommodations. And I'm not referring to the accommodations for the zapatista delegation, but those for all the people who, from the states of the Republic and from other parts of the world, are going to participate in the march along with us. An idea: that organizations and groups which can offer places to put people up please advise the Zapatista Information Center, and the "pilgrims" can then be informed.

Concerning the technological breakthroughs, I am informing you that the Web page is now functioning. The address is: http://www.ezlnaldf.org. I am taking the opportunity to make a request of all the web pages that already exist, or which refer to the zapatones and their movement: please put in a "link" or "pass", or whatever it's called, so that those visiting your pages can also have access to the one about the current mobilization. We also have our e-mail address now. The address is: ciz@ezlnaldf.org

Good, that's how things are up to now. We'll be passing along more information to you in the next one.

Vale. Salud, and may peace come soon dot com.

> *From the mountains of the Mexican Southeast,*
> *Subcomandante Insurgente Marcos.*
> *Mexico, January of 2001.*

100. WHILE THEY DISCUSS SKI-MASKS OR NO SKI-MASKS

January 24, 2001
Zapatista Army of National Liberation
Mexico
To the national and international press

Here we are sending you the detailed route and the scheduled dates. There is also a letter which is being sent to an Hidalgo indigenous community, accepting their hospitality.

We humbly accept the undeserved praise given to us by the business sector.

While they discuss ski-masks or no ski-masks up there, down here they are already organizing to receive and accompany the caravan. There is a national outcry demanding the constitutional recognition of indigenous rights and culture.

Vale. Salud and, if they're going to arrest us, we're asking that they put us in the high (hah!) security prison in Puente Grande, Jalisco. Because then one might just feel like going out to eat some cakes in Guadalajara.

From the mountains of the Mexican Southeast,
Subcomandante Insurgente Marcos.
Mexico, January of 2001.

101. To the Community of Tephe

January 24, 2001
Zapatista Army of National Liberation
Mexico
To the community of Tephe, municipality of Ixmiquilpan, Hidalgo, Mexico

Indigenous brothers and sisters of Tephe,

We were greatly moved when we read the letter you sent us, inviting our delegation to pass through your community during the trip it will be making to Mexico City. We are including your words here so that other brothers and sisters might know them:

"We know you are soon going to be coming to our state of Hidalgo, we want you to come and have your meeting here in the indigenous community of Tephe, here in Ixmiquilpan, we have a spa and a hotel so you can sleep a bit and bathe if you are tired. We also want to hear what you say here also. The indigenous community of Tephe is expecting you soon."

Then, brothers and sisters of Tephe, we would like to tell you that it would be a great honor for us to be able to share shelter and food with you on our trip. We, like you and like all honest men and women in Mexico, want peace and the recognition of the rights which we have as the Mexican indigenous we are. That is why we are making this trip, and that is why we are most sincerely grateful for the help you are giving us.

We are letting you know that we will be arriving in your community on February 28, 2001. We are 24 delegates, 5 are women and 19 are men. We do not need anything special for sleeping or eating. Your solidarity with us is enough shelter to cover us, and your words shall be enough food to nurture us.

Salud brothers and sisters of Tephe, Ixmiquilpan, Hidalgo. We shall meet on February 28, 2001.

From the mountains of the Mexican Southeast,
Subcomandante Insurgente Marcos.
Mexico, January of 2001.

102. TO THE CYBERNAUTS

January 27, 2001
Zapatista Army of National Liberation
Mexico

Brother and Sister Cybernauts,

The EZLN rose up in arms on January 1, 1994 in demand, among other things, of respect and recognition for the Indian peoples of Mexico. As of January 12, 1994, the zapatistas, listening to the voices of national and international civil society, suspended their armed actions and entered into a process of dialogue, seeking a negotiated solution to their demands. After 2 years, in February of 1996, the EZLN and the Mexican government signed the first San Andres Accords (taking the name of the seat of dialogue, San Andres Sakamchen de Los Pobres, a Tzotzil municipality in Los Altos of Chiapas). These first Accords were on indigenous rights and culture. The Mexican government committed itself, among other things, to constitutionally recognizing the rights and cultures of the Indian peoples of Mexico. In response to the government's failure to honor its word, a group of Mexican legislators from the Commission of Concordance and Peace (Cocopa), drew up a legislative proposal in the month of December, in 1996, what has subsequently been referred to as the "Cocopa Law". Up until the end of the end of the administration of Ernesto Zedillo Ponce de Leon, the government had refused to carry out the Accords, and the EZLN kept the dialogue suspended.

When Vicente Fox's government took office, and he offered the fulfillment of the pending Accords and a negotiated solution to the conflict, the EZLN responded, demonstrating their willingness to walk the road of peace, making it clear that it was demanding a serious, respectful and real dialogue. The EZLN asked the Fox government for 3 signals which would indicate the government's commitment to dialogue and negotiation.

With these signals, the EZLN was waiting for a response to 3 questions which are fundamental for the success of the peace process: Is Fox in charge of the federal army, and is he willing to abandon the military route as a solution to the conflict? Does the government recognize that the zapatistas are social fighters and not criminals? And, will there be no repetition of the history of humiliation, contempt and racism against the Mexican indigenous?

Up to this moment, Fox's government has responded that it is and is not willing to abandon the military route, or that it is more or less willing. This is because it has withdrawn only 4 of the 7 positions which were demanded, and it has attached conditions for fulfilling the remaining 3. Concerning the zapatista prisoners, only 19 of the more than 100 who are in the country's jails have been released. They are continuing to be used as hostages, and, keeping them imprisoned means that the government is still thinking about using the police-military option. Concerning the constitutional recognition of indigenous rights and culture, the so-called "Cocopa Law" is already in the Congress of the Union. In order to secure its approval, the EZLN has decided to send a delegation to Mexico City for the purpose of engaging in dialogue with federal legislators.

Fox's government has resorted to a publicity strategy in order to build an image of peacemaker, and to project the image of an intransigent EZLN, arguing its fear that the zapatistas, when they see the signals fulfilled, are going to ask for more and to draw out the conflict. The zapatistas do indeed keep their word. If they have asked for only those 3 signals, they will not add more. As soon as they are fulfilled, they will sit down to dialogue.

Regarding the zapatista march to Mexico City, the country's powerful (the high clergy, the political class, businesspersons and the army) have wanted to supplant the discussion with trivialities: for example, concerning ski-masks and weapons. Concerning the ski-masks, the EZLN has made it clear that they form part of their zapatista selves, and they will go with them in place. Concerning weapons, the EZLN has said, time and time again, that it respects the Law for Dialogue, and the trip will be made unarmed.

In some areas of government, the threat has been used that the zapatistas will be apprehended because the law protects them only in Chiapas. This is false. The law allows travel throughout national territory, and the zapatista march is, therefore, legitimate and legal. There is no legal argument against it.

The EZLN has repeated in its last communiqués that it will go to Mexico City to engage in dialogue with the Congress of the Union, that it will engage in dialogue along its route with civil society, primarily with the Indian peoples and the National Indigenous Congress, and that its objective is the constitutional recognition of indigenous rights and culture.

Regarding the military positions which have yet to be withdrawn, the EZLN has made it clear that their dismantling would in no way affect the military capacity of the federal Army. That there are no civil populations whatsoever who are demanding that government troops remain in those places. And that the number is 7 because it is a symbolic number for the zapatistas.

The EZLN will not make contact with the government until the signals are completed, because it does not want dialogue to again be a deception. The zapatistas want dialogue to take place and for it to be successful so there can, in that way, be an end to the war, to the causes which led to it, and in order to be able to engage in politics like any other Mexican citizen.

Vale. Salud and may those who make history finally find a place in it.

From the mountains of the Mexican Southeast,
Subcomandante Insurgente Marcos.
Mexico, January of 2001.

103. RECIPIENTS OF THE WORLD, UNITE

January 27, 2001
Zapatista Army of National Liberation
Mexico

Sir, Madame, Young Man, Young Lady, Boy, Girl,

If you happen to find yourself reading... Excuse me. I should begin again. Our best wishes to you. I am writing to you in the name of the men, women, children and old ones of the Zapatista Army of National Liberation.

Now. If you happen to find yourself reading these lines, it is owing to two reasons which have to do with each other - or which are mutually, reciprocally related - or with coming and going, as when one says the one goes with the other and vice versa. It's like a table leg, which is a table leg because there is a table which has legs, which, if it didn't, then the table would fall down and it would just be a table on the floor (or in the mud, because here the floor and the mud are reciprocal, if you follow me). Or also like the paddle for a raft, which is a paddle because there's a raft which needs paddles (I already know that there are rafts without paddles, but I'm talking about a raft with paddles, so stop your rhetorical games). I know!! I've come up with a verrry illustrative example! It's like a recipient who has a sender, because if there is no sender, then the recipient would be very sad, like Garcia Marquez Colonel, whom no one wrote to. And if the sender doesn't have a recipient, then the sadness would be no less. To whom would he write? Fine, I think we're beginning to understand each other. So forget about legs, tables, paddles and rafts, and concentrate on the sender and the recipient. Ya? Fine, there's no problem here because the mystery has been cleared up: you are the recipient, and we are the senders. The only unknowns remaining are the two reasons which will explain why you are reading these lines. Great, I've already forgotten them. But I'll remember in just a second... Mmm... mmm... Oh, yes! Here they go:

It so happens that, as you most certainly already know (if not, then you would-n't be reading this letter), we zapatudos have decided to send a delegation to the Mexican capital. The purpose of the trip is to engage in dialogue with the legisla-tors in order to achieve the constitutional recognition of indigenous rights and cul-ture. Fine, it so happens, then, that we are like tables without legs, like rafts with-out paddles, like senders without recipients (and vice versa), like knights without horses, like _____ without _____ (you fill in the blanks. This is an interac-tive letter.com). In short, we need your financial help in order to carry out this trip which, it is quite clear, has no other goal than peace with justice and dignity. And so there are the two reasons: We are writing you because we trust you, and because we know you will understand what we are so confusingly saying to you (I hope).

Don't worry, you can help with anything. We are accepting all the currencies of the world and the galaxies (always and when they come from honest people like you), and we will not speculate with the exchange rate.

What? All that talk just for that? Perhaps, but we didn't even know, for exam-ple, if this letter was going to reach you, because we don't even have anything for postage stamps. And just think how sad you would be if you were a recipient with-out a sender... Right? Good, and so we are putting our trust in you.

Vale. Salud and, as no one has, of yet, said, Recipients of the World, Unite (or was it "senders"?)

> *From the mountains of the Mexican Southeast,*
> *Subcomandante Insurgente Marcos.*
> *Mexico, January-February of 2001.*
>
> Ah?! I forgot. The bank account is:
> Bancomer Branch 437 Account #5001060-5
> Name: Senora Ma. Del Rosario Ibarra,
> San Cristobal de Las Casas Chiapas, Mexico

104. FAQ ON MARCH

February of 2001

Dear Cybernauts,

The following questions, asked by journalists and people from civil society, have reached the EZLN through this web page and by email. Subcomandante Marcos, military chief and spokesperson for the zapatistas, is responding, and will continue to respond, as far as possible, to the most general questions. We are now presenting this section, updated as of February 9, 2001. As far as possible, we will be adding more questions, expanding upon and updating our answers. The words presented here are the EZLN's official position on each issue addressed.

The questions have been grouped in five areas:

1) CURRENT POLITICAL DEBATE

2) THE THREE SIGNALS

3) COCOPA LAW

4) EN ROUTE

5) STAY IN MEXICO CITY

1. Current Political Debate

1. Is Marcos going to Mexico City at the invitation of President Vicente Fox?

No, the zapatista delegation is going to Mexico City on its own initiative and for the purpose of engaging in dialogue with the Congress of the Union, that is, with Deputies and Senators. The purpose of that dialogue is to seek approval of the so-called "Cocopa legislative proposal," which, taken to the constitutional level, will mean the fulfillment of the agreements reached at Table One of the San Andre's Dialogues and will be a very important step on the path to peace in Chiapas. During its march to Mexico City, the zapatista delegation will engage in dialogue with civil society and the Indian peoples of 12 Mexican states. It will also be participating in the work of the Third National Indigenous Congress. All of this for the purpose of promoting the constitutional recognition of indigenous rights and culture.

2. Has the EZLN had direct contact or correspondence with the government commissioner, Luis H. Alvarez?

No, the EZLN has said, as long as long as the three signals we have demanded for dialogue are not carried out, it will not make direct contact with the federal government. As soon as they are carried out, we will establish contact. Meanwhile, we are making it clear that there has not even been an exchange of correspondence. The conflicting information on this point has, we believe, been deliberately orchestrated by the federal government in order to confuse people. On the other hand, we continue to view Senor Luis H. Alvarez with respect, and, as soon as the three minimal signals we are asking for take place, we will make direct contact with him.

3. *Has the EZLN had direct contact or correspondence with the Cocopa or with any of its members?*

No. There has been no exchange of correspondence nor have there been direct contacts.

4. *Has the EZLN not felt pressured by the publicity deployed by Fox government concerning the actions it has undertaken in Chiapas? Do they not feel that the people can ask them to sit down now?*

We feel that the people also want the government to offer these signals. We don't feel pressured, because they aren't telling us "to sit down now". That's what the government is saying. The people, in any case, want the two parties to commit ourselves seriously to the peace process. As far as we are concerned, the government's seriousness will be demonstrated with the fulfillment of the three minimal signals. And, on our part, seriousness will consist in our not asking for new signals in order to begin dialogue. On the other hand, the people have always made us feel that they understand us. It's obvious that when we say "the people", we aren't referring to the powerful, to the One'cimos or to the Loyolas, but to civil society in general.

5. *Are the zapatista delegates who will be travelling to Mexico City going armed?*

No. The zapatistas will be travelling unarmed, as and how established by law. In this undertaking, we are not leaving to make war, but to engage in dialogue. When we engage in dialogue, we do not need weapons.

6. *Are the 24 zapatista delegates going to be travelling with their faces covered with ski-masks? Why?*

Yes, they will be going with ski-masks. Because ski-masks are now a symbol of zapatismo. The ski-masks point out that the government does not look at the indigenous when they show themselves, and, now that they conceal themselves, they do see them. It's also an invitation for everyone to feel part of this struggle.

7. *Can the zapatista delegates be detained?*

No, because the so-called "Law for Dialogue, Reconciliation and Dignified Peace in Chiapas" protects the zapatistas from any legal action against them. The law states that the suspension of legal actions continues while dialogue is in effect. The law points out that weapons should not be carried in places of dialogue and negotiation. The Cocopa has already publicly pointed out its position in this regard: the dialogue continues in effect, and therefore the law which guarantees respect for the zapatistas' freedom of movement and safety is in effect. Since we will be going without weapons, we cannot be detained.

8. *What does the indigenous issue mean to the EZLN? Do they want to separate from Mexico?*

The EZLN is a primarily indigenous organization that rose up in arms for Democracy, Liberty and Justice for all Mexicans. Of all the Mexican peoples, the indigenous is the most forgotten. That's why the EZLN raised the recognition of indigenous rights and culture as an important demand. This demand found echo throughout the country and in the entire world. The indigenous issue signifies, for the EZLN, an unfinished debt of Mexico, and we should not have to wait any longer for its resolution. We do not want independence from Mexico, we want to be part of Mexico, to be Mexican indigenous. Up until now, they've treated us as second-class citizens, or as a hindrance for the country. We want to be first-class citizens and to be part of the country's development, but we want to be so without ceasing to be indigenous.

9. *Why has the EZLN not signed the peace?*

Because Zedillo's government did not carry out the accords it signed with the EZLN. In order for peace to be real, it must be built on accords that are fulfilled. If it's not so, then it's not peace, but pretense. The EZLN has wanted peace for seven years, but not just any peace, one with justice and dignity. We are continuing on that path.

10. *What do the zapatista indigenous want after the end of the PRI?*

For the Mexican nation to recognize indigenous rights and culture in the Constitution. That it works to resolve the serious condition of marginalization of the Indian peoples of Mexico, taking them into account. For democracy to become a reality for all Mexicans, all the time. For the indigenous woman to have a special place in Mexican society. And for the zapatistas to be able to go out and engage in politics like any other citizen, that is, for neither ski-masks nor weapons to be necessary any longer.

11. *After seven years of militarization and siege, how has the situation changed for the peoples of Chiapas?*

Now there is hope that the past will not be repeated, that the indigenous self will no longer be the cause for shame or pain, that we can improve the condition of our lives, that we will never again have to make war in order for them to hear us. The fundamental change, in short, is that we are not alone now.

12. *What expectations are there concerning the Vicente Fox government, which is not PRI, now?*

We hope the Fox government understands that the country has changed now. That the Indian people cannot continue to be kept in oblivion. That the people should, and want, to participate in decision-making. That peace with justice and dignity is a national and international demand. We hope that it gives clear signals as to its willingness to dialogue, that it engages in dialogue, that it reaches accords and that it carries them out. We hope that it decides to seek peace.

13. *What will happen to Subcomandante Marcos if peace is signed?*

Along with all the zapatista companeros and companeras, he will fight for democracy, liberty and justice along new paths.

14. *How does the EZLN respond to those who attack them and speak badly of the zapatistas?*

That we aren't attacking anyone, we don't want to take anything away from anyone. What we want is a dignified place for the indigenous of Mexico. Those who are attacking us are attacking a demand for justice which everyone, throughout the world, supports and recognizes. We are only afraid of those who prefer to see the indigenous dead.

15. Are there political groups, drug traffickers or foreign interests behind the EZLN?

No. The EZLN is a completely Mexican organization. It didn't have any foreign financing, and its decisions and actions are answerable to the orders of the zapatista indigenous communities. We are independent of all national and international political organizations. Not only are we not dependent on drug trafficking, but we have fought it since our creation. In the zapatista indigenous communities, the use, planting and trafficking of narcotics is prohibited. No country or organization maintains the EZLN economically. The EZLN supports itself through its own resources, that is, with the support of the communities. That is why we are a poor army.

16. Why does the EZLN say "army"?

Because it is organized as an army, and it fulfills all international regulations for recognition as an army. When the war began, the EZLN did so fulfilling international conventions: it formally declared war, it has recognizable uniforms, ranks and insignias, it respects the civil population and neutral bodies. The EZLN has weapons and military organization and discipline.

17. Why does the EZLN say it seeks to disappear?

Because the EZLN is fighting so that it will no longer be necessary to be clandestine and to be armed in order to fight for justice, liberty and democracy. When the EZLN achieves what it is seeking, then the EZLN will no longer be necessary. That is why we say we are fighting in order to disappear.

18. Why does the EZLN say it isn't fighting for Power?

Because from the time of our first public appearance we have never proposed the taking of Power. We are not interested in having government positions, but in the people participating and their voice being listened to and heeded. We think it's not important who's in government. What is important is that it "govern obeying", or that the people compel those governing to carry out their work in accordance with the people's interest, and not in accordance with the interest of a party or of an economic or religious group.

19. Are there women in the EZLN? And in the delegation?

Yes. There are women in the EZLN at all levels: there are women who are support bases, there are militia, there are insurgents, there are officers, there are local and regional "responsables", and there are comandantes. In the delegation going to Mexico City there are four comandantes. There names are Susana, Yolanda, Esther and Fidelia. There are more women in the Clandestine Revolutionary Indigenous Committee, which is the top leadership of the EZLN, but only 4 of them are going on this trip.

20. Are there children in the EZLN?

No, there are no children fighters in the EZLN, or no child soldiers. There are zapatista children, but they are support bases.

21. Is Marcos willing to meet with Fox personally?

The EZLN does not think that the war in Chiapas will be resolved by a meeting between two people, but that a process of dialogue and serious, respectful and responsible negotiation is necessary. When the three signals are fulfilled, the EZLN will name a group of its leaders, among whom may or may not be Marcos, in order to engage in dialogue and to negotiate with the federal government. The Fox government has already named the person who will be in charge of negotiation, Senor Luis H. Alvarez. The zapatistas will, therefore, engage in dialogue with him when the process begins.

2. The Three Signals

1. If Vicente Fox's government carries out the three signals demanded by the EZLN in order to begin dialogue, will the EZLN demand more conditions? What is the guarantee that, if Fox carries out the three signals, the zapatistas won't ask for more?

Upon the fulfillment of the three signals, the EZLN will make contact with the Commissioner for Peace, and it will jointly set the day, place, hour and agenda for the first meeting. There will not be any more conditions. The guarantee the EZLN is offering is its word, which we have never broken.

2. Will the zapatistas go to Mexico City even if the Fox government does not carry out the three signals for dialogue?

Yes, as we have already explained, the purpose of the trip is dialogue with the Congress of the Union, with the Indian peoples of Mexico and with civil society, not with the federal executive. Even if Fox has not carried out the three signals, the dialogue with Congress, the indigenous and civil society will take place.

3. Is it true that Fox has already withdrawn the army from Chiapas?

No. The Fox government had some of the checkpoints and control points on the roads withdrawn, and he ordered the withdrawal of troops from 4 positions out of the 259 military camps which have invaded chiapaneco lands.

4. Is the EZLN demanding complete demilitarization in order to sit down to talks? Does it recognize the troop withdrawal?

No, the EZLN is only asking that they close 7 military positions. The federal army will still be keeping 252 positions inside the so-called "conflict zone". By asking for the closing of 7 positions, the EZLN is asking the Fox government to respond to the question: "Are you in charge of the federal army, and are you willing to abandon the military option as a means of resolving the conflict?" By asking for 7 positions, the EZLN is using 7 as a symbol. The closing of those positions does not mean the demilitarization of the conflict zone. The federal army will maintain, even without these 7 positions, its military capacity. The closing of the 7 positions will not in any way affect the correlation of forces between the federal army and the EZLN. The EZLN recognizes that only 4 of the 7 positions have been closed. The reluctance to close the remaining 3 means that the Fox government has not decided to abandon military means, or that it's not in charge of the federal army, and their orders are not being fully complied with.

5. *At what point is the process of the release of zapatistas who are imprisoned in different jails in the country?*

Up to now, only 25 zapatista prisoners have been released. The 25 have been released by the government of the state of Chiapas. The federal government has not released one single one. In addition to Chiapas, there are imprisoned zapatistas in Tabasco and in Queretaro. The governor of Queretaro has said he will not let the 2 zapatistas who are being kept in prison go. With this, and with his statements asking for the death penalty for us, the governor of Queretaro has become one of the obstacles preventing the recognition of Indian rights and progress in dialogue.

6. *Are the zapatistas satisfied with Vicente Fox's having sent the Cocopa law to the Congress of the Union? What is still needed for the fulfillment of this first signal?*

No, the sending of the "Cocopa law" to the Congress of the Union is not sufficient. It's necessary for this proposal to be turned into law, that is, into constitutional reform. The "Cocopa law" has a three-fold importance: it is important because it recognizes the rights of the very first residents of Mexico. It is important because it will be a fundamental signal for the reopening of dialogue and for reaching peace. And it is important because it will demonstrate that dialogue and negotiation are indeed the means for resolving conflicts. What remains for the fulfillment of this signal is for the federal executive - Fox, that is - to work with Deputies and Senators in search of consensus for its approval. The Cocopa needs to work with the parliamentary groups of the various parties represented in the legislature. The Congress of the Union needs to listen and to heed the clamor of the Indian peoples represented in the CNI and the EZLN.

3. Cocopa Law

1. Who made the "Cocopa Law", and what does this law say?

The so-called "Cocopa law" was drawn up in December of 1996 by legislators from the Commission of Concordance and Peace (Cocopa). The legislators belonged to the 4 most important political parties: the PRI, the PAN, the PRD and the PT. The zapatistas did not make this legislative proposal, rather the legislators did: those who make the laws in Mexico. The so-called "Cocopa law" takes up the most important of the first San Andre's Accords, signed by the government and the EZLN in February of 1996: it recognizes the right of the indigenous peoples to inclusionary autonomy (that is, that their difference is recognized, but they continue to be Mexicans), without breaking national unity and respecting human rights, especially those of indigenous woman. It also notes that the indigenous peoples should be taken into account in decision-making which affects them. That their culture should be respected and promoted. And that there should be guarantees that their voice is listened to and heeded, and that they have the right to have representation in the Congress of the Union and in the state Congresses. Fundamentally, the "Cocopa Law" constitutionally recognizes a reality: the Indian peoples are part of Mexico, and they have their own forms of social and political organization. That is, they have the right to be indigenous and to be Mexicans.

2. *Is it true that the EZLN is not willing to have any period or comma of the "Cocopa Law" changed?*
   In the current debate no one is suggesting that the problem with the "Cocopa Law" has to do with periods and commas. The attacks on the law are directed at its fundamental aspects (autonomy of the Indian peoples, territoriality, collective rights), not at mere problems of wording. By defending the "Cocopa Law", the EZLN is defending the San Andre's Accords, which reflect the demands of the Indian peoples of Mexico.

3. *What is the Cocopa's position regarding the law that they themselves made, and which is, today, as important as peace itself?*
   The Cocopa has not, as a legislative body, made any pronouncement. Its members have, speaking personally, made contradictory statements. The current Cocopa will thus have to take a position regarding the legislative proposal they drew up.

4. *Is the Cocopa Law supported by the country's indigenous groups, or just by the zapatistas?*
   The Cocopa's legislative proposal is supported by representatives of indigenous organizations of all Mexico's ethnic groups, grouped in the National Indigenous Congress. In addition, it has been analyzed and discussed over the last four years in many of the indigenous communities throughout the country. Over the last few years no legislative proposal has received such analysis, debate and backing by Mexican citizens, primarily indigenous.

5. *Does the recognition of all indigenous uses and customs not represent risks for the nation?*
   There are uses and customs which do not serve the indigenous communities, primarily those having to do with the segregation of women in decision-making, but they are being fought by the communities themselves, basically by organized indigenous women. We are not demanding the recognition of a bad custom which we ourselves are striving to change. What we are demanding is the recognition of our different selves, of our culture, of our history, of our language, of our forms of governance, of our form of social organization. Apart from that, returning to the case of indigenous women, the Cocopa law itself puts emphasis on respect for the integrity of women and their political participation. It is for that reason, among other things, that we want this law to be approved in Congress.

4. En Route

1. *Who are the 24 delegates who are going to Mexico City?*

   Comandante David, Comandante Tacho, Comandante Zebedeo, Comandante Susana, Comandante Javier, Comandante Yolanda, Comandante Isaias, Comandante Bulmaro, Comandante Abel, Comandante Moises, Comandante Esther, Comandante Maxo, Comandante Ismael, Comandante Eduardo, Comandante Gustavo, Comandante Sergio, Comandante Omar, Comandante Filemon, Comandante Abraham, Comandante Daniel, Comandante Mister, Comandante Fidelia, Comandante Alejandro and Subcomandante Insurgente Marcos. In the EZLN al DF web page you will find the names of the delegates, their photographs and a text concerning each one of them.

2. *Will the EZLN address each and every one of the invitations from civil society, from social organizations, from NGOs and other groups who want to meet with the zapatistas?*

   The zapatista delegation will answer invitations from civil society as far as possible. The time necessary for covering the route makes it impossible, unfortunately, to respond affirmatively to all the invitations. When we reject an invitation, we're not doing so because of a lack of interest, a lack of courtesy, or because we don't consider it important to attend to it, but because we have limited time and an agenda to meet. In passing, let me say that there are, in the Zapatista Information Center, hundreds of invitations from the twelve states through which we'll be passing and from the Federal District.

3. *What people do you want to count on for the mobilization to Mexico City?*

   On everyone, without regard to their sex, their political affiliation, their ideology, their religious beliefs, their size, their weight, their social position, etcetera. Indigenous groups which want to meet with us will, obviously, have a special place.

4. *Who is organizing the mobilization?*

   The EZLN, through an office called the "Zapatista Information Center". This CIZ is receiving proposals from civil society and channeling them to the EZLN. Through the CIZ, the EZLN is informing civil society of the plans they are making and the details for the mobilization to take place.

5. *During the route of the march, will the EZLN be meeting only with the CNI?*

   No. Although the CNI and the Indian peoples are very important in the march, the EZLN knows that the struggle for the recognition of indigenous rights and culture does not belong only to the Indian peoples, but to all honest Mexican men and women, and to all the people of the 5 continents who are struggling for peace, justice and dignity for all human beings.

6. *Who is organizing the Third Indigenous Congress in Nurio, Michoacan?*

   The people of Nurio are organizing it directly, along with the CNI. More information can be obtained about the Congress in the following places: UCEZ. Telephone-fax: (014) 314-13-94 E-mail:encuentromor@latinmail.com in Morelia. La Casa Hotel del maestro.

Telephone-fax: (014) 324-00-01, in Morelia. Graciela Contreras (01715) 3-75-89, in Zita'cuaro. Alfonso Vargas Romero Telephone-fax: (01452) 5-09-40, in Paracho.

7. Who is going to be financing the zapatista's delegation to Mexico City?

National and international civil society. The EZLN is asking for financial support for all those persons who can and want to help in the struggle for the recognition of indigenous rights and culture. That is why the EZLN has asked Senora Rosario Ibarra de Piedra to open a bank account so that people can make their financial donations. The bank account number is: Bancomer. Branch 437. Account #5001060-5 In the name of Senora Ma. Del Rosario Ibarra. San Cristobal de Las Casas, Chiapas, Mexico.

The Zapatista Information Center is operating through the funds being collected, and they will cover the costs of the trip for the delegation.

8. Should deposits be made into this same account in support of the work of the Third Indigenous Congress?

The organization of the Third CNI is an enormous effort, which is also dependent on everyone's efforts. The infrastructure for the meeting, the feeding of the thousands of delegates and all the fitting out and adjustments being made in the community of Nuri'o need financial contributions from the entire world. The CNI maintains the following bank account: Bancomer. Branch 463. Account #1029446-9 In the name of Alfonso Vargas Romero Uruapan, Michoacan, Mexico.

9. If the zapatista delegation is not going to be passing through my area, how can I participate in this mobilization?

In several ways. One is by becoming informed about the delegation's route, so that you can see where the EZLN delegation will be holding public events, and you can make plans to be present. Another is by joining the zapatista caravan, whether from when it leaves Chiapas, or during the journey, or during its arrival in Mexico City. Another is by holding informative events in your area, simultaneous with the march. On the CIZ web page you can find the la test information concerning the objectives of the march and what is happening every day.

10. If I'm in another country, what can I do to support the mobilization?

We have suggested to the international community that they accompany us on the march, in the Federal District or in their own countries. Any of these three forms of accompaniment would be equally important for us. They can also help the zapatista march financially through Dona Rosario Ibarra de Piedra's bank account, or in the National Indigenous Congress bank account (described above).

11. What is the zapatista delegation's agenda in the state of Chiapas?

The zapatista delegates will travel to the city of San Cristobal de Las Casas on February 24, departing from the Aguascalientes of Oventic, La Garrucha and La Realidad, in addition to the community of Moises Gandhi. The EZLN is expecting to be accompanied by national and international civil society from these four points.

In addition, the date for the farewell event for the delegation has been confirmed. The event will be held in the central plaza of the city of San Cristo'bal de Las Casas this February 24 in the afternoon.

The delegation will spend the night in San Cristobal, and it will leave this city on the morning of February 25 for Juchitan, Oaxaca, stopping briefly in Tuxtla Gutierrez to greet the people gathered there.

12. What is the zapatista delegation's agenda in the state of Oaxaca?

We will be leaving San Cristobal de Las Casas, Chiapas on the morning of February 25, heading towards the municipality of Juchitan. The delegation will be greeting the companeros and companeras gathered at the entrance to Oaxaca lands. Further along it will be participating in an event organized in front of the Juchitan municipal palace, where Zapotec, Huave, Zoque, Chontal and Mixe brothers and sisters will be gathered.

The delegation will spend the night in this municipality, and on the morning of the 26th it will leave for the city of Oaxaca, where it will be holding a main event with Mixtec, Amuzgo, Cuicatec, Zapotec, Chatino, Chocholtec, Triqui and Chinantec brothers and sisters.

Following this event, the delegation will be spending the night in this city, and on the morning of the 27th it will leave for the city of Puebla.

13. What is the zapatista delegation's agenda in its travels through Orizaba, Veracruz?

On February 27, en route to Puebla, we will stop off to participate in a brief event organized in the municipality of Orizaba.

14. What is the zapatista delegation's agenda in the state of Puebla?

The zapatista delegation will arrive in the city of Puebla this February 27, and they will hold an event there in the central plaza, prior to participating in an event with people gathered in Tehuacan (Puebla) and in Orizaba (Veracruz).

The delegation will stay over in the city of Puebla, and on February 28, during the morning, it will leave, headed for the state of Hidalgo.

15. What is the zapatista delegation's agenda in the state of Hidalgo?

The zapatista delegation will arrive in the state of Hidalgo on February 28, and they will be holding a main event there, in the municipality of Ixmiquilpan, with a brief prior stopover to greet the people of Emiliano Zapata, Ciudad Sahagun, Pachuca, Actopan, Francisco I. Madero and Tepatepec, who can either remain in their areas or travel to the main event in Ixmiquilpan (or, even better, do both). The delegation will spend the night in the community of Tephe, and on the morning of March 1, it will leave for Michoacan.

16. What is the zapatista delegation's agenda in the state of Queretaro?

On the first of March the delegation will be participating, along with our brothers and sisters of Queretaro, in a brief event organized in the state capital. When the event is over, the zapatistas will continue on their way to Michoacan (with a prior stop in Acambaro, Guanajuato).

17. What is the zapatista delegations' agenda in the state of Guanajuato?

It will be an honor for the 24 zapatista delegates to greet the people gathered in the municipality of Acambaro on March 1. After this greeting, the delegation will continue on its way to Michoacan.

18. What is the zapatista delegation's agenda in the state of Michoacan?

The zapatista delegation will be arriving in the state of Michoacan on March 1, specifically in the community of Nurio, stopping previously and briefly to greet the people of Zinapecuaro, Morelia, Patzcuaro and Uruapan.

We will be staying in Nurio on March 2, 3 and 4, participating in the work of the Third Congress of the CNI. On the morning of the 5th we'll be leaving for the state of Mexico, participating in a previous event planned in the municipality of Morelia.

19. What is the zapatista delegation's agenda in the state of Mexico?

The zapatista delegation will arrive in the Toluca Valley on March 5, and they will hold an event in the city, and another in the municipality of Temoaya, belonging to the Otomi' region of the state. After sharing food and shelter with our brothers and sisters from the "Andres Molina Enriquez" residential complex, known as "La Pila" (in the municipality of Metepec), we will be departing on the morning of March 6 for the state of Morelos.

20. What is the zapatista delegation's agenda in the state of Morelos?

The 24 zapatista delegates and the caravan accompanying them will arrive in the municipality of Tepoztlan on March 6. A public event will be held there, and food and shelter will be shared with the brothers and sisters of Tepoztlan, following a previous stop in the city of Cuernavaca, where we will briefly greet the people gathered there.

On March 7 we will be leaving Tepoztlan headed for Iguala, Guerrero, without making any stops. In Iguala we will be participating in a joint event with Guerrero companeros gathered in this municipality. We'll return to spend the night in Cuautla that same day, March 7.

On March 8 we'll be spending the greatest part of the day in the state of Morelos, and, following the route of our General Emiliano Zapata, we'll leave that same day, heading for the delegation of Milpa Alta, where we'll arrive in the afternoon.

21. What is the zapatista delegation's agenda in the state of Guerrero?

Responding to the call of the Guerrero indigenous people and civil society, the zapatista delegation will be holding a main event in the municipality of Iguala, Guerrero, on March 7. After participating in the act, the 24 delegates will return to Cuautla, Morelos to spend the night.

22. What is the zapatista delegation's agenda in Milpa Alta and in Mexico City?

The zapatista delegation will arrive in Milpa Alta in the afternoon of March 8. They'll be spending the night there, and on the morning of the 9th, an event will be held in the historic zapatista barracks in San Pablo Oxtotepec. They'll also be spending this night in Milpa Alta.

23. What is the zapatista delegation's agenda in Xochimilco?

On March 10 a main event will be held in Xochimilco. The zapatista delegation will spend the night there, and the following day they'll set off for the Zo'calo in Mexico City. The event is currently being organized.

24. What are the zapatista delegates going to be travelling in?

In a bus. If it breaks down, we'll look for a bicycle, a burro or, if not, then on foot.

5. Stay in Mexico city

1. How long is the zapatista delegation going to be in Mexico City?

As long as it takes to enter into dialogue with the Congress of the Union and with civil society.

2. On what day are you going to enter the Zocalo in Mexico City?

On Sunday, March 11, 2001.

3. Where is the EZLN going to be meeting with civil society during its stay in Mexico City?

The EZLN will release the places, dates and hours in advance of the public events in which it will be participating. We'll be having public events and private meetings.

4. Does the EZLN have any representation in Mexico City?

No. The EZLN doesn't have any outside representation, neither in Mexico City nor any place else.

5. Will the EZLN be going to the UNAM?

As I already explained in an interview, prior to responding, we'd have to have an invitation from the university community (students, workers and academics). Up to now we've only received invitations from students.

6. What issues will the zapatista delegation be addressing during their stay in Mexico City?

The zapatistas will be concentrating on the issue of Indigenous Rights and Culture, the San Andres Accords, the law which the Cocopa has made and the peace process in Chiapas. We'll be talking about these issues (which are, in fact, one) with legislators, indigenous and campesino organizations, unions, NGOs, students, teachers, neighbors, intellectuals, journalists and everyone who wants to meet with us.

Vale. Salud and we'll be seeing you soon.

From the mountains of the Mexican Southeast,
Subcomandante Insurgente Marcos.
Mexico, February of 2001.

105. THE DEVILS OF THE NEW CENTURY

To the boys and girls of Guadalupe Tepeyac in Exile

> *"Miguel Kantun, of Lerma is Canek's friend. He wrote him a letter and sent it to his son in order to make him a man. Canek answered him, saying he would make his son an Indian."*
> - Ermilo Abreu Gomez, Canek - History and Legend of a Mayan Hero

This is not a political text. It is about zapatista boys and girls, about those who were, about those who are, and about those who are to come. It is, therefore, a text of love... and war.

Children can make wars and loves, meetings and misunderstandings. Unpredictable and unwitting magicians, children play and go about creating the mirror which the world of adults avoids and detests. They have the power to change their environment, and to turn, for example, an old frayed hammock into a modern airplane, into a cayuco, into a car in order to go to San Cristo'bal de Las Casas. A simple doodle, traced with the pencil which La Mar provides them with for these occasions, gives them the artillery for recounting a complicated history in which "last night" can encompass hours or months, and "in a bit" could mean "the next century," in which (is anyone in doubt?) they are heroes and heroines. And they are, but not just in their fictitious histories, but also, and above all, in the fact of their being indigenous boys and girls in the mountains of the Mexican southeast.

Nine are the circles of Dante's inferno. Nine the prisons which confine indigenous children in Mexico: hunger, ignorance, illness, work, mistreatment, poverty, fear, forgetting and death.

In the indigenous communities of Chiapas, childhood malnutrition reaches 80%. 72% of the children do not even manage to complete the first year of primary education. And, in all indigenous homes, boys and girls, from the age of 4, must cut down and carry fire wood in order to eat. In order to break those circles, they must fight very much, always, even from the time they are children. They must fight fiercely. Sometimes they must make war, a war against the forgetting.

I have said that this is a text about boys and girls who were. Since it is "ladies first" with horses and gentlemen, I will begin with this memory which hopes not to be repeated.

I am talking about "Paticha." I have spoken of her before, and, through her, about all the neverborn of Mexico's basement.

Much has been written, for better or worse, about the causes of the zapatista uprising. I am taking advantage of the opportunity here to propose another point of departure: the zapatista neverborn, that is, a good part of the zapatista children. It is the rare indigenous family in Mexico that does not have 3 or 4 children dead before the age of 5. Thousands in the mountains of the Mexican southeast, tens of thousands in that attic abandoned by the reigning "modernity": the Indian peoples, the native inhabitants of these lands.

When she was less than five years old, Paticha died of a fever, a temperature burned up her years and her dreams.

Who was responsible for her death? What conscience was enriched with her disappearance? What doubt was resolved? What fear overcome? What bravery flourished? What hand was armed? How many deaths like Paticha's made possible the war which began in 1994?

The questions are important, because the death of Paticha was a hidden death. I said before that she was not even considered to be deceased, since, as far as the Powers were concerned, she was never born. And there was more, the neverborn called Paticha died in the darkness of the night, in the forgetting.

Obscurities like her death are, nonetheless, those which illuminated the imperfect night of this country, in 1994...

I.

And, speaking of fertile obscurities, there should be a scientific explanation in order to understand how a dark cloud can give way to the powerful glitter of a lightning flash. There are many ideological explanations, but even before a man realizes, in ceremonies, books and colloquiums, the miracle of a night storm, obscurity has already created clarity, night has given way to day, and the fiercest fire had already become a fresh wind.

And so it is that this is an especially dark dawn. Nonetheless, to the surprise of the most brilliant meteorologists (or simply in order to contradict them), rays were streaming through the eastern horizon, dry branches of light falling from the luminous tree which the night conceals behind it. The night is a black mirror in that way, a shadow breaking into yellow and orange. A mirror. The frame is formed by the four cardinal points of a horizon of up and down, trees and gray dark. A mirror seen from the dark side of the mirror. The dark side of a mirror, warning of what is behind it, promising it...

All histories are peopled with shadows. In the zapatista history, there have not been a few delineated by our light. We are full of silent footsteps which have, nonetheless, made the shouts possible. There have been many who have kept silent so that the movement may walk. Many vague faces which have allowed other faces to be made clear. Someone said that zapatismo was successful because it knew how to weave nets. Yes, but behind ours there are many weavers of skillful hands, of great ingenuity, of prudent steps. And, while an incandescent and brief light is raised above every knot of the rebel net of the forgotten of the world, they are still weaving new strokes and embraces in the shadows...

And, speaking of weavers and of embraces, I tore myself away from La Mar's warmth and cool in bed, and got up to take just a short walk, in this dawn in which February repeats its delirium and announces the arrival of the March hare. And just there, where the mountain is the land of the night of below, some fireflies were becoming excited by the humid warmth which announces a storm.

A small shadow was sobbing close to the hammock. I drew near until I was able distinguish a small little man, squat, mustachioed and rather advanced both in years and in weight. Two beat up wings made of red cardboard, a pair of small horns and a tail which ended in an arrow point made him look like the devil.

Yes, a devil. A fairly ill-treated devil. A poor devil...

"'Poor devil' like hell!" the diminutive figure muttered.

I wasn't intimidated. Even though my head and legs were telling me to run far away from here, I am the man of the house (okay, of the hut, but I believe you understand me), and I should not be abandoning La Mar, who is the woman of the house. After so many movies by Pedro Infante I have been steeled to protecting the house, and, since "Martin Corona" and "Here Comes Martin Corona," I must check my impulse to take flight. Well, at least not without warning La Mar who is, as I said previously, the woman of the house of which I am the man of the house.

And so I did not attempt any "strategic withdrawal," and, as I always do when seized by terror, I lit my pipe and started talking. I made some idle comments about the unsettled weather, and, seeing that there was no response, I ventured...

"Since you're listening to what I think..."

"You might as well be shouting," responded the little man.

"And don't call me little man!" he screeched.

"Luzbel, call me Luzbel," he hastened to interrupt my thoughts.

"Luzbel? That sounds like, like... Isn't that the angel who rebelled in pride against the Christian god, and as punishment they sent him to hell?" I said.

"That mess. But it wasn't like that. History, my unhappy mortal, is written by the victors. God, in this case. What happened was, in reality, a problem over salaries and work conditions. A union, no matter how angelic it might be, was not part of the divine plan, so God opted to invoke the exclusion clause. The mercenary scribes took it upon themselves to vilify our just fight, and so we went..." said Luzbel, getting comfortable and sitting down at the foot of a Huapac.

At that point I realized how small he was, but I didn't say anything. I suppose my silence encouraged him to continue talking, and that is what in effect happened, because Luzbel began recounting a history - fitting for a devil - of terrible horror and cruelty. His story seemed to be tragedy, comedy, or part of war...

II.

Luzbel remained silent for a bit... Except for the stars of above and those of below (the fireflies), nothing else was about in the outside night. I lit my pipe again. More to take advantage of the light from the lighter and to look at the figure of the little devil, than out of a desire to smoke. Nine circles of smoke came out of the pipe. When the last of them had dispersed, he spoke.

The history which Luzbel recounted to me might wound the sensibilities of the good and of conscientious Christians, something which is not very advisable, especially during these times when the high clergy is struggling to turn back the clock of history. But, as I am not competing for indulgences - and I have already known the hell which the Powers impose on the poor - I have nothing to worry about. In any case, I have done my duty by warning the readers, and in reminding them that I am merely transcribing what Luzbel told me, to wit:

"The God of the rich and of the ledgers was very satisfied with the Free Trade Agreement, the steps towards the first world, economic globalization and all that rubbish, which seemed more the product of hell than of the divine, since we, the devils, wouldn't be capable of such horrors."

"Anyway, what happened was that God had assigned, as he should, a guardian angel to care for each of the children of the Free Trade Agreement generation. There aren't many angels, and working as a guardian angel for children is very poorly paid. But someone called Gabriel, a pro-management leader, an archangel to be more specific, forced the wage scale in order to meet the quota. There were some protests, but not many. And so each child of NAFTA would have his guardian angel."

"But it so happened that you, the zapatistas, decided to rise up in arms on that first of January of 1994 and change everything, even divine memory. Because it just so happened that God had not remembered about the indigenous children. It's not that he hadn't had them in mind, or that he was thinking of getting rid of them, he was simply unaware of their existence."

"The God of the ledgers and the rich is an employer like any other, but very old-school. And so he believed that, while neoliberalism was seeing to dispatching all zapatista children to another world, he would have to fulfill his divine duties and to assign a guardian angel to every zapatista child."

"But, as there were no longer any guardian angels available, he then began rehabilitating devils. In order to achieve this, he forced us to sign a humiliating commercial treaty that was damaging to hell's diabolical sovereignty. Hell had been having economic problems, and someone called Saint Peter had taken advantage of our difficulties in order to grant us a financial credit which had, as one might imagine, a diabolical clause."

"Anyway, the fact was that God was able to have the infernal work force at his disposal, under unfair conditions, and without it affecting the migration restrictions imposed on us devils if we cross the celestial border. Without our hardly being aware of it, we were suddenly second-class employees, under orders from the one who had expelled us." Luzbel broke off, in what seemed like a sob. Then he continued...

"And so, from the extra-territoriality of his financial power, God put us to work as 'guardian angels' of those who had been forgotten in the First World euphoria, the indigenous children. And now, instead of inciting good consciences to sin, of perverting innocent souls, of sponsoring business leaders, of 'inspiring' the PAN governor of Queretaro, of advising Bishop Onesimo Cepeda, or of devising Fox's post-election campaign, now we are taking care of the children of the basement, under miserable working conditions."

"So now we are 'guardian devils'!"

"Really! At a miserable salary, God (who, one mustn't forget it, is God of all creation, even of hell) is forcing us to guard zapatista children. And to think that there are still those who boast of divine goodness...!"

III.

Luzbel was silent for a moment, and I took advantage of it to scribble a few words. And believe me, I was surprised myself. So much so that I immediately wrote Don Eduardo Galeano some lines, so that he could recount this in one of his books:

"Date: The beginning of the third millennium.

Don Galeano:

In neoliberal Mexico at the beginning of the 21st century, zapatista children are so poor that they do not even have guardian angels. Instead, they have devils with them, a little guardian devil.

During the stormy nights in the mountains of the Mexican southeast, the children are praying: "Little Guardian Devil, sweet companion, do not abandon me, neither by night or by day," and so it goes...

Vale. Salud and nada de mate.

The Sup."

(end of letter to Galeano).

Okay, I'm not going to drive the editorial staff crazy with any more dialogue punctuation, so I'll just recount what made this "guardian devil" unhappy.

IV.

It happened that it fell to Luzbel to be head of a squadron of "guardian devils." I don't know how many squadrons are necessary to guard all the zapatista children (who are a goodly number), but an infernal, horrific, diabolical job fell to Luzbel. He had to care for: Beto, Heriberto, Ismita, El Andulio, Nabor, Pedrito, Tonita, Eva, Chelita, Chagua, Mariya, Regina, Yeniperr, and, lastly - horror of horrors! - Olivio and Marcelo.

When it fell to him to be Beto's "guardian devil," Luzbel became desperate. And it wasn't the hectic life of this child-soldier, who challenged an armored vehicle with his slingshot, a Hummer with grenade launchers, as well as a "Black Hawk" helicopter of the NAFTA generation. Nor was it his tireless climbing up and down hills and ravines, looking for firewood for his house. No, what exasperated Luzbel (and made him ask for a custody change) were Beto's questions:

"How far away is the big city? Is it bigger than Ocosingo? How wide is the sea? What is so much water for? How do the people live who live in the sea? How big is the slingshot that can kill a helicopter? If the soldier's house and family is some-place else, why does he come to take away our houses from us and to persecute us? If the sea is as big as the sky, why don't we turn them upside down so that the government helicopters and planes will drown?"

Questions such as those were what motivated Luzbel's change in work. But it didn't go any better for him, because then they assigned him to care for Heriberto...

"It was terrible," Luzbel confessed. "That child hates school as if he were a Secretary of Public Education, and the teachers like a pro-management union leader. He prefers to play and to hunt for sweets and chocolate. You should see how you have to run after him when he hears a chocolate wrapper!"

After Heriberto, Luzbel went on to care for Ismita.

Luzbel recounted to me that one day Ismita had some trouble with Marikerr (that's what the girl is called, don't blame me), because he said she had broken a branch off Ismita's nance (fruit tree). "But how could she break it if she was so small and the tree so big?" Luzbel asked him. "She grabbed it and broke the branch," Ismita said, and looked reprovingly at Marikerr, who was bent on a children's assault on the "Aguascalientes" store. The assault had been organized by Luzbel because, he said, "the children should prepare themselves for anything, even to govern." Ismita must be about 10 years ago, but chronic malnutrition has granted him the stature of a 4 year old child. Ismita compensates for his lack of physical height with moral greatness. He not only pardoned Marikerr for breaking the branch of his nance, he also offered him some soft drink and cookies he had gotten during the assault on the store. "No one shares," Ismita told Luzbel when the latter had objected.

Generosity does not provoke the passion of hell, so Luzbel went to care for Andulio.

After walking a great distance, Luzbel reached the home of Andulio, he of the brilliant smile. We met Andulio during those terrible days of the 1995 persecution. May was a hot wind then, burning days and nights, and Andulio stayed up all night in a tree, trying to imitate a turkey with his song. He didn't approach us often, but we discovered he had accepted us when, one afternoon, he asked for a record player, and, to the rhythm of a corrido, he began dancing. La Mar asked him then, in front of a poster, where the Sup was. Andulio hesitated, and a split-second later, turned around and pointed to me. The Sup couldn't be in the poster and in the doorway at the same time, and so, as he pointed me out in the flesh, he repeated his philosophical materialism. I had forgotten to mention that Andulio was born without hands, a genetic malformation left stumps on the ends of his arms.

"That child may not have hands, but he does have a smile that's too angelic," Luzbel said, justifying his new change. And so he came to be with Nabor.

It wasn't any better with Nabor. With 3 years behind him, Nabor has a libido that would put Casanova to shame. Luzbel could do nothing but blush, and he immediately went to another community. And so he came to Guadalupe Tepeyac in exile.

In this Tojolabal community, dislocated from their homes by the Mexican federal army, it fell to him to be "guardian angel," - excuse me, "guardian devil" - for Pedrito. Pedrito is a Guadalupe child born in exile. When the First Interc-onti-nental Meeting for Humanity and Against Neoliberalism opened, his mother gave birth to him. With 3 years behind him, Pedrito is Lino's friend, another Guadalupe child. Lino was born on February 9, 1995, and he was barely a few hours old when he was expelled from his home by soldiers.

Returning to Pedrito, it so happens that he didn't want to go to school. I had already threatened to take his case to the community assembly, but no way. I warned him that if he didn't go, I was going to denounce him in a communiqué directed to the people of Mexico and to the peoples and governments of the world. Pedrito just looked at me, shrugged his shoulders and said: "Send it, I don't even know how to read." La Mar defended him, saying that he was barely 3 years old, and Pedrito just stared at her, sighing, in love. But that is another history, we are now with Luzbel taking care of Pedrito.

It so happened that Pedrito decided to play horses. You imagine rightly if you are imagining that it fell to Luzbel to be the horse. And you guess correctly if you are guessing that Luzbel resigned.

"That child made the belt too tight," he said in justification.

V.

After Pedrito, Luzbel decided to switch to a more mild-mannered gender, and he devoted himself to caring for a zapatista girl: Tonita.

Luzbel wasn't bothered by Tonita's tendency to look down on love, which "hurts a lot" (to my outrage, he characterized her tendency as "healthy"). Not by that, nor by having been dressed up like a doll by a Tonita who was determined to cut off his wings.

"You wouldn't have been the only one to have had them cut off," I said resentfully.

The "guardian devil" put up with all of that, but he could not tolerate that constant breaking and mending of teacups which is the life of zapatista girls...

And so Tonita's "guardian devil" resigned and went on to care for Eva. He didn't last long. When he was watching "School for Vagabonds" for the umpteenth time, he fell asleep and Eva took the opportunity to embroider little flowers and a "Viva the EZLN" on his wings. The shame forced Luzbel to emigrate.

After Eva, Chelita followed. A dark-haired girl of 6 or 7, with black eyes like stars. The same thing happened to Luzbel that happened to everyone, when Chelita looked at him he was left frozen (not an adequate temperature for a devil), she made him fly through the skies (not an advisable direction, given the expulsion, etcetera) and she let out with an "Ave Maria Purisima!" that was, quite certainly, too much. Luzbel felt as if they had ripped out his soul - excuse me, as if they had ripped off his wings - when they took him away from caring for Chelita and ordered him to be with Chagua.

Chagua, as her name indicates, is not called "Chagua," but Rosaura, but no one calls her as she is called. She must be about 8 years old. In a small gang of warlike children, the one who is the leader is not a boy, but a girl, Chagua. She is the first and fastest in climbing trees in order to catch cicadas, she is the fiercest and most accurate in fights with stones and mud, she is the first to throw herself into the fray, and, up until now, no one has ever heard her ask for mercy. However, when she approaches us, something strange happens: Chagua is a tender and sweet girl who embraces La Mar and asks her to tell her a story or to fix her hair, or she just hugs her and stays quiet, sighing from time to time.

Luzbel did not resign because of the confusion provoked by Chagua's "tender fury," but because he was hit on the head with a rock during an altercation, and the bump it created on his skull left him with a third horn which did not suit him at all. And so Luzbel went to care for another girl, Mariya.

Mariya must be about 7 years old, and in her village she is the one who has the best aim with a slingshot. We discovered this, we and the village, during one of our travels through those lands.

After walking for several hours, La Mar and I collapsed under the lintel of a hut. We had not even caught our breath when Huber, Saul, Pichito, and an indeterminate number of children of equally indeterminate names, arrived. All of them had brought their slingshots, and they asked to have a contest to see who had the best aim. Mariya was already sitting next to La Mar, and she didn't say anything. Without getting up, I organized the turns, and I indicated that they should set up a can 10 steps away. Each and every one of them took their turn, and the can remained in place.

When I asked if everyone had had their turn, La Mar said: "Mariya hasn't."

To everyone's outrage, Mariya joined in and borrowed a slingshot.

A murmur of disapproval went through the group of men (I wasn't among them, not because I wanted to be seen as a feminist, but because I didn't have the strength to get up and support my gender).

Mariya gave the boys a swift look of contempt, and that was enough for them to stay quiet. A silence reigned, which had little to do with mockery and much with expectation...

Mariya drew the slingshot, closed one eye - as and how mandated by slingshot manuals - fired, and the can leapt with a metallic crash.

Mariya and La Mar broke into cries of jubilation: "The women won!"

We boys were left shocked, contrite and open-mouthed. "Don't worry," I told them in consolation, "We'll have the contest without Mariya next time." I don't think I convinced anyone.

Luzbel has been educated in the "old-school," that is: slingshots are not for girls. And so he had what we call a "crisis of macho conscience," which came over him when Mariya won in the rough and (formerly) masculine sport of firing at cans with a slingshot. And that is how Luzbel came to go elsewhere.

In other communities, Luzbel looked after Regina, a child of about 9 or 10 years of age who behaved as if she were 30. Mature and responsible, Regina is sister and mother to her little brothers and sisters, bodyguard of the insurgents, the best tortilla maker in the barrio, and a sun when she smiles. Despite his experience in infernal burnings, Luzbel resigned when he couldn't tolerate the burning of his fingers when he turned the tortillas on the stove.

"It wasn't the burns," Luzbel told me, "but that I had to get up at 4 in the morning to make the fire, grind the maize and make the tortillas. And that was just to start the day."

Lacking sleep, and with his fingers burned, Luzbel went to care for Yeniperr.

Yeniperr is an excellent example of the bird who conquers the machine. When the helicopters make low overflights above the community, Yeniperr chases them with questions. In the face of such fierce projectiles, the warlike machines withdraw, and Yeniperr continues to flutter about amidst lovebirds and hummingbirds. When Yeniperr flies, she often gets lost and has nothing to fear, unless Capirucho and Capirote are anywhere close by.

Luzbel lasted barely a few days with Yeniperr. According to what he told me, it wasn't the fear of government helicopters and planes that made him ask for a change in work.

"I've never been into this flying. That's why I'm a fallen angel," Luzbel said, rubbing his backside.

They should never have done it, but it so happened that they assigned Luzbel, owing to a lack of personnel, to care for two children: Olivio and Marcelo, that is, Capirucho and Capirote.

VI.

Olivio, or the self-styled "Sergeant Capirucho," has confessed to me that, when he is big, he is going to be "Sup." "And, you, Sup, what are you going to be?", he asked me, knowing that the fulfillment of his aspirations would leave me without a job. "Me?" I asked, in order to gain time. "I'm going to be a horse, a child horse, and I'm going to go there, very far away," and I pointed to an indefinite point on the horizon. "You can be Sergeant," Olivio consoled me, while he discovered a little turtledove who was fluttering about, oblivious to Capirucho's hierarchical aspirations and to the fearsome slingshot hanging from his belt.

"Corporal Capirote," Marcelo answered when they ask him what he is called. Without any shame whatsoever, and perhaps making use of the military privilege of his rank, he went wherever he pleased and would start looking for sweets and chocolates, recounting incredible histories, or he would he would set about spying on the women while they were bathing.

Olivio and Marcelo, Capirucho and Capirote. These two boys play at confusing each other when they recite poetry. Four poems make up their repertoire, and they always devise ways to mix them up with each other. The result? It doesn't matter, if, in the end, they get a piece of candy or a chocolate, if they can sketch "little marbles," or go hunting, always unsuccessfully, for rooks. Capirucho and Capirote believe that there is no better remedy for lack of love than a good rook to eat together.

These two dwarves, excuse me, children, have overcharged batteries. They are about 7 years old, and they broaden their radius of activity every day. They pursue the "erello" (a species of salamander up to a meter in length) among thorns and acahuales, but they don't get very close to it. They have taken Luzbel from one end to the other, his wings were full of thorns and scratches, they filled his pockets with pebbles (for the slingshot), and they "fried his brain" with their constant blather. The nights were not enough to allow for Luzbel's recuperation, and he would have to follow behind them early in order to fish for conch, crab and shrimp, to go to the coffee fields, to be stung by ants, bees or by any of the community's "wild" animals, to kick a deflated ball, to eat everything they found within their grasp and their height, and to listen to them recount exploits which had never occurred. But what depressed Luzbel the most was that they made him a target for practicing with the slingshot.

Luzbel is old now, his age goes back to the beginning of time. I am saying this not so you will pity him, but so you will understand him. I know Capirucho and Capirote, and I am certain that the work of caring for them would leave God himself (who, incidentally, is not young either) exhausted.

That is why Luzbel did not surprise me when he told me he was definitively resigning from taking care of zapatista boys and girls.

"I'd be better off going to Kosovo or Rwanda or any place else where the UN is carrying out its mission to promote wars," Luzbel said, sitting up. "There's bound to be more calm there."

And, as he got ready to walk away, he added:

"Or the Diocese of Ecatepec or the upper echelons of Mexican business, which is turning into the same thing. There is corruption there, lies, outrages, theft and all those evils more appropriate for orthodox devils such as myself."

I understand Luzbel's desperation and despair. I am certain that he would have rather not have tried to organize an angelic union if he had known that, in the course of time, he was going to have to be following after these children.

By the light of a firefly, I added a postscript to the letter to Eduardo Galeano,

"P.S. Which Provides More Details. - Don Eduardo: In the indigenous mountains of Mexico, God is not alive. Nor the devil, not even if they pay him..."

It was almost dawn now, and so I said farewell to Luzbel and returned to La Mar.

VII.

The majority of the indigenous boys and girls of Guadalupe Tepeyac in exile were born and raised away from their homes. There is another political party in government in Mexico, and these children continue to be held hostage (now by those self-styled "promoters of change") in order to impose surrender on them. What has changed for these children? The history of their native town seems like a story to them, it is so far away in time and space that it seems to them to be a very long trip to return to it. Complicated and petty political calculations and a stupid pride are what expelled them from their village, and what is refusing to return to them what belongs to them.

Not only in this nomadic village, but in all zapatista communities, boys and girls are growing up and becoming youngsters and adults in the midst of a war. But, contrary to what might be thought, the teachings they receive from their towns are not of hate and vengeance, even less of desperation and sadness. No, in the mountains of the Mexican southeast, the children are growing up learning that "hope" is a word spoken collectively, and they are learning to live dignity and respect for the different. Perhaps one of the differences between these children and those from other areas, is that these are learning from the time they are little to see the morning.

More and more boys and girls will continue to be born in the mountains of the Mexican Southeast. They will be zapatistas, and, as such, they will not manage to have a guardian angel. We, "poor devils," will have to care for them until they are big. Big like us, the zapatistas, the most small...

From the mountains of the Mexican Southeast,
Subcomandante Insurgente Marcos.
Mexico, February of 2001.

106. To the Boys and Girls of the Isidro Favela Neighborhood

March 18, 2001

To the Boys and Girls of the Isidro Favela Neighborhood

Through my voice the voice of the Zapatista Army of National Liberation is not speaking.

Yes, you heard the "is not speaking the voice of etcetera" right, and it so happens that I was gazing at the walls in the room where we were staying yesterday, and I was looking for an idea or something that would wind me up to say a few words which would simultaneously be analysis, reflection, gratitude, invitation, etcetera-tion, or something better than one of those games where everybody participates and there's joy and songs and dances, or at least as good.

But nothing. What came out was like that radio program where they say "youngsters" or something would just occur to me, like the way Fox's image advisors tell him, to imitate what we do, I could go out with a statement that I'm willing to fulfill the three signals or that I don't want to replace peace with commercials, or something along those lines.

That's what I was up to, when the lights went out. The most incomplete darkness reigned around me. And I say "incomplete" because almost immediately there appeared, under the doorjamb, a kind of miniaturized Christmas tree, laboriously moving. I checked the calendar, and it told me "We are in March, there are no little Christmas trees in March."

Panic took over me, but I pulled myself together, since, given that stuff about us zapatistas being very brave, it wouldn't look good if I were to panic. And so you guys won't be able to go around saying that I'm afraid of the dark, given that we children are in fact afraid of the dark. Which is why we zapatistas are fighting so that all us children can have light, but okay, that's another story.

I'm telling you that, from under my door, something appeared that looked like a little Christmas tree, advancing towards me. When it got close, I was able to realize that it wasn't a little Christmas tree, but one of those strings of colored lights that was being dragged by something that looked like a little dented car or a little deflated ball or...

"Little dented car your mama, and little deflated ball your mama!" screamed that thing that looked like a little deflated ball or a little dented car. I happen to like my mama very much so I turned on the lights in order to give... whatever it was!... its just desserts.

When I turned on the lights, surprise! - I discovered that it was nothing more and nothing less than a cantankerous beetle who calls himself "Don Durito of the Lacandona," although his real name is Nebuchadnezzar. He allows his friends to call him "Durito."

"Excuse me, Durito," I said to him. "But I didn't expect to see you here. Why are you dragging that string of Christmas lights? Don't you know we're just barely into March?"

"Of course I know! If you really were a zapatista, then you'd know that we zapatistas are fighting so that children can have Christmas whenever they want, whether in March or July, or a Christmas for every month of the year..."

"Okay, okay. Why are you bringing those Christmas lights?"

"Because I've come in disguise."

"And what are you disguised as?"

"As a patrol car."

"As a patrol car?"

"Yes, I'm in charge of looking after security for the zapatista delegation, and I disguised myself as a patrol car so no one would realize that I am the great, the incomparable, the supreme Don Durito of the Lacandona! Completely digitized, guaranteed, and with batteries included!"

"Digitized, guaranteed and with batteries included?" I asked.

Durito answered: "Yes, I'm into business excellence now." And he continued:

"And tell me, dented carrot nose, what are you doing?"

"A message or greeting to the children of the neighborhood where we are, in order to thank them for having us."

"Fine, to one side. This is a job for the unbreakable Durito. I'm going to dictate a story to you. You'll read it to them, and it's going to be the delight of the small and the large."

"But Durito!" I tried to protest.

"It's not negotiable! Write this:

The Story of the Little Dented Car

"Once upon a time there was a little wind-up car that no longer had a cord. Or, it did have one, but no one wound it up. And no one wound it up because it was an old little car, completely dented. It was missing a tire and, when it did work, it just went round and round.

The children didn't pay it much attention because they were into transformers and pokemon and zodiac knights and other things.

And so the little dented wind-up car didn't have anyone to wind it up. And then the lights went out in the great city, because the one who governed had privatized the electricity industry, and the rich had taken away the light to other countries, and the transformers and pokemon and zodiac knights wouldn't run anymore. And then the little dented car said: I have a cord but I don't have anyone to wind it up. And a little boy heard him and wound him up and the little car began turning round and round, and the little boy said And now? Not like that, said the little car. Turn me upside down. The child did so, and he asked: And now? Put a rubber band on the motor there. And the little boy did, and the little car said now pull my cord and you will see that light is going to be generated, and, yes, the little boy did, and there was light once again. And this was repeated in all the homes where they had a little dented wind-up car, and, where they didn't, they continued without light. And in the end the little car said: That's exactly how you have to do things. Turn things upside down so that the world will have light once again. Tan-tan."

Moral: Better that the electricity industry not be allowed to be privatized, because what if everyone doesn't have a little dented wind-up car?

> *From the Isidro Favela Neighborhood,*
> *Don Durito of the Lacandona (batteries included).*
> *Mexico, March of 2001.*

"Durito," I protested.

"What?"

"No one's going to like that story!"

"Why not? It's lovely, substantial, it doesn't need batteries and it's unbreakable. And I'm leaving now, because there goes Fernandez de Cevallos and I brought a razor along with me."

And so this is the story, boys and girls of the Isidro Favela neighborhood. I hope you have enjoyed it and that you understand now that the voice of the EZLN is not speaking through my voice, but, in this case, the voice is speaking of a beetle by the name of "Don Durito of the Lacandona," who, he says, is devoted to helping the poor and challenging the powerful.

Vale. Salud and, if you see him around here, tell him to give me back the tobacco he took without letting me know.

The Sup, sneezing.

107. OUR WORD FOR EVERYONE

March 28, 2001
Message from Subcomandante Insurgente Marcos to civil society gathered in front of the Chamber of Deputies

We would like to tell you that with this act - and I am referring to this act we are participating in right now - we are marking the end of a mobilization begun with the Fifth Declaration of the Selva Lacandona.

A mobilization which began in 1998, and which, in 1999, two years ago, in March, achieved one of its greatest shining moments with the Consulta.

We would like to thank the three million persons who voted that day for the recognition of indigenous rights and culture.

Thank you to those who mobilized then, and thank you to the millions who are mobilizing now.

I would like to give special thanks to my companero chiefs, the Comandantes and Comandantas of the Clandestine Revolutionary Indigenous Committee.

We would also like to send our appreciation, in a greeting which is quite far away in distance, but very close in our hearts, to our zapatista peoples, to the support bases, the men, women, children and old ones of the EZLN.

We would especially also like to thank the indigenous brothers in all the corners of the Republic who came here - the people from civil society of Chiapas, Oaxaca, Puebla, Veracruz, Tlaxcala, Hidalgo, Queretaro, Guanajuato, Michoacan, the State of Mexico, Morelos, Guerrero, the Federal District and Mexico City - who accompanied us throughout this final phase of the mobilization which is called the March of the Color of the Earth.

We want to thank them... we are finished now. Tomorrow we are going to pack our knapsacks and leave for our return journey back to our place.

We want to tell you something, we want to ask you to go to your homes, to your workplaces, and tell your friends, your families, that, thanks to you, a boy called Pedro - Pedrito, we say - is going to be able to return to his house after six years and one month of living in the mountains.

Thanks to you the Tojolabal indigenous community of Guadalupe Tepeyac will no longer have "in exile" as its last name, and now it will once again be just Guadalupe Tepeyac, zapatista.

We would also like to thank the artists and intellectuals who helped us organize this event: the teacher Oscar Chavez, the teacher Gabino Palomares? - they said Gabino Barrera on the radio here, does anyone know? - and all those who have helped us. Like it says in that Oscar Chavez song, who agreed to my request to sing it, that "along with you we were able to make the world in another way, but it is not done being changed, many things are going to have to be done for it to turn out well, but at least it's not like it was before." We're going.

We can return now, brothers of the National Indigenous Congress. We are not going with empty hands. We are going with them full of all the hands we reached out for. The hands we saluted close up or from a distance, the hands which entwined themselves in the security hands in order to protect us. Those which went to great effort to prepare our food, those which built and equipped the places we spent the night in. Those which wrote us letters and words of support and encouragement. Those which cared for us during the nights and in the dawns, those which were lifted high on that March 11 this year in the capital Zocalo. Those which were made indignant when the stubbornness of a few tried to close the path of dialogue. The ones which voted yes during the March 22 sessions in the Chamber of Deputies and the Senate. Those which we did not see, but which became tense with anxiety, sharing ours, and which are now applauding, sharing our joy. Our hands are full with your hands, and hands - everyone knows - are the shape which hearts take on when they meet.

Thank you brother, thank you sister, thank you compa, thank you brother, thank you bud, thank you nero, thank you nera, thank you papa, thank you mama, thank you son, thank you daughter, thank you uncle, thank you aunt, thank you brother-in-law, thank you cousin, nephew, niece, godmother, godson and goddaughter.

Thank you Mexico. We're going, really.

108. Words of the EZLN In Juchitan

March 31, 2001

The afternoon is flickering out in the heat of the night. Shadows come down from the great Ceiba, the mother tree and sustenance of the world, picking any spot in which to put their mysteries to bed. Along with the afternoon, March is also going out, and not this one which surprises us today, going about with the many. I am speaking of another afternoon, in another time and in another land, ours. Old Antonio had returned from hoeing the field, and he sat down in the doorway of his hut. Inside, Dona Juanita was preparing tortillas and words. And, as she did so, she was passing them to Old Antonio, putting some in and taking others out, Old Antonio was muttering, while he smoked his rolled cigarette...

The History of the Search

Our most ancient wise men recount that the very first gods, those who birthed the world, had created almost all things, and they did not make everything, because they were aware that a goodly number should be created by men and women. That is why the gods who birthed the world, the most first, went away when the world was not yet complete. They did not go away without finishing it out of laziness, but because they knew that it was up to a few to begin, but finishing is the work of everyone. The most ancient of our most old also recount that the most first gods, those who birthed the world, had a knapsack where they had been keeping all the undone things they were leaving in their work. Not in order to do them later, but in order to have memory of what must come when men and women have finished the world which had been born incomplete.

And the gods who birthed the world, the most first, went away then. They left like the afternoon, as if putting themselves out, as if covering themselves in shadows, as if they were not there even though they were there. Then the rabbit, who was angry with the gods because they had not made him big even though he had carried out the tasks they had assigned him (monkeys, tigers, lizards), went and nibbled at the gods' knapsack, but he was noisy and the gods noticed and they pursued him in order to punish him for the crime he had committed. The rabbit ran quickly. That is why rabbits do indeed eat as if they had committed a crime and run away quickly if anyone sees them. The fact is that, even though he was unable to entirely rip open the knapsack of the most first gods, the rabbit always does manage to make a hole. Then, when the gods who had birthed the world went away, all the undone things fell out of the hole in the knapsack. And the most first gods did not even realize it, and then one came whom they called wind and it took to blowing and blowing, and the undone things went in one direction and the other, and, since it was night, no one knew where they had gone so they could stop those undone things which were the things which had to be created in order for the world to be complete.

When the gods became aware of the mess, they made a huge racket and they became very sad and they say that some even wept. That is why they say that, when it is going to rain, first the sky makes much noise and then the water comes. The men and women of maize, the true ones, heard the bawling, because when the gods cry it can indeed be heard far away. The men and women of maize then went to see why the most first gods were crying, those who birthed the world, and then, between sobs, the gods recounted to them what had happened. And then the men and women of maize said: "Do not cry anymore. We are going to look for the undone things which were lost, because we already know that there are things undone, and that the world will not be complete until everything is made and fixed up." And the men and women of maize went on to say: "Then let us ask you, most first gods, those who birthed the world, whether you remember a bit of the undone things which were lost, so that we may then know if what we find are undone things, or if they are something new which are already being birthed."

The most first gods did not reply then, because their bawling was preventing them even from speaking. And then, later, while they were rubbing their eyes in order to clean away their tears, they said: "An undone thing is each person finding themselves."

That is why our most ancient say that when we are born, we are born lost, and then, as we grow up, we go about seeking ourselves, and that living is seeking, looking for ourselves.

And, more calmed down now, the gods who birthed the world, the most first, went on to say: "All those things yet to be born in the world have to do with this, which we are telling you, with each person finding himself. That is how you will know if what you find is something yet to be born in the world, if it helps you find yourselves."

"That is good," said the true men and women, and they set about seeking everywhere the undone things which must be created in the world and which would help them find themselves.

Old Antonio finished the tortillas, the cigarette and the words. He remained still for a while, looking at a corner of the night. After a few minutes, he said: "Since then, we go about seeking, seeking ourselves. We seek when we are working, when we are resting, when we are eating and when we are sleeping, when we are loving and when we are dreaming. When we live seeking ourselves and seeking ourselves seeking when we have already died. In order to find ourselves we seek ourselves, in order to find ourselves we live and we die."

"And how does one go about finding oneself?" I asked.

Old Antonio kept looking at me, and he said to me, while rolling another cigarette:

"An old wise Zapotec told me how. I am going to tell you, but in Spanish, because only those who have found themselves can speak the Zapoteca tongue well, which is the flower of the word, and my word is barely seed, and there are others which are stem and leaves and fruit, and the one who is complete finds that. The father Zapotec said:

'First you shall walk all the paths of all the peoples of the earth, before finding yourself.' (Niru zazalu' guira'xixe neza guidxilayu' ti ganda guidxelu' lii)"

I took note of what Old Antonio told me that afternoon, in which March and the afternoon were putting themselves out. Since then, I have walked many paths, but not all, and I am still seeking the face which will be seed, stem, leaf, flower and fruit of the word. I seek myself with everything and in everything in order to be complete.

A light was smiling in the night above, as if she would find herself in the shadow below.

March is going. But hope is arriving.

Subcomandante Insurgente Marcos.
Juchitan, Oaxaca.
Mexico, March 31, 2001.

109. Marcos Reports Back in Oventik

April 1, 2001
Support bases of the Zapatista Army of National Liberation
Local and regional Committees of Los Altos region of Chiapas
Clandestine Revolutionary Indigenous Committee Los Altos region

Companero, companera,
I am here returning our Committee chiefs to you.
That is exactly the order which you gave us.
They are returning a bit pleased, because we carried out the work with which you entrusted us.
You entrusted me with the mission of taking them and taking care of them.
In order to be able to carry this out, you told me to ask for help from other indigenous and non-indigenous brothers and sisters, mostly Mexicans, and some from other countries.
They cared for us the entire time. They did not leave us alone for one single

moment, and they gave us everything we needed, and they also gave us what we did not need.

They gave us shelter and food.

They covered us when we were cold, and they refreshed us when we were hot.

They gave us drink when we thirsty, and when we were hungry they gave us food.

When we encountered deaf ears, they uncovered the ears of the powerful with their strength, and when our words seemed small, they lifted them up, and the zapatista word shone very brightly, your word companero, companera.

They are these people we call civil society who took us and treated us well. And so I am telling you quite clearly, companero, companera, that it was not I, it was these men and women from civil society, who did all the work, and they did it very well, and they did not receive any payment for that work. They did it because their hearts are very large and generous.

Some of these persons are present here, but not all of them. There are many more who are not here in body, but they were, and are, always, in their hearts.

That is why I am asking you, companero, companera, for us to salute all the persons who took us and treated us well.

We also have to say that the media workers walked with us from one side to the other, and our word almost always arrived exactly as it is, without traps or deception. Only a few twisted our words, but their tongues are already twisted. But the great majority of the press did indeed say exactly what was happening and what we were saying, and what others were saying, and all of that was also important so that we could go and return well.

Then, companero, companera, I am asking you for us to salute the honest press, and that our salute may serve for them to know that we, the zapatistas, recognize their work, and we hope that their spaces will always be open for those of us who are beneath everything.

Companero, companera, the greatest part of this work with which you entrusted us was for us to be able to be next to our brothers and sisters from the National Indigenous Congress. They helped us greatly with their wisdom and their firmness. The Indian peoples of all of Mexico joined in our struggle.

Companero, companera,

37 days we walked. 6000 kilometers. In that journey we passed through 13 states of the Mexican Republic, and we then entered into the land which grows upwards, Mexico City. And so we passed through Chiapas, Oaxaca, Puebla, Veracruz, Tlaxcala, Hidalgo, Queretaro, Guanajuato, Michoacan, the State of Mexico, Morelos, Guerrero and the Federal District.

In the journey we held 77 public events where we took 7 times 7 your word so that it could be heard.

The brother, the sister, who carries blood dark like ours for 4 times 7, gave us their word which walked in ours: 7 ceremonial staffs we carried on February 25, with 28 ceremonial staffs we entered Mexico City.

In the House of the Purepecha we met with other brothers and sisters. We met with 44 Indian peoples there, and we follow our path together now.

And so are named the brothers and sisters who, like us, have the color we are of the earth:

Tenek. Tlahuica. Tlapaneco. Tojolabal. Totonaco. Triqui. Tzeltal. Tzotzil. Wixaritari. Yaqui. Zapoteco. Zoque. Maya. Kumiai. Mayo. Mazahua. Mazateco. Mixe. Amuzgo. Cora. Cuicateco. Chinanteco. Chocholteco. Chol. Pericuri. Guaycuri. Cochimi. Chontal. Guarijio. Huasteco. Huave. Kikapu. Kukapa. Mame. Matlatzinca. Mixteco. Nahuatl. O'Odham. Pame. Popoluca. Purepecha. Raramuri.

Companero, companera,

We have now returned. You gave us the order to carry the name of zapatistas with dignity, and with dignity we carried it.

To the arrogant, we were defiant, and with the humble we were humble.

We poked fun at the one who offered us jail and death.

The one who offered us listening and true word received our respect.

You told us to carry upwards the demand for the recognition of our rights and culture, and that we did. Now the wind and the times augur well for that pain, which is all which we are, to begin to end.

Much remains, companero, companera, but there is less now.

Now you will never again lower your head in front of the one who wishes to humiliate you.

Now our color will no longer be a source of shame.

Now there will no longer be mockery of our culture.

Now to say "Indian" will be to say "dignified."

Now the one who looks at you will have to look at straight ahead at you, never again downwards.

Now the place we have wanted, needed and deserved is in the hearts of everyone.

But it remains for the law to recognize that place.

In order to achieve that we now have the support of millions of Mexicans and of thousands from other countries.

The one who makes the laws will have to listen to those millions and, along with them, will have to open the door to dialogue, to peace.

This we did, companeros, companeras. I am now bringing you the news that your strength is greater because it has known to be wise and generous. Your name is now a reason to be respected, and many have learned the lesson of dignified resistance which you have given.

As far as we can see, today war is a little further away, and peace with justice and dignity is a bit more near.

Today, dialogue is closer, and confrontation more distant.

That is why we are calling on all of those for whom Chiapas is the ground and sky of their lives, to be responsible, and to not cause these first steps to be lost once again in confrontation, division, lies, deception or forgetting.

Peace has not arrived, that is true, but it could arrive. And it is that possibility which me must care for.

In the next few days we will be preparing a good report of all that took place on this journey we have made. You will see it, and you will tell us then if our steps were good or bad, and you will also decide what steps are to follow and how and when and where.

I am returning the ceremonial staff to you, companero, companera. We will await your orders.

Companero, companera,

I want you to know that serving you has been the greatest honor which we, the insurgents, have ever had. We shall continue doing so.

We, your guerreros and guerreras, have received another lesson over these last few days from you, and which we shall know how to learn: your patient wisdom.

Companero, companera, murcielago men and women,

Chiapas will no longer be the word for misfortune, poverty, crime, impotence, impunity, shamelessness.

Chiapas is now, for millions, the word for dignity.

Chiapas has been, is, and will be, the cry of...

Democracy!

Liberty!

Justice!

From the mountains of the Mexican Southeast,
Subcomandante Insurgente Marcos.
Mexico, April of 2001.

110. We Are in Silence - and the Silence Is Not Being Broken

September of 2002

Zapatista Army of National Liberation

Mexico

For: Fernando Ya'nez Munoz, Architect

From: Subcomandante Insurgente Marcos

Big Brother,

Please accept the usual greetings, almost as usual as the cold which will soon be clothing the mountains of the Mexican southeast.

As you will remember, it has now been 18 years since I arrived in the mountains of the Mexican southeast, that is, I have reached the age of majority. This is an excellent excuse for writing you, for greeting you and, in passing, for congratulating you, since I have found out that you graduated with honors, which is how zapatistas graduate.

I received the letter where you told me about the project of Professor Sergio Rodriguez Lascano, the teacher Adriana Lopez Monjardin and Javier Elorriaga, that of making a magazine whose name, as I understand it, will be Rebeldia.

Regarding that, I would like to let you know that we can do nothing less than applaud that intellectual effort and say how good that it is zapatistas who are undertaking that task.

If that magazine, Rebeldia, does not follow the path of the publications of the left, it is likely that they will even publish more than one copy and, one fine day, they will launch it publicly, so that the entire world (that is, those who make it and their friends and family) will know of it.

I have never been to a magazine launch, but I imagine that there is a table where those who are presenting the magazine will sit, and they look at each other, asking themselves, not unblushingly, why there are more people at the table than in the audience.

But that is, in fact, assuming that the project doesn't stay shelved.

And, speaking of assumptions, the outlandish idea has occurred to me that you might be present at the improbable launch of Rebeldia, and, if so, our voice would be represented in your voice.

After all, it will be a magazine made by zapatistas, and we should be present in some form.

As we are in silence - and the silence is not being broken, but tended - we shall not be able to attend (indeed, I'm taking it as a given here that those who are making the magazine would have the tact to invite us, although I doubt that they'll do so, not out of a lack of courtesy, but because of terror that we would speak of their publication).

If they do not invite us, make yourself the victim and, singing that song of Aute's that says, "passing by here," slam the door and, when they are yawning, ask to speak and come out with one of those lectures that leave wounds. They'll definitely be asleep, but at least they'll have nightmares instead of dreams.

Since I already know that you are asking yourself what you can talk about since we are in silence, I'm sending you some thoughts here that can be used for your presentation.

The problem is that they are written in that sparkling and playful style which is the joy of young and old, and not in the stilted and serious style of the anthropologists, but you can compose them into something very very formal.

Here, then, are the thoughts (bear in mind they I have been very careful to not refer to anything current or to the indigenous law; concerning these topics, the word will come that comes; you also take care not to break the silence).

ONE. The intellectual work of the left should, above all else, be a critical and self-critical exercise.

Since self-criticism is always postponed for the next number, critique, then, becomes the sole motor of thought.

In the case of the left in Mexico, that intellectual work now has, among others, one central objective, the critique of politics and culture, and of history.

TWO. In present-day Mexico, the practice of politics and culture are full of myths.

Ergo, the critique by the left should combat those myths. And there are not a few myths which inhabit the culture.

But there are myths and myths.

There is, for example, the cultural myth which chants: "Enrique Krauze is an intellectual," when we all know that he's nothing but a mediocre businessman.

Or that other one which says: "Maria Felix was a diva," when the truth is she was just a professional of herself.

There is the myth that "Viana sells cheaper," when you can get a better price and better quality from any street vendor.

There are also myths in politics:

There is the myth that "The National Action Party is a party of the right."

Actually, it is not a party of the center or the left either.

The PAN is, in reality, nothing more than a placement agency for management positions.

There is also that other myth that "The Democratic Revolutionary Party is a left alternative."

Nor on the other hand, is it an alternative of the center or of the right. The PRD is, simply, not an alternative of anything.

Or you have the myth: "The Institutional Revolutionary Party is a political party." The PRI is, in reality, a cave with 40 thieves who are fruitlessly waiting for their Ali Baba. Or that other myth, so beloved by the stagnant left, that chants: "Going against globalization is like going against the law of gravity."

Opposed to that, throughout the world, are the marginalized of all colors who are defying both of them, and neither physics nor the International Monetary Fund can prevent them.

And there is the myth for which the federal and the Chiapas state governments are paying, and paying dearly, that says: "The zapatistas are finished," when the only thing that the zapatistas are finished with is patience.

I am sure there are other myths I have missed, but I am only mentioning a few.

And I am certain that Rebeldia magazine will unclothe them more radically.

And I am not doing it like that, because it is already known that the zapatistas are famous for being "moderate" and "reformist."

That is what the alleged "ultras" of the CGH called us, who are today undoubtedly lining up at the doors of the PRD closest to their hearts, and their wallets, waiting for the chance to run in the next election.

THREE. The rebel is, if you will permit the image, a human being beating himself against the walls of the labyrinth of history. And, so that there is no misinterpretation, it is not that he is pummeling himself in order to look for the path which will lead him to the way out.

No, the rebel beats at the walls because he knows that the labyrinth is a trap, because he knows that there is no way out other than by breaking down the walls.

If the rebel uses his head as a club, it is not because it is a hard head (which it is, have no doubt), but because breaking down the traps of history, along with their myths, is a job that is done with the head, that is, it is an intellectual work.

And so, as a consequence, the rebel suffers from a headache that is so severe and continuous that it makes him forget about the most severe migraine.

FOUR. Among the traps of history is the one which says "all previous times were better."

When the right says that, it is confessing to its reactionary nature. When it is the parliamentary left which puts it forward, it is demonstrating the capitulations of its present.

When it is the center which is speaking, then someone is delirious, because the center does not exist. When the institutional left looks at itself in the mirror of Power and says: "I am a responsible and mature left," it is in reality saying, "I am a left which the right finds agreeable."

When the right looks at itself in the mirror of Power and says "what beautiful clothes I am wearing!", it forgets that it is naked.

When the center looks for itself in the mirror of Power, it does not find anything.

FIVE. Neither the forms of struggle nor the times are for the exclusive use of one social sector. Neither autonomy nor resistance are forms of organization and struggle which concern only the Indian peoples.

And let me tell you something here: It is said that the EZLN is an example of the construction of autonomy and resistance.

And yes. For example, every zapatista insurgent is a kind of autonomous municipality, or he does what he wants to do.

And what better resistance than the one which opposes carrying out orders. And all of that is a defect, but it is also a virtue.

There you have the enemy intercepting our communications and finding out that the command is calling for a meeting at the G-spot (note that my double entendres are now in the sublime).

The enemy does his work and sets up an ambush... but no one arrives.

What happened? Was it sexual incompetence? Did the zapatista counterintelligence services function perfectly?

No, if one thoroughly investigates, it would be found that Pa'nfilo did not arrive because he thought it would be better to meet on the other side. Clotilde thought yes, but another day. And Eufrosino did not think, because he was studying a sex education manual in order to see where the G-spot was (by the way, your companera is still waiting for you to find it).

Are these not magnificent examples of zapatista autonomy and resistance used as weapons against the enemy?

And, speaking of the G-spot, allow me another digression, since this letter will not be made public.

The new disc by Joaquin Sabina will have, in addition to the song that is not a song that the Sup wrote, another cut which is called 69 G-spot.

I am told that the record will sell like hotcakes (the 69 and the G-spot being the hot), and not because it's a song by the Sup but, rather - between us here - in spite of that.

Now I'm remembering another myth, the one that says "Sabina and the Sup are in love," when the one they both love is Panchito Varona.

But fine, what I want to tell you, about Sabina, is that the other day I was in a village, cutting a blue carnation for the princess, and a support base companera arrived in order to show me her son.

"He is called Sabino," she told me.

I made a face like "Sabino?", but I didn't say anything.

The companera understood my gesture and clarified: "Yes, Sabino, like the Sabina you're making the songs for. But since this one is male, he came out Sabino and not Sabina."

What?

About my making the songs for Sabina.

If they find out, they won't give us even one percent of the royalties.

Where was I?

Ah yes! In myths, in politics and in culture, in the continuous headaches of the rebels in their zeal for breaking the traps of history.

SIX. The fundamental myth for why the Power is what it is, is in history.

Not in history as such, but in the one it invents for its convenience.

In that history, in the history of Power, the struggle of those of below, for example, is made up of nothing but defeats, betrayals and capitulations.

You know very well that we are full of scars that do not close. Some of them, the minority, are those bestowed by heartlessness.

The majority are those of our history, that of below, and, in our case, that of the most below, the underground, the clandestine.

It is not that there have been no defeats and betrayals there, but not only those.

The river which carries it has more heroism and generosity than meanness and egoism.

And, speaking of history, I'm now remembering when I met you, 22 years ago, you and Lucha, in the house we called La Mina.

And it was La Mina not because it contained a treasure, but because it was dark and damp as a cave.

At that time Lucha was determined to make me eat, and you were determined to teach me so many things which, you said, would be useful someday.

I believe that I was not a good guest nor a good student, but I well remember the little figure of Che which you gave me on my birthday, and in which you wrote, in your own hand, those words of Jose Marti that go, more or less: "The true man does not look at which side lives better, but on which side duty lies."

Duty, brother, that kind tyrant which governs us.

During our history, I have had the good fortune of knowing men and women for whom duty is their entire life and, in not a few cases, their entire death.

And that leads me to reflection number...

SEVEN. Given the need to choose between anything at all and duty, the rebel always chooses duty. And so it goes.

I believe, big brother, that you should also regale them, those who are listening to you on the day of the magazine launch, with that very phrase, but made current. And I would say something like...

"Man, woman, homosexual, lesbian, child, youth, old one, that is, the true human being, does not look at which side lives better, but on which side duty lies."

Those words sum up better than anything else what the rebel's vocation is, and they surpass anything I could say to you or to anyone on the subject.

Good, then, brother, now I'll say goodbye. All the companeros and companeras send you greetings. They hope, as do I, that you are well physically, because we already know that morally you are, as ever, strong and firm.

Vale. Salud and, if they press you, tell them that rebellion is just a headache which is not worth being cured of... ever.

From the mountains of the Mexican Southeast,
Subcomandante Insurgente Marcos.
Mexico.
It is September of 2002 and the rain has not been able to hurt the skin of the sun.

P.S. It can be expected that there will be one or another member of the Zapatista Front of National Liberation in the audience. Give them our greetings. We already know that they are working hard to give themselves a new face, a new profile.

ANOTHER P.S. And now I'm remembering another myth which says that "the EZLN doesn't love the frentistas," when it's clear that it's the frentistas we don't love. No, that's not true. We do indeed love all of them, what happens is that they also, in their own way, are practicing autonomy and resistance... in front of us.

Because there are organized rebellions, as it is assumed should grow in the FZLN, and disorganized rebellions, like the ones we experience in the EZLN, and so we go.

P.S. The last one and we're going. A favor: when you read something of mine during the presentation of the magazine, cough from time to time. That is in order to promote another myth, the one that says that I am very very sick. I hope they send me nuts.

P.S. Yes indeed the last one. (Note: this postscript heading voids the previous postscript heading).

It can now be seen that, for being in silence, we are talking quite a bit.

It is probably owing to the fact that we are zapatistas. Because in Mexico, "REBELDIA" is written with a "Z" for "nuez" and for "zapatista."

Vale de nuez de la India.

The very very sick (Ha!) Sup dreaming that Shadow-Light will finally walk and that the horizon can already be seen.

111. EZLN SENDS GREETINGS TO THE MADRID AGUASCALIENTES

October 12, 2002
EZLN sends greetings to the Aguascalientes
Zapatista Army of National Liberation, Mexico
For: Angel Luis Lara, "the Russian"
From: Subcomandante Marcos

Russian, brother,

First, a hug. Second, a bit of advice: I think that you would have done well to change the pseudonym, so that you won't be confused by the Chechens. If so, good-bye Aguascalientes and goodbye to one of the best rockers of our time.

The date (the 12th of October) in which I begin to write you these lines is not accidental (nothing is it accidental for the Zapatistas), nor is it an absurd bridge, on this day, that tries to stretch to the place where you are working to prepare for the inception of the Aguascalientes in Madrid.

I am sure that it will go very well for you and that the absence of the imbecile from Aznar (who, as his name indicates, is only missing the bray) and of the constipated little king Juan Carlos will go unnoticed until the magazine comes. Hello!

But tell each and everyone that those who are with you in this heroic project will not pay for it in hell. A magazine (deported, for sure) is about to come out that is named Defiance that, and do not doubt it, will have a "Social" section where you guys will be able to insert a review that puts the marriage of the princess in the category of "child weddings."

Moreover, the famous magazine Defiance will surely be consistent and the first that they make will rebel against spelling, so that they do not invest much in the paid insertion. Certainly, if it has photos it will be more expensive (unless they are porn) and the price, I lament to inform you, is not in Euros, but in Marks, since over there they prefer a strong currency.

There will be no whimpers if the royalty doesn't attend. On the other hand, I think that men, women, children and elderly, not only of the Iberian peninsula, but all over, will abound. If they are there everything will be a success. But, I should let you know that following the success of those at the bottom always appears the police. Because those at the bottom should only cry and be resigned, this is what the edict says, I do not know which number, that the crown sent out, I don't know when, but by the rhythm of the batons of the Civil Guard they all march with your Aguascalientes to the prison, or to the cemetery, which is the place that Spanish "democracy" has for the Iberian rebels.

I know well that it is not only from the Spanish state that will there be people who attend the fiesta of the rebellion that this Aguascalientes signifies, but it will be the majority of the people.

Transatlantic Kayaks

We can't go, but we plan to invade Europe soon and, as you might imagine, everyone here already has luggage ready (of course, their luggage could be called two bundles of tortillas, a plate of rancid beans, two bottles of pozol and chile at your discretion) and, however, no one has life preservers at hand.

The most cautious carry pills for the sickness and ask, naively, if we're going to have "bathroom stops."

But this isn't the worst, as it turns out I can't convince them that with kayaks (canoes made with a tree trunk) we aren't going to get very far.

Clearly there's no need to make much of the detail that Chiapas has no outlet onto the Atlantic ocean, and that of course we have nothing with which to pay the Panama Canal toll; we will have to turn towards the Pacific, skirt the Philippines, India, and Africa and end up at the Canary Islands.

Because it would be undesirable to arrive by land. We would have to cross Mongolia, the debris of the USSR - where we'd have to take care saying that we were going to see the "Russian" and hope that they would correct us - Western Europe, pass through France to supply ourselves with "Chateau Neuf Du Pape, harvested in 69", (I already joked with the wines), turn towards Italy and stuff ourselves with pasta, and afterwards cross the Pyrennees. It's not that the long walk tires us, but with so much bustle, the uniform gets messed up.

Meanwhile, the enthusiasm among the future crew is almost as abundant as the vomit (by the way, I saw a comrade "chewing" and asked him why he is vomiting if we haven't yet embarked). "It is that I'm training myself," he says to me with that indisputable logic that comes from in the Southeast mountains of Mexico.

What was I saying? Oh yes - That we are not going to be able to go to the inauguration of the Aguascalientes because we're "training ourselves," as the comrade says, for the expedition.

It's important that you don't tell anyone that we're going to invade the Iberian Peninsula (the first pass by Lanzarote, where we will have ourselves a cup of coffee with Saramago and Pilar) because you already know how the monarchy is, again and again it gets nervous and for the nervousness gives itself a vacation with the infants and buffoons (or it could be that I refer to Felipillo Gonzalez and to Pepillo Aznar, who, I repeat, carry penitence in their names).

Besides, to speak badly of the monarchy can cost you; at minimum, they oust you from the area. What has occurred to them is to make the Aguascalientes in an "occupied location," because the headquarters should belong to the decent people; no one doubts that there is more nobility in any occupied house than in El Escorial.

Damn! Already I have inserted myself again into royalty, but I shouldn't do it, because when one puts himself in a bucket of trash he ends up smelling like shit, and that odor doesn't come off, even with bottles of adulterated perfume that they sell in the English court.

Fine, say yes to the piracy but not to the dispersion, so I retake the thread of this monologue that has the great advantage that you can't speak or be pious, as when you're in front of the Benemérita Civil Guard that, if you will permit me to say so, neither is a guard nor is it civil, but it's already known that the world of power is full of incoherence.

What? Did I go off on a tangent? You're right, shit, it's just that the prospective of losing the reheated Gallego broth that they will be distributing because they haven't got a penny left for something more, makes me, let's say, restless.

I said that the date of this letter is not accidental, that if this writing begins October 12 to salute the Aguascalientes project it means something.

In some sectors people have the erroneous idea that the situation of the Indian people of Mexico is due to the Spanish Conquest. And it's not that Hernan Cortés and other scoundrels of armor and cassocks that accompanied him have been benevolent, but that compared to the neo-liberal governors of today, they are brothers of charity.

From the men and women of dignified Spain we have only received brotherly words, unconditional solidarity, attentive ears, helping hands that salute, that embrace.

So pardon me Father Hidalgo, but we Zapatistas shout: "Down with neo-liberals! Up with Spaniards!"

I imagine that over there must be a group from Catalonia that plays a mean ranchero, but in the job there's nobody to carry the rhythm. And also should come those from Galicia, from Asturias, from Cantabria, from Andalucia, from Murcia, from Extremadura, from Valencia, from Aragón, from La Rioja, from Castilla-León, from Castilla-La Mancha, from Navarra, from the Islas Baleares, from the Canary Islands and from Madrid. Give all of them a hearty embrace for our part, that is for all of us. Because with so many brothers and sisters, and all of them so big, our arms have grown by the force of our affection for you.

What? I have left out the Basque country? No, I don't want to ask you to permit me to make a special mention of these brothers and sisters.

Well I know that that grotesque clown, the self-named judge Garzón, from the hand of the Spanish political class (which is as ridiculous as the court, but without this discrete charm that we get from). Yes, the clown Garzón has declared the political struggle of the Basque Country illegal. After ridiculously catching Pinochet with that tall tale (the only thing he did is take expenses-paid vacations), he demonstrates his true fascist vocation by denying the Basque people the right to fight politically for a legitimate cause.

And I won't say anything more because... But that here we have seen many Basque brothers and sisters. They were in our peace camps. They did not come to tell us what to do, nor did they teach us to make bombs, nor to plan attacks.

Because here the only bombs are Chiapans that, unlike the Yucatan's, never rhyme.

Because here Olivio comes and tells me that if I give him a few walnut chocolates that they gave me because, they gossip, I am veeerry sick, then he will recite me a bomb.

"Fine," I tell him as I see that the chocolates are already moldy. And Olivio raises his voice when he recites: "Bomb, bomb: in the patio at my house there is an orange bush, how cute your sister is."

I don't get too offended by the bit about my sister, but by the lack of rhyme, and I give Olivio the chocolates anyway... but in the head, because I throw them while chasing him until I'm exhausted, which is after the first few steps.

What's more, here the only attempts against good musical taste are when I get hold of a guitar and intone, with my unmatchable baritone, something that goes "whenever I get drunk, it's said that something happens to me, I go straight to see you, and I end up in the wrong hammock."

I'm sure that if Manu Chao hears me he'll hire me. That is, provided that I don't pay for two strings I broke when, hand to hand with the insurgents I was singing that one about the Schizophrenic Cow. Or was it Crazy Cow? Anyway, if you go by there give a hand to Manu and tell him nothing more than that we'll pardon him about the strings when we meet in the next station which, as it's known, is called "Hope."

And if Manu doesn't hire me, then I'll go to the group from Amparo. Although they might have to change their name, and instead of "Amparonoia" I would call it "Amparophobia," by that which any one of my critics also globalizes.

In the end, what terrorists lack more than anything is vocation and no means.

But, well, it so happens that here there have been brothers from the Basque country and they have carried themselves with dignity, which is how Basques themselves act.

And I don't know if Fermin Muguruza is around your way, but I remember that one time when he was here they asked him where he was from and he said "Basque," and they asked again: "Basque of Spain or Basque of France?" And Fermin didn't even bat an eyelid when he responded "Basque from the Basque country."

And I was looking for something in Basque to send as a greeting to the brothers and sisters of that country, and I didn't find much, but I don't know if my dictionary is good because I looked up how to say "dignity" in Basque, and the Zapatista dictionary said "Euskal Herria." Ask them if that's right for me, or even better, I'll go back.

Finally, what neither Garzón nor his cronies know is that there are times when dignity becomes a hedgehog, and ouch! from there they attempt to smash it.

Fiesta of the Rebellion

Well, I told you before that the Aguascalientes should be a fiesta of rebellion, a thing that none of the political parties like...

"They are a fraud!" Durito interrupts me.

"But... wait, Durito, I'm not even talking about Mexican political parties."

"I'm not talking about those frauds, but Internet porn pages."

"But Durito, in the jungle we don't have Internet."

"We don't have it? It sounds like the European Union. I have it. With a little ingenuity and another little thing I've converted one of my antennas into a powerful satellite modem."

"And you must know, walking postmodern gentleman, why the Internet porn pages are frauds?"

"Well because there's not a single photo with lady scarabs in it, not even nude, damn, not even with one of those knickers of 'dental floss', as they say."

"Knickers?"

"Sure! Fuck! Aren't you writing to those spanishistas?" Durito says and asks while he jams on a beret.

"Knickers?" I repeat, trying to avoid the inevitable, being that Durito gets a hand into what I'm writing, because for this he's got too many hands and too much impertinence.

"Let's see, hmm hmm," murmurs Durito already leaning over my shoulder.

"Russian? Are you writing to Putin? I wouldn't recommend it, don't let it happen that he sends one of those gases, not even the ones you lay when you eat too many beans."

I protest:

"Look, Durito, let's not start revealing intimate things, because right here I have a letter that the Pentagon sent you asking you for the formula for the development of ultratoxic gases."

"Ah! But I denied it. Because my gas, like my love, is neither bought nor sold, but I give it as a gift, because I am detached and I give things without looking to see if people deserve them," Durito says with an Andalucian accent that must fuck him up.

After a pause, he adds:

"And what is the subject of your writing, lad?"

"And nothing, uncle, of what it's going to be, on rebellion and an Aguascalientes that they're going to open near Madrid," I respond, infected by the flamenco that spreads in the country.

"Madrid? Which Madrid? The one of Aznar and the Benemérita? Or irreverent Madrid?"

"Irreverent Madrid, of course. Although it wouldn't be strange that Aznar wants to get his hooves in on it."

"Magnificent!" applauds and dances Durito in a way that revives Federico Garcia Lorca and is made up of the little-known and unedited Sole of the Epileptic Scarab.

When he finishes his dance, Durito orders:

"Write! I will dictate you my report."

"But Durito, you're not in the program. Not even if they have invited you."

"Sure, that's why the Russians don't like me. But it doesn't matter. Go, write. The title is 'Rebellion and Chairs'."

"Chairs? Durito, don't come out with another of your..."

"Shut up! The idea comes from something Saramago and I wrote at the end of the last century and it's called 'Chairs'."

"Saramago? Do you mean José Saramago, the writer?" I ask, perplexed.

"Of course. What, is there another? Well, it so happens that that day we drank to the point of falling out of said chair, and on the ground, with that perspective and lucidity of the underdogs, I say: 'Pepe, this little wine hits harder than Aznar's mule' and he didn't say anything because he was looking for his glasses."

And then I say to him: "Something's happening to me, quickly José, the ideas are like beans with sausage, if you stop worrying another will come and we'll have brunch."

"Saramago finally found his glasses and together we gave shape to that story, if I remember correctly, early in the eighties. Of course in the credit only his name appears, because we scarabs battle a lot over the rights of the author."

I want to abbreviate Durito's anecdotes so I urge: "The title's already there, what more?"

"Well, it's about how the attitude that a human being assumes towards chairs is what defines them politically. The Revolutionary (like that, with capitals) looks with detachment at common chairs and says and says: 'I don't have time to sit down, the weighty mission with which History (like that, with capitals) has entrusted me impedes me from distracting myself with silliness.' This is the way he passes his life until he arrives in front of the seat of Power, knocks it down with a shot so that he can sit in it, and he sits with a knitted brow, as if he were constipated, and says and says, 'History (like that, with capitals) has completed itself. Everything, absolutely everything, acquires meaning. I am in The Chair (like that, with capitals) and I am the culmination of our times.' From there he continues until another Revolutionary (like that, with capitals) arrives, knocks him off and history (like that, with lower-case) repeats itself.

The rebel (like that, with lower-case), on the other hand, when he looks at a chair, common and average, he analyzes it fixedly, and afterwards goes and nears another chair, and another, and another, and, within a short time, it looks like a book club because more rebels (like that, with lower-case) have arrived and begin to swarm with coffee, tobacco and words, and then, precisely when they begin to feel comfortable, they become restless, as if they had worms in the cauliflower, and nobody knows if it was the effects of the coffee or the tobacco or the words, but they all rise up and continue on their way. Until they encounter another common and average chair and history repeats itself.

There is only one variation, when the rebel comes across the Seat of Power (like that, with upper-case), looks at it fixedly, analyzes it, but instead of sitting he goes for a file of the type for nails and, with heroic patience, he files the legs until, as he understands it, they are left so fragile that they will break when someone sits, which happens almost immediately. So, so."

"So, so? But Durito..."

"Nothing, nothing. I already know that it is too arid and that theory should be velvety, but mine is the metatheory. I could be that they accuse me of being an anarchist, but value my report as a humble homage to the old Spanish anarchists, that there are those who silence their heroism and don't shine less for it."

Durito goes, although I'm sure that he would prefer to come back.

Well, let's leave joking to the side. Where was I before that armor-plated impertinence interrupted me.

Ah!, in that the Aguascalientes is a fiesta of rebellion.

And then, my dear Chechen, all that's missing to define is rebellion.

It could be enough for you to take a look at all the men and women that put it upon themselves to erect that Aguascalientes, and at all those who will attend its inauguration (not to the closing ceremony, because I'm sure the police will do that) so that obtain a definition, but since this is a letter, I should attempt to do it with words that, as eloquent as they may be, will never be forceful as seeing.

So, searching for a text that would serve me for this, I found a book that Javier Elorriaga lent me.

The little book is called New Ethiopia, and it is by a Basque poet named Bernardo Atxaga. There is a poem there called "Reggae of the Butterflies," which speaks of butterflies that fly in the inner sea and that will not have a place to land because the sea has neither islands nor rocks.

Well, I hope you pardon me, Bernardo if the synthesis is not as fortunate as your reggae, but it helps me with what I want to say to you.

Rebellion is like that butterfly that guides its flight towards this sea without islands or rocks.

No to logic!

No to prudence!

No to immobility!

No to conformity!

And nothing, absolutely nothing, will be as marvelous as seeing the journey of that flight, to estimate the challenge that it represents, to feel like it begins to stir the wind and see how, with those airs, it is not the leaves of the trees that tremble, but the knees of the powerful that until then naively thought that the butterflies died in the sea.

Well, yes, in my Muscovite appraisal, it is known that the butterflies, as is the rebellion, are contagious.

And there are butterflies, like rebels, in all colors.

Those who are blue are painted such that they are confused with the sky and the sea.

Those who are yellow are painted such that they are embraced by the sun.

The red ones are painted with rebellious blood.

The brown carry in waves the color of the land

The green, like always are painted with the hope.

And all are skin, skin that shines without importance the color that it is painted.

And there are flights of each color.

And there are times that butterflies of all colors and from all parts get together and then there is a rainbow.

And the work of the butterflies, which is said in whatever encyclopedia, is to bring the rainbow down in a way that all the children can learn to fly.

And, speaking of butterflies and rebellions, it occurred to me that when they are all in a circle, or in their tribe, in front of the clown Garzon, and they ask them what they were doing in the Aguascalientes, you can respond, flying.

Although, they send you flying deported to Chechnya, the laughter will be heard until the mountains of Southeast Mexico.

And a laugh, brother, that will be enjoyed as much as music.

And speaking of music, I know the dance of the crab that has been the manner of the governments of Mexico, Spain, Italy and France, and it consists, in a gross way, of moving the hips and arms in the inverse fashion of hands of a clock.

And since we are the hands of a clock, if you see Manuel Vazquez Montalban, give his hands a squeeze for us.

Tell him that I already learned that The Fox asked him if he knew why Marcos and the Zapatistas were in silence, and that he answered him: "They aren't in silence, what is happening is that you don't hear."

In passing, tell him that pork sausages are not like diamonds, that is to say, that they are not eternal, and that the ones that he sent, were finished some time ago, and that if he doesn't get handsome, let's say with some 5 kilograms, then we are going to take him and Pepe Carvahlo as hostages.

No, better not. Because they are not going to take us for terrorists and Bush, from the hand of the United Nations, strews us to the wind with another "humanitarian" war. Better that you send pork sausages, and in return I'll send the recipe for Marco's Special, for which - not for nothing - the chef of its majesty has asked me with useless insistence.

Now I say goodbye. Keep letting me know which jail they throw them into, for when we pass by there.

No, don't think that it will be to free them; it will be to assure ourselves that they are well enclosed, because all of you are crazy. It appears that, to inaugurate an Aguascalientes in Madrid... The only thing missing is that they make an autonomous community inside a jail.

Anyway, we won't be able to send you cigars. But we can send tortillas and pozol; just as worthy as you.

Health to you. If it is a matter of reigning, then reign the rebellion.

> *From the Southeast Mexican mountains,*
> *Insurgent Subcommander Marcos.*
> *Mexico, October 2002.*

P.S. As Eva said, if in the Spanish state (she said it like this, I think) they have videotapes because she wants to carry her collection of Pedro Infante movies. I told her that they have another system there. She asked me: "You're kidding, they don't have a neo-liberal government there?" I didn't respond, but I say to her now: "Commander Eva, what else could it do?"

Another P.S. Don't think that I don't know that the Aguascalientes Rebels will also go to Italy, France, Greece, Switzerland, Germany, Denmark, Sweden, England, Ireland, Portugal, Belgium, Holland and etc. Greet them all and tell them that, if they behave badly, we will also... invade. We're going to globalize the moldy tortilla and the rancid alcohol. We're going to see how the number of globalophobes grows geometrically.

Thanks again.

> *The Subcomandante is being trained for the trip, that is to say "chewing" the choco-*
> *late with moldy walnuts that the Olivio left thrown on the ground.*

112. THE BASQUE COUNTRY: PATHS

December 7, 2002

Marcos accepts Garzón's gauntlet

Zapatista Army of National Liberation

Mexico

To: Señor Fernando Baltasar Garzón Real

Magistrate-Judge of the No. 5 Central Trial Court of the Supreme Court

Calle Garcia Gutiérrez 1 28.004

Madrid, Spain

Senor Baltasar Garzón,

I read the letter which you addressed to me, dated this December 3, 2002 and which was published on the 6th in the Mexican newspaper El Universal. In it, in addition to allowing yourself to insult me with all kinds of labels, you challenged me to a debate at the place and time of my choosing.

I am informing you that I accept the challenge and (as mandated by the laws of knight-errantry), given that I am the man challenged, it is up to me to set the conditions of the meeting.

These are the conditions:

First. The debate will be held in the Canary Islands, more specifically on Lanzarote, from April 3 to 10, 2003.

Second. Señor Fernando Baltasar Garzón Real shall secure the necessary and sufficient guarantees and safe-conduct, from the Spanish government as well as from the Mexican, so that the knight who has been challenged and six of his gallants can attend the duel and return home safely. The expenses for the trip and accommodations for Subcomandante Insurgente Marcos and his delegation will be borne by the EZLN, which are coyucos, tostadas, beans and pozol. In addition, insofar as spending the night, the knight-errant (or seafaring-knight) will need no roof other than the dignified Canary sky.

Third. In the same place as the debate, parallel to but not simultaneously, a meeting will be held between all the political, social and cultural actors in the Basque problem who so desire. The theme of the meeting will be "The Basque Country: Paths."

Fourth. Señor Baltasar Garzón Real shall attend that meeting, in order to speak and to listen. He should also make a great effort to convince the Spanish government to contribute, through détente measures, to creating a favorable atmosphere for the event. He should also urge them to send a delegation to the meeting, regardless of their decision making capacity, since they are only being asked to listen and to talk.

Fifth. The knight Subcomandante Insurgente Marcos shall attend said meeting, but only to listen, because the issue is something which is the responsibility of the sovereignty of the Basque people alone.

Subcomandante Insurgente Marcos shall, in addition, address the Basque organization Euskadi Ta Askatasuna (better known by its initials: ETA), asking them for a unilateral truce for 177 days, during which time the ETA shall not carry out any offensive military actions. The ETA truce shall begin on the dawn of December 24, 2002.

Subcomandante Insurgente Marcos shall, similarly, address Basque political and social organizations, and the Basque people as a whole, inviting them to organize and to carry out the above mentioned meeting.

Subcomandante Insurgente Marcos shall also address Spanish and Basque civil society, asking them to mobilize for the "An Opportunity For the Word" campaign, whose purpose is to pressure the Spanish government and the ETA to create, throughout the entire Iberian peninsula, suitable conditions for the meeting.

Sixth. The winner of the debate will be chosen by a panel of judges made up of seven persons, all of them from the Spanish State. Subcomandante Insurgente Marcos yields to Señor Fernando Baltasar Garzón Real the privilege of naming four of the members of the panel of judges and of designating who shall preside over it and, in the case of a draw by way of abstention, of deciding through casting a tie breaking vote, who is the winner in the joust. The other three members of the panel of judges shall be invited by the EZLN.

Seventh. If Señor Fernando Baltasar Garzón Real defeats Subcomandante Insurgente Marcos fairly and squarely, he will have the right to unmask him once, in front of whomever he wishes. Subcomandante Insurgente Marcos shall, in addition, publicly apologize and will be subjected to the actions of Spanish justice so that they may torture him (just like they torture the Basques when they are detained) and he may answer to the charges which abound in Señor Garzón Real's latter dated April 3, 2003.

If, on the other hand, Señor Fernando Baltasar Garzón Real is fairly defeated, he will commit himself to legally advising the EZLN on the charges which; as perhaps the last peaceful zapatista recourse, and in front of international legal bodies; will be presented in order to demand the recognition of indigenous rights and culture, which, in violation of international laws and common sense, have not been recognized by the three branches of the Mexican government.

This is owing to the fact that charges will also be presented for crimes against humanity by Señor Ernesto Zedillo Ponce de Leon, responsible for the Acteal killing (perpetrated in the mountains of the Mexican southeast in December of 1997), where 45 indigenous children, women, men and old ones were executed. As will be remembered, Señor Zedillo was recently awarded by Señor José Maria Aznar, the head of the Spanish government, for his participation in the killings.

Charges will similarly be presented against the heads of state of the Spanish government who, during Señor Zedillo's administration in Mexico, were his accomplices in that, and other, attacks against the Mexican Indian peoples.

These conditions are not negotiable, and Señor Fernando Baltasar Garzón Real shall respond, in a reasonable time period, as to whether or not he accepts them. The details of the debate, on the other hand, can be agreed to by the teams of seconds of the challenger and the challenged.

Señor Fernando Baltasar Garzón Real: as you can see in the copies of the letters I am attaching, I have already begun the task of carrying out the part that I am responsible for.

You have the opportunity to choose: either putting your knowledge and skills at the service of a just and noble cause (and, incidentally, of demonstrating that international justice does not serve only to endorse wars and hide criminals), or of continuing where you are, receiving strokes from those who are above because they are on top of the blood and pain of those of below.

Vale. Salud, and may all this serve to give the word a chance.

From the mountains of the Mexican Southeast,
Subcomandante Insurgente Marcos.
December of 2002.

P.S. Know, Your Honor, that all the insults you lavished on me in your letter left me practically u-n-m-o-v-e-d. What did hurt me, a lot, was the remark about the "ridiculous pipe." That's why I'm carving a new one now. You'll see, it will be all the rage when it shows up on the Gran Via or La Ramblas. By the way, can you smoke in front of the Cibeles?

ANOTHER P.S. That stuff about the "boat adrift" has me worried. You mean that the coasts which are looming now aren't those of El Hierro island (considered to be the end of the world until the discovery of America), but those of the island of Java? I already said, when we passed along one side of Krakatoa, that, as usual and in honor the "zapatistas," we had chosen the longest path. Sigh.

Letters to Basque and Spanish civil society and to ETA on a projected encuentro in Lanzarote, simultaneous with the projected duel/debate with Garzón.

(The following are a series of 4 letters, or communiqués, from Subcomandante Insurgente Marcos, to ETA, and to Basque and Spanish civil society, in explanation

and support of an encuentro, to be held in Lanzarote this April, for all those parties affected by, and interested in, the Basque issue. It is to be held simultaneously, but not concurrently, with the projected duel/debate between Marcos and Judge Garzón)

1.

Monday, December 7, 2002
Zapatista Army of National Liberation
To: Euskadi Ta Askatasuna (ETA) political-military organization
Basque Country
From: Subcomandante Insurgente Marcos
Mexico

Ladies and Gentlemen,

I am writing you in the name of the children, old ones, women and men of the Zapatista Army of National Liberation, of Mexico.

As you perhaps know, we recently, in a letter that was read on Spanish territory, referred to the struggle of the Basque people for their sovereignty. Despite the fact that the text clearly made reference to the Basque political struggle, and not the military one, the words were intentionally ambiguous regarding the activities of your organization, ETA.

The purpose of the ambiguity was to provoke what we did, in fact, provoke. We are not unaware that we placed the moral capital at risk which the zapatistas have won throughout the world, in particular in the Iberian peninsula, but it was necessary then.

You and we know quite well that the EZLN has not merely not carried out any military action against civilians. You also know that we condemn those types of attacks, which usually claim the greatest number of victims among persons who do not even know what the issue is about.

Your actions have caused not a few civilian victims. Among them are persons who sympathized with our cause and who, like the rest of the civilian victims, died with the anguish of not knowing why.

We believe that the struggle of the Basque people for their sovereignty is just and legitimate, but neither that noble cause, nor any other, is justification for the sacrifice of civilian lives. It not only does not produce any political gain whatsoever, but, even if it were to produce it, the human cost is irredeemable. We condemn military actions which harm civilians. And we condemn them equally, whether they come from the ETA or the Spanish State, from Al Qaeda or from George W. Bush, from Israelis or Palestinians, or from whomever, under different names or initials - whether in the name of reasons of State, or ideological or religious ones -

claims its victims among children, women, old ones and men who have nothing to do with the matter.

I also know that that the thousands of Basques who have been executed, tortured and disappeared by the State forces are not included among the calculations of dead and wounded made by the Spanish government. I am not, however, writing to you in order to compare numbers of dead. We would surpass some, since there have been millions of Mexican indigenous who have, since the Spanish conquest, fallen. And we shall not set our dead up to be compared with anyone.

No, I am not writing to you to speak of what has happened before.

A few days ago, the Spanish Judge, Fernando Baltasar Garzón Real, challenged me to a debate. I have responded affirmatively to him, and I have set as a condition, among others, that an encuentro be held among all the political, social and cultural forces which are involved or interested in the problems of the Basque Country, so that they can talk about, and listen to, the Basque paths.

Similarly, in the name of all my companeros and companeras, I am asking you to declare a unilateral truce for a period of 177 days, beginning at dawn on December 24, 2002. I am also asking you to publicly commit yourselves to not carrying out any offensive military operation during that period, and thus contribute to creating an atmosphere which is conducive for that encuentro, that is, in order to give the word a chance.

It would be good if Euskadi Ta Askatasuna could send one or several delegates to speak and to listen - not to negotiate or to agree to anything - to The Basque Country: Paths encuentro. I know they would be taking risks, but, if you are willing to die or to be taken prisoner in military actions you carry out, I do not see why you would not be willing to suffer the same in a political action.

That is what I am asking of you, not to surrender, not to abandon your arms or convictions. I am only asking that you give the word a chance, and thus honor the great risk which we zapatistas have, and will be, taking. In case you do not accept, I am offering myself up personally as an opportune victim for your next attack. You could accuse me of "collaborating" with the Spanish State (which would be quite paradoxical, since Spanish officials are accusing me of being an "apologist for terrorism"). The argument is the least of the problem. There will be no reproaches or reprisals on our part, since I, at least, will then know why I died. I await your response.

Vale. Salud, and an opportunity for peace.

From the mountains of the Mexican Southeast,
Subcomandante Insurgente Marcos.
Mexico, December of 2002.

2.

December 7, 2002

Zapatista Army of National Liberation

Mexico

To all the political, social, cultural and religious forces of the Basque Country, regardless of their ideology

From Subcomandante Insurgente Marcos

Ladies, Gentlemen and Children,

I am writing you in the name of the Zapatista Army of National Liberation, in order to invite you to join together and embrace the "AN OPPORTUNITY FOR THE WORD" mobilization, which is an attempt to secure a suitable atmosphere from ETA and the Spanish government for the holding of "The Basque Country: Paths" encuentro.

This encuentro is to be held on the island of Lanzarote, in the Canary Islands, from April 3 through 7 of 2003, and its only purpose is to try and change the war-like logic that abounds throughout the world.

We are also asking you to embrace that encuentro, to organize it and to participate in it, in the time and manner you find most suitable.

The encuentro is meant to be one of the conditions we set for the holding of the debate to which Judge Baltasar Garzón challenged us. If it is not held, however, or if some misfortune or contretemps prevents the joust from being celebrated, we are respectfully asking you to somehow hold that encuentro at the place and date that is most convenient for you.

I shall not go on any further so that I do not repeat what is already in the letters I am attaching.

We are certain that this initiative, if successful, will become a ray of hope for all the peoples of the earth.

May I reiterate our greetings, our respect and our admiration.

Vale. Salud, and is it not worthwhile giving the word a chance?

From the mountains of the Mexican Southeast,
Subcomandante Insurgente Marcos.
Mexico, December of 2002.

3.

December 7, 2002
Zapatista Army of National Liberation
Mexico
To Spanish and Basque Civil Society
Iberian Peninsula
Planet Earth
From Subcomandante Insurgente Marcos
Mexico

Ladies, gentlemen and children,

I am writing you in the name of the old ones, women, children and men of the Zapatista Army of National Liberation, of Mexico, in order to extend our greetings.

Recently, a letter of ours, read in the Madrid Aguascalientes, unleashed a polemic and a condemnation of us, because the missive was ambiguous regarding the activities of the ETA Basque organization. Despite the fact that, at the beginning of the epistle, it warned that "nothing is by chance with the zapatistas," and the fact that we clearly referred to the political, and not the armed, struggle, of the Basque people, there was an attempt to interpret the lack of an explicit condemnation of terrorism as support by the EZLN for ETA and their actions.

I should tell you that the ambiguity was intentional, as well as the entire tone of the letter. We sought to provoke the Spanish temperament of a man, and to thus set in motion a noble and honest initiative, which, insofar as the part which concerns us, represents perhaps the last opportunity for achieving a peaceful, dignified resolution of our demands, which are, as everyone knows, the recognition of indigenous rights and culture.

You know quite well that we do not practice terrorism, and that we have, on numerous occasions, in written and spoken statements, condemned terror, from wherever it comes. And, if we did not make it explicit this time, it was for reasons which will soon be clearly discerned.

For the victims of ETA and of the Spanish State, among whom are not a few sympathizers with our cause, our sincere apologies if we were lacking in respect for your pain through that ambiguity. We desire, with all our hearts, for you to understand us, and for you, someday, to forgive us for our part.

We also regret that your suffering has been manipulated by the Spanish government in order to distract, and in that way cover up, their criminal inefficiency in the ecological catastrophe which is befalling the noble Galician people, who have demonstrated that they can organize and resolve their problem while those who govern are appearing in the social pages of the Madrid newspapers.

As you know, Judge Fernando Baltasar Garzón Real has challenged me to a public debate on various issues. We have decided to accept the debate and to set, as one of the conditions, that an encuentro be held among those interested in and affected by the Basque problem, so that they can talk and listen, without bombs, bullets and arrest warrants. The theme of the encuentro is The Basque Country: Paths.

In order to carry out this encuentro, I have already addressed the Basque organization ETA, through a letter, in order to ask them to declare a 177 day unilateral truce (beginning this December 24), and, therefore, foster a suitable environment for the encuentro to be held.

We feel that something should be done in order to change the criminal framework which is currently being imposed in the entire sphere. Terror can be fought with terror, but it cannot win. Legal arguments can be used to justify torture, disappearances, assassinations, but they do not do away with those who, with ideological or religious arguments, justify the deaths of others.

We are presented in today's world with a syllogistic option which, like all syllogistic options, is a trap. It forces us to choose between one terror and another, and criticizing one implies supporting the other. In this case, it forces us to choose between the terrorism of ETA or the terrorism of the Spanish State, and, if we distance ourselves from one, then we are accomplices of the other. You and we know that the alternative is not one thing or the other, but what is built as a new path, a new world.

It would be beautifully just and instructive if - in the midst of a polarized world, where death and destruction vary only in their arguments and their injustices (where condemning the punitive actions of Bush equals supporting Bin Laden's fundamentalist madness) - it were to be the Iberian peninsula where a space would be opened in order to give an opportunity for the word.

It would be marvelous if it were Iberian dignity which would be the one to tell the entire world that it is possible, and necessary, to give the word a chance.

For all of this, we are calling on you to mobilize throughout Hispanic soil, in order to demand exactly that of the Spanish government and ETA: an opportunity for the word.

From the mountains of the Mexican Southeast,
Subcomandante Insurgente Marcos.
Mexico, December of 2002.

4.

December 7, 2002
Zapatista Army of National Liberation
To the Basque political, social and cultural organizations of the left
Basque Country
From Subcomandante Insurgente Marcos

Brothers and sisters,

I am writing you in the name of the children, old ones, women and men of the Zapatista Army of National Liberation of Mexico, and I greet all of you with respect and admiration.

I believe I would not be in error to assume that you are well aware of the polemic which has been unleashed because of the zapatista letter which was read in the Madrid Aguascalientes in late November of this year.

As you shall see in the attached letter, I have accepted the challenge to debate, which Judge Baltasar Garzón leveled at me. Given that I am the challenged, and it is up to me to set the conditions, I have answered him that one of those conditions is that an encuentro be held, parallel with the debate, among all the political and cultural forces involved in the problem of the Basque Country which are so willing. I have also written to the ETA, asking them to declare a unilateral truce for 177 days beginning this December 24, for the purpose of creating conditions suitable for holding this encuentro.

There then, that is a brief summary. You can see more details in the letters I mentioned. But I am writing specifically to you for several reasons.

In addition to inviting you to participate in the encuentro, I am writing you in order to ask you to join in the petition I am making to ETA, since you have the moral authority and prestige which I lack in that regard.

I am also asking you, with inclusion and tolerance, to gather together the greatest forces possible in order to organize and to hold the event. I am asking you because, historically, the left has always shown itself to be more organized than the right. The themes, pace and other issues of the encuentro should be decided by all those forces which wish to give the word a chance.

I am well aware that you, unlike the Mexican parliamentary left, do indeed have an alternative political program, not only in order to fight for Basque sovereignty, but also for the building of a system that is more just, more democratic and more free, that is, more human. That is why I am turning to you, to your experience, to your decision to struggle, to your heroism and to the moral authority which, I have no doubt, have been built within the noble Basque people. I have no doubt that there are still hitherto unknown paths for winning Basque sovereignty.

And nor do I have any doubt that those paths are now closed by the terror which is being encouraged on one side and the other.

That is why I am asking you to speak and to listen, to speak to each other and to listen to each other. Not to renounce your convictions and programs, but, instead, to have them be known in a space which should be fought for, that yes, along with all honest men and women.

I am asking you to make that space a reality. No one has anything to lose (except us, the zapatistas, but that is our specialty), and they do have much to gain.

I am asking you to dedicate your best efforts towards giving the word a chance.

Another thing (yes, I know that now I'm starting to annoy), I am asking you, even if everything goes against you and nothing turns out as you would have liked, to open that space however you can, and to call on all those who want to, to speak and to listen to what everyone has to say and hear.

Vale. Salud, and I already know that it sounds like a slogan from a street demonstration, but the word must be given a chance.

> From the mountains of the Mexican Southeast,
> Subcomandante Insurgente Marcos.
> Mexico, December of 2002.

113. The Zapatistas Can, and Should, Speak Only About the Indigenous Question?

December 29, 2002
Zapatista Army of National Liberation
Mexico
To Whom It May Concern

Greetings. Yes, the cold and rain are encircling us in their embrace, and not even a bonfire made up of all the criticisms they have sent me (us) can manage to even moderately warm one up. It must be because most of them are so mediocre.

Of course, they are varied and sundry. Some are making great efforts to get us to apologize. And not for any purported sympathy towards ETA (which anyone with a modicum of vision and shame knows is nonexistent, either in theory or in practice). No. What they want is for us to apologize for having got off the subject in which

THEY have pigeonholed us, to wit: the zapatistas can, and should, speak only about the indigenous question. We are banned from any other subject, national or international. And, since we got off (got off?) the indigenous issue in the last seven letters, we should, ergo, apologize to the neo-commissars of "good manners." The only thing that remains for them to tell us, in the same arrogant and scolding tone, is to not put our elbows on the table and to not belch in the presence of his majesty.

And, indeed, we should apologize after all. But not to them, not to the little king, not to Aznar or to Felipillo (to Garzon, but only if he wins the debate). If apologies must be made to anyone it is to the noble people of Navarre, who, through an error when the letter - which has provoked so much enthusiasm among Mexican and Hispanic intellectuals - was being transcribed, were left out of the Basque people. And so, to the people of Navarre, our sincere apologies: Navarre is Basque. Gora Nafarroa! Gora Euzkera! Gora Iparralde! Gora Hegoalde!

Not all of them are like that, nor is that all of them. Because it is only fair to say: not all Mexican intellectuals are busily engaged in patting themselves on the back and congratulating each other ("I even sent a copy of my column to Felipe. I'm sure he'll be putting me on the list of candidates for the Prince of Asturias prize. Yes? Sure, but my etceteras against the masked one of cotton seemed quite superior to me..."). No, some people do indeed realize what is going on around them, and they know, just like that, by turning that corner, resentment and despair begin to mount. They know that terror (that of above and that of below) feeds on that combination. They know that when that happens, there will be no declaration of war, nor communiqué's, nor twe and/or melodramatic letters, nor anyone to scold for being badly educated or disrespectful.

Ah, the intellectuals of Power! Always striving to understand and absolve those of above and to judge and condemn those of below.

But there are intellectuals in Mexico and the Iberian peninsula who avoid the traps set by Power. Just like the United States intellectuals who courageously denounce Bush's insane bellicosity, even though they are accused of sympathizing with Bin Laden. Or the Israelis who refuse to support the massacres perpetrated by their country's army, without that meaning support for the actions of the Palestinians.

Of course, in the troubled waters of the moment (how many comandantes have left me!), the scoldings and calls to behave well (all useless) by intellectuals and columnists, the Mexican government has been injecting itself, and now it's trying to dislocate several villages which, driven by war and poverty, have found themselves forced to settle in the so-called Montes Azules. And there, also, they are not all them, nor are they all that there are.

For example, there are some 160 zapatistas living in the new town called 12 de Diciembre (a clearly subversive name). Their history has not merited any letters in support of good manners. They are from the village of Salina Cruz. On November 2, 2000, militants from that organization called MOCRI assassinated Manuel Mendez Sanchez and Gloria Mendez Sanchez. They ambushed them, shot them and, when they were already dead, they hacked them with machetes.

The motive? At that time the MOCRI leaders were engaged in a torrid romance with El Croquetas Albores, and they were a part of that failed Zedillo strategy of buying consciences. Manuel and Gloria were, are, zapatistas and, as such, they were promoting resistance. Using the argument of words, Gloria and Manuel convinced the community to resist and to not accept government charity. That went against the MOCRI leaders' economic premises, and they gave their support to the assassination. The MOCRI people also threatened the rest of the zapatistas in the same style which the government used for the recent "peaceful dislocation," which merited so much coverage in the Mexican press: either you stop being zapatistas or you'll meet the same fate as Manuel and Gloria did.

The companeros and companeras preferred being displaced to letting themselves be shot by MOCRI and thus be party to one of so many histories of confrontations between indigenous. The crime will not go unpunished. And it will not be by enforcing Talion's Law [an eye for an eye], nor by using the "humanitarian" methods of the Chiapas government. Justice will be served, but with wisdom and in calm. Perhaps it will also serve to teach Garzon that terror is not defeated by that other terror which hides behind laws and judges, which tortures prisoners and which makes ideas illegal.

12 de Diciembre is not the only zapatista village being threatened with dislocation (I am not going to mention the names of those that are zapatista, so as not to uncover those which are not zapatista), but all the zapatistas who are in the same predicament are there, not because they lack land or take morbid pleasure in destroying the Selva, but because they have found themselves forced to leave everything so as not to swell the ranks of the silence with which the Power and the intellectuals bury the misfortune and deaths of the Mexican indigenous.

We have spoken with the representatives of those zapatista villages and with the authorities of the Autonomous Municipalities to which they belong. They have communicated to us their decision to stay there, even at the cost of their own lives, as long as the zapatista demands are not met.

We have replied to them that we completely support them.

And so it is good that everyone know in advance: in the case of the zapatista villages, there will be no "peaceful dislocation."

Returning to the sudden proliferation of experts on the Basque question, I don't know why they are getting so upset: the persons in question (except Garzon) haven't been affected in the least. As for the king, for example, I just saw a recent photograph, and he still has the same face. Aznar, despite the postscript he got from the Prestige, continues braying with marked enthusiasm. And Felipillo, well, he did get angry, he gagged the Iberian press and mobilized all his homeboys in this Mexican Republic, which would be a monarchy if it were not for a few of this country's intellectuals.

Even so, I ask forgiveness from all those intellectuals who are enthusiasts of the Spanish crown (and of their literary prizes). I did not wish to be lacking in respect for his majesty or anything like that. What I, in fact, wanted to say, to put it, more than anything, in Spanish terms, is that I don't give a damn about the monarchy.

Because know that for us there are no worldly kings other than those in a deck of cards (Spanish, to be more precise), nor any queens other than those who, from time to time, rob us of our sleep with barely a glance and then leave us.

But fine, given that they have been allowed to ramble on about the EZLN's unlikely sympathy for terrorism, here are some other subjects for them (conveniently disguised as questions):

Why does the EZLN want to begin its so-called march through Europe (Ah! So it's a European march?) in the Spanish state and not, for example, in Italy, where there are many imprisoned and free zapatistas (almost as many of both as there are in Mexico)? Why did the zapatistas choose such a difficult and complicated subject as the Basque one, about which there has been a complicit and widespread silence in order to avoid the accusation of being "terrorists"?

Is the EZLN going to try and refute Fox's statements in the European Parliament that there is peace in Mexico?

Doesn't the EZLN know that in Europe, and in the world, the right is the government, and it is more belligerent than ever?

Why is the EZLN trying to exhaust the peaceful path to a resolution of the war, instead of rushing the World Trade Center with a horse (we only have paper airplanes) loaded with explosives and in that way provide the columnists with a topic on the zapatista "sympathies" for Al Qaeda's methods?

When it visits France, will the EZLN attend one of the presentations of Zorro', el Zapato, which the children from the poor barrios are presenting under heroic conditions? Will the EZLN speak with Chirac and Le Pen or with those Sans Papiers? Will they revisit the Latin Quarter? Will they go to Place Pigalle?

Will the EZLN be wearing proper clothing for withstanding the inclement weather in the Nordic countries, in Switzerland, in Holland, in Belgium, in Germany? Will they visit rebel Greece? Will they make gestures of elegant contempt at the monarchs of Sweden, thus losing the opportunity for a Nobel Prize?

Does the EZLN assume that their cayucos will be able to satisfactorily cross the English Channel and disembark in Great Britain, thus emulating "D" Day, but in reverse? Will they go to Ireland to pay homage to the San Patricio Battalion?

In sum, they are subjects which still fall in the category of the hypothetical.

There are more, but this letter is already turning out to be quite long, and the postscripts are yet to come.

Right then, last but not least, the purpose of this letter is to wish you a Happy New Year.

And, as everyone knows, one will be happy if one does not stop fighting for what one believes in.

Vale. Salud and, as you can now see, there are globalizations and globalizations.

> *From the mountains of the Mexican Southeast,*
> *Subcomandante Insurgente Marcos.*
> *Mexico, December of 2002.*

P.S. WRAPPED UP AS A GIFT: Following its custom of serving its kind clientele, the Recurring Postscript recommends to its readers the following gifts for - joining in the intellectual enthusiasm for the crown - the upcoming King's Day, January 6: for little king Juan Carlos, a laxative (they exist in various forms); for Pepillo Aznar, a flute; for Felipillo (that dark object of desire who is fought over by Nexos and Letras Vencidas), a protection order (for the unlikely day in which Spanish justice calls him to account for sponsoring the terrorist group GAL).

P.S. WITH BERET PULLED DOWN AND CIGARETTE IN LIPS: Viva the Republic! Down with the monarchy! Long live the Workers Committees! Down with returned Francos! Viva republican Spain! Viva the International Brigade! Viva Spain! Gora Euskera! Gora Zapata! Viva life! Death to death! Long live the ghosts that will again walk Europe!

P.S. FOR BERLUSCONI: Don't laugh, because you're next. Remember that "all roads lead to Rome."

ILLEGAL P.S. It would appear that we insist on not respecting the laws of good behavior. The only Law which deserves our respect is the musical group of the same name (I even think it's Chilean), and that only when they're accompanied by the Mexican Ely Guerra in the song titled El duelo, and, if not, then not even that law.

P.S. WHICH INSISTS ON GETTING OFF TOPIC: Argentina is still generous. Previously they gave the world Che, now they're giving an entire world action plan. Because that "Everyone out!" is not just a slogan. Viva the Argentine rebellion!

LATIN AMERICAN P.S. Respect for the sovereignty of Venezuela!

MASOCHISTIC P.S. Keep beating us! More journalistic punches! Like that! More! Oh! Yes! More! More! Oh my god! Ahhh! (Mmh, I love it when you get angry).

114. I Shit on All the Revolutionary Vanguards of This Planet

January 9 to 12, 2003

Zapatista National Liberation Army

To: the Basque political-military organization Euskadi Ta Askatasuna Basque Country

From: the Zapatista National Liberation Army Mexico

Ladies and Gentlemen,

We received the letter that, dated January 1st, 2003, you sent us through news agencies, newspapers, web pages, etc. We knew of your letter's existence on January 6th, but not in the complete version until it came out in the Mexican newspaper La Jornada. This is the version we are referring to. The news came in the way all news arrives here. I was in the latrine, thinking about what would happen if ETA took my word and fulfilled my desires just as I would be completing necessities that are known as philosophy. I could already see the newspapers headlines the next day: "The Sup Dies, A Victim of his Big Mouth", and later the gun shot (it's a journalistic term, not what you think): "He left the shit he made" (ok, well the journalists who keep good manners and preserve the good customs could say "He left the poop he made"). And all the dailies would publish a centerfold, signed by the clearest minds and most elegant of Mexico and Spain that would say, "We always said that this uncle was a shit."

In the end, I was in reflections of this type (that Salater and the CIA enthuse about so much) and returning to the commandancia (Command) when the commandantes Tacho, Mister, and Brus Li (and not Bruce Lee like they put in the news) came looking for me and told me:

"We heard in the news that the ETA has responded."

"Oh yeah? And what did they say?"

"They scolded you."

"Great, this is already an international sport. And how is it 'they scolded you'? It would be 'they scolded us', isn't it 'from my voice speaks the voice of the EZLN'?"

"No, they scolded you. This is the deal: They directed the scolding to you and the greeting and congratulations to us," said Mister. He added: "Maybe someone sent the complete letter." This took a really long time, seeing that we are supposed to be "postmodern" guerillas with all the advanced technology and that we "surf" cyberspace.

With the letter finally in hand, they read it and later passed it to me with a sarcastic "Uy!" Tacho asked: "Why would they say 'we know that you haven't always guessed right?'" Omar responded, smiling: "I think it is because we didn't guess right when we put the Sup as the spokesperson." The side-splitting laughter should have been heard all the way in Basque Country. Comandante David came close to me and consoled me: "Don't take it seriously, they're joking." Comandante Ester tried to say something but the laughter got in her way. For a change, Comandante Fidelia offered to prepare me a tea and told me: "There has to be a response, about all the children of the EZLN". "Also about this," Tacho said and marked for me some parts of your letter with a pen that once belonged to the General of the Division Absalon Castellanos (General of the Mexican Federal Army, famous for assassinating indigenous and persecuting, torturing, jailing, and killing dissident voices; he was taken prisoner by Zapatista forces in 1994, judged and condemned to the punishment of carrying with him for the rest of his life the pardon of those who were his victims). It goes like this:

FIRST- I'll clarify that the children of the EZLN don't understand everything without words, as you incorrectly suppose in your letter. We treat the children like children. It is the powerful with their war that treats them like they are adults. We talk to them. We teach them that the word, together with love and dignity, is what makes us human beings. We don't teach them how to fight. Well, yes, but only how to fight with their words. They learn. They know that the reason we are in all this is so that they won't have to do the same. And they talk and they also listen. Contrary to what you say, we teach the children that words don't kill but that yes it is possible to kill words and, along with them, the act of being human.

We teach them that there are so many words like colors and that there are so many thoughts because within them is the world where words are born. That there are different thoughts and we should respect them. That there are those who pretend their way of thinking should be the only way and they persecute, jail, and kill (always hidden behind the reasons of the State, illegitimate laws, or "just causes") thoughts that are different then their own. And we teach them to speak the truth, that is to say, to speak with their hearts. Because the lie is another form of killing words. In the language of the bat men, those that in talking orient their paths, the Tzotziles, to speak with the truth they say "YALEL TA MELEI". We teach them to speak and also to listen. Because when people only talk and don't listen, they end up thinking that what they say is the only thing that is worth anything. In the language of the Tzotziles, those that in listening orient their paths, to listen with their hearts they say "YATEL TAJLOK EL COONTIC". Speaking and listening to words is how we know who we are, where we come from, and where our steps are going. Also it's how we know about others, their steps, and their world. Speaking and listening to words is like listening to life.

SECOND- I see that you have a sense of humor and that you have uncovered us: we the Zapatistas, who have never had the attention of the national or international press, we wanted to "use" the Basque conflict that, as is evident, gets great press. Furthermore, since the day that we publicly referred to the political struggle in Euskal Herria, the positive comments about the Zapatistas, in the streets and in the national and international press, have been growing. In respect to how you don't want to be part of any type of "pantomime" or "opera", I understand this. You prefer the tragedies. About how you refuse to be the "next fashionable T-shirt on the main street in Madrid", well this spoils our plans of putting a Zapatista souvenir stall on that street (this is how we were thinking about covering the costs of our trip). What's more, I doubt someone would dare to wear a shirt with the ETA cause (and not because you lack sympathizers - you have them, we don't forget this - rather because if they make Batasuma illegal because it does not condemn the armed struggle of ETA, imagine what they would do to someone with a T-shirt that said "Gora ETA"). Apart from that, we didn't think we would ask for autographs or fight with anyone to share the stage with you. That the meeting would be something serious would be guaranteed because we wouldn't be the ones organizing it (we only specialize in zarzuelas [Spanish comic opera] or absurd theater), rather we proposed that Basque social and political forces organize it and make it happen even when it wouldn't be possible to have a debate with Garzon, whether it would be for obstacles from the Mexican or Spanish governments or from him or ETA.

THIRD- "The public manner, without prior consulting," in that we put forth our initiative of AN OPPORTUNITY TO THE WORD is how the Zapatistas do things. We don't previously agree "in the dark" so that we later feign to propose things that were already agreed upon beforehand. What's more, we don't have the means, or the interest, or the obligation to "consult" ETA before speaking. Because the Zapatistas have won the right to the word: to say what we want to, about what we want to, when we want to. And for this we do not have to consult with or ask permission from anyone. Not from Aznar, nor the king Juan Carlos, nor the judge Garzon, nor ETA.

FOURTH- About us "lacking respect for the Basque people"; this is something that Garzon has also accused us of (which, consequently, he should auto-declare illegal because ETA is coinciding with his positions) along with all the Spanish and Basque right wing. This is due to the fact that to suggest giving an opportunity to the word goes against the interests of those that, from apparently contrary positions, have made their alibis and business out of the death of the word. Because the Spanish government kills the word when it attacks the Basque language Euskera or the Navarrorum tongue, when it harasses or jails journalists that "dare" to talk about the Basque theme and include all points of view, and when it tortures prisoners so that they "confess" to whatever will be useful to Spanish "justice". And ETA kills the word when it assassinates those that attack with words and not weapons.

FIFTH- In respect to the fact that ETA is willing to "do everything possible so that the EZLN is better informed about the Basque conflict with the French and Spanish states", we reject your disposition. We are not asking that anyone inform us. We are informed, and better than a lot of people suppose. If we don't express this information, which is also an opinion, it is because one of our principles is that the matters of each nation correspond to each people which is why we point out that would not speak at the forum "An opportunity to the word". But now that you are ready to inform, I think those that you should inform are the Basque people. We ask for an opportunity for the word. We should have directed this to various actors in the Basque conflict. We did it because we owe it, not because we are impassioned about writing to Garzon or ETA. In one form or another, from distinct points on the Mexican, Spanish, or Basque political spectrum (you included) they have taken this opportunity and they have talked (even though the majority of it has been to scold us). And so, even though it is grumbling and preaching, they are already giving an opportunity to the word. And this is the point.

SIXTH- The matter about representation. The judge Garzon claims to represent the Spanish and Basque people (and unites with the representation of the king, Pepillo, and Felipillo) and says that if I offend these said people then I offend all the Basque and Spanish people. ETA claims to represent the Basque people and if we offend them by proposing an opportunity to the word then we offend all the Basque people. I don't know if the Basque or Spanish people agree with being represented by one or the other. It is up to them to decide, not us. Contrary to judge Garzon and you, we do not claim to represent anyone, only ourselves. We don't represent the Mexican people (there are many political and social organizations in this country). We don't represent the Mexican left (there are other consistent leftist organizations). We do not represent Mexican armed struggle (where there are at least 14 other armed political-military organizations on the left). Nor do we represent all the Indian people of Mexico (there are, fortunately, many indigenous organizations in Mexico, some better organized than the EZLN). So we have never said that the stupidities that you have dedicated to us have offended "the Mexican people" or "the Indian people". They concern us and we don't hide ourselves behind those we supposedly represent who, in the majority of cases, don't even realize they are being "represented".

SEVENTH- We know that the Zapatistas don't have a place in the (dis)agreement of the revolutionary and vanguard organizations of the world, or in the rearguard. This doesn't make us feel bad. To the contrary, it satisfies us. We don't grieve when we recognize that our ideas and proposals don't have an eternal horizon, and that there are ideas and proposals better suited than ours. So we have renounced the role of vanguards and to obligate anyone to accept our thinking over another argument wouldn't be the force of reason.

Our weapons are not used to impose ideas or ways of life, rather to defend a way of thinking and a way of seeing the world and relating to it, something that, even though it can learn a lot from other thoughts and ways of life, also has a lot to teach. We are not those who you have to demand respect from. It's already been seen how we are a failure of "revolutionary vanguards" and so our respect wouldn't be useful for anything. Your people are those you have to win respect from. And "respect" is one thing; another very distinct thing is "fear". We know you are angry because we haven't taken you seriously, but it is not your fault. We don't take anyone seriously, not even ourselves. Because whoever takes themselves seriously has stopped with the thought that their truth should be the truth for everyone and forever. And, sooner or later, they dedicate their force not so that their truth will be born, grow, be fruitful and die (because no earthly truth is absolute and eternal) rather they use it to kill everything that doesn't agree with this truth.

We don't see why we would ask you what we should do or how we should do it. What are you going to teach us? To kill journalists who speak badly about the struggle? To justify the death of children for reason of the "cause"? We don't need or want your support or solidarity. We already have the support and solidarity of many people in Mexico and the world. Our struggle has a code of honor, inherited from our guerilla ancestors and it contains, among other things: respect of civilian lives (even though they may occupy government positions that oppress us); we don't use crime to get resources for ourselves (we don't rob, not even a snack store); we don't respond to words with fire (even though many hurt us or lie to us). One could think that to renounce these traditionally "revolutionary" methods is renouncing the advancement of our struggle. But, in the faint light of our history it seems that we have advanced more than those that resort to such arguments (more to demonstrate their radical nature and consequences than to effectively serve their cause). Our enemies (who are not just a few nor just in Mexico) want us to resort to these methods. Nothing would be better for them then the EZLN converting into a Mexican and indigenous version of ETA. In fact, ever since we have used the word to refer to the struggle of the Basque people they have accused us of this. Unfortunately for them, it is not like this. And it never will be. By the way, in the tongue of the night warriors "To fight with honor" they say "PASC OP TA SCOTOL LEQUILAL".

Ok, "Salud" and we don't try to tell anyone what they should do, we only ask for an opportunity to the word. If you don't want to give it one, too bad.

From the mountains of Southeast Mexico,

in the name of the girls, boys, men, women, and elders of the EZLN,
Subcomandante Insurgente Marcos,
Headquarters of the Zapatista National Liberation Army.
Mexico, January 2003.

P.S. Before I forget (Tacho has reminded me) in respect to your final "!Viva Chiapas Libre!" (Long Live a Free Chiapas!): We don't ask for your respect, rather a familiarity with geography. Chiapas is a state in Southeastern Mexico. No organization or individual has posed themselves to liberate Chiapas (well, one time the Chiapan PRI bothered, because the Mexican federal army didn't dedicate itself to annihilating us), much less the Zapatistas. We don't want to make ourselves independent from Mexico. We want to be a part of it, but without leaving who we are: indigenous. So, figuring in that we struggle for Mexico, for the Indian peoples of Mexico, for all the men and women of Mexico no matter if they are Indian or not, the ending should say: Long live a Mexico with its' Indigenous!

P.S. "Accidental" Something should have happened, in the past, in the dates that I began and ended this letter.

Another P.S. It should already be evident, but I want to remark: I shit on all the revolutionary vanguards of this planet...

115. Durito and One About False Options

Durito says that all the multiple options being offered by the Powers conceal a trap.

"Where there are many paths, and we're presented with the chance to choose, something fundamental is forgotten: all those paths lead to the same place. And so, liberty consists not in choosing the destination, the pace, the speed and the company, but in merely choosing the path. The liberty which the Powerful are offering is, in fact, merely the liberty to choose who will walk representing us," Durito says.

And Durito says that, in reality, the Power offers no liberty other than that of choosing among multiple options of death. You can choose the nostalgic model, that of the forgetting. That is the one which is being offered, for example, to the Mexican indigenous as being the most suitable for their idiosyncrasies.

Or you can also choose the modernizing model, that of frenetic exploitation. This is the one which is being offered, for example, to the Latin American middle classes as being most suitable for their patterns of consumption.

Or, if not, you can choose the futuristic model, that of 21st century weapons.

This is the one, for example, being offered by the guided missiles in Iraq and which, so that there may be no doubt as to their democratic spirit, kill Iraqis as well as North Americans, Saudi Arabians, Iranians, Kurds, Brits and Kuwaitis (the nationalities which have accrued in just one week).

There are many other models, one for almost every taste and preference. Because if there is anything neoliberalism is able to pride itself on, it is on offering an almost infinite variety of deaths. And no other political system in the history of humanity can say that.

Then Durito puts a vase with water on the little table, which is made of sticks, tied together with liana, and he says: "The Powers tell us, for example, that we have to choose between being optimists or pessimists. The pessimist sees the glass as being half empty, the optimist sees the glass as half full. But the rebel realizes that neither the vase, nor the water which it contains, belong to them, and it is someone else, the powerful, who fills it and empties it at his whim. The rebel, on the other hand, sees the trap. But he also sees the spring from which the water issues forth."

"And so, when the rebel faces the option of choosing between various paths, he looks further ahead and he looks twice: he sees that those routes lead to the same place, and he sees that there is no path to the place where he wishes to go. Then the rebel, instead of agonizing over polls which say that one path is better than the other because such and such a percent cannot be wrong, begins building a new path," says Durito, while handing out many "NOs" on little pieces of paper of all colors in front of North American embassies throughout the world, which, as everyone knows, look suspiciously like plastic burger shops.

> *From the mountains of the Mexican Southeast,*
> *Subcomandante Insurgente Marcos.*
> *Mexico, March of 2003.*

116. Chiapas: The Thirteenth Stele

Part One: A Conch

Dawn in the mountains of the Mexican Southeast.

Slowly, with an unhurried but continuous movement, the moon allows the dark sheet of night to slip off her body and to finally reveal the erotic nudity of her light. She then reclines across the length of the sky, desirous of looking and being looked at, that is, of touching and being touched. If light does anything, it delineates its opposite, and so, down below, a shadow offers the cloud its hand while murmuring:

"Come with me, look with your heart at what my eyes show you, walk in my steps and dream in my arms. Up above, the stars are making a shell, with the moon as origin and destiny. Look and listen. This is a dignified and rebel land. The men and women who live it are like many men and women in the world. Let us walk, then, in order to look at and listen to them now, while time hovers between night and day, when dawn is queen and lady in these lands.

Take care with that puddle and the mud. Better to follow the tracks which, like in so many other things, are the most knowing. Do you hear that laughter? It is from a couple who are repeating now the ancient rite of love. He murmurs something, and she laughs, she laughs as if she were singing. Then silence, then sighs and muted moans. Or perhaps the other way around, first sighs and moans, afterwards murmurs and laughter. But let's continue on ahead, because love needs no witnesses other than glances turned flesh, and, since it is sunlight regardless of the hour, it also undresses shadows.

Come. Let us sit for a bit and let me tell you things. We are in rebel lands. Here live and fight those who are called "zapatistas". And these zapatistas are very otherly... and they despair of more than one of them. Instead of weaving their history with executions, death and destruction, they insist on living. And the vanguards of the world tear at their hair, because, as for "victory or death", these zapatistas neither vanquish nor die, but nor do they surrender, and they despise martyrdom as much as capitulation. Very otherly, it's true. And then there is the one who is said to be their leader, one Sup Marcos, whose public image is closer to that of Cantinflas and Pedro Infante than to Emiliano Zapata's and Che Guevara's. And it's a waste of time to say that no one will take them seriously that way, because they themselves are the first to joke about their being so otherly.

They are rebel indigenous. Breaking, thus, the traditional preconception, first from Europe and afterwards from all those who are clothed in the color of money, that was imposed on them for looking and being looked at.

And so they do not adapt to the "diabolical" image of those who sacrifice humans to appease the gods, nor to that of the needy indigenous, with his hand extended, expecting crumbs or charity from he who has everything. Nor that of the good savage who is perverted by modernity, nor that of the infant who entertains his elders with gibberish. Nor that of the submissive peon from all those haciendas which lacerated the history of Mexico. Nor that of the skillful craftsperson whose products will adorn the walls of he who despises him. Nor that of the ignorant fool who should not have an opinion about what is further than the limited horizon of his geography. Nor that of someone who is fearful of heavenly or earthly gods.

Because you must know, my blue repose, that these indigenous become angry even at those who sympathize with their cause. And the fact is that they do not obey. When they are expected to speak, they are silent. When silence is expected, they speak. When they are expected to move forward, they go back. When they are expected to keep going back, they're off on another side. When it's expected that they just speak, they break out talking of other things. When they're expected to be satisfied with their geography, they walk the world and its struggles.

Or it's that they're not content with anyone. And it doesn't seem to matter to them much. What does matter to them is for their heart to be content, and so they follow the paths shown by their heart. That's what they seem to be doing now. Everywhere there are people on paths. They are coming and going, barely exchanging the usual greetings. They are spending long hours in meetings or assemblies or whatever. They go in with frowning faces, and they leave, smiling in complicity.

Mmh...

Whatever it is, I am sure that many people will not like what they are going to do or say. In addition, as the Sup says, the zapatistas' specialty is in creating problems and then seeing later who is going to solve them. And so one shouldn't expect much from those meetings other than problems...

Perhaps we might guess what it is about if we look carefully. The zapatistas are very otherly endash; I don't know if I already told you that endash; and so they imagine things before those things exist, and they think that, by naming them, those things will begin to have life, to walk... and, yes, to create problems. And so I am sure they have already imagined something, and they are going to begin to act as if that something already exists, and no one is going to understand anything for some time, because, in effect, once named, things begin to take on body, life and a tomorrow.

Then we could look for some clue... No, I don't know where to look... I believe their way is looking with their ears and listening with their eyes. Yes, I know it sounds complicated, but nothing else occurs to me. Come, let's keep on walking.

Look, the stream is turning into a whirlpool there, and in its center the moon is shimmering its sinuous dance. A whirlpool... or a shell.

They say here that the most ancient say that other, earlier ones said that the most first of these lands held the figure of the shell in high esteem. They say that they say that they said that the conch represents entering into the heart, that is what the very first ones with knowledge said. And they say that they say that they said that the conch also represents leaving the heart in order to walk the world, which is how the first ones called life. And more, they say that they say that they said that they called the collective with the shell, so that the word would go from one to the other and agreement would be reached. And they also say that they say that they said that the conch was help so that the ear could hear even the most distant word. That is what they say that they say that they said. I don't know. I am walking hand in hand with you, and I am showing you what my ears see and my eyes hear. And I see and hear a shell, the puy, as they say in their language here.

Ssh. Silence. The dawn has already yielded to day. Yes, I know it's still dark, but look how the huts are filling, little by little, with light from the fire in the stoves. Since now we are shadows in the shadow, no one sees us, but if they did see us, I am sure they would offer us a cup of coffee, which, with this cold, would be appreciated. As I appreciate the pressure of your hand in my hand.

Look, the moon is already slipping away to the west, concealing its pregnant light behind the mountain. It is time to leave, to shelter the journey in the shadow of a cave, there, where desire and weariness are soothed with another, more pleasant weariness. Come, here, I will murmur to you with flesh and words:

> "And, ay, how I would wish to be
> a joy among all joys,
> one alone, the joy you would take joy in!
> A love, one single love:
> the love you would fall in love with.
> But, I am nothing more than what I am."
> -Pedro Salinas, La voz a ti debida

We will no longer be looking at each other there, but, in the half-sleep of desire, moored in a safe harbour, we will be able to listen to that activity which is stirring these zapatistas now, those who insist on subverting even time, and who are once again raising, as if it were an external flag, another calendar... that of resistance."

Shadow and light go. They have not noticed that in a hut a faint light has been kept up all through the night. Now, inside, a group of men and women are sharing coffee and silence, as they shared the word previously.

For several hours these humans with their dusk-colored hearts have traced, with their ideas, a great shell. Starting from the international, their eyes and their thoughts have turned within, passing successively through the national, the regional and the local, until they reached what they call "El Votan". The guardian and heart of the people, the zapatista people. And so, from the shell's most external curve, they thought words like "globalization", "war of domination", "resistance", "economy", "city", "countryside", "political situation", and others which the eraser has been eliminating after the usual question: "Is it clear or are there questions?" At the end of the path from outside in, in the center of the shell, only some initials remain: "EZLN". Afterwards, there are proposals, and they paint, in thought and in heart, windows and doors which only they see (among other reasons, because they still don't exist). The disparate and scattered word begins to make common collective path. Someone asks: "Is there agreement?" "There is," the now collective voice responds affirmatively. The shell is traced again, but now in the opposite path, from inside out. The eraser also continues the reverse path until only one sentence remains, filling the old chalkboard, a sentence which is madness to many, but which is, to these men and women, a reason for struggle: "A world where many worlds fit." A little bit later, a decision is made.

Now is silence and waiting. A shadow goes out into the night rain. A spark of light barely illuminates the eye. Once again smoke rises from his lips in the darkness. With his hands behind his back, he begins a coming and going without destination. A few minutes ago, there, inside, a death has been decided...

From the mountains of the Mexican Southeast,
Subcomandante Insurgente Marcos.
Mexico, July of 2003.

117. A Death has been Decided

CHIAPAS: The Thirteenth Stele
Part Two: A Death

A few days ago, the Zapatista Army of National Liberation decided on the death of the so-called "Aguascalientes" of La Realidad, Oventik, La Garrucha, Morelia and Roberto Barrios. All of them located in rebel territory. The decision to disappear the "Aguascalientes" was made after a long process of reflection...

On August 8, 1994, during the Democratic National Convention held in Guadalupe Tepeyac, Comandante Tacho, in the name of the Clandestine Revolutionary Indigenous Committee-General Command of the Zapatista Army of National Liberation, inaugurated, before some 6000 persons from various parts of Mexico and the world, the so-called "Aguascalientes", and he handed it over to national and international civil society.

Many people did not know that first "Aguascalientes", whether because they couldn't go, or because they were very young in that year (if you are 24 now, or turning 25, you would have been 14 then, or turning 15), was a formidable ship. Run aground on the side of a hill, its huge white sails hoped to travel the 7 seas. The flag, with its ferocious skull and crossbones, waved fiercely and defiantly above the bridge. Two huge national flags were unfurled at the sides, like wings. It had its library, infirmary, lavatories, showers, piped music (which alternated obsessively between "red bow" and "marked cards"), and, it is said, even a place for attacks. The layout of the buildings looked, as I have related once, like a huge conch, thanks to what we called the "crooked house". The "crooked house" wasn't crooked, it had a crack that appeared at first glance to be an architectural error, but which, from above, allowed one to observe the spiral formed by the buildings. The crew of the first "Aguascalientes" was made up of individuals without face, clear transgressors of maritime and terrestrial laws. And their captain was the most handsome pirate who has ever sailed the oceans: a patch over his missing right eye, a black beard glistening with strands of platinum, a pronounced nose, hook in one hand, saber in the other, a leg of flesh and one of wood, pistol in his belt and pipe in his mouth.

The process that led to the building of that first "Aguascalientes" was fortuitous... and painful. And I am not referring to the physical construction (which was carried out in record time and without television "spots"), but to the conceptual construction. Let me explain:

We, after having prepared ourselves for 10 years for killing and dying, for handling and firing weapons of all kinds, for making explosives, for executing strategic and tactical military maneuvers, in sum, for making war... after the first days of combat, we found ourselves invaded by a genuine army. First an army of journalists, but later one of men and women from the most diverse social, cultural and national backgrounds. It was after those "Cathedral Dialogues", in February-March of 1994. The journalists continued to appear intermittently, but what we call "civil society" - in order to differentiate it from the political class, and so as not to categorize it in social classes - was always constant.

We were learning, and, I imagine, civil society was as well. We learned to listen and to speak, the same, I imagine, as civil society. I also imagine that the learning was less arduous for us.

After all, that had been the EZLN's fundamental origin: a group of "illuminati" who came from the city in order to "liberate" the exploited and who looked, when confronted with the reality of the indigenous communities, more like burnt out light bulbs than "illuminati". How long did it take us to realize that we had to learn to listen, and, afterwards, to speak? I'm not sure, not a few moons have passed now, but I calculate some two years at least. Meaning that what had been a classic revolutionary guerrilla war in 1984 (armed uprising of the masses, the taking of power, the establishment of socialism from above, many statues and names of heroes and martyrs everywhere, purges, etcetera, in sum, a perfect world), by 1986 was already an armed group, overwhelmingly indigenous, listening attentively and barely babbling its first words with a new teacher: the Indian peoples.

I believe I have already related previously, several times, this part of the EZLN's formation (or "re-founding"). But, if I'm repeating it now, it's not in order to overwhelm you with nostalgia, but in order to try and explain how we got to the building of the first "Aguascalientes", and their later proliferation in zapatista, that is, rebel, lands. What I mean by this is that the main founding act of the EZLN was learning to listen and to speak. I believe, at that time, we learned well and we were successful. With the new tool we built with the learned word, the EZLN quickly turned into an organization not just of thousands of fighters, but one which was clearly "merged" with the indigenous communities. To put it another way, we ceased to be "foreigners", and we turned into part of that corner forgotten by the country and by the world: the mountains of the Mexican Southeast.

A moment arrived, I can't say precisely just when, in which it was no longer the EZLN on one side and the communities on the other, but when we were all simply zapatistas. I'm simplifying, necessarily, when remembering this period. There will be another occasion, I hope, and another means, for going into details about that process which, in broad terms, was not without contradictions, setbacks and backsliding.

The fact is, that's how we were, still learning (because, I believe, learning is never done), when the now "newly appeared" Carlos Salinas de Gortari (then President of Mexico, thanks to a colossal election fraud) had the "brilliant" idea of making reforms which did away with the campesinos' right to the land.

The impact in the communities which were already zapatista was, to say the least, brutal. For us (note that I no longer distinguish between the communities and the EZLN), the land is not merchandise, but it has cultural, religious and historic connotations which don't need to be explained here. And so, our regular ranks grew, quickly and exponentially.

And there was more. Poverty also grew and, along with it, death, especially of infants under the age of 5. As part of my responsibilities, it was up to me at that time to check in with the now hundreds of villages by radio, and there wasn't a day when someone didn't report the death of a little boy, of a little girl, of a mother. As if it was a war. Afterwards, we understood that it was, in fact, a war. The neoliberal model which Carlos Salinas de Gortari commanded in such a cynical and carefree fashion was, for us, an authentic war of extermination, an ethnocide, given that it was entire Indian peoples who were being destroyed. That is why we know what we are talking about when we speak of the "neoliberal bomb".

I imagine (there are serious studies here that will recount with precise figures and analysis) that this took place in all the indigenous communities in Mexico. But the difference was that we were armed and trained for a war. Mario Benedetti says, in a poem, that one doesn't always do what one wants, that one can't always, but he has the right to not do what he doesn't want. And, in our case, we did not want to die... or, more accurately, we didn't want to die like that.

Previously I have already spoken of the importance memory has for us. And, therefore, death by forgetting was (and is) the worst of deaths for us. I know it will sound apocalyptic, and that more than one person will search for some touch of martyrdom in what I am saying, but, in order to put it in simple terms, we found ourselves then facing a choice, but not between life or death, rather between one kind of death or the other. The decision, collective and in consultation with each one of the then tens of thousands of zapatistas, is already history, and it was the spark for that dawn of the first of January of 1994.

Mmh. It seems to me as if I'm wandering, because what this is about here is informing you that we have decided to kill off the zapatista "Aguascalientes". And not only to inform you, but also to try and explain why. Ah well, be generous and keep reading.

Cornered, we left on that dawn in 1994 with only two certainties: one was that they were going to tear us to shreds. The other was that the act would attract the attention of good persons towards a crime that was no less bloody because it was silent and removed from the media: the genocide of thousands of Mexican indigenous families. And, like I said, it could sound as if we were inclined to being martyrs who sacrificed themselves for others.

I would lie if I said yes. Because even though, looking at it coldly, we had no chance militarily, our hearts weren't thinking of death, but of life, and, given that we were (and are) zapatistas and, ergo, our doubts include ourselves, we thought we could be wrong about being torn to shreds, perhaps the entire people of Mexico would rise up. But our doubts, I should be sincere, didn't extend so far as imagining that what actually happened could have happened.

And what happened was precisely what gave rise to the first "Aguascalientes", and, then, to the ones which followed. I don't believe it's necessary to repeat what happened. I'm almost sure (and I'm not usually sure about anything) that anyone reading these lines had something, or much, to do with what happened.

And so make an effort and put yourself in our place: entire years preparing ourselves for firing weapons, and it so happens that it's words which have to be fired. When it's said like that, and now that I read what I just wrote, it seems as if it was almost natural, like one of those syllogisms they teach in high school. But believe me, at that time nothing was easy. We struggled a lot... and we continue to do so. But it so happens that a guerrero doesn't forget what he learns, and, as I explained earlier, we learned to listen and to speak. And so then history, as someone I don't know said, grew tired of moving and repeated itself, and we were once again like we were in the beginning. Learning.

And we learned, for example, that we were different, and that there were many who were different than ourselves, but there were also differences among they themselves. Or, almost immediately after the bombs ("they weren't bombs, but rockets", those connected intellectuals - the ones who criticize the press when it talks of "bombing indigenous communities" - will then hasten to clarify), a multiplicity fell on top of us that made us think, not a few times, that it would have been better, effectively, if they had torn us to shreds.

A fighter defined it, in very zapatista terms, in April of that 1994. He came to report to me about the arrival of a caravan from civil society. I asked him how many there were (they had to be put up somewhere) and who they were (I didn't ask each one of their names, but what organization or group they belonged to). The rebel considered the question first, and then the answer he would give. That generally took a while, so I lit my pipe. After considering, the companero said: "They're a chingo, and they're absolute chaos." I believe it is useless to expound on the quantitative universe embraced by the scientific concept of "a chingo", but the rebel wasn't using "absolute chaos" disapprovingly, or as a means of characterizing the state of mind of those who were arriving, but rather of defining the composition of the group. "What do you mean, absolute chaos?" I asked him. "Yes," he answered. "There's everything, there's... it's absolute chaos," he ended up saying, insisting that there was no scientific concept whatsoever which could better describe the multiplicity that had taken rebel territory by storm. The storm was repeated again and again. Sometimes they were, in effect, a chingo. Other times they were two or three chingos. But it was always, to use the neologism utilized by the rebel, "utter chaos".

We intuited then that, no way, we had to learn, and this learning must be for the most possible. And so we thought about a kind of school, where we would be the students and the "absolute chaos" would be the teacher. This was already June of 1994 (we weren't very quick at realizing we had to learn), and we were about to make public the "Second Declaration of the Selva Lacandona" which called for the creation of the "National Democratic Convention" (CND).

The history of the CND is a matter for another story, and I'm only mentioning it now in order to orient you in time and space. Space. Yes, that was part of the problem with our learning. That is, we needed a space in order to learn and to listen and to speak with that plurality that we call "civil society". We agreed then to build the space and to name it "Aguascalientes", given that it would be the seat of the National Democratic Convention (recalling the Convention of the Mexican revolutionary forces in the second decade of the 20th century). But the idea for the "Aguascalientes" went further. We wanted a space for dialogue with civil society. And "dialogue" also means learning to listen to the other and learning to speak with him.

The "Aguascalientes" space, however, had been created linked to a current political initiative, and many people assumed that, once that initiative had run its course, the "Aguascalientes" would lose meaning. A few, very few, returned to the "Aguascalientes" of Guadalupe Tepeyac. Later came Zedillo's betrayal on February 9, 1995, and the "Aguascalientes" was almost totally destroyed by the federal army. They even built a military barracks there.

But if anything characterizes zapatistas, it's tenacity ("stupidity", more than one person might say). And so not even a year had passed before new "Aguascalientes" arose in various parts of rebel territory: Oventik, La Realidad, La Garrucha, Roberto Barrios, Morelia. Then, yes, the "Aguascalientes" were what they should be: spaces for encuentro and dialogue with national and international civil society. In addition to being the headquarters for great initiatives and encuentros on memorable dates, they were the place where "civil society" and zapatistas met everyday.

I told you that we tried to learn from our encuentros with national and international civil society. But we also expected them to learn. The zapatista movement arose, among other things, in demand of respect. And it so happened that we didn't always receive respect. And it's not that they insulted us. Or at least not intentionally. But, for us, pity is an affront, and charity is a slap in the face. Because, parallel with the emergence and operation of those spaces of encuentro that were the "Aguascalientes", some sectors of civil society have maintained what we call "the Cinderella syndrome".

I'm taking out of the chest of memories right now some excerpts from a letter I wrote more than 9 years ago: "We are not reproaching you for anything (to those from civil society who came to the communities), we know that you are risking much to come and see us and to bring aid to the civilians on this side. It is not our needs which bring us pain, it's seeing in others what others don't see, the same abandonment of liberty and democracy, the same lack of justice. (...) From what our people received in benefit in this war, I saved an example of "humanitarian aid" for the chiapaneco indigenous, which arrived a few weeks ago: a pink stiletto heel, imported, size 6 1/2... without its mate. I always carry it in my backpack in order to remind myself, in the midst of interviews, photo reports and attractive sexual propositions, what we are to the country after the first of January: a Cinderella. (...) These good people who, sincerely, send us a pink stiletto heel, size 6 1/2, imported, without its mate... thinking that, poor as we are, we'll accept anything, charity and alms. How can we tell all those good people that no, we no longer want to continue living Mexico's shame. In that part that has to be prettied up so it doesn't make the rest look ugly. No, we don't want to go on living like that."

That was in April of 1994. Then we thought it was a question of time that the people were going to understand that the zapatista indigenous were dignified, and they weren't looking for alms, but for respect. The other pink heel never arrived, and the pair remained incomplete, and piling up in the "Aguascalientes" were useless computers, expired medicines, extravagant (for us) clothes, which couldn't even be used for plays ("senas", they call them here) and, yes, shoes without their mate. And things like that continue to arrive, as if those people were saying: "Poor little things, they're very needy. I'm sure anything would do for them, and this is in my way."

And that's not all. There is a more sophisticated charity. It's the one that a few NGOs and international agencies practice. It consists, broadly speaking, in their deciding what the communities need, and, without even consulting them, imposing not just specific projects, but also the times and means of their implementation. Imagine the desperation of a community that needs drinkable water and they're saddled with a library. The one that requires a school for the children, and they give them a course on herbs.

A few months ago, an intellectual of the left wrote that civil society should mobilize in order to achieve the fulfillment of the San Andres Accords because the zapatista indigenous communities were suffering greatly (not because it would be just for the Indian peoples of Mexico, but so that the zapatistas wouldn't suffer any more deprivation).

Just a moment. If the zapatista communities wanted, they could have the best standard of living in Latin America. Imagine how much the government would be willing to invest in order to secure our surrender and to take lots of pictures and make a lot of "spots" where Fox or Martita could promote themselves, while the country fell apart in their hands. How much would the now "newly appeared" Carlos Salinas de Gortari have given in order to end his term, not with the burden of the assassinations of Colosio and Ruiz Massieu, but with a picture of the rebel zapatistas signing the peace, and the Sup handing over his weapon (the one God gave him?) to the one who plunged millions of Mexicans into ruin? How much would Zedillo have offered in order to cover up the economic crisis in which he buried the country, with the image of his triumphal entrance into La Realidad? How much would the "croquetas" Albores have been willing to give so that the zapatistas would accept the ephemeral "redistricting" he imposed during his tragicomic administration?

No. The zapatistas have received many offers to buy their consciences, and they keep up their resistance nonetheless, making their poverty (for he who learns to see) a lesson in dignity and generosity. Because we zapatistas say that "For everyone everything, nothing for us," and, if we say it, it is what we live. The constitutional recognition of indigenous rights and culture, and the improvement of living conditions, is for all the Indian peoples of Mexico, not just for the zapatista indigenous. The democracy, liberty and justice to which we aspire are for all Mexicans, not just for us.

We have emphasized to not a few people that the resistance of the zapatista communities is not in order to engender pity, but respect. Here, now, poverty is a weapon which has been chosen by our peoples for two reasons: in order to bear witness that it is not welfare that we are seeking, and in order to demonstrate, with our own example, that it is possible to govern and to govern ourselves without the parasite that calls itself government. But fine, the issue of resistance as a form of struggle isn't the purpose of this text either.

The support we are demanding is for the building of a small part of that world where all worlds fit. It is, then, political support, not charity.

Part of indigenous autonomy (to which the "Cocopa Law" certainly speaks) is the capacity for self governance, that is, for conducting the harmonious development of a social group. The zapatista communities are committed to this effort, and they have demonstrated, not a few times, that they can do it better than those who call themselves the government. Support for the indigenous communities should not be seen as help for mental incompetents who don't even know what they need, or for children who have to be told what they should eat, at what time and how, what they should learn, what they should say and what they should think (although I doubt that there are children who would still accept this). And this is the reasoning of some NGOs and a good part of the financing bodies of community projects.

The zapatista communities are in charge of the projects (not a few NGOs can testify to that), they get them up and running, they make them produce and thus improve the collectives, not the individuals. Whoever helps one or several zapatista communities is helping not just to improve a collective's material situation, it is helping a much simpler, but more demanding project: the building of a new world, one where many worlds fit, one where charity and pity for another are the stuff of science fiction novels... or of a forgettable and expendable past.

With the death of the "Aguascalientes", the "Cinderella syndrome" of some "civil societies" and the paternalism of some national and international NGOs will also die. At least they will die for the zapatista communities who, from now on, will no longer be receiving leftovers nor allowing the imposition of projects.

For all these reasons, and for other things which will be seen later, on this August 8, 2003, the anniversary of the first "Aguascalientes", the well "deceased" death of the "Aguascalientes" will be decreed. The fiesta (because there are deaths which must be celebrated) will be in Oventik, and all of you are invited who, over these ten years, have supported the rebel communities, whether with projects, or with peace camps, or with caravans, or with an attentive ear, or with the companera word, whatever it may be, as long as it not with pity and charity.

On August 9, 2003, something new will be born. But I will tell you of that tomorrow. Or, more accurately, in a bit, because it is dawn here now, in the mountains of the Mexican Southeast, dignified corner of the patria, rebel land, lair of the transgressors of the law (including the one of seriousness) and small piece of the great world jigsaw puzzle of rebellion for humanity and against neoliberalism.

From the mountains of the Mexican Southeast,
Subcomandante Insurgente Marcos.
Mexico, July of 2003.

118. Each Caracol Now has a Name Assigned

CHIAPAS: The Thirteenth Stele
Part Three: A Name

It's raining. As it does here in July, the seventh month of the year. I'm shivering next to the stove, turning around and around, as if I were a chicken on a rotisserie, to see if I can dry off like that a bit. It so happened that the meeting with the committees ended quite late, at dawn, and we were camped a good distance from where the meeting took place. It wasn't raining when we left, but, as if it were waiting for us, an almighty downpour was unleashed right when we were halfway there, when it would have been the same distance to go back or to keep on going. The rebels went to their respective huts to change out of their wet uniforms. I didn't, not out of bravery, but out of idiocy, because it so happens that, seeking to lighten the weight of my backpack, I wasn't carrying a change of clothes. And so, here I am, making like a "Sinaloa style chicken". Uselessly, to boot, because, for some reason, which I'm not able to fathom, my cap acts like a sponge, absorbing the water when it rains and exuding it only when its inside. The fact is, inside the hut where the stove is, I have my own personal rain. These absurdities don't astonish me. After all, we're in zapatista lands, and here the absurd is as frequent as the rain, especially in the seventh month of the year. Now I've really thrown too much wood on the fire, not figuratively, and now the flames are threatening to burn the roof. "There's no bad that can't get worse," I say to myself, remembering one of Durito's refrains, and it's best that I leave.

Outside there isn't any rain above, but there's a deluge under my cap. I'm trying to light a pipe with the bowl turned down when Major Rolando arrives. He just watches me. He looks at the sky (which, at this altitude, is already completely clear and with a moon that looks, believe me, like a noonday sun). He looks at me again. I understand his confusion and say: "It's the cap." Rolando says "Mmh," which has come to mean something like "Ah." More rebels come over and, of course, a guitar (and, yes, that's dry), and they start singing. Rolando and yours truly burst into a duet, "La Chancla", in front of a confused public, because the "hit parade" here leans towards cumbias, folk songs and nortenas.

Having seen a repeat of my failed launch as a singer, I withdrew to a corner and followed the wise counsel of Monarca, who, just like Rolando, kept looking at me, looked at the sky, looked at me again and just said: "Take off your cap, Sup." I took it off and, of course, my private rain stopped. Monarca went over to where the others were. I told Captain Jose Luis (who acts as my bodyguard) to go rest, that I wasn't going to be doing anything now. The Captain went, but not to rest, rather to join in with the singing.

And so I was left alone. Still shivering, but now without rain over me. I went back to trying to light my pipe, now with the bowl turned up, but then I discovered that my lighter had gotten wet, and it wouldn't even flicker. I murmured: "Son of a bitch, now I can't even light my pipe," certain that my "sex appeal" would be going to hell. I was searching in my pants' pockets (and there's quite a few), not for a paperback edition of the Kamasutra, but for a dry lighter, when a flame was lit quite close to me.

I recognized the face of Old Antonio behind the light, I moved the bowl of my pipe to the lit match and, still puffing, I said to Old Antonio: "It's cold."

"It is," he responded, and he lit his hand rolled cigarette with another match. By the light of the cigarette, Old Antonio kept looking at me, then he looked at the sky, then he looked at me again, but he didn't say anything. I didn't either, certain that Old Antonio was already accustomed, as I was, to the absurdities which inhabit the mountains of the Mexican Southeast. A sudden wind put out the flame, and we were left with just the light of a moon that was like an axe, jagged from use, and smoke scratching at the darkness. We sat down on the trunk of a fallen tree. I believe we were silent for a time, I don't remember very well, but the fact is that, without me hardly noticing, Old Antonio was already recounting to me...

The History of the Upholder of the Sky

"According to our earliest ones, the sky must be held up so that it does not fall. The sky is not simply firm, every once in a while it becomes weak and faints, and it just lets itself fall like the leaves fall from the trees, and then absolute disasters happen, because evil comes to the milpa and the rain breaks everything and the sun punishes the land and it is war which rules and it is the lie which conquers and it is death which walks and it is sorrow which thinks.

Our earliest ones said that it happens like this because the gods who made the

world, the most first, put so much effort into making the world that, after they finished it, they did not have much strength left for making the sky, the roof of our
home, and they just put whatever they had there, and so the sky is placed above the
earth just like one of those plastic roofs. Thus the sky is not simply firm, at times it
comes loose. And you must know that when this happens, the winds and waters are
disrupted, fire grows restless, and the land gets up and walks, unable to find peace.

That is why those who came before we did said that four gods, painted in different
colors, returned to the world. They placed themselves at the four corners of the world
in order to grab hold of the sky so that it would not fall and it would stay still and good
and even, so sun and moon and stars and dreams could walk without difficulty.

However, those of the first steps on these lands recount, by times one or more of
the bacabes, the upholders of the sky, would start to dream or would be distracted by
a cloud, and then he would not hold up his side of the earth's roof tightly, and then
the sky the roof of the world, would come loose and would want to fall over the earth,
and the sun and the moon would not have an even path and nor would the stars.

That is how it happened from the beginning, that is why the first gods, those
who birthed the world, left one of the upholders of the sky in charge, and he had
to stay alert, in order to read the sky and to see when it began coming loose, and
then this upholder had to speak to the other upholders in order to awaken them,
so they would tighten up their side and put things straight again.

And this upholder never sleeps, he must always be alert and watchful, in order to
awaken the others when evil falls on the earth. And the most ancient of journey and
word say that this upholder of the sky carries a caracol [conch] hanging from his
chest, and he listens to the sounds and silences of the world with it, and he calls the
other upholders with it so that they do not sleep or in order to awaken them.

And those who were the very first say that this upholder of the sky, so that he
would not sleep, came and went inside his own heart, by way of the paths he carried in his chest, and those ancient teachers say that this upholder taught men and
women the word and its writing, because they say that while the word walks the
world it is possible for evil to be quieted and for the world to be just right, they say.

That is why the word of the one who does not sleep, of he who is alert to evil
and its wicked deeds, does not travel directly from one side to the other, instead he
walks towards himself, following the lines of reason, and the knowledgeable ones
from before say that the hearts of men and women have the shape of a caracol, and
those of good heart and thoughts walk from one side to the other, awakening the
gods and men so that they will be alert to whether the world is just right... That is
why the one who stays awake when the others are sleeping uses his caracol, and he

uses it for many things, but most especially in order to not forget."

With his last words, Old Antonio had taken a wand and sketched something in the dirt. Old Antonio goes, and I go as well. The sun is just barely peeking through the horizon in the east, as if it were just looking, as if checking to see if the one who is staying awake has not gone to sleep, and if there is someone staying alert for the world to become fine again.

I returned there at the hour of pozol, when the sun had already dried the earth and my cap. At one side of the fallen trunk, I saw the sketch which Old Antonio had made on the ground. It was a firmly traced spiral, it was a caracol.

The sun was halfway through its journey when I returned to the meeting with the committees. The death of the "Aguascalientes" having been decided the previous dawn, now being decided was the birth of the "Caracoles", with other functions in addition to the ones the now dying "Aguascalientes" had.

And so the "Caracoles" will be like doors for going into the communities and for the communities to leave. Like windows for seeing us and for us to look out. Like speakers for taking our word far, and for listening to what is far away. But, most especially, for reminding us that we should stay awake and be alert to the rightness of the worlds which people the world.

The committees of each region have met together in order to name their respective caracoles. There will be hours of proposals, discussions on translations, laughter, anger and voting. I know that takes a long time, so I withdraw and tell them to let me know when an agreement has been reached.

In the barracks now, we are eating, and then, sitting around the table, Monarca says that he has found a really "fantastic" pool for bathing and he doesn't know what all else. The fact is that Rolando, who doesn't bathe even in his own self-defense, gets enthusiastic and says: "Let's go."

I've been listening with some skepticism (it wouldn't be the first time that Monarca has been up to tricks), but, since we have to wait anyway for the committees to reach agreement, I say "Let's go" as well. Jose Luis stays in order to catch up with us later, because he hasn't eaten, and so the three of us - Rolando, Monarca and me - leave first. We cross a pasture, and nothing. We cross a milpa, and nothing. I told Rolando: "I think we're going to arrive when the war is already over." Monarca replies that "We're just about there."

We finally arrive. The pool is in a ford of the river where cattle cross and is, therefore, muddy and surrounded with cow and horse dung. Rolando and I protest in unison. Monarca defends himself: "It wasn't like this yesterday." I say: "Besides, it's cold now. I don't think I'm going to bathe." Rolando, who lost his enthusiasm during the walk, remembers that dirt, like Piporro put it so well, also protects against bullets, and he joins in with a "I don't think I will either." Monarca lets out then with a speech about duty and I don't know what all else and says that "Privations and sacrifices don't matter." I ask him what duty has to with his bloody pool, and then he delivers a low blow, because he says: "Ah, then you're backing out."

He shouldn't have said it. Rolando was grinding his teeth like an angry boar while he was taking his clothes off, and I was chewing my pipe as I undressed completely, down to completely revealing my "other average personal details". We dove into the water, more out of pride than desire. We bathed somehow, but the mud left our hair in such a state that we would have been the envy of the most radical punk. Jose Luis arrived and said: "The water's a mess." Roland and I said to him, in stereo: "Ah, then you're backing out." And so Jose Luis also got into the muddy pool. When we got out, we realized that no one had brought anything to dry ourselves off with. Rolando said: "Then we'll dry off in the wind." And so we only put on our boots and our pistols, and we started back, absolutely stark naked, with our minutiae exposed, drying ourselves in the sun.

Suddenly Jose Luis, who was marching in the vanguard, alerted us, saying: "People coming!" We put on our ski-masks and continued on ahead. It was a group of companeras who were going to wash clothes in the river. Of course they laughed and someone said something in their language. I asked Monarca if he'd heard what they said, and he told me "There goes the Sup." Hmm... I say they recognized me by the pipe, because, believe me, I haven't given them any reason to have recognized me from the "other" average personal details.

Before we got to the barracks, we got dressed, even though we were still wet, because we didn't want to disturb the rebels either. They advised us then that the committees had already finished. Each caracol now had a name assigned:

The Caracol of La Realidad, of Tojolabal, Tzeltal and Mame zapatistas, will be called "Madre de los Caracoles del Mar de Nuestros Suenos" (Mother of Caracoles of the Sea of Our Dreams), or "SNAN XOCH BAJ PAMAN JA TEZ WAY-CHIMEL KUUNTIC".

The Caracol of Morelia, of Tzeltal, Tzotzil and Tojolabal zapatistas, will be called "Torbellino de Nuestras Palabras" (Whirlwind of Our Words), or "MUCUL PUY ZUTUIK JUUN JCOPTIC".

The Caracol of La Garrucha, of Tzeltal zapatistas, will be called "Resistencia Hacia un Nuevo Amanecer" (Resistance for a New Dawn), or "TE PUY TAS MALIYEL YAS PAS YACHIL SACAL QUINAL".

The Caracol of Roberto Barrios, of Chol, Zoque and Tzeltal zapatistas, will be called "El Caracol Que Habla Para Todos" (The Caracol Which Speaks For All), or "TE PUY YAX SCOPJ YUUN PISILTIC" (in Tzeltal), and "PUY MUITITAN

CHA AN TI LAK PEJTEL" (in Chol).

The Caracol of Oventik, of Tzotziles and Tzeltales, will be called "Resistencia y Rebeldia Por la Humanidad" (Resistance and Rebellion for Humanity), or "TA TZIKEL VOCOLIL XCHIUC JTOYBAILTIC SVENTA SLEKILAL SJUNUL BALUMIL".

That afternoon it didn't rain, and the sun was able to come out without any problems, traveling through a level sky, towards the house it has behind the mountain. The moon came out then, and, even though it seems incredible, the dawn warmed the mountains of the Mexican Southeast.

From the Mountains of the Mexican Southeast,
Subcomandante Insurgente Marcos.
Mexico, July of 2003.

119. WE ARE MEXICANS... BUT WE ARE ALSO INDIGENOUS

CHIAPAS: The Thirteenth Stele
Part Four: A Plan

The zapatista indigenous communities have been committed for several years now to a process of building autonomy. For us, autonomy is not fragmentation of the country or separatism, but the exercise of the right to govern and govern ourselves, as established in Article 39 of the political Constitution of the United Mexican States.

From the beginning of our uprising, and even long before, we zapatista indigenous have insisted that we are Mexicans... but we are also indigenous. This means that we demand a place in the Mexican nation, but without ceasing to be what we are.

The purported zapatista project for a "Mayan Nation" exists solely in the papers of some of the stupidest military persons in the Mexican Federal Army who, knowing that the war they are waging against us is illegitimate, are using this poor argument in order to convince their troops that, by attacking us, they are defending Mexico. The high military command and their intelligence services know, however, that the aim of the EZLN is not to separate itself from Mexico, but, as its initials say, for "national liberation".

The separatist project for the Mexican Southeast does indeed exist, on the other hand, in the implementation of the neoliberal doctrine in our lands, and it is being directed by the federal government. The now ill-fated "Plan Puebla Panama" was nothing more than a plan for fragmenting the country, assigning the Mexican

Southeast the function of "reserve" for world capital.

In the fragmentation project which is being operated by the government (this is the real agenda of the political parties and the three branches of the government, not the one which appears in the press), Mexico will be divided in three parts: the North, with its states incorporated into the economic and commercial framework of the American Union; the Center, as provider of consumers with middle and high level purchasing power; and the South-Southeast, as a territory to be conquered for the appropriation of natural resources which, in the globalized destruction, are increasingly more important: water, air and land (wood, oil, uranium... and people).

Being simple and laconic, we would hold that the plan is to make the North into a great maquila, the center into a gigantic mall and the South-Southeast into a large finca.

But plans on paper are one thing, and reality is another. Big capital's voracity, the corruption of the political class, the inefficiency of public administration and the increasing resistance of groups, collectives and communities, have all prevented the plan from being fully implemented. And, where it is able to be established, it demonstrates the solidity of a shaky cardboard stage set.

Since "suicides" seem to be fashionable for Power of late, we might say that there is no better concept for defining the plan that politicians and businesspersons have for our country: it's a suicide.

The globalization of Capital needs the destruction of the Nation State. For some time the Nation State has been (among other things) the trench where local capital has taken refuge in order to survive and grow. But there is only a bit of rubble left of the trench.

In the countryside, small and mid-size producers have been succumbing in the face of large agro-industry. They will soon be followed by the large national producers. In the cities, the "malls", the commercial centers, are not only destroying small and mid-size businesses, they are also "swallowing up" the large national companies. Not even to mention national industry, which is already in its last death throes.

In response to this, the strategy of national capital has been naive, if not stupid. It has been distributing coins on one side and the other of the spectrum of the political parties, thus ensuring (or at least believing) that it does not matter what color (party) is governing, because it will always be at the service of the color of money. And so big Mexican businessmen finance the PRI, the PAN and the PRD equally, as well as any political party which might have a chance in the governmental and parliamentary rackets.

During their meetings (like in the times of the mafia in North America, weddings are generally a pretext for the great gentlemen to sign agreements and settle conflicts), the Mexican gentlemen of money congratulate each other. They have the entire national political class on the payroll.

But I regret to have to give them some bad news: as the now silenced scandal of the "Friends of Fox" demonstrated, the heavy duty money comes from the other side. If the one who pays, governs, the one who pays more governs more. And so those politicians will promote laws commensurate with the checks they receive. Sooner or later, big foreign capital will be appropriating everything, starting by bankrupting and absorbing those who have the most. And all of this with the protection of "ad hoc" laws. Politicians are now, and have been for some time, docile employees... of whomever pays more. National businessmen are quite wrong if they think that foreign capital will be satisfied with the electricity industry and oil. The new power in the world wants everything. And so there will be nothing left of national capital but nostalgia and, if they're lucky, some minor positions on the boards of directors.

Dying national capital, in its historical blindness, looks at any form of social organization with terror. The houses of rich Mexicans are protected with complicated security systems. They fear that the hand which is going to snatch what they have away from them is going to come from below. By exercising their right to schizophrenia, rich Mexicans are revealing not only the real source of their prosperity, but also their shortsightedness. They will be dispossessed, yes, but not by improbable popular rage, rather by an avarice that is even larger than theirs: those who are indeed rich where the wealth is. Misfortune will not enter by assaulting the great mansions at dawn, but through the front door and during office hours. The thief will not have the physique of the destitute, but of the prosperous banker.

The one who will be stripping everything from Slim, the Zambranos, Los Romo, the Salinas Pliegos, the Azcarragas, the Salinas de Gortaris, and the other surnames from the limited universe of wealthy Mexicans, do not speak Tzeltal, Tzotzil, Chol or Tojolabal, nor do they have dark skin. They speak English, their skin is the green of the color of money, they studied in foreign universities, and they are thieves with cultivated manners.

That is why armies and police forces will be of no use to them. They are preparing and entrenching themselves in order to fight against rebel forces, but their greatest enemy, the one which will annihilate them completely, practices the same ideology: savage capitalism.

The traditional political class, for its part, has already begun to be displaced. If the State is viewed as a business, it is better if managers, not politicians, run it. And in the "nation-state.com" neo-business, the art of politics is of no use.

The politicians of yesteryear have now realized that, and they are positioning themselves for ambush in their respective regional or local trenches. But the neoliberal hurricane will also go there to seek them out.

Meanwhile, national capital will continue with their sumptuous feasts. And they might never realize that one of their guests will be their gravedigger.

That is why those who are longing for the defense of the Nation State to come from national businessmen, from politicians or from "the institutions of the Republic", are waiting in vain. The one, the other and the other have all been intoxicated by the hologram of national power, and they do not realize that they will soon be thrown out of the mansion they now have.

We, the zapatistas, have referred on some occasions to the so-called "Plan Puebla Panama" as something already extinct. This has been for various reasons:

One is that the plan has already been undermined, and even the attempt at its implementation will do nothing but worsen social uprisings.

Another is that the plan expects us to accept that things have already been decided in the north and center of the country and that no one is opposed. This is false. The routes of resistance and rebellion cross the entire national territory, and they are also surfacing there, where modernity seems to have completely triumphed.

Another reason is that, at least in the mountains of the Mexican Southeast, its implementation will not, for any reason, be permitted.

We have no problem if Derbez and Taylor continue conning businessmen with the Plan, or if some officials earn a salary for working on a corpse. We have done our duty by letting them know, and everyone can believe whatever they wish.

The government's main plan is not the "Plan Puebla Panama". That is only useful for entertaining a part of the state bureaucracy and so that national businessmen will fall for the idea that now the government will, yes, be doing something to improve the economy.

The main plan of the presidential couple, on the other hand, involves something completely separate from the "PPP": dismantling all of the already weak defenses of the national economy, handing it over completely to globalized disorder and lessening, just a bit, with sermons and handouts, the brutal impact of a world war which has already devastated several nations.

If Carlos Salinas de Gortari's post-administration plan was "Pronasol" (remember that the "solidarity party" was even beginning to be formed), for Fox it is the "Let's Go Mexico Foundation" which Martha Sahagun de Fox directs. "Pronasol" was nothing but institutionalized handouts. "Let's Go Mexico" has, in addition, a strong odor of rancid gossip.

Government plans are generally complicated and grandiose, but the only thing which is concealed by so many words are the high salaries of its officials. These plans serve only to have offices, release press communiques and give the impression that something is being done for the people.

Those who govern governing have forgotten that the virtue of a good plan is that it should be simple.

And so, in response to the "Plan Puebla Panama" in particular, and against all global plans for the fragmentation of the Mexican Nation in general, the Zapatista Army of National Liberation is now launching the... "Plan La Realidad-Tijuana" (or "RealiTi").

The Plan involves linking all the resistances in our country and, along with them, rebuilding the Mexican nation from below. There are men, women, children and old ones in all the states of the federation who do not surrender and who, even though they go unnamed, are fighting for democracy, liberty and justice. Our plan involves speaking with them and listening to them.

The "La Realidad-Tijuana" plan has no budget whatsoever, nor officials, nor offices. It has only those people who, in their place, in their time and in their way, are resisting dispossession, and who remember that the patria is not a business with branch offices, but a common history. And history is not something which is just the past. It is also, and above all, the future.

Like the Corrido of the White Horse, but in Shadow-Light and departing one Sunday from La Realidad (and not from Guadalajara), the zapatista word and ear will cross the entire national territory, from Cancun and Tapachula, to Matamoros and La Paz, it will arrive in Tijuana at the light of day, it will pass through Rosarito, and it will not back off until it sees Ensenada.

And not just that. Given that our modest aim is to contribute in some way to the building of a world where many worlds fit, we also have a plan for the five continents.

For the north of the American continent, we have the "Morelia-North Pole Plan", which includes the American Union and Canada.

For Central America, the Caribbean and South America, we have the "La Garrucha-Tierra del Fuego Plan".

For Europe and Africa, we have the "Oventik-Moscow Plan" (traveling to the east and passing through Cancun this September).

For Asia and Oceania, we have the "Roberto Barrios-New Delhi Plan" (traveling to the west).

The plan is the same for the five continents: fighting against neoliberalism and for humanity.

And we also have a plan for the galaxies, but we still don't know what name to give it (the "Earth-Alpha Centauri Plan"?). Our intergalactic plan is as simple as the previous ones, and it involves, in broad strokes, in it not being shameful to call oneself a "human being".

It is obvious that our plans have several advantages: they are not onerous, they do not have any directors and they can be carried out without ribbon cuttings, without boring ceremonies, without statues and without the music group having to repress its desire to play - now to the rhythm of the cumbia and while the respectable kick up their heels - the one that goes "the horizon can now be seen..."

> *From the Mountains of the Mexican Southeast,*
> *Subcomandante Insurgente Marcos.*
> *Mexico, July of 2003.*
> *Chiapas, Mexico, American Continent, Planet Earth, Solar System, Galaxy...*
> *Galaxy... What is our galaxy called?*

P.S. Speaking of evil plans, this July 25 it will be 9 years since the attack on the procession of the then candidate for Governor of Chiapas, Amado Avendano Figueroa, in which social activists Agustin Rubio, Ernesto Fonseca and Rigoberto Mauricio, lost their lives. Justice is still pending. I don't know about you, but we have not forgotten.

120. THE HISTORY OF THE REBEL ZAPATISTA AUTONOMOUS MUNICIPALITIES

CHIAPAS: The Thirteenth Stele
Part Five: A History

The history of the rebel zapatista Autonomous Municipalities is relatively young; it is 7 years old, going on 8. Although they were declared at the time the December 1994 siege was broken, the rebel zapatista Autonomous Municipalities (the MAREZ) still took a while to become reality.

Today, the exercise of indigenous autonomy is a reality in zapatista lands, and we are proud to say that it has been led by the communities themselves. The EZLN has been engaged in this process only in order to accompany, and to intervene when there have been conflicts or deviations. That is why the EZLN's spokesperson has not been the same as the Autonomous Municipalities'. The Autonomous Municipalities themselves have directly communicated their denuncias, requests, agreements, "twinnings" (not a few rebel zapatista Autonomous Municipalities maintain relationships with municipalities in other countries, primarily in Italy). If the autonomous have now asked the EZLN to fulfill the duties of spokesperson, it is because they have entered into a higher stage of development and, having broadened, announcements are not the purview of one, or several, municipalities. That is the reason for the agreement that the EZLN would announce these current changes.

The problems of the autonomous authorities, in the period which is now over, can be divided into two types: those having to do with their relationship with national and international civil society, and those having to do with self-governance, that is, with relations with zapatista and non-zapatista communities.

In their relationship with national and international civil society, the primary problem has been an unbalanced development of the Autonomous Municipalities, of the communities located within them, and, even, of the zapatista families who live there. Those Autonomous Municipalities which are most well known (like those which were the seats of the now defunct "Aguascalientes") or closer at hand (closer to urban centers or with highway access), have received more projects and more support. The same thing has taken place with the communities. The most well known and those along the highway receive more attention from "civil societies".

In the case of zapatista families, what happens is that, when civil society visits the communities or works on projects or sets up a peace camp, they usually build special relationships with one or more families in the community. Those families will, obviously, have more advantages - assignments, gifts or special attention - than the rest, even though they are all zapatistas. Nor is it unusual for those who interact with civil society because of the position they occupy in the community, in the Autonomous Municipality, in the region or in the area, to receive special attention and gifts which often give rise to talk in the rest of the community and do not follow the zapatista criterion of "to each according to his needs".

I should clarify that it is not a bad relationship, nor what someone proudly called "well intentioned counterinsurgency", but rather something natural in human relations. It can, however, produce imbalances in community life if there are no counterbalances to that privileged attention.

Regarding the relationship with zapatista communities, the "govern obeying" has been administered without distinction. The authorities must see that communities' agreements are carried out, their decisions must be regularly informed, and the collective "weight", along with the "word of mouth" which functions in all the communities, become a kind of monitoring which is difficult to avoid. Even so, instances take place of persons managing to get around this and to become corrupt, but it does not get very far. It is impossible to conceal illicit enrichment in the communities. The guilty party is punished by being compelled to do collective work and to repay to the community whatever he wrongfully took.

When the authority goes amiss, becomes corrupt or, to use a local term, "is a shirker", he is removed from his position, and a new authority replaces him. In the zapatista communities, the position of authority is not remunerated at all (during the time that the person is in authority, the community helps to support him). It is conceived as work in the collective interest, and it is rotated. It is not infrequently enforced by the collective in order to punish laxness or indifference of some of its members, such as, when someone misses a lot of the community assemblies, they are punished by being given a position such as municipal agent or ejidal commissioner.

This "form" of self-governance (of which I am giving just the sketchiest summary) is not an invention or contribution of the EZLN. It comes from further back in time. When the EZLN was born, it had already been operating for a good while, although only at the level of each community.

It was because of the enormous growth of the EZLN (as I have already explained, this was at the end of the 80s), that this practice moved from the local to the regional. Functioning with local responsables (that is, those in charge of the organization in each community), regional ones (a group of communities) and area ones (a group of regions), the EZLN saw that those who did not discharge their duties were, in a natural fashion, replaced by another. Although here, given that it is a political-military organization, the command makes the final decision.

What I mean by this is that the EZLN's military structure in some way "contaminated" a tradition of democracy and self-governance. The EZLN was, in a manner of speaking, one of the "undemocratic" elements in a relationship of direct community democracy (another anti-democratic element is the Church, but that's a matter for another paper).

When the Autonomous Municipalities began operating, self-governance did not move just from the local to the regional, it also emerged (always tendentially) from the "shadow" of the military structure. The EZLN does not intervene at all in the designation or removal of autonomous authorities, and it has limited itself to only pointing out that, given that the EZLN, by principle, is not fighting for the taking of power, none of the military command or members of the Clandestine Revolutionary Indigenous Committee can occupy a position of authority in the community or in the Autonomous Municipalities. Those who decide to participate in the autonomous governments must definitively resign from their organizational position within the EZLN.

I am not going to expand much on the operations of the Autonomous Councils. They have their own methods of acting ("their way," as we say) as guarantor, and there are not a few witnesses (national and international "civil societies", who have seen them functioning and who work with them directly).

I do not, however, want to leave the impression that it is something perfect or that it should be idealized. The "govern obeying" in zapatista territories is a tendency, and it is not exempt from ups and downs, contradictions and errors, but it is a dominant tendency. Its having managed to survive in conditions of persecution, harassment and poverty that have rarely existed in the history of the world speaks to the fact that it has benefited the communities. In addition, the autonomous councils have managed to carry forward, with the fundamental support of "civil societies", a colossal labor: the building of the material conditions for resistance.

Charged with governing a territory in rebellion, that is, without any institutional support and under persecution and harassment, the autonomous councils have focused their efforts on two fundamental aspects: health and education.

In health, they have not limited themselves to building clinics and pharmacies (always helped by "civil societies", it must not be forgotten), they also train health workers and maintain constant campaigns for community health and disease prevention.

One of those campaigns came very close, once, to costing me being criticized in assembly (I don't know if you know what it's like being criticized in an assembly, but, if not, it's enough to tell you that hell must be something like that) and being "looked at" by the community (the people "look" at you, but with one of those looks which make you tremble, in sum, a kind of purgatory). It so happened that, I think I was in La Realidad, I was passing through, and I spent the night in one of the huts the compas have for these cases. The community's "health committee" was going around checking out the latrines in each house (there was an agreement that the latrines had to be regularly blocked with lime or ash in order to prevent the spread of disease). Our latrine, of course, had neither lime nor ash. The "health committee" told me, kindly: "Companero Subcomandante Insurgente Marcos, we're checking out the latrines by agreement of the community, and your latrine doesn't have lime or ash, so you have to put it in, and we're going to come tomorrow to see if it has it then." I began babbling something about the trip, the lame horse, the communiques, military movements, the paramilitaries and I don't remember what all else. The "health committee" listened patiently until I stopped talking and said only: "That's all companero Subcomandante Insurgente Marcos." When the "health committee" came by the next day, the latrine, of course, had ash, lime, sand, but not cement, only because I couldn't find any and seal the latrine up forever...

Regarding education - in lands where there had been no schools, let alone teachers - the Autonomous Councils (with the help of "civil societies", I will not tire of repeating) built schools, trained education promoters and, in some cases, even created their own curricula. Literacy manuals and textbooks are created by "education committees" and promoters, accompanied by "civil societies" who know about those subjects. In some areas (not in all, it's true), they have managed to see to it that girls - who have been traditionally deprived of access to learning - go to school. Although they have also seen to it that women are no longer sold and may freely choose their mate, what feminists call "gender discrimination" still exists in zapatista lands. The "women's revolutionary law" still has a long way to go in being fulfilled.

Continuing with education, in some places the zapatista bases have made agreements with teachers from the democratic section of the teachers' union (those who aren't with Gordillo) that they will not do counterinsurgency work and will respect the curricula recommended by the Autonomous Councils. Zapatistas in fact, these democratic teachers accepted the agreement, and they have fully complied with it.

Neither the health nor the educational services take in all the zapatista communities, it's true, but a large number of them, the majority, now have a means of obtaining medicine, of being treated for an illness and for having a vehicle for taking them to the city in case of illness or serious accident. Literacy and primary education are hardly widespread, but one region already has an autonomous secondary school which, incidentally, recently "graduated" a new generation made up of men and, ojo, indigenous women.

A few days ago, they showed me the diplomas and school-leaving certificates from the Rebel Autonomous Zapatista Secondary School. My humble opinion is that they should have made them out of chewing gum, because at the top they have "EZLN - Zapatista Army of National Liberation", and then they read (in Castillo and in Tzotzil): "The Rebel Autonomous Zapatista Educational System of National Liberation (referring to how it operates in Los Altos, because there are other educational systems in other areas) certifies that student so-and-so has satisfactorily completed the three grades of the Autonomous Secondary School, in accordance with the Zapatista Plans and Programs in ESRAZ, Primero de Enero of 1994 Rebel Autonomous Zapatista Secondary School, obtaining an average of _____. Therefore our Educational System recognizes your efforts, your contributions to the resistance struggle and invites you to share with our peoples what the people have given you." And it then says: "For a liberating education! For a scientific and popular education! I put myself at the service of my people." And so, in the event of persecution, the student will not only be unable to show it, she will also have to eat it, that's why it would be better if it were chewing gum. There is also the report card (which appears as "Recognition"), and there you can read the subjects (in reality, they aren't subjects, but "areas") which were completed: Humanism, Sports, Arts, Reflection on Reality, Social Sciences, Natural Sciences, Reflections on the Mother Language, Communication, Mathematics and Productions and Services to the

Community. There are only two assessments: "A" ("area approved") and "ANA" ("area not approved"). I know that the "Anas" of the world are going to be offended, but there's nothing I can do, because, like I say, autonomies are autonomies...

Education is free, and the "education committees" go to great efforts (I repeat: with the support of "civil societies") to see that each student has his own notebook and her pencil, without having to pay for it.

In health, efforts are being made to see that it is free as well. In some zapatista clinics, they no longer charge the companeros, not for the consult, not for the medicine, not for the operation (if it's necessary and able to be performed in our circumstances), and in the others only the cost of the medicine is charged, not the cónsult nor the medical care. Our clinics have the help and direct participation of specialists, surgeons, doctors, nurses from national and international civil society, as well as from students and assistants in medicine and odontology from UNAM, from UAM and from other institutions of higher education. They do not charge one single peso, and, not infrequently, they pay out of their own pockets.

I know that some of you will be thinking that this is starting to look like a government report, and the only thing missing is my saying "the number of poor have been reduced" or some other "Fox-ism", but no, the number of poor have increased here, because the number of zapatistas have increased, and one thing goes with the other.

That is why I want to emphasize that all of this is taking place under conditions of extreme poverty, shortages and technical and information limitations, in addition to the fact that the government does everything possible to block those projects which come from other countries.

A short time ago, I was talking with some "civil societies" about the suffering they had to go through in order to bring a freezer that worked off solar energy. The project involved vaccinating children, but the majority of the communities do not have electricity or, if they do have it, they don't have a refrigerator. And so the freezer would allow the vaccine to be maintained until it was administered to those who needed it. Fine, it so happened that, in order to bring the freezer, they had to go through an infinity of bureaucratic procedures and, according to their investigation, there was only one organization which could bring what they wanted in from the outside expeditiously: Martha Sahagun de Fox's "Let's Go Mexico Foun-dation". They did not, of course, resort to that publicity agency. They carried out all the procedures, and the freezer will be installed, although late, and there will be vaccinations.

In addition to education and health, the Autonomous Councils look at problems with land, work and trade, where they are making a little progress. They also look at the issues of housing and food. Where we are in our infancy. Where things are doing a bit well is in culture and information. In culture, the defense of language and cultural traditions is being promoted above all. In information, news in local languages is being transmitted through the various zapatista radio stations. Also being regularly transmitted, alternating with music of all kinds, are messages recommending that men respect the women, and calling for women to organize themselves and to demand respect for their rights. And, it may not be much, but our coverage on the war in Iraq was very superior to CNN's (which, strictly speaking, isn't saying much).

The Autonomous Councils also administer justice. The results are erratic. In some places (in San Andres Sacamchen de los Pobres, for example) even the PRIs go to the autonomous authorities because, as they say: "They do take care of it and resolve the problem." In others, as I will explain now, there are problems.

If the relationship between the Autonomous Councils and the communities is full of contradictions, the relationship with non-zapatista communities has been one of constant friction and confrontation.

In the offices of non-governmental human rights defenders (and in the Comandancia General of the EZLN), there are a fair few denuncias against zapatistas for alleged human rights violations, injustices and arbitrary acts. In the case of the denuncias which the Comandancia receives, they are turned over to the committees in the region in order to investigate their veracity and, when the results are positive, to resolve the problem, bringing the parties together in order to come to agreement.

But in the case of human rights defenders organizations, there is doubt and confusion, because there has been no definition as to whom they should be directed. To the EZLN or to the Autonomous Councils?

And they are right (the human rights defenders), because there is no clarity on this matter. There is also the problem of differences between statute law and "uses and customs" (as the jurists say) or "path of good thinking" (as we say). The resolution of the latter belongs to those who have made the defense of human rights their lives. Or, as in the case of Digna Ochoa (whom the special prosecutor regarded as nothing more than an office worker - as if being an office worker was somehow less - but who was, and is, a defender for the politically persecuted), their death. Regarding a clear definition of whom one should direct oneself to in order to process those denuncias, it belongs to the zapatistas. It will be made known soon how they will try to resolve them.

In sum, there are not a few problems confronting indigenous autonomy in zapatista lands. In order to try and resolve some of them, important changes have been made in its structure and operation. But I will tell you of these later, now I just want to give a brief sketch of where we're at.

This long explication is owing to the fact that indigenous autonomy has not been the work of just the zapatistas. If the process has been carried out exclusively by the communities, its realization has had the support of many and many more.

If the uprising of January 1, 1994 was possible because of the conspiratorial complicity of tens of thousands of indigenous, the building of autonomy in rebel lands is possible because of the complicity of hundreds of thousands of persons of different colors, different nationalities, different cultures, different languages, in short, of different worlds.

They, with their help, have made possible (for the good, because the bad is our responsibility alone), not the resolution of the demands of the rebel zapatista indigenous, but their being able to improve their living conditions a bit, and, above all, to survive and make grow one more, perhaps the smallest, of the alternatives in the face of a world which excludes all the "others", that is, indigenous, young people, women, children, migrants, workers, teachers, campesinos, taxi drivers, shopkeepers, unemployed, homosexuals, lesbians, transsexuals, committed and honest religious persons, artists and progressive intellectuals and _____ (add whatever is missing).

There should also be a diploma for all of them (and those who are not them), which says: "The Zapatista Army of National Liberation and the Rebel Zapatista Indigenous Communities certify that _____ (name of the accomplice in question) is our brother/sister and has, in these lands and with us, a dusk-colored heart as home, dignity as food, rebellion as flag, and, for tomorrow, a world where many worlds fit. Given in zapatista lands and skies at such and such a day of such and such a month of the year, etcetera." And it would be signed by those zapatistas who know how to do so, and those who can't would leave their mark. In a corner I would put:

From the mountains of the Mexican Southeast,
Subcomandante Insurgente Marcos.
Mexico, July of 2003.

121. A GOOD GOVERNMENT

CHIAPAS: The Thirteenth Stele
Part Six: A Good Government

In each one of the five "Caracoles" which are being created in rebel territory, they are working at top speed to see that everything is ready. Well, like a compa committee member told me: "It's going to be a bit ready, but not nearly, but a bit enough." With more enthusiasm than wisdom, they are constructing, painting (or repainting) buildings, cleaning, straightening up, reordering. A constant hammering-sawing-digging-planting is resounding in the mountains of the Mexican Southeast, with background music that varies from one place to the other. There, for example, are "Los Bukis" and "Los Temerarios". Someplace else, "Los Tigres del Norte" and "El Dueto Castillo". Over there, "Filiberto Remigio", "Los Nakos", "Gabino Palomares", "Oscar Chavez". Over that way, "Maderas Rebeldes" (which is a zapatista group which, surprisingly, has been climbing the local "hit parade" by leaps and bounds - but I haven't found out if they're climbing up or down).

And, in each "Caracol", a new building, the "Casa de la Junta de Buen Gobierno" [House of the Good Government Junta] can be made out. As far as can be seen, there will be a "Good Government Junta" in each region, and it involves an organizing effort on the part of the communities, not only to confront the problems of autonomy, but also to build a more direct bridge between them and the world. So...

In order to counteract unbalanced development in the Autonomous Municipalities and the communities.

In order to mediate conflicts which might arise between Autonomous Municipalities, and between Autonomous Municipalities and government municipalities.

In order to deal with denuncias against Autonomous Councils for human rights violations, protests and disagreements, to investigate their veracity, to order Rebel Zapatista Autonomous Councils to correct these errors and to monitor their compliance.

In order to monitor the implementation of projects and community work in the Rebel Zapatista Autonomous Municipalities, making sure that they are carried out in the time frames and methods which were agreed by the communities; in order to promote support for community projects in the Rebel Zapatista Autonomous Municipalities.

In order to monitor the fulfillment of those laws which, by common agreement with the communities, are operative in the Rebel Zapatista Municipalities.

In order to serve and guide national and international civil society so that they can visit communities, carry out productive projects, set up peace camps, carry out research (those which provide benefits for the communities) and any other activity permitted in the rebel communities.

In order to, in common accord with the CCRI-CG of the EZLN, promote and approve the participation of companeros and companeras of the Rebel Zapatista Autonomous Municipalities in activities or events outside the rebel communities; and in order to choose and prepare those companeros and companeras.

In short, in order to see to it that, in rebel zapatista lands, governing, governing obeying, the "Good Government Juntas" will be formed on August 9, 2003.

They shall be seated in the "Caracoles", with one junta for each rebel region, and it will be formed by 1 or 2 delegates from each one of the Autonomous Councils of that region.

The following will continue to be the exclusive government functions of the Rebel Zapatista Autonomous Municipalities: the provision of justice; community health; education; housing; land; work; food; commerce; information; culture; and local movement.

The Clandestine Revolutionary Indigenous Committee in each region will monitor the operations of the Good Government Juntas in order to prevent acts of corruption, intolerance, injustice and deviation from the zapatista principle of "Governing by Obeying".

Each Good Government Junta has its own name, chosen by the respective Autonomous Councils:

The Selva Border Good Government Junta (which encompasses Marques de Comillas, the Montes Azules region, and all the border municipalities with Guatemala to Tapachula), is called "Hacia la Esperanza" ["Towards Hope"], and takes in the Autonomous Municipalities of "General Emiliano Zapata", "San Pedro de Michoacan", "Libertad de los Pueblos Mayas" and "Tierra y Libertad".

The Tzots Choj Good Government Junta (which encompasses part of those lands where the government municipalities of Ocosingo, Altamirano, Chanal, Oxchuc, Huixtan, Chilon, Teopisca and Amatenango del Valle are located), is called "Corazon del Arcoiris de la Esperanza" ["Heart of the Rainbow of Hope"] (in local language, "Yotan te xojobil yuun te smaliyel"), and includes the Autonomous Municipalities of "17 de Noviembre", "Primero de Enero", "Ernesto Che Guevara", "Olga Isabel", "Lucio Cabanas", "Miguel Hidalgo" and "Vicente Guerrero".

The Selva Tzeltal Good Government Junta (which encompasses part of the land where the government municipality of Ocosingo is located), is called "El Camino del Futuro" ["Path of the Future"] (in local language: "Te sbelal lixambael"), and includes the Autonomous Municipalities of "Francisco Gomez", "San Manuel", "Francisco Villa" and "Ricardo Flores Magon".

The Northern Region Good Government Junta (which encompasses part of those lands where the municipal governments of the north of Chiapas are found, from Palenque to Amatan), is called "Nueva Semilla Que Va a Producir" ["New Seed Which Shall Bring Forth"] (in Tzeltal: "Yachil ts unibil te yax batpoluc"; and in Chol: "Tsi Jiba Pakabal Micajel Polel"), and includes the Autonomous Municipalities of "Vicente Guerrero", "Del Trabajo", "La Montana", "San Jose en Rebeldia", "La Paz", "Benito Juarez" and "Francisco Villa".

Los Altos of Chiapas Good Government Junta (which encompasses part of those lands where the government municipalities of Los Altos of Chiapas are found and which extends to Chiapa de Corzo, Tuxtla Gutierrez, Berriozabal, Ocozocuatla and Cintalapa), is called "Corazon Centrico de los Zapatistas Delante del Mundo" ["Central Heart of the Zapatistas in Front of the World"] (in local language: "Ta olol yoon zapatista tas tukil sat yelob sjunul balumil"), and includes the Autonomous Municipalities of "San Andres Sacamchen de los Pobres", "San Juan de la Libertad", "San Pedro Polho", "Santa Catarina", "Magdalena de la Paz", "16 de Febrero" and "San Juan Apostol Cancuc".

Among the Good Government Juntas' first regulations are the following:

ONE.- Donations and help from national and international civil society will no longer be allowed to be earmarked to anyone in particular or to a specific community or Autonomous Municipality. The Good Government Junta shall decide, after evaluating the circumstances of the communities, where that help most needs to be directed. The Good Government Junta will impose the "brother tax", which is 10% of the total cost of the project, on all projects. In other words, if a community, municipality or collective receives economic support for a project, it must give the 10% to the Good Government Junta, so that it can earmark it for another community which is not receiving help. The objective is to balance somewhat the economic development of the communities in resistance. Leftovers, charity and the imposition of projects shall, of course, not be accepted.

TWO.- Only those persons, communities, cooperatives and producers and marketing associations which are registered in a Good Government Junta shall be recognized as zapatistas. In that way, persons shall be prevented from passing as zapatistas who are not only not zapatistas, but are even anti-zapatista (such is the case with some organic coffee producers and marketing cooperatives). Surpluses or bonuses from the marketing of products from zapatista cooperatives and societies shall be given to the Good Government Juntas in order to help those companeros and companeras who cannot market their products or who do not receive any kind of aid.

THREE.- It is not unusual for dishonest people to deceive national and international civil society, presenting themselves in cities as "zapatistas", purportedly sent "on secret or special missions" to ask for money for sick people, projects, trips or things of that nature. Sometimes they even go so far as to offer training in purported, and false, EZLN "safe houses" in Mexico City. In the former case, intellectuals, artists and professional persons, and not a few local government officials, have been deceived. In the latter, it has been young students who have been the victims of the lie. The EZLN is emphasizing that it does not have any "safe house" in Mexico City, and it does not offer any training whatsoever. These bad persons, according to our reports, are involved in banditry, and the money they receive, which they are supposedly requesting for the communities, is used for their own personal benefit. The EZLN has now begun an investigation in order to determine who is responsible for usurping their name and for swindling good and honest people. Since it is difficult to contact the Comandancia General of the EZLN in order to confirm whether such and such a person is part of the EZLN or their support bases, and whether what they are saying is true or not, now they will just have to get in contact with the Good Government Juntas (the one in the region where the "swindler" says he is from), and in a matter of minutes they will be told if it is true or not, and whether or not he is a zapatista. To this end, the Good Government Juntas will be issuing certifications and accreditations which should, however, still be corroborated.

These and other decisions will be taken by the Good Government Juntas (which are so called, I want to make clear, not because they are already "good", but in order to clearly differentiate them from the "bad government").

And so, "civil societies" will now know with whom they must reach agreement for projects, peace camps, visits, donations and etcetera. Human rights defenders will now know to whom they should turn over the denuncias they receive and from whom they should expect a response. The army and the police now know whom to attack (just bearing in mind that we, meaning the EZLN, have already gotten involved there). The media, which say what they're paid to say, now know whom to slander and/or ignore. Honest media now know where they can go in order to request interviews or stories on the communities. The federal government and its "commissioner" now know what they have to do to not exist. And the Power of Money now knows who else they should fear.

The noise and activity continue. Someplace someone turns the radio dial and, suddenly, one can clearly hear: "This is Radio Insurgente, Voice of those Without Voice, transmitting from somewhere in the mountains of the Mexican Southeast," and then a marimba sounds the unmistakable rhythms of "The horizon can now be seen". The companeros and companeras stop their work for a moment and begin exchanging comments in indigenous language. Just for a moment. Once again the celebration of work resumes.

It's odd. It has suddenly occurred to me that these men and women do not appear to be building a few houses. It seems as if it is a new world which is being raised in the middle of all this bustle. Perhaps not. Maybe they are, in effect, just a few buildings, and it's been nothing but the effect of shadow and light which the dawn is extending across the communities where the "caracoles" are being drawn, which made me think it was a new world that was being built.

I slip away to a corner of the dawn, and I light my pipe and uncertainty. Then I hear myself, clearly, saying to myself: "Perhaps not... but perhaps yes..."

From the mountains of the Mexican Southeast,
Subcomandante Insurgente Marcos
Mexico, July of 2003.

122. A Postscript

CHIAPAS: The Thirteenth Stele
Seventh and Last Part: A Postscript

Here it is again! It's back! After a tragic period when it didn't delight us with its incomparable style! The much longed for! The... Recurring... Postscript! Yes!!! Yippee!!!! Hurray!!!!! Bravo!!!!!! Cheers!!!!!!! (It may be assumed that at this point the audience is erupting in joyful applause).

P.S. Which Extends the Hand and the Word.

It's official: you are formally invited to the celebration of the death of the "Aguascalientes", and to the fiesta for naming the "Caracoles" and the beginning of the "Juntas of Good Government". It will be in Oventik, San Andres Sacamchen de Los Pobres Autonomous Municipality, Zapatista and Rebel Chiapas, on August 8, 9 and 10 of 2003. Or, as we say here, arrival is on the 8th, the fiesta on the 9th and departure on the 10th. There is a sign at the entrance to the Caracol of Oventik that reads: "You are in Rebel Zapatista Territory: here the people govern, and the government obeys." (I want to put a similar one up in our camps, but it would say: "Here the Sup governs, and everyone can do whatever they like." Sigh.).

P.S. Which Reveals Classified Information.

Attending the fiesta, as revealed by our intelligence services (who are, at the end of the day, not so intelligent, because they still haven't found my sock that I lost the other day), will be the Autonomous Councils of ALL the rebel zapatista municipalities, the Clandestine Revolutionary Indigenous Committee-Comandancia General of the EZLN, and some thousands of support bases. There will be few speeches and many songs. There have been persistent rumors that zapatista musical groups will be there from various regions, and they will present a hyper-mega-magna-super duper concert for no reason other than the joy of continuing to be alive and rebel - compared to this, any techno concert would be nothing but a snack with a pinata, little hats and tiny packets of sweets.

In the unlikely event that you decide to attend and to share this joy with the transgressors of the law, you would do well to listen to the following recommendations:

P.S. Which Blows Its Own Horn Because It Says Still an Umbrella (For the Rain, You Understand).

In zapatista lands, the ground, in addition to being dignified and rebel, is cold, wet and muddy. The fiestas are generally so lively that the rain can't contain itself, and it has to participate, extremely heavily, right in the middle of dances and heartfelt words. That's why it wouldn't be a bad idea to bring, in addition to light feet for dancing, an umbrella, nylon, plastic, a raincoat (or, if lost, a magazine), in order to cover yourself from above and below. One of those horrid "sleeping bags" would be of great use to you if you wish to have the good fortune of being able to interpose something between you and the rain, and between you and the ground.

P.S. Which Makes the Sign of the Cross.

In zapaton soil, the only roof which is guaranteed is the one that the supporter of the sky holds up (Old Antonio dixit), and, given what was explained in the previous postscript, it rains during these days and nights as if it were thirst, and not dignity, that abounded here. Because of that, you should be willing to sleep (ave Maria purisima) with many and many more, under the same roof and in such promiscuity that would render Roman orgies mere "children's parties". Or you should bring one of those tents (which are quite practical, because they're the first to become shipwrecked in the rain and the mud) in order to pass countless moments of silence and tranquility.

P.S. Which Is Preparing a "Marco's Special" Sandwich.

Under zapatudo skies, the only food which abounds and redounds is hope. Given that, according to scientific studies, a balanced diet is necessary in order to complete hope with calories, carbohydrates, vitamins, hydrocarbons, and other similar things, it would be good if you were to bring an adequate portion of canned food, junk food, rolls, biscuits and cookies (if they're "pancrema", they'll be seized), or something of that nature, because the only thing you're likely to find here is tortillas (and maybe not even that).

P.S. Which Tunes In.

If you have one, bring your short-wave radio (or "borrow" one, but don't buy it unless it's from a stall seller or a small shop - they work better than those from the big malls), because on August 9, at a time we still haven't decided, the first intergalactic broadcast of "Radio Insurgente" will be heard. Even if you decide to punish us with the whip of your disdain, wherever you are you will be able to tune us in. The exact band and frequency are: band of 49 meters, at 5.8 megahertz, on short-wave. Since it is to be expected that the supreme will interfere with the transmission, move the dial with the same swinging of hips like in a cumbia, and search until you find us.

P.S. Which Cheers.

During the momentous event, there will also be a hard fought basketball tournament. The best team will rise to the victory (Note: Any foreign team which dares to defeat the locals - the zapatistas - will be taken prisoner, forced to listen, completely, to the "Fox With You" program, and declared "illegal", therefore voiding his victory). Participate! Support your favorite team! (Note: Any demonstration of support or sympathy by the spectators towards any team other than the locals - the zapatistas - will be remanded to the closest assembly in order to be criticized and "looked at"). There will be teams from all over the planet: United States, Euzkal Herria, the Spanish State, France, Italy, UNAM, UAM, POLI, ENAH, "Civil Societies", "Absolute Chaos, S.A. of (i)R. (i)L, of C.V." and others, including the "dream team" of the "Primero de Enero de 1994 Rebel Autonomous Zapatista Secondary School" (by the time they finish saying their name, the opposing team will already be asleep!). It's almost certain that the final will be between the EZLN and the EZLN (in order to guarantee it, generous portions of sour pozol will be distributed to the other teams). It has been rumored that there's been a fierce fight among the large multinational sports news consortiums for broadcasting rights, but it would appear that the Zapatista System of Intergalactic Television has the exclusive. It is also said that the betting in Las Vegas is 7 times 7 to 0.0001 (in favor of the zapatudos, of course).

Vale. Salud and, if you can't come, don't worry, you'll still be with us.

From the mountains of the Mexican Southeast,
Subcomandante Insurgente Marcos.
Mexico, July of 2003.

123. The Death Train of the WTO

September 12, 2003

Brothers and sisters of Mexico and the world, who are gathered in Cancun in a mobilization against neoliberalism, greetings from the men, women, children and elderly of the Zapatista National Liberation Army. It is an honor for us that, amid your meetings, agreements and mobilizations, you have found time and place to hear our words.

The world movement against the globalization of death and destruction is experiencing one of its brightest moments in Cancun today. Not far from where you are meeting, a handful of slaves to money are negotiating the ways and means of continuing the crime of globalization.

The difference between them and all of us is not in the pockets of one or the other, although their pockets overflow with money while ours overflow with hope.

No, the difference is not in the wallet, but in the heart. You and we have in our hearts a future to build. They only have the past which they want to repeat eternally. We have hope. They have death. We have liberty. They want to enslave us.

This is not the first time, nor will it be the last, that the people who think themselves the owners of the planet have had to hide behind high walls and their pathetic security forces in order to put their plans in place.

As if at war, the high command of the multinational army that wants to conquer the world in the only way possible, that is to say, to destroy it, meets behind a system of security that is as large as their fear.

Before, the powerful met behind the backs of the world to scheme their future wars and displacements. Today they have to do it in front of thousands in Cancun and millions around the world.

That is what this is all about. It is war. A war against humanity. The globalization of those who are above us is nothing more than a global machine that feeds on blood and defecates in dollars.

In the complex equation that turns death into money, there is a group of humans who command a very low price in the global slaughterhouse. We are the indigenous, the young, the women, the children, the elderly, the homosexuals, the migrants, all those who are different.

That is to say, the immense majority of humanity.

This is a world war of the powerful who want to turn the planet into a private club that reserves the right to refuse admission. The exclusive luxury zone where they meet is a microcosm of their project for the planet, a complex of hotels, restaurants, and recreation zones protected by armies and police forces.

All of us are given the option of being inside this zone, but only as servants. Or we can remain outside of the world, outside life. But we have no reason to obey and accept this choice between living as servants or dying. We can build a new path, one where living means life with dignity and freedom. To build this alternative is possible and necessary. It is necessary because on it depends the future of humanity.

This future is up for grabs in every corner of each of the five continents. This alternative is possible because around the world people know that liberty is a word which is often used as an excuse for cynicism.

Brothers and sisters, there is dissent over the projects of globalization all over the world. Those above, who globalize conformism, cynicism, stupidity, war, destruction and death. And those below who globalize rebellion, hope, creativity, intelligence, imagination, life, memory and the construction of a world that we can all fit in, a world with democracy, liberty and justice.

We hope the death train of the World Trade Organization will be derailed in Cancun and everywhere else.

> *From the Mountains of the Mexican Southeast,*
> *Subcomandante Insurgente Marcos.*
> *Mexico, September of 2003.*

124. Launch of "EZLN: 20&10: Fire and Word" Campaign

October 26, 2003
To Rebeldia Magazine

Brothers and sisters,

I am writing you in the name of the children, old ones, women and men of the... What? But, Durito! Oh, alright...

I'm writing you in the name of the children, old ones, women, men and beetles of the Zapatista Army of National Liberation.

We received the letter where you told us about your organizing the "EZLN: 20 and 10, Fire and Word" campaign, which is going to be held from November 10 of this year through January 12, 2004.

We welcome that initiative, and we appreciate the honor you are bestowing on us. We are also grateful, of course, for the invitation that accompanied your letter and which included, in detail, the following program (I hope "everything's included"):

1. The beginning of the campaign on November 10 in the Casa Lamm, where the book-chronology of the 10 years will also be presented. We accept the invitation, and I'm letting you know that we will be sending a delegation to that event.

2. For the Graphic Art presentation (which will be on November 11 in the Jesus Reyes Heroles Casa de la Cultura at 6 p.m.) and raffle, we will be sending one of our "works of art", in a medium that we shall call "mixed", since we don't exactly know how to define it (because it doesn't exist yet, for one thing). In anticipation of the possibility that no one will buy raffle tickets for that painting (which, incidentally, is so dented it looks round) and we end up looking like idiots, we are asking you NOT to print any tickets for that... "thing", and, when some scatterbrain (and there are those) asks to enter that drawing, try to look serious and say "we're sorry, those have already run out".

3. The dance is on November 14, to the rhythm of the salsa, in the Los Angeles Salon. We are accepting the invitation, and we are advising you (or warning you) that we shall be sending a beetle, who is, as far as I know, only familiar with the tomato variety of salsa and... What?... It's not tomato salsa? If you don't stop eating Pancrema cookies, I'm not going to understand what you're saying! Mexican salsa? Fine then: Durito says he's going to shake his stuff to a rhythm that will leave the hottest salsa in the "low calorie sweetener" category. It will leave the women breathless (Godard dixit), it will make the men like salsa verde, and musical historians will have to change the books and note that the salsa was invented by beetles. (I've always said that this beetle is quite mean...) Where was I? Oh, yes, the program!

4. The photographic and poster exhibition in the Chopo (by the way, greetings to the stallholder raza), which will be on November 25 at 6 p.m.. I'll be sending a photograph, part of my personal archive called "Los patos le tiran a las escopetas" (that's what the archive is called, not the photo).

5. We will be attending the presentations of music CDs, of communiques and of photographs in spirit (unless, of course, you're brave enough to put up with the impertinences of a "Pancrema-cookie-eating" beetle).

6. Our Comandantes and Comandantas of the CCRI-CG of the EZLN will, however, be sending our words to the roundtables.

7. We will also be participating, with messages from the CCRI-CG of the EZLN, in the November 17 fiesta.

Lastly, I'm letting you know that that we will be informing the Good Government Juntas about the objective of this initiative: that the money which is collected will be for the programs of the indigenous rebel communities.

Vale. Salud and there's no birthday party without the birthday boy! So we'll be there.

In the name of the Birthday Boy, that is, the EZLN,
Subcomandante Insurgente Marcos.
Mexico, October of 2003.

P.S. Which notes, indulgently, serious shortcomings in the program.

And the cake? And the bags of sweets? And the little hats? And the pinata? And the "open them, open them" (the presents, you understand)? And the water balloons?

P.S. Which, as usual, pokes its nose into other people's business.

In my humble opinion, the cake should be mocha; the bags of sweets should have few sweets and a lot of pecans; no little hats or gorrones; the pinata should have Bush's face; it would be good if a few dozen Torton could be gotten for the presents; and the water balloons should be like dignity: of all colors.

125. FIRE AND WORD

November 10, 2003

(Message sent by Subcomandante Insurgente Marcos to the opening of the "EZLN 20 & 10, Fire and Word" campaign and to the presentation of the book of the same name, written by Gloria Munoz Ramirez.)

Good morning, good afternoon, good evening. Sup Marcos speaking to you. Welcome, everyone.

We are here in order to begin the celebration of a history and in order to present a book which recounts a good part of that history. Although you might think the opposite, the history which is to be celebrated and recounted is not about the 20 and 10 years of the EZLN. I mean, it's not only about that. Many people will feel that they have been participants in those 20 and those 10. And I'm not referring just to the thousands of indigenous rebel peoples, but also to the thousands of men, women, children and old ones of Mexico and of the world. The history which we are beginning to celebrate today is also the history of all of those people.

The words which I am now writing and speaking are directed to all those persons who, without having joined the ranks of the EZLN, have shared, lived and struggled with us for an idea: the building of a world where all worlds fit. This could also be expressed by saying that we want a birthday where all the birthday boys and girls fit.

And so we are beginning the fiesta just like birthday parties have been begun in the mountains of the Mexican Southeast for the last 20 years, that is, by recounting histories. According to our calendar, there were, prior to the start of the war, 7 stages in the history of the EZLN.

The first of them was when we selected those persons who would form part of the EZLN. This was around 1982. Practices were organized for one or two months in the selva, during which the performance of those in attendance was evaluated in order to see who could "make the cut". The second stage is the one which we call the "establishment", the actual founding of the EZLN.

Today is November 10, 2003. I ask you to imagine, if you will, that on a day like today, but 20 years ago, in 1983, a group of people were preparing, in some safe house, the tools they would need to be taking to the mountains of the Mexican Southeast. Perhaps, twenty years ago, the day went by in checking on the impedimenta, gathering reports on roads, alternative routes, weather, detailing itineraries, orders, devices. Twenty years ago, perhaps at this very hour, they would have been getting into a vehicle and beginning the trip to Chiapas. If we could have been there, perhaps we might have asked those persons what it was they were going to do. And they certainly would have answered: "Establish the Zapatista Army of National Liberation." They had been waiting to say those words for 15 years.

Let us assume, then, that they started their trip on November 10, 1983. A few days later, they reached the end of a dirt road, got their things out, said goodbye to the driver with a "hasta luego" and, after adjusting their knapsacks, began the ascent of one of the sierras, sloping to the west, which cross the Selva Lacandona. After walking for many hours, with some 25 kilos of weight on their backs, they set up their first camp, right in the middle of the sierra. Yes, it might have been cold that day, and even rainy.

On that day, twenty years ago, night had come early under the large trees and, with the aid of lanterns, these men and women were putting up a plastic roof, using a cord as crossbar, hanging up their hammocks, looking for dry firewood and, setting fire to a plastic bag, lighting the bonfire. The commander was writing in his campaign diary, by the light of the bonfire, something like: "November 17, 1983. So many meters above sea level. Rainy. We set up camp. All quiet." On the upper left hand corner of the page on which he was writing, the name appears which they had given to this first station in a trip which they all know was going to be very long. There hadn't been any special ceremony, but on that day and at that hour, the Zapatista Army of National Liberation had been formed. Someone probably proposed a name for that camp, we don't know. What we do know is that the group was made up of 6 persons. The first 6 insurgents, five men and one woman. Of those 6, three were mestizos and three indigenous. The proportion, of 50% mestizos and 50% indigenous, has not been repeated in the 20 years of the EZLN, nor the proportion of women (less than 20% in those first days). Currently, twenty years after that November 17, the percentage must be around 98.9% indigenous and 1% mestizos. The proportion of women is close to 45%.

What was that first EZLN camp called? Those first 6 insurgents don't agree on the subject. As I later learned, the names of the camps were picked without any logic, naturally and without affectations, avoiding apocalyptic or prophetic names. None of them was called, for example, "First of January of 1994". According to those first 6, one day they sent an insurgent to explore a site in order to see if it was suitable for encampment. The insurgent returned, saying that the place "was a dream". The companeros marched in that direction, and, when they arrived, they found a swamp. They then told the companero: "This isn't a dream, it's a nightmare." Ergo, the camp was then called "The Nightmare." It must have been in the first months of 1984. The name of that insurgent was Pedro. Later he would be a Second Lieutenant, Lieutenant, Second Captain, First Captain and Subcomandante. It was while holding that rank, and as head of the zapatista General Staff, ten years later, that he fell in combat on the first of January of 1994, during the capture of Las Margaritas, Chiapas, Mexico.

The third stage, still prior to the uprising, was when we were given over to the tasks of survival, that is, hunting, fishing, gathering fruits and forest plants. At this time, we applied ourselves to knowledge of the terrain, to orientation, hiking and topography. And during that period we were studying military strategies and tactics in the manuals of the North American and Mexican federal armies, as well as the use and care of various firearms, in addition to the so-called "martial arts". We were also studying Mexican history, and we were, of course, leading a very intense cultural life.

I arrived in the Selva Lacandona during this third stage, in 1984, around August-September of that year, some 9 months after the first group had gotten there. I arrived with two other companeros: a Chol indigenous companera and a Tzotzil indigenous companero. If I remember correctly, the EZLN had 7 support base members when I arrived, and two others who "went up and down" to the city with mail and for supplies. They crossed into the villages by night, disguised as engineers.

The camps at that stage were relatively simple: they had a quartermaster's area, or kitchen, dormitories, an exercise area, sentry post, the 25 and 50 area and the fields of fire for defense. Perhaps some of you, who are listening to me, might be asking yourselves what the hell the "25 and 50 area" is. Well, it so happened that, in order to meet those needs which are referred to as "primary", one had to move away a certain distance from the camp. In order to go and urinate, one had to withdraw 25 meters, in order to defecate, 50 meters, in addition to making a hole with the machete and then covering up the "product". These regulations were, of course, when we were, as they say, a handful of men and women, not more than 10. Later on, we would build latrines in more distant areas, but the terms "25" and "50" remained. There was a camp that was called "The Stove", because that was where we built the first one. Prior to that, the fire had been made level with the ground, and the pots (two: one for beans and the other for the animal which we had hunted or fished) hung from a crossbar tied together with liana. But there were more of us then, and we entered the "era of the stove". There were 12 fighters in the EZLN at that time. Some time later, in a camp called "Recruits" (because that's where our new combatants were trained), we entered the "era of the wheel". We carved a wooden wheel with a machete, and we made a wheelbarrow to carry rocks for the trenches. It must have been the times, because the wheel was quite square, and we ended up carrying the rocks in the mud. Another camp was called "Baby Doc", in honor of the one who terrorized, with the blessings of the United States, Haitian lands. It so happened that we were on the move, with a column of recruits, in order to set up camp near a village. We ran into a pair of jabali, a ton of wild pigs, along the road. The guerrilla column deployed with discipline and skill. The one who was in the front yelled "pigs", and, fuelled and driven by panic, he climbed a tree with a skill we've never seen since. Others ran bravely... but to the opposite side from where the enemy, the wild boar, were. Some took aim, and they realized there were two wild boars. During the enemy retreat - when the pigs left - a piglet, barely the size of a domestic cat, was left abandoned. We adopted him, and we named him "Baby Doc", because Papa Doc had died at that time, bequeathing the slaughter to his offspring. We encamped there, in order to dress the meat and eat. The piglet became very attached to us, I think because of the smell. Another camp during those years was called "De la Juventud", because that was where the first group of insurgent youth, called "Rebel Youth of the South", was formed. The young insurgents met once a week in order to dance, read, and to participate in sports and contests. The first time we celebrated the anniversary of the EZLN was on November 17, 1984, 19 years ago. There were 9 of us. I believe it was a camp called "Margaret Thatcher", because we had hung a hog there, which, I swear, was the clone of the "Iron Lady". One year later, in 1985, we celebrated in a camp called "Watapil", because that was the name of a plant whose leaves we used to make a shed for storing food. I was Second Captain, we were in the "Sierra del Almendro", and the mother column had stayed in another mountain range. I had 3 insurgents under my command. If I have my math right, there were 4 of us in that camp. We celebrated with tostadas, coffee, pinole with sugar and a cojo-la we'd killed that morning. There were songs and poems. One of us would sing or recite, and the other three applauded with a level of boredom worthy of a better cause. When it was my turn, I told them - in a solemn speech, without any arguments other than the mosquitoes and solitude which surrounded us - that one day there would be thousands of us, and that our word would go round the world. The other three agreed that the tostada was moldy, that it had most certainly sickened me and that was why I was delirious. I remember that it rained that night.

In what we call the fourth stage, the first contacts were made with the villages in the area. First we would talk with one person, and then he would talk with his family. From the family, it went to the village. From the village, to the region. And so, little by little, our presence turned into an open secret and into a massive conspiracy. During this stage, which ran parallel in time with the third, the EZLN was no longer what we had thought when we had arrived. By then we had already been defeated by the indigenous communities, and, as a consequence of that defeat, the EZLN began to grow exponentially and to become "very otherly". The wheel continued, dented, until, at last, it was round and able to do what a wheel is supposed to do, to roll.

The fifth stage was that of the EZLN's explosive growth. Owing to the political and social conditions, we grew beyond the Selva Lacandona, and we reached Los Altos and the North of Chiapas. The sixth was the voting on war and the preparations, including the "Battle of Corralchen", in May of 1993, when we engaged in the first combat with the federal army.

Two years ago, during the March of Indigenous Dignity, in one of the places we passed through, I saw a kind of fat bottle, like a pot with a narrow neck. It was made of clay, and it was covered with little pieces of mirror. As it reflected the light, each little mirror of the pot-bottle returned a unique image. Everything around it had its singular reflection and, at the same time, the whole resembled a rainbow of images. It was as if many small histories had joined together in order, without losing its distinctive self, to form a larger history. I thought the history of the EZLN might be recounted, looked at and analyzed like that bottle-pot.

Today, November 10, 2003, twenty years after that trip begun by the founders of our organization, a campaign is getting under way, an initiative of Rebeldia magazine, to celebrate the twentieth birthday of the EZLN and the tenth anniversary of the beginning of the war against forgetting. And this book called "EZLN: 20 & 10, Fire and Word", by Gloria Munoz Ramirez, is being presented. If this book could be summed up in an image, nothing would seem better to me than the pot-bottle covered in little pieces of mirror.

In one part of the book, Gloria has gathered statements from some support base companeros, responsables, committees and insurgents, who talked about their little piece of mirror during the 5 stages prior to the uprising, stages 3, 4, 5, 6 and 7. It is the first time that companeros, who have been engaged in the struggle for more than 19 years, have opened their hearts and their memories on those years of silence.

And so Gloria has managed to turn those little pieces of mirror into little pieces of crystal, which allow one to have a bit of a look at the first 10 years of the EZLN.

In this way, another history can be seen, one that is very different from the one constructed by the governments of Carlos Salinas de Gortari and Ernesto Zedillo. Theirs was built with lies, with police reports altered to their convenience, and with the complicity of intellectuals who, under the cover of supposedly "serious" research, concealed the check and the strokes they received from the Powers in order to pay for their "scientific objectivity".

With the little pieces of mirror and crystal which Gloria has found, the reader will realize that he is looking at just a few parts of an immense jigsaw puzzle. A jigsaw puzzle whose key piece is in the first day of the year of 1994, when Mexico entered the First World via the North American Free Trade Agreement.

Prior to that first of January, just before it, was the seventh stage of the EZLN. I remember that on the night of December 30, 1993, I found myself on the Ocosingo-San Cristobal de las Casas highway. On that day, I had been at the positions we were maintaining around Ocosingo. I had checked by radio on the situation of our troops who were concentrating along various points next to the highway, throughout the canadas of Patiwitz, from Monte Lobano and Las Tazas. These troops belonged to the Third Infantry Regiment. There were 1500 combatants. The third regiment's mission was to take Ocosingo. But prior to that they were, "in passing", going to take over the fincas in the area and get their hands on the armaments that belonged to the finqueros' white guards. They reported to me that a federal army helicopter was circling the town of San Miguel, undoubtedly alerted by the enormous number of vehicles that were concentrating in that town. Starting at the dawn of the 29th, none of the vehicles entering left: all of them were "borrowed" in order to mobilize the troops of the Third Regiment. The Third Regiment was made up, in its entirety, of Tzeltal indigenous.

In passing, I had checked the positions of Battalion #8 (which formed part of the Fifth Regiment), that was in charge of taking the municipal seat of Altamirano in a first movement. Afterwards, on the march, it would take Chanal, Oxchuc and Huixtan and then participate in the attack on the Rancho Nuevo barracks, outside San Cristobal. The Eighth was a reinforced battalion. It would have some 600 combatants for the taking of Altamirano, some of whom were to remain in the seized plaza. It would incorporate more companeros in its advance, reaching Rancho Nuevo with some 500 troops. The Eighth Battalion was composed in the great majority by Tzeltals.

While still on the highway, I made a stop at one of the highest areas, making radio contact with Battalion 24 (also part of the Fifth Regiment), whose mission was the seizure of the municipal seat of San Cristobal de Las Casas and the joint attack (in conjunction with Battalion #8) of the Rancho Nuevo military barracks. The Twenty-fourth was also a reinforced battalion. Its troops numbered almost 1000 combatants, all from the region of Los Altos and all Tzotzil indigenous.

Upon reaching San Cristobal, I skirted the city and headed for the position where the headquarters of the General Command of the EZLN was to be. From there, I communicated by radio with the head of the First Regiment, Subcoman-dante Insurgente Pedro, Chief of the zapatista General Staff and second in command of the EZLN. His mission was to take the municipal seat of Las Margaritas and to advance and to attack the military barracks in Comitan. 1200 combatants strong, the First Regiment was mostly made up of Tojolabales.

In addition, there was a battalion in the so-called "Second Strategic reserve", made up of Chol indigenous, in the depths of our launch bases, and 3 battalions were at the ready in the Tzeltal, Tojolabal and Chol regions, in the "First Strategic Reserve". Yes, the EZLN came to public light with more than 4500 combatants in the first lines of fire, the Twenty-first Zapatista Infantry Division, and some 2000 combatants remained in reserve.

On the dawn of December 31, 1993, I confirmed the attack, the date and the hour. In sum: the EZLN would simultaneously attack 4 municipal seats and another 4 "in passing". It would overpower the police and military troops in those plazas, and afterwards it would march to attack two large federal army barracks. The date: December 31, 1993. The time: midnight. The morning of the 31st was spent vacating the urban positions which were being maintained in some places. Around 2 p.m. the different regiments confirmed to the Comandancia General by radio that they were ready. The countdown was begun at 5 p.m.: That hour was dubbed "Minus 7". From that point on, all communication was cut with the regiment. The next radio contact was planned for "Plus 7", 7 a.m. on January 1, 1994... with those who were still alive. What happened afterwards, if you don't know, can be found in this book. And if you already know it, you can remember it.

In it, the pot-bottle turns into a huge tapestry, fortunately sketched in its broad lines by Gloria, full of those little pieces of mirror and crystal which are composed of the different moments of the EZLN over the last 10 years, the period from January 1, 1994 to August 1, 2003. I'm sure many of you will find the mirror and crystal that belongs to you. I wrote the following in the Introduction, thinking just about that: ...a woman, a journalist by profession, ended up leaping, not without difficulties, the complicated and thick wall of zapatista skepticism, and she stayed and lived in the indigenous rebel communities. From that time on, she shared with the companeros the dream and the sleepless nights, the joys and the sorrows, the food and its absence, the persecutions and the respites, the deaths and the lives. Little by little, the companeros and companeras came to accept her and to make her part of their daily lives. I am not going to recount her history. Among other things, because she has preferred to recount the history of a movement, the zapatista one, and not hers.

This person's name is Gloria Munoz Ramirez. During the period from 1994 to 1996, she worked for the Mexican newspaper "Punto", for the German news agency DPA, for the North American newspaper "La Opinion", and for the Mexican daily "La Jornada". In 1995, on the morning of February 9 and along with Hermann Bellinghausen, she carried out what might have been the last interview with Subcomandante Insurgente Marcos. In 1997, she left her work, her family, her friends (in addition to things that only she knows), and she came to live in the zapatista communities. She did not publish anything during those 7 years, but she continued to write, and she did not abandon her journalistic keenness. She wasn't a journalist anymore, of course, or she wasn't just a journalist any longer. Gloria was learning a new way of looking, the one that is far from the glare produced by the spotlights, from the pandemonium of the bandstands, from the pushing and shoving behind the news, from the fight for the exclusive. The way of looking which is learned in the mountains of the Mexican Southeast. With patience worthy of an embroiderer, she was compiling fragments of the inside and outside reality of zapatismo during those, now 10, years of the EZLN's public life.

We didn't know it. It wasn't until the announcement of the birth of the Caracoles and the creation of the Good Government Juntas, when we received a letter from her, presenting that embroidery of words, dates and memories, and putting it at the disposal of the EZLN. We read the book, well, it wasn't a book then, but rather a vast and multicolored tapestry, whose vision helped considerably in portraying the complicated silhouette of zapatismo from 1994 to 2003, the Zapatista Army of National Liberation's 10 years of public life. And so we liked it. We do not know of any other material that has been published with such attention to detail and which is so complete. We responded to Gloria just like we respond, that is, with a "Hmm, and?" Gloria wrote again, and she talked about the double anniversary (20 years of the EZLN and 10 years since the beginning of the war against the forgetting), about the stage that was starting with the creation of the Caracoles and the Good Government Juntas, something about a plan for celebrations by "Rebeldia" magazine, and I don't remember how many other things. Among so much chatter, one thing was clear: Gloria was proposing to publish the book so that young people of today could learn more about zapatismo.

"Young people of today?" I wondered, and I asked Major Moises: "Aren't we the young people of today?" "We are," Major Moises answered me, without stopping saddling up his horse, while I kept on oiling my wheelchair and cursing the fact that Viagra hadn't been included in the field kit...

Where was I? Oh, yes, the book that wasn't a book yet. Gloria wasn't waiting for us to say yes or who knows, or, in the purest zapatista style, not to respond. On the contrary, Gloria attached to the tapestry, or the rough draft of the book that wasn't a book, a request to complete the material with interviews. I went to the committee, and I stretched out the tapestry (the rough draft of the book) on the muddy September ground. They saw. I mean the companeros saw themselves. Aside from being a tapestry, it was a mirror. They didn't say anything, but I understood that there would be more people, many more people, who might also see and see themselves. We responded to Gloria: "Carry on." That was in August or September of this year, I don't remember, but it was after the fiesta of the Caracoles. I do remember that it was raining a lot, that I was going up a hill, repeating Sisyphus' curse with each step, and that Monarca was determined that we were going to finish a remix of "La del Mono Colorado" on Radio Insurgente, "The Voice of Those Without Voice". When I turned around to tell Monarca that he was going to have to go over my head in order to do that, I slipped for the umpteenth time, but then I went and fell on a pile of sharp rocks, and I cut my leg. While I was recounting my injuries, Monarca, just like that, went over my head. That afternoon we broadcast a version of "La del Mono Colorado" on Radio Insurgente, "The Voice of Those Without Voice", which, judging by the calls we received to the radio, was a resounding success. I sighed, what else could it have been?

The book which the reader now has in his or her hands is that tapestry-mirror, but disguised as a book. You cannot put it up on the wall or hang it in your boudoir, but you can approach it and seek us and seek yourself. I am certain that you will find us and you will find yourself.

The "EZLN: 20 & 10, Fire and Word" book, written by Gloria Munoz Ramirez, has been edited through two efforts, that of "Rebeldia" magazine and that of the Mexican newspaper, "La Jornada", which is run by Carmen Lira. Hmm. Another woman. Editorial design is by Efrain Herrera, and the illustrations are by Antonio Ramirez and Domi. Hmm... more women. The photographs are by Adrian Meland, Angeles Torrejon, Antonio Turok, Araceli Herrera, Arturo Fuentes, Caros Cisneros, Carlos Ramos Mamahua, Eduardo Verdugo, Eniac Martinez, Francisco Olvera, Frida Hartz, Georges Bartoli, Heriberto Rodriguez, Jesus Ramirez, Jose Carlo Gonzalez, Jose Nunez, Marco Antonio Cruz, Patricia Aridjis, Pedro Valtierra, Simona Granati, Victor Mendiola and Yuriria Pantoja. Yuriria Pantoja was in charge of photographic editing, and Priscila Pacheco carried out the editorial care.

Hmm... women once again. If the reader notices that women are in the majority, do what I do - scratch your head and say: "No way."

It is my understanding (I am writing this at a distance), that the book is in three parts. In one of them, there are interviews with support base companeros, committees and insurgent soldiers. In the interviews, the companeros and companeras talk about the 10 years prior to the uprising. I should tell you that it is not a global image, but snippets of a memory that must still wait to be joined together and presented. These pieces help a great deal, nonetheless, in understanding what comes next, in the second part. This contains a kind of compass lens of zapatismo's public activities, from the beginning of the war on the dawn of the first of January of 1994, to the birth of the Caracoles and the creation of the Good Government Juntas. It is, from my point of view, the most complete coverage of what has been the EZLN's public activity. The reader can find many things in this tour, but one leaps into sight: the principled nature of a movement. In the third part, an interview with me appears. They sent it to me in writing, and I had to respond in front of a little tape player. I've always thought that the "rewind" on tape players was "record", and so I tried to make an assessment of the 10 years, in addition to reflecting on other things. As I was responding, alone, in front of the tape recorder, it was raining outside, and one of the Good Government Juntas was giving the "shout of independence". It was the dawn of September 16, 2003.

I believe that the three parts tie together quite well. Not just because it was the same pen which created them. Also because they have a way of looking which helps to look, to look at us. I am certain that, like Gloria, many people, by looking at us, will look at themselves. And I am also certain that she, and many others along with her, will find themselves the better. And that is what this is all about, about being better.

That was in the introduction, because in the prologue to the book I wrote the following: Ten years ago, on the dawn of the first of January of 1994, we rose up in arms for democracy, liberty and justice for all Mexicans. In a simultaneous action, we took 7 municipal seats in the Southeastern Mexican state of Chiapas, and we declared war on the federal government, on its army and police. Since then the world has known us as the "Zapatista Army of National Liberation".

But we had already been calling ourselves that before. The EZLN was founded on November 17, 1983, 20 years ago, and we began, as the EZLN, walking the mountains of the Mexican Southeast, carrying a small flag with a black background and a five-pointed red star with the letters "EZLN", also in red, under the star. I still carry that flag. It has been often mended and much abused, but it still waves gracefully in the Comandancia General of the Zapatista Army of National Liberation. Our souls have also been patched up, carrying wounds which we assume have healed, but which open up when we least expect it. For more than 10 years we prepared for those first minutes of 1994. January of 2004 can be seen there. Soon it will have been 10 years of war. 10 years of preparation and 10 years of war. 20 years. But I am not going to speak about the first 10 years, nor about the ones that followed, nor about the 20 added together.

I am not even going to speak about years, about dates, about calendars. I am going to talk about a man, an insurgent soldier, a zapatista. I am not going to talk much. I cannot. Not yet. His name was Pedro, and he died fighting. He held the rank of Subcomandante, and he was, at the time that he fell, the chief of the EZLN General Staff and my second in command. I am not going to say that he has not died. He is indeed dead, and I did not want him to be dead. But Pedro, like all of our dead, walks here, and every once in a while he appears and he talks and jokes and gets serious and asks for more coffee and lights his umpteenth cigarette. He's here now. It is October 26, and it's his birthday. I say to him: "Greetings, birthday boy." He lifts his little cup of coffee and says: "Greetings, Sub." I don't know why I called myself "Marcos" if no one calls me that, everyone calls me "Sub" or its equivalent. Pedro calls me "Sub". We chat with Pedro. I tell him things, and he tells me things. We remember. We laugh. We get serious. Sometimes I tell him off. I scold him for being undisciplined, because I didn't order him to die and he died. He didn't obey. And so I tell him off. He just opens his eyes wide and tells me: "No way." Yes, no way. Then I show him a map. He just likes to look at maps. I point out to him how we've grown. He smiles.

Josue comes over, says hello tells him: "Congratulations, companero Subcomandante Insurgente Pedro." Pedro laughs and says: "Jesus, man, by the time you finished saying all that, I've already had another birthday." Pedro looks at him, and Josue looks at me. I silently agree.

Suddenly we're no longer celebrating the birthday boy. The three of us are going up a hill. During a break, Josue says: "It's coming up on 10 years since the start of the war." Pedro doesn't say anything, he just lights a cigarette. Josue adds: "And 20 years since the EZLN was born. There has to be a big dance." "20 and 10," I repeat slowly, and add, "and those yet to come..."

By this time, we had reached the top of the hill. Josue set his knapsack down. I lit my pipe and waved into the distance. Pedro looked at where I was pointing and said, said to himself, said to us: "Yes, the horizon can be seen now..." And yes, that's just how it is: we have to continue...

What was I saying to you? Ah, yes! We were born 20 years ago, and 10 years ago we rose up in arms for democracy, liberty and justice. We are known by the name of the "Zapatista Army of National Liberation", and our souls, though full of mends and scars, continue to wave like that old flag which can be seen above, that one with the five-pointed red star on a black background and the letters "EZLN".

We are the zapatistas, the most small, the ones who cover our faces in order to be gazed upon, the dead who die in order to live. And that is all because 10 years ago, a first of January, and 20 years ago, a November 17, in the mountains of the Mexican Southeast...

That is where the prologue ends and Gloria Munoz Ramirez' words begin, as my words are ending today, and the "EZLN: 20 & 10, Fire and Word" campaign is beginning with the presentation of a book which is by times a pot-bottle covered with mirrors and crystals, which is by times a tapestry, and which is always a history which must not be forgotten because, by forgetting it, we forget our very selves.

Now, yes, it's official: congratulations to everyone who, during these 20 and 10, have contributed the fire and the word. Those are all my words. If you were bored, go tomorrow, November 11, to the graphic art exhibition which will be raffled in the Jesus Reyes Heroles Casa de Cultura and to the dance in the Los Angeles Salon on the 14th. If you're still bored, then you have the makings of a deputy, to be a senator or a candidate for the Mexican presidency.

Fine, I'm going now because I hear the first chords of "Cartas Marcadas", and I'm sure they're going to get me up with the cake and the little bags of candy.

Vale. Salud and may everyone find us and find themselves.

From the mountains of the Mexican Southeast,
Subcomandante Insurgente Marcos.
Mexico, November of 2003.

The Sup blowing up water balloons just so they won't say I don't get it up anymore.

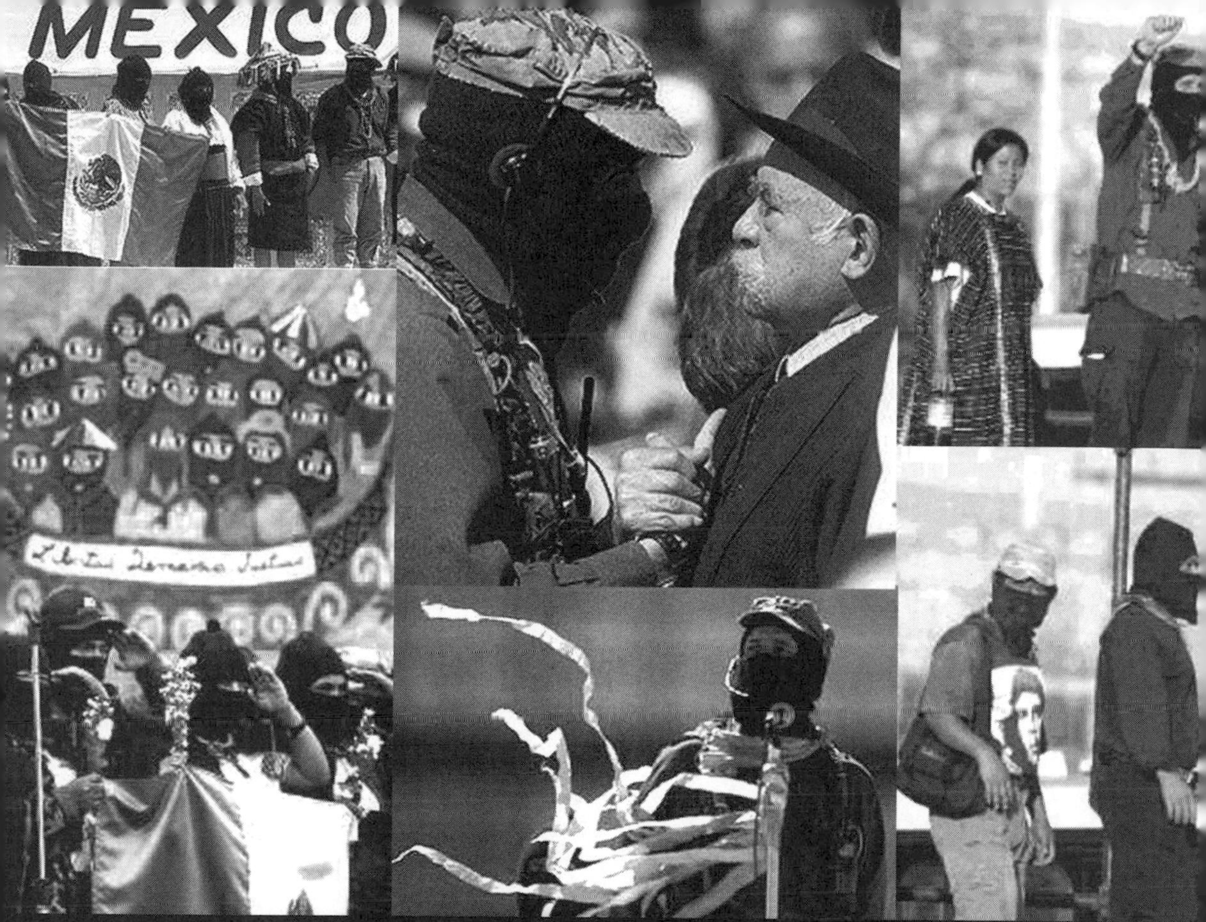

CHAPTER IV: EZLN Communiqués

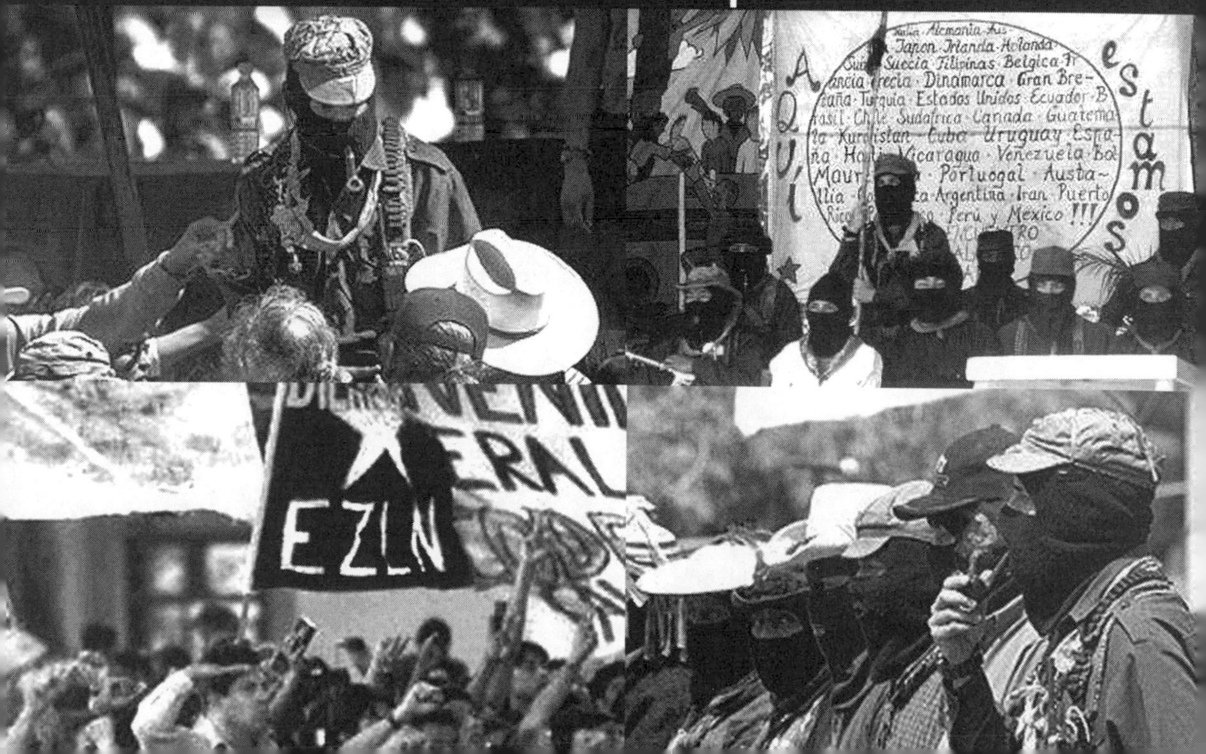

1. First Declaration from the Lacandon Jungle

January 1, 1994

EZLN's Declaration of War

"Today we say 'enough is enough!' (Ya Basta!)"

To the people of Mexico

Mexican Brothers and Sisters,

We are a product of 500 years of struggle: first against slavery, then during the War of Independence against Spain led by insurgents, then to avoid being absorbed by North American imperialism, then to promulgate our constitution and expel the French empire from our soil, and later the dictatorship of Porfirio Diaz denied us the just application of the Reform laws and the people rebelled and leaders like Villa and Zapata emerged, poor men just like us. We have been denied the most elemental preparation so they can use us as cannon fodder and pillage the wealth of our country. They don't care that we have nothing, absolutely nothing, not even a roof over our heads, no land, no work, no health care, no food nor education. Nor are we able to freely and democratically elect our political representatives, nor is there independence from foreigners, nor is there peace nor justice for ourselves and our children.

But today, we say ENOUGH IS ENOUGH.

We are the inheritors of the true builders of our nation. The dispossessed, we are millions and we thereby call upon our brothers and sisters to join this struggle as the only path, so that we will not die of hunger due to the insatiable ambition of a 70 year dictatorship led by a clique of traitors that represent the most conservative and sell-out groups. They are the same ones that opposed Hidalgo and Morelos, the same ones that betrayed Vicente Guerrero, the same ones that sold half our country to the foreign invader, the same ones that imported a European prince to rule our country, the same ones that formed the "scientific" Porfirsta dictatorship, the same ones that opposed the Petroleum Expropriation, the same ones that massacred the railroad workers in 1958 and the students in 1968, the same ones the today take everything from us, absolutely everything.

To prevent the continuation of the above and as our last hope, after having tried to utilize all legal means based on our Constitution, we go to our Constitution, to apply Article 39 which says:

"National Sovereignty essentially and originally resides in the people. All political power emanates from the people and its purpose is to help the people. The people have, at all times, the inalienable right to alter or modify their form of government."

Therefore, according to our constitution, we declare the following to the Mexican federal army, the pillar of the Mexican dictatorship that we suffer from, monopolized by a one-party system and led by Carlos Salinas de Gortari, the maximum and illegitimate federal executive that today holds power.

According to this Declaration of War, we ask that other powers of the nation advocate to restore the legitimacy and the stability of the nation by overthrowing the dictator.

We also ask that international organizations and the International Red Cross watch over and regulate our battles, so that our efforts are carried out while still protecting our civilian population. We declare now and always that we are subject to the Geneva Accord, forming the EZLN as our fighting arm of our liberation struggle. We have the Mexican people on our side, we have the beloved tri-colored flag highly respected by our insurgent fighters. We use black and red in our uniform as our symbol of our working people on strike. Our flag carries the following letters, "EZLN," Zapatista National Liberation Army, and we always carry our flag into combat.

Beforehand, we refuse any effort to disgrace our just cause by accusing us of being drug traffickers, drug guerrillas, thieves, or other names that might by used by our enemies. Our struggle follows the constitution which is held high by its call for justice and equality.

Therefore, according to this declaration of war, we give our military forces, the EZLN, the following orders:

First: Advance to the capital of the country, overcoming the Mexican federal army, protecting in our advance the civilian population and permitting the people in the liberated area the right to freely and democratically elect their own administrative authorities.

Second: Respect the lives of our prisoners and turn over all wounded to the International Red Cross.

Third: Initiate summary judgments against all soldiers of the Mexican federal army and the political police that have received training or have been paid by foreigners, accused of being traitors to our country, and against all those that have repressed and treated badly the civil population and robbed or stolen from or attempted crimes against the good of the people.

Fourth: Form new troops with all those Mexicans that show their interest in joining our struggle, including those that, being enemy soldiers, turn themselves in without having fought against us, and promise to take orders from the General Command of the Zapatista National Liberation Army.

Fifth: We ask for the unconditional surrender of the enemy's headquarters before we begin any combat to avoid any loss of lives.

Sixth: Suspend the robbery of our natural resources in the areas controlled by the EZLN.

To the People of Mexico,

We, the men and women, full and free, are conscious that the war that we have declared is our last resort, but also a just one. The dictators are applying an undeclared genocidal war against our people for many years. Therefore we ask for your participation, your decision to support this plan that struggles for work, land, housing, food, health care, education, independence, freedom, democracy, justice and peace. We declare that we will not stop fighting until the basic demands of our people have been met by forming a government of our country that is free and democratic.

JOIN THE INSURGENT FORCES OF THE ZAPATISTA NATIONAL LIBERATION ARMY.

General Command of the EZLN.

2. Second Declaration from the Lacandon Jungle

June 10, 1994

"Today we say: We will not surrender!"

"... Those who bear swords aren't the only ones who lose blood or who shine with the fleeting light of military glory. They aren't the only ones who should have a voice in designating the leaders of the government of a people who want democracy; this right to choose belongs to every citizen who has fought in the press or in the courts. It belongs to every citizen who identifies with the ideals of the Revolution and who has fought against the despotism that has ignored our laws. Tyranny isn't eliminated just by fighting on the battlefield; dictatorships and empires are also overthrown by launching cries of freedom and terrible threats against those who are executing the people... Historical events have shown us that the destruction of tyranny and the overthrow of all evil governments are the work of ideas together with the sword. It is therefore an absurdity, an aberration, an outrageous despotism to deny the people the right to elect their government. The people's sovereignty is formed by all those people in society who are conscious of their rights and who, be they civilians or armed, love freedom and justice and who work for the good of the country."
- Paulino Martinez, Zapatista delegate to the Revolutionary Sovereignty Convention, Aguascalientes, Mexico, on behalf of Emiliano Zapata, October 27, 1914

To the people of Mexico
To the peoples and governments of the world

Brothers and Sisters,

The Zapatista National Liberation Army, on a war footing against the government since January 1, 1994, addresses itself to you in order to make known its opinion:

Mexican Brothers and Sisters,

In December, 1993, we said, "Enough!" On January 1, 1994, we called on the legislative and judicial powers to assume their constitutional responsibility and to restrain the genocidal policies that the federal executive imposes on our people. We base our constitutional right in the application of Article 39 of the Political Constitution of the United Mexican States:

"National sovereignty essentially and originally resides in the people. All political power emanates from the people and its purpose is to help the people. The people have, at all times, the inalienable right to alter or modify their form of government."

The government responded to this call with a policy of extermination and lies. The powers in Mexico ignored our just demand and permitted a massacre. However, this massacre only lasted 12 days. Another force, a force superior to any political or military power, imposed its will on the parties involved in the conflict. Civil society assumed the duty of preserving our country. It showed its disapproval of the massacre and it obliged us to dialogue with the government. We understand that the ascendancy of the political party that has been in power for so long cannot be allowed to continue. We understand that this party, a party that has kept the fruits of every Mexican's labor for itself, cannot be allowed to continue. We understand that the corruption of the presidential elections that sustains this party impedes our freedom and should not be allowed to continue. We understand that the culture of fraud is the method with which this party imposes and impedes democracy. We understand that justice only exists for the corrupt and powerful. We understand that we must construct a society in which those who lead do so with the will of the people. There is no other path.

This is understood by every honest Mexican in civil society. Only those who have based their success on the theft of the public trust, those who protect criminals and murderers by prostituting justice, those who resort to political murder and electoral fraud in order to impose their will, are opposed to our demands.

These antiquated politicians plan to roll back history and erase the cry from the national consciousness that was taken up by the country after January 1, 1994: "Enough!"

We will not permit this. Today we do not call on those weak powers in Mexico that refuse to assume their constitutional duties and which permit themselves to be controlled by the federal executive. If the legislature and the judges have no dignity, then others who do understand that they must serve the people, and not the individual, will step forward. Our call transcends the question of presidential terms or the upcoming election. Our sovereignty resides in civil society. Only the people can alter or modify our form of government. It is to them that we address this...

Second Declaracion from the Lacandon Jungle

First: We have respected the international conventions of warfare while we have carried out our military actions. These conventions have allowed us to be recognized as a belligerent force by national and foreign forces. We will continue to respect these conventions.

Second: We order all of our regular and irregular forces, both inside national territory and outside the country, to continue to obey the unilateral offensive cease-fire. We will continue to respect the cease-fire in order to permit civil society to organize in whatever forms they consider pertinent toward the goal of achieving a transition to democracy in our country.

Third: We condemn the threats against civilian society brought about by the militarization of the country, both in terms of personal and modern repressive equipment, during this time leading up to the federal elections. Without a doubt, the Salinas government is trying to impose its will by fraud. We will not permit this.

Fourth: We propose to all independent political parties that are suffering from intimidation and repression of political rights - the same intimidation and repression that our people have suffered for the last 65 years - that they declare themselves in favor of a government of transition toward democracy.

Fifth: We reject the manipulation and the attempts to separate our just demands from the demands of the Mexican people. We are Mexicans, and we will not put aside our demands nor our arms until we have democracy, freedom, and justice for all.

Sixth: We reiterate our disposition toward finding a political solution to the transition to democracy in Mexico. We call upon civil society to re-take the protagonist's role that it first took up in order to stop the military phase of the war. We call upon civil society to organize itself in order to direct the peaceful efforts towards democracy, freedom, and justice. Democratic change is the only alternative to war.

Seventh: We call on all honest sectors of civil society to attend a National Dialogue for Democracy, Freedom and Justice.

For this reason we say:

Brothers and Sisters,

After the start of the war in January, 1994, the organized cry of the Mexican people stopped the fighting and called for a dialogue between the contending forces. The federal government responded to the just demands of the EZLN with a series of offers that didn't touch on the essential problem: the lack of justice, freedom, and democracy in Mexican territory.

The offers with which the federal government responded to the demands of the EZLN are limited by the system of the political party in power. This system has made possible the continuation of certain sectors in the Mexican countryside that have superseded the power of the Constitution, and whose roots have maintained the party in power. It is this system of complicity that has made possible the existence and belligerence of the caciques, the omnipotent power of the ranchers and businessmen, and the spread of drug-trafficking. Just the fact that the government offered us the so-called Proposals for a Dignified Peace in Chiapas provoked tremendous agitation and an open defiance by these sectors. The single-party political system is trying to maneuver within this reduced horizon. It can't alienate these sectors without attacking itself, yet it can't leave things as they are without having to face the anger of the campesinos and Indigenous peoples. In other words, to go through with the proposals would necessarily mean the death of the state party system. By suicide or execution, the death of the current Mexican political system is a necessary precondition, although it is not sufficient, for the transition to democracy in our country. There will be no real solutions in Chiapas until the situation in Mexico as a whole is resolved.

The EZLN understands that the problem of poverty in Mexico isn't due just to a lack of resources. Our fundamental understanding and position is that whatever efforts are made will only postpone the problem if these efforts aren't made within the context of new local, regional, and national political relationships - relationships marked by democracy, freedom, and justice. The problem of power is not a question of who rules, but of who exercises power. If it is exercised by a majority of the people, the political parties will be obligated to put their proposals forward to the people instead of merely relating to each other.

Looking at the problem of power within the context of democracy, freedom, and justice will create a new political culture within the parties. A new type of political leader will be born and, without a doubt, new types of political parties will be born as well.

We aren't proposing a new world, but something preceding a new world: an antechamber looking into the new Mexico. In this sense, this revolution will not end in a new class, faction of a class, or group in power. It will end in a free and democratic space for political struggle. This free and democratic space will be born on the fetid cadaver of the state party system and the tradition of fixed presidential succession. A new political relationship will be born, a relationship based not in the confrontation of political organizations among themselves, but in the confrontation of their political proposals with different social classes. Political leadership will depend on the support of these social classes, and not on the mere exercise of power. In this new political relationship, different political proposals (socialism, capitalism, social democracy, liberalism, Christian democracy, etc.) will have to convince a majority of the nation that their proposal is the best for the country. The groups in power will be watched by the people in such a way that they will be obligated to give a regular accounting of themselves, and the people will be able to decide whether they remain in power or not. The plebiscite is a regulated form of confrontation among the nation, political parties, and power, and it merits a place in the highest law of the country.

Current Mexican law is too constricting for these new political relationships between the governed and the governors. A National Democratic Convention is needed from which a provisional or transitional government can emerge, be it by the resignation of the federal executive or by an electoral route.

This National Democratic Convention and transitional government should lead to the creation of a new constitution, and, in the context of this new constitution, new elections should be held. The pain that this process will bring to the country will be less than the damage that would be caused by a civil war. The prophecy of the Southeast is valid for the entire country. We can learn from what has already occurred so that there is less pain during the birth of the new Mexico.

The EZLN has its idea of what system and proposal are best for the country. The political maturity of the EZLN as a representative of a sector of the nation is shown by the fact that it doesn't want to impose its proposal on the country. The EZLN demands what is shown by their example: the political maturity of Mexico and the right for all to decide, freely and democratically, the course that Mexico must take. Not only will a better and more-just Mexico emerge from this historic synthesis, but a new Mexico as well. This is why we are gambling our lives: so that the Mexicans of the future can inherit a country in which it isn't shameful to live...

The EZLN, in a democratic exercise without precedent in an armed organization, consulted its component bases about whether or not to sign the peace accords presented by the federal government. The Indigenous bases of the EZLN, seeing that the central demands of democracy, freedom and justice have yet to be resolved, decided against signing the government's proposal.

Under siege and under pressure from different sectors that threatened us with extermination if the peace accords weren't signed, we Zapatistas reaffirmed our commitment to achieve a peace with justice and dignity. In our struggle, the dignified struggle of our ancestors has found a home. The cry of dignity of the insurgent Vincente Guererro, "Live for the country or die for freedom," once again sounds from our throats. We cannot accept an undignified peace.

Our path sprang out of the impossibility of struggling peacefully for our ele-mental rights as human beings. The most valuable of these rights is the right to decide, freely and democratically, what form the government will take. Now the possibility of a peaceful change to democracy and freedom confronts a new test: the electoral process that will take place this August, 1994. There are those who are betting on the outcome of the elections and the post-election period. There are those who are predicting apathy and disillusionment. They hope to profit from the blood of those who fall in the struggles, both violent and peaceful, in the cities and in the countryside. They found their political project in the conflict they hope will come after the elections. They hope that the political demobilization will once again open the door to war. They say that they will save the country.

Others hope that the armed conflict will restart before the elections so that they can take advantage of the chaotic situation to keep themselves in power. Just as they did before, when they usurped popular will with electoral fraud, these people hope to take advantage of a pre-electoral civil war in order to prolong the agony of a dictatorship that has already lasted decades. There are others, sterile nay-sayers, who reason that war is inevitable and who are waiting to watch their enemy's cadaver float by... or their friend's cadaver. The sectarians suppose, erroneously, that just the firing of a gun will bring about the dawn that our people have waited for since night fell upon Mexican soil with the death of Villa and Zapata.

Every one of these people who steals hope supposes that behind our weapons are ambition and an agenda that will guide us to the future. They are wrong. Behind our weapons is another weapon: reason. Hope gives life to both of our weapons. We won't let them steal our hope.

The hope that came with the trigger came about at the beginning of the year. It is precisely now that the hope that comes with political mobilizations takes up the protagonist's role that belongs to it by right and reason. The flag is now in the hands of those who have names and faces, good and honest people who have the same goal that we yearn for. Our greetings to these men and women. You have our greetings and our hope that you can carry the flag to where it should be. We will be standing there waiting for you with dignity. If the flag should fall, we will be there to pick it up again...

Now is the time for hope to organize itself and to walk forward in the valleys and in the cities, as it did before in the mountains of the Southeast. Fight with your weapons; don't worry about ours. We know how to resist to the end. We know how to wait... And we know what to do if the doors through which dignity walks close once again.

This is why we address our brothers and sisters in different non-governmental organizations, in campesino and Indigenous organizations, workers in the cities and in the countryside, teachers and students, housewives and squatters, artists and intellectuals, members of independent political parties, Mexicans.

We call all of you to a national dialogue with the theme of democracy, freedom, and justice. For this reason, we put forward the following invitation to a National Democratic Convention:

We, the Zapatista National Liberation Army, fighting to achieve the democracy, freedom, and justice that our country deserves, and considering that:

One: The supreme government has usurped the legality that we inherited from the hero of the Mexican Revolution.

Two: The Constitution that exists doesn't reflect the popular will of the Mexican people.

Three: The resignation of the federal executive usurper isn't enough and that a new law is necessary for the new country that will be born from the struggles of all honest Mexicans.

Four: Every form of struggle is necessary in order to achieve the transition to democracy in Mexico.

Considering these things, we call for a sovereign and revolutionary National Democratic Convention from which will come a transitional government and a new national law, a new constitution that will guarantee the legal fulfillment of the people's will.

This sovereign revolutionary convention will be national in that all states of the federation will be represented. It will be plural in the sense that all patriotic sectors will be represented. It will be democratic in the way in which it will make decisions by national consultations.

The Convention will be presided over, freely and voluntarily, by civilians, prestigious public figures, regardless of their political affiliation, race, religion, sex, or age.

The Convention will be launched by local, state, and regional committees in every ejido, settlement, school, and factory. These committees of the Convention will be in charge of collecting the people's proposals for the new constitution and the demands to be completed by the new government that comes out of the Convention.

The convention should demand free and democratic elections and should fight for the people's will to be respected.

The Zapatista National Liberation Army will recognize the National Democratic Convention as the authentic representative of the interests of the Mexican people in their transition to democracy.

The Zapatista National Liberation Army is now to be found throughout national territory and is in a position to offer itself to the Mexican people as an army to guarantee that the people's will is carried out.

For the first meeting of the National Democratic Convention, the EZLN offers as a meeting-place a Zapatista settlement with all of the resources to be found there.

The date and place of the first session of the National Democratic Convention will be announced when it is appropriate to do so.

Mexican Brothers and Sisters,

Our struggle continues. The Zapatista flag still waves in the mountains of the Mexican Southeast and today we say: We will not surrender!

Facing the mountains we speak to our dead so that their words will guide us along the path that we must walk.

The drums sound, and in the voices from the land we hear our pain and our history.

"Everything for everyone," say our dead.

"As long as this is not true, there will be nothing for us."

"Find in your hearts the voices of those for whom we fight. Invite them to walk the dignified path of those who have no faces. Call them to resist. Let no one receive anything from those who rule. Ask them to reject the handouts from the powerful. Let all the good people in this land organize with dignity. Let them resist and not sell out."

"Don't surrender! Resist! Resist with dignity in the lands of the true men and women! Let the mountains shelter the pain of the people of this land. Don't surrender! Resist! Don't sell-out! Resist!"

Our dead spoke these words from their hearts. We have seen that the words of our dead are good, that there is truth in what they say and dignity in their counsel. For this reason we call on our brother Mexicans to resist with us. We call on the Indigenous campesinos to resist with us. We call on the workers, squatters, housewives, students, teachers, intellectuals, writers, on all those with dignity, to resist with us. The government doesn't want democracy in our land. We will accept nothing that comes from the rotting heart of the government, not a single coin nor a single dose of medication, not a single stone nor a single grain of food. We will not accept the handouts that the government offers in exchange for our dignity.

We will not take anything from the supreme government. Although they increase our pain and sorrow, although death may accompany us, although we may see others selling themselves to the hand that oppresses them, although everything may hurt and sorrow may cry out from the rocks, we will not accept anything. We will resist. We will not take anything from the government. We will resist until those who are in power exercise their power while obeying the people's will.

Brothers and Sisters,

Don't sell out. Resist with us. Don't surrender. Resist with us. Repeat along with us, "We will not surrender! We will resist!" Let these words be heard not only in the mountains of the Mexican Southeast, but in the North and on the peninsulas. Let it be heard on both coasts. Let it be heard in the center of the country. Let it cry out in the valleys and in the mountains. Let it sound in the cities and in the countryside. Unite your voices, brothers. Cry out with us: "We will not surrender! We will resist!"

Let dignity break the siege and lift off of us the filthy hands with which the government is trying to strangle us. We are all under siege. They will not let democracy, freedom, and justice enter Mexican territory. Brothers, we are all under siege. We will not surrender! We will resist! We have dignity! We will not sell-out!

What good are the riches of the powerful if they aren't able to buy the most valuable thing in these lands? If the dignity of the Mexican people has no price, then what good is the power of the powerful?

Dignity will not surrender!

Dignity will resist!

Democracy!

Freedom!

Justice!

From the mountains of the Mexican Southeast,
Clandestine Revolutionary Indigenous Committee
-General Command of the Zapatista National Liberation Army.
Mexico June, 1994.

3. THIRD DECLARATION FROM THE LACANDON JUNGLE

The EZLN calls for the formation of a National Liberation Movement

One year after the Zapatistas uprising, today we say:

"The motherland lives! And she is ours! We have been disgraced, it is true; our luck has been bad many times, but the cause of Mexico, which is the cause of the people's rights and justice, has not succumbed; it has not died and it will not die because there still exist committed Mexicans, in whose hearts burns the sacred fire of patriotism. Wherever in the Republic weapons are clenched and the national banner flies, there, as well as here, will exist, with vitality and energy, the protest of Right against Force. Understanding well the gullible man who has accepted the sad mission of being the instrument for enslaving a free people: his vacillating throne does not rest on the

free will of the nation, but rather on the blood and cadavers of thousands of Mexicans who have been sacrificed without reason and only because they defend their freedom and their rights.

Mexicans: those who have the disgrace to live under the dominion of the usurpers, do not resign yourselves to putting up with the yoke of oppression that weighs on you. Do not delude yourselves with the perfidious insinuations of the followers of the consummated deeds, because they are and have been always the followers of despotism. The existence of arbitrary power is a permanent violation of people's rights and Justice, which neither the passage of time nor arms can ever justify, and whose destruction is necessary to honor Mexico and humanity.

I declare myself: in action and deeds, just as resolute as in the first day."

- Benito Juarez, January 1865, Chihuahua

To the people of Mexico
To the peoples and governments of the world

Brothers and Sisters,

The first day of January of 1994 we released the "First Declaration of the Lacandon Jungle". The 10th of June of 1994 we released the "Second Declaration of the Lacandon Jungle". First one and then the other were inspired by the fervor of the struggle for democracy, liberty and justice for all Mexicans.

In the first one we called upon the Mexican people to take up arms against the bad government, as the principal obstacle to the transition to democracy in our country. In the second one we called Mexicans to a civic and peaceful effort. This was the National Democratic Convention, which was to achieve the profound changes that the nation demanded.

While the supreme government demonstrated its falseness and haughtiness, we, by one gesture after another, dedicated ourselves to showing the Mexican people our social base, the justness of our demands and the dignity that motivated our struggle. Our weapons were laid down, and were put aside so that the legal struggle could demonstrate its possibilities... and limitations. In the "Second Declaration of the Lacandon Jungle" the EZLN attempted, by all means, to avoid the re-initiation of hostilities and to look for a political, dignified and just solution to resolve the demands contained in the 11 points of our program for struggle: housing, land, work, food, health, education, justice, independence, liberty, democracy and peace.

The pre-electoral process in August 1994 brought hope to many sectors of the country, that the transition to democracy was possible by means of the electoral process. Knowing that elections are not, in the current conditions, the road to democratic change, the EZLN accepted being put to one side in order to give legal political opposition forces the opportunity to struggle. The EZLN pledged its word and its effort, then, to seeking a peaceful transition to democracy. In the National Democratic Convention the EZLN sought a civic and peaceful force. One which, without opposing the electoral process, would also not consumed by it, and that would seek new forms of struggle which would include more democratic sectors in Mexico as well as linking itself with democratic movements in other parts of the world. August 21 ended the illusions of an immediate change through peaceful means. An electoral process that is corrupt, immoral, unfair and illegitimate culminated in a new mockery of the good will of the citizens.

The party-State system reaffirmed its anti democratic vocation and imposed, in all parts and at all levels, its arrogance. In the face of an unprecedented level of voter participation, the Mexican political system opted for imposition and cut off, therefore, the hopes for the electoral process.

Reports from the National Democratic Convention, the Civic Alliance, and the Commission for Truth brought to light what the mass media had hidden, with shameful complicity: a gigantic fraud. The multitude of irregularities, the inequity, the corruption, the cheating, the intimidation, the robbery and the lying - they made the elections the dirtiest ones in Mexico's history. The high absentee rates in the local elections in Veracruz, Tlaxcala, and Tabasco showed that skepticism would reign within civil society in Mexico. Not satisfied with this, the Party/State system repeated the fraud of August, imposing governors, mayors and local congresses. As at the end of the 19th century, when the traitors held "elections" to justify the French intervention, today it is said that the nation greets with approval the continuation of an authoritarian imposition. The electoral process of August 1994 is a State crime. They should be judged as criminals and held responsible for this mockery.

On the other side, gradualism and hesitation appear in the lines of the opposition who accept a perception of this great fraud as a series of small "irregularities". A great dilemma in the struggle for democracy in Mexico reappears: the civic struggle bets upon a transition "without pain", a final blow which will light the road to democracy, and only prolongs the agony.

The case of Chiapas is only one of the consequences of this political system. Ignoring the longings of the people of Chiapas, the government repeats its dosage of imposition and domination.

Confronted by a broad movement of repudiation, the Party/State system opts to repeat to society the lie of its triumph and to exacerbate the confrontations. The present polarization in southeastern Mexico is the responsibility of the government and demonstrates its incapacity to resolve, at their roots, the political and social problems of Mexico. Through corruption and repression they try to resolve a problem that can only be solved when the legitimate triumph of the will of the people of Chiapas is recognized. The EZLN has maintained itself, until now, at the margins of the popular mobilizations, even though they have been subjected to a great campaign of defamation and indiscriminate repression.

Waiting for signs of the government's willingness to accept a political, just and dignified solution to the conflict, the EZLN watched, powerlessly, as the best sons and daughters of the dignity of Chiapas were assassinated, jailed and threatened. The EZLN watched as their indigenous brothers in Guerrero, Oaxaca, Tabasco, Chihuahua and Veracruz were repressed and received mockery as an answer to their demands for a solution to their living conditions.

During all of this period the EZLN resisted not only the military blockade and the threats and the intimidations by federal forces; but also resisted a campaign of slander and lies. As during the first days of 1994, they accused us of receiving foreign military support and financing; they tried to force us to give up our flags in exchange for money and government posts; they tried to delegitimize our struggle by reducing the national problem to a local indigenous context.

Meanwhile the supreme government prepared a military solution for the indigenous rebellion in Chiapas and in the nation despair and impatience arose. Covered by an expressed desire for dialogue that only hid the desire to liquidate the Zapatista movement through asphyxiation, the bad government let time and death run rampant through the indigenous communities in the country.

Meanwhile the Revolutionary Institutional Party, the political arm of organized crime and drug traffickers, went into its most acute phase of decomposition, by resorting to assassination as the method of solving its internal conflicts. Incapable of a civilized dialogue within its own party, the PRI bloodied the national soil. The shame of seeing the national colors usurped by the emblem of the PRI continues for all Mexicans.

The government and the country again forgot the original inhabitants of these lands. Cynicism and laziness returned to take possession of the sentiments of the Nation. Along with their rights to the minimal conditions of life with dignity, the indigenous peoples were denied the right to govern and govern according to their own reason and will. The deaths of our members become useless. Seeing that they did not leave us with any other alternative, the EZLN risked breaking the military blockade that surrounded it, and marched with the help of other indigenous brothers, who were fed up with the despair and misery and tired of the peaceful means. Seeking at all costs to avoid bloodying Mexican soil with the brothers' blood, the EZLN saw itself obliged to call the Nation's attention anew to the grave conditions of Mexican indigenous life. We called attention especially to those who supposedly had received government help, and yet continue living in the misery that they inherited, year after year, for more than five centuries. With the offensive in December 1994, the EZLN sought to show, to Mexico and to the world, its proud indigenous essence and the impossibility of resolving the local situation without simultaneous profound changes in the political, economic and social relations throughout the country.

The indigenous question will not have a solution if there is not a RADICAL transformation of the national pact. The only means of incorporating, with justice and dignity, the indigenous of the Nation, is to recognize the characteristics of their own social, political and cultural organization. Autonomy is not separation; it is integration of the most humble and forgotten minorities of contemporary Mexico. This is how the EZLN understood the issue since its founding, and this is how the indigenous communities who make up the leadership of our organization have defined it.

Today we repeat: OUR STRUGGLE IS NATIONAL!

We have been criticized for asking for too much. We, the Zapatistas, it is said, should be satisfied with the handouts that the bad government offers us. Those who are willing to die for a just and legitimate cause have the right to ask for everything. We Zapatistas are willing to give up the only thing we have, life, to demand democracy, liberty and justice for all Mexicans.

Today we reaffirm: FOR EVERYONE EVERYTHING, NOTHING FOR US!

At the end of 1994 the economic farce with which Salinas had deceived the Nation and the international economy exploded. The nation of money called the grand gentlemen of power and arrogance to dinner, and they did not hesitate in betraying the soil and sky in which they prospered with Mexican blood. The economic crisis awoke Mexicans from the sweet and stupefying dream of entry into the first world. The nightmare of unemployment, scarcity and misery will now be even more wearing for the majority of Mexicans.

1994, the year that has just ended, has just shown the real face of the brutal system that dominates us. The economic, political, social and repressive program of neo-liberalism has demonstrated its inefficiency, its deceptions, and the cruel injustice that is its essence. Neoliberalism as a doctrine and as a reality should be flung into the trash heap of national history.

Brothers and Sisters,

Today, in the middle of this crisis, decisive action by all honest Mexicans is necessary in order to achieve a real and profound change in the destinies of the Nation.

Today, after having called first to arms and later to a civic and peaceful struggle, we call the people of Mexico to struggle BY ALL MEANS, AT ALL LEVELS, AND IN ALL PARTS OF THE COUNTRY, for democracy, liberty and justice, by means of this...

Third Declaration of the Lacandon Jungle

We call upon all social and political forces of the country, to all honest Mexicans, to all of those who struggle for the democratization of the national reality, to form a National Liberation Movement, including the National Democratic Convention and ALL forces, without distinction by religious creed, race or political ideology, who are against the system of the State party. This National Liberation Movement will struggle from a common accord, by all means, at all levels, for the installation of a transitional government, a new constitutional body, a new constitution, and the destruction of the system of the Party-State. We call upon the National Democratic Convention and citizen Cuahtemoc Cardenas Solorzano to head up this National Liberation Movement, as a broad opposition front.

We call upon the workers of the Republic, the workers in the countryside and the cities, the neighborhood residents, the teachers and students of Mexico, the women of Mexico, the young people of the whole country, the honest artists and intellectuals, the responsible religious members, the community-based militants of the different political organizations, to take up the means and forms of struggle that they consider possible and necessary, to struggle for the end of the Party-State system, incorporating themselves into the National Democratic Convention if they do not belong to a party, and to the National Liberation Movement if they are active in any of the political opposition forces.

For now, in keeping with the spirit of this III. DECLARATION OF THE LACANDON JUNGLE, we declare:

First- That from the federal government custody of the Motherland be taken The Mexican flag, the justice system of the Nation, the Mexican Hymn, and the National Emblem - they will now be under the care of the resistance forces until legality, legitimacy and sovereignty are restored to all of the national territory.

Second- The original Political Constitution of the United Mexican States is declared valid, as written on the 5th of February of 1917, with the incorporation of the Revolutionary Laws of 1993 and inclusion of the Statutes of Autonomy for the indigenous regions, and will be held as valid until a new constitutional body is installed and a new constitution is written.

Third- We call for the people of Mexico to struggle for recognition for "the transitional governments to democracy". These shall be social and political organizations, as they are defined by the distinct communities for themselves, which maintain the federal pact agreed upon in the 1917 Constitution, and which are included, without regard for religious creed, social class, political ideology, race, or sex, in the National Liberation Movement.

The EZLN will support the civilian population in the task of restoring the legality, order, legitimacy and national sovereignty, and in the struggle for the formation and installation of a national transitional government for democracy with the following characteristics:

1. The liquidation of the system of Party-State and really separates the government from the PRI.

2. The reform of the electoral law in terms that guarantees: clean elections, legitimacy, equity, non-partisan and non-governmental citizen participation, recognition of all national, regional and local political forces, and that convenes new general elections in the federation.

3. The convening of a constitutional body for the creation of a new constitution.

4. The recognition of the particularities of the indigenous groups, recognizing their right to inclusive autonomy and citizenship.

5. The re-orientation of the national economic program, putting aside lies and deceptions, and favoring the most dispossessed sectors in the country, the workers and the peasants, who are the principal producers of the wealth that others appropriate.

Brothers and Sisters,

Peace will come hand in hand with democracy, liberty and justice for all Mexicans. Our path cannot find a peace with justice which our dead demand, if it is at the cost of our Mexican dignity. The earth does not rest; it walks in our hearts. The mockery to our dead demands that we struggle to wash away their shame. We will resist. The oppression and the arrogance will be overthrown.

As with Benito Juarez in the face of French intervention, the Motherland marches today at the side of the patriotic forces, against the anti-democratic forces and authorities. Today we say:

The Motherland lives! And she is ours!

Democracy!

Liberty!

Justice!

From the mountains of Southeastern Mexico,
Clandestine Indigenous Revolutionary Committee
-General Command of the Zapatista National Liberation Army.
Mexico, January 1995.

4. FOURTH DECLARATION FROM THE LACANDON JUNGLE

January 1, 1996

"Today we say: we are here, we are rebel dignity, the forgotten of the homeland."

"All those communities, all those who work the land, all whom we invite to stand on our side so that together we may give life to one sole struggle, so that we may walk with your help.

We must continue to struggle and not rest until the land is our own, property of the people, of our grandfathers, and that the toes of those who have paws of rocks which have crushed us to the shadow of those who loom over us, who command us; that together we raise with the strength of our heart and our hand held high that beautiful banner of the dignity and freedom of we who work the land. We must continue to struggle until we defeat those who have crowned themselves, those who have helped to take the land from others, those who make much money with the labor of people like us, those who mock us in their estates. That is our obligation of honor, if we want to be called men of honesty and good inhabitants of our communities.

Now then, somehow, more than ever, we need to be united, with all our heart, and all our effort in that great task of marvelous and true unity, of those who began the struggle, who preserve purity in their heart, guard their principles and do not lose faith in a good life.

We beg that those who receive this manifesto pass it on to all the men and women of those communities."

- Reform, Liberty, Justice and Law Chief General of the Southern Liberation Army Emiliano Zapata (original Zapatista manifesto written in Nahuatl)

I.

To the People of Mexico
To the peoples and governments of the world

Brothers and Sisters,

The flower of the word will not die. The masked face which today has a name may die, but the word which came from the depth of history and the earth can no longer be cut by the arrogance of the powerful. We were born of the night. We live in the night. We will die in her. But the light will be tomorrow for others, for all those who today weep at the night, for those who have been denied the day, for those for whom death is a gift, for those who are denied life. The light will be for all of them. For everyone everything. For us pain and anguish, for us the joy of rebellion, for us a future denied, for us the dignity of insurrection. For us nothing.

Our fight has been to make ourselves heard, and the bad government screams arrogance and closes its ears with its cannons.

Our fight is caused by hunger, and the gifts of the bad government are lead and paper for the stomachs of our children.

Our fight is for a roof over our heads which has dignity, and the bad government destroys our homes and our history.

Our fight is for knowledge, and the bad government distributes ignorance and disdain.

Our fight is for the land, and the bad government gives us cemeteries.

Our fight is for a job which is just and dignified, and the bad government buys and sells our bodies and our shames.

Our fight is for life, and the bad government offers death as our future.

Our fight is for respect for our right to sovereignty and self-government, and the bad government imposes laws of the few on the many.

Our fight is for liberty of thought and walk, and the bad government builds jails and graves.

Our fight is for justice, and the bad government consists of criminals and assassins.

Our fight is for history and the bad government proposes to erase history.

Our fight is for the homeland, and the bad government dreams with the flag and the language of foreigners.

Our fight is for peace, and the bad government announces war and destruction.

Housing, land, employment, food, education, independence, democracy, liberty, justice and peace. These were our banners during the dawn of 1994. These were our demands during that long night of 500 years. These are, today, our necessities.

Our blood and our word have lit a small fire in the mountain and we walk a path against the house of money and the powerful. Brothers and sisters of other races and languages, of other colors, but with the same heart now protect our light and in it they drink of the same fire.

The powerful came to extinguish us with its violent wind, but our light grew in other lights. The rich dream still about extinguishing the first light. It is useless, there are now too many lights and they have all become the first.

The arrogant wish to extinguish a rebellion which they mistakenly believe began in the dawn of 1994. But the rebellion which now has a dark face and an indigenous language was not born today. It spoke before with other languages and in other lands. This rebellion against injustice spoke in many mountains and many histories. It has already spoken in nahuatl, paipai, kiliwa, cucapa, cochimi, kumiai, yuma, seri, chontal, chinanteco, pame, chichimeca, otomi, mazahua, matlatzinca, ocuilteco, zapoteco, solteco, chatino, papabuco, mixteco, cucateco, triqui, amuzzgo, mazateco, chocho, ixcaateco, huave, tlapaneco, totonaca, tepehua, populuca, mixe, zoque, huasteco, lacandon, mayo, chol, tzeltal, tzotzil, tojolabal, mame, teco, ixil, aguacateco, motocintleco, chicomucelteco.

They want to take the land so that our feet have nothing to stand on. They want to take our history so that our word and we will be forgotten and die. They do not want Indians. They want us dead.

The powerful want our silence. When we were silent, we died, without the word we did not exist. We fight against this loss of memory, against death and for life. We fight the fear of a death because we have ceased to exist in memory.

When the homeland speaks its Indian heart, it will have dignity and memory.

Brothers and Sisters,

On January 1 of 1995, after breaking the military blockade with which the bad government pretended to submerge us in surrender and isolation, we called upon the different citizen forces to construct a broad opposition front which would unite those democratic voices which exist against the State-Party System: the National Liberation Movement. Although the beginning of this effort at unity encountered many problems, it lives still in the thoughts of those men and women who reject conformity when they see their Homeland under the rule of the Powerful and foreign monies. This broad opposition front, after following a route filled with difficulty, regressions and misunderstandings, is about to concretize its first Aproposals and agreements for coordinated action. The long process of maturity of this organizing effort will bear fruit this new year. We Zapatistas, salute the birth of this Movement for National Liberation and we hope that, among those who form it there will always be a zeal for unity and respect for differences.

Once the dialogue with the supreme government began, the commitment of the EZLN to its search for a political solution to the war begun in 1994 was betrayed. Pretending to want to dialogue, the bad government opted for a cowardly military solution, and with stupid and clumsy arguments, unleashed a great military and police persecution which had as its supreme objective the assassination of the leadership of the EZLN. The armed rebel forces of the EZLN met this attack with serene resistance tolerating the blows of thousands of soldiers assisted by the sophisticated death machinery and technical assistance of foreigners who wanted to end the cry for dignity which came out of the mountains of the Mexican Southeast. An order to retreat allowed the Zapatista forces to conserve their military power, their moral authority, and their political force and historic reason which is the principal weapon against crime made government. The great mobilizations of national and international civil society stopped the treacherous offensive and forced the government to insist upon the path of dialogue and negotiation. Thousands of innocent civilians were taken prisoners by the bad government and still remain in jail utilized as hostages of war by the terrorists who govern us. The federal forces had no other military victory other than the destruction of a library, an auditorium for cultural events, a dance floor and the pillage of the few belongings of the indigenous people of the Lacandon jungle. This murderous attempt was covered up by the governmental lie of recuperating national sovereignty.

Ignoring Article 39 of the Constitution which it swore to uphold on December 1, 1994, the supreme government reduced the Mexican Federal Army to the role of an army of occupation. It gave it the task of salvaging the organized crime which has become government, and deployed it to attack its own Mexican brothers.

Meanwhile, the true loss of national sovereignty was concretized in the secret pacts and public economic cabinet with the owners of money and foreign governments. Today, as thousands of federal soldiers harass and provoke a people armed with wooden guns and the word of dignity, the high officials finish selling off the wealth of the great Mexican Nation and destroy the little which was left.

Once it took up that dialogue for peace again, forced by the pressure of international and national civil society, the government delegation once again took the opportunity to demonstrate clearly its true motivation for the peace negotiations. The neo-conquerors of the indigenous people headed by the negotiating team of the government have distinguished themselves by their prepotent attitude, their arrogance, their racism and their constant humiliation which pursues failure after failure in the different sessions of the Dialogue of San Andres. It bet upon the exhaustion and frustration of the Zapatistas, and the government delegation placed all its energies to breaking the dialogue, confident that it would then have all the arguments in its favor for the use of armed force, securing what reason could not secure.

Once the EZLN understood that the government refused to concentrate seriously on the national conflict which the war represented, it took a peace initiative in an attempt to unravel the dialogue and negotiations. It called civil society to a national and international dialogue in its search for a new peace, it called for the PLEBISCITE FOR PEACE AND DEMOCRACY in order to hear national and international opinion about its demands and future.

With the enthusiastic participation of the members of the National Democratic Convention, the disinterested volunteerism of thousands of disorganized citizens with democratic hopes, the mobilization of international solidarity groups and groups of young people, and the invaluable help of the brothers and sister of National Civic Alliance during the months of August and September of 1995 a civic and unprecedented experiment was carried out. Never before in the history of the world or the nation had a peaceful civil society dialogued with a clandestine and armed group.

More than a million three hundred thousand dialogues were realized in order to verify this encounter with democratic wills. As a result of this plebiscite, the legitimacy of the Zapatista demands were ratified, a new push was given to the broad opposition front which had become stagnated and clearly expressed the will to see the Zapatistas participating in the civic political life of the country. The massive participation of international civil society called attention to the necessity to construct those spaces where the different aspirations for democratic change could find expression even among the different countries. The EZLN considers the results of this national and international dialogue very serious and will now begin the political and organizational work necessary in order to comply with those messages.

Three new initiatives were launched by the Zapatistas as responses to the success of the PLEBISCITE FOR PEACE AND DEMOCRACY.

An initiative for the international arena expresses itself in a call to carry out an intercontinental dialogue in opposition to neoliberalism. The two other initiatives are of a national character: the formation of civic committees of dialogue whose base is the discussion of the major national problems and which are the seeds of a non-partisan political force; and the construction of the new Aguascalientes as places for encounters between civil society and Zapatismo.

Three months after these three initiatives were launched, the call for the intercontinental dialogue for humanity and against neoliberalism is almost complete, more than two hundred civic committees of dialogue have been organized in all of the Mexican republic, and today, 5 new Aguascalientes will be inaugurated: one in the community of La Garrucha, another in Oventic, Morelia, La Realidad, and the first and last one in the hearts of all the honest men and women who live in the world. In the midst of threats and penuries, the indigenous Zapatista communities and civil society have managed to raise these centers of civic and peaceful resistance which will be a gathering place for Mexican culture and cultures of the world.

The new National Dialogue had its first test under the rationale for Discussion Table Number One in San Andres. While the government discovered its ignorance in regards to the original inhabitants of these lands, the advisors and guests of the EZLN began such a new and rich dialogue that it overwhelmed the limitations of the Discussion Table in San Andres and it had to be re-located to its rightful place: the nation. The indigenous Mexicans, the ones always forced to listen, to obey, to accept, to resign themselves, took the word and spoke the wisdom which is in their walk. The image of the ignorant Indian, pusillanimous and ridiculous, the image which the Powerful had decreed for national consumption, was shattered, and the indigenous pride and dignity returned to history in order to take the place it deserves: that of complete and capable citizens.

Independently of what arises as a result of the first negotiation of the agreements of San Andres, the dialogue begun by the different ethnic groups and their representatives will continue now within the Indigenous National Forum, and it will have its rhythm and achievements which the indigenous people themselves will agree upon and decide.

On the national political scene, the criminality of Salinismo was re-discovered and it destabilized the State-Party System. The apologists for Salinas, who reformed and altered the Constitution now have amnesia and are among the most enthusiastic persecutors of the man under whom they acquired their wealth. The National Action Party, the most faithful ally of Salinas de Gortari, began to demonstrate its real possibilities of replacing the Institutional Revolutionary Party (PRI) in the summit of political power and demonstrate its repressive, intolerant and reactionary nature. Those who see hope in the rise of neo-PANism forget that a substitution in a dictatorship is not democracy. They applaud the new inquisition, which through a democratic facade, pretends to sanction with moralistic blows the last remains of a country which was once a world wonder and today provides the material for chronicles of police action and scandals. A constant presence within the exercise of government was repression and impunity; the massacres of indigenous people in Guerrero, Oaxaca, and the Huasteca ratify government policy towards indigenous peoples; the authoritarianism in the UNAM toward the movement of those students wishing to democratize the College of Sciences and Humanities is a manifestation of the corruption which seeps into academia from politics; the detention of the leaders of El Barzon is another manifestation of treachery as a method of dialogue; the bestial repression of the regent Espinoza rehearses street fascism in Mexico City; the reforms to the Social Security law repeat the democratization of misery, and the support for the privatization of the banks secure the unity between the State-Party System and money. These political crimes have no solution because they are committed by those who are supposed to prosecute; the economic crisis makes corruption even more prevalent in government spheres. Government and crime, are today synonymous and equivalent.

While the legal opposition dedicated itself to find the center in a dying nation, large sectors of the population increased their skepticism towards political parties and searched, without finding it still, for an option for new political work, a political organization of a new kind.

Like a star, the dignified and heroic resistance of the indigenous Zapatista communities illuminated 1995 and wrote a beautiful lesson in Mexican history. In Tepoztlan, in the workers of SUTAUR-100, in El Barzon, just to mention a few places and movements, popular resistance found representatives with great dignity.

In summary, 1995 was characterized by the definition of two national projects completely different and contradictory.

On the one hand, the national project of the Powerful, a project which entails the total destruction of the Mexican nation; the negation of its history; the sale of its sovereignty; treachery and crime as supreme values; hypocrisy and deceit as a method of government; destabilization and insecurity as a national program; repression and intolerance as a plan for economic development. This project finds in the PRI its criminal face and in the PAN its pretense of democracy.

On the other hand, the project of a transition to democracy, not a transition within a corrupt system which simulates change in order for everything to remain the same, but the transition to democracy as a reconstruction project for the nation; the defense of national sovereignty; justice and hope as aspirations; truth and government through obedience as a guide for leadership; the stability and security given by democracy and liberty; dialogue, tolerance and inclusion as a new way of making politics. This project must still be created and it will correspond, not to a homogeneous political force or to the geniality of an individual, but to a broad opposition movement capable of gathering the sentiments of the nation.

We are in the midst of a great war which has shaken Mexico at the end of the 20th century. The war between those who intend to perpetuate a social, cultural and political regime which is the equivalent to the crime of treachery to the nation; and those who struggle for a democratic, just, and free change. The Zapatista war is only a part of that great war which is the struggle between a history which aspires for a future and an amnesia which has foreign vocation.

A plural, tolerant, inclusive, democratic, just, free and new society is only possible today, in a new nation. The Powerful will not be the ones to construct it. The Powerful are only the salesmen of the remains of a destroyed country, one devastated by the true subversives and destabilizers: those who govern.

Those projects which belong to the new opposition lack something which today has become decisive. We are opposed to a national project which implies its destruction, but we lack a proposal for a new Nation, a proposal for reconstruction.

Part, but certainly not all its vanguard, has been and is the EZLN in its effort for a transition to democracy. In spite of the persecution and the threats, beyond the lies and deceits, the EZLN has remained legitimate and accountable and forges ahead in its struggle for democracy, liberty and justice for all Mexicans.

Today, the struggle for democracy, liberty and justice in Mexico is a struggle for national liberation.

II.

Today, with heart of Emiliano Zapata and having heard the voice of all our brothers and sisters, we call upon the people of Mexico to participate in a new stage of the struggle for national liberation and the construction of a new nation, through this...

Fourth Declaration of the Lacandon Jungle

...in which we call upon all honest men and women to participate in the new national political force which is born today: THE ZAPATISTA FRONT OF NATIONAL LIBERATION (FZLN) a civic and peaceful organization, independent and democratic, Mexican and national, which will struggle for democracy, liberty and justice in Mexico. The Zapatista Front of National Liberation is born today and we invite the participation of the workers of the Republic, the workers in the field and in the city, the indigenous people, the squatters, the teachers and students, Mexican women, the youth in all the nation, honest artists and intellectuals, religious people who are accountable, all those Mexican citizens who do not want Power but democracy, liberty, and justice for ourselves and for our children.

We invite national civic society, those without a party, the citizen and social movement, all Mexicans to construct this new political force.

A new political force which will be national. A new political force based in the EZLN.

A new political force which forms part of a broad opposition movement, the National Liberation Movement, as a space for citizen political action where there may be a confluence with other political forces of the independent opposition, a space where popular wills may encounter and coordinate united actions with one another.

A political force whose members do not exert nor aspire to hold elective positions or government offices in any of its levels. A political force which does not aspire to take power. A force which is not a political party.

A political force which can organize the demands and proposals of those citizens and is willing to give direction through obedience. A political force which can organize a solution to the collective problems without the intervention of political parties and of the government. We do not need permission in order to be free. The role of the government is the prerogative of society and it is its right to exert that function.

A political force which struggles against the concentration of wealth in the hands of a few and against the centralization of power. A political force whose members do not have any other privilege than the satisfaction of having fulfilled its commitment.

A political force with local, state and regional organization which grows from the base, which is its social force. A political force given birth by the civic committees of dialogue.

A political force which is called a FRONT because it incorporates organizational efforts which are non-partisan, and has many levels of participation and many forms of struggle.

A political force called ZAPATISTA because it is born with the hope and the indigenous heart which, together with the EZLN, descended again from the Mexican mountains.

A political force with a program of struggle with 13 points. Those contained in the First Declaration of the Lacandon Jungle and added throughout the past two years of insurgency. A political force which struggles against the State-Party System. A political force which struggles for a new constituency and a new constitution. A political force which does not struggle to take political power but for a democracy where those who govern, govern by obeying.

We call upon all those men and women of Mexico, the indigenous and those who are not indigenous, we call upon all the peoples who form this Nation; upon those who agree to struggle for housing, land, work, bread, health, education, information, culture, independence, democracy, justice, liberty and peace; to those who understand that the State-Party System is the main obstacle to a transition to democracy in Mexico; to those who know that democracy does not mean substituting those in absolute power but government of the people, for the people and by the people; for those who agree with the need to create a new Magna Carta which incorporates the principal demands of the Mexican people and the guarantees that Article 39 be complied with through plebiscites and referendums; to those who do not aspire or pretend to exercise public privileges or elected posts; to those who have the heart, the will and the wisdom on the left side of their chest; to those who want to stop being spectators and are willing to go without pay or privilege other than participation in national reconstruction; to those who want to construct something new and good, to become a part of the FZLN.

Those citizens without a party, those social and political organizations, those civic committees of dialogue, movements and groups, all those who do not aspire to take Power and who subscribe to this FOURTH DECLARATION OF THE LACANDON JUNGLE commit themselves to participate in a dialogue to formulate its organic structure, its plan of action, and its declaration of principles for this FZLN.

Today, this January 1 of 1996, the Zapatista Army of National Liberation signs this FOURTH DECLARATION OF THE LACANDON JUNGLE. We invite all the people of Mexico to subscribe to it.

III.

Brothers and Sisters,

Many words walk in the world. Many worlds are made. Many worlds are made for us. There are words and worlds which are lies and injustices. There are words and worlds which are truths and truthful. We make true words. We have been made from true words.

In the world of the powerful there is no space for anyone but themselves and their servants. In the world we want everyone fits.

In the world we want many worlds to fit. The Nation which we construct is one where all communities and languages fit, where all steps may walk, where all may have laughter, where all may live the dawn.

We speak of unity even when we are silent. Softly and gently we speak the words which find the unity which will embrace us in history and which will discard the abandonment which confronts and destroys one another.

Our word, our song and our cry, is so that the most dead will no longer die. So that we may live fighting, we may live singing.

Long live the word.

Long live Enough is Enough!

Long live the night which becomes a soldier in order not to die in oblivion. In order to live the word dies, its seed germinating forever in the womb of the earth. By being born and living we die. We will always live. Only those who give up their history are consigned to oblivion.

We are here.

We do not surrender.

Zapata is alive, and in spite of everything, the struggle continues.

From the mountains of the Mexican Southeast,
Subcomandante Insurgente Marcos.
Indigenous Clandestine Revolutionary Committee
-General Command of the Zapatista Army of National Liberation Mexico.
January of 1996.

5. Fifth Declaration from the Lacandon Jungle

"Today we say: We are here! We are resisting!"

"We are the avengers of death.
Our lineage will never be extinguished as long as
there is light in the morning star."
- Popul Vuh

Brothers and sisters,

Ours is not the house of pain and misery. That is how he who robs and deceives us has painted us.

Ours is not the land of death and anguish. Ours is not the treason nor does our way have room for the forgetting.

Ours are not the empty ground and the hollow sky.

Ours is the house of light and joy. That is how we created it, that is how we struggle for it, that is how we nurture it.

Ours is the land of life and hope.

Ours is the path of peace which is planted with dignity and harvested with justice and liberty.

I. Resistance and Silence

Brothers and sisters,

We understand that the struggle for the place which we deserve and need in the great Mexican Nation, is only one part of everyone's great struggle for democracy, liberty and justice, but it is a fundamental and necessary part. Time and again, since the beginning of our uprising on January 1, 1994, we have called on all the peoples of Mexico to struggle together, and by all means possible, for the rights which the powerful deny us. Time and again, since we saw and spoke with all of you, we have insisted on dialogue and meeting as the path for us to walk. For more than four years, the war has never come from our side. Since then the war has always come from the mouth and the steps of the supreme governments. From there have come the lies, the deaths, the miseries.

Along the path that you asked us to walk, we held talks with the powerful and we reached agreements which would mean the beginning of peace in our lands, justice for the indigenous of Mexico and hope for all honest men and women in the country.

These agreements, the San Andres Accords, were not the product of only our will, nor were they created alone. Representatives from all the Indian peoples arrived at San Andres, their voice was represented there, and their demands were expressed there. Their struggle, which is lesson and path, was shining, their word spoke and their heart defined.

The zapatistas and their accords were not alone there. The zapatistas were, and are, next to and behind the Indian peoples. Like now, then we were only a small part of the great history with face, word and heart of the nahuatl, paipai, cucapa, cochimi, kumiai, yuma, seri, chontal, chinanteco, pame, chichimeca, otomi, mazahua, matlazinca, ocuilteco, zapoteco, solteco, chatino, papabuco, mixteco, cuicateco, triqui, amuzgo, mazateco, chocho, izcateco, huave, tlapaneco, totonaca, tepehua, popoluca, mixe, zoque, huasteco, lacandon, maya, chol, tzeltal, tzotzil, tojolabal, mame, teco, ixil, aguacateco, motocintleco, chicomucelteco, kanjobal, jacalteco, quiche, cakchiquel, ketchi, pima, tepehuan, tarahumara, mayo, yaqui, cahita, opata, cora, huichol, purepecha y kikapu.

As we did then, we now continue walking together with all the Indian peoples in their struggle for recognition of their rights. Not as vanguard or guide, only as a part.

We keep our word of seeking a peaceful solution.

But the supreme government did not keep their word and broke the first fundamental accord which we had reached: recognition of indigenous rights.

To the peace which we offered, the government countered with their stubborn war.

Since then, the war against us and all the Indian peoples has continued.

Since then, the lies have grown.

Since then they have deceived the country and the entire world, feigning peace and making war against all the indigenous.

Since then they have tried to forget the breaking of the governmental word and they have wanted to hide the treason which governs Mexican lands.

Against the war, not another war, but the same dignified and silent resistance.

While the government unveils to Mexico and the world their desire for death and destruction, the zapatistas do not respond with violence, nor do we enter into the evil competition to see who can inflict the most deaths and misery on the other side.

While the government piles up hollow words and hastens to argue with a rival that constantly slips away, the zapatistas make a weapon of struggle out of silence, which they do not understand and against which they can do nothing, and time and again they oppose our silence with sharp lies, bullets, bombs, blows. Just as we discovered the weapon of words after the combat in January of 1994, now we do it with silence. While the government offered everyone threats, death and destruction, we could learn from ourselves, teach ourselves and teach another form of struggle, and that, with reason, truth and history, one could fight and win...

While the government handed out bribes and lied with economic supports to buy loyalties and break convictions, the zapatistas made out of our dignified rejection of the powerful's charity, a wall which protected us and made us stronger.

While the government baited with corrupt wealth and imposed hunger in order to force surrender and to conquer, the zapatistas made our hunger into food, and our poverty into the wealth that we deserved and were entitled to.

Silence, dignity and resistance were our strengths and our best weapons. With them, we fight and defeat an enemy which is powerful but whose cause lacks right and justice. From our experience and from the long and shining history of indigenous struggle which we inherited from our ancestors, the first inhabitants of these lands, we pick up these weapons again and convert our silences into soldiers, our dignity into light, and our walls into resistance.

Despite the fact that, during the time our remaining quiet lasted, we kept away from direct participation in the primary national problems with our position and proposals; although our silence allowed the powerful to create and to spread rumors and lies about internal divisions and ruptures within the zapatistas, and they tried to dress us in the cloth of intolerance, intransigence, weakness and renunciation; despite the fact that some grew discouraged from the lack of our words and that others took advantage of their absence to pretend to be our spokespersons, despite those sorrows, and also because of them, we have taken, and are taking, great steps forward.

We saw that our dead could no longer remain silent, the dead speak of our dead, the dead accuse, the dead shout, the dead live again. Our dead will never die again. Our dead are always ours and of all of those who struggle.

We saw dozens of us confront thousands of modern weapons with hand and nail, we saw ourselves taken prisoner, we saw ourselves rise up with dignity and resist with dignity, We saw members of civil society taken prisoner for being close to the indigenous and for believing that peace has to do with art, education and respect. We saw them, their fighting hearts now with ours, and so we saw them as brothers.

We saw the war come from above with its thunder, and we saw them think that we would respond, and we saw them absurdly turn our responses into arguments to step up their crimes. And the government brought war and received no response at all, but their crime continued. Our silence unclothed the powerful, and showed him exactly as he is: a criminal beast. We saw that our silence kept the death and destruction from growing. This way the assassins were unmasked who were hiding behind the robes that they call the "state of law." The veil was torn away from what they were hiding, the half-hearted and faint-hearted were revealed, those who play with death for profit, those who see in the blood of others a staircase, those who kill because the matador is applauded and underhanded... And the government's ultimate and hypocritical robe was removed. "The war is not against the indige-nous," they said while persecuting, imprisoning and assassinating indigenous. Their own and personal war accused them of murder while our silence was accusing them.

We saw our powerful government become irritated when it could find neither rival nor surrender, we saw them then turn against others and strike out against those who do not walk our same path but who raised the same banners: honest indigenous lead-ers, independent social organizations, mediators, like-minded non-governmental organizations, international observers, any citizens who wanted peace. We saw all these brothers and sisters beaten and we saw them not surrender. We saw the govern-ment lash out at everyone and, wanting to take away strength, add enemies we saw.

We also saw that the government is not one, nor is the vocation of death, which their chief flaunts, unanimous. We saw that within it there are people who want peace, who understand it, who see it as necessary, who see it as essential. Being quiet, we saw other voices from within the war machine speaking to say no to its path.

We saw the powerful refuse to keep their own word and send the legislators a proposal for a law that did not resolve the demands of the very first of these lands, which distanced peace, and which disappointed hopes for a just solution that would end the war. We saw them sit down to the table of money, and announce their treachery there, and seek the support which those from below deny them. From the money the powerful received applause, gold and the order to eliminate those who speak mountains. "Let those who must die, die, thousands if necessary, but get rid of this problem," so spoke the money to the ear of he who says he governs. We saw this proposal break with what had already been agreed, with our right to govern and to govern ourselves as part of this nation.

We saw this proposal want to break us into pieces, want to take away our histo-ry, want to erase our memory, and forget the will of all the Indian peoples who joined together at San Andres. We saw this proposal bring division in its hand, destroy bridges and erase hope.

We saw our silence was joined by the will of good people and persons who, in the political parties, raised their voices and organized forces against the lie, and in that way they could stop the injustice and pretense that paraded as a constitution-al law for Indian rights and was no more than a law for war.

We saw that, being quiet, we could better hear voices and winds from below, and not just the cruel voice of the war from above.

We saw that while we were being quiet, the government buried the legitimacy which is conferred by a desire for peace and reason as route and step. The space cre-ated by our absent word pointed out the empty and sterile word of he who orders by ordering, and they convinced others to not listen to us and to look at us with distrust. And so the need for peace with justice and dignity as surnames was confirmed in many.

We saw all of those who are others like us, look to themselves and look for other forms for the peace to return to the lands of possible hopes, we saw the building and undertaking of initiatives, we saw them grow. We saw them arrive in our communities with help, letting us know that we are not alone. We saw them marching in protest, signing letters, banners, painting, singing, writing, reaching us. We also saw them proposing dialogue, true dialogue, with them, not that which is simulated by the will of the powerful. We also saw some of them discredited through intolerance by those who should be more tolerant.

We saw others whom we had not seen before. We saw new and good people, join the struggle for peace, not us, men and women who, able to opt for cynicism and apathy, chose commitment and mobilization.

In silence we saw everyone, in silence we greet those who seek and open doors, and in silence we construct this response.

We saw men and women born in other lands join the struggle for peace. We saw some extend the long bridge of "you are not alone" from their own countries, we saw them mobilize and repeat "Ya basta!", at first we saw them imagine and make complaints of justice, march as they sang, write as they shout, speak as they could march. We saw all of those sparks bounce across the heavens and arrive in our lands with all the names that Joseph had named, with all the faces of all who in all the worlds want a place for all.

We saw others cross the long bridge and, from their lands, arrive in ours after crossing borders and oceans, to observe and to condemn the war. We saw them come to us to let us know that we are not alone. We saw them being persecuted and harassed like us. We saw them being beaten like us. We saw them being vilified like us. We saw them resisting like us. We saw them staying even when they left. We saw them in their lands speaking of what their eyes had seen and showing what their ears had heard. We saw them continuing to struggle.

We saw that, being quiet, our people's resistance spoke more strongly against deceit and violence.

We saw that in silence we also spoke what we truly are, not like he who brings the war, but like he who speaks peace, not like he who imposes his will, but as he who longs for a place where everyone belongs, not like he who is alone and pretends to have crowds by his side, but as he who is everyone even in the silent solitude which resists.

We saw that our silence was shield and sword which wounded and exhausted what the war wanted and imposed. We saw our silence make the power which simulates peace and good government slip time and again, and make their powerful death machine crash time and again against the silent wall of our resistance. We saw that with each new attack they won less and lost more. We saw that by not fighting, we were fighting.

And we saw that the will for peace being quiet also affirms, demonstrates and convinces.

II. San Andres: A National Law for all the Indigenous and a Law for Peace

A national indigenous law should respond to the hopes of the indigenous peoples in the entire country. Representatives of Mexico's indigenous, and not just zapatistas, were at San Andres. The signed accords are with all the indigenous peoples, and not just with the zapatistas. For us, and for millions of indigenous and non-indigenous Mexicans, a law which does not carry out San Andres is only a pretense, it is a door to war and a precedent for indigenous rebellions which, in the future, will have to pay the bill which history so regularly exacts from the lies.

A constitutional reform in matters of indigenous rights and culture should not be unilateral, it should incorporate the San Andres Accords and in that way recognize the fundamental nature of the Indian peoples demands: autonomy, territoriality, Indian peoples, sets of regulations. In the Accords, the right to indigenous autonomy and territoriality is recognized, in accordance with Convention 169 of the OIT, signed by the Senate of the Republic. No legislation which tries to shrink the Indian peoples by limiting their rights to communities, promoting in that way their fragmentation and their dispersal which will make their annihilation possible, can assure the peace and the inclusion in the Nation of the very first Mexicans. Any reform which tries to break the bonds of historical and cultural solidarity which exist among the indigenous, is condemned to failure and is, simply, an injustice and an historical denial.

Although it does not incorporate all the San Andres Accords (one more proof that we are not intransigent, we accept the coadvisory work and we respect it), the law initiative drawn up by the Commission of Concordance and Peace is a proposal for a law which was created through the negotiation process and, therefore, in the spirit of lending dialogue continuity and a reason for being, it is a firm foundation which can herald the peaceful solution to the conflict, it becomes an important help in canceling the war and proceeding to peace. The so-called "Cocopa law" was built on the foundation of what was produced by the Indian peoples from below, it recognizes a problem and sets the bases for its solution, it reflects another way of doing politics, that which aspires to make itself democratic, it responds to a national demand for peace, it unites social sectors and allows them to continue forward in the agenda of the great national problems. For this today we reaffirm that we support the law initiative drawn up by the Commission of Concordance and Peace, and we demand that it be elevated to a constitutional level.

III. Dialogue, Negotiation, Possible if Real

Concerning dialogue and negotiation, we say that they have three great enemies which must be defeated so that they can be built on a path that is viable, effective and credible. These enemies are the absence of mediation, the war and the lack of carrying out of the accords. And the lack of mediation, the war and the breaking of word are the responsibility of the government.

Mediation in the negotiation of a conflict is essential, without it is not possible for dialogue to exist between two opposing sides. By destroying the National Commission of Intermediation with their war, the government destroyed the only bridge that existed for dialogue, they destroyed an important obstacle to violence and they provoked the emergence of a question: national or international mediation?

Dialogue and negotiation will have relevance, viability and effectiveness when, in addition to having mediation to count on, confidence and credibility are restored. Meanwhile, it can only be a farce in which we are not inclined to participate. We are not going to enter into dialogue for that. We will enter into it to seek peaceful means, not to gain time betting on political swindles. We cannot be accomplices in a sham.

Nor can we be cynical and feign a dialogue only to avoid persecution, imprisonment and the assassination of our leaders. The zapatista flags were not just born with our leaders, nor will they die with them. If our leaders are assassinated or jailed, it will not be able to be said that it was for being inconsistent or traitorous.

We did not rise up and we did not become rebels in order to believe ourselves stronger or more powerful. We rose up demanding democracy, liberty and justice because we have the right and the dignity of history on our side. And with this in our hands and in our hearts, it is impossible to remain impassive in front of the injustices, betrayals and lies which are now a "style of governing" in our country.

Reason has always been a weapon of resistance in front of the stupidity which now, but not for much longer, seems so overwhelming and omnipotent. Whether we be zapatistas or not, peace with justice and dignity is a right which honest Mexicans, indigenous or not, will continue to struggle for.

IV. We Resist, We Continue

Brothers and sisters,

The EZLN has managed to survive one of the fiercest offensives which has been unleashed against it. Its military capacity is preserved intact, its social base has been expanded, and it has been strengthened politically by demonstrating the justice of its demands. The indigenous nature of the EZLN has been reinforced, and it continues to be an important driving force in the struggle for the rights of the Indian peoples. The indigenous are national actors today, and their destinies and their platforms form part of the national discussion. The words of the first inhabitants of these lands now hold a special place in public opinion, the indigenous are no longer tourism and crafts, but rather the struggle against poverty and for dignity. We zapatistas have extended a bridge to other social and political organizations, and to thousands of persons without party, and we have received respect from all of them, and we have corresponded with them all. And we have also, together with others, extended bridges to the entire world and we have contributed to the creation (alongside men and women of the 5 continents) of a great network which struggles through peaceful means against neoliberalism, and resists fighting for a new and better world. We have also contributed something to the creation of a new and fresh cultural movement which struggles for a new man and new worlds.

All of this has been possible thanks to our companero and companera bases of support, the greatest weight of our struggle has fallen to them, and they have confronted it with firmness, decision and heroism. The support from Indian peoples in the entire country has also been important, from our indigenous brothers who have taught us, who have listened to us, and who have spoken to us. National civil society has been the fundamental factor for the just demands of the zapatistas and the indigenous in the entire country to continue through the path of peaceful mobilizations. International civil society has been sensitive and has kept ears and eyes attentive so that the responses to the demands would not be more deaths or prisons. The independent political and social organizations have accepted us as brothers, and in this way our resistance has been filled with inspiration. Everyone has supported us in resisting the war, no one in making it.

Today, with all of those who walk within us and at our side, we say: We are here! We are resisting!

In spite of the war which we are suffering, of our death and prisoners, the zapatistas do not forget why we are struggling or the nature of our primary flag in the struggle for democracy, liberty and justice in Mexico: that of the recognition of the rights of the Indian peoples.

For the commitment made since the first day of our uprising, today again we put in first place, from within our suffering, from within our problems, from within our difficulties, the demand that the rights of the indigenous be recognized with a change in the Political Constitution of the Mexican United States, which will assure for everyone the respect and possibility of struggle for what belongs to them: land, roof, bread, medicine, education, democracy, justice, liberty, national independence and dignified peace.

V. It is the Hour of the Indian Peoples, Civil Society and the Congress of the Union

Brothers and sisters,

The war has already spoken its thunderous noise of death and destruction.

The government and its criminal mask have already spoken.

It is the time for the silent weapons which we have carried for centuries to flourish in words again. It is the time for peace to speak, it is the time for the word of life.

It is our time.

Today, with the indigenous heart which is the dignified root of the Mexican nation, and having listened long enough now to the voice of death which comes from the government's war, we call on the People of Mexico and on the men and women of the entire planet to unite their steps and their efforts with us in this stage of the struggle for liberty, democracy and justice, through this...

Fifth Declaration of the Lacandon Jungle

...In which we call on all honest men and women to struggle for the: "Recognition of the rights of the Indian peoples and for an end to the war of extermination."

There will be no transition to democracy, nor State reform, nor real solutions to the primary problems of the national agenda, without the Indian peoples. A better and new country is necessary and possible with the indigenous. Without them there is no future at all as a Nation.

This is the hour of the Indian peoples of all Mexico. We call on them so that, together, we can continue struggling for the rights that history, reason and the truth have given us. We call on them so that, together, reclaiming the inheritance of struggle and resistance, we will mobilize across the entire country and we will let everyone know, through civil and peaceful means, that we are the roots of the Nation, its dignified foundation, its struggling present, its inclusive future. We call on them so that, together, we will struggle for a place of respect alongside all Mexicans. We call on them so that, together, we will demonstrate that we want democracy, liberty and justice for everyone. We call on them to demand to be recognized as a dignified part of our Nation. We call on them so that, together, we will stop the war which the powerful are making against everyone.

It is the hour of National Civil Society and independent political and social organizations. It is the hour of the campesinos, of the workers, of the teachers, of the students, of the professionals, of the religious men and women, of the journalists, of the neighbors, of the small shopkeepers, of the debtors, of the artists, of the intellectuals, of the disabled, of the sero-positives, of the homosexuals, of the lesbians, of the men, of the women, of the children, of the young people, of the old persons, of the unions, of the cooperatives, of the campesino groups, of the political organizations, of the social organizations. We call on them, together with the Indian peoples and with us, to struggle against the war and for the recognition of indigenous rights, for the transition to democracy, for an economic model which serves the people and does not serve itself, for a tolerant and inclusive society, for respect for difference, for a new country where peace with justice and dignity will be for everyone.

This is the hour of the Congress of the Union. After a long struggle for democracy, headed by the opposition political parties, there is, in the chambers of Deputies and Senators, a new relationship of forces which hampers the presedentialism's own injustices and points, with hope, to a true separation and independence of the powers of the Union. The new political make-up of the lower and upper chambers presents the challenge of dignifying legislative work, the expectation of converting it into a space of service to the Nation, and not to the acting president, and the hope of making a reality of the "Honorable" which proceeds the collective names by which the federal senators and deputies are known. We call on the deputies and senators of the Republic from all the political parties of record, and on the independent congressional members, to legislate on the behalf of all Mexicans. That they govern, obeying. That they carry out their duty supporting peace and not war. Making the separation of powers effective, making the federal Executive stop the war of extermination which it is carrying out against the indigenous peoples of Mexico. With full respect for the powers granted to them by the Political Constitution, listening to the voice of the Mexican people and making that what directs them at the moment of legislating. Supporting firmly and fully the Commission of Concordance and Peace, so that this legislative commission can discharge their coadvisory work effectively and efficiently in the peace process. Responding to the historical call which demands full recognition of the rights of the Indian peoples. Passing into national history as a Congress which stopped obeying and serving the one, and carried out their obligation to obey and serve all.

This is the hour of the Commission of Concordance and Peace. In their hands and competence is the stopping of the war, the completing of what the Executive refuses to carry out, the opening of hope for a just and dignified peace, and the creating of conditions for the peaceful coexistence of all Mexicans. It is the hour for legally complying with the law dictated for dialogue and negotiation in Chiapas. It is the hour to respond to the confidence which has been invested in this Commission, not just by the Indian peoples who attended the table at San Andres, but also by all the people who demand for the given word be kept, a halt to the war and the necessary peace.

This is the hour for the struggle for the rights of the Indian peoples, as a step towards democracy, liberty and justice for all.

As part of this struggle which we are calling for in this Fifth Declaration of the Lacandon Jungle for the recognition of indigenous rights and for an end to the war, reaffirming our "For everyone, everything, nothing for ourselves," the Zapatista Army of National Liberation announces that it will directly and in all Mexico carry out a National Consultation concerning the initiative of the indigenous law of the commission of concordance and peace and for and end to the war of Extermination.

In order to accomplish this, we propose to carry the initiative of the law of the Commission of Concordance and Peace to a national consultation in all the municipalities in the country so that all Mexican men and women can express their opinion on this initiative. The EZLN will send a delegation of their own to each one of the municipalities in the entire country to explain the contents of this initiative of Cocopa's, and to participate in the carrying out of this consultation. For this, the EZLN will address, at their opportunity and publicly, national civil society and political and social organizations in order to let them know the exact announcement.

We call on,

The Indian peoples of all Mexico to, together with the zapatistas, mobilize and demonstrate, demanding the recognition of their constitutional rights.

The brothers and sisters of the National Indigenous Conference to participate, together with the zapatistas, in the work of consulting with all Mexican men and women on the initiative of the Cocopa law.

To the workers, campesinos, teachers, students, housewives, neighbors, small business owners, small shopkeepers and businesses, retired persons, disabled, religious men and women, young people, women, old persons, homosexuals and lesbians, boys and girls, to, individually or collectively, participate directly with the zapatistas in the promotion, support and carrying out of this consultation, as one more step towards peace with justice and dignity.

To the scientific, intellectual and artistic community to join with the zapatistas in the work of organizing the consultation across all the national territory.

To the social and political organizations to, with the zapatistas, work in the carrying out of the consultation.

To the honest Political Parties, committed to popular causes, to lend all the support necessary to this national consultation. For this, the EZLN will address, at their opportunity and publicly, the national leadership of the political parties in Mexico.

To the Congress of the Union, to assume their commitment to legislate on behalf of the people, to contribute to the peace and not to the war, supporting the carrying out of this consultation. For this, the EZLN will address, at their opportunity and publicly, the coordinators of the parliamentary wings and the independent legislators in the chambers of Deputies and Senators.

To the Commission of Concord and Peace to, carrying out their coadvisory work in the peace process, smooth the path for the realization of a national consultation on their initiative. For this, the EZLN will address, at their opportunity and publicly, the legislative members of the Cocopa.

VI. Time for the Word of Peace

Brothers and sisters,

The time has now passed for the war of the powerful to speak, we will not let it speak more.

It is now the time for peace to speak, which we all deserve and need, peace with justice and dignity.

Today, July 19, 1998, the Zapatista Army of National Liberation endorses this Fifth Declaration of the Lacandon Jungle. We invite everyone to know it, to disseminate it and to join in the efforts and the work which it demands.

Democracy!

Liberty!

Justice!

From the mountains of Southeast Mexico,
Clandestine Revolutionary Indigenous Committee
-General Command of the Zapatista Army of National Liberation.
Mexico, July of 1998.

Acknowledgments

Public acknowledgments can be risky and even dangerous, since you almost always leave somebody out... So at this point I would like to thank everyone who has helped me in anyway throughout the whole process of producing this book. But to few people and organizations I should thank for their extra help individually.

First and foremost, my profound thanks go to Subcomandante Insurgente Marcos and other "masked" compañeros in Chiapas and all around the world, for inspiration and guidance in our struggle for a better world, and above all, for their contribution to win it.

Special thanks go to Enlace Civil and Centro de Información Zapatista in San Cristóbal de las Casas, Chiapas, Mexico, for their help, support and cooperation in this project. Thank you for sharing Marcos' stories and thus trusting us with precious memories, experiences and truths.

My sincerest thanks go to Prof. Howard Zinn, Prof. Noam Chomsky, Naomi Klein and Tom Hayden, for generously contributing their reflections on the Zapatista uprising, and also for their commitment to the struggle for human rights that has been inspiration to all of us. No words can express my gratitude for the strength and wisdom you bring to the world and also to this book. Thanks also to Fences and Windows Fund (www.fencesfund.org), founded by Naomi Klein to raise money for activist legal defense and popular education about global democracy, which unselfishly ceded its part of this book's proceeds to the people in Chiapas.

I'm deeply indebted to everyone at AK Press, who gave me this great opportunity to release ¡Ya Basta! also in the Americas. I'm grateful and honored to become a part of AK Press family. Rock on!

A big thanks also to Jaka Modic (for all the work he did instead of me...) and Darij Zadnikar @ Dost je!, Igor Brlek @ Studentska zalozba and Andrej Kosec @ Reuters, for their help and commitment in publishing ¡Ya Basta!.

Thanks to comrades @ The Utopian Collective, ON, Canada, for contributing the "visual part" of the book, and to other dedicated people, who keep translating the Zapatista communiqués and thus keeping the Chiapas issue ever-present.

And finally, heartfelt thanks and hugs to my family and my lovely girlfriend Tjasa. Thank you for your sincerest support, ideas, inspiration and limitless patience through long periods of neglect. I owe you everything...

About the Contributors

Subcomandante Insurgente Marcos is a spokesperson and strategist for the Zapatistas, an indigenous insurgency movement based in Chiapas, Mexico. He is the author of several books translated in English, including Shadows of Tender Fury (Monthly Review Press) which featured early letters and communiqués, and a children's book Story of the Colors (Cinco Puntos), which won a Firecracker Alternative Book Award. Marcos lives and works in "the mountains of the Mexican Southeast" in the state of Chiapas.

Noam Chomsky is universally accepted as one of the preeminent public intellectuals of the modern era. He writes extensively and lectures around the world on linguistics, philosophy, international affairs, US foreign policy, and human rights. He is listed among the ten most cited writers in the humanities, and is the only living member of the top ten. An internationally acclaimed philosopher, scholar and political activist, he is Institute Professor at the Massachusetts Institute of Technology, Department of Linguistics and Philosophy.

Naomi Klein is an award-winning journalist and author of the international bestsellers, No Logo: Taking Aim at the Brand Bullies, and Fences and Windows. No Logo has been translated in 25 languages - The New York Times called it "a movement bible". Naomi Klein's articles have appeared in numerous publications including The Nation, The Guardian, and The New York Times. For the past six years, Ms. Klein has traveled throughout North America, Asia, Latin America and Europe, tracking the rise of anti-corporate activism. She is a frequent media commentator and has guest lectured at Harvard, Yale, New York University, London School of Economics. She lives and works in Toronto, Canada. You can visit her Web site at www.nologo.org.

The Utopian Collective is an autonomous, anti-capitalist collective of concerned individuals located in Cambridge, ON, Canada. Their goal is to raise awareness and nourish a critical understanding of issues relating to capitalist-globalization. Their efforts include the distribution of pamphlets, direct-actions, guerrilla theatre, side-walk chalking, group debates, and facilitating the formation of new collectives. You can visit their Web site at www.angelfire.com/realm/u_c/. Keep an eye on them. More importantly, participate.

Permissions

About the Editor

Žiga Vodovnik is a publicist, activist and postgraduate student at University of Ljubljana, Department of Social Sciences (FDV). Currently he is writing a Ph.D. thesis and finishing his second book, this time a children's booklet about the possibility of building a better world through global (r)evolution. He lives in a small town, Črna na Koroškem.

Ordering Information

AK Press
674-A 23rd Street,
Oakland, CA 94612-1163,
USA

Phone: (510) 208-1700
E-mail: akpress@akpress.org
URL: www.akpress.org
Please send all payments (checks, money orders, or cash at your own risk) in U.S. dollars. Alternatively, we take VISA and MC.

AK Press
PO Box 12766,
Edinburgh, EH8 9YE,
Scotland

Phone: (0131) 555-5165
E-mail: ak@akedin.demon.co.uk
URL: www.akuk.com
Please send all payments (cheques, money orders, or cash at your own risk) in U.K. pounds. Alternatively, we take credit cards.

For a dollar, a pound or a few IRC's, the same addresses would be delighted to provide you with the latest complete AK catalog featuring several thousand books, pamphlets, zines, audio products and stylish apparel published & distributed by AK Press. Alternatively, check out our websites for the complete catalog, latest news and updates, events, and secure ordering.

Other Titles from AK Press

Books

MARTHA ACKELSBERG—Free Women of Spain

KATHY ACKER—Pussycat Fever

MICHAEL ALBERT—Moving Forward: Program for a Participatory Economy

JOEL ANDREAS—Addicted to War: Why the U.S. Can't Kick Militarism

ALEXANDER BERKMAN—What is Anarchism?

HAKIM BEY—Immediatism

JANET BIEHL & PETER STAUDENMAIER—Ecofascism: Lessons From The German Experience

BIOTIC BAKING BRIGADE—Pie Any Means Necessary: The Biotic Baking Brigade Cookbook

JACK BLACK—You Can't Win

MURRAY BOOKCHIN—Anarchism, Marxism, and the Future of the Left

MURRAY BOOKCHIN—Social Anarchism or Lifestyle Anarchism: An Unbridgeable Chasm

MURRAY BOOKCHIN—Spanish Anarchists: The Heroic Years 1868-1936, The

MURRAY BOOKCHIN—To Remember Spain: The Anarchist and Syndicalist Revolution of 1936

MURRAY BOOKCHIN—Which Way for the Ecology Movement?

DANNY BURNS—Poll Tax Rebellion

CHRIS CARLSSON—Critical Mass: Bicycling's Defiant Celebration

JAMES CARR—Bad

NOAM CHOMSKY—At War With Asia

NOAM CHOMSKY—Language and Politics

NOAM CHOMSKY—Radical Priorities

WARD CHURCHILL—On the Justice of Roosting Chickens: Reflections on the Consequences of U.S. Imperial Arrogance and Criminality

HARRY CLEAVER—Reading Capital Politically

ALEXANDER COCKBURN & JEFFREY ST. CLAIR (ed.)—Politics of Anti-Semitism, The

ALEXANDER COCKBURN & JEFFREY ST. CLAIR (ed.)—Serpents in the Garden

DANIEL & GABRIEL COHN-BENDIT—Obsolete Communism: The Left-Wing Alternative

EG SMITH COLLECTIVE—Animal Ingredients A-Z (3rd edition)

VOLTAIRINE de CLEYRE—Voltairine de Cleyre Reader

HOWARD EHRLICH—Reinventing Anarchy, Again

SIMON FORD—Realization and Suppression of the Situationist International: An Annotated Bibliography 1972-1992, The

YVES FREMION & VOLNY—Orgasms of History: 3000 Years of Spontaneous Revolt

DANIEL GUERIN—No Gods No Masters

AGUSTIN GUILLAMON—Friends Of Durruti Group, 1937-1939, The

ANN HANSEN—Direct Action: Memoirs Of An Urban Guerilla

WILLIAM HERRICK—Jumping the Line: The Adventures and Misadventures of an American Radical

FRED HO—Legacy to Liberation: Politics & Culture of Revolutionary Asian/Pacific America

STEWART HOME—Assault on Culture

STEWART HOME—Neoism, Plagiarism & Praxis

STEWART HOME—Neoist Manifestos / The Art Strike Papers

STEWART HOME—No Pity

STEWART HOME—Red London

STEWART HOME—What Is Situationism? A Reader

JAMES KELMAN—Some Recent Attacks: Essays Cultural And Political

KEN KNABB—Complete Cinematic Works of Guy Debord

KATYA KOMISARUK—Beat the Heat: How to Handle Encounters With Law Enforcement

NESTOR MAKHNO—Struggle Against The State & Other Essays, The

G.A. MATIASZ—End Time

CHERIE MATRIX—Tales From the Clit

ALBERT MELTZER—Anarchism: Arguments For & Against

ALBERT MELTZER—I Couldn't Paint Golden Angels

RAY MURPHY—Siege Of Gresham

NORMAN NAWROCKI—Rebel Moon

HENRY NORMAL—Map of Heaven, A

HENRY NORMAL—Dream Ticket

HENRY NORMAL—Fifteenth of February

HENRY NORMAL—Third Person

FIONBARRA O'DOCHARTAIGH—Ulster's White Negroes: From Civil Rights To Insurrection

DAN O'MAHONY—Four Letter World

CRAIG O'HARA—Philosophy Of Punk, The

ANTON PANNEKOEK—Workers' Councils

BEN REITMAN—Sister of the Road: the Autobiography of Boxcar Bertha

PENNY RIMBAUD—Diamond Signature, The

PENNY RIMBAUD—Shibboleth: My Revolting Life

RUDOLF ROCKER—Anarcho-Syndicalism

RON SAKOLSKY & STEPHEN DUNIFER—Seizing the Airwaves: A Free Radio Handbook

ROY SAN FILIPPO—New World In Our Hearts: 8 Years of Writings from the Love and Rage Revolutionary Anarchist Federation, A

ALEXANDRE SKIRDA—Facing the Enemy: A History Of Anarchist Organisation From Proudhon To May 1968

ALEXANDRE SKIRDA—Nestor Mahkno—Anarchy's Cossack
VALERIE SOLANAS—Scum Manifesto
CJ STONE—Housing Benefit Hill & Other Places
ANTONIO TELLEZ—Sabate: Guerilla Extraordinary
MICHAEL TOBIAS—Rage and Reason
JIM TULLY—Beggars of Life: A Hobo Autobiography
TOM VAGUE—Anarchy in the UK: The Angry Brigade
TOM VAGUE—Great British Mistake, The
TOM VAGUE—Televisionaries
JAN VALTIN—Out of the Night
RAOUL VANEIGEM—Cavalier History Of Surrealism, A
FRANCOIS EUGENE VIDOCQ—Memoirs of Vidocq: Master of Crime
GEE VOUCHER—Crass Art And Other Pre-Postmodern Monsters
MARK J WHITE—Idol Killing, An
JOHN YATES—Controlled Flight Into Terrain
JOHN YATES—September Commando
BENJAMIN ZEPHANIAH—Little Book of Vegan Poems
BENJAMIN ZEPHANIAH—School's Out
HELLO—2/15: The Day The World Said NO To War
DARK STAR COLLECTIVE —Beneath the Paving Stones: Situationists and the Beach, May 68
DARK STAR COLLECTIVE —Quiet Rumours: An Anarcha-Feminist Reader
ANONYMOUS —Test Card F
CLASS WAR FEDERATION —Unfinished Business: The Politics of Class War

CDs

THE EX—1936: The Spanish Revolution
MUMIA ABU JAMAL—175 Progress Drive
MUMIA ABU JAMAL—All Things Censored Vol.1
MUMIA ABU JAMAL—Spoken Word
FREEDOM ARCHIVES—Chile: Promise of Freedom
FREEDOM ARCHIVES—Prisons on Fire: George Jackson, Attica & Black Liberation
JUDI BARI—Who Bombed Judi Bari?
JELLO BIAFRA—Become the Media
JELLO BIAFRA—Beyond The Valley of the Gift Police
JELLO BIAFRA—High Priest of Harmful
JELLO BIAFRA—I Blow Minds For A Living
JELLO BIAFRA—If Evolution Is Outlawed
JELLO BIAFRA—Machine Gun In The Clown's Hand
JELLO BIAFRA—No More Cocoons
NOAM CHOMSKY—American Addiction, An
NOAM CHOMSKY—Case Studies in Hypocrisy
NOAM CHOMSKY—Emerging Framework of World Power
NOAM CHOMSKY—Free Market Fantasies
NOAM CHOMSKY—New War On Terrorism: Fact And Fiction

NOAM CHOMSKY—Propaganda and Control of the Public Mind
NOAM CHOMSKY—Prospects for Democracy
NOAM CHOMSKY/CHUMBAWAMBA—For A Free Humanity: For Anarchy
WARD CHURCHILL—Doing Time: The Politics of Imprisonment
WARD CHURCHILL—In A Pig's Eye: Reflections on the Police State, Repression, and Native America
WARD CHURCHILL—Life in Occupied America
WARD CHURCHILL—Pacifism and Pathology in the American Left
ALEXANDER COCKBURN—Beating the Devil: The Incendiary Rants of Alexander Cockburn
ANGELA DAVIS—Prison Industrial Complex, The
JAMES KELMAN—Seven Stories
TOM LEONARD—Nora's Place and Other Poems 1965-99
CHRISTIAN PARENTI—Taking Liberties: Policing, Prisons and Surveillance in an Age of Crisis
UTAH PHILLIPS—I've Got To know
DAVID ROVICS—Behind the Barricades: Best of David Rovics
ARUNDHATI ROY—Come September
VARIOUS—Better Read Than Dead
VARIOUS—Less Rock, More Talk
VARIOUS—Mob Action Against the State: Collected Speeches from the Bay Area Anarchist Bookfair
VARIOUS—Monkeywrenching the New World Order
VARIOUS—Return of the Read Menace
HOWARD ZINN—Artists In A Time of War
HOWARD ZINN—Heroes and Martyrs: Emma Goldman, Sacco & Vanzetti, and the Revolutionary Struggle
HOWARD ZINN—People's History of the United States: A Lecture at Reed College, A
HOWARD ZINN—People's History Project
HOWARD ZINN—Stories Hollywood Never Tells

DVDs

NOAM CHOMSKY—Distorted Morality
ARUNDHATI ROY—Instant Mix Imperial Democracy